I0592054

Monier Williams

A Practical Grammar of the Sanskrit Language Arranged with Reference to the Classical Languages of Europe

For the Use of English Students

Monier Williams

A Practical Grammar of the Sanskrit Language Arranged with Reference to the Classical Languages of Europe
For the Use of English Students

ISBN/EAN: 9783741178764

Manufactured in Europe, USA, Canada, Australia, Japa

Cover: Foto ©Paul-Georg Meister /pixelio.de

Manufactured and distributed by brebook publishing software (www.brebook.com)

Monier Williams

A Practical Grammar of the Sanskrit Language Arranged with Reference to the Classical Languages of Europe

A

PRACTICAL GRAMMAR

OF THE

SANSKṚIT LANGUAGE,

ARRANGED WITH REFERENCE TO

THE CLASSICAL LANGUAGES OF EUROPE,

FOR THE USE OF

ENGLISH STUDENTS.

BY

MONIER WILLIAMS, M.A.

BODEN PROFESSOR OF SANSKṚIT IN THE UNIVERSITY OF OXFORD, ETC.

THIRD EDITION,

MUCH ENLARGED AND IMPROVED.

Oxford:

AT THE CLARENDON PRESS.

M.DCCC.LXIV.

PREFACE

TO THE THIRD EDITION.

IN putting forth this third edition of my Sanskṛit Grammar I am bound to confess that the great general development of Sanskṛit learning, since the last edition, has compelled me almost to re-write the work for the third time. Any one who compares the present Grammar with its predecessor will see at once the difference between the two, not indeed in its structure and arrangement, nor even in the numbering of the rules*, but in the fuller and more complete explanation of points of detail. Thanks to the criticisms of other scholars, (generally tendered in that tone of courtesy and spirit of humility which always characterize true learning,) I have been enabled to correct the errors which, notwithstanding all my efforts, unassisted as I was in the work of revision, crept into my last edition. But I dare not even now hope to have attained the standard of perfection. Sanskṛit is far too vast and intri-

* In some few instances I have been forced to vary slightly the numbering of the rules; but as my edition of 'the Story of Nala' is more than half exhausted, and as Professor Johnson's references to my Grammar in his new 'Hitopadeśa' are to my present edition, the variation will not be of much importance.

cate a subject, and has still too many untrodden fields of labour, to admit of such pretensions. All I can with truth affirm is, that I have done what I could to bring the present edition up to the level of the scholarship of the day; and that if my life be spared to complete any further editions that may be required, it will be my duty to apply my energies again towards the same object.

In deference to the increasing attention given by Continental scholars to the study of the Veda, I have introduced more notices of Vedic peculiarities in the present work; and I have to thank my friend Dr. Kielhorn for his aid in adding to these notices, and in revising the proof-sheets as they issued from the press. Respect for the views of German scholars, to whose laborious research we English students of Sanskṛit cannot be too grateful, has also induced me to make more references to the great native grammarian Páṇini, and generally to add more allusions to the technical phraseology of Indian grammatical writers than in my last edition.

Nevertheless, I do not venture to hope, that my method of teaching Sanskṛit, addressing itself especially to the English mind, will ever approve itself to Continental students, any more than the Sanskṛit Grammars published by German scholars commend themselves to my judgment. But doctors may disagree and yet respect each other's opinions. The public, at least, must be the sole judge of the merits of opposite systems; and harsh censure of each other's statements in publications which are competing for public favour, is not only unproductive of good, and unbefitting the character of true scholars, but discreditable to the quarter whence such censure emanates.

I therefore decline all controversy; nor will I enter on the profitless task of defending my own theories against the attacks of rival grammarians, but simply say that my sole aim as Boden Professor is the promotion of a more general and critical knowledge of the Sanskṛit language among my own fellow-countrymen, to whose rule a vast Eastern Empire has been committed, and who cannot hope, except through Sanskṛit, to know the spoken dialects of India, or to understand the mind, read the thoughts, and reach the very heart and soul of the Hindús themselves.

M. W.

Oxford, June 1864.

PREFACE

TO THE PREVIOUS EDITION*.

In 1846 I published a Grammar of the Sanskrit language, which I entitled 'An elementary Grammar, arranged according to a new Theory.' This work is now out of print, and a new edition is required. The increasing experience which, during the subsequent ten years, I have derived from my duties as Sanskrit Professor at the East-India College, where every student without exception is compelled by statute to acquire this language, has led me to modify some of the views I expressed in my first Grammar respecting the Indian grammatical system. I have consequently felt myself called upon to re-write the book; and although I have seen no reason to depart materially from the arrangement originally adopted, yet I am confident that the present enlarged and more complete work will be found even better adapted than its predecessor to the practical wants of the European student.

At the best, a grammar is regarded by an European as a necessary evil, only to be tolerated because unavoidable. Especially must it be so in the case of a language confessedly more copious, more elaborate and artificial, than any other language of the world, living or dead. The structure of such a language must of necessity be highly complex. To the native of Hindústán this complexity is a positive recommendation. He views in it an evidence and

---

* I have slightly abridged this Preface.

a pledge of the sacred and unapproachable character of the tongue which he venerates as divine. To him the study of its intricate grammar is an end, complete and satisfying in itself. He wanders with delight in its perplexing mazes; and values that grammar most which enters most minutely into an abstract analysis of the construction of the language, apart from its practical bearing on the literature or even on the formation of his own vernacular dialect. But the matter-of-fact temperament of an European, or at least of an Englishman, his peculiar mental organization, his hereditary and educational bias, are opposed to all such purely philosophical ideas of grammatical investigation. A Sanskṛit grammar intended for his use must be plain, straightforward, practical; not founded on the mere abstract theory of native grammarians, not moulded in servile conformity to Indian authority, but constructed independently from an examination of the literature, and with direct reference to the influence exercised by Sanskṛit on the spoken dialects of India and the cognate languages of Europe. To the English student, as a general rule, all grammatical study is a disagreeable necessity—a mere means to an end—a troublesome road that must be passed in order that the goal of a sound knowledge of a language may be attained. To meet his requirements the ground must be cleared of needless obstacles, its rough places made smooth, its crooked places straight, and the passage over it facilitated by simplicity and perspicuity of arrangement, by consistency and unity of design, by abundance of example and illustration, by synoptical tables, by copious indices, by the various artifices of typography.

Before directing attention to the main features of the plan adopted in the present volume, and indicating the principal points in which it either differs from or conforms to the Indian system of grammatical tuition, I will endeavour to explain briefly what that system is; on what principles it is based; and in what relation it stands to the literature.

It might have been expected that in Sanskrit, as in other languages, grammatical works should have been composed in direct subservience to the literature. But without going the length of affirming that the rules were anterior to the practice, or that grammarians in their elaborate precepts aimed at inventing forms of speech which were not established by approved usage, certain it is that in India we have presented to us the curious phenomenon of a vast assemblage of purely grammatical treatises, the professed object of which is not so much to elucidate the existing literature, as to be studied for their own sake, or as ancillary to the study of the more abstruse work of the first great grammarian, Páṇini. We have, moreover, two distinct phases of literature; the one, simple and natural—that is to say, composed independently of grammatical rules, though of course amenable to them; the other, elaborate, artificial, and professedly written to exemplify the theory of grammar. The Vedas, indeed, the earliest parts of which are generally referred back to the 12th or 13th century B.C., abound in obsolete and peculiar formations, mixed up with the more recent forms of grammar with so much irregularity as to lead to the inference, that the language at that time was too unsettled and variable to be brought under subjection to a system of strict grammatical rules; while the simplicity of the style in the code of Manu and the two epic poems is a plain indication that a grammar founded on and intended to be a guide to the literature as it then existed, would have differed from the Páṇiníya Sútras as a straight road from a labyrinth.

What then was the nature of Páṇini's extraordinary work? It consisted of about four thousand Sútras or aphorisms, composed with the symbolic brevity of the most concise *memoria technica*. These were to the science of Sanskṛit grammar what the seed is to the tree, the bud to the full-blown flower. They were the germ of that series of grammatical treatises which, taking root in them, speedily germinated and ramified in all directions. Each aphorism, in itself more dark and mystic than the darkest and most mystical of oracles, was pregnant with an endless progeny of interpretations and commentaries, sometimes as obscure as the original. About one hundred and fifty grammarians and annotators followed in the footsteps of the great Father of Sanskṛit grammar *, and, professing to explain and illustrate his dicta, made the display of their own philological learning the paramount aim and purpose of their disquisitions.

It cannot be wondered, when all the subtlety of the Indian intellect expended itself in this direction, that the science of Sanskṛit grammar should have been refined and elaborated by the Hindús to a degree wholly unknown in the other languages of the world. The highly artificial writings of later times resulted from such an elaboration, and were closely interwoven with it; and although much of the literature was still simple and natural, the greater part was affected by that passion for the display of philological erudition which was derived from the works of Páṇini and his disciples. Poetry itself became partially inoculated with the mania. Great poets, like Kálidása, who in the generality of their writings were remarkable for majestic simplicity and vigour, condescended in some

---

* It should be stated here, that Yáska, the well known explainer of the Vedic dialect, was doubtless earlier than Páṇini, who is himself now generally placed in the middle of the 4th century B. C. Páṇini, moreover, mentions the names of at least ten grammarians older than himself. The most illustrious followers of Páṇini were, 1. Kátyáyana, who wrote the Várttikas or Supplementary Rules. 2. Patanjali, who wrote the great commentary on Páṇini (Mahá-bháshya), in which he often criticises the criticisms of his predecessor Kátyáyana. 3. Kaiyaṭa, who, in his turn, commented on Patanjali. Vopadeva, a great authority in Bengal, lived probably in the 13th century of our era.

of their works to humour the taste of the day by adopting a pedantic and obscure style; while others, like Bhaṭṭi, wrote long poems, either with the avowed object of exemplifying grammar, or with the ill-concealed motive of exhibiting their own familiarity with the niceties and subtleties of speech.

Indeed it is to be regretted that the Paṇḍits of India should have overlaid their system, possessing as it does undeniable excellences, with a network of mysticism. Had they designed to keep the key of the knowledge of their language, and to shut the door against the vulgar, they could hardly have invented a method more perplexing and discouraging to beginners. Having required, as a preliminary step, that the student shall pass a noviciate of ten years in the grammar alone, they have constructed a complicated machinery of signs, symbols, and indicatory letters, which may have been well calculated to aid the memory of native teachers when printing was unknown, but only serves to bewilder the English tyro. He has enough to do, in conquering the difficulties of a strange character, without puzzling himself at the very threshold in a labyrinth of symbols and abbreviations, and perplexing himself in his endeavour to understand a complicated cipher, with an equally complicated key to its interpretation. Even Colebrooke, the profoundest Sanskṛit scholar of his day, imbued as he was with a predilection for every thing Indian, remarks on the eight lectures or chapters, which, with four sections under each, comprise all the celebrated Páṇinīya Sútras, and constitute the basis of the Hindú grammatical system;—'The outline of Páṇini's arrangement is simple, but numerous exceptions and frequent digressions have involved it in much seeming confusion. The first two lectures (the first section especially, which is in a manner the key of the whole grammar) contain definitions; in the three next are collected the affixes by which verbs and nouns are inflected. Those which appertain to verbs occupy the third lecture; the fourth and fifth contain such as are affixed to nouns. The remaining three lectures treat of the changes which roots and affixes undergo in special cases, or by general rules of orthography, and which are all effected by the addition or by the substitution of one or more elements. The apparent simplicity of the design vanishes in the perplexity of the structure. The endless pursuit of exceptions and limitations so disjoins the general precepts, that the reader cannot keep in view their intended connexion and mutual relation. He wanders in an intricate maze, and the clue of the labyrinth is continually slipping from his hand.' Again; 'The studied brevity of the Páṇiníya Sútras renders them in the highest degree obscure; even with the knowledge of the key to their interpretation, the student finds them ambiguous. In the application of them, when understood, he discovers many seeming contradictions; and, with every exertion of practised memory, he must experience the utmost difficulty in combining rules dispersed in apparent confusion through different portions of Páṇini's eight lectures.'

That the reader may judge for himself of the almost incredible brevity and hopeless obscurity of these grammatical aphorisms, we here present him with the closing Sútra at the end of the eighth lecture, as follows: 'अ अ *a a*.' Will it be believed that this is interpreted to mean, 'Let short *a* be held to have its organ of utterance contracted, now that we have reached the end of the work, in which it was necessary to regard it as being otherwise?'

My aim has been, in the present work, to avoid the mysticism of Indian grammarians, without ignoring the best parts of their system, and without rejecting such of their technical symbols as I have found by experience to be really useful in assisting the memory.

With reference to my first chapter, the student will

doubtless be impatient of the space devoted to the explanation of the alphabet. Let him understand at the outset, that a minute and accurate adjustment of the mutual relationship of letters is the very hinge of the whole subject of Sanskṛit grammar. It is the point which distinguishes the grammar of this language from that of every other. In fact, Sanskṛit, in its whole structure, is an elaborate process of combining letters according to prescribed rules. Its entire grammatical system, the regular formation of its nouns and verbs from crude roots, its theory of declension and conjugation, and the arrangement of its sentences, all turn on the reciprocal relationship and interchangeableness of letters, and the laws which regulate their euphonic combination. These laws, moreover, are the key to the influence which this language has exercised on the study of comparative philology. Such being the case, it is scarcely possible for a Sanskṛit grammar to be too full, luminous, and explicit in treating of the letters, their pronunciation, classification, and mutual affinities.

With regard to the second chapter, which contains the rules of Sandhi or euphonic combination, I have endeavoured as far as possible to simplify a part of the grammar which is the great impediment to the progress of beginners. There can be little doubt that the necessity imposed on early students of conquering these rules at the commencement of the grammar, is the cause why so many who address themselves energetically to the study of the language are compelled after the first onset to retire from the field dispirited, if not totally discomfited. The rules for the combination and permutation of letters form, as it were, a mountain of difficulty to be passed at the very beginning of the journey; and the learner cannot be convinced that, when once surmounted, the ground beyond may be more smooth than in other languages, the ingress to which is comparatively easy. My aim has been to facilitate the comprehension of these rules, not indeed by omission or abbreviation, but by a perspicuous method of arrangement, and by the exhibition of every Sanskṛit word with its equivalent English letters. The student must understand that there are two distinct classes of rules of Sandhi, viz. those which affect the final or initial letters of complete words in a sentence, and those which relate to the euphonic junction of roots or crude bases with affixes and terminations. Many of the latter class come first into operation in the conjugation of the more difficult verbs. In order, therefore, that the student may not be embarrassed with these rules, until they are required, the consideration of them is reserved to the middle of the volume. (See p. 147.)

As to the chapter on Sanskṛit roots and the formation of nominal bases, the place which it occupies before the chapter on declension, although unusual, scarcely calls for explanation; depending as it does on the theory that nouns as well as verbs are derived from roots, and that the formation of a nominal base must precede the declension of a noun, just as the formation of a verbal base must be anterior to the conjugation of a verb. Consistency and clearness of arrangement certainly require that an enumeration of the affixes by which the bases of nouns are formed should precede their inflection. The early student, however, may satisfy himself by a cursory observation of the eight classes under which these affixes are distributed. Some of the most uncommon, which are only applicable to single words, have been omitted. Moreover, in accordance with the practical character of the present Grammar, the servile and indicatory letters of Indian grammarians, under which the true affix is often concealed, if not altogether lost, have been discarded. For example, the adjective *dhana-vat*, 'rich,' is considered in the following pages to be formed by the affix *vat*, and not, as in native Grammars, by *matup*; and the substantive *bhoj-ana*, 'food,' is considered to be formed with the affix *ana*, and not, as in native Grammars, by *lyuṭ*.

In my explanation of the inflection of the base of both nouns and verbs, I have, as before, treated both declension and conjugation as a process of *Sandhi*; that is to say, *junction* of the crude base, (as previously formed from the root,) with the terminations. But in the present Grammar I have thought it expedient to lay more stress on the general scheme of terminations propounded by native grammarians; and in the application of this scheme to the base, I have referred more systematically to the rules of euphonic combination, as essential to a sound acquaintance with the principles of nominal and verbal inflection. On the other hand, I have in the present work deviated from the Indian system by retaining स् *s* as a final in the declension of nouns and conjugation of verbs, for the practical reason of its being more tangible and easy to apprehend than the symbol *Visarga* or *ḥ*, which is less perceptible in pronunciation. (See the observations under changes of final *s*, p. 40.) Even in native Grammars those terminations, the finals of which are afterwards changed to Visarga, are always regarded as originally ending in स् *s*; and the subsequent resolution of *s* into *ḥ*, when the termination is connected with the base, is a source of confusion and uncertainty. Thus *s* is said to be the termination of the nominative case; but the nominative of अग्नि *agni*, 'fire,' would according to the Indian system be written अग्निः *agniḥ*, which an Englishman would scarcely distinguish in pronunciation from the base *agni*. In the following pages, therefore, the nominative is given *agnis*; and the liability of *agnis* to become *agniḥ* and *agnir* is explained under the head of changes of final *s* (at pp. 40, 41). This plan has also the advantage of exhibiting the resemblance between the system of inflection in Sanskrit and Latin and Greek.

The difficulty experienced in comprehending the subject

of Sanskrit conjugation has led me to give abundant examples of verbs conjugated at full. I have of course deviated from the Indian plan of placing the third person first. I have, moreover, deemed it advisable to exhibit the English equivalents of Sanskrit words in the principal examples under each declension and conjugation, knowing by experience the thankfulness with which this aid is received by early students, not thoroughly familiar with the Devanágarí character. The numerous examples of verbs, primitive and derivative, will be found to include all the most useful in the language. In previous Grammars it has been usual to follow the native method of giving only the 3d pers. sing. of each tense, with an occasional indication of any peculiarities in the other persons. The present Grammar, on the other hand, exhibits the more difficult tenses of *every verb in full*, referring at the same time for the explanation of every peculiar formation to the rule, in the preceding pages, on which it depends. This is especially true of the 2d and 3d preterite (or perfect and aorist), as these constitute the chief difficulty of the Sanskrit verb; and I have constantly found that even advanced students, if required to write out these tenses, will be guilty of inaccuracies, notwithstanding one or two of the persons may have been given for their guidance.

In the chapter on compound words I have again endeavoured, without ignoring the Indian arrangement, to disembarrass it of many elements of perplexity, and to treat the whole subject in a manner more in unison with European ideas. The explanations I have given rest on actual examples selected by myself from 'the Hitopadeśa' and other standard works in ordinary use. Indeed this chapter and that on syntax constitute the most original part of the present volume. In composing the syntax, the literature as it exists has been my only guide. All the examples are taken from classical authors, so as to serve the purpose of an easy delectus, in which the learner may exercise himself before passing to continuous translation. The deficiency of native Grammars on this important subject is only to be accounted for on the supposition that their aim was to furnish an elaborate analysis of the philosophical structure of the language, rather than a practical guide to the study of the literature.

The exercises in translation and parsing, in the last chapter of this volume, will, it is hoped, facilitate the early student's first effort at translation.

In regard to the general scope of the book, it remains to state that my aim has been to minister to the wants of the earliest as well as the more advanced student. I have therefore employed types of two different sizes; the larger of which is, of course, intended to attract the eye to those parts of the subject to which the attention of the beginner may advantageously be confined. The smaller, however, often contains important matter which is by no means to be overlooked on a second perusal.

Under the conviction that the study of Sanskṛit ought to possess charms for the classical scholar, independently of its wonderful literature, I have taken pains to introduce in small type the most striking comparisons between this language and Latin and Greek. I am bound to acknowledge that I have drawn nearly all the materials for this important addition to the book from the English translation of Bopp's 'Comparative Grammar,' by my friend and colleague Professor Eastwick.

One point more remains to be noticed. The want of an Index was felt to be a serious defect in my first Grammar. This omission is now supplied. Two full Indices have been appended to the present work, the one English, and the other Sanskṛit. The latter will enable the student to turn at once to any noun, verb, affix, idiom or peculiar formation explained in the foregoing pages.

In conclusion, I desire to take this opportunity of expressing to the Delegates of the Oxford University Press my grateful and respectful sense of the advantages the volume derives from their favour and patronage*.

M. W.

EAST-INDIA COLLEGE, HAILEYBURY,
January 1857.

---

* Not the least of these advantages has been the use of a press which, in its appointments and general efficiency, stands unrivalled. The judgment and accuracy with which the most intricate parts of my MS. have been printed, have excited a thankfulness in my mind, which those only can understand who know the toil of correcting the press, when much Oriental type is interspersed with the Roman, and when a multitude of minute diacritical points, dots, and accents have to be employed to represent the Deva-nágarí letters.

CONTENTS.

INTRODUCTORY REMARKS.

SANSKṚIT is the classical and learned language of the Hindús, in which all their literature is written, and which bears the same relation to their vernacular dialects that Greek and Latin bear to the spoken dialects of Europe. It is one of the family called by modern philologists Arian * or Indo-European; that is to say, it is derived, in common with the languages of Europe, from that primeval but extinct type, once spoken by a tribe in Central Asia, partly pastoral, partly agricultural, who afterwards separated into distinct nationalities, migrating first southwards into Áryávarta or Upper India—the vast territory between the Himálaya and Vindhya mountains—and then northwards and westwards into Europe.

In all probability Sanskṛit approaches more nearly to this primitive type than any of its sister-tongues; but, however this may be, comparative philology has proved beyond a doubt its community with Greek, Latin, Persian †, Gothic, Lithuanian, Slavonic, Keltic, and through some of these with Italian, French, Spanish, Portuguese, German, and our own mother-tongue.

The word Sanskṛit (संस्कृत *sanskṛita* or *saṃskṛita*, see 6. *f*) is made up of the preposition *sam* (सम् = *σύν*, *con*), 'together,' and the passive participle *kṛita* (कृत = *factus*), 'made,' an euphonic *s* being inserted (see 53. *a*. and 6. *b*. of the following Grammar). The compound means 'carefully constructed,' 'symmetrically formed' (*confectus*, *constructus*). In this sense it is opposed to Prákṛit (प्राकृत

* More properly written *Áryan*, from the Sanskṛit आर्य *árya*, 'noble,' 'honourable,' 'venerable,' the name assumed by the race who immigrated into Northern India, thence called *Áryávarta*, 'the abode of the Áryans.'

† Especially old Persian. Zand (or Zend), which is closely connected with old Persian, might be added to the list, although the reality of this language as any thing more than the vehicle of the sacred writings called *Zand-Avastá* (affirmed by the Parsí priests of Persia and India to be the composition of their prophet Zoroaster) has been disputed. Comparative philologists also add Armenian.

prákrita), 'common,' 'natural,' the name given to the vulgar dialects which gradually arose out of it, and from which most of the languages now spoken in Upper India are more or less directly derived. It is probable that Sanskṛit, although a real language—once the living tongue of the Áryan or dominant races, and still the learned language of India, preserved in all its purity through the medium of an immense literature—was never spoken in its most perfect and systematized form by the mass of the people. For we may reasonably conjecture, that if the language of Addison differed from the vulgar and provincial English of his own day, and if the Latin of Cicero differed from the spoken dialect of the Roman plebeian, much more must the most polished and artificial of all languages have suffered corruption when it became the common speech of a vast community, whose separation from the educated classes was far more marked. To make this hypothesis clearer, it may be well to remind the reader, that, before the arrival of the Sanskṛit-speaking immigrants, India was inhabited by a rude people, called 'barbarians' or 'outcastes' (*Mlećchas, Nishádas, Dasyus*, &c.) by Sanskṛit writers, but probably the descendants of various Scythian hordes who, at a remote period, entered India by way of Bilúćistán * and the Indus. The more powerful and civilised of these aboriginal tribes appear to have retired before the Áryans into Southern India, and there to have retained their independence, and with their independence the individuality and essential structure of their vernacular dialects. But in Upper India the case was different. There, as the Áryan race increased in numbers and importance, their full and powerful language forced itself on the aborigines. The weak and scanty dialect of the latter could no more withstand a conflict with the vigorous Sanskṛit, than a puny dwarf the aggression of a giant. Hence the aboriginal tongue gradually wasted away, until its identity became merged in the language of the Áryans; leaving, however, a faint and skeleton-like impress of itself on the purer Sanskṛit of the educated classes, and disintegrating it into Prákṛit, to serve the purposes of ordinary speech †.

* The Brahui, a dialect of Bilúćistán, still preserves its Scythian character.

† The cerebral letters in Sanskṛit, and words containing cerebral letters, are probably the result of the contact of Sanskṛit with the language of the Scythian

Prákṛit, then, was merely the natural process of change and corruption which the refined Sanskṛit underwent in adapting itself to the exigencies of a spoken dialect*. It was, in fact, the provincial Sanskṛit of the mass of the community; whilst Sanskṛit, properly so called, became, as it is to this day, the language of the Bráhmaṇs and the accomplishment of the learned†.

This provincial Sanskṛit assumed of course different modifications, according to the circumstances of the district in which the corruption took place; and the various modifications of Prákṛit are the intermediate links which connect Sanskṛit with the dialects at present spoken by the natives of Hindústán.

They have been analyzed and assorted by Vararući, the ancient grammarian, who was to Prákṛit what Páṇini was to Sanskṛit grammar. The most noticeable varieties were the *Mágadhí*, spoken in Magadha or Bihár; the *Maháráshṭrí*, spoken in a district stretching from Central to Western India; and the *Śauraseni*, spoken on the banks of the Jamná, in the neighbourhood of the ancient Mathurá‡. These patois modifications of Sanskṛit are employed as the language of the inferior characters in all the Hindú dramas which have come

tribes: and a non-Sanskṛit, or, as it may be called, a Scythian element, may be traced with the greatest clearness in the modern dialects of Hindústán. In all of these dialects there is a substratum of words, foreign to Sanskṛit, which can only be referred to the aboriginal stock. See the last note at the bottom of p. xxii.

* It would be interesting to trace the gradual transition of Sanskṛit into Prákṛit. In a book called the *Lalita-vistara*, the life and adventures of Buddha are narrated in pure Sanskṛit. It is probably of no great antiquity, as the Buddhists themselves deny the existence of written authorities for 400 years after Buddha's death (about B. C. 543). But subjoined to the Sanskṛit version are *gáthás* or songs, which repeat the story in a kind of mixed dialect, half Sanskṛit, half Prákṛit. They were probably rude ballads, which, though not written, were current among the people soon after Buddha's death. They contain Vedic as well as more modern formations, interspersed with Prákṛit corruptions (e. g. शृणुहि for शृणु, which is Vedic; and भोति for भवति, which is Prákṛit), proving that the language was then in a transition state.

† The best proof of this is, that in the Hindú dramas all the higher characters speak Sanskṛit, whilst the inferior speak various forms of Prákṛit. It is idle to suppose that Sanskṛit would have been employed at all in dramatic composition, had it not been the spoken language of a section of the community.

‡ Arrian (ch. VIII) describes the *Suraseni* as inhabiting the city of Methoras.

down to us, some of which date as far back as the 2d century B. C., and the first of them is identical with *Páli*, the sacred language of the Ceylon Buddhists *. Out of them arose *Hindí* (termed *Hindústání* or *Urdú*, when mixed with Persian and Arabic words), *Maráthí*, and *Gujaráthí*—the modern dialects spread widely over the country. To these may be added, *Bengálí*, the language of Bengal, which bears a closer resemblance to its parent, Sanskṛit, than either of the three enumerated above; *Uriya*, the dialect of Orissa, in the province of Cuttack; *Sindhí*, that of Sindh; *Panjábí*, of the Panjáb; *Kásmírian*, of Kásmír; and *Nipálese*, of Nipál †.

The four languages of Southern India, viz. 1. Tamil ‡, 2. Telugu (the Ándhra of Sanskṛit writers) §, 3. Kanarese (also called Kannaḍi or Karṇáṭaka), and 4. Malayálam (Malabar) ‖, although drawing largely from Sanskṛit for their literature, their scientific terms, their religion, their laws, and their social institutions, are proved to be distinct in their structure, and are referred, as might have been expected from the previous account of the aborigines, to the Scythian, or, as it is sometimes termed, the Tatar or Turanian type ¶.

---

* Páli, which is identical with the Mágadhi Prákṛit, is the language in which the sacred books of the Buddhists of Ceylon are written. Buddhist missionaries from Magadha carried their religion, and ultimately (after the decay of Buddhism in India) their language, into that island. Páli (meaning in Singhalese 'ancient') is the name which the priests of Ceylon gave to the language of the *old* country, whence they received their religion.

† For an account of some of these dialects, see Prof. H. H. Wilson's very instructive Preface to his 'Glossary of Indian Terms.'

‡ Often incorrectly written Tamul, and by earlier Europeans erroneously termed Malabar. The cerebral *l* at the end has rather the sound of *rl*.

§ Sometimes called Gentoo by the Europeans of the last generation.

‖ A fifth language is enumerated, viz. Tuḷu or Tuḷuva, which holds a middle position between Kanarese and Malayálam, but more nearly resembles the former. It is spoken by only 150,000 people. Added to this, there are four rude and uncultivated dialects spoken in various parts of Southern India, viz. the Tuda, Kôta, Gônd, and Ku or Khood; all of which are affiliated with the Southern group.

¶ This is nevertheless consistent with the theory of a remote original affinity between these languages and Sanskṛit and the other members of the Indo-European family. The various branches of the Scythian stock, which spread themselves in all directions westward, northward, and southward, must have radiated from a common centre with the *Aryans*, although the divergence of the latter took place at a much

Sanskrit is written in various Indian characters, but the character which is peculiarly its own is the Nágarí or Deva-nágarí, i. e. that of 'the divine, royal, or capital city.' The earliest form of this character can scarcely be traced back to a period much anterior to the 3d century B. C.*; and the more modern, which is one of the most perfect, comprehensive, and philosophical of all known alphabets, is not traceable for several centuries *after* Christ. The first is the corrupt character of the various inscriptions which have been discovered on pillars and rocks throughout India, written in Mágadhí Prákrit, spoken at the time of Alexander's invasion over a great part of Hindústán. These inscriptions are ascertained to be addresses from the Buddhist sovereigns of Magadha to the people, enjoining the practice of social virtues and reverence for the priests. They are mostly in the name of Piya-dasi † (for Sanskrit Priya-darśí), supposed to be an epithet of Aśoka, who is known to have reigned at some period between the 2d and the 3d century B. C. by his being the grandson of Candra-gupta, probably identical with Sandrakottus, described by Strabo as the most powerful Rájá, immediately succeeding Alexander's death. He was one of the kings of Magadha (Bihár), whose court was at Páli-bothra or Páṭali-putra (Patna), and who claimed the title of Samráṭs or universal monarchs; not without reason, as their addresses are found in these inscriptions at Delhi, and at Kuttack in the south, and again as far west as Gujarát, and again as far north as the Panjáb. The imperfect form of Nágarí which the corrupt character exhibits is incompatible with Sanskrit orthography. It may therefore be conjectured that a more perfect alphabet existed, which bore the same relation to the corrupt form that Sanskrit bore to Prákrit.

---

later period. It is to be observed, that in the South-Indian dialects the Scythian element constitutes the bulk of the language. It may be compared to the warp, and the Sanskrit admixture to the woof. In the Northern dialects the grammatical structure and many of the idioms and expressions are still Scythian, but the whole material and substance of the language is Sanskrit. See, on this subject, the able Introduction of the Rev. R. Caldwell to his 'Comparative Grammar of the Drávidian or South-Indian Languages,' lately published.

* Mr. James Prinsep placed the earliest form as far back as the 5th century B.C.

† The regular Prákrit form would be Pia-dassi. Probably the spoken Prákrit of that period approached nearer to Sanskrit than the Prákrit of the plays.

Nor does it militate against this theory that the perfect character is not found in any ancient inscription, as it is well known that the Bráhmans, who alone spoke and understood the pure Sanskṛit, and who alone would therefore need that character, never addressed the people, never proselytized, and never cared to emerge from the indolent apathy of a dignified retirement.

An interesting table of the various modifications of the Deva-nágarí alphabet, both ancient and modern, from the date of the earliest inscriptions to the present time, may be seen in Mr. Edward Thomas' edition of Prinsep's 'Indian Antiquities,' vol. II. p. 52*. The perfection of the modern character, and the admirable manner in which it adapts itself to the elaborate and symmetrical structure of the Sanskṛit language, will be apparent from the first chapter of the present Grammar.

* This table, by the kind permission of Mr. Thomas, was lent to me by Mr. Stephen Austin of Hertford, the printer of the above work, and inserted in my second edition; but as the table is more interesting to scholars generally than useful to the student of Sanskṛit grammar, and as the increase of matter in the present volume makes space an object, I have preferred referring to the table as exhibited in Prinsep's 'Indian Antiquities.'

NOTICE TO THE STUDENT.

The publication at the Oxford University Press of 'the Story of Nala' (confessedly the best reading-book for beginners), as a companion to the present volume, with full vocabulary and copious grammatical references, has almost superseded the need for the exercises in translation and parsing appended to the previous editions of the Grammar. They have, therefore, been much abridged in the following edition.

When the Sanskrit-English Dictionary, now being printed under the patronage of the Delegates of the Oxford Press, is completed, the student will be supplied with such facilities for translating the literature that a delectus at the end of the Grammar will be rendered unnecessary.

Observe—'The Sanskṛit Manual,' by the author of the present work, contains a complete series of progressive exercises intended to be used in connexion with the rules in the following Grammar, and adapted to facilitate its study. This Manual may be obtained from W. H. Allen & Co., London, or any bookseller.

SANSKṚIT GRAMMAR.

CHAPTER I.

LETTERS.

1. THE Deva-nágarí character, in which the Sanskṛit language is written, is adapted to the expression of almost every known gradation of sound; and every letter has a fixed and invariable pronunciation.

There are fourteen vowels (or without *ḷṛí* * thirteen) and thirty-three simple consonants. To these may be added the nasal symbol, called *Anusvára*, and the symbol for a final aspirate, called *Visarga* (see rule 6). They are here exhibited in the dictionary order †. All the vowels, excepting *a*, have two forms; the first is the initial, the second the medial or non-initial.

VOWELS.

अ *a*, आ ा *á*, इ ि *i*, ई ी *í*, उ ु *u*, ऊ ू *ú*, ऋ ृ *ṛi*, ॠ ॄ *ṛí*, ऌ ॢ *ḷṛi*, ॡ ॣ *ḷṛí**, ए े *e*, ऐ ै *ai*, ओ ो *o*, औ ौ *au*.

Nasal symbol, called *Anusvára*, ं *ṃ*. Symbol for the final aspirate, called *Visarga*, ः *ḥ*.

CONSONANTS.

Gutturals,	क *k*	ख *kh*	ग *g*	घ *gh*	ङ *ṅ*
Palatals,	च *ć* ‡	छ *ćh*	ज *j*	झ *jh*	ञ *ñ*
Cerebrals,	ट *ṭ*	ठ *ṭh*	ड *ḍ*	ढ *ḍh*	ण *ṇ*
Dentals,	त *t*	थ *th*	द *d*	ध *dh*	न *n*
Labials,	प *p*	फ *ph*	ब *b*	भ *bh*	म *m*
Semivowels,	य *y*	र *r*	ल *l*	व *v*	
Sibilants,	श *ś*	ष *sh*	स *s*		
Aspirate,	ह *h*				

---

* See rule 3. *b*.

† The character ळ *ḷ* is not given, as being peculiar to the Vedas. See 16. *a*.

‡ In the previous editions this letter was represented by *ch*, out of deference to

The compound or conjunct consonants (see rule 5) may be multiplied to the extent of four or five hundred. The most common are given here; and a more complete list will be found at the end of the volume.

THE MORE COMMON OF THE COMPOUND OR CONJUNCT CONSONANTS.

क्क *kk*, क्त *kt*, क्र or क्र *kr*, क्ल *kl*, क्व *kv*, क्ष *ksh*, ख्य *khy*, ग्न *gn*, ग्र *gr*, ग्ल *gl*, घ्र *ghr*, ङ्क *ṅk*, ङ्ग *ṅg*, च्च *ćć*, च्छ *ććh*, च्य *ćy*, ज्ज *jj*, ज्ञ *jñ*, ज्व *jv*, ञ्च *ñć*, ञ्छ *ñćh*, ञ्ज *ñj*, ट्ट *ṭṭ*, ट्य *ṭy*, ड्ग *ḍg*, ड्य *ḍy*, ण्ट *ṇṭ*, ण्ठ *ṇṭh*, ण्ड *ṇḍ*, ण्ण *ṇṇ*, ण्य *ṇy*, त्त *tt*, त्थ *tth*, त्न *tn*, त्म *tm*, त्य *ty*, त्र or त्र *tr*, त्व *tv*, त्स *ts*, थ्य *thy*, द्ग *dg*, द्ध *ddh*, द्भ *dbh*, द्म *dm*, द्य *dy*, द्र *dr*, द्व *dv*, ध्य *dhy*, ध्व *dhv*, न्त *nt*, न्द *nd*, न्न *nn*, न्य *ny*, प्त *pt*, प्य *py*, प्र *pr*, प्ल *pl*, ब्ज *bj*, ब्द *bd*, ब्य *by*, ब्र *br*, भ्य *bhy*, भ्र *bhr*, म्भ *mbh*, म्म *mm*, म्य *my*, म्ल *ml*, य्य *yy*, र्क *rk*, र्म *rm*, ल्प *lp*, ल्ल *ll*, व्य *vy*, व्र *vr*, श्च *ść*, श्य *śy*, श्र *śr*, श्ल *śl*, श्व *śv*, ष्ट *shṭ*, ष्ठ *shṭh*, ष्ण *shṇ*, ष्य *shy*, स्क *sk*, स्ख *skh*, स्त *st*, स्थ *sth*, स्न *sn*, स्म *sm*, स्य *sy*, स्र *sr*, स्व *sv*, स्स *ss*, ह्म *hm*, ह्य *hy*, ह्ल *hl*, क्त्य *kty*, क्त्र *ktr*, क्त्व *ktv*, क्ष्ण *kshṇ*, क्ष्म *kshm*, क्ष्य *kshy*, ग्न्य *gny*, ग्भ्य *gbhy*, ग्र्य *gry*, ङ्क्त *ṅkt*, ङ्क्य *ṅky*, च्छ्य *ććhy*, च्छ्र *ććhr*, ण्ड्य *ṇḍy*, त्त्न *ttn*, त्म्य *tmy*, त्र्य *try*, त्स्य *tsy*, त्त्र *ttr*, त्त्व *ttv*, द्द्य *ddy*, द्ध्य *ddhy*, द्भ्य *dbhy*, द्र्य *dry*, न्त्य *nty*, म्ब्य *mby*, र्द्र *rdr*, र्य्य *ryy*, र्व्व *rvv*, ष्ट्र *shṭr*, स्थ्न *sthn*, स्त्य *sty*, स्त्र *str*, त्स्म्य *tsmy*, स्त्र्य *stry*, र्त्स्य *rtsy*, र्त्स्न्य *rtsny*.

The letters (except *r*) have no names like the names in Hebrew or Greek, but the consonants are enunciated with *a*; and it is usual in designating any letter to add the word कार *kára*; thus, अकार *a-kára* 'the letter *a*,' ककार *ka-kára* 'the letter *ka*.' The letter र *r*, however, is called रेफ *repha*.

Observe—In reading the following pages for the first time, it is recommended that the attention be confined to the large type.

OF THE METHOD OF WRITING THE VOWELS.

2. The short vowel अ *a* is never written unless it begin a word, because it is supposed to be inherent in every consonant. Thus, *ak* is written अक्, but *ka* is written क; so that in such words as कनक *kanaka*, नगर *nagara*, &c., no vowel has to be written. The

---

the usage of English Orientalists. In an essay 'on the use of the Roman character' prefixed to my edition of the *Bagh o Bahár*, published in 1859 (p. xxviii), I have explained my reasons for preferring *ć*.

mark ् under the *k* of इक्, called Virâma (see rule 9), indicates a consonantal stop, that is, the absence of any vowel, inherent or otherwise, after the consonant.

a. The other vowels, if written after a consonant, take the place of the inherent *a*. They assume two forms, according as they are initial or not initial. Thus, *ik* is written इक्, but *ki* is written कि.

b. Observe here, that the *short* vowel ि *i*, when *initial*, is written in its right place, but when *not initial*, is always written *before* the letter *after* which it is pronounced. Hence, in order to write such a word as *iti*, the letters would have to be arranged in Sanskṛit thus, *iit* इति.

c. It is difficult to assign a reason for this peculiarity. The top of the non-initial ि *i*, if written in its right place, might occasionally interfere with a subsequent compound letter, but this tells both ways; as in the word तर्हि *tarhi*, where the *i* would come more conveniently in its right position. Possibly the peculiarity may be intended to denote a slight drawing back of the breath, in the pronunciation of short *i*; or it may be merely a method of marking more decidedly the difference between the short and the long vowel. In the Bengáli character this artifice for distinguishing more forcibly between the length of vowel sounds is not confined to *i*.

3. The long vowels ा *á* and ी *í*, not initial, take their proper place after a consonant. The vowels *u*, *ú*, *ṛi*, *ṛí*, *lṛi*, not initial, are written *under* the consonants after which they are pronounced; as, कु *ku*, कू *kú*, कृ *kṛi*, कॄ *kṛí*, कॢ *klṛi*; except when *u* or *ú* follows र *r*, in which case the method of writing is peculiar; thus, रु *ru*, रू *rú*.

a. The vowels *ṛi*, *ṛí*, *lṛi* and *lṛí* are peculiar to Sanskṛit. See rule 11. *c*. ऌ *lṛi* only occurs in the root कॢप्, 'to make,' and its derivatives.

b. The long ॡ *lṛí* is not found except in technical grammatical phraseology; strictly it has no existence, and is useless except as contributing to the completeness of the alphabetical system.

c. The vowels *e* and *ai*, not initial, are written above the consonants after which they are pronounced; thus, के *ke*, कै *kai*. The vowels *o* and *au* (which are formed by placing ` and ^ over ा *á*), like ा *á*, take their proper place after their consonants; thus, को *ko*, कौ *kau*.

OF THE METHOD OF WRITING THE CONSONANTS.

4. The consonants have only one form, whether initial or not initial. And here note this peculiarity in the form of the Devanágarí letters. In every consonant, except those of the cerebral

class, and in some of the initial vowels, there is a perpendicular stroke; and in all the consonants without exception, as well as in all the initial vowels, there is a horizontal line at the top of the letter. In two of the letters, ध *dh* and भ *bh*, this horizontal line is broken; and in writing rapidly, the student should form the perpendicular line first, then the other parts of the letter, and lastly the horizontal line. The natives, however, sometimes form the horizontal line first.

OF THE COMPOUND CONSONANTS.

5. Every consonant is supposed to have the vowel अ *a* inherent in it, so that it is never necessary to write this vowel, excepting at the beginning of a word. Hence when any simple consonants stand alone in any word, the short vowel अ *a* must always be pronounced after them; but when they appear in conjunction with any other vowel, this other vowel of course takes the place of short अ *a*. Thus such a word as कलानलया would be pronounced *kalánalayá*, where long आ *á* being written after *l* and *y* takes the place of the inherent vowel. But supposing that instead of *kalánalayá* the word had to be pronounced *klánlyá*, how are we to know that *kl* and *nly* have to be uttered without the intervention of any vowel? This occasions the necessity for compound consonants. *Kl* and *nly* must then be combined together thus, क्ल, न्ल्य, and the word is written क्लान्ल्या. And here we have illustrated the two methods of compounding consonants; viz. 1st, by writing them one above the other; 2dly, by placing them side by side, omitting in all, except the last, the perpendicular line which lies to the right. Observe, however, that some letters change their form entirely when combined with other consonants. Thus र, when it is the *first* letter of a compound consonant, is written above the compound in the form of a semicircle, as in the word कूर्म *kúrma*; and when the *last*, is written below in the form of a small stroke, as in the word क्रमेण *krameṇa*. So again in क्ष* *ksha* and ज्ञ† *jña* the simple elements क ष and ज ञ are hardly traceable. In some compounds the simple letters slightly change their form;

* Sometimes formed thus क्ष, and pronounced *ky* in Bengálí. In Greek and Latin it often passes into ξ and *x*: compare दक्षिण, dexter, δεξιός. But not always: compare κτείνω, *kshaṇomi*; χθών, *ksham* (*kshamá*); oculus, *akshi*.

† This compound is sometimes pronounced *gya* or *nya*, though it will be more convenient to represent it by its proper equivalent *jña*.

as, श ś becomes श in श्च śca; द् d with य y becomes द्य dya; द् d with ध dh becomes द्ध ddha; द् d with भ bh becomes द्भ dbha; त t with र् r becomes त्र tra or त्र tra; क् k with त t becomes क्त kta.

a. Observe, that when र् r comes in the middle of a conjunct consonant, it takes the same form as at the end; thus, ग्र्य gry, ग्र gr: and that in one or two words, where it precedes the vowel ṛi, it is written above the initial form of that vowel in the crescent shape; thus, निर्ऋति nirṛiti, 'the goddess of destruction.' When conjunct consonants commencing with ॅ are followed by the vowels i, ī, e, ai, o, au, or by a nasal symbol (see 6), then ॅ is properly written on the right of all; thus, र्पि rpi, र्पी rpī, र्के rke, र्कौ rkau, र्कं rkaṃ.

b. In a few words initial vowels follow other vowels; e. g. गोअग्र, प्रउग, तितउ.

THE SYMBOLS ANUSVĀRA, ANUNĀSIKA, AND VISARGA.

6. *Anusvāra* (ं ṃ), i. e. 'after-sound,' always belongs to a preceding vowel, and can never be used like a nasal consonant to begin a syllable. It is denoted by a simple dot, which ought to come either over the vowel after which the nasalization is sounded, or on the right of the vowel-mark; thus, कं kaṃ, कुं kuṃ, किं kiṃ, कीं kīṃ. It properly denotes a weaker and less distinct nasal sound than that of the five nasal consonants. These latter are actual and full consonants, which may be followed by vowels, whereas Anusvāra is rather the symbol of the nasalization of the vowel which precedes it. It should be noted, however, that it partakes of the nature of a consonant, inasmuch as in conjunction with a following consonant it imparts prosodial length to a preceding short vowel.

a. Observe, that Anusvāra must take the place of a final म् m when the three sibilants श् ś, ष् sh, स् s, and the aspirate ह् h (see *f.* and 7. *b.* next page) follow; and also generally when र् r follows (except सम्राज् *sam-rāj*, 'a sovereign;' and see *c.* next page), being then expressible by ṃ; thus, तं शत्रुं *taṃ śatrum*, तं राजानं *taṃ rājānam*.

b. Anusvāra is also sometimes used as a short substitute for any of the five nasal consonants ङ् ṅ, ञ् ñ, ण् ṇ, न् n, म् m, when no vowel intervenes between these and a following consonant *in the middle of the same word* (thus the syllables *iṅk*, *iñc*, *aṇḍ*, *int*, *imp* are correctly written इङ्क्, इञ्च्, अण्ड्, इन्त्, इम्प्; and sometimes more shortly इंक्, इंच्, अंड्, इंत्, इंप्); but Anusvāra is more usually substituted for these nasals *when final* and resulting from the euphonic adaptation of the final *m* of accus. cases sing., nom. cases neut., some adverbs and persons of the verb to a following word; see 59.

c. Anusvāra is even used, though less correctly, for the final म् m of such words when they stand in a pause (i. e. are not followed by another word); and has often been so used in this grammar for the convenience of typography.

d. But Anusvára is not admitted as a substitute for the original final न् *n* of a *pada* or inflected word (as in accus. cases plur., loc. cases of pronominals, the 3d pers. plur. and pres. part. of verbs, &c., see 54), unless the next word begin with *ć, ṭ, t*, or their aspirates, when, by 53, a sibilant is interposed before the initial letter.

e. And in the case of *roots* ending in न् *n* or म् *m*, these final nasals, if not dropped, pass into Anusvára before terminations or affixes beginning with a sibilant or *h*, *but are not changed before semivowels;* thus मन् + स्यते = मंस्यते, हन् + से = हंसे (617), यम् + स्यति = यंस्यति, गम् + य = गम्य (602), नम् + र = नम्र.

f. Hence it appears that Anusvára is peculiarly the nasal of the three sibilants श् *ś*, ष् *sh*, स् *s*, and the aspirate ह् *h;* and that the true Anusvára always occurs before these letters. When it so occurs *in the middle* of simple words, as in अंश, अंहति, it would be better to represent it in English type by *n;* thus, *anśa, anhati*, not *amśa, amhati*. In order, however, not to multiply perplexing distinctions we have preferred in the grammar to make *ṃ* the equivalent for Anusvára both in the middle and end of words (except only in the word Sanskrit, which is now Anglicised).

7. That Anusvára is less peculiarly the nasal of the semivowels is evident from *e.* above. Hence, before *y, l*, and *v*, म् *m* final in a word (not a root) may either pass into Anusvára or assimilate itself to these letters; thus सम् + यम = संयम or सय्ँयम, सम् + लोके = सं लोके or सल्ँलोके; but in the latter case the nasal origin of the first member of the double letter is denoted by another nasal symbol called *Anunásika* (i. e. 'through the nose,' sometimes called *Ćandra-vindu*, 'the dot in the crescent'), which is also applied to mark the nasality of a final ल् *l* deduced from a final न् *n* when followed by initial ल् *l*, see 56.

a. And this *Anunásika* ँ is not only the sign of the nasality of य् *y*, ल् *l*, and व् *v*, in the preceding cases, but also marks the nasality of vowels, though in a less degree than Anusvára, see 11. *g*.

b. Observe—A final म् *m* before ह्म *hm*, ह्न *hn*, ह्य *hy*, ह्ल *hl*, ह्व *hv*, may either be changed to Anusvára or undergo assimilation with the second letter of the initial compound; thus किं ह्मलयति or किम् ह्मलयति, किं ह्नुते or किन् ह्नुते, किं ह्यः or किय्ँ ह्यः, &c. (see 7. above).

8. The symbol *Visarga*, 'rejection,' (called so as symbolising the rejection or suppression of a letter in pronunciation,) usually written thus :, but more properly in the form of two small circles ः, is used to represent a weaker aspiration than the letter ह् *h*, and that generally, but not always, at the end of a word*. It expresses an euphonic transition of final स् *s* and र् *r* into a kind of breathing. This symbol Visarga is never the

* Visarga is, of course, liable to appear in the middle of compound words. Nor can it be called final in the loc. plur. of nouns in *s;* as, मनःसु. See p. 95.

representative of ह् *h*, but rather of a final aspirate, which, under certain circumstances, takes the place of final *s* and *r*. It may be conveniently represented by the English *ḥ*. At the same time it should be borne in mind that Visarga (*ḥ*) is less than *h*, and is in fact no consonant, but only a symbol for *s* and *r* whenever the usual consonantal sound of these letters is deadened at the end of a sentence or through the influence of a *k*, *p*, or a sibilant commencing the next word. Observe, however, that all those inflections of nouns and persons of verbs, which as standing separate from other words are by some made to end in Visarga, may most conveniently be allowed to retain their final स् *s*; only bearing in mind that this *s* is liable at the end of a sentence, or when followed by certain consonants, to pass into a weak breathing, as in the French *les* or the English *isle*, *viscount*; in all which cases it might be expressed by Visarga, thus ले: &c. So again, in French infinitives, such as *aller*, the final *r* is silent; and in many English words, such as *bar*, *tar*, the sound of *r* is very indistinct; and these also might be written in Sanskṛit with Visarga, अले: *alleḥ*, बा: *báḥ*, &c.

a. An *Ardha-visarga*, 'half-visarga,' or modification of the symbol Visarga, in the form of two semicircles ✕, is sometimes employed before *k*, *kh*, and *p*, *ph*. Before the two former letters this symbol is properly called *Jihvá-múlíya*, and the organ of its enunciation said to be the root of the tongue. Before *p* and *ph* its proper name is *Upadhmáníya*, and its organ of utterance is then the lips.

b. The Ardha-visarga is very rarely, if ever, seen in classical Sanskṛit. In the Vedas the Upadhmáníya occurs, but only after an Anusvára or Anunásika: thus, नृं✕ पाहि or नॄँ✕ पाहि, and in this case also the symbol Visarga may be used for it.

The following are other marks:

9. The *Virámа*, 'pause' or 'stop,' placed under a consonant (thus क् *k*), indicates the absence of the inherent अ *a*, by help of which the consonant is pronounced.

Observe—Virámа properly means the pause of the voice at the end of a sentence. By the natives it is employed like a mark of punctuation at the close of a sentence ending with a quiescent consonant, while the mark । is the only means of denoting the close of a sentence ending in a vowel, all the preceding words being written without separation, because supposed to be pronounced without pause. When, however, by simply extending the functions of the Virámа we can make Sanskṛit typography conform to modern European ideas so as to enable proper spaces to be left between distinct words in such a sentence as the following; *sakṛid duḥkhakarâv âdyâv antimas tu pade pade;* it seems better to break through the native rule which however theoretically correct would oblige us to write the first five words of the same sentence thus, *sakṛiddụḥkhakarâvâdyâvantimastu*. See r. 26.

10. The mark ऽ (*Avagraha*, sometimes called *Ardhâkâra*, half the letter *a*), placed between two words, denotes the elision or suppression (*abhinidhâna*) of an initial अ *a* after ए *e* or ओ *o* final preceding. It corresponds to our apostrophe in some analogous cases. Thus, तेऽपि *te 'pi* for ते अपि *te api*.

a. In books printed in Calcutta the mark ऽ is sometimes used to resolve a long *â* resulting from the blending of a final *â* with an initial *a* or *â*; thus यथाऽवहं for यथा अवहं, usually written यथावहं. Sometimes a double mark ऽऽ denotes an initial long आ. The mark ऽ is also used in the Veda as the sign of a hiatus between vowels, and in the *pada* text to separate the component parts of a compound or of other grammatical forms.

b. The half pause । is a stop or mark of punctuation, usually placed at the end of the first line of a couplet or stanza.

c. The whole pause ॥ is placed at the end of a couplet like a full stop.

d. The mark of repetition ° indicates that a word or sentence has to be repeated. It is also used to abbreviate a word, just as in English we use a full point; thus प° stands for पर्वं, as *chap.* for *chapter*.

PRONUNCIATION OF SANSKṚIT VOWELS.

11. The vowels in Sanskṛit are pronounced for the most part as in Italian or French, though occasional words in English may exemplify their sound.

a. Since अ *a* is inherent in every consonant, the student should be careful to acquire the correct pronunciation of this letter. There are many words in English which afford examples of its sound, such as *vocal*, *cedar*, *zebra*, *organ*. But in English the vowel *u* in such words as *fun*, *bun*, *sun*, more frequently represents this obscure sound of *a*; and even the other vowels may occasionally be pronounced with this sound, as in *her*, *sir*, *son*.

b. The long vowel आ *â* is pronounced as *a* in the English *father*, *bard*, *cart*; इ *i* as the *i* in *pin*, *sin*; ई *î* as the i in *marine*, *police*; उ *u* as the *u* in *push*; ऊ *û* as the *u* in *rude*.

c. The vowel ऋ *ṛi*, peculiar to Sanskṛit, is pronounced as the *ri* in *merrily*, where the *i* of *ṛi* is less perceptible than in the syllable *ri*, composed of the consonant *r* and the vowel *i* *. ॠ *ṛī* is pronounced nearly as the *ri* in *chagrin*, being hardly distinguishable from the syllable री; but in the case of the vowels *ṛi* and *ṛī* there is a mere vibration of the tongue in the direction of the upper gums, whereas in pronouncing the consonant *r*, the tongue should actually touch them (compare 19 and 20): ए *e* as the *e* in *prey*; ओ *o* as in *so*; ऐ *ai* as *ai* in *aisle*; औ *au* as *au* in the German *baum* or as *ou* in the English *our*. ऌ *lṛi* and ॡ *lṛī* do not differ in sound from the letter ल *l* with the vowels *ṛi* and *ṛī* annexed, but as before remarked the vowel ऌ *lṛi* only occurs in one root, viz. क्लृप् *klṛip*, 'to make;' and its long form is not found in any word in the language. As to the Vaidik ळ *ḷra* or *ḷa*, see 16. *a*.

d. Hence it appears that every simple vowel in Sanskrit has a short and a long form, and that each vowel has one invariable sound; so that the beginner can never be in doubt what pronunciation to give it, as in English, or whether to pronounce it long or short, as in Latin.

e. Note, however, that Sanskrit possesses no short *ĕ* and *ŏ* in opposition to the long diphthongal sounds of *e* and *o*.

f. In comparing Sanskrit words with Greek and Latin, it will be found that the Sanskrit अ *a* usually answers to the Greek ε as well as to α (especially in vocative cases); and rarely to ο. In Latin, the Sanskrit अ *a* is represented by *u* as well as by *a*, *e*, and *o*. Again, the Sanskrit आ *ā* is generally replaced by the Greek η or ω, rarely by a long alpha. In Latin it is represented by long *a* or even by long *e*.

g. Although for all practical purposes it is sufficient to regard vowels as either short or long, it should be borne in mind that native grammarians give eighteen different modifications of each of the vowels *a*, *i*, *u*, *ṛi*, and twelve of *lṛi*, which are thus explained:—Each of the first four vowels is supposed to have three prosodial lengths, a short (*hrasva*), a long (*dīrgha*), and a prolated (*pluta*); the long being equal to two, and the prolated to three short vowels. Each of these three modifications may be uttered with a high tone, or a low tone, or a tone between high and low; or in other words, may have the acute, or the grave, or the circumflex accent. This gives nine modifications to *a*, *i*, *u*, *ṛi*; and each of these again may

---

* That there is not, practically, much difference between the pronunciation of the vowel *ṛi* and the syllable रि *ri* may be gathered from the fact that some words beginning with ऋ are also found written with रि, and *vice versâ*; thus, रिषि and ऋषि, रिष्टि and ऋष्टि, रिक्थ and ऋक्थ. Still the distinction between the definition of a vowel and consonant at 19 and 20 should be borne in mind. There is no doubt that in English the sound of *ri* in the words *merrily* and *rich* is different, and that the former approaches nearer to the sound of a vowel.

be regarded either as nasal or non-nasal, according as it is pronounced with the nose and mouth, or with the mouth alone. Hence result eighteen varieties of every vowel, excepting *ḷṛi*, *e*, *ai*, *o*, *au*, which have only twelve, because the first does not possess the long and the last four have not the short prosodial time. A prolated vowel is marked with three lines underneath or with ३ on one side, thus आ or आ३.

PRONUNCIATION OF SANSKṚIT CONSONANTS.

The arrangement of most of the consonants in the table at page 1 under the five heads of gutturals (*kaṇṭhya*), palatals (*tálavya*), cerebrals (*múrdhanya*), dentals (*dantya*), and labials (*oshṭhya*), refers of course to the organ principally employed in pronouncing them, whether the throat, the palate, the top of the palate, the teeth, or the lips. This classification is more fully explained at 18.

12. क *ka*, च *ća*, ज *ja*, प *pa*, ब *ba* are pronounced as in English. Observe that च *ća* is a simple consonantal sound, although represented in English words by *ch*. It is a modification or softening of *ka*, just as *ja* is of *ga*, the organ of utterance being in the palate, a little in advance of the throat. Hence, in Sanskṛit and its cognate languages, the palatals *ć* and *j* are often exchanged with the gutturals *k* and *g*. See note †, p. 15.

a. ग *ga* has always the sound of *g* in *gun*, *give*, never of *g* in *gin*.

b. त *ta*, द *da* are more dental than in English, *t* being something like *t* in *stick*, and *d* like *th* in *this*; thus *veda* ought to be pronounced rather like *vetha*. But in real fact we have no sound exactly equivalent to the Indian dentals *t* and *d*. The sound of *th* in *thin*, *this*, is really dental, but, so to speak, *over-dentalised*, the tongue being forced *through* the teeth instead of *against* them. Few Englishmen acquire the correct pronunciation of the Indian dentals. They are said to be best pronounced by resting the end of the tongue against the inside of the front teeth and then suddenly removing it.

13. ट *ṭa*, ड *ḍa*. The sound of these cerebral letters is in practice hardly to be distinguished from the sound of our English *t* and *d*. Properly, however, the Sanskṛit cerebrals should be uttered with a duller and deeper intonation, produced by keeping the tongue as far back in the head (*cerebrum*) as possible—that is, it should strike the palate rather above the front gums, not as in English, the gums themselves. A Hindú, however, would always write any English word or name containing *t* and *d* with the cerebral letters. Thus such words as *trust*, *drip*, *London* would be written ट्रस्ट्, ड्रिप्, लण्डन्.

a. Observe—The cerebral letters have probably been introduced into Sanskrit through the aboriginal dialects with which it came in contact. In Bengal the cerebral ड *ḍa* and ढ *ḍha* have nearly the sound of a dull *r*. Thus विडालः *viḍālaḥ*, 'a cat,' is pronounced *virālah*. In fact in some words both ड and ढ seem interchangeable with र and ल; thus खोड्, 'to be lame,' may also be written खोट्, खोर्, खोल्. In corruptions of Sanskrit (especially in Prákrit) cerebral letters often take the place of dentals. In Sanskrit the cerebrals are rarely found at the beginning of words.

14. ख *kha*, घ *gha*, छ *ćha*, झ *jha*, ठ *ṭha*, ढ *ḍha*, थ *tha*, ध *dha*, फ *pha*, भ *bha*. These are the aspirated forms of the preceding consonants. In pronouncing them the sound of *h* must be distinctly added to the unaspirated consonantal sound. Thus ख is pronounced like *kh* in *ink-horn*, not like the Greek χ; थ as *th* in *ant-hill*, not as in *think*; फ as *ph* in *uphill*, not as in *physic*. Care must be taken not to interpolate a vowel before the aspirate. Indeed it is most important to acquire the habit of pronouncing the aspirated consonants distinctly. *Dá* and *dhá*, *prishṭa* and *prishṭha*, *stamba* and *stambha*, *kara* and *khara* have very different meanings, and are pronounced very differently. Few Englishmen pay sufficient attention to this, although the correct sound is easily attainable. The simple rule is to breathe hard while uttering the aspirated consonant, and then an aspirated sound will come out with the consonant before the succeeding vowel.

a. The Sanskrit थ *th* may be represented by τ in Greek, and ध *dh* by θ, while छ *ćh* may answer to σκ, भ *bh* to φ and *f*, or sometimes in Latin (in declension) to *b*.

b. With a view to the comparison of Sanskrit words with Greek and Latin, it is important to remember that the aspirates of the different classes are easily interchangeable in different languages; thus *dh* and *bh* in Sanskrit may be *f* (or *ph*) in Latin; *gh* in Sanskrit may be θ in Greek &c.

15. ङ *ṅa*, ञ *ña*, ण *ṇa*, न *na*, म *ma*. Each of the five classes of consonants in Sanskrit has its own nasal sound, represented by a separate nasal letter. In English and most other languages the same fivefold division of nasal sounds might be made, though we have only one nasal letter to express the guttural, palatal, cerebral, and dental nasal sounds. The truth is, that in all languages the nasal letters take their sound from the organ employed in uttering the consonant that follows them. Thus in English it will be found that guttural, palatal, cerebral, dental, and labial nasals are followed by consonants of the same classes, as in *ink*, *sing*, *inch*, *under*, *plinth*, *imp*. If such words existed in Sanskrit, the distinction of nasal

sounds would be represented by distinct letters; thus, रङ्, सिङ्, रन्, बन्नर्, सिन्न्, रम्. Compare 6.

a. It should be observed, however, that the guttural nasal ङ, which is rarely found by itself at the end of a word in Sanskrit, never at the beginning, probably has, when standing alone, the sound of *ng* in *sing*, where the sound of *g* is almost imperceptible. So that the English *sing* might be written सिङ्. This may be inferred from the fact that words like प्राञ्च् (r. 176) make in the nominative case not प्राङ्क् or प्राङ्ग्, but प्राङ्. The palatal ञ is only found in conjunction with palatal consonants, as in ञ्च *ñć*, ञ्ज *ñj*, च्ञ *ćñ*, and ज्ञ *jñ*. This last may be pronounced like *ny*, or like *gn* in the French *campagne*. In Bengal, however, it always has the sound of *gy*; thus राज्ञा is pronounced *rágyá*. The cerebral nasal ण *ṇ* is found at the beginning of words and before vowels, as well as in conjunction with cerebral consonants. It is then pronounced, as the other cerebrals, by turning the tip of the tongue rather upwards. The dental and labial nasals न *na* and म *ma* are pronounced with the same organs as the class of letters to which they belong. (See 21.)

16. य *ya*, र *ra*, ल *la*, व *va* (*antaḥstha*, see r. 22) are pronounced as in English. Their relationship to and interchangeableness with (*samprasáraṇa*) the vowels *i*, *ṛi*, *ḷṛi*, *u*, respectively, should never be forgotten. See rule 22. *a.* When व *v* is the last member of a conjunct consonant it is pronounced like *w*, as द्वार is pronounced *dwára*; but not after *r*, as सर्व *sarva*. To prevent confusion, however, व will *in all cases* be represented by *v*, thus द्वार *dvára*.

a. The character ळ *ḷa* (represented by *ḷ*) is peculiar to the Vedas. It appears to be a mixture of the ल *l* and र *r*, representing a liquid sound formed like the cerebrals by turning the tip of the tongue upwards; and it is often in the Veda a substitute for the cerebral ड when between two vowels, as ईळे is for ईडे.

b. The semivowels are so soft and vowel-like in their nature that they readily flow into each other. Hence *l* and *r* are sometimes exchangeable.

17. श *śa*, ष *sha*, स *sa*, ह *ha* (called in native grammars *úshmáṇas*). Of these, श *śa* is a palatal sibilant, and is pronounced like *sh* or like *s* in *sure*; (compounded with *r* it is sounded more like *s* in *sun*, but the pronunciation of *ś* varies in different provinces and different words.) ष *sha* is a cerebral, rather softer than our *sh*, but that its pronunciation is hardly to be distinguished from that of the palatal is proved by the number of words written indiscriminately with श or ष; as, कोश or कोष. The dental स *sa* is pronounced as the common English *s*. The same three sibilants exist in English, though represented by one character, as in the words *sure*, *session*, *sun*. ह *ha* is pronounced as in English, and is guttural.

a. The guttural origin of ह *ha* is proved by its passing into *k* at the end of Sanskrit words, and answering to χ, κ, and *c*, in Greek and Latin; as, हृदय, καρδία, *cor*. It is probably not an original letter in Sanskrit, but arose out of the soft aspirates घ, ध, भ; thus in the Veda ग्रभ् is used for ग्रह्, and in classical Sanskrit the rules of euphony frequently require the change of ह् to a soft aspirated consonant.

b. Note that श *śa*, although a palatal, might be called half a guttural. It is certainly guttural in its origin, as all the palatals are. This is well illustrated by its constantly answering to κ and *c* in Greek and Latin words. Compare अश्रु δάκρυ, अश्व *equus*, श्वन् κύων. It is moreover interchanged with क *k* in Sanskrit words.

c. According to Professor Benfey, the following are the letters of the Sanskrit alphabet, which are probably *original*, the others being either derived from them, in the development of the phonetic system, or introduced from other languages,— अ, इ, उ; क, ख, ग, घ; त, थ, द, ध; प, फ, ब, भ; न, म; य, र, व; स.

OF THE CLASSIFICATION OF LETTERS.

18. In the first arrangement of the alphabet all the consonants, excepting the semivowels, sibilants, and *h*, were distributed under the five heads of gutturals, palatals, cerebrals, dentals, and labials. We are now to show that *all the forty-seven* letters, vowels, semivowels, and consonants, may be referred to one or other of these five grand classes, according to the organ principally concerned in their pronunciation, whether the throat, the palate, the upper part of the palate, the teeth, or the lips.

a. We are, moreover, to point out that all the letters may be regarded according to another principle of division, and may be all arranged under the head of either HARD or SOFT, according as the effort of utterance is attended with expansion (*vivára*), or contraction (*saṃvára*), of the throat.

b. The following tables exhibit this twofold classification, the comprehension of which is of the utmost importance to the study of Sanskrit grammar.

Gutturals	अ *a* आ *á*	क *ka* ख *kha*	ग *ga* घ *gha*	ङ *n·a*	ह *ha*	
Palatals	इ *i* ई *í* ए *e* ऐ *ai*	च *ća* छ *ćha*	ज *ja* झ *jha*	ञ *ña*	य *ya*	श *śa*
Cerebrals	ऋ *ṛi* ॠ *ṛí*	ट *ṭa* ठ *ṭha*	ड *ḍa* ढ *ḍha*	ण *ṇa*	र *ra*	ष *sha*
Dentals	ऌ *lṛi* ॡ *lṛí*	त *ta* थ *tha*	द *da* ध *dha*	न *na*	ल *la*	स *sa*
Labials	उ *u* ऊ *ú* ओ *o* औ *au*	प *pa* फ *pha*	ब *ba* भ *bha*	म *ma*	व *va*	

The first two consonants in each of the above five classes and the sibilants are hard; all the other letters are soft, as in the following table:

HARD OR SURD LETTERS.		SOFT OR SONANT LETTERS.			
क ka* ख kha*		अ a आ á	ग ga* घ gha*	ङ ṅa	ह ha
च ća* छ ćha*	श śa	इ i ई í ए e ऐ ai	ज ja* झ jha*	ञ ña	य ya
ट ṭa* ठ ṭha*	ष sha	ऋ ri ॠ rí	ड ḍa* ढ ḍha*	ण ṇa	र ra
त ta* थ tha*	स sa	ऌ lri ॡ lrí	द da* ध dha*	न na	ल la
प pa* फ pha*		उ u ऊ ú ओ o औ au	ब ba* भ bha*	म ma	व va

Note.—Hindú grammarians begin with the letters pronounced by the organ furthest from the mouth, and so take the other organs in order, ending with the lips. This as a technical arrangement is perhaps the best, but the order of creation would be that of the Hebrew alphabet; 1st, the labials; 2d, the gutturals; 3d, the dentals.

c. Observe, that although ए *e*, ऐ *ai*, are more conveniently connected with the palatal class, and ओ *o*, औ *au*, with the labial, these letters are really diphthongal, being made up of *a* + *i*, *á* + *í*, *a* + *u*, *á* + *ú*, respectively. Their first element is therefore guttural.

d. Note also, that it is most important to observe which hard letters have kindred soft letters, and *vice versa*. The kindred hard and soft are those in the same line marked with a star in the above table; thus *g*, *gh*, are the corresponding soft letters to *k*, *kh*; *j*, *jh*, to *ć*, *ćh*, and so with the others.

In order that the foregoing classification may be clearly understood, it is necessary to remind the student of the proper meaning of the term vowel and consonant, and of the relationship which the nasals, semivowels, and sibilants, bear to the other letters.

19. A vowel is defined to be a vocal emission of breath from the lungs, modified or modulated by the play of one or other of five organs, viz. the throat, the palate, the tongue, the teeth, or the lips †, but not interrupted or stopped by the actual *contact* of any of these organs.

a. Hence अ *a*, इ *i*, उ *u*, ऋ *ri*, ऌ *lri*, with their respective long forms, are simple vowels, belonging to the guttural, palatal, labial,

† See Proposals for a Missionary Alphabet, by Prof. Max Müller.

cerebral, and dental classes respectively, according to the organ principally concerned in their modulation. But ए *e*, ऐ *ai*, ओ *o*, औ *au*, are diphthongal or compound vowels, as explained above at 18. *c*.* So that *e* and *ai* are half guttural, half palatal; *o* and *au* half guttural, half labial.

b. The vowels are of course considered to be soft letters.

20. A consonant is not the modulation, but the actual stoppage, of the vocal stream of breath by *the contact* of one or other of the five organs, and cannot be enunciated excepting in conjunction with a vowel.

a. All the consonants, therefore, are arranged under the five heads of gutturals, palatals, cerebrals, dentals, and labials, according to the organ concerned in *stopping* the vocal sound.

b. Again, the first two consonants in each of the five classes, and the sibilants, are called *hard* or *surd*, because the vocal stream is abruptly and completely interrupted, and no murmuring sound (*aghosha*) allowed to escape: while all the other letters are called *soft* or *sonant*, because the vocal sound is less suddenly and completely arrested, the effect of stopping it being attended with a low murmur (*ghosha*).

c. Observe, that as the palatal stop is only a modification of the guttural, the point of contact being moved a little more forward from the throat towards the palate †; so the cerebral (*múrdhanya*) stop is a modification of the dental, the difference being, that whereas in the dental consonantal sound the tip of the tongue is brought into direct contact with the back of the front teeth; in the cerebral it is kept more back in the mouth and curled slightly upwards, so as to strike the gums or palate above the teeth, thus producing a more obtuse sound.

d. The name *cerebral* is retained in deference to established usage. Perhaps a more correct translation of *múrdhanya* would be *supernal*, as *múrdhan* here denotes the *upper part of* the palate, and not the head or brain, which is certainly

---

* If the two vowels *a* and *i* are pronounced rapidly they naturally form the sound *e* pronounced as in *prey*, or as *a* and *i* in *sail*; and so with the other diphthongs. The sound of *ai* in *aisle* may readily be resolved into *á* and *i*, and the sound of *ou* in *out* into *á* and *u*.

† The relationship of the palatal to the guttural letters is proved by their frequent interchangeableness in Sanskrit and in other languages. See 17. *b*. and 176, and compare *church* with *kirk*, Sanskrit *čatvár* with Latin *quatuor*, Sanskrit *ča* with Latin *que* and Greek *καί*, Sanskrit *jánu* with English *knee*, Greek *γόνυ*, Latin *genu*. Some German scholars represent the palatals च and ज by *k'* and *g'*.

not the organ of enunciation of any letter. But the inaccuracy involved in the word *cerebral* hardly justifies a change of name. As these letters are pronounced chiefly with the help of the tongue, they are more appropriately called *linguals*.

21. A nasal or narisonant letter is a soft letter, in the utterance of which the vocal stream of breath incompletely arrested, as in all soft letters, is forced through the nose instead of the lips. As the soft letters are of five kinds, according to the organ which interrupts the vocal breathing, so the nasal letters are five, guttural, palatal, cerebral, dental, and labial. See 15.

22. The semivowels *y*, *r*, *l*, *v* (called *antaḥstha* because in the first arrangement of the alphabet they *stand between* the other consonants and the sibilants) are formed by a vocal breathing, which is only half interrupted, the several organs being only slightly touched by the tongue. They are, therefore, soft or sonant consonants, approaching nearly to the character of vowels; in fact, half vowels, half consonants.

a. Each class of soft letters (excepting the guttural) has its own corresponding semivowel to which it is related. Thus the palatal soft letters इ *i*, ई *í*, ए *e*, ऐ *ai*, ज *j*, have य y for their kindred semivowel. (Compare Sanskṛit *yuvan* with Latin *juvenis* &c.) Similarly र *r* is the kindred semivowel of the cerebral soft letters ऋ *ṛi*, ॠ *ṛí*, and ड *ḍ*; ल *l* of the dentals ऌ *lṛi*, ॡ *lṛí*, and द *d* *; and व *v* of उ *u*, ऊ *ú*, ओ *o*, औ *au*, and ब *b*. The guttural soft letters have no semivowel in Sanskṛit, unless the aspirate ह *h* be so regarded.

23. The sibilants or hissing sounds (called *winds* by the native grammarians) are hard letters, which, nevertheless, strictly speaking, have something the character of vowels. The organs of speech in uttering them, although not closed, are more contracted than in vowels, and the vocal stream of breath in passing through the teeth experiences a friction which causes sibilation.

a. Sanskṛit does not recognise any guttural sibilation, though the palatal sibilant is really half a guttural. See 17. *a*. The aspirate ह *h* might perhaps be regarded as a guttural *flatus* or wind without sibilating sound. The labial sibilation denoted by the letter *f*, and the soft sibilation denoted by *z*, are unknown in Sanskṛit.

b. In the *Śiva-sútras* of native grammars the letters are arranged in fourteen

---

* That ल *l* is a dental, and kindred to द *d*, is proved by its interchangeableness with *d* in cognate languages. Thus *lacryma*, δάκρυμα. Compare also दीप् with λάμπω.

groups: thus, *a i u ṇ—ṛi ḷṛi k—e o ṅ—ai au c—h y v r ṭ—l ṇ—ñ m ṅ ṇ n m—jh bh ñ—gh ḍh dh sh—j b g ḍ d ś—kh ph ch ṭh th c ṭ t v—k p y—ś sh s r—h l*. By taking the first letter of any series and joining it to the last of any other series various classes of letters are designated; thus *al* is the technical name for the whole alphabet; *hal* for all the consonants; *ac* the vowels; *ak* all the simple vowels; *aṇ* the vowels *a*, *i*, *u*, short or long; *ec* the diphthongs; *yaṇ* the semivowels; *jaś* the soft consonants *g*, *j*, *ḍ*, *d*, *b*; *jhaś* the same with their aspirates; *jhash* the soft aspirates alone; *yar* all the consonants except *h*; *jhal* all the consonants except the nasals and semivowels; *jhar* all the consonants except the aspirate, nasals, and semivowels.

ACCENTUATION.

24. Accentuation in Sanskṛit is only marked in the Vedas. Only three names for the accents are generally recognised by grammarians; viz. 1. *Udátta*, 'raised,' i. e. the elevated or high tone, marked in Roman writing by the acute accent; 2. *Anudátta*, 'not raised,' i. e. the low or grave tone; 3. *Svarita*, 'sounded,' i. e. the sustained tone, neither high nor low, but a combination of the two (*samáhára*, Páṇ. I. 2. 32) which is thus produced. In pronouncing the syllable immediately following the high-toned syllable, the voice unable to lower itself abruptly to the level of the low intonation, is sustained in a tone not so high as the *udátta*, and yet not so low as the *anudátta*. A syllable uttered with this sustained mixed intonation is said to be *svarita*, 'sounded.' These three accents, according to native grammarians, are severally produced, through intensifying, relaxing, and sustaining or throwing out the voice (*áyáma visrambha ákshepa*); and these operations are said to be connected with an upward, downward, and horizontal motion (*tiryag-gamana*) of the organs of utterance, which may be illustrated by the movements of the hand in conducting a musical performance *.

But although there are only three recognised names for the accents, there are in reality four tones. This may be proved (as Prof. Roth observes) by any one who tries to adjust the exact relationship between the sounds of the three accents above described. If they are arranged in regular musical series or progression, one link will be found wanting. The *udátta* and *svarita* are names for (so to speak) positive sounds, and the *anudátta* for negative; but the neutral, general, accentless sound, which may be compared to a flat horizontal line, and lies as it were between the positive and negative, remains undesignated.

Those grammarians, such as Páṇini, who recognise only three names for the accents, apply the name *anudátta* to this neutral accentless sound also. Hence this name becomes unsuited to the low tone, properly so called, i. e. the tone which immediately precedes the high and is lower than the flat horizontal line taken to represent the general accentless sound. The fact is that the exertion

---

* In native grammars the *udátta* sound of a vowel is said to result from employing the upper half of the organs of utterance, and the *anudátta* from employing the lower half.

required to produce the high tone (*udátta*) is so great that in order to obtain the proper pitch, the voice is obliged to lower the tone of the preceding syllable as much below this flat line as the syllable that bears the *udátta* is raised above it; and Páṇini himself explains this lower tone by the term *sannatara* (for which the commentators have substituted the expression *anudáttatara*), while he explains the neutral accentless tone by the term *eka-śruti* (called in the Prátiśákhyas *pracaya* or *pracita*), i. e. the one monotonous sound in which the ear can perceive no variation. We have therefore really *four* tones in Sanskṛit, and *four* expressions are now usually adopted to correspond. The name *anudátta* is confined to the neutral, indifferent, accentless or monotonous tone represented by the flat horizontal line. The expression *anudáttatara* has been adopted to designate the lowest sound of all or that immediately preceding the *udátta*, while the *svarita* (which in some respects corresponds with the Greek circumflex) denotes the mixed sustained sound which follows the *udátta*.

25. The three accents are thus marked in the Ṛig-veda.

When a syllable having a horizontal mark underneath (*anudáttatara*) is followed by one bearing no mark, the one bearing no mark is *udátta*; and when followed by two syllables, bearing no mark, both are *udátta*.

The *svarita* accent is denoted by a small perpendicular stroke above the syllable. Thus in the word [illegible] the syllable [illegible] is *anudáttatara*, [illegible] is *udátta*, and [illegible] is *svarita*.

In the Pada text (if *anudáttatara* be admitted) the horizontal stroke under a syllable may mark both the *anudátta* or neutral tone, and the *anudáttatara* or low tone; and if it extend under all the syllables of the same word, the whole word is *anudátta* accentless, thus [illegible]. In the Saṃhitá, the stroke underneath marks the *anudáttatara* and all such *anudátta* syllables as precede the first *anudáttatara* syllable, but in the remainder of the sentence the absence of accent (*anudátta*) is denoted by the absence of all mark after the *svarita* until the next *anudáttatara*.

In fact all the syllables (in a word or sentence) which follow the *svarita* are supposed to be pronounced in the accentless tone until the *anudáttatara* mark under a syllable appears again; so that the absence of mark may denote both *udátta* and *anudátta*. Properly, therefore, the *anudáttatara* mark is the beginning of a series of three accents, of which the *svarita* is the end; the appearance of this mark preparing the reader for an *udátta* immediately following, and a *svarita*. The latter, however, may sometimes be retarded by a new *udátta* syllable. Moreover, the *svarita* mark does not always imply an *anudáttatara* mark preceding, as in the word [illegible] at the beginning of a line, where the *svarita* merely shows that the first syllable is *udátta*. Again, in the Pada, where each word stands separately, there may be no *svarita* following an *udátta*, as [illegible] । [illegible]. It must also be borne in mind that where a *svarita* is immediately followed by an *udátta* syllable, the *svarita* becomes changed to *anudáttatara*: thus in दिवा [illegible] the *svarita* of [illegible] becomes so changed, because of the *udátta* following.

Again, as to the *svarita* mark, it may either indicate a dependent *svarita*, or an independent, i. e. either a *svarita* produced by an *udátta* immediately preceding, or a *svarita* produced by the suppression of a syllable bearing the *udátta*, as in कन्या contracted from कनिया, where the middle syllable is properly *udátta*. In the latter case, if the syllable bearing the *svarita* is long, and another word follows beginning with an *udátta*, then that syllable and all preceding syllables in the same word receive the *anudáttatara* mark, and the figure ३ is inserted to carry the *svarita*, having also the *anudáttatara* mark beneath; thus कन्या ३ सम. If the syllable bearing the independent *svarita* be short, then the figure १ carries the *svarita*, with an *anudáttatara* under it; thus अप्स्व१न्तर्.

Observe—The accent in Sanskrit is not confined to the last three syllables of a word, as in Greek and Latin. Observe also, that although the Sanskrit independent *svarita* is in some respects similar to the Greek circumflex, it should be borne in mind, that the latter is confined to long syllables, whereas the *svarita* may also be applied to short *.

OF THE INDIAN METHOD OF WRITING.

26. According to Hindú grammarians every syllable ought to end in a vowel †, and every final consonant ought to be attracted to the beginning of the next syllable; so that where a word ends in a consonant, that consonant ought to be pronounced with the initial letter of the next word. Hence in some Sanskrit MSS. all the syllables are separated by slight spaces, and in others all the words are joined together without any separation. Thus the two words आसीद् राजा *ásíd rájá* would in some books be written आ सी द्रा जा and in others आसीद्राजा. In Sanskrit works printed in Europe, the common practice is to separate only those words the final or initial letter of which are not acted on by the rules of combination. In such books *ásíd rájá* would be written together, आसीद्राजा, because the final द् is the result of an euphonic change from त्, caused by the following र् *r*. There seems, however, but little reason for considering the mere spaces left between the words of a sentence to be incompatible with the operation of euphonic laws; especially as the

* See on the subject of Vedic accentuation, Roth's preface to the Nirukta: two treatises by Whitney in the Journal of the American Oriental Society, vol. IV. p. 195 etc., and V. p. 387 etc.; *Aufrecht*, de accentu compositorum Sanscriticorum, Bonnae, 1847; reviewed by *Benfey*, Göttinger Gelehrte Anzeigen, 1848, p. 1995—2010.

† Unless it end in Anusvára or Visarga *ḥ*, which in theory are the only consonantal sounds allowed to close a syllable. That Anusvára is not a full consonant is proved by the fact that it does not impede the operation of rule 70.

absence of such spaces must always cause more or less impediment even to the fluent reader. Therefore in many books recently printed in Europe, every uncompounded word capable of separation by the use of the Viráma is separated. Thus *pitur dhanam ádadáti* is written पितुर् धनम् आददाति, and not पितुर्धनमाददाति. The only cases in which separation is undesirable, are where the final vowel of one word blends with the initial vowel of the next into one long similar or dissimilar vowel, and where final *u* and *i* are changed into their corresponding semivowels *v* and *y*.

The following words and passages in the Sanskṛit and English character, are given that the Student, before proceeding further in the Grammar, may exercise himself in reading the letters and in transliteration; that is to say, in turning Sanskṛit letters into the English equivalents, and *vice versa*.

To be turned into English letters.

अक, अज, अण, आस, आप, इल, इष, ईड, ईर, उख, उच, ऊह, ऋण, ऋज, एध, ओख, कण, कित, कुमार, क्षम, क्षिप, क्षुध, क्षै, क्लृप, खन, खिद, गाह, गुज, गृध, गॄ, घृण, घुष, चकास, चक्ष, चित, छिद, छो, जीवा, झष, टीका, ठः, डीनं, ढौक, णिद, तापः, तडागः, दया, दमकः, दशरथः, दुरालापः, देव, धूमिका, धृतः, नदः, नील, नेम, परिदानं, पुरुषस्, पौरः, पौरु-षेयी, पुरोडाशः, बहुः, बालकस्, भोगः, भोजनं, मुखं, मृगः, मेदस्, मेदिनी, यकृत्, योगः, रेणु, रेचक, रै, रैवत, रुजा, रूपं, रुरुदिषु, लोह, वामः, वैरं, शक्, शौरः, षट्, साधुः, हेमकूटः, हेमन्.

To be turned into Sanskṛit letters.

Ada, asa, ali, ádi, ákhu, ágas, iti, íśah, íhá, uddra, upanishad, uparodha, úru, úsha, ṛishi, eka, kakud, kaṭu, koshaḥ, gaura, ghaṭa, ćaitya, ćet, ćhalam, jetṛi, jhirí, ṭagara, ḍamara, ḍhála, ṇama, talas, tathá, tṛiṇa, tushára, deha, daitya, dhavala, nanu, nayanam, nidánam, pitṛi, bhauma, bheshajam, marus, mahat, yuga, rush, rádhis, śauka, vivekas, śatam, shoḍaśan, sukhin, hṛidaya, tatra, adya, buddhi, arka, kratu, aṃsa, aṅ-ka, aṅ-ga, aṅćala, añjana, kaṇṭha, aṇḍa, anta, manda, sampúrṇa.

The following story has the Sanskrit and English letters interlineated.

अस्ति हस्तिनापुरे विलासो नाम रजकः । तस्य गर्द-
asti hastinápure viláso náma rajakaḥ tasya garda-

भो ऽतिभारवाहनाद् दुर्बलो मुमूर्षुर् अभवत् । ततस् तेन
bho 'tibháraváhanád durbalo mumúrshur abhavat tatas tena

रजकेनासौ व्याघ्रचर्मणा प्रच्छाद्यारण्यसमीपे शस्यक्षेत्रे
rajakenásau vyághraćarmaṇá praćhádyáraṇyasamípe śasyakshetre

मोचितः । ततो दूराद् अवलोक्य व्याघ्रबुद्ध्या क्षेत्रप-
moćitaḥ tato dúrád avalokya vyághrabuddhyá kshetrapa-

तयः सत्वरं पलायन्ते । अथ केनापि शस्यरक्षकेण धूसर-
tayaḥ satvaraṃ paláyante atha kenápi śasyarakshakeṇa dhúsara-

कम्बलकृततनुत्राणेन धनुःकाण्डं सज्जीकृत्यावनतकायेन
kambalakṛitatanutráṇena dhanuḥkáṇḍam sajjíkṛityávanatakáyena

एकान्ते स्थितं । ततस् तं च दूरे दृष्ट्वा गर्दभः पुष्टाङ्गो
ekánte sthitam tatas tam ća dúre dṛishṭvá gardabhaḥ pushṭáṅ-go

गर्दभीयमिति मत्वा शब्दं कुर्वाणस् तदभिमुखं धावितः ।
gardabhíyamiti matvá śabdam kurváṇas tadabhimukham dhávitaḥ

ततस् तेन शस्यरक्षकेण गर्दभो ऽयमिति ज्ञात्वा लीलयैव
tatas tena śasyarakshakeṇa gardabho 'yamiti jñátvá líayaiva

व्यापादितः ॥
vyápáditaḥ

The following story is to be turned into Sanskrit letters.

Asti śríparvatamadhye brahmapurákhyam nagaram. Tatra śaila-śikhare ghaṇṭákarṇo náma rákshasaḥ prativasatíti janapraváḍaḥ śrú-yate. Ekadá ghaṇṭám ádáya paláyamánaḥ kaśćić ćauro vyághreṇa vyápáditaḥ. Tatpáṇipatitá ghaṇṭá vánaraiḥ práptá. Te vánarás táṃ ghaṇṭám anukshaṇam vádayanti. Tato nagarajanair manushyaḥ khádito dṛishṭaḥ pratikshaṇaṃ ghaṇṭáravaśća śrúyate. Anantaraṃ ghaṇṭákarṇaḥ kupito manushyán khádati ghaṇṭáṃ ća vádayati ity-uktvá janáḥ sarve nagarát paláyitáḥ. Tataḥ karálayá náma kuṭṭinyá vimṛiśya markaṭá ghaṇṭáṃ vádayanti svayaṃ vijñáya rájá vijñápitaḥ. Deva yadi kiyaddhanopakshayaḥ kriyate tadáham enaṃ ghaṇṭákarṇaṃ sádhayámi. Tato rájñá tushṭena tasyai dhanaṃ dattam. Kuṭṭinyá ća maṇḍalaṃ kṛitvá tatra gaṇeśádigauravaṃ darśayitvá svayaṃ vánarapriyaphaláṇyádáya vanam praviśya phaláṇyákírṇáni. Tato ghaṇṭám parityajya vánaráḥ phalásaktá babhúvuḥ. Kuṭṭiní ća ghaṇṭáṃ gṛihítvá nagaram ágatá sakalalokapújyábhavat.

Observe, that Anusvára at the end of a word, when a consonant follows, is most conveniently transliterated by ṃ, and *vice versâ*; thus, *brahmapurábhyaṃ nagaraṃ* ब्रह्मपुराभ्यं नगरं. Strictly, however, the ṃ, being influenced by the following n, is equivalent in sound to n, and the two words might have been written *brahmapurá-bhyan nagaraṃ* ब्रह्मपुराभ्यन् नगरं. Similarly, *pratikshaṇaṃ* before *ghaṇṭáravas* is written प्रतिक्षणं *pratikshaṇaṃ*, though equivalent in sound to प्रतिक्षणङ् *pratiksha-ṇaṅ*, in consequence of the following घ.

CHAPTER II.

SANDHI OR EUPHONIC COMBINATION OF LETTERS.

We are accustomed in Greek and Latin to certain euphonic changes of letters. Thus *rego* makes, in the perfect, not *regsi*, but *reksi* (*rexi*), the soft *g* being changed to the hard *k* before the hard *s*. Similarly, *veho* becomes *veksi* (*vexi*). In many words a final consonant assimilates with an initial; thus *συν* with *γνώμη* becomes *συγγνώμη*; *ἐν* with *λάμπω*, *ἐλλάμπω*. *Suppressus* is written for *subpressus*; *appellatus* for *adpellatus*; *immensus* for *inmensus*; *affinitas* for *adfinitas*; *offero* for *obfero*, but in perfect *obtuli*; *colloquium* for *conloquium*; *irrogo* for *inrogo*. These laws for the euphonic junction of letters are applied throughout the whole range of Sanskṛit grammar; and that, too, not only in uniting different parts of one word, but in combining words in the same sentence. Thus, if the sentence "*Rara avis in terris*" were Sanskṛit, it would require, by the laws of Sandhi or combination, to be written *Rarávir ins terriḥ*; and might even be joined together thus, *Raráviriṁsterriḥ*. The learner must not be discouraged if he is unable to understand *all* the laws of combination at first. He is recommended, after reading those that are printed in large type, to pass at once to the declension of nouns and conjugation of verbs. To attempt to commit to memory a number of rules, the use of which is not fully seen till he comes to read and construct *sentences*, must only lead to a loss of time and patience.

Sect. I.—CHANGES OF VOWELS.

27. It is to be observed that there are two distinct classes of rules of Sandhi; viz. 1. Those affecting the final or initial letters of complete words in a sentence; 2. Those which take effect in the *formation* of words by the junction of roots or crude bases with affixes or terminations. Of the latter, those which come into operation in the formation of *verbs*, are reserved till they are wanted (see rule 294), but those which come into immediate application in the formation and declension of nouns will be explained here; and amongst these, the changes of vowels called Guṇa and Vṛiddhi should be impressed on the memory, before another step is taken in the study of the Grammar. When the vowels इ *i* and ई *í* are changed to ए *e*, this is called the Guṇa change, or *qualification*; when *i* and *í* are changed to ऐ *ai*, this is called the Vṛiddhi change, or *increase* *. Similarly, उ *u* and ऊ *ú* are often changed to their Guṇa ओ *o*, and Vṛiddhi औ *au*; ऋ *ṛi* and ॠ *ṛí* to their Guṇa अर् *ar*, and Vṛiddhi आर् *ár*; and अ *a*, though it have no corresponding Guṇa change, has a Vṛiddhi substitute in आ *á*.

a. Observe—Native grammarians consider that *a* is already a Guṇa letter, and on that account can have no Guṇa substitute. Indeed they regard *a*, *e*, *o* as the only Guṇa sounds, and *á*, *ai*, *au* as the only Vṛiddhi; *a* and *á* being the real Guṇa and Vṛiddhi representatives of the vowels ऋ and ऌ. It is required, however, that *r* should always be connected with *a* and *á* when these vowels are substituted for *ṛi*; and *l*, when they are substituted for *ḷṛi*.

28. Let the student, therefore, never forget the following rules.

---

* गुण *guṇa* in Sanskṛit means 'quality,' and वृद्धि *vṛiddhi*, 'increase.' It will be convenient to Anglicise these words.

There is no Guṇa substitute for अ *a*, but आ *á* is the Vṛiddhi substitute for अ *a*; ए *e* is the Guṇa, and ऐ *ai* the Vṛiddhi, for इ *i* and ई *í*; ओ *o* is the Guṇa, and औ *au* the Vṛiddhi, for उ *u* and ऊ *ú*; अर् *ar* is the Guṇa, and आर् *ár* the Vṛiddhi, for ऋ *ṛi* and ॠ *ṛí*; अल् *al* is the Guṇa, and आल् *ál* the Vṛiddhi, for ऌ *lṛi* and ॡ *lṛí*. Moreover, ऐ *ai* is the Vṛiddhi of the Guṇa ए *e*, and औ *au* the Vṛiddhi of the Guṇa ओ *o*.

a. Observe—It will be convenient in describing the change of a vowel to its Guṇa or Vṛiddhi substitute, to speak of that vowel as *gunated* or *vriddhied*.

b. But in the formation of bases, whether for declension or conjugation, the vowels of roots cannot be gunated or vriddhied, if they are followed by double consonants, i. e. if they are long by position; nor can a vowel long by nature be so changed, *unless it be final*. The vowel अ *a* is of course incapable of Guṇa. See 27. *a*.

29. Again, let him bear in mind that the Guṇa sounds ए *e*, ओ *o* are diphthongal, that is, composed of two simple vowel sounds. Thus, ए *e* is made up of अ *a* and इ *i*; ओ *o* of अ *a* and उ *u*; so that a final अ *a* will naturally coalesce with an initial इ *i* into ए *e*; with an initial उ *u* into ओ *o*. Again, अर् *ar* may be regarded as made up of अ *a* and ऋ *ṛi*; so that a final अ *a* will blend with an initial ऋ *ṛi* into अर् *ar*. Compare 18. *c*.

a. Similarly, the Vṛiddhi diphthong ऐ *ai* is made up of *a* and *e*, or (which is really the same) *á* and *i*; and औ *au* of *a* and *o*, or (which is really the same) *á* and *u*. Hence, a final *a* will naturally blend with an initial ए *e* into ऐ *ai*; and with an initial ओ *o* into औ *au*. Compare 18. *c*; and see the note to the table in the next page. It is to be observed, that the simple vowels in their diphthongal unions are not very closely combined, so that *e*, *o*, *ai*, *au* are constantly liable to be resolved into their constituent simple elements.

b. If *ai* is composed of *á* and *i*, it may be asked, How is it that long *á* as well as short *a* blends with *i* into *e* (see 32), and not into *ai*? In answer to this, Professor Bopp (Comparative Grammar, p. 2) maintains that a long vowel at the end of a word naturally shortens itself before an initial vowel. His opinion is, that the very meaning of Guṇa is the prefixing of short *a*, and the very meaning of Vṛiddhi, the prefixing of long *á*, to a simple vowel. He therefore holds that the Guṇa of *i* is originally *a i*, though the two simple vowels blend afterwards into *e*. Similarly, the original Guṇa of *u* is *a u*, blending afterwards into *o*; the original Guṇa of *ṛi* is *a ṛi*, blending into *ar*.

c. Hence it appears, that, since the Sanskṛit *a* answers to the Greek ε or ο (see 11. *f*), the practice of gunating vowels is not peculiar to Sanskṛit alone. The Sanskṛit एमि *emi*, 'I go,' which in the plural becomes इमस् *imas*, is originally *a i mi*, corresponding to the Greek εἶμι and ἴμεν. Similarly in Greek, the root φυγ (ἔφυγον) is in the present φεύγω. Compare also the Sanskṛit *veda* (*vaida*), 'he knows,' with Greek οἶδα; and compare λέλοιπα, perfect of λιπ, with the Sanskṛit 2d preterite.

30. Again, let him never forget that य *y* is the kindred semivowel of इ *i*, ई *í*, ए *e*, and ऐ *ai*; व *v* of उ *u*, ऊ *ú*, ओ *o*, and औ *au*; र *r* of ऋ *ṛi* and ॠ *ṛí*; and ल *l* of ऌ *ḷṛi* and ॡ *ḷṛí*. So that *i*, *í*, *e*, *ai*, at the end of words, when the next begins with a vowel, may often pass into *y*, *y*, *ay*, *áy*, respectively; *u*, *ú*, *o*, *au*, into *v*, *v*, *av*, *áv*; and *ṛi*, *ṛí*, into *r*; just as in English we often use *y* for *i* in *holy*, and *w* for *u* in *cow*, *now*, &c. [NB. *ḷṛí* is not found as a final.]

In order to impress the above rules on the mind, the substance of them is embodied in the following table:

Simple vowels,	*a* or *á*	*i* or *í*	*u* or *ú*	*ṛi* or *ṛí*	*ḷṛi* or *ḷṛí*
Guṇa substitute,		*e*	*o*	*ar*	*al*
Vṛiddhi substitute,	*á*	*ai*	*au*	*ár*	*ál*
Simple vowels,		*i* or *í*	*u* or *ú*	*ṛi* or *ṛí*	*ḷṛi* or *ḷṛí*
Corresponding semivowel,		*y*	*v*	*r*	*l*
Guṇa,		*e*	*o*		
Guṇa resolved,		*a* + *i*	*a* + *u*		
With semivowel substitute,		*ay*	*av*		
Vṛiddhi,		*ai*	*au*		
Vṛiddhi resolved,		*a* + *e*	*a* + *o*		
		a + *a* + *i*	*a* + *a* + *u*		
		**á* + *i*	**á* + *u*		
With semivowel substitute,		*áy*	*áv*		

* Since *e* = *a* + *i* and *o* = *a* + *u*, therefore *a* + *e* will equal *a* + *a* + *i* or *á* + *i* and *a* + *o* will equal *a* + *a* + *u* or *á* + *u*.

The succeeding rules will now explain themselves. They all result from the law that euphony abhors a hiatus between vowels; see, however, note to r. 66.

31. अ *a* or आ *á*, followed by the similar vowels अ *a* or आ *á*, blends into one long similar vowel: thus

न + अस्ति *na* + *asti* becomes नास्ति *násti*, 'there is not.'

जीवा + अन्त *jívá* + *anta* = जीवान्त *jívánta*, 'the end of life.'

a. The same rule applies to the other vowels, इ *i*, उ *u*, ऋ *ṛi*, short or long: thus

अधि + ईश्वर *adhi* + *íśvara* becomes अधीश्वर *adhíśvara*, 'the supreme lord.'

ऋतु + उत्सव *ṛitu* + *utsava* = ऋतूत्सव *ṛitútsava*, 'the festival of the season.'

पितृ + ऋद्धि *pitṛi* + *ṛiddhi* = पितृद्धि *pitṛiddhi*, 'the father's prosperity.'

32. अ *a* or आ *á*, followed by the dissimilar vowels इ *i*, उ *u*, ऋ *ṛi*, short or long, blends with *i* or *í* into the Guṇa ए *e*; with *u* or *ú* into the Guṇa ओ *o**; with *ṛi* or *ṛí* into the Guṇa अर् *ar*: thus

परम + ईश्वर *parama* + *íśvara* becomes परमेश्वर *parameśvara*, 'the mighty lord.'

हित + उपदेश *hita* + *upadeśa* = हितोपदेश *hitopadeśa*, 'friendly instruction.'

गङ्गा + उदक *gangá* + *udaka* = गङ्गोदक *gan-godaka*, 'Ganges-water.'

तव + ऋद्धि *tava* + *ṛiddhi* = तवर्द्धि *tavarddhi*, 'thy growth.'

महा + ऋषि *mahá* + *ṛishi* = महर्षि *maharshi*, 'a great sage.'

Similarly, तव + ऌकार *tava* + *ḷikára* becomes तवल्कार *tavalkára*, 'thy letter ḷi.'

33. अ *a* or आ *á*, followed by the dissimilar vowels ए *e*, ओ *o*, ऐ *ai*, or औ *au*, blends with *e* into the Vṛiddhi *ai*; with *ai* also into *ai*; with *o* into the Vṛiddhi *au*; with *au* also into *au*: thus

पर + एधित *para* + *edhita* becomes परैधित *paraidhita*, 'nourished by another.'

विद्या + एव *vidyá* + *eva* = विद्यैव *vidyaiva*, 'knowledge indeed.'

देव + ऐश्वर्य *deva* + *aiśvarya* = देवैश्वर्य *devaiśvarya*, 'divine majesty.'

* The blending of *a* and *i* into the sound *e* is recognised in English in such words as *sail*, *nail*, &c.; and the blending of *a* and *u* into the sound *o* is exemplified by the French *faute*, *baume*, &c.

अल्प + ओजस् *alpa + ojas* = अल्पौजस् *alpaujas*, 'little energy.'

गङ्गा + ओघ *gangá + ogha* = गङ्गौघ *gangaugha*, 'the torrent of the Ganges.'

ज्वर + औषध *jwara + aushadha* = ज्वरौषध *jwaraushadha*, 'fever-medicine.'

34. इ *i*, उ *u*, ऋ *ṛi* (short or long), followed by any dissimilar vowel, pass into their kindred semivowels; viz. *i* or *í* into *y**; *u* or *ú* into *v**; *ṛi* or *ṛí* into *r*: thus

अग्नि + अस्त्र *agni + astra* becomes अग्न्यस्त्र *agnyastra**, 'fire-arms.'

प्रति + उवाच *prati + uváća* = प्रत्युवाच *pratyuváća*, 'he spoke in reply.'

तु + इदानीम् *tu + idáním* = त्विदानीम् *twidáním**, 'but now.'

मातृ + आनन्द *mátṛi + ánanda* = मात्रानन्द *mátránanda*, 'the mother's joy.'

35. Final ए *e* and ओ *o*, followed by अ *a*, *initial in another word*, remain unchanged, and the initial अ *a* is cut off: thus

ते + अपि *te + api* becomes तेऽपि *te'pi*, 'they indeed.' (See 10.)

सो + अपि *so + api* = सोऽपि *so'pi*, 'he indeed.'

36. But followed by any other vowel (except अ *a*), *initial in another word*, are changed to *ay* and *av* respectively; and the *y* of *ay*, and more rarely the *v* of *av*, may be dropped, leaving the *a* uninfluenced by the following vowel: thus

ते + आगताः *te + ágatáḥ* becomes तयागताः *tayágatáḥ*, and then त आगताः *ta ágatáḥ*, 'they have come.'

Similarly, विष्णो + इह *vishṇo + iha* becomes विष्णविह *vishṇaviha*, and then विष्ण इह *vishṇa iha*, 'O Vishṇu, here!'

a. And in the case of ए *e* and ओ *o* followed by vowels *in the same word*, &c., even though the following vowel be अ *a* or ए *e* or ओ *o*, then *e* must still be changed to *ay*, and *o* to *av*, and both *y* and *v* must be retained: thus

जे + अति *je + ati* becomes जयति *jayati*, 'he conquers†.'

अग्ने + ए *agne + e* = अग्नये *agnaye*, 'to fire.'

---

* So in English we pronounce a word like *million* as if written *millyon*; and we write *evangelist* for *euangelist*.

† In English we respect this law in writing, though not in pronouncing such words as *saying*, *playing*, &c.

भो + अति *bho + ati* = भवति *bhavati*, 'he is.'

गो + ईश्वर *go + íśvara* = गवीश्वर *gavíśvara*, 'owner of kine.'

गो + ओकस् *go + okas* = गवोकस् *gavokas*, 'the abode of cattle.'

37. ऐ *ai* and औ *au*, followed by any vowel, similar or dissimilar, are changed to *áy* and *áv* respectively: thus

कस्मै + अपि *kasmai + api* becomes कस्मायपि *kasmáyapi*, 'to any one whatever.'

रै + अः *rai + aḥ* = रायः *ráyaḥ*, 'riches.'

ददौ + अन्नं *dadau + annam* = ददावन्नं *dadávannam*, 'he gave food.'

नौ + औ *nau + au* = नावौ *návau*, 'two ships.'

a. If both the words be complete words, the *y* and *v* are occasionally dropped, but not so usually as in the case of *e* at 36: thus कस्मा अपि *kasmá api* for कस्मायपि *kasmáyapi*, and ददा अन्नं *dadá annam* for ददावन्नं *dadávannam*.

38. There are some exceptions (usually called *pragṛihya*, 'to be taken out') to the above rules. The most noticeable is that of the dual, whether of nouns or verbs, ending in *í*, *ú*, or *e*. These are not acted on by following vowels: thus

हरी एतौ *harí etau*, 'these two Haris.'

विष्णू इमौ *vishṇú imau*, 'these two Vishṇus;' अमू आसाते 'these two are present;' पचेते इमौ 'these two cook;' शेवहे आवां 'we two lie down.'

The same applies to अमी *amí*, nom. pl. m. of the pronoun अदस्.

Prolated vowels remain unchanged, as आगच्छ कृष्ण ३ अत्र 'Come, Kṛishṇa, here,' &c.

a. A vocative case in *o*, when followed by the particle *iti*, may remain unchanged, as विष्णो इति *vishṇo iti*, or may follow 36.

b. Particles, when simple vowels, and आ *á* and ओ *o*, as the finals of interjections, remain unchanged, as इ इन्द्र *i indra*, 'O, Indra!' उ उमेश *u umeśa*, 'O, lord of Umá!' आ एवं *á evam*, 'Ah, indeed!' अहो इन्द्र *aho indra*, 'Ho, Indra!'

c. The ओ *o* of गो *go*, 'a cow,' may become अव *ava* in certain cases, as गो + इन्द्र *go+indra* becomes गवेन्द्र *gavendra*, 'lord of kine;' and अव् *av* in others, as गव्य *gavya*, 'relating to cows.'

d. Except the following from r. 32: अक्ष + ऊहिनी = अक्षौहिणी 'a complete army;' प्र + ऊह = प्रौह 'a good argument;' प्र + ऊढ = प्रौढ 'proud;' सुख + ऋत = सुखार्त 'influenced by joy' [but सुखेन + ऋत = regularly सुखेनर्त]; प्र + ऋण = प्रार्ण 'principal debt.' Similarly, कम्बल + ऋण 'debt of a blanket;' वसन + ऋण 'debt of a cloth;' ऋण + ऋण 'debt of a debt, compound interest.'

e. Except also from r. 32, प्र + ऋच्छति = प्रार्च्छति 'he goes on,' and उप + ऋच्छति = उपार्च्छति 'he approaches.' Compare 260. *a.*

f. The ऊ *ú* which takes the place of the वा of वाह् in the acc. pl. of such words as प्रष्ठवाह्, 'a steer training for the plough,' requires Vṛiddhi after *a*, as प्रष्ठौहः.

g. The उ *u* of किमु may remain or be changed to व् *v* before a vowel, as किमु उक्तं or किम्वुक्तं 'whether said.'

h. According to Śákalya, *a, i, u, ṛi* (short or long), final in a word, may optionally either remain unchanged (but a long vowel must be shortened) before a word beginning with ऋ or follow the usual rule, thus ब्रह्म + ऋषि or even ब्रह्मा + ऋषि 'a Brahman who is a Ṛishi' may be either ब्रह्मऋषि or ब्रह्मर्षि, but in no case ब्रह्मा ऋषि. So in the case of *í* or *ú* or *ṛí*, final in a word, followed by dissimilar vowels, thus चक्री + अत्र is either चक्रिअत्र or चक्र्यत्र 'the discus armed here.' But compounded words follow the usual rule, as नदी + उदक = नद्युदक 'the water of the river.'

i. Verbs beginning with ए or ओ do not generally blend these vowels with the final *a* of a preceding preposition, but cut it off; see rule 783. *k.* and *p.* [But उप + एति makes regularly उपैति 'he approaches,' and उप + एधते = उपैधते 'he increases.']

j. The particle इव when it denotes uncertainty is said to have the same effect on a preceding final *a*.

k. The words ओतु 'a cat' and ओष्ठ 'the lip' may optionally have the same effect, and दिव + ओकस् may be either दिवौकस् or दिवोकस् 'a deity.'

l. So also the sacred syllable ओम् and the preposition आ *á* may have the same effect, as शिवाय + ओं नमः = शिवायों नमः 'Om! reverence to Śiva,' and शिव + एहि (i. e. आ with इहि) = शिवेहि 'O Śiva, come!'

m. The following words illustrate the same irregularity: शक + अन्धु = शकन्धु 'a pot-herb;' कर्क + अन्धु = कर्कन्धु 'jujube;' लाङ्गल + ईषा = लाङ्गलीषा 'plough-handle;' मार्त + अण्ड = मार्तण्ड 'the sun;' मनस् + ईषा = मनीषा 'intellect.'

The following table exhibits all the combinations of vowels at one view. Supposing a word to end in *í*, and the next word to begin with *au*, the student must carry his eye down the first column (headed "final vowels") till he comes to *í*, and then along the top horizontal line of "initial vowels," till he comes to *au*. At the junction of the perpendicular column under *au* and the horizontal line beginning *í*, will be the required combination, viz. *y au*.

INITIAL VOWELS.	1 a	2 á	3 i	4 í	5 u	6 ú	7 ṛi	8 ṛí	9 e	10 ai	11 o	12 au
FINAL VOWELS.												
a or á	á 31	á 31	e 32	e 32	o 32	o 32	ar 32	ar 32	ai 33	ai 33	au 33	au 33
i or í	y a 34	y á 34	í 31. a.	í 31. a.	y u 34	y ú 34	y ṛi 34	y ṛí 34	y e 34	y ai 34	y o 34	y au 34
u or ú	v a 34	v á 34	v i 34	v í 34	ú 31. a.	ú 31. a.	v ṛi 34	v ṛí 34	v e 34	v ai 34	v o 34	v au 34
ṛi or ṛí	r a 34	r á 34	r i 34	r í 34	r u 34	r ú 34	ṛí 31. a.	ṛí 31. a.	r e 34	r ai 34	r o 34	r au 34
e 35, 36	e ’	a á	a i	a í	a u	a ú	a ṛi	a ṛí	a e	a ai	a o	a au
36. a.	ay a	ay á	ay i	ay í	ay u	ay ú	ay ṛi	ay ṛí	ay e	ay ai	ay o	ay au
ai 37	áy † a	áy á	áy i	áy í	áy u	áy ú	áy ṛi	áy ṛí	áy e	áy ai	áy o	áy au
o 35, 36	o * ’	av † á	av i	av í	av u	av ú	av ṛi	av ṛí	av e	av ai	av o	av au
au 37	áv † a	áv á	áv i	áv í	áv u	áv ú	áv ṛi	áv ṛí	áv e	áv ai	áv o	áv au

Observe, that in the above table the final letter, in its changed state, has been printed, for greater clearness, separate from the initial; except in those cases where the blending of the two vowels made this impossible.

* If the initial a belong to a termination, affix, &c., and not to a complete word, then a is not cut off, and o becomes av before it. See 36. a.

† If both the words are complete words, the y and v may be dropped throughout, but not so usually as in the case of e.

Sect. II.—CHANGES OF CONSONANTS.

39. Before proceeding to the combination of consonants, let the letters be again regarded as divided into two grand classes of Hard and Soft, as explained at 20. *b*.

HARD OR SURD.			SOFT OR SONANT.							
k	*kh*		*g*	*gh*	*ṅ*	*h*	*a*	*á*		
ć	*ćh*	*ś*	*j*	*jh*	*ñ*	*y*	*i*	*í*	*e*	*ai*
ṭ	*ṭh*	*sh*	*ḍ*	*ḍh*	*ṇ*	*r*	*ṛi*	*ṛí*		
t	*th*	*s*	*d*	*dh*	*n*	*l*	*ḷri*	*ḷrí*		
p	*ph*		*b*	*bh*	*m*	*v*	*u*	*ú*	*o*	*au*

Note—In the following rules it may generally be observed, that final consonants have a tendency to adapt themselves to initial, rather than initial to final.

GENERAL RULES.

40. If two hard or two soft consonants come in contact, there is generally no change; and similarly, if a soft consonant ends a word, when a vowel follows: thus

विद्युत् प्रकाशते *vidyut prakáśate*, 'the lightning shines.'
कुमुद् विकसति *kumud vikasati*, 'the lotus blossoms.'
दृषद् अधोगच्छति *dṛishad adhogaćchhati*, 'the rock descends.'
विद्युत् + सु *vidyut* + *su* = विद्युत्सु *vidyutsu*, 'in lightnings.'

a. Observe, however, that the unaspirated form of a final letter is substituted for the aspirated, as चित्रलिख् + करोति *ćitralikh* + *karoti* becomes चित्रलिक् करोति *ćitralik karoti*, 'the painter forms;' and similarly, if two aspirated letters come in contact, the first must be written in the unaspirated form (see 5. *a*).

41. If any hard letter ends a word when any soft initial letter follows, the hard (unless affected by some special rule) is changed to its own unaspirated soft (but see paragraph *b*, next page): thus

वाक् + देवी *vák* + *deví* becomes वाग्देवी *vágdeví*, 'the goddess of eloquence.'
वाक् + ईश *vák* + *íśa* = वागीश *vágíśa*, 'the lord of speech.'

चित्रलिख् + लिखति *ćitralikh + likhati* = चित्रलिग् लिखति *ćitralig likhati*, 'the painter paints.'

विट् + भव *viṭ + bhava* = विड्भव *viḍbhava*, 'generated by filth.'

प्राट् + विवाक *práṭ + viváka* = प्राड्विवाक *práḍ-viváka*, 'a judge.'

a. There is an option allowed before nasals; that is, when two words come together, the initial of the second word being a nasal, then the final of the first word is usually (though not necessarily *) changed to the nasal of its own class: thus

वाच् + मय *vák + maya* becomes वाङ्मय *váṅ-maya*, 'full of words.'

विट् + मय *viṭ + maya* = विण्मय *viṇmaya*, 'full of filth.'

चित् + मय *ćit + maya* = चिन्मय *ćinmaya*, 'formed of intellect.'

तत् + मात्रं *tat + mátram* = तन्मात्रं *tanmátram*, 'that element.'

तत् + नेत्रं *tat + netram* = तन् नेत्रं *tan netram*, 'that eye.'

अप् + मूलं *ap + múlam* = अम्मूलं *ammúlam*, 'water and roots.'

b. Observe particularly—Rule 41 applies to terminations of nouns beginning with consonants, but not to terminations beginning with vowels. In the latter case, the final hard consonant is supposed to attract the initial vowel, and thus, losing its character of a final letter, is not made soft: thus वाच् + भिस् *vák + bhis* becomes वाग्भिस् *vágbhis*, 'by words;' but वाच् + आ *váć + á* remains वाचा *vá-ćá*, 'by a speech' (not वाजा *váj-á*). सरित् + भिस् *sarit + bhis* = सरिद्भिस् *sa-rid-bhis*, 'by rivers;' but सरित् + आ *sarit + á* remains सरिता *sari-tá*, 'by a river' (not सरिदा *sarid-á*). चित्रलिख् + सु *ćitralikh + su* is चित्रलिक्षु *ćitralik-su*, 'in painters;' but चित्रलिख् + आ *ćitralikh + á* remains चित्रलिखा *ćitrali-khá*, 'by a painter' (not *ćitralig-á*).

c. Similarly, in the case of *verbal* terminations beginning with vowels attached to roots ending in hard letters, rule 41 does not apply: thus पत् + अति *pat + ati* remains पतति *patati*, and क्षिप् + अति remains *kshipati*. And even in the case of *verbal* terminations beginning with *m*, *v*, or *y*, rule 41 does not generally apply: thus *vać + mi* remains *vaćmi*, *ćekship + vas* remains *ćekshipvas*, and *kship + yati* remains *kshipyati*; but *ćekship + dhi* becomes regularly *ćekshibdhi*.

d. Of course, rule 41 does not apply to final sibilants, as they have no corresponding soft letters. The rules for sibilants are given at 61.

e. In the case of षष् 'six,' followed by the termination *nám*, the final nasal being

---

* According to the Laghu-kaumudí (77) it is necessarily changed when the next word is a *pratyaya* or affix like *maya*.

a cerebral affects also an initial *n* coming in contact with it; thus षण्णाम्. The same applies to षट् + नवति, which is written षण्णवति 'ninety-six.' Similarly, षण्णगर्यः 'six cities.' Compare r. 58. *b*.

42. If a soft letter ends a word, root, or crude base, when any hard initial letter follows, the soft is changed to its own unaspirated hard: thus कुमुद् + सु *kumud + su* becomes कुमुत्सु *kumutsu*, loc. pl. of *kumud*, 'a lotus;' समिध् + सु *samidh + su* = समित्सु *samitsu*, loc. pl. of *samidh*, 'fuel.'

Note—Similarly in Latin, a soft guttural or labial often passes into a hard before *s* and *t*; thus *reg + si* becomes *reksi* (*rexi*), *scrib + si* = *scripsi*, *reg + tum* = *rektum*, &c.

a. The same may optionally take place at the end of a sentence or before a pause, as फुल्लति कुमुत् *phullati kumut* or *kumud*. See Pāṇini VIII. 4. 56. It is usual, however, to write the hard unaspirated form in such cases.

b. Soft letters, which have no corresponding hard, such as the nasals, semi-vowels, and ह् *h*, are changed by special rules.

c. If the final be an aspirated soft letter, and belong to a root whose initial is ग् *g* or ड् *ḍ*, द् *d* or ब् *b*, then the aspiration, which is suppressed in the final, is transferred back to the initial letter of the root; as बुध् + सु *budh + su* becomes भुत्सु *bhutsu*, loc. pl. of *budh*, 'one who knows.' Similarly, दध् + तस् *dadh + tas* becomes धत्तस् *dhattas*, 'they two place;' and see 306. *a*, 299. *a*. *b*, 664.

Note—Greek recognises a similar principle in τρέχω, θρέξομαι; τρυφ, θρύπτω: *cf*. also the nom. θρίξ, i. e. θρικ-ς from the crude form τριχ-.

43. The following consonants are not allowed to remain unchanged at the end of words*, that is to say, they undergo modifications without reference to the following letters in a sentence; and when they are combined with the initial letters of succeeding words, or with the initial *strong consonants* of affixes (see *f*. next page), these modifications must take place before 41 and 42 are applied. 1st, A conjunct quiescent consonant (with few exceptions); 2d, an aspirated quiescent consonant; 3d, the aspirate ह् *h*; 4th, the palatal letters च् *ć*, छ् *ćh*, ज् *j*, झ् *jh* (when radical, and not the result of the changes of final त् *t* and द् *d* at 47); 5th, the sibilants श् *ś* and ष् *sh*.

a. With regard to 1, as a general rule, a compound quiescent consonant at the end of a word is reduced to a simple one, and when a word ends in a single or conjunct quiescent consonant, and a termination to be affixed consists of a quiescent consonant, then, to avoid the concurrence of such consonants at the end, the first only is allowed to remain, and the termination is dropped: thus चरन्त् + स् *ćarant + s* leaves चरन् *ćaran*, 'going;' अवेद् + स् *aved + s* becomes *avets* and then *avet*. (So ἔτυπτεν for ἔτυπτοντ; and analogously, *mulsi* for *mulg-si*, *sparsi* for *sparg-si*, &c.)

* Of course, however, roots and crude forms are first cited in their unchanged state; and are so found in dictionaries and vocabularies.

Observe, however, that a radical क्, ट्, त्, or प्, preceded by र् *r*, remains; as, ऊर्क् nom. of ऊर्ज् 176. *b*.

But in the case of such a word as *abibhar* at p. 231, the affix *t* in the third person is dropped, as not being radical.

And in such a word as चिकीर्ष् (nom. चिकीः 'desirous of doing'), the final quiescent sibilant, though belonging to the base, is dropped after *r*. See 166. *a*.

b. With regard to 2, the unaspirated form is substituted for the aspirated.

c. With regard to 3, a final ह् *h* is usually changed either to क् *k* or ट् *ṭ*. See 182, 305, 306, 17. *a*. (So in Arabic ة *h* becomes ت *t*.)

d. With regard to 4, palatals, as being derived from gutturals (see 20. *c*), generally revert to their originals; i. e. final च् *c* and झ् *jh* are usually changed to क् (see 12), but छ् *ch* may become ट् *ṭ* (176); ज् *j* becomes क् *k* or ग् *g*, but sometimes ट् *ṭ* or ड् *ḍ*. (So in cognate languages *ch* is often pronounced as *k*, or passes into *k*. Compare 'archbishop,' 'archangel,' 'church,' 'kirk,' &c. Again, 'nature' is pronounced like 'nachure,' and *g* in English is often pronounced as *j*.)

e. With regard to 5, final श् *ś* and ष् *sh* usually pass into either क् *k* or ट् *ṭ*. See 181, 17. *b*; and compare 'parish,' 'parochial,' 'nation' for 'nashun,' &c.

f. The above changes must hold good, whatever may be the initial letter of a following word; but rules 41 and 42 must be afterwards applied. They also hold good before all *terminations* or *affixes* beginning with strong consonants (i. e. all consonants except nasals and semivowels); but before vowels (except the affix *a* at 80. I) and weak consonants (i. e. nasals and semivowels) the finals remain unchanged. See 41. *b*, and *vāc* at 176, and *vac* at 650.

SPECIAL RULES.

44. The special rules for the changes of consonants are very numerous, but since comparatively few words in Sanskrit end in any other consonants than त् *t* and द् *d*, the nasals न् *n* and म् *m*, the dental sibilant स् *s*, and the semivowel र् *r*, it will be sufficient for all practical purposes to notice these special rules under four heads:

1st, Changes of final त् and द्.

2d, Changes of the nasals, especially न् and म्.

3d, Changes of final स्.

4th, Changes of final र्.

CHANGES OF FINAL त् *t* AND द् *d*.

45. By the general rule (41), final त् *t* becomes द् *d* before soft consonants, and before vowels; as मरुत् + वाति *marut + vāti* becomes मरुद् वाति *marud vāti*, 'the wind blows.' But see exception, r. 41. *b*.

a. Except, also, bases ending in *t* followed by the affixes *vat*, *mat*, *vin*, *vala*; as, *vidyut-vat*, 'possessed of lightning;' *garut-mat*, 'possessed of wings.'

b. There is an exception also in the case of verbal terminations beginning with *m*, *v*, *y*; see 41. *c*, and compare 554.

46. And, by 42, final द् *d* generally becomes त् *t* before hard consonants; as, दृषद् + पतन becomes *dṛishat-patana*, 'the fall of a stone.'

47. And, by 41. *a*, final त् *t* or द् *d* may become न् *n* before *n* or *m*.

But there are certain special rules relating to त् *t* or द् *d*, and incidentally to other consonants, which must be given under this head.

48. If त् *t* or द् *d* ends a word, when an initial च *ć*, ज *j*, or ल *l*, follows, then त् *t* or द् *d* assimilates with these letters: thus भयात् + लोभात् + च *bhayát* + *lobhát* + *ća* becomes *bhayál lobháć ća*, 'from fear and avarice;' तद् + जीवनम् *tad* + *jívanam* = *taj jívanam*, 'that life.'

a. A final त् *t* or द् *d* also assimilates with a following छ *ćh* or झ *jh*, but by 43. *b*. the result will then be *ć ćh*, *j jh*; thus तत् + छिनत्ति = तच् छिनत्ति 'he cuts that,' तद् + झषः = तज्झषः 'the fish of him.'

b. Final त् *t* or द् *d* assimilates in the same way with ट *ṭ*, ड *ḍ*, and their aspirates: thus तद् + टीका = तट्टीका; तद् + डीनं = तड्डीनं; तद् + ढक्का = तड्ढक्का.

Observe—The converse does not take place in the contact of complete words; thus षट् ते, not षत् ते 'those six;' but ईट् + ते = ईट्टे 'he rules.' see 325.

Final त् *t* or द् *d* may also assimilate with initial श *ś* and ष *ṣ*.

c. When छ *ćh* is between two vowels in a simple word, त् *t*, changeable by 48. *a*. to च् *ć*, must be inserted; thus the root प्रछ् *praćh* with vowel *a* following must be written प्रच्छ *praććha* (as in पृच्छति at 631).

The same holds good when छ *ćh* is initial and a previous syllable either of an inflected word, or of a crude form preceding in a compound, or of a prefix ends in a short vowel; as, शिलछाया or शिलच्छाया 'the shadow of a rock:' so also, चि* + छेद = चिच्छेद 'he cuts;' अ* + छिनत् = अच्छिनत् 'he was cutting.'

The same is obligatory after the preposition आ and the particle मा; as, आ + छन्न = आच्छन्न 'covered;' मा + छिदत् = मा च्छिदत् 'let him not cut.'

In other cases after long vowels the insertion of च् *ć* is optional; as, बदरीछाया or बदरीच्छाया 'the shadow of a fig-tree;' सा छिनत्ति or सा च्छिनत्ति 'she cuts.'

d. After final ट् *ṭ*, before initial स् *s*, an augment त् *t* may be inserted; as, षट् सन्तः or षट् त्सन्तः 'being six.'

49. If त् *t* or द् *d* ends a word and the next begins with श *ś* immediately followed by a vowel, semivowel, or nasal, then *t* or *d* is changed to च् *ć*, and the initial श *ś* is usually changed to छ *ćh*;

* चि *ći* is the syllable of reduplication to form the perfect of छिद् *ćhid*, अ *a* the augment to form the imperfect of all verbs; but in the paradigms, words like अच्छिनत् are, for the convenience of typography, printed अछिनत्, &c. See p. 286.

thus तत् + श्रुत्वा *tat + śrutvá* = तच् छ्रुत्वा *tać ćhrutvá*, 'having heard that,' but तच् श्रुत्वा is allowable.

a. Similarly, the change of initial श *ś* to छ *ćh* is optional after a final क्; thus वाक् शत may either remain so or be written वाक् छत. Again, after a final ट् *ṭ* and प् *p* this rule is said to be optional; but examples are not likely to occur: though in Ṛig-veda III. 33. 1, we have विपाट्छुतुद्री *for* विपाट् + शुतुद्री the names of two rivers in the Panjáb.

50. If त् *t* ends a word, when initial ह *h* follows, the final त् *t* is changed to द् *d* (by 41), and the initial ह *h* optionally to ध *dh*: thus तत् + हरति *tat + harati* becomes तद् धरति (or तद्धरति) *tad dharati*, 'he seizes that;' but तद् हरति *tad harati* is allowable.

51. By a similar rule, and on the same principle, any consonant (except a nasal, semivowel, or sibilant) followed by ह, must be softened if hard, and its soft aspirate optionally substituted for the initial ह; thus वाक् + हरति *vák + harati* becomes वाग् घरति *vág gharati*, 'speech captivates.' Similarly, अच् + ह्रस्वः *ać + hrasvaḥ* = अज्झ्रस्वः *ajjhrasvaḥ*, 'a short vowel.'

CHANGES OF THE NASALS.

52. If the letter न् *n*, preceded by a *short* vowel, ends a word, when the next begins with any vowel, the *n* is doubled: thus आसन् + अत्र *ásan + atra* becomes *ásann atra*, 'they were there;' तस्मिन् + उद्याने *tasmin + udyáne* = *tasminn udyáne*, 'in that garden.'

a. This applies equally to final ङ् *ṅ* and ण् *ṇ* (as प्रत्यङ् + आत्मा = प्रत्यङ्ङात्मा 'the soul evidently existent'); but these, especially the last, can rarely occur as finals.

53. If न् *n* ends a word, when an initial च *ć*, ट *ṭ*, or त *t*, (or their aspirates,) follows, a sibilant is inserted between the final and initial letter, according to the class of the initial letter; and the न् *n* then passes into Anusvára, see 6. *b*: thus कस्मिन् + चित् *kasmin + ćit* becomes कस्मिंश्चित् *kasmiṇśćit*, 'in a certain person;' अस्मिन् + तडागे *asmin + taḍáge* = अस्मिंस्तडागे *asmiṇs taḍáge*, 'in this pool;' महान् + टङ्कः *mahán + ṭaṅ-kaḥ* = महांष्टङ्कः *maháṇsh ṭaṅ-kaḥ*, 'a large axe.'

The same holds good before छ *ćh* (as, तांश्छादयति 'he covers them'), and before ठ *ṭh*, थ *th*: but the two latter are not likely to occur.

If *s* immediately follows *t* in a conjunct consonant, as in the word त्सरु 'a sword-hilt,' there is no change: thus तन् त्सरुः.

a. A similar euphonic *s* is inserted between the prepositions *sam*, *ava*, *pari*, *prati*, and certain words which begin with *k*, as संस्कार *saṃskára*, परिष्कार *parishkára*, प्रतिष्कार *pratishkára*, &c. (see 70); just as in Latin, between the prepositions *ab* and *ob*, and *c*, *q*, and *p*. Also, between पुम् 'a male,' and a word beginning with a hard consonant, as कोकिल 'a cuckoo,' thus पुंस्कोकिलः; also when कान्, 'whom?' is repeated, thus कांस्कान् 'whom?' 'whom?' 'which of them?'

b. न् *n* at the end of a root, or incomplete word, is not amenable to this rule: thus हन् + ति *han* + *ti* is हन्ति *hanti*, 'he kills.'

c. Except, also, प्रशान् *praśān* (nom. of *praśām*, see 179. *a*); as, प्रशान् तनोति 'the peaceful man spreads;' प्रशान् चिनोति 'the peaceful man collects.'

54. Rule 53 describes the only cases in which न् *n*, when originally the final of a word, can pass into Anusvāra: thus in classical Sanskrit combinations like तान् करोति or तान् ददाति must not be written तां करोति, तां ददाति.

55. If न् *n* ends a word, when the next begins with श् *ś*, then न् *n* and श् *ś* may be combined in either of the two following ways: 1st, the final न् *n* may be changed to ञ् *ñ*; thus महान् + शूरः *mahān* + *śūraḥ* may be written महाञ् शूरः 'a great hero;' 2dly, the initial श् *ś* may be changed to छ् *ch*; thus महाञ् छूरः.

a. Observe, that according to native authorities an augment *t*, changeable to *c*, may be inserted in both cases, thus महाञ्च् शूरः or महाञ्च् छूरः, but this is rarely done; and in practice, both न् and श् are often left unchanged against the rule.

b. Final ङ् *ṅ* may optionally insert an augment क् *k* when any sibilant begins the next word. Similarly, final ण् *ṇ* may insert ट् *ṭ*. So final न् *n* may insert त् *t* before स् *s*. Hence प्राङ् शेते may be either प्राङ्क् शेते (or प्राङ्क् षेते by 49. *a*) or may remain unchanged; the loc. pl. of सुगण्, 'a good reckoner,' is सुगण्षु or सुगण्ट्सु; and सन् सः, 'he being,' may be सन्त् सः; and some say the inserted letters may optionally be aspirated. The insertion of त् between a final न् and initial स् is common in the Veda; but in later Sanskrit these insertions are not usual.

56. If न् *n* ends a word, when the next begins with ल् *l*, the *n* assimilates with the *l*, and the mark ँ is placed over the *l*, derived from *n*, to denote its nasality: thus पक्षान् + लुनाति *pakshān* + *lunāti* becomes पक्षाँल्लुनाति or पक्षाँल् लुनाति 'he clips the wings;' see 7. Similarly, ἐν + λάμπω = ἐλλάμπω; *con* + *ligo* = *colligo*.

a. Final न् *n*, before ज् *j* or झ् *jh*, and ञ् *ñ*, is properly written in the palatal form ञ्, but in practice is often allowed to remain unchanged against the rule.

b. Final न् *n*, before ड् *ḍ*, ढ् *ḍh*, and ण् *ṇ*, should be written in the cerebral form ण्.

c. But final न् *n*, before ष् *sh*, remains unchanged; as, तान् षट् 'those six.'

57. न् *n* as the final of crude bases is rejected before terminations and affixes beginning with consonants: thus धनिन् + भिस् *dhanin* + *bhis* becomes धनिभिस् *dhanibhis*, 'by rich people;' धनिन् + त्व *dhanin* + *tva* = धनित्व *dhanitva*, 'the state of being rich.'

a. As the final of a root it is rejected before those terminations beginning with consonants (excepting nasals and semivowels) which have no indicatory P (see 307 and 323): thus हन् + *ti*P is हन्ति, but हन् + *tas* is हतस्, see 654.

b. Also, when a word ending in न् *n* is the first (or any but the last) member of a compound word, even though the next member of the compound begins with a vowel: thus राजन् + पुरुष *rājan* + *purusha* becomes राजपुरुष *rāja-purusha*, 'the king's servant;' राजन् + इन्द्र *rājan* + *indra* = राजेन्द्र *rājendra*, 'the chief of kings;' स्वामिन् + अर्थम् *svāmin* + *artham* = स्वाम्यर्थम् *svāmy-artham*, 'on account of the master.' Similarly, *svāmin* + *vat* = *svāmivat*, 'like the master.'

58. If न् n (*not final*, and having immediately after it a simple vowel, diphthong, or one of the consonants न् n, म् m, य् y, व् v) follows any one of the three cerebral letters ऋ ṛi (short or long), र् r, ष् sh, *in the same word* (*samána-pade*), then न् n must be changed to the cerebral ण् ṇ, even though a simple vowel or diphthong or any of the guttural and labial letters क् k, ग् g, प् p, ब् b, (or their aspirates,) or Anusvára, or any of the letters ह् h, य् y, व् v, ञ् ṅ, म् m, either singly or combined together or with any vowel, intervene: thus क्षिप् + आनि = क्षिपाणि (635); ब्रह्मन् + आ = ब्रह्मणा (152); मृग + इन = मृगेण (107); बृंह + अण = बृंहण 'causing to grow fat;' शृङ्गिन् + आ = शृङ्गिणा 'horned;' क्षिप् + नु = क्षिप्णु 'diffusive.' Observe—In a word like कुर्वन्ति, 'they do,' *t* immediately after *n*, prevents the change. Similarly, कृत्स्नम्, p. 288.

न् *n* final in a word is not so changed; thus रामान् p. 83, not रामाण्.

a. And the intervention of any of the five palatal, cerebral, or first four dental consonants at page 1, (viz. च् *ch*, छ् *chh*, ज् *j*, झ् *jh*, ञ् *ñ*, ट् *ṭ*, ठ् *ṭh*, ड् *ḍ*, ढ् *ḍh*, ण् *ṇ*, त् *t*, थ् *th*, द् *d*, ध् *dh*,) or of ल् *l* or of श् *ś* or of स् *s*, prevents the operation of this rule, as in वर्त्मानि 'roads' (n. pl. of वर्त्मन्); अर्चना 'worship;' अर्जन 'abandoning;' क्रीडन 'playing;' शृगालेन 'by a jackal' (149).

Even the intervention of a guttural or palatal *if conjunct* with the न् *n* may in some cases preclude any change, as in तृप्नोति 'he satisfies;' प्राप्नोति 'he obtains;' क्षुभ्नाति 'he shakes' (694); क्षिप्नु 'casting;' वृक्न 'cut' (630); रुग्न 'broken;' ब्रह्मघ्न, वृत्रघ्न (157). In the Veda, however, तृप्णोति is found; and क्षिप्णु, वृक्ण, and रुग्ण are by some considered the more correct forms, see 541, 544. It is certain that the intervention of nasals, semivowels, or *h*, though conjunct with the न्, do not prevent this rule, as in ब्रह्मण्य (157).

b. If two न् *n*'s follow the letters causing the change, then the first alone becomes ण, as in प्रणीन[*], unless the two न *n*'s are conjunct, when they both become ण, as in विषण्ण *vishaṇṇa*† (540).

c. Even in compound words where ऋ, ॠ, ष, र are in the first member of the compound, and न occurs in the second member, the change to ण may sometimes take place (especially when the separate ideas inherent in each word are lost sight of in a single object denoted), and sometimes is optional. When, however, the words do not, so to speak, merge their individuality in a single object, no change is generally allowed, but even in these cases it is impossible to lay down a precise rule. The following are a few examples: रामायण 'the Rámáyana,' वार्ध्रीणसः 'an

---

[*] Except a word like प्राणिणत् redup. aorist of अन् 'to breathe,' with प्र.

† The whole rule 58 is thus expressed in the first two Sútras of Páṇini VIII. 4, रषाभ्यां नो णः समानपदे । अट्कुप्वाङ्नुम्व्यवायेऽपि. The vowel *ṛi* is supposed to be included in र. अट् stands for the vowels, diphthongs, *y*, *r*, *v*, and *h*; कु for the guttural class; पु for the labial; आङ् for the preposition आ; नुम् for Anusvára, singly or combined.

animal' (?), either 'a Rhinoceros' or 'a goat,' खरणसः 'having a sharp nose,' but चर्मनासिका 'a whip,' and सर्वनामन् 'a pronoun,' स्वर्णदी or स्वर्नदी 'the Ganges of heaven,' पुष्पवाहन 'a plant' (where पुष्पवाहण might be expected), गिरिनदी or गिरिणदी 'a mountain-stream,' आम्रवणं 'a mango-grove,' ब्रह्मघ्नं (acc. of ब्रह्महन्) 'the killer of a Bráhman,' सर्वाह्णः 'the whole day.' See Páṇ. VIII. 4. 3, &c.

d. Again, the prepositions अन्तर्, निर्, परा, परि, and प्र generally cerebralise a following न, even when the preposition नि intervenes, but not always; thus परिणय, पर्याणय, प्रणाम, प्रणमति, प्रणेय, अन्तर्णय (but अन्तर्नय 'name of a country,' परिनिंसन, प्रणमन, निर्णय); and when a root ending in a consonant encloses any other vowel than *a* or *á*, the change appears to be optional, as प्रकोपण or प्रकोपन 'provocation.' An intervening preposition नि is usually cerebralised, as in प्रणिपात, प्रणिपतति, प्रणिहित, परिणिवपन; but not invariably, as परिनिविष्ट. In this way final म् may be changed to न् at the end of a word, as in प्रशान् formed from rt. *śam*.

59. If म् *m* ends a word, when any consonant follows, then म् *m* may pass into Anusvára, but ought more properly, before those consonants which have a corresponding nasal, to be changed to this nasal: thus गृहम् + जगाम *gṛiham* + *jagáma* is written either गृहं जगाम or गृहञ् जगाम 'he went home:' so also सम् + डीन becomes either संडीन or सण्डीन 'flight;' सम् + चय either संचय or सञ्चय 'collection;' सम् + त्याग either संत्याग or सन्त्याग 'abandonment.' But although म् *m* may in these cases be represented by Anusvára, the latter must always take the sound of the nasal to which it should euphonically be changed.

a. The final म् *m* of a root is changed to न् *n* or ण् *ṇ* before affixes beginning with any consonant except *y, r, l, s*: thus जगम् + वि = जगन्वि (see 709). So also चक्रम् + वहे = चक्रण्वहे (see 58).

b. Before श, ष, स, ह, a final म् is represented by Anusvára; also generally before the semivowels, but see 6. *e*, 7. 7. *b*.

60. When the next word begins with a vowel, then म् *m* must always be written: thus गृहमागच्छति or गृहम् आगच्छति 'he comes home.'

CHANGES OF FINAL स् *s*.

61. Nearly every nominative case, and many other cases of nouns, in Sanskṛit, besides many inflections of verbs, end in स् *s*, which is changeable to ष् *ṣ* and श् *sh*, and is liable to be represented by Visarga (:, i.e. the symbol for a final aspirate), or to pass into र् *r*, or to be liquefied into उ *u*, or to be dropped altogether, according to the nature of the initial letter following and the vowel preceding *. *At*

* In a few Latin words *s* passes into *r* in declension. Thus *flos* becomes in the genitive *floris*; *genus* becomes *generis*: and other words, such as *labor*, *robur*, were originally written either *labor* or *labos*, *robur* or *robus*. Again, the initial aspirate in many Greek words is represented in Latin by *s*; as, ἕξ, *sex*, &c.

every step these changes will meet the eye: therefore let the student master the following five rules, before he attempts to read a single sentence of the most elementary Sanskrit work.

Observe—The following rules are designated by other grammarians, "rules for the changes of Visarga." It seems, however, a simpler and preferable course (the result being in the end equivalent) to start from the tangible character स् *s*, which Visarga, under certain circumstances, represents; or, in other words, to regard Visarga as no letter at all, but a mere symbol for final स् *s*, and, as we shall afterwards see at 71, for final र् *r*, when these letters are pronounced as aspirates (compare rule 8), before क *k*, प *p*, स *s*, श *ś*, ष *sh*, and at the end of a sentence.

First Rule.—*When does the final sibilant remain unrejected?*

62. Before त *t*, च *ć*, and ट *ṭ*, and their aspirates, respectively. Before त *t*, and its aspirate, स् *s* remains unchanged. Before च *ć*, and its aspirate, स् *s* passes into the palatal sibilant श् *ś*. Similarly, before ट *ṭ*, and its aspirate, स् *s* passes into the cerebral sibilant ष् *sh*. But this latter change can rarely occur.

a. Final स् *s* is also allowed to remain unchanged before initial स *s*, and to assimilate with initial श *ś* and ष *sh**. More commonly, however, it is in these cases represented by Visarga; see rule 63.

b. So also, the final स् *s of a root* must always remain unchanged before the terminations *si*, *se*: thus शास् + से = शास्से; वस् + से = वस्से; see 304. *a*.

Second Rule.—*When does final* स् *s pass into Visarga* (:)?

63. Before क *k*, प *p*, and their aspirates, and generally (but see 62. *a*) before the three sibilants स *s*, श *ś*, and ष *sh*†.

a. Before a pause, i. e. at the end of a sentence.

b. Observe—When a word stands by itself, final *s* properly passes into Visarga; and this is why, in native grammars, the terminations of nouns and verbs, which appear first in the tabular scheme, as ending in *s*, are made to end in Visarga, when they appear again in declension and conjugation. In the following pages, however, *s* will be preserved as a final, in declension and conjugation, for two reasons: 1st, because it is more tangible, and easy to apprehend, than a symbol which as representing a mere breathing is less perceptible in pronunciation; 2dly, because it enables the classical student to keep in view the resemblance between Sanskrit and Greek and Latin terminations.

---

* The assimilation of स् with an initial ष will of course be very rare, but त्रयष्षष्टि offers an example.

† Examples of the change to Visarga before initial ष (which can only occur rarely) are त्रयःषष्टि and चतुःषष्टि.

THIRD RULE.—*When does final* अस् *as become* o?

64. Before all *soft* consonants.

a. Similarly, before short अ *a*, which *a* is then cut off.

This rule is more properly, but less simply, stated thus. When does final स् *s* blend with a preceding *a* into the vowel *o*? Before all *soft* consonants final स् *s* is treated as if liquefied into *u* *.

FOURTH RULE.—*When does final* स् *s become* र् *r*?

65. When preceded by any other vowel but अ *a* or आ *ā*, and before all *soft* letters, consonants or vowels.

a. Unless र् *r* itself be the soft letter following, in which case, to avoid the conjunction of two *r*'s, final स् *s* is dropped, and the vowel preceding it (if short) is lengthened.

FIFTH RULE.—*When is final* स् *s rejected?*

66. When preceded by short अ *a*, before any other vowel except short अ *a* †. NB. The अ *a*, which then becomes final, opens on the initial vowel without coalition ‡.

a. When preceded by long आ *ā*, before any soft letter, consonant or vowel. NB. If the initial letter be a vowel, the आ *ā*, which then becomes final, opens on it without coalition.

b. When preceded by any other vowel but अ *a* or आ *ā*, before the letter *r*, as noticed at 65. *a*.

c. Observe—Although it simplifies the subject to speak of final *s* as dropped in these cases, yet, according to native grammarians, it would be more correct to say that final *s* first passes into Visarga, which is then dropped: otherwise the term

---

* That is, it is first changed to *r*, as at 65, and *r* is then liquefied into a vowel; just as *l* is often changed to *u* in French. The plural of *animal* is *animaux*, not *animals*.

† That is, it blends with *a* into *o*, as in 64; and *o* becoming *av* before any vowel but *a*, the *v* is rejected by 36. Indian grammarians hold that final *s* or Visarga here becomes *y*, which would also be rejected by 36. This, however, seems rather to apply to 66. *a*.

‡ This is one of the three cases in which a hiatus of two vowels is admissible in Sanskrit. The three cases are, 1. when final *s* is rejected from *as* or *ās* (66); 2. when a complete word, ending in *e*, is followed by any other vowel but *a* (see 36); 3. when the dual terminations ई *ī*, ऊ *ū*, ए *e*, are followed by vowels (see 38). In the middle of a word a hiatus is never allowed, except in one or two rare instances, as तितउ *tita-u*, 'a sieve.'

Visarga is without meaning. Indian grammarians, however, hold that Visarga undergoes another change before it is dropped, viz. to *y*; and that this *y* is rejected in accordance with 36, 37.

d. The interjections भोस्, भगोस्, and अघोस् drop their final *s* before a vowel or soft consonant.

The above five rules are illustrated in the following table, in which the nominative cases नरस् *naras*, 'a man;' नरास् *narás*, 'men;' हरिस् *haris*, 'the god Vishṇu;' रिपुस् *ripus*, 'an enemy;' and नौस् *naus*, 'a ship'—are joined with the verbs *karoti*, 'he does;' *kurvanti*, 'they do;' *khanati*, 'he digs;' *khananti*, 'they dig;' *paćati*, 'he cooks;' *paćanti*, 'they cook;' *sarati*, 'he goes;' *śoćati* 'he grieves;' *tarati*, 'he crosses;' *ćarati*, 'he moves;' *gaććhati*, 'he goes;' *jayati*, 'he conquers;' *rakshati*, 'he preserves;' *atti*, 'he eats;' *adanti*, 'they eat;' *eti*, 'he goes;' *áyáti*, 'he comes;' *edhate*, 'he prospers.'

First Rule. Final sibilant remains unrejected.	Second Rule. Final स् s passes into Visarga.	Third Rule. Final अस् as becomes ओ o.	Fourth Rule. Final स् s becomes र् r.	Fifth Rule. Final स् s is rejected.
नरस् तरति *naras tarati* नरास् तरन्ति *narás taranti* हरिस् तरति *haris tarati* नौस् तरति *naus tarati* नरश् चरति *naraś ćarati* नराश् चरन्ति *naráś ćaranti* हरिश् चरति *hariś ćarati* नौश् चरति *nauś ćarati* Final *s* rarely remains unchanged before स *s*, and assimilates with श *ś*: thus, नरस् सरति *naras sarati* नरास् सरन्ति *narás saranti* हरिस् सरति *haris sarati* नरश् शोचति *naraś śoćati* नराश् शोचन्ति *naráś śoćanti* हरिश् शोचति *hariś śoćati*	नरः करोति *naraḥ karoti* नराः कुर्वन्ति *naráḥ kurvanti* हरिः करोति *hariḥ karoti* नरः खनति *naraḥ khanati* नराः खनन्ति *naráḥ khananti* हरिः खनति *hariḥ khanati* नरः पचति *naraḥ paćati* नराः पचन्ति *naráḥ paćanti* हरिः पचति *hariḥ paćati* नरः सरति *naraḥ sarati* नराः सरन्ति *naráḥ saranti* हरिः सरति *hariḥ sarati* नरः शोचति *naraḥ śoćati* नराः शोचन्ति *naráḥ śoćanti* हरिः शोचति *hariḥ śoćati* Before a pause, करोति नरः *karoti naraḥ*	नरो गच्छति *naro gaććhati* नरो जयति *naro jayati* नरो याति *naro yáti* नरो रक्षति *naro rakshati* Similarly, final *s* preceded by *a*, before all soft consonants: and also before अ *a*, which अ *a* is then cut off: thus, नरोऽत्ति *naro 'tti* for *nara atti*	हरिर् अत्ति *harir atti* रिपुर् अत्ति *ripur atti* नौर् आयाति *naur áyáti* हरिर् एति *harir eti* रिपुर् एति *ripur eti* नौर् एति *naur eti* हरिर् गच्छति *harir gaććhati* रिपुर् गच्छति *ripur gaććhati* नौर् गच्छति *naur gaććhati* हरिर् याति *harir yáti* रिपुर् याति *ripur yáti* नौर् याति *naur yáti* Similarly, final *s* preceded by any vowel but *a* or *á*, before all soft letters excepting *r*, when final *s* also becoming *r* is rejected, and the preceding vowel lengthened: thus, हरी रक्षति *harí rakshati* रिपू रक्षति *ripú rakshati*	नर आयाति *nara áyáti* नरा अदन्ति *nará adanti* नर ईक्षते *nara íkshate* नरा ईक्षन्ते *nará íkshante* नर एधते *nara edhate* नरा एधन्ते *nará edhante* नरा गच्छन्ति *nará gaććhanti* नरा यान्ति *nará yánti* नरा रक्षन्ति *nará rakshanti* Similarly, final *s* preceded by अ *a*, before all vowels excepting अ *a*; and, final *s* preceded by *á*, before all soft letters, consonants or vowels.

67. There is one common exception to 62, 63, 64: सस् *sas*, 'he,' and एषस् *eshas*, 'this,' the nominative case masc. of the pronouns तद् *tad* and एतद् *etad* (220, 223), drop the final *s* before any *consonant*, hard or soft; as, स करोति *sa karoti*, 'he does;' स गच्छति *sa gaććhati*, 'he goes;' एष पचति *esha paćati*, 'this (man) cooks.' But rules 64. *a*, 66, and 63. *a*, are observed: thus, सोऽपि *so 'pi*, 'he also;' स एषः *sa eshaḥ*, 'he himself.' Sometimes (but only पादपूरणे to fill up a verse or suit the metre) *sa* may blend with a following vowel, as सैषः for स एषः.

A remarkable agreement is observable here in the Greek ὁ for ὅς. Compare also the Latin *qui* for *quis*, and *ille*, *iste*, *ipse*, for *illus*, *istus*, *ipsus*. Bopp considers that the reason why *sa* dispenses with the termination *s* is, that this termination is itself derived from the pronoun *sa*.

a. With regard to the second rule, there is an option allowed when an initial sibilant is compounded with another hard consonant. In that case, the preceding final *s* may be dropped; as, हरि स्कन्दति *hari skandati*, 'Hari goes.'

b. A rare exception to the first rule occurs, when an initial त् *t* is compounded with a sibilant. In that case, the preceding final *s* becomes Visarga; as, हरिः त्सरुं गृह्णाति *hariḥ tsarum gṛihṇāti*, 'Hari grasps the hilt of (his) sword.'

68. The preceding rules are most frequently applicable to स् *s*, as the final of the cases of nouns and inflections of verbs; but they come equally into operation in substantives or adjectives, whose *base* or *crude form* ends in अस् *as*, इस् *is*, and उस् *us*; thus, by 65, चक्षुस् + ईक्षते *ćakshus* + *īkshate* becomes चक्षुर् ईक्षते *ćakshur īkshate*, 'the eye sees;' and चक्षुस् + भिस् *ćakshus* + *bhis* = चक्षुर्भिस् *ćakshurbhis*, 'by eyes.' Similarly, by 64, मनस् + जानाति *manas* + *jānāti* = मनो जानाति *mano jānāti*, 'the mind knows;' and मनस् + भिस् *manas* + *bhis* = मनोभिस् *manobhis*, 'by minds.'

a. Observe—All nouns ending in इस् *is* and उस् *us* may be regarded as ending in इष् *ish* and उष् *ush*, which is the form they necessarily assume in declension before the terminations beginning with vowels (see 70, and compare 41. *b*): thus चक्षुस् + आ *ćakshus* + *ā* becomes चक्षुषा *ćakshushā*, 'by the eye;' but before consonants they must be treated as ending in the dental sibilant. See 165.

69. स् *s* at the end of the first member of a *compound word*, before hard letters of the guttural or labial classes (क् *k*, प् *p*, or their aspirates), may follow 63, but is more usually retained, passing sometimes into ष् *sh*, according to 70: thus तेजस् + कर *tejas* + *kara* becomes either तेजस्कर or तेजःकर 'causing light;' प्रादुस् + कृत *prādus* + *kṛita* becomes प्रादुष्कृत *prādushkṛita*, 'made manifest;' दिवस् + पति *divas* + *pati* = दिवस्पति 'the lord of day.'

a. Again, in opposition to 64 and 65, a final स् *s* is usually retained before affixes beginning with व् *v* and म् *m*, passing sometimes into ष् *sh*, according to 70: thus तेजस् + विन् *tejas* + *vin* becomes तेजस्विन् *tejasvin*, 'full of light;' भास् + वर *bhās* + *vara* = भास्वर *bhāsvara*, 'radiant;' and अर्चिस् + मत् *arćis* + *mat* = अर्चिष्मत् *arćishmat*, 'possessing flame.'

b. An augment स् *s* is inserted after सम्, in combination with कृ and its derivatives, as in संस्कार, संस्कृत, &c.

70. स *s*, *not final*, passes into ष *sh* when preceded by any other vowel but अ *a* or आ *á*; also when preceded by the semivowel र् *r*, or by क् *k*: thus अग्नि + सु *agni* + *su* becomes अग्निषु *agnishu*, 'in fires;' करो + सि *karo* + *si* = करोषि *karoshi*, 'thou doest;' बिभर् + सि *bibhar* + *si* = बिभर्षि *bibharshi*, 'thou bearest;' वाक् + सु *vák* + *su* = वाक्षु *vákshu*, 'in words.' See 69. and 69. *a*.

a. An intervening Anuswára or Visarga does not prevent the operation of this rule: thus, हवींषि, चक्षूंषि, हविःषु (or हविष्षु), चक्षुःषु.

b. In accordance with this rule, roots and their derivatives beginning with स will change their initials to ष after the prepositions अभि, अधि, नि, निः, परि, प्रति, वि, अनु, अपि; thus परिषिच् from परि and सिच्, निष्णा from नि and स्ना; and the change may even be preserved though the augment अ *a* intervenes, as in न्यषेधत् from सिध् with नि, अभ्यष्ठात् from स्था with अभि; and even in the reduplication of the 2d pret., as अधितष्ठौ (but not always in either case, as अभ्यस्थात्, अनुतस्थौ).

c. The root स्तम्भ् changes its initial to ष after अव, as अवष्टभ्नाति.

d. In a few roots the change is optional, as परिस्कन्दति or परिष्कन्दति, विस्फुरति or विष्फुरति.

e. Even in compounds the initial *s* of the 2d member of the compound may be affected by rule 70, especially if a single object is denoted, as in हरिषेण, a proper name, अग्निषद 'a frying-pan.' So also in अग्निष्टोम, पितृष्वसृ, दुःषम, &c.

f. In compounds formed with सह् (rt. सह्), the initial becomes ष where ह् is changed to a cerebral (ढ्, ड्, or ट्). See 182. *f*.

g. The स् of the affix सात् is not changed, as अग्निसात्कृ 'to consume by fire.'

CHANGES OF FINAL र् *r*.

71. Most of the changes of final र् *r* are the same as those of final स् *s*.

a. Thus, by 63. प्रातर् + काल *prátar* + *kála* becomes प्रातःकाल *prátaḥkála*, 'the time of morning;' and प्रातर् + स्नान *prátar* + *snána* = प्रातःस्नान *prátaḥsnána*, 'morning ablution.' But *r* as the final of a root, or as a radical letter, remains unchanged before a sibilant: thus, चर् + सु = चर्षु (70); बिभर् + सि = बिभर्षि; चतुर् + सु = चतुर्षु, see 203.

b. By 62. प्रातर् + तु *prátar* + *tu* becomes प्रातस्तु *prátastu*; and प्रातर् + च *prátar* + *ća* = प्रातश्च *prátaśća*.

Note, that the transition of *r* into *s* before *t* is exemplified in Latin by *gestum* from *gero*, *ustum* from *uro*, &c. On the other hand, *r* in the middle of words is preserved before *t* in Sanskrit, as in *kartum*, &c.

c. By 65. निर् + उक्त *nir* + *ukta* remains निरुक्त *nirukta*, 'described;' निर् + इच

nir+daya remains निर्दय *nirdaya*, 'without pity;' and निर्+रस *nir+rasa* is नीरस *nīrasa*, 'without flavour.'

d. After the analogy of 65. *a*, final *ar* before initial *r* drops its own *r*, and lengthens the preceding *a*; as पुनर्+रक्षति *punar+rakshati* becomes पुना रक्षति *punā rakshati*, 'again he preserves.'

e. But in opposition to 64 and 66, final अर् *ar*, unlike अस् *as*, remains unchanged before any soft letter (consonant or vowel): thus प्रातर्+आश *prātar+āśa* remains प्रातराश *prātarāśa*, 'morning meal;' पुनर्+याति *punar+yāti* remains पुनर् याति *punar yāti*, 'again he goes.'

72. र् *r* at the end of the first member of a compound, before क *k*, प *p*, and their aspirates, may either become Visarga, by 63, or more usually follows 69, and passes into स् *s*, which is liable to become ष *sh* by 70: thus निर्+फल *nir+phala* becomes निष्फल *nishphala*, 'without fruit.' In the case of दुर्+ख *dur+kha*, दुःख is more common than दुष्ख.

73. र् *r* may optionally double any consonant, except ह *h*, that immediately follows it: thus निर्+दय *nir+daya* may be written either निर्दय *nirdaya* or निर्द्दय *nirddaya*, 'merciless;' but it does not double a sibilant followed by a vowel, as in वर्षं 71. *e*. It is said that *h* may have the same effect as *r* in doubling a consonant immediately following; but this is not observed in practice.

a. The doubling of consonants, when they come in contact with others, is constantly allowable in Sanskrit, though not usual in practice. Thus, in any conjunction of two (or even more) consonants preceded by a short vowel (or even occasionally a long vowel), especially if a semivowel be the last letter in the compound, the first letter, provided it be not र or ह, may be doubled; thus पुत्त्र may be written for पुत्र, मद्ध्य for मध्य (see 40. *a*), इत्यात्तद्भ्यो for इत्यादभ्यो, but the more simple form is preferable.

The following table exhibits the more common combinations of consonants at one view. Observe, that in the top line of initial letters the aspirated consonants have been omitted, because it is an universal rule, that whatever change takes place before any consonant, the same holds good before its aspirate.

INITIAL VOWELS AND CONSONANTS.	1 अ a	2 आ, इ, ā, i, &c.	3 क k	4 ग g	5 च c	6 ज j	7 त t	8 द d	9 न n	10 प p	11 ब b	12 म m	13 य y	14 र r	15 ल l	16 व v	17 श ś	18 स s	19 ह h
FINAL CONSONANTS.																			
क् k or ग् g	g a	g ā g i	k k	g g	k c	g j	k t	g d	ṅ n g n 41.a.	k p	g b	ṅ m g m 41.a.	g y	g r	g l	g v	k ś	k s	g gh 50
त् t or द् d	d a	d ā d i	t k	d g	c c 48	j j 48	t t	d d	n n d n 41.a.	t p	d b	n m d m 41.a.	d y	d r	l l	d v	c ch 49	t s	d dh 50
न् n	nn* a 52	nn* ā n i	n k	n g	ṃś c 53	ñ† j	ṃs t 53	n d	n n	n p	n b	n m	n y	n r	l l	n v	ñ† ś or ñ† ch 55	n s	n h
अस् as	o ' 64.a.	a ā a i 66	aḥ k 63	o g 64	aś c 62	o j	as t 62	o d	o n	aḥ p 63	o b	o m	o y	o r	o l	o v	aḥ ś 63	aḥ s 63	o h
आस् ās	ā a 66.a.	ā ā ā i 66.a	āḥ k 63	ā g 66.a.	āś c 62	ā j 66.a.	ās t 62	ā d	ā n	āḥ p 63	ā b	ā m	ā y	ā r	ā l	ā v	āḥ ś 63	āḥ s 63	ā h
इस् is, ईस् īs उस् us, ऊस् ūs एस् es, ऐस् ais ओस् os, औस् aus	ir a 65 ur a &c.	ir ā 65 ur ā &c.	iḥ k 63 uḥ k &c.	ir g 65 ur g &c.	iś c 62 uś c &c.	ir j 65 ur j &c.	is t 62 us t &c.	ir d ur d &c.	ir n ur n &c.	iḥ p 63 uḥ p &c.	ir b ur b &c.	ir m ur m &c.	ir y ur y &c.	ī r 65.a. ū r &c.	ir l ur l &c.	ir v ur v &c.	iḥ ś 63 uḥ ś &c.	iḥ s 63 uḥ s &c.	ir h ur h &c.
र् r, preceded by any vowel.	r a 17.c.	r ā &c.	ḥ k 71	r g 71	ś c 71	r j	s t	r d	r n	ḥ p	r b	r m	r y	r	r l	r v	ḥ ś	ḥ s	r h

* n is only doubled if preceded by a short vowel.

† A final n before ś and j is often allowed to remain unchanged.

CHAPTER III.

ON SANSKṚIT ROOTS, AND THE FORMATION OF THE CRUDE BASES OF NOUNS.

BEFORE treating of Sanskṛit nouns (संज्ञा or नामन्), it will be advisable to point out in what respect the peculiar system adopted in their formation requires an arrangement of the subject different from that to which we are accustomed in other languages.

74. In Sanskṛit nouns (including substantives, adjectives, pronouns, and numerals) there is this great peculiarity, that every one of them has two distinct states prior to the formation of the nominative case; viz. 1st, a root (*dhátu*); 2dly, coming directly from the root, a state which is called *the crude form* or *crude base* (*prátipadika*); that is to say, a state antecedent to inflection, and anterior to any of the cases, even the nominative. This crude form or crude base of the noun is sometimes termed *the inflective base*, because it generally coincides with this inflective base or *an-ga* * (Páṇ. I. 4, 13), i. e. with that changed form of the root, which serves as the basis for the construction of the case †.

In the first place, then, let us inquire what is the root?

There are in Sanskṛit about two thousand elementary sounds (*dhátu*), out of which, as out of so many blocks, are carved and fashioned, not only all the nouns, but all the verbs which exist in the language.

a. Though the root may be compared to a rough block, or to the raw material, out of which nouns and verbs are constructed, yet the student must understand that in the dialect of the Vedas, and even in modern classical Sanskṛit, roots are not unfrequently used by themselves as substantives and adjectives, and are very commonly so used at the end of compounds. See 84, 87, and 172.

---

* The *an-ga* or inflective base though often identical with the crude form or crude base is not always so; thus, in the model of the 1st class of nouns masculine, the crude base is *śiva*, but the inflective base is not only *śiva*, but also *śivá*, *śive*, and *śiván*.

† The crude word, before declension, is called *prátipadika* (or sometimes *śabda*), whereas *pada* is the name for the *inflected* word, or base and case-affix together.

b. Every one of these roots or primary sounds conveys some simple idea, which appears under different modifications in the derivatives from it. Thus—to mention a few of the most common—the root क्षिप् *kship* conveys the idea of 'throwing;' कृ *kṛi*, of 'doing,' 'making;' क्री *krí*, of 'buying;' हृ *hṛi*, of 'seizing,' 'taking;' युज् *yuj*, 'joining;' अस् *as*, वृत् *vṛit*, 'being;' भू *bhú*, 'becoming;' जीव् *jív*, 'living;' नी *ní*, 'leading;' जि *ji*, 'conquering;' गम् *gam*, या *yá*, चर् *ćar*, क्रम् *kram*, इ *i*, सृ *sṛi*, स्कन्द् *skand*, 'going;' वद् *vad*, वच् *vać*, ब्रू *brú*, 'speaking;' बुध् *budh*, ज्ञा *jná*, 'knowing;' दृश् *dṛiś*, 'seeing;' इष् *ish*, कम् *kam*, 'wishing;' मृ *mṛi*, 'dying;' दा *dá*, 'giving;' जन् *jan*, 'producing;' धा *dhá*, 'placing;' अद् *ad*, भुज् *bhuj*, भक्ष् *bhaksh*, 'eating;' पा *pá*, 'drinking;' पच् *pać*, 'cooking;' हन् *han*, 'killing;' पत् *pat*, 'falling;' वस् *vas*, 'dwelling;' विश् *viś*, 'entering;' स्था *sthá*, 'standing;' श्रु *śru*, 'hearing;' स्पृश् *spṛiś*, 'touching;' सिध् *sidh*, साध् *sádh*, 'accomplishing;' कुप् *kup*, क्रुध् *krudh*, 'being angry;' चि *ći*, 'collecting;' घ्रा *ghrá*, 'smelling;' ख्या *khyá*, 'relating;' नश् *naś*, 'perishing;' त्यज् *tyaj*, रह् *rah*, 'quitting;' द्विष् *dvish*, 'hating;' निन्द् *nind*, 'blaming;' द्रु *dru*, 'running;' द्युत् *dyut*, दीप् *díp*, भा *bhá*, शुभ् *śubh*, 'shining;' पू *pú*, 'purifying;' प्रच्छ् *prachh*, 'asking;' आप् *áp*, लभ् *labh*, 'obtaining;' स्तु *stu*, शंस् *śaṇs*, 'praising;' यत् *yat*, 'striving;' यम् *yam*, 'restraining;' शक् *śak*, 'being able;' तप् *tap*, 'heating;' दह् *dah*, 'burning;' मुच् *muć*, 'liberating;' मुह् *muh*, 'being foolish;' युध् *yudh*, 'fighting;' रुह् *ruh*, 'growing;' हस् *has*, 'laughing;' स्वप् *svap*, 'sleeping;' हृष् *hṛish*, नन्द् *nand*, ह्लाद् *hlád*, 'being glad;' स्ना *sná*, 'bathing;' रभ् *rabh*, 'beginning;' स्वर् *svar*, 'sounding;' सह् *sah*, वह् *vah*, 'bearing;' स्मृ *smṛi*, 'remembering;' अर्च् *arć*, 'honouring.'

c. Observe, that it will be convenient, in the following pages, to express the idea contained in the root by prefixing to it the Infinitive sign *to*. But the student must not suppose that the sound *kship* denotes any thing more than the mere idea of 'throwing;' nor must he imagine that in deriving nouns from it, we are deriving them from the infinitive, or from any part of the verb, but rather from a simple original sound, which is the common source of both nouns and verbs.

75. A cursory glance at the above list of common roots will serve to shew that there are two particulars in which they all agree. Every one of them is monosyllabic, and every one of them contains a single vowel, and no more. In other respects they offer considerable diversity. Some consist of a single vowel only; some begin with one or two consonants, and end in a vowel, but none end in

either अ *a* or औ *au*; some begin with a vowel, and end in one or two consonants *; and some begin and end with one or two consonants †, inclosing a medial vowel; so that a root may sometimes consist of only one letter, as इ *i*, 'to go;' and sometimes of five, as स्कन्द् *skand*, 'to move;' प्रच्छ् *praćh*, 'to ask.' It is probable that those roots which consist of simple letters, such as भू, भृ, इ, विद्, बुध्, &c., are the most ancient; and that those which have compound consonants, such as स्कन्द् &c., are less so. Those which have cerebral letters, such as लुड् 'to roll,' are probably derived from the aboriginal language of India.

a. There are a few polysyllabic words recognised as roots, but they are generally the result of the accidental conjunction of a preposition with a monosyllabic root; that is to say, the preposition has been so constantly used in conjunction with the root, that it has at length come to be regarded as part of the root: thus in the roots संग्राम् *san-grām*, 'to fight,' and अवधीर् *avadhīr*, 'to despise,' the prepositions सं *sam* and अव *ava* have combined with the root in this manner. A few other polysyllabic roots are the result of a reduplication of the radical syllable; (as, दरिद्रा *daridrā*, 'to be poor;' जागृ *jāgṛi*, 'to be awake;' चकास् *ćakās*, 'to shine;' वेवी *vevī*, 'to go,' 'pervade;') and a few are derived from nouns; as, कुमार् 'to play,' from कुमार *kumāra*, 'a boy.'

b. न *n* and स *s* at the beginning of a root are liable, according to 58 and 70, to be changed to ण *ṇ* and ष *sh*. Hence most of these roots ‡ are exhibited in Native Grammars as beginning with ण and ष, because the Indian system requires that in exhibiting any general type of a class of words, that *form* should be taken which may occur even under the rarest circumstances. But in this Grammar, roots of which the initials are न *n* and स *s* will be exhibited as beginning with these letters, by reason of their more frequent occurrence.

c. According to Indian grammarians, roots are either *uddātta* or *anudātta* (see r. 24). *Uddātta* roots take the inserted इ *i* in certain tenses (see r. 391), *anudātta* roots reject this inserted vowel (Pāṇini VII. 2, 10). Modern native grammarians attach to roots certain symbolical letters or syllables (called *anubandhas*, 'appendages,' or technically इत् *it*) to indicate peculiarities in their conjugation,

* Rule 43, which requires that if a word ends in a conjunct consonant, the last member shall be rejected, is not applicable to roots, unless they are used as complete words in a sentence. Nevertheless, in the case of roots ending in a consonant, preceded by a nasal, the latter is often euphonically dropped, as स्रंस् becomes स्रस्.

† One root, श्च्युत् *śćyut*, 'to drop,' begins with three consonants.

‡ But not all, ex. gr. the स of roots containing ऋ, ॠ, or र generally remains, as in सृप्, स्तृ; as also the स of सृज्, सम्, स्वप्, and a few others; and a few may be written with either स or ष.

which *anubandhas* or *its* may either have the *udátta* accent to shew that the verb takes the Parasmai-pada (243) terminations only (such verbs being then called *udáttetaḥ*); or the *anudátta* to shew that it takes the Átmane-pada only (such verbs being *anudáttetaḥ*); or the *svarita* to shew that it takes both (such verbs being *svaritetaḥ*). See Páṇini I. 3, 12, 72, 78. The following is a list of Páṇini's *anubandhas* (with one or two added by Vopadeva): आ indicates that the past participle affixes (530. 553. called *nishṭhá* in native grammars) do not take the inserted *i*, P. VII. 2, 16. इ that a nasal is inserted before the last letter of the root in all the tenses; thus *nid i* shews that the present is *nindámi* &c., P. VII. 1, 58. इर् that the 3d pret. is formed in two ways, either with form I (418) or form II (435); thus *ghush ir* shews that the 3d pret. is either *aghoshisham* &c. or *aghusham* &c., and *dṛiś ir* that the 3d pret. is either *adrákshan* or *adarśam*. ई that the past participle (530, 553) is formed without *i*, P. VII. 2, 14. उ that the indeclinable participle (555) may optionally reject *i*, while the past part. always rejects it, P. VII. 2, 56, 15. ऊ that *i* may optionally be inserted in the non-conjugational tenses, P. VII. 2, 15. ऋ that in the caus. 3d pret. the radical long vowel must not be shortened, P. VII. 4, 2. ॠ that the vowel may be either lengthened or shortened in the caus. 3d pret. ऌ that the 3d pret. takes form II (435) in the Parasmai, P. III. 1, 55. ए that Vṛiddhi is not admitted in the 3d pret. Parasmai, P. VII. 2, 5. ओ that the past pass. part. is formed with *na* instead of *ta*, P. VIII. 2, 45. औ that a root is *anudátta*, i. e. that it rejects the inserted *i*. ङ that a root is inflected in the Átmane, P. I. 3, 12. ञ that a root is inflected in the Parasmai and Átmane, P. I. 3, 72. ञि that the past part. has a present signification, P. III. 2, 187. टु that a noun with the affix *athu* may be formed from the root; thus *ṭu-kshu* indicates that *kshavathu* may be formed from *kshu*, P. III. 3, 89. डु that a noun with the affix *trima* may be formed from the root; thus *ḍu kṛi* indicates that *kṛitrima* may be formed from *kṛi*, P. III. 3, 88. म indicates that the vowel *a* must not be lengthened in forming the causal, that in the 3d sing. 3d pret. pass. (technically called *ćiṇ*, 475) and indec. part. of repetition (567, technically named *ṇamul*) the vowel can be optionally lengthened or shortened, and that nouns of agency in *a* (580) can be formed from causal bases having short radical vowels, P. V. 4, 92, 93, 94. ष that a noun may be formed from the root by adding the affix *a* (80. XXII), P. III. 3, 104.

76. The learner is recommended to study attentively the commonest of these roots, or elementary sounds, as given at 74. *b*. He may rest assured, that by pausing for a time at the root, his progress afterwards will be more rapid, when he ascends to the branches which spring from it. For it must never be forgotten, that every word in Sanskṛit, whether substantive, adjective, verb, or adverb, stands in close filial relationship to some radical sound. In fact, every root is a common bond of union for a large family of

words, which might otherwise appear unconnected; and words which, when viewed apart from the root, are isolated symbols, demanding a separate effort of memory for each separate idea which they express, fasten themselves readily on the mind when regarded as so many parts of one original idea, so many branches of a common stock.

Thus, to take any one of the foregoing roots — as, for example, *budh*, 'to know'— we shall find that from it may be drawn out with great regularity, 1st, a set of simple substantives; 2dly, of simple adjectives; 3dly, of simple verbs: thus, *bodha* or *bodhana*, 'knowledge;' *buddhi*, 'intellect;' *bodhaka*, 'an informer;' *bauddha*, 'a Buddhist;' *budha*, 'wise;' *buddhimat*, 'intellectual;' and the following verbs, *bodhati*, 'he knows;' *budhyate*, 'it is known;' *bodhayati*, 'he informs;' *bubhutsate* or *bubodhishati*, 'he wishes to know;' *bobudhyate*, 'he knows well.' And the simple idea contained in the root may be endlessly extended by the prefixing of prepositions; as, *prabodha*, 'vigilance;' *prabudhyate*, 'he awakes,' &c.

77. In the next place we are to inquire what is the base or crude form of the noun. The student should understand, at the outset, the meaning and use of this form. It is an intermediate state between the root and nominative case, the naked form of the noun, which serves as the basis on which to construct its eight cases, beginning with the nominative. In a Greek or Latin dictionary we look for the noun under the nominative case; but in Sanskrit we look for it under its crude state. Thus, *bodha*, *bodhana*, *tat*, *pathin*, *bhavat*, are the crude bases under which the nominative cases *bodhas*, *bodhanam*, *sas*, *panthá*, *bhaván*, are to be sought. And here it may be observed, that the base of a noun is no mere grammatical invention. It is, perhaps, more practically useful than the cases derived from it. It is that form of the noun which is always used in the formation of compound words, and in this respect may be regarded as the most general of cases. And since every Sanskrit sentence contains more compound words than simple, it may with truth be said, that the crude base is the form under which the noun most usually appears.

We may conceive it quite possible that Greek and Latin grammarians might have proceeded on a similar plan, and that they might have supposed a root λεγ, from which was drawn out the nouns λέξις, λεξικὸς, λεκτὸς, καταλογὴ, ἔλλογος, and the verbs λέγω, καταλέγω, ἐλλογέω: so also, a root *scrib*, from which was derived the nouns *scriptio*, *scriptum*, *scriptor*, *scriptura*; and the verbs *scribo*, *perscribo*, *ascribo*: or a root *nav*, from which would come *nauta*, *navis*, *nauticus*, *navalis*, *navigo*, &c. Again, they might have supposed a crude base to each of these nouns, as well as a root; as, for instance, λεξι and λεξικο of λέξις and λεξικὸς, and *navi* of *navis*; and they might have required the student to look for λέξις under λεξι, λέγω under λεγ, *navis* under *navi*, and *navigo* under *nav*. Further than this, they might have shewn that the base was the form used in the formation of compound words, as in λεξικογράφος and *naviger*. But Greek and Latin are too uncertain in their construction to admit of such an analysis being completely carried out.

78. It will be perceived from the foregoing remarks that the consideration of Sanskṛit nouns must divide itself into two heads: 1st, the formation of the base; 2dly, the inflection or declension of the base; that is, the adaptation of the crude base or modified root to a common scheme of case-terminations.

a. In fact, it will appear in the sequel, that the same system applies both to nouns and verbs. As in verbs (see 248) the formation of a verbal base from a root precedes the subject of verbal inflection or conjugation, so in nouns it is necessary to the clear elucidation of the subject that the method of forming the nominal base from the root should be explained antecedently to declension.

b. Indeed, it must be remembered that nouns, substantive and adjective, in Sanskṛit are classified into separate declensions, according to the finals of their crude *bases*, not according to the finals of their cases; and it becomes essential to determine the form of the final syllable of the nominal base before the various declensions can be arranged.

79. The crude bases of nouns are formed either by adding certain affixes to the root, the vowel of which is liable, at the same time, to be gunated or vriddhied (which nouns are called *kṛidanta*, primary derivatives); or by adding certain affixes to the bases of nouns already formed (which nouns are then called *taddhita*, secondary derivatives). When, however, the root itself is used as a noun, no affix is required, but the root is then also the base. Hence it follows that the final syllable of nominal bases will end in almost any letter of the alphabet. Those bases, however, that end in vowels may be conveniently separated under four classes, each class containing masc., fem., and neuter nouns; the 1st ending in अ *a*, आ *á*, and ई *í*; the 2d in इ *i*; the 3d in उ *u*; and the 4th in ऋ *ṛi*. Those that end in consonants may also be arranged under four classes; the 1st, 2d, and 3d, ending in त् *t* (and द् *d*), न् *n*, and स् *s*, respectively (compare 44); and the 4th comprising all other final consonants.

a. It will be afterwards shewn, that the first class of nouns, comprising bases in *a*, *á*, and *í*, is by far the most numerous; just as the first group of verbs, comprising bases ending in *a* and *á*, is the most numerous and important. See 109.

Bearing in mind, therefore, that Sanskṛit declension consists in building up a system of cases on a base, by attaching the case-terminations to that base—bearing in mind, moreover, that the whole distinction of declensions depends on the distribution of the bases of nouns under eight classes, according to their final syllables—we are now to explain more precisely, under each of these classes, the method of forming the nominal crude base by regular derivation from the root.

Observe—It is not intended that the student should dwell long on the following pages printed in small type. He is recommended to read them over rapidly, and to note carefully the final letters of the base under each of the eight classes.

Observe, moreover, that although all the bases of Sanskṛit nouns, without exception, are derived from roots, there are many in which the connection between the noun and its source, either in sense or form, is not very obvious *. The following rules have reference only to those bases whose formation proceeds on clear and intelligible principles.

FORMATION OF THE CRUDE FORM OR BASE OF NOUNS.

80. FIRST CLASS.—*Comprising Masculine and Neuter bases in* अ a; *Feminine in* आ á *and* ई í.

Formed by adding to ROOTS—

[Note—Primary derivatives from roots are called in native grammars *kṛidanta*, while those from nouns already formed, or secondary derivatives, are called *taddhita*.]

1. अ *a*, *forming*, 1st (nom. *-as*), after Vṛiddhi of medial *a* of a root, and Guṇa

* This applies especially to nouns formed with the *uṇádi* affixes, so called from the affix uṇ (i. e. u with an indicatory ṇ), by which the words *kárú*, *váyu*, &c., are formed in the first Sútra. The import of these derivatives is not generally in accordance with the radical meaning, and even when it is so, usually receives an individual signification; thus *kárú*, though it involves the general idea of *doing*, means especially 'an artizan.' It is difficult to acquiesce in the derivation of some of these *uṇádi* words: thus *purusha*, 'a man,' is said to come from *pur*, 'to precede;' *náku*, 'an ant-hill,' from *nam*, 'to bend;' *kapila*, 'tawny,' from *kam*, 'to love,' &c.

of any other vowel, a large class of masculine substantives; as, from the root *div*, 'to shine,' *deva*, 'a deity.' If a root ends in *c* or *j*, these letters are changed to *k* and *g* respectively; as, from *pac*, 'to cook,' *pāka*, 'cooking;' from *yuj*, 'to join,' *yoga*, 'joining.' See 43. *d*.

II. अ *a*, forming, 2dly (nom. masc. *-as*, fem. *-ā*, neut. *-am*), after Guṇa of a final, and sometimes Guṇa of a medial vowel, nouns of agency and adjectives; as, from *plu*, 'to swim,' *plava*, 'what swims;' from *sṛip*, 'to creep,' *sarpa*, 'what creeps.' See 580. Adjectives of this form generally occur at the end of compounds; as, *ari-dama*, 'foe-taming;' *bhayan-kara*, 'fear-causing.' Compare corresponding formations in Greek and Latin; as, ἱππό-δαμος, *veri-dicus*, *grandi-loquus*, *omni-vorus*, &c. When सु *su* and दुस् δυς are prefixed to these adjectives, they are susceptible of a passive sense, both in Sanskrit and Greek; as, सुकर 'easy to be done;' दुष्कर 'hard to be done,' &c. Similarly, εὔφορος, δύσφορος, δύστομος, &c.

III. र *ra*, forming, 3dly (nom. *-as*, *-ā*, *-am*), adjectives: as, from *śubh*, 'to shine,' *śubhra* 'beautiful.' Sometimes there is great variation from the root; as in *śiva*, 'propitious,' from शी *śī*, 'to sleep;' *sundara*, 'beautiful,' from दृ *dṛi*, 'to respect:' and sometimes the feminine may be formed in *ī*; as, *sundarī*. There are very few adjectives formed with this affix.

IV. अक *aka* (nom. *-akas*, *-akā* or *-ikā*, *-akam*), after Vṛiddhi of a final vowel or medial *a*, and Guṇa of any other vowel. Still more common than *a* to form adjectives and nouns of agency (see 582. *b*); as, from *tap*, 'to burn,' *tāpaka*, 'inflammatory;' from *kṛi*, 'to do,' *kāraka*, 'a doer,' 'acting.' Observe, *-akā* is generally taken for the feminine of the adjectives, and *-ikā* for the feminine of the agents; as, *tāpakā*, *kārikā*. Compare Greek forms like φύλακες.

V. अन *ana* (nom. *-anam*), after Guṇa of the root, forming, 1st, a large class of neuter substantives; as, from *nī*, 'to guide,' *nayana*, 'the eye,' 'guidance;' from *dā*, 'to give,' *dāna*, 'a gift;' from *dṛip*, 'to make proud,' *darpaṇa*, 'a mirror.' Compare analogous Greek formations in ανο; as, ὄργανον, δρέπανον, &c.

अन *ana*, forming, 2dly (nom. *-anas*, *-anā*, *-anam*), nouns of agency (see 582. *c*) and adjectives; as, from *nṛit*, 'to dance,' *nartana*, 'a dancer;' from *śubh*, 'to shine,' *śobhana*, 'bright.' Compare Greek forms like ἱκανός, &c. The feminine of the agents is sometimes in *-anī*.

VI. न *na*. A few abstract nouns are formed with *na*; as, *yajña*, 'sacrifice,' from *yaj*; *yatna*, 'effort,' from *yat*; *svapna*, 'sleep,' from *svap*. Compare ὕπνος, *somnus*.

VII. त्र *tra* (nom. *-tram*), after Guṇa of the root; as, from पा *pā*, 'to drink,' *pātra*, 'a vessel;' from श्रु *śru*, 'to hear,' *śrotra*, 'the organ of hearing.' Sometimes the vowel *i* is inserted; as, from खन् 'to dig,' *khanitra*, 'a spade.' This affix is used to form neuter nouns denoting some instrument or organ, and corresponds to the Latin *trum* in *aratrum*, *plectrum*, &c.; and the Greek τρον, θρον in νίπτρον, βάκτρον, βάθρον, &c.

VIII. There are other uncommon affixes to roots to form adjectives and a few substantives in अ *a* (nom. *-as*, *-á*, *-am*); as, र *ra*, ल *la*, आल *ála*, अर *ara*, वर *vara*, मर *mara*, इल *ila*, इर *ira*, उर *ura*, उल *ula*, म *ma*, व *va*, त्र *tra*, आलु *álu*, वर *vra*, उक *uka*, आक *áka*, क *ka*. The following are examples of nouns formed with these affixes: *dípra*, 'shining' (compare Greek formations like λάμπ-ρος, &c.; and Latin *pu-rus*, &c.); *čandra*, 'the moon;' *śukla*, 'white;' *čapala*, 'fickle;' *tarala*, 'tremulous' (compare Greek forms like τρόχ-αλος, τρέμ-ελος; and Latin *tremulus*, &c.); *asthira*, 'unsteady' (compare Greek forms like φάνερος, &c.); *sthávara*, 'stationary;' *ghasmara*, 'voracious;' *anila*, 'wind;' *pathila*, 'a traveller' (compare Latin forms like *agilis*, &c.); *čhidira*, 'an axe;' *bhidura*, 'brittle;' *kurabala*, 'a lover;' *bhíma*, 'terrible;' *gharma*, m., 'heat;' *yugma*, n., 'a pair;' *dhúma*, m., 'smoke' (compare forms like θύ-μος, ἄνεμ-ος, *fumus*, *animus*, &c.); *aśva*, m., 'a horse' (*equus*, ἵππος); *čitra*, 'variegated;' *jalpáka*, 'talkative' (compare forms like *loquax*, i.e. *loquac-s*, *loquac-o*; and φέναξ, i.e. φένακς for φένακος); *patvara*, 'moving;' *varshuka*, 'rainy;' *jágarúka*, 'watchful,' *úka* being added (especially to frequentative or reduplicate forms; as, from *vávad*, 'to speak often,' *vávadúka*, 'loquacious'); *śushka*, 'dry' (from *śush*, 'to dry.' Compare Latin *siccus*).

Formed by adding to the bases of NOUNS—

IX. त्व *tva* (nom. *-tvam*), forming neuter abstract substantives from any noun in the language; as, from *purusha*, 'a man,' *purushatva*, 'manliness.' In adding this affix to bases ending in nasals, the nasal is rejected; as, from *dhanin*, 'rich,' *dhanitva*, 'the state of being rich.' (See 57.)

X. य *ya*, forming, 1st (nom. *-yam*), neuter abstract substantives and a few collectives, the first syllable of the noun taking Vṛiddhi; as, from सुहृद् *suhṛid*, 'a friend,' सौहृद्य *sauhṛidya*, 'friendship.' When the base ends in a vowel, this vowel is rejected before *ya*; and when in *an* and *in*, these syllables are rejected; as, from *vičitra*, 'various,' *vaičitrya*, 'variety;' from *rájan*, 'a king,' *rájya*, 'kingdom;' from *svámin*, 'a lord,' *svámya*, 'lordship.'

XI. य *ya*, forming, 2dly (nom. *-yas*, *-yá*, *-yam*), adjectives expressing some relationship to the noun; as, from *dhana*, 'wealth,' *dhanya*, 'wealthy.' Sometimes Vṛiddhi takes place; as, from *soma*, 'the moon,' *saumya*, 'lunar.' In this case the fem. is *-yí*. Compare Greek adjectives in ιος, and Latin in *ius*.

XII. अ *a* (nom. *-as*, *-í*, *-am*), after Vṛiddhi of the first syllable of the noun, forming innumerable adjectives expressing some relationship to the noun. When the base ends in *a*, no further affix is required, and the only change is the Vṛiddhi of the first syllable; as, from *purusha*, 'a man,' पौरुष *paurusha*, 'manly;' from *Vasishṭha*, *Vásishṭha*, 'a descendant of Vasishṭha.' When in *á* or *í*, this *á* or *í* must be rejected; as, from *sikatá*, 'sand,' *saikata*, 'sandy.' When in *u*, this *u* is gunated, and becomes *av* before this and the three following affixes; as, from *Vishṇu*, 'the god Vishṇu,' *Vaishṇava*, 'a worshipper of Vishṇu;' from *dáru*, 'wood,' *dárava*, 'wooden;' from *manu*, *mánava*, 'a descendant of Manu.'

When the initial letter of a word is compounded with *v* or *y*, followed by *a* or *á*, then *v* and *y* are generally resolved into *uv* and *iy*, which are vriddhied; as, सौवर

sauvara, 'relating to sound,' from *svara*, 'a note;' वैयाघ्र *vaiyāghra*, 'relating to a tiger,' from *vyāghra*, 'a tiger.' This applies to the next two affixes also; but the rule is not universal unless the *v* and *y* are the result of the euphonic change of an original *u* and *i*, as in *vaiyākaraṇa*, 'grammatical,' from *vyākaraṇa*, 'grammar.'

Sometimes the neuter form of these adjectives is taken as an abstract substantive; thus, nominative case, *paurusham*, 'manliness,' from *purusha*, 'a man;' *śaiśavam*, 'childhood,' from *śiśu*, 'a child;' or, as a collective; thus, *kshaitram*, 'fields,' collectively, from *kshetra*. Observe—This applies to the next two affixes also.

XIII. इक *ika* (nom. *-ikas*, *-ikī*, *-ikam*), after Vṛiddhi of the first syllable of the noun, forming numerous adjectives. Before this affix is added, the final vowel of the base must be rejected; as, from *dharma*, 'religion,' *dhārmika*, 'religious;' from *veṇu*, 'a flute,' *vainavika*, 'a flute-player;' from *dvāra*, 'a door,' *dauvārika*, 'a porter;' from श्वस् *śvas*, 'to-morrow' (an euphonic *t* being inserted), शौवस्तिक *śauvastika*, 'relating to to-morrow.' Compare Latin forms like *bellicus*, *rusticus*, &c.; and Greek πολεμικός, &c.

XIV. एय *eya* (nom. *-eyas*, *-eyī*, *-eyam*), after Vṛiddhi of the first syllable of the noun, forming many adjectives. The final vowel of the base must be rejected; as, from *purusha*, 'a man,' *paurusheya*, 'manly;' from *agni*, 'fire,' *āgneya*, 'fiery.' Compare forms like λεόντειος, λεόντεος; and Latin *igneus*, &c.

XV. ईय *īya* (nom. *-īyas*, *-īyā*, *-īyam*), without any change of the noun, except the rejection of final *a*; as, from *parvata*, 'a mountain,' *parvatīya*, 'mountainous.' Sometimes there is Vṛiddhi; as, from *sukha*, 'pleasure,' *saukhīya*, 'pleasurable.' When the final of the base remains, *k* is prefixed to this and the last affix; as, from *para*, 'another,' *parakīya*, 'belonging to another.'

XVI. There are other uncommon affixes to nouns forming adjectives in अ *a* (nom. *-as*, *-ā*, *-am*); such as *īna*, *ina*, *vala*, *tana*, *titha*; forming, from *grāma*, 'a village,' *grāmīṇa*, 'rustic;' from *ratha*, 'a chariot' (Lat. *rota*), *rathina*, 'having a chariot;' from *śikhā*, 'a crest,' *śikhāvala*, 'crested;' from *śvas*, 'to-morrow,' *śvastana*, 'future;' from *bahu*, 'many,' *bahutitha*, 'manieth.' This last answers to the Latin *tinus*, and has reference to *time*. Compare *crastinus*, &c.

XVII. क *ka* (nom. *-kas*, *-kā*, *-kam*), added to words to form adjectives and collective nouns, or to express depreciation: thus, *madhuka*, 'sweet,' from *madhu*, 'honey;' *aśvaka*, 'a hack,' from *aśva*, 'a horse.' Observe—*Ka* is often redundant.

XVIII. मय *maya* (nom. *-mayas*, *-mayī*, *-mayam*), added to words to denote 'made of,' 'full of;' as, from *loha*, 'iron,' *lohamaya*, 'made of iron;' from *tejas*, 'light,' *tejomaya*, 'full of light' (by r. 64).

XIX. तर *tara* (nom. *-taras*, *-tarā*, *-taram*), तम *tama* (nom. *-tamas*, *-tamā*, *-tamam*), इष्ठ *ishṭha* (nom. *-ishṭhas*, *-ishṭhā*, *-ishṭham*), added to adjectives to express the degrees of comparison. See 191, 192.

XX. दघ्न *daghna* (nom. *-daghnas*, *-daghnī*, *-daghnam*; cf. Hindi تک), द्वयस *dvayasa* (*-dvayasas*, *-dvayasī*, *-dvayasam*), and मात्र *mātra* (*-mātras*, *-mātrī*, *-mātram*; cf. μέτρον, metre), added to words to denote 'measure' or 'height;' as, *jānu-daghnam jalam*, 'water up to the knees.'

XXI. देशीय *deśīya* (nom. *-deśīyas*, *-deśīyā*, *-deśīyam*) and कल्प *kalpa* (nom. *-kalpas*, *-kalpā*, *-kalpam*), added to words to denote 'similitude,' but with some inferiority; as, *kavi-kalpa* or *kavi-deśīya*, 'a sort of poet:' or denoting 'nearly,' 'about;' as, *mṛita-kalpa*, 'nearly dead;' *viṃśati-varsha-deśīya*, 'about twenty years of age.'

a. Observe—The affixes त *ta* and इत *ita* and न *na* (nom. *-as*, *-ā*, *-am*), forming innumerable passive participles—as, *jita*, 'conquered,' from *ji*, 'to conquer,' &c.—fall under the first class of bases. See 530.

b. So also many other participles formed with *māna*, *āna*, *tavya*, *anīya*, *ya*, &c. See 526, 527, 568.

c. इत *ita* is said to be added to nouns to form adjectives; as, *phalita*, 'fruitful,' from *phala*, 'fruit;' but these may be regarded as passive participles from nominal verbs. See 551.

Feminine bases in आ *ā and* ई *ī.*

By adding to ROOTS—

XXII. आ *ā* (nom. *-ā*), with no change of the root, forming feminine substantives; as, from *jīv*, 'to live,' *jīvā*, 'life;' from स्पृह् *spṛih*, 'to desire,' स्पृहा *spṛihā*, 'desire.' Compare Greek formations like φορά, φυγή: and Latin *fuga*, &c. Occasionally there is Guṇa; as in *lekhā*, 'a line,' from *likh*, 'to write;' *jarā*, 'old age,' from *jṛī*, 'to grow old.' This affix is frequently added to the desiderative form of a root; as, from *pipās*, 'to desire to drink,' *pipāsā*, 'thirst;' and rarely to the frequentative or intensive; as, from *loluy*, 'to cut much,' *loluyā*, 'cutting much.'

A few abstract nouns are formed with णा *ṇā*; as, *tṛishṇā*, 'thirst,' from *tṛish*: compare Greek nouns in νη, as ζώνη, φερνή.

By adding to the bases of NOUNS—

XXIII. ता *tā* (nom. *-tā*), forming feminine abstract substantives; as, from *purusha*, 'a man,' *purushatā*, 'manliness.' This affix may be added to any noun in the language, and corresponds to the Latin *tas* in *celeritas*, &c.; and the Greek τηs in κακότης, πλαστότης (पुरुषता).

Also forming collectives; as, बन्धुता 'a number of relations,' from बन्धु 'a relation.'

XXIV. त्रा *trā* (nom. *-trā*), forming a few substantives, and like neuters in *tra* (see VII) denoting 'the instrument' or 'means;' as, दंष्ट्रा 'a tooth,' 'the instrument of biting,' from *daṃś*, 'to bite;' यात्रा 'provisions,' 'the means of going,' from *yā*, 'to go.'

XXV. ई *ī* (nom. *-ī*), forming a large class of feminine substantives, usually derived from masculines in *a*, by changing *a* to *ī*; as, from *nada*, 'a river,' fem. *nadī*; from *putra*, 'a son,' fem. *putrī*; from *nartaka*, 'a dancer,' fem. *nartakī*. An affix *ānī* is used to denote 'the wife of;' as, from *Indra*, इन्द्राणी (58) 'the wife of Indra.' Compare the Greek αινα in θέαινα, &c.

XXVI. ई *í* (nom. *-í*), forming, 2dly, the feminine of nouns of agency, like दात्री *dátrí* from दातृ *dátri*, 'a giver' (129. *b*), and *káriṇí* from *kárin*, 'a doer' (160).

XXVII. ई *í* (nom. *-í*), forming, 3dly, the feminine of many adjectives; as of *tanu*, 'thin' (118. *a*), of *dhanavat*, 'rich,' and *dhímat*, 'wise' (140. *b*); of *dhanin*, 'rich' (160), and of comparative degrees like *balíyas* (167). Observe—The feminine of some adjectives formed with the affixes *a*, *ya*, *ika*, and *eya* (XI. XII. XIII. XIV), and of some adjectives like *sundara*, 'beautiful,' is also formed with *í*.

XXVIII. A few roots standing by themselves as substantives, or with prepositions prefixed, or at the end of compounds, may come under this class; as, *bhí*, 'fear,' *ájñá*, 'an order,' from ज्ञा 'to know;' *senání*, 'a general,' from *sená*, 'an army,' and *ní*, 'to lead,' &c. It will be more convenient, however, to consider the declension of monosyllabic nouns in *í* under the 2d class. See 123, 126.

81. Second Class.—*Masculine, Feminine, and Neuter bases in* इ i.

Formed by adding to roots—

I. इ *i*, forming, 1st (nom. *-is*), a few masculine substantives; as, *agni*, 'fire' (derivation doubtful); *kavi*, 'a poet,' from *ku*, 'to sound;' *ahi*, 'a snake' (ἔχις, *anguis*), from *aṃh*, 'to move;' *dhvani*, 'sound,' from *dhvan*; *pavi*, 'a thunderbolt,' from *pavh*, 'to crush,' &c. When this affix is added to the root *dhá*, 'to place,' 'to hold,' *á* is dropped, and various prepositions are prefixed; as in *sandhi*, *vidhi*, *nidhi*, &c. Observe—A feminine noun of this kind formed from *dhá* is *oshadhi*, 'an annual plant' (also *oshadhí*).

Also a few feminine nouns; as, *kṛishi*, 'ploughing,' from *kṛish*; *lipi*, 'writing,' from *lip*, &c. Compare Greek forms like χάρις, ἐλπίς, μῆτις (मति).

II. इ *i*, forming, 2dly (nom. *-i*), one or two neuter substantives; as, from *vṛi*, 'to surround,' *vári*, 'water;' from *aksh*, 'to pervade,' *akshi*, 'the eye' (*oculus*, ὄσσε).

III. इ *i*, forming, 3dly (nom. *-is*, *-is*, *-i*), a few adjectives; as, from *śuc*, 'to be pure,' *śuci*, 'pure;' from *budh*, 'to know,' *budhi*, 'wise.'

IV. मि *mi* (nom. *-mis*), forming a few nouns; as, *bhúmi*, f., 'the earth,' from *bhú*, 'to be' (*humus*); *raśmi*, m., 'a ray,' &c.

V. ति *ti* (nom. *-tis*), forming abstract substantives feminine. This affix bears a great analogy to the passive participle at 531. The same changes of the root are required before it as before this participle; and, in fact, provided the passive participle does not insert *i*, this substantive may always be formed from it, by changing *ta* into *ti*. But if *i* is inserted before *ta*, no such substantive can be formed: thus, from *vad*, 'to speak,' *ukta*, 'spoken,' *ukti*, 'speech;' from *man*, 'to imagine,' *mata*, 'imagined,' *mati*, 'the mind;' from *dá*, 'to give,' *datta*, 'given,' *datti*, 'a gift;' from *pṛí*, 'to fill,' *púrta*, 'filled,' *púrti*, 'fulness.' And when *na* is substituted for *ta* of the passive participle, *ni* is generally substituted for *ti*; as, from *glai*, 'to be weary,' *gláua*, 'wearied,' *gláni*, 'weariness;' from *lú*, 'to cut,' *lúna*, 'cut,' *lúni*, 'cutting.' This affix corresponds to the *tio* of the Latin,

I 2

added in the same way to passive participles; as, *actus*, *actio*; *junctus*, *junctio* (*yuktis*). Greek exhibits analogous forms in ζεῦξις, πίστις, δόσις.

a. A few masculine nouns are formed with *ti*; as, *yati*, 'a sage,' from *yam*, 'to restrain;' *jñāti*, 'a relation,' from *jñā*; *pati*, 'a husband' (for *pāti*), from *pā*.

Formed by adding to the bases of a few NOUNS ending in *a*—

VI. इ *i* (nom. -*is*), after Vṛiddhi of the first syllable, and after rejection of the final vowel. This affix forms a few patronymics; as, दौष्यन्ति *daushyanti*, 'the son of Dushyanta,' from दुष्यन्त *dushyanta*.

82. Third Class.—*Masculine, Feminine, and Neuter bases in* उ u.

Formed by adding to ROOTS—

I. उ *u*, forming, 1st (nom. -*us*), substantives of the masculine, and one or two of the feminine gender; as, from *bandh*, 'to bind,' *bandhu*, m., 'a kinsman;' from *kṛi*, 'to do,' *kāru*, m., 'an artificer;' from *bhid*, 'to cleave,' *bhidu*, m., 'a thunderbolt;' from *tan*, 'to stretch,' *tanu*, f., 'the body.'

II. उ *u*, forming, 2dly (nom. -*u*), one or two neuter substantives; as, *dāru*, 'wood' (also m.), from *dṛī*, 'to cleave' (δόρυ); *madhu*, 'honey' (μέθυ), &c.

III. उ *u*, forming, 3dly (nom. -*us*, -*us* or -*vī*, -*u*), sometimes with change of the root, a few adjectives; as, from *svad*, 'to taste,' *svādu*, 'sweet' (ἡδύ); from *tan*, 'to stretch,' *tanu*, 'thin' (compare ταναύ); from *langh*, 'to spring,' *laghu*, 'light' (ἐλαχύ); from *prath*, 'to extend,' *pṛithu*, 'broad' (πλατύ). This affix is often added to desiderative roots to form adjectives; as, from *pipās*, 'to desire to drink,' *pipāsu*, 'thirsty;' from जिजीविष 'to desire to live,' जिजीविषु 'desirous of living.'

Latin has added an *i* to all adjectives formed with *u* in the cognate languages; as, *tenuis* for *tanus*; *gravis* (*garuis*) for *gurus* (comparative *garīyas*), βαρύς. It has, however, substantives in *u*; as, *currus*, *acus*, &c.

IV. नु *nu* (nom. -*nus*, -*nus*, -*nu*), forming adjectives and substantives; as, from *tras*, 'to fear,' *trasnu*, 'timid;' from *bhā*, 'to shine,' *bhānu*, m., 'the sun;' from *dhe*, 'to drink,' *dhenu*, f., 'a cow;' from *sū*, 'to bear,' *sūnu*, m., 'a son.' (Compare Greek forms like λιγνύς.)

V. इष्णु *ishṇu* (nom. -*ishṇus*, -*ishṇus*, -*ishṇu*), with Guṇa of the root, forming adjectives; as, from *kshi*, 'to perish,' *kshayishṇu*, 'perishing.'

VI. There are many other affixes to roots, forming nouns in *u* (nom. -*us*, -*us*, -*u*); as, रु *ru*, नु *nu*, आरु *āru*, लु *lu*, आलु *ālu*, इत्नु *itnu*, तु *tu*, अथु *athu*, यु *yu*. The following nouns afford examples of these affixes: *bhīru*, 'timid;' *aśru*, n., 'a tear' (for *daśru*, from *daṃś*, 'to bite;' compare δάκρυ, *lacryma*); *śayālu*, 'sleepy;' *sthāṇu*, 'firm;' *śarāru*, 'noxious;' *gadayitnu*, 'loquacious;' *jantu*, m., 'an animal;' *gantu*, m., 'a traveller;' *vepathu*, m., 'trembling;' *manyu*, m., 'wrath' (μένος); and *mṛityu*, m., 'death.'

There are a few nouns in long *ū*, which may conveniently be placed under this class. They consist chiefly of roots standing by themselves as substantives, or as the end of compounds: thus, भू f. 'the earth,' स्वयंभू m. 'the self-existent,' &c. See 125. a, 126. b.

83. Fourth Class.—*Masculine, Feminine, and Neuter bases in* ऋ ṛi.

Formed by adding to roots—

I. तृ *tṛi*, forming, 1st (nom. *-tá*, *-trí*, *-tṛi*), nouns of agency of three genders, the same change of the root being required which takes place in the first future, and the same euphonic changes of *t* (see 386 and 581): thus, from *kship*, 'to throw,' *kshepṭṛi*, 'a thrower;' from *dá*, 'to give,' *dátṛi*, 'a giver;' from *budh*, 'to know,' *boddhṛi*, 'a knower;' from *sah*, 'to bear,' *soḍhṛi*, 'patient.' This corresponds to the Latin affix *tor*, and the Greek τηρ and τορ: compare *dator*, δοτήρ.

II. तृ *tṛi*, forming, 2dly (nom. *-tá*), nouns of relationship, masculine and feminine; as, *pitṛi*, 'a father,' *mátṛi*, 'a mother.'

84. Fifth Class.—*Masculine, Feminine, and Neuter bases in* त् t (*and* द् d).

Formed by adding to roots—

I. त् *t* (nom. *-t*, in all genders), if the root ends in a *short vowel*: forming nouns of agency, substantives and adjectives, of three genders; as, from *kṛi*, 'to do,' *kṛit*, 'a doer;' from *ji*, 'to conquer,' *jit*, 'a conqueror.' This class of nouns are rarely used, except as the last member of compounds: thus, *karmakṛit*, 'a doer of work.'

Roots already ending in *t* or *d*, taken to form adjectives or nouns of agency, fall under this class; as, from *vid*, 'to know,' *dharmavid*, 'one who knows his duty;' from अद् 'to eat,' क्रव्याद् 'an eater of flesh.' There are also a few nouns falling under this class, formed by prefixing prepositions to roots ending in *t* or *d* or a short vowel; as, from विद् *vid*, 'to know,' संविद् f. 'an agreement;' from द्युत् *dyut*, 'to shine,' *vidyut*, f., 'lightning;' from पद् *pad*, 'to go,' *sampad*, f., 'success;' उपनिषद् f., 'a mystical philosophical work,' from सद् *sad*. So also, *samit*, f., 'conflict,' from *i*, 'to go,' with prep. *sam*.

One or two roots ending in त् or द् may stand by themselves as substantives: thus, मुद् *mud*, f., 'joy;' चित् *chit*, f., 'the mind.'

The practice of using roots at the end of compounds prevails also in Greek and Latin; as in χέρ-νιψ (-νιβ), βου-πλήξ (-πληγ), &c., *arti-fex* (-*fic*), *carni-fex* (-*fic*), *præ-ses* (-*sid*), &c. And there is a very remarkable agreement between Sanskṛit and Latin in the practice of adding *t* to roots ending in short vowels: thus, *com-it* (*comes*), 'a goer with;' *equ-it* (*eques*), 'a goer on horseback;' *al-it* (*ales*), 'a goer with wings;' *super-stit* (*superstes*), 'a stander by,' &c. Greek adds a similar *t* to roots with a long final vowel; as, ἀ-γνώτ, ἀ-πτώτ, &c. (See Bopp's Comparative Grammar, 2d edition, 907, 910.)

II. इत् *it* (nom. -*it*, in all genders), after Guṇa of the root, forming a few substantives and adjectives; as, from सृ *sṛi*, 'to flow,' सरित् *sarit*, f., 'a stream;' from हृ 'to seize,' हरित् 'green,' 'Vishṇu.'

III. There are a few other nouns in त् *t* and द् *d*, of uncertain derivation; as, मरुत् m. 'the wind,' शरद् f. 'autumn,' दृषद् or दृशद् f. 'a stone,' कुमुद् n. 'a lotus.'

By adding to the base of NOUNS—

IV. वत् *vat* (nom. -*vān*, -*vatī*, -*vat*), if the base ends in *a* or *ā**, forming innumerable adjectives; as, from *dhana*, 'wealth,' *dhanavat*, 'possessed of wealth.' This and the next affix are universally applicable, and are of the utmost utility to form adjectives of possession. Sometimes *vat* is added to bases in *s* and *t*; as in तेजस्वत् *tejasvat* (compare 69. *c*) and *vidyutvat* (see 45. *s*). Compare Greek forms in εις (for Fεις), εντ; as, χαρίεις, χαρίεντ, δακρυόεις, δακρυόεντ, &c.

V. मत् *mat* (nom. -*mān*, -*matī*, -*mat*), if the base ends in *i*, *ī*, or *u*, to form adjectives like the preceding; as, from *dhī*, 'wisdom,' *dhīmat*, 'wise;' from *aṃśu*, 'a ray,' *aṃśumat*, 'radiant.'

85. SIXTH CLASS.—*Masculine, Feminine, and Neuter bases in* अन् an *and* इन् in.

Formed by adding to ROOTS—

I. अन् *an* (nom. -*ā*), forming a few masculine nouns; as, *rājan*, 'a king,' from *rāj*, 'to be glorious;' *takshan*, 'a carpenter,' from *taksh*, 'to cleave;' *ukshan*, 'a bull' (compare English OXEN), from *uksh*, 'to impregnate;' *snehan*, 'a friend,' from *snih*, 'to love,' &c. Greek and Latin have similar formations in ων, εν, ην, ον, *on* and *in*; as, τεκτων = तक्षन् (τέκτων), *εἰκον* (-*κών*), *homin* (*homo*), &c.

II. मन् *man* (nom. -*ma*), after Guṇa of the root, forming neuter substantives; as, from *kṛi*, 'to do,' *karman*, 'a deed.' This affix corresponds to the Latin *men*, in *regimen*, *agmen*, *stamen*, &c.; and to the Greek μον, in μνήμον, τλῆμον, &c.: but adjectives in *man*, like सुशर्मन् 'prosperous,' are rare in Sanskṛit. A few nouns in *man* are masculine; as, *ātman*, 'soul' (nom. -*mā*); ऊष्मन् 'the hot season;' शुष्मन् 'fire;' पाप्मन् 'sin;' सीमन् 'a border;' अश्मन् 'a stone.'

III. वन् *van* (nom. -*vā*, -*varī*, -*va*), forming a few substantives and adjectives; as, दृश्वन् 'seeing,' 'a looker,' from *dṛiś*, 'to see.'

By adding to roots or to the base of NOUNS—

IV. इमन् *iman* (nom. -*imā*), forming masculine abstract substantives. If the noun ends in *a* or *u*, these vowels are rejected; as, from *kāla*, 'black,' *kāliman*, 'blackness;' from *laghu*, 'light,' *laghiman*, 'lightness;' from *mṛidu*, 'soft,'

---

* *Vat* is not often found added to feminine bases. It occurs, however, occasionally; as, भार्यावत् 'having a wife,' शिखावत् 'crested.'

mradiman, &c. If it ends in a consonant, this consonant, with its preceding vowel, is rejected; as, from *mahat*, 'great,' *mahiman*, 'greatness.' A medial *ṛi* before a simple consonant is changed to *ra*, but not before a double consonant; as, from कृष्ण 'black,' कृष्णिमन् 'blackness.' A final *ṛi* is gunated; as, *ariman*, 'going,' from *ṛi*, 'to go;' *stariman*, 'a bed,' from *stṛī*, 'to spread' (compare *stramen*); *hariman*, 'time,' from *hṛi*, 'to seize,' &c. *Iman* is generally added to *adjectives*, and the same changes generally take place before it, that take place before the affixes *īyas* and *ishṭha* (see 192): thus, *gariman*, 'weight;' *preman*, 'affection;' *drāghiman*, 'length;' *bhūman*, 'much;' *prathiman*, 'largeness,' &c.

By adding to ROOTS—

V. इन् *in* (nom. *-ī*, *-inī*, *-i*), after Vṛiddhi of a final vowel and medial *a*, and Guṇa of any other medial vowel, forming nouns of agency of three genders (see 82. *b*); as, from *kṛi*, 'to do,' *kārin*, 'a doer.' Compare Greek and Latin formations in *ων* and *on*; as, τέκτων (-ονος), *edon* (*edo*), &c.

By adding to the base of NOUNS—

VI. इन् *in* (nom. *-ī*, *-inī*, *-i*), forming innumerable adjectives of possession. The final of a base is rejected before this affix; as, from *dhana*, 'wealth,' *dhanin*, 'wealthy;' from *mālā*, 'a garland,' *mālin*, 'garlanded;' from *vrīhi*, 'rice,' *vrīhin*, 'having rice.' Compare Greek and Latin formations in *ων* and *on*; as, *γνάθ-ων*, 'having cheeks;' *nason* (*naso*), 'having a nose.'

VII. विन् *vin* (nom. *-vī*, *-vinī*, *-vi*), if the base ends in *ā* or *as*, forming a few adjectives; as, from *medhā*, 'intellect,' *medhāvin*, 'intellectual;' from *tejas*, 'splendour,' *tejasvin*, 'splendid.' Compare 69. *a*.

VIII. मिन् *min* (nom. *-mī*, *-minī*, *-mi*); as, from *vāć*, 'speech,' *vāgmin*, 'eloquent;' from *go*, 'a cow,' *gomin*, 'rich in herds;' from *sva*, 'own' (with lengthening of the final), *svāmin*, 'owner.'

86. Seventh Class.—*Masculine, Feminine, and Neuter bases in* अस् as, इस् is, *and* उस् us.

Formed by adding to ROOTS—

I. अस् *as* (nom. *-as*), after Guṇa, forming a great many neuter substantives; as, from *man*, 'to think,' *manas*, 'the mind;' from *sṛi*, 'to go,' *saras*, 'water.' It also forms one or two masculine and feminine nouns; as, *vedhas*, m., 'Brahmā;' *ćandramas*, m., 'the moon;' *apsaras*, f., 'a nymph;' *ushas*, f., 'the dawn,' from *ush*, 'to glow;' but in these the nominative is long (*-ās*).

II. इस् *is* or उस् *us* (nom. *-is*, *-us*). In place of *as*, the neuter affixes *is* or *us* are occasionally added; as, from *hu*, 'to offer,' *havis*, 'ghee;' from *ćaksh*, 'to look,' *ćakshus*, 'the eye.' See 68. *a*. With *as* compare the Latin *es* in *nubes* (नभस् *nabhas*), *sedes* (सदस् *sadas*), &c.; but especially the *us* and *ur* of words like *genus*, *scelus*, *robur*. Compare also the Greek formations *πάθ-ος*, *εἶδ-ος*, *μέν-ος*, *ψεῦδ-ος*, &c.; and such compounds as *εὐμενής*, neut. *εὐμενές*, &c.

87. Eighth Class.—*Masculine, Feminine, and Neuter bases in any Consonant, except* त् t *and* द् d, न् n, स् s.

Formed by using roots as adjectives, substantives, or nouns of agency—

Any root may be used to form an adjective or a noun of agency, provided it be the last member of a compound word: thus, from शक् 'to be able,' *sarva-śak*, 'omnipotent.' Those roots which end in *t* or *d*, or in a short vowel, having *t* affixed, have been already noticed as falling under the fifth class. This eighth class is intended to comprise all other roots, ending in *any consonant*; as, भुज् *bhuj* (nom. भुक् 'an eater'); राज् *rāj*, m. (nom. राट् 'a king'); प्राछ् (nom. प्राट् 'an asker'); बुध् (nom. भुत् 'a knower'); पुर् f. (nom. पूः 'a city'); गिर् f. (nom. गीः 'a voice'); दिव् f. (nom. द्यौः 'the sky'); स्पृश् (nom. स्पृक् 'one who touches'); विश् (nom. विट् 'one who enters'); लिह् (nom. लिट् 'one who licks'); दुह् (nom. धुक् 'one who milks'). Similarly, the desid. base, पिपक्ष् (nom. पिपक् 'one who wishes to cook'). There are also a few other nouns derived from roots falling under this class; as, तृष्णज् 'thirsty' (nom. तृष्णक्); ऋत्विज् m. 'a priest' (nom. ऋत्विक्); असृज् n. 'blood' (nom. असृक्); and a few substantives formed by prefixing prepositions to roots; as, समिध् f. 'fuel' (nom. समित्), from the root इन्ध् 'to kindle' (see 43 and 75. with note).

A *few roots* standing by themselves as substantives may fall under this class: thus, युध् f. 'battle' (nom. युत्); क्षुध् f. 'hunger' (nom. क्षुत्); वाच् f. 'speech' (nom. वाक्), from *vac*, 'to speak,' the medial *a* being lengthened. Greek and Latin use a few monosyllabic roots in the same manner; as, ὤψ (ὀπ), φλόξ (φλογ), &c.; and Latin *vox* (*voc*), *lex* (*leg*), *dux* (*duc*).

CHAPTER IV.

DECLENSION; OR INFLECTION OF THE BASE OF NOUNS, SUBSTANTIVE AND ADJECTIVE.

GENERAL OBSERVATIONS.

88. Having explained how the crude base of nouns is generally formed, we have now to shew how it is inflected.

As, in the last chapter, nouns, substantive and adjective, were arranged under eight classes, according to the final of their bases (the first four classes comprising those ending in vowels, the last four those ending in consonants), so it will be the object of the present chapter to exhibit their declension or inflection under the same eight classes. Moreover, as every class comprises adjectives as well as substantives, so it is intended that the declension of a masculine, feminine, and neuter substantive, exhibited under each, shall serve as the model for the declension of masculine, feminine, and neuter adjectives coming under the same class.

89. The learner will have already gathered that the noun has three genders, and that the gender is, in many cases, determinable from the termination of the base. Thus, nearly all bases in *á*, *í*, and those formed with the affix *ti* (r. 81. V), are feminine: nearly all nouns whose crudes end in *ana*, *tva*, *ya*, *tra* (see under 80), *as*, *is*, *us* (86), and *man* (85. II), are neuter; those in *iman* (85. IV) are generally masculine; but those in *a*, *i*, *u*, and *ṛi*, are not reducible to rule. The nominative case is, however, in the first of these instances a guide to the gender; as, *devas*, 'a deity,' is masculine; but *dánam*, 'a gift,' neuter. And in other cases the meaning of the word; as, *pitṛi*, 'a father,' is masculine; and *mátṛi*, 'a mother,' feminine.

90. In Sanskṛit, nearly all the relations between the words in a sentence are expressed by inflections. A great many prepositions exist in the language, but in the later or classical Sanskṛit they are not often used alone in government with any case, their chief use being as prefixes to verbs and nouns. This leads to the necessity for eight cases, which are regularly built upon the base. These are called, 1. nominative (*prathamá* or *kartṛi*); 2. accusative (*dvitíyá* or *karma*); 3. instrumental (*tṛitíyá* or *karaṇa*); 4. dative (*ćaturthí* or *sampradána*); 5. ablative (*panćamí* or *apádána*); 6. genitive (*shashṭhí* or *sambandha*); 7. locative (*saptamí* or *adhikaraṇa*); 8. vocative (*sambuddhi*) *. Of these, the third and seventh are new to the classical student. The *instrumental* denotes the instrument or agent by which or by whom a thing [illegible]; as, *tena kṛitam*, 'done by him.' The *locative* generally refers to the place or time in which any thing is done; as, *Ayodhyáyám*, 'in *Ayodhyá*;' *púrvakále*, 'in former time;' *bhúmau*, 'on the ground †.' Hence it follows that the *ablative* is generally

* These cases will sometimes be denoted by their initial letters. Thus N. will denote nominative; I., instrumental.

† Both these cases are used to denote various other relations. See the Chapter on Syntax, r. 805, 817.

restricted to the sense *from*, and can rarely be used, as in Latin and Greek, to express other relations, such as *by*, *with*, *in*, &c. See 812.

91. According to the Indian system of teaching, each of these eight cases has three numbers, singular (*ekavaćana*), dual (*dvivaćana*), and plural (*bahuvaćana*); and to each belongs a termination which is considered to be peculiarly its own, serving alike for masculine (*puṃ-liṅ-ga*), feminine (*strí-liṅ-ga*), and neuter gender (*klíva* or *napuṃsaka-liṅ-ga*). Again, according to the native system, some of the terminations may be combined with memorial letters to aid pronunciation or assist the memory. Thus the proper termination of the nominative singular is स् *s* (expressible by Visarga: before *k*, *kh*, *p*, *ph*, and the sibilants, or at the end of a sentence, see 63); but the memorial termination is *su*, the letter *u* being only memorial. Similarly, the termination of the nominative plural is *jas*, the *j* being memorial. The two schemes of termination (*vibhakti*, Páṇ. I. 4, 104), with and without the memorial letters, are here exhibited. The first is given in small type, as being of no importance excepting as subservient to the second.

Terminations with memorial letters.

(Observe—The memorial or servile letters are printed in capitals.)

	SING.	DUAL.	PLURAL.
Nom.	सु *sU* *	औ *au*	जस् *Jas*
Acc.	अम् *am*	औट् *auṬ* *	शस् *Śas*
Inst.	टा *Ṭá*	भ्याम् *bhyám*	भिस् *bhis*
Dat.	ङे *Ṅ·e*	भ्याम् *bhyám*	भ्यस् *bhyas*
Abl.	ङसि *Ṅ·asI*	भ्याम् *bhyám*	भ्यस् *bhyas*
Gen.	ङस् *Ṅ·as*	ओस् *os*	आम् *ám*
Loc.	ङि *Ṅ·i*	ओस् *os*	सुप् *suP*

* The vowel *u*, which is of course merely memorial or servile, to enable the *s*, which is the real termination, to be pronounced, may possibly be used, in preference to any other vowel, to indicate that final *s*, in certain positions, is liable to be liquefied into *u*. The object of the ट् of औट् in the acc. du. is to enable a *pratyáhára* सुट् (or before soft letters सुड्) to be formed, denoting the first five inflections or strong cases.

The same terminations without memorial letters.

	SING.	DUAL.	PLURAL.
Nom.	स् *s*	औ *au*	अस् *as*
Acc.	अम् *am*	— *au*	— *as*
Inst.	आ *á*	भ्याम् *bhyám*	भिस् *bhis*
Dat.	ए *e*	— *bhyám*	भ्यस् *bhyas*
Abl.	अस् *as*	— *bhyám*	— *bhyas*
Gen.	— *as*	ओस् *os*	आम् *ám*
Loc.	इ *i*	— *os*	सु *su*

92. Observe—The vocative is not given in the above general scheme, as it is held to be a peculiar aspect of the nominative, and coincides with the nom. in the dual and plural. In the singular it is sometimes identical with the base, sometimes with the nominative, and sometimes differs from both *.

a. Observe also—The terminations beginning with vowels will sometimes be called *vowel-terminations;* and those beginning with consonants, including the nom. sing., *consonantal-terminations.*

Similarly, those cases which take the vowel-terminations will sometimes be called *vowel-cases;* and those which take the consonantal, *consonantal-cases.*

See also the division into strong, middle, and weak cases at 135. *b.*

93. Having propounded the above scheme, which for convenience will be called *the memorial scheme of terminations,* as the general type of the several case-affixes in the three numbers, Indian grammarians proceed to adapt them to every noun, substantive and adjective, in the language, as well as to pronouns, numerals, and participles, whether masculine, feminine, or neuter. In fact, their theory is, that there is but one declension in Sanskṛit, and that the base of a noun being given, and the regular case-terminations being given, the base is to be joined to those terminations according to the usual rules for the combination of final and initial letters, as in the following examples of the two bases, नौ *nau*, f., 'a ship' (*navi, nau*), and हरित् *harit*, m. f., 'green.'

* In the first or commonest class of nouns the crude base stands alone in the vocative, just as the termination is dropped from the 2d sing. imperative in the first group of conjugations, see 247.

94.

	SINGULAR.	DUAL.	PLURAL.
Nom. voc.	नौस् *naus* *nau* + *s*	नावौ *návau* *nau* + *au*. See 37.	नावस् *návas* *nau* + *as*. 37.
Acc.	नावम् *návam* *nau* + *am*. 37.	— *návau*	— *návas*
Inst.	नावा *nává* *nau* + *á*. 37.	नौभ्याम् *naubhyám* *nau* + *bhyám*	नौभिस् *naubhis* *nau* + *bhis*
Dat.	नावे *náve* *nau* + *e*. 37.	— *naubhyám*	नौभ्यस् *naubhyas* *nau* + *bhyas*
Abl.	नावस् *návas* *nau* + *as*. 37.	— *naubhyám*	— *naubhyas*
Gen.	नावस् *návas* *nau* + *as*. 37.	नावोस् *návos* *nau* + *os*. 37.	नावाम् *návám* *nau* + *ám*. 37.
Loc.	नावि *návi* *nau* + *i*. 37.	— *návos*	नौषु *naushu* *nau* + *su*. 70.

95.

	SINGULAR.	DUAL.	PLURAL.
Nom. voc.	हरित् *harit* *harit* + *s*. See 43. *a*.	हरितौ *haritau* *harit* + *au*. 41. *b*.	हरितस् *haritas* *harit* + *as*. 41. *b*.
Acc.	हरितम् *haritam* *harit* + *am*. 41. *b*.	— *haritau*	— *haritas*
Inst.	हरिता *haritá* *harit* + *á*. 41. *b*.	हरिद्भ्याम् *haridbhyám* *harit* + *bhyám*. 41.	हरिद्भिस् *haridbhis* *harit* + *bhis*. 41.
Dat.	हरिते *harite* *harit* + *e*. 41. *b*.	— *haridbhyám*	हरिद्भ्यस् *haridbhyas* *harit* + *bhyas*. 41.
Abl.	हरितस् *haritas* *harit* + *as*. 41. *b*.	— *haridbhyám*	— *haridbhyas*
Gen.	— *haritas*	हरितोस् *haritos* *harit* + *os*. 41. *b*.	हरिताम् *haritám* *harit* + *ám*. 41. *b*.
Loc.	हरिति *hariti* *harit* + *i*. 41. *b*.	— *haritos*	हरित्सु *haritsu* *harit* + *su*. 40.

96. Unfortunately, however, it happens, that of nouns whose bases end in vowels, नौ *nau*, 'a ship,' is nearly the only one that admits of this regular junction of the base with the case-endings; and, although nouns whose bases end in consonants are numerous, and are generally declined as regularly as *harit*, yet they are numerically insignificant, compared with nouns in *a*, *á*, *i*, *í*, *u*, and *ṛi*, whose declension requires frequent changes in the final of the base, and various modifications, or even substitutions, in the terminations.

97. Thus in the first class of nouns ending in *a* (which will be found to comprise almost as many nouns as the other seven classes together; compare 80 with 81—87), not only is the final *a* of the base liable to be lengthened and changed to *e*, but also the termination *ina* is substituted for *á*, the proper termination of the instrumental sing. masc.; *ya* for *e* of the dative; *t* for *as* of the ablative; *sya* for *as* of the genitive; *n* for *as* of the accus. plural; *ais* for *bhis* of the instrum. plural. And in many other nouns particular changes and substitutions are required, some of which are determined by the gender. (Compare the first group of verbal bases at 257. *a*.)

The annexed table exhibits synoptically the terminations, with the most usual substitutions, throughout all the classes of nouns.

	SINGULAR.	DUAL.	PLURAL.
N.	स् (m.f.), म्* (n.)	औ (m.f.), ई (n.)	अस् (m.f.), इ (n.)
Ac.	अम् (m.f.), म्* (m.f.n.)	औ (m.f.), ई (n.)	अस्, स् (m.f.), न्* (m.), इ (n.)
I.	आ (m.f.n.), इन* (m.n.)	भ्याम् (m.f.n.)	भिस् (m.f.n.), ऐस्* (m.n.)
D.	ए (m.f.n.), य* (m.n.)	भ्याम् (m.f.n.)	भ्यस् (m.f.n.)
Ab.	अस् (m.f.n.), स्, उर् (m.f.), त्* (m.n.)	भ्याम् (m.f.n.)	भ्यस् (m.f.n.)
G.	अस् (m.f.n.), स्, उर् (m.f.), स्य* (m.n.)	ओस् (m.f.n.)	आम् (m.f.n.)
L.	इ (m.f.n.), आम् (f.), औ (m.f.)	ओस् (m.f.n.)	सु (m.f.n.)

Observe—Those substitutions marked * are mostly restricted to nouns ending in *a*, and are therefore especially noticeable.

a. Comparing the above terminations with those of Latin and Greek, we may remark that *s* enters into the nom. sing. masc., and *m* or *n* into the neuter, in all three languages. In regard to the Sanskrit dual *au*, the original termination was *á*, as found in the Vedas; and *á* equals the Greek α, ω, and ε. In nom. pl. masc. the *s* appears in many Latin and Greek words. In acc. sing., Sanskrit agrees with Latin, and frequently with Greek, as the Sanskrit *m* may be euphonically changed to *n* (ν), if influenced by a dental following (see observation, p. 22). In the acc. pl. *s* appears in all three languages; and when the Sanskrit ends in *n*, as in the first class of nouns, this *n* is probably for *ns*, since a preceding *a* is lengthened to compensate for the rejection of *s*. Compare some Vedic acc. plurals; cf. also Bopp's Comp. Gr. § 236, ἵππανς acc. pl. in the Cretic dialect; and Gothic forms, such as *balgins*, *sununs*. In inst. pl. *bhis* is preserved in the Latin *nobis*, *vobis*, and the Greek φι(ν) for φις (ναῦ-φιν = *naubhis*). The *ais* which belongs to Sanskrit nouns in *a* is probably a contraction of *ābhis*, since in the Vedas *ebhis* for *ābhis* is found for *ais*, as *vṛikebhis* for *vṛikais*, &c. &c. The termination *ais* probably answers to the Latin dat. and abl. plural in *is*, just as *bhis* and *bhyas* answer to the Latin *bus*. In the gen. sing. all three languages have preserved the *s* (*nāvas*, *navis*, νηός for νηFος); and in the gen. pl. *ām* is equivalent to the Greek ων, and the Latin *um* (पदां = ποδῶν, *pedum*). In loc. sing. the Sanskrit *i* is preserved in the dative of Greek and Latin words (निशि = νυκτί—Compare the expression τῇ αὐτῇ νυκτί —नावि = *navi*). In loc. pl. *su* answers to the Greek σι (नौषु = ναυσί). Sanskrit bases in *a* prefix *i* to *su*; so that *vṛikeshu* (29. *b*) = λυκοῖσι. The voc. sing. in Greek is generally identical with the base, and the voc. dual and pl. with the nom., as in Sanskrit: thus λόγε is the voc. sing. of λόγος, τριήρες of τριήρης, χαρίεν of χαρίεις, βασιλεῦ of βασιλεύς, &c.

98. In the following pages no attempt will be made to bring back all nouns to the general scheme of terminations by a detailed explanation of changes and substitutions in every case. But under every one of the eight classes a model noun for the masculine, feminine, and neuter, serving for adjectives as well as substantives, will be declined at full; and under every case of every noun the method of joining the final letter of the base with the proper terminations will be indicated in English letters.

99. The student must, however, understand, that the division into eight classes, which here follows, is not meant to imply the existence of eight separate declensions in the sense understood by the classical scholar, but is rather intended to shew, that the final letters of the crude bases of nouns may be arranged under four general heads for vowels, and four for consonants; and that all Sanskrit nouns, whatever may be the final of their bases, are capable of adaptation to one common scheme of nearly similar case-terminations.

a. In the same manner it will appear in the sequel, that the ten classes into which verbs are divided do not imply ten different conjugations, but rather ten different ways of adapting the bases of verbs to one common scheme of tense-terminations; and just as in nouns the commonest declension is formed by bases in *a* and *ā*, so in verbs the commonest conjugation or group of conjugations (see 257) is formed by bases in *a* and *ā*. There is no reason why the same system of generalisation should not have been carried out by Latin and Greek grammarians, had the formation of nouns and verbs from roots and crude bases been traceable with equal clearness in these languages.

100. The classical scholar may, if he please, satisfy his own ideas of declension, by regarding masculine and neuter nouns in *a*, like *śiva* of the first class, as his 1st declension; feminine nouns in *ā* and *ī*, like *śivā* and *nadī* of the first class, as his 2d declension; masculine and feminine nouns in *i* and *u*, like *kavi*, *mati*, *bhānu*, and *dhenu*, of the second and third classes, as his 3d declension; and all the remaining nouns, including the neuters of those in *i* and *u*, and all those contained in the last five classes, as his 4th declension. These four declensions may be traced in regular order in the following pages, and will be denoted by the capital letters A at 103; B at 105; C at 110; D at 114.

101. Observe, that in declining the model nouns, under every inflection, the base with the sign +, and after it the termination, will be exhibited in English letters. Moreover, the number of the rule of Sandhi which must come into operation in joining the final of the base with the initial of the termination will generally be indicated. For it is most important to remember, that the formation of every case in a Sanskrit noun supposes the application of a rule of Sandhi or 'junction;' and that *declension* in Sanskrit is strictly 'junction,' i. e. not a divergence from an upright line (*rectus*), but a *joining together* of a base with its terminations.

102. Not unfrequently, however, before this *joining together* takes place, the original final of the base is changed to its Guṇa or Vṛiddhi equivalent (see 27), or to some other letter (see 43. *b*. *c*. *d*. *e*), so that the *inflective* base often varies from the original crude; and not unfrequently the original termination of the scheme is changed for some other termination, as indicated at 97.

In order, therefore, that the student, without forgetting the original final of the crude base, or the original termination of the memorial scheme, may at the same time observe, 1st, whether in any particular instances the final of the base undergoes any or what modification—2dly, whether the original termination suffers any change—it will be desirable that, whenever in exceptional cases the final vowel of the base is to be gunated or vriddhied, or otherwise changed (whenever, in fact, the *inflective* base differs from the *crude* base), this changed form of the crude base be exhibited in place of the original form: thus, at 103, under the genitive dual *śivayos*, *śive* + *os* denotes, that before the base *śiva* is joined to the termination *os*, the final letter *a* is to be changed to *e*; and the number indicates the rule of Sandhi which must come into operation in joining *śive* and *os* together. Similarly, whenever the original termination has to be modified, it will be desirable that the termination be exhibited in its altered form; thus, at 103, under the accus. sing., *śiva+m* denotes, that the base is to be joined with *m*, substituted for the original termination *am*. See the table, page 69.

SECTION I.

INFLECTION OF NOUNS, SUBSTANTIVE AND ADJECTIVE, WHOSE BASES END IN VOWELS, OR OF THE FIRST FOUR CLASSES OF NOUNS.

FIRST CLASS OF NOMINAL BASES INFLECTED.

Masculine and neuter bases in अ *a; feminine bases in* आ *á and* ई *í.*

Note, that this class comprises by far the greater number of nouns, substantive and adjective, in the language. It answers to a common class of Latin and Greek words in *us* and *ος*, *um* and *ον*, *a* and *α*; such as *lupus*, λύκος (= Sans. *vṛikas*, nom. of *vṛika*); *donum*, δῶρον; *terra*, χώρα (= धरा); and to adjectives like *bonus*, ἀγαθός, &c.

103. (A; see r. 100.) Masculine bases in *a*, declined like शिव *śiva*, m., 'the god Śiva,' or as an adjective, 'prosperous.'

The final of the base is lengthened in D. Ab. sing., I. D. Ab. du., G. pl.; and changed to *e* in G. L. du., D. Ab. L. pl.; *n* is euphonically affixed to the final in G. pl. Hence the four inflective bases *śiva*, *śivá*, *śive*, *śiván*.

N.	शिवस् *śivas* *śiva+s*	शिवौ *śivau* *śiva+au*. See 33.	शिवास् *śivás* *śiva+as*. See 31.
Ac.	शिवम् *śivam* *śiva+m*	— *śivau*	शिवान् *śivân* *śivá+n*. 31.
I.	शिवेन *śivena* *śiva+ina*. 32.	शिवाभ्याम् *śivábhyám* *śivá+bhyám*	शिवैस् *śivais* *śiva+ais*. 33.
D.	शिवाय *śiváya* *śivá+ya*	— *śivábhyám*	शिवेभ्यस् *śivebhyas* *śive+bhyas*
Ab.	शिवात् *śivát* *śivá+t*. 31.	— *śivábhyám*	— *śivebhyas*
G.	शिवस्य *śivasya* *śiva+sya*	शिवयोस् *śivayos* *śive+os*. 36.	शिवानाम् *śivánám* *śiván+ám*
L.	शिवे *śive* *śiva+i*. 32.	— *śivayos*	शिवेषु *śiveshu* *śive+su*. 70.
V.	शिव *śiva* *śiva* (*s* dropped). 92.	शिवौ *śivau* *śiva+au*. 33.	शिवास् *śivás* *śiva+as*. 31.

104. Neuter bases in *a*, declined like शिव *śiva*, n., 'prosperous.'

The final of the base is lengthened and assumes *n* in N. Ac. V. pl.

N. Ac.	शिवम् *śivam* *śiva + m*. 97.	शिवे *śive* *śiva + í*. 32.	शिवानि *śiváni* *śivá + n + i*

The vocative is शिव *śiva*, शिवे *śive*, शिवानि *śiváni*; all the other cases are like the masculine.

105. (B; see r. 100.) Feminine bases in *á*, declined like शिवा *śivá*, f., 'the wife of Śiva,' or as an adjective, 'prosperous.'

The final of the base is changed to *e* in I. sing., G. L. du.; *yá* is inserted in D. Ab. G. L. sing.; and *n* in G. pl. Hence the inflective bases *śivá*, *śive*.

N.	शिवा *śivá* *śivá* (*s* rejected)	शिवे *śive* *śivá + í*. 32.	शिवास् *śivás* *śivá + as*. 31.
Ac.	शिवाम् *śivám* *śivá + am*. 31.	— *śive*	— *śivás*
I.	शिवया *śivayá* *śive + á*. 36.	शिवाभ्याम् *śivábhyám* *śivá + bhyám*	शिवाभिस् *śivábhis* *śivá + bhis*
D.	शिवायै *śiváyai* *śivá + yá + e*. 33.	— *śivábhyám*	शिवाभ्यस् *śivábhyas* *śivá + bhyas*
Ab.	शिवायास् *śiváyás* *śivá + yá + as*. 31.	— *śivábhyám*	— *śivábhyas*
G.	— *śiváyás*	शिवयोस् *śivayos* *śive + os*. 36.	शिवानाम् *śivánám* *śivá + n + ám*
L.	शिवायाम् *śiváyám* *śivá + yá + ám*. 31.	— *śivayos*	शिवासु *śivásu* *śivá + su*
V.	शिवे *śive* *śivá + i*. 32.	शिवे *śive* *śivá + í*. 32.	शिवास् *śivás* *śivá + as*. 31.

106. Feminine bases in *í*, declined like नदी *nadí*, f., 'a river.'

The final of the base becomes *y* before the vowel-terminations, by 34; *á* is inserted in D. Ab. G. sing.; the final of the base is shortened in V. sing.; and *n* is inserted in G. pl.

N.	नदी *nadí* *nadí* (*s* rejected)	नद्यौ *nadyau* *nadí + au*. 34.	नद्यस् *nadyas* *nadí + as*. 34.
Ac.	नदीम् *nadím* *nadí + m*	— *nadyau*	नदीस् *nadís* *nadí + s*
I.	नद्या *nadyá* *nadí + á*. 34.	नदीभ्याम् *nadíbhyám* *nadí + bhyám*	नदीभिस् *nadíbhis* *nadí + bhis*.

D.	नद्यै *nadyai* *nadī+ā+e.* 33.	नदीभ्याम् *nadībhyām*	नदीभ्यस् *nadībhyas* *nadī+bhyas*
Ab.	नद्यास् *nadyās* *nadī+ā+as.* 31.	— *nadībhyām*	— *nadībhyas*
G.	— *nadyās*	नद्योस् *nadyos* *nadī+os.* 34.	नदीनाम् *nadīnām* *nadī+n+ām*
L.	नद्याम् *nadyām* *nadī+ā+ām.* 34.	— *nadyos*	नदीषु *nadīshu* *nadī+su.* 70.
V.	नदि *nadi* *nadi* (final shortened)	नद्यौ *nadyau* *nadī+au.* 34.	नद्यस् *nadyas* *nadī+as.* 34.

The classical student will recognise in the terminations of *śiva*, *śivā*, and *nadī* many resemblances to Latin and Greek terminations, remembering that Sanskrit *a* corresponds to Latin *u* and Greek *o*; Sanskrit *m* to Latin *m* and Greek *ν*; Sanskrit *ā* to Latin *a* and Greek *η* or *α*, or in gen. plur. to *ω*; Sanskrit *ī* to Greek and Latin *i*; Sanskrit *bh* or *bhy* to Latin *b*. See 11. *f*. and 97. *a*.

107. In accordance with 58, such words as मृग *mṛiga*, m., 'a deer;' पुरुष *purusha*, m., 'a man;' भार्या *bhāryā*, f., 'a wife;' कुमारी *kumārī*, f., 'a girl'—must be written, in the inst. sing. m. and the gen. pl. m. f., with the cerebral ण *ṇ*: thus, मृगेण *mṛigeṇa*, पुरुषेण, मृगाणां, पुरुषाणां, भार्याणां, कुमारीणां. When *n* is final, as in the acc. pl. m., it remains unchanged, in accordance with 58.

a. Observe, monosyllabic nouns in ई *ī*, like श्री f. 'fortune,' भी f. 'fear,' &c., vary from *nadī* in the manner explained at 123.

b. Observe also, that feminine nouns in ऊ *ū*, like वधू f. 'a wife,' are declined analogously to *nadī*, excepting in the nom. sing., where *s* is not rejected. See 125.

108. When a feminine noun ending in *ā* is taken to form the last member of a compound adjective, it is declined like *śiva* for the masculine and neuter. Thus, from *vidyā*, 'learning,' *alpa-vidyas, alpa-vidyā, alpa-vidyam*, 'possessed of little learning.' Similarly, a masculine noun takes the fem. and neut. terminations; and a neuter noun, the masc. and fem.

a. When roots ending in *ā*, such as *pā*, 'to drink' or 'to preserve,' are taken for the last member of compound words, they form their neuter like the neuter of *śiva*. For their masculine and feminine they assume the memorial terminations regularly, rejecting, however, the final of the base in the Ac. pl. and remaining weak or vowel-cases: thus, सोमपा *soma-pā*, m. f., 'a drinker of Soma juice;' N. V. -पास्, -पौ, -पास्; Ac. -पां, -पौ, -पस्; I. -पा, -पाभ्यां, &c.; D. -पे, &c. Similarly, विश्वपा 'protector of the universe' and शङ्खध्मा 'a shell-blower.'

b. हाहा *hāhā*, m., 'a Gandharba' or 'celestial minstrel,' assumes the terminations with the regular euphonic changes, but the Ac. pl. ends in न्: thus, N. V. हाहास्, हाहौ, हाहास्; A. हाहां, हाहौ, हाहान्; I. हाहा, &c.; D. हाहै, &c.; Ab. हाहास्, &c.; G. हाहास्, हाहौस्, हाहां; L. हाहे, &c.

c. The voc. cases of अम्बा *ambá*, अक्का *akká*, and अल्ला *allá*, all signifying 'mother,' are अम्ब, अक्क, अल्ल, 'O mother!'

d. जरा *jará*, f. 'decay,' forms some of its cases optionally from *jaras*, see 171.

e. दन्त m. 'a tooth,' मास m. 'a month,' पाद m. 'a foot,' यूष m. n. 'soup,' आस्य n. 'the face,' हृदय n. 'the heart,' उदक n. 'water,' शीर्ष n. 'the head,' मांस n. 'flesh,' निशा f. 'night,' नासिका f. 'the nose,' पृतना f. 'an army,' may substitute दत्, मास्, पद्, यूषन्, आसन्, हृद्, उदन्, शीर्षन्, मांस्, निश्, नस्, पृत्, in the acc. pl. and remaining cases. In the neut. nouns, the nom. pl. does not admit the same substitute as the acc. pl. according to most grammarians. Thus, उदक will be Ac. pl. उदकानि or उदानि; I. sing. उदकेन or उद्ना. Again, नासिका in I. du. will be नासिकाभ्यां or नोभ्यां; and मांस, मांसाभ्यां or मान्भ्यां.

109. To convince the student of the absolute necessity of studying the declension of this first class of nouns, he is recommended to turn back to rule 80. He will there find given, under twenty-eight heads, the most usual forms of nouns, substantive and adjective, which follow this declension. All the masculine and neuter substantives in this list are declined like *śiva*, and all the feminine either like *śivá* or *nadí*. Again, all the adjectives in this list follow the same three examples for their three genders. Again, according to *śiva* masc. and neut., and *śivá* fem., are declined all present participles, Átmane-pada (see 526, 527, 528); all passive past participles, which are the most common of verbal derivatives (see 530); all future passive participles (see 568); all participles of the second future, Átmane (see 578); many ordinals, like *prathama* (208). Lastly, according to *nadí* feminine, are also declined the *feminines* of innumerable adjectives, see 80. XIII. XIV; the feminines of participles, like *kritavat* (553, and 140. *a*) and *vividvas* (see 554 and 168); the feminines of many ordinals, like *ćaturtha* (209).

SECOND AND THIRD CLASSES OF NOMINAL BASES INFLECTED.

The declension of the 2d and 3d classes of nouns (see 81 and 82) is exhibited together, that their analogy may be more readily perceived.

2d class—Masculine, feminine, and neuter bases in इ *i*.

3d class—Masculine, feminine, and neuter bases in उ *u*.

Note, that the 2d class answers to Latin and Greek words like *ignis*, *turris*, πόλις, πίστις, *mare*, μέλι; and the 3d, to words like *gradus*, βότρυς, ἡδύς, μέθυ.

110. (C.) Masculine bases in इ *i*, declined like अग्नि *agni*, m. (*ignis*), 'fire.'

The final of the base is gunated in D. Ab. G. V. sing., N. pl.; lengthened in

N. Ac. V. du., Ac. G. pl.; dropped in L. sing., or, according to Páṇini, changed to *a*; *n* is inserted in I. sing., G. pl. Hence the inflective bases *agni, agní, agne, agn*.

N.	अग्निस् *agnis* *agni+s*	अग्नी *agní* *agní* (*au* rejected)	अग्नयस् *agnayas* *agne+as*. 36.
Ac.	अग्निम् *agnim* *agni+m*	— *agní*	अग्नीन् *agnín* *agní+n*
I.	अग्निना *agniná* *agni+n+á*	अग्निभ्याम् *agnibhyám* *agni+bhyám*	अग्निभिस् *agnibhis* *agni+bhis*
D.	अग्नये *agnaye* *agne+e*. 36.	— *agnibhyám*	अग्निभ्यस् *agnibhyas* *agni+bhyas*
Ab.	अग्नेस् *agnes* *agne+s*	— *agnibhyám*	— *agnibhyas*
G.	— *agnes*	अग्न्योस् *agnyos* *agni+os*. 34.	अग्नीनाम् *agnínám* *agní+n+ám*
L.	अग्नौ *agnau* *agn* (*i* dropped)+*au*	— *agnyos*	अग्निषु *agnishu* *agni+su*. 70.
V.	अग्ने *agne* *agne* (*s* rejected)	अग्नी *agní* *agní* (*au* rejected)	अग्नयस् *agnayas* *agne+as*. 36.

111. Masculine bases in उ *u*, declined like भानु *bhánu*, m., 'the sun.'

The inflective base varies as in the last. Páṇini makes it in L. sing. *bhána*. Perhaps the locative was originally *bhánavi* (such a form actually occurring in the Veda); and *i* being dropped, *bhánav* would become *bhánáv* (*bhánau*).

N.	भानुस् *bhánus* *bhánu+s*	भानू *bhánú* *bhánú* (*au* rejected)	भानवस् *bhánavas* *bháno+as*. 36.
Ac.	भानुम् *bhánum* *bhánu+m*	— *bhánú*	भानून् *bhánún* *bhánú+n*
I.	भानुना *bhánuná* *bhánu+n+á*	भानुभ्याम् *bhánubhyám* *bhánu+bhyám*	भानुभिस् *bhánubhis* *bhánu+bhis*
D.	भानवे *bhánave* *bháno+e*. 36.	— *bhánubhyám*	भानुभ्यस् *bhánubhyas* *bhánu+bhyas*
Ab.	भानोस् *bhános* *bháno+s*	— *bhánubhyám*	— *bhánubhyas*
G.	— *bhános*	भान्वोस् *bhánvos* *bhánu+os*. 34.	भानूनाम् *bhánúnám* *bhánú+n+ám*
L.	भानौ *bhánau* *bhán* (*u* dropped)+*au*	— *bhánvos*	भानुषु *bhánushu* *bhánu+su*. 70.
V.	भानो *bháno* *bháno* (*s* rejected)	भानू *bhánú* *bhánú* (*au* rejected)	भानवस् *bhánavas* *bháno+as*. 36.

112. Feminine bases in इ *i*, declined like मति *mati*, f., 'the mind.'

The final of the base is gunated in D. Ab. G. V. sing., N. pl.; lengthened in N. Ac. V. du., Ac. G. pl.; dropped in L. sing. (unless the termination be आम्); *n* is inserted in G. pl. Hence the inflective bases *mati*, *matí*, *mate*, *mat*.

N.	मतिस् *matis* *mati*+*s*	मती *matí* *matí* (*au* rejected)	मतयस् *matayas* *mate*+*as*. 36.
Ac.	मतिम् *matim* *mati*+*m*	— *matí*	मतीस् *matís* *matí*+*s*
I.	मत्या *matyá* *mati*+*á*. 34.	मतिभ्याम् *matibhyám* *mati*+*bhyám*	मतिभिस् *matibhis* *mati*+*bhis*
D.	मतये *mataye* or मत्यै * *mate*+*e*. 36.	— *matibhyám*	मतिभ्यस् *matibhyas* *mati*+*bhyas*
Ab.	मतेस् *mates* or मत्यास् * *mate*+*s*	— *matibhyám*	— *matibhyas*
G.	— *mates* or मत्यास् *	मत्योस् *matyos* *mati*+*os*. 34.	मतीनाम् *matínám* *matí*+*n*+*ám*
L.	मतौ *matau* or मत्याम् * *mat* (*i* dropped)+*au*	— *matyos*	मतिषु *matishu* *mati*+*su*. 70.
V.	मते *mate* *mate* (*s* dropped)	मती *matí* *matí* (*au* rejected)	मतयस् *matayas* *mate*+*as*. 36.

113. Feminine bases in उ *u*, declined like धेनु *dhenu*, f., 'a milch cow.'

The inflective base varies as in the last.

N.	धेनुस् *dhenus* *dhenu*+*s*	धेनू *dhenú* *dhenú* (*au* rejected)	धेनवस् *dhenavas* *dheno*+*as*. 36.
Ac.	धेनुम् *dhenum* *dhenu*+*m*	— *dhenú*	धेनूस् *dhenús* *dhenú*+*s*
I.	धेन्वा *dhenvá* *dhenu*+*á*. 34.	धेनुभ्याम् *dhenubhyám* *dhenu*+*bhyám*	धेनुभिस् *dhenubhis* *dhenu*+*bhis*
D.	धेनवे *dhenave* or धेन्वै † *dheno*+*e*. 36.	— *dhenubhyám*	धेनुभ्यस् *dhenubhyas* *dhenu*+*bhyas*
Ab.	धेनोस् *dhenos* or धेन्वास् † *dheno*+*s*	— *dhenubhyám*	— *dhenubhyas*
G.	— *dhenos* — †	धेन्वोस् *dhenvos* *u*+*os*. 34.	धेनूनाम् *dhenúnám* *dhenú*+*n*+*ám*
L.	धेनौ *dhenau* or धेन्वाम् † *dhen* (*u* dropped)+*au*	— *dhenvos*	धेनुषु *dhenushu* *dhenu*+*su*. 70.
V.	धेनो *dheno* *dheno* (*s* dropped)	धेनू *dhenú* *dhenú* (*au* rejected)	धेनवस् *dhenavas* *dheno*+*as*. 36.

* The D. may also be *matyai*; the Ab. and G. *matyás*; the L. *matyám*.

† The D. may also be *dhenvai*; the Ab. and G. *dhenvás*; and the L. *dhenvám*.

114. (D.) Neuter bases in इ *i*, declined like वारि *vári*, n., 'water' (Lat. *mare*).

The base inserts *n* before the vowel-terminations, and the final is lengthened in N. Ac. pl. Hence the inflective bases *vári*, *várí*.

N.	वारि *vári* *vári*	वारिणी *váriṇí* *vári+n+í.* See 58.	वारीणि *váríṇi* *várí+n+i.* See 58.
Ac.	— *vári*	— *váriṇí*	— *váríṇi*
I.	वारिणा *váriṇá* *vári+n+á.* 58.	वारिभ्याम् *váribhyám* *vári+bhyám*	वारिभिस् *váribhis* *vári+bhis*
D.	वारिणे *váriṇe* *vári+n+e.* 58.	— *váribhyám*	वारिभ्यस् *váribhyas* *vári+bhyas*
Ab.	वारिणस् *váriṇas* *vári+n+as.* 58.	— *váribhyám*	— *váribhyas*
G.	— *váriṇas*	वारिणोस् *váriṇos* *vári+n+os.* 58.	वारीणाम् *váríṇám* *várí+n+ám.* 58.
L.	वारिणि *váriṇi* *vári+n+i.* 58.	— *váriṇos*	वारिषु *várishu* *vári+su.* 70.
V.	वारि *vári* or वारे *váre* *vári* or *váre.* 92.	वारिणी *váriṇí* *vári+n+í.* 58.	वारीणि *váríṇi* *várí+n+i*

115. Neuter bases in उ *u*, declined like मधु *madhu*, n., 'honey' (μέθυ).

The inflective base varies as in the last.

N.	मधु *madhu* *madhu*	मधुनी *madhuní* *madhu+n+í*	मधूनि *madhúni* *madhú+n+i*
Ac.	— *madhu*	— *madhuní*	— *madhúni*
I.	मधुना *madhuná* *madhu+n+á*	मधुभ्याम् *madhubhyám* *madhu+bhyám*	मधुभिस् *madhubhis* *madhu+bhis*
D.	मधुने *madhune* *madhu+n+e*	— *madhubhyám*	मधुभ्यस् *madhubhyas* *madhu+bhyas*
Ab.	मधुनस् *madhunas* *madhu+n+as*	— *madhubhyám*	— *madhubhyas*
G.	— *madhunas*	मधुनोस् *madhunos* *madhu+n+os*	मधूनाम् *madhúnám* *madhú+n+ám*
L.	मधुनि *madhuni* *madhu+n+i*	— *madhunos*	मधुषु *madhushu* *madhu+su.* 70.
V.	मधु *madhu* or मधो *madho* *madhu* or *madho.* 92.	मधुनी *madhuní* *madhu+n+í*	मधूनि *madhúni* *madhú+n+i*

116. Neuter nouns in *i* and *u* follow the analogy of nouns in *in* at 159, except in G. plur. and V. sing. सानु n., 'summit,' substitutes स्नु, according to r. 108. *e*.

117. Although there are not many substantives declined like *agni* and *vári* (81), yet nouns like *mati* are numerous (81. V). Moreover, adjectives like *śuci*, and compound adjectives ending in *i*, are declined like *agni* in the masc.; like *mati* in the fem.; and like *vári* in the neuter.

118. Again, although there are but few substantives declined like *dhenu* and *madhu*, yet it is important to study their declension, as well as that of the masc. noun *bhánu*; for all simple adjectives like *tanu*, and all like *pipásu* (82), and all other simple adjectives in *u*, and all compound adjectives ending in *u*, are declined like *bhánu* in the masc.; *dhenu* in the fem.; and *madhu* in the neut.

a. Many adjectives in *u*, however, either optionally or necessarily follow the declension of *nadí* in the fem.; as, *tanu*, 'thin,' makes its nom. fem. either *tanus* or *tanví*; मृदु, 'tender,' makes nom. f. मृद्वी *mridví*; and गुरु, 'heavy,' makes गुर्वी *gurví*: and some optionally lengthen the *u* in the feminine; as, *bhíru*, 'timid,' makes fem. भीरु or भीरू, declinable like nouns in *ú*, 125.

119. When feminine nouns ending in *i* and *u* are taken to form the last member of a compound adjective, they must be declined like *agni* in the masc., and *vári* in the neut. Thus the compound adjective *alpa-mati*, 'narrow-minded,' in the acc. plur. masc. would be *alpa-matín*; fem. *alpa-matís*; neut. *alpa-matíni*. Similarly, a masc. or neut. noun, as the last member of a compound, may take the feminine form.

a. Although adjectives in *i* and *u* are declined like *vári* and *madhu* for the neuter, yet in the D. Ab. G. L. sing., and in the G. L. du., they may optionally follow the masculine form: thus the adjectives *śuci* and *tanu* will be, in the D. sing. neut., शुचिने or शुचये, तनुने or तनवे; and so with the other cases.

120. There are some useful irregular nouns in इ *i*, declined as follows: सखि m. 'a friend:' N. सखा, सखायौ, सखायस्; Ac. सखायं, सखायौ, सखीन्; I. सख्या, सखिभ्यां, &c.; D. सख्ये, &c.; Ab. सख्युस्, &c.; G. सख्युस्, सख्योस्, &c.; L. सख्यौ, &c.; V. सखे, सखायौ, &c. Hence it appears that *sakhi* in some cases assumes the memorial terminations at 91 more regularly than *agni*. In the rest it follows *agni*.

121. पति m. 'a master,' 'lord' (πόσις), when not used in a compound word, follows *sakhi* at 120 in I. D. Ab. G. L. sing. (thus, I. पत्या, D. पत्ये, Ab. G. पत्युस्, L. पत्यौ); in the other cases, *agni*. But this word is generally found at the end of a compound, and then follows *agni* throughout (thus, भूपतिना 'by the lord of the earth').

122. A few neuter nouns, अस्थि n. 'a bone' (ὀστέον), अक्षि n. 'an eye' (*oculus*, ὄκος), सक्थि n. 'a thigh,' दधि n. 'curd,' drop their final *i* in I. sing. and remaining weak or vowel-cases, and are declined in those cases as if derived from obsolete forms in *an*; such as अस्थन्, &c. (compare 149): thus, N. V. Ac. अस्थि, अस्थिनी, अस्थीनि; I. अस्थ्ना, अस्थिभ्यां, &c.; D. अस्थ्ने, अस्थिभ्यां, &c.; Ab. अस्थ्नस्, &c.; G. अस्थ्नस्, अस्थ्नोस्, अस्थ्नां; L. अस्थ्नि or अस्थनि, अस्थ्नोस्, अस्थिषु.

Hence, according to 58, अक्षि *akshi* will make in I. sing. अक्ष्णा; in D. अक्ष्णे, &c.

Nouns ending in ई *ī and* ऊ *ū.*

We have already shewn that feminine bases of more than one syllable ending in *ī*, generally derived from masculines or forming the feminines of numerous adjectives and participles, are declined like *nadī* at 106: thus, नटी 'an actress,' पुत्री 'a daughter,' देवी 'a goddess,' सखी 'a female friend,' नारी 'a woman,' व्याघ्री 'a tigress,' धनिनी or धनवती 'a rich woman,' and numerous others all follow *nadī*.

123. There are a *few* common monosyllabic words in long ई *ī primitively feminine*, (i. e. not derived from masculine substantives, see *nadī* and *patnī* at 80. XXV, and not the feminine forms of adjectives or participles, 80. XII. &c.,) whose declension must be noticed separately. They vary from the declension of नदी (106) by forming the nom. with स्, and using the same form for the voc., and by changing the final *ī* to *iy* before the vowel-terminations: thus, श्री f. 'prosperity:' N.V. श्रीस्, श्रियौ, श्रियस्; Ac. श्रियं, श्रियौ, श्रियस्; I. श्रिया, श्रीभ्यां, श्रीभिस्; D. श्रिये or श्रियै, श्रीभ्यां, श्रीभ्यस्; Ab. श्रियस् or श्रियास्, श्रीभ्यां, श्रीभ्यस्; G. श्रियस् or श्रियास्, श्रियोस्, श्रियां or श्रीणां; L. श्रियि or श्रियां, श्रियोस्, श्रीषु.

a. Similarly are declined भी f. 'fear,' ह्री f. 'shame,' and धी f. 'understanding:' thus, N. V. भीस्, भियौ, भियस्; Ac. भियं, &c.; I. भिया, &c.; D. भिये or भियै, &c.

b. स्त्री f., 'a woman,' follows नदी in N. V. sing., and varies also in other respects from श्री; thus, N. स्त्री, स्त्रियौ, स्त्रियस्; V. स्त्रि, स्त्रियौ, स्त्रियस्; Ac. स्त्रीं or स्त्रियं, स्त्रियौ, स्त्रीस् or स्त्रियस्; I. स्त्रिया, स्त्रीभ्यां, स्त्रीभिस्; D. स्त्रियै, स्त्रीभ्यां, स्त्रीभ्यस्; Ab. स्त्रियास्, स्त्रीभ्यां, स्त्रीभ्यस्; G. स्त्रियास्, स्त्रियोस्, स्त्रीणां; L. स्त्रियां, स्त्रियोस्, स्त्रीषु. As the last member of a compound adjective, it shortens its final, and in some of its cases follows *agni* and *mati*; e. g. अतिस्त्रि m. f. n. 'surpassing a woman:' N. masc. -स्त्रिस्, -स्त्रियौ, -स्त्रयस्; Ac. -स्त्रिं or -स्त्रियं, -स्त्रियौ, -स्त्रीन् or -स्त्रियस्; I. -स्त्रिणा, -स्त्रिभ्यां, &c.; D. -स्त्रये, &c.; Ab. -स्त्रेस्, &c.; G. -स्त्रेस्, -स्त्रियोस्, -स्त्रीणां; L. -स्त्रौ, &c.; V. -स्त्रे, &c. The fem. form is like the masc., but Ac. pl. -स्त्रीस् or -स्त्रियस्; I. -स्त्रिया; D. -स्त्रियै or -स्त्रये; Ab. -स्त्रियास् or -स्त्रेस्, &c. For neut., see 126.

124. There are a *few* primitively feminine words *not* monosyllabic, such as लक्ष्मी 'the goddess of prosperity,' तन्त्री 'a lute-string,' तरी 'a boat,' which, like श्री, take *s* in the nom. sing., but in other respects follow नदी; thus, N. लक्ष्मीस्, लक्ष्म्यौ, लक्ष्म्यस्; Ac. लक्ष्मीं, &c.; V. लक्ष्मि. But गौरी f. 'the brilliant (goddess),' as a derivative fem. noun, is N. sing. गौरी.

125. Feminine nouns, not monosyllabic, ending in long ऊ *ū*, like वधू 'a wife,' are declined analogously to primitively feminine nouns of more than one syllable, ending in ई *ī*, i. e. like लक्ष्मी, they follow the analogy of *nadī* except in N. sing., where *s* is retained. In the other cases ऊ *ū* becomes *v*, wherever ई *ī* is changed to *y* (see 34): thus, N. वधूस्, वध्वौ, वध्वस्; Ac. वधूं, वध्वौ, वधूस्; I. वध्वा, वधूभ्यां,

वधूभिस्; D. वध्वै, वधूभ्यां, वधूभ्यस्; Ab. वध्वास्, वधूभ्यां, वधूभ्यस्; G. वध्वास्, वध्वोस्, वधूनां; L. वध्वां, वध्वोस्, वधूषु; V. वधु, वध्वौ, वध्वस्. Similarly, चमू f. 'a host;' श्वश्रू f. 'a mother-in-law.'

a. Again, monosyllabic words in *ú* primitively feminine are declined analogously to श्री f. at 123; *ú* being changed to *uv*, wherever *í* is changed to *iy*: thus, भू f. 'the earth:' N. V. भूस्, भुवौ, भुवस्; Ac. भुवं, भुवौ, भुवस्; I. भुवा, भूभ्यां, भूभिस्; D. भुवे or भुवै, भूभ्यां, भूभ्यस्; Ab. भुवस् or भुवास्, भूभ्यां, भूभ्यस्; G. भुवस् or भुवास्, भुवोस्, भुवां or भूनां; L. भुवि or भुवां, भुवोस्, भूषु. Similarly, भ्रू f. 'the eye-brow' (ὀφρύς): N. V. भ्रूस्, भ्रुवौ, भ्रुवस्, &c. Observe—The voc. is like the nom.

126. Roots of one syllable ending in *í* and *ú*, used as masc. or fem. nouns, follow the declension of monosyllabic words in *í* and *ú*, such as श्री at 123 and भू at 125. *a*; but in the D. Ab. G. L. sing., G. pl., they take only the first inflection: thus, क्री m. f., 'one who buys,' makes D. क्रिये only for m. and f., and लू m. f., 'a reaper,' makes D. लुवे only for m. and f.

a. The same generally holds good if they have adjectives prefixed to them: thus, परमक्री m. f. 'the best buyer' (N. V. -क्रीस्, -क्रियौ, -क्रियस्; Ac. -क्रियं, &c.).

b. And when they are compounded with another noun as a dependent or subordinate term they generally change their final *í* and *ú* to *y* and *v*, before vowel-terminations, and not to *iy* and *uv* (unless *í* and *ú* are preceded by a double consonant, as in यवक्री 'a buyer of barley'), thus conforming more to the declension of polysyllables; e. g. जलपी (for जलपा) m. f., 'a water-drinker,' makes N. V. जलपीस्, -प्यौ, -प्यस्; Ac. जलप्यं, -प्यौ, -प्यस्; I. जलप्या, -पीभ्यां, &c.; D. जलप्ये, &c.; Ab. जलप्यस्, &c.; G. जलप्यस्, -प्योस्, &c.; L. जलप्यि (in opposition to r. 31. *a*), &c. So also, खलपू m. f. 'a sweeper:' N. V. खलपूस्, -प्वौ, -प्वस्; Ac. खलप्वं, &c.; I. खलप्वा, &c.; L. खलप्वि, &c.: and सुलू 'one who cuts well;' N. V. सुलूस्, -ल्वौ, -ल्वस्.

c. Similarly, वर्षाभू m. f. 'a frog,' दृन्भू m. 'a thunderbolt,' करभू m. 'a finger-nail,' पुनर्भू m. f. 'born again' (N. V. पुनर्भूस्; Ac. -र्भ्वं, &c.; I. -र्भ्वा; D. -र्भ्वे; Ab. G. -र्भ्वस्, -र्भ्वि. But if the sense is limited to a distinct female object, as 'a virgin widow remarried,' the D. will be -र्भ्वै; Ab. G. -र्भ्वास्; L. -र्भ्वां, like वधू).

d. Similarly also, सेनानी m. 'a general,' ग्रामणी m. f. 'the chief of a village;' but these, like नदी, take *ám* for the termination of the L. sing. even in the masc.: thus, N. V. सेनानीस्, -न्यौ, -न्यस्; Ac. -न्यं, &c.; I. -न्या; L. सेनान्यां, सेनान्योस्, सेनानीषु, &c. This applies also to the simple noun नी m. f. 'a leader,' but the final becomes *iy* before vowel-terminations.

e. But स्वयम्भू and स्वभू m. 'self-existent,' as a name of Brahmá, follow भू at 125. *a*, taking only the first inflections: thus, D. -भुवे; Ab. -भुवस्, &c.

f. Masculine non-compounds in *í* and *ú* of more than one syllable, like पपी m. 'who drinks' or 'cherishes,' 'the sun,' हूहू m. 'a Gandharba,' follow जलपी and खलपू at 126. *b*, except in Ac. sing. and plur.: thus, N. V. पपीस्, पप्यौ, पप्यस्; Ac. पपीं, पप्यौ, पपीन्; and in L. sing. the final *í* combines with the *i* of the termination into *í* (31. *a*), not into *yi*: thus, L. sing. पपी (but हूह्वि from हूहू). Again, वातप्रमी m., 'an antelope' (surpassing the wind), as a compound, may follow जलपी; but

Vopadeva makes Ac. sing. and pl. follow नदी. When such nouns have a feminine, the Ac. plur. ends in *s*: thus बभ्रू m. f., 'tawny,' makes बभ्रूस् for the Ac. pl. f.

g. A word like प्रधी f. 'superior understanding' (formed from the compound verb प्रध्यै), when used as a fem. noun, is treated as a polysyllable, and follows यवक्री, except in D. Ab., &c., where it takes the second inflections (D. sing. प्रध्यै, &c.). But when used adjectively, in the sense 'having superior understanding,' it follows यवक्री throughout, both for masc. and fem., but may optionally for the fem. be declined like the fem. substantive. The voc. fem. may be प्रधीस् or प्रधि. Two rare nouns, सुखी 'one who loves pleasure' and सुती 'one who wishes for a son,' also follow यवक्री, but in Ab. G. sing. make सुख्युस्, सुत्युस्.

h. Monosyllabic nouns primitively feminine (like श्री f., धी f., भी f., at 123, भ्रू f. 'the eye-brow'), forming the last member of a compound adjective, still follow the declension of monosyllables, but use the first inflections only in the D. Ab. G. L. cases and G. plur., for the masc., and may optionally use them for the fem.: thus, N. गतभीस् m. f., 'fearless,' is गतभिये only in D. sing. m., -भिये or -भियै in D. sing. f. So also, सुधी m. f. 'intelligent,' शुद्धधी m. f. 'having pure thoughts,' दुर्धी m. f. 'stupid,' सुश्री m. f. 'having good fortune,' सुभ्रू m. f. 'having beautiful brows:' thus, N. V. सुभ्रूस्, -भ्रुवौ, -भ्रुवस्; Ac. सुभ्रुवं, &c. According to Vopadeva, the voc. f. may be सुभ्रु, but this alternative is generally restricted to those compounds which have one consonant before the final vowel: thus, सुधी; V. fem. सुधीस् or सुधि.

i. When primitively feminine nouns, *not* monosyllabic, occur at the end of compounds they preserve their fem. terminations (except in acc. pl.) though used as masc. adjectives (i. e. according to Páṇ. I. 4, 3, they retain their *nadī* character); thus बहुश्रेयसी, m. 'a man of many excellences,' is thus declined: N. बहुश्रेयसी, -स्यौ, -स्यस्; V. -सि, &c.; Ac. -सीं, -स्यौ, -सीन्; I. -स्या, -सीभ्यां, &c.; D. -स्यै, &c.; Ab. G. -स्यास्, &c.; L. -स्यां, &c. Similarly (but N. sing. will end in स्), अतिलक्ष्मी m. f. 'one who has surpassed Lakshmī,' निर्लक्ष्मी m. f. 'deprived of fortune,' अतिचमू m. f. 'victorious over hosts' (N. अतिचमूस्, -म्वौ, -म्वस्; V. -मु; Ac. -मूं, -म्वौ, -मून्, Ac. pl. f. -मूस्; I. -म्वा, -मूभ्यां, &c.; D. -म्वै, &c.; Ab. -म्वास्, &c.); but the last three may follow Vopadeva's declension of यवक्री at 126. *f.*

j. All adjectives ending in *ī* and *ū* shorten the final vowel for the neuter gender, and follow the declension of *vāri*; but in the I. D. Ab. G. and L. cases they may optionally take the masc. terminations: thus, N. V. sing. neut. गतभि; I. गतभिना or गतभिया; D. गतभिने or गतभिये, &c. N. V. Ac. sing. खलपु; I. खलपुना or -प्वा, &c. N. V. Ac. सुलु; I. -लुना or -ल्वा. N. V. Ac. बहुश्रेयसि; I. -श्रेयसिना or -श्रेयस्या; D. -श्रेयसिने or -श्रेयस्यै, &c. N. V. Ac. ग्रामणि; I. -णिना or -ण्या.

FOURTH CLASS OF NOMINAL BASES INFLECTED.

Masculine, feminine, and neuter bases in ऋ *ṛi*.

127\. Masculine bases in *ṛi*, declined like दातृ *dātṛi*, m., 'a giver,' and पितृ *pitṛi*, m., 'a father.' The former is the model of nouns of agency (83); the latter, of nouns of relationship.

In nouns of agency like *dátṛi* the final *ṛi* is vriddhied (28), and in nouns of relationship like *pitṛi* (except *naptṛi*, 'a grandson,' and *svasṛi*, 'a sister') gunated, in the strong cases (see p. 86); but the *r* of *ár* and *ar* is dropped in N. sing., and to compensate in the last case *a* is lengthened. In both, the final *ṛi* is gunated in L. V. sing., and *ur* is substituted for final *ṛi* and the initial *a* of *as* in Ab. G. sing. In Ac. G. pl. final *ṛi* is lengthened, and assumes *n* in G. pl. Hence the inflective bases *dátṛi*, *dátár*, *dátar*, *dátṝ*, *dátur*; and *pitṛi*, *pitar*, *pitṝ*, *pitur*.

This class answers to δοτήρ, πατήρ, *pater*, &c.; *ṛi* being equivalent to *ar*; and it is remarkable, that *dátáram*, *dátáras*, &c., bear the same relation to *pitaram*, *pitaras*, &c., that δοτῆρα, δοτῆρες, δοτῆρι, &c., bear to πατέρα, πατέρες, πατέρι, &c. Compare also the Latin *datoris* from *dator* with *patris* from *pater*.

a. Note—There is elision of *s* at the end of a conjunct consonant after *r*; hence in Ab. G. *dáturs* and *piturs* become *dátur* and *pitur*. Compare 43. *a*.

N.	दाता *dátá* *dátá* (*rs* rejected)	दातारौ *dátárau* *dátár+au*	दातारस् *dátáras* (δοτῆρες) *dátár+as*
Ac.	दातारम् *dátáram* *dátár+am*	— *dátárau*	दातॄन् *dátṝn* *dátṝ+n*
I.	दात्रा *dátrá* *dátṛi+á*. 34.	दातृभ्याम् *dátṛibhyám* *dátṛi+bhyám*	दातृभिस् *dátṛibhis* *dátṛi+bhis*
D.	दात्रे *dátre* *dátṛi+e*. 34.	— *dátṛibhyám*	दातृभ्यस् *dátṛibhyas* *dátṛi+bhyas*
Ab.	दातुर् *dátur* *dátur+s* (*s* rejected)	— *dátṛibhyám*	— *dátṛibhyas*
G.	— *dátur*	दात्रोस् *dátros* *dátṛi+os*. 34.	दातॄणाम् *dátṝṇám* *dátṝ+n+ám*
L.	दातरि *dátari* *dátar+i*	— *dátros*	दातृषु *dátṛishu* *dátṛi+su*. 70.
V.	दातर् *dátar* *dátar*	दातारौ *dátárau* *dátár+au*	दातारस् *dátáras* *dátár+as*

128.

N.	पिता *pitá* *pitá* (*rs* rejected)	पितरौ *pitarau* *pitar+au*	पितरस् *pitaras* (πατέρες) *pitar+as*
Ac.	पितरम् *pitaram* *pitar+am*	— *pitarau*	पितॄन् *pitṝn* *pitṝ+n*
I.	पित्रा *pitrá* *pitṛi+á*. 34.	पितृभ्याम् *pitṛibhyám* *pitṛi+bhyám*	पितृभिस् *pitṛibhis* *pitṛi+bhis*
D.	पित्रे *pitre* *pitṛi+e*. 34.	— *pitṛibhyám*	पितृभ्यस् *pitṛibhyas* *pitṛi+bhyas*
Ab.	पितुर् *pitur* *pitur+s* (*s* rejected)	— *pitṛibhyám*	— *pitṛibhyas*

G.	पितुर् *pitur*	पित्रोस् *pitros*	पितॄणाम् *pitṛīṇām*
	pitar + *s* (*s* rejected)	*pitṛi* + *os*. 34.	*pitṛi* + *n* + *ām*
L.	पितरि *pitari*	— *pitros*	पितृषु *pitṛishu*
	pitar + *i*		*pitṛi* + *su*. 70.
V.	पितर् *pitar*	पितरौ *pitarau*	पितरस् *pitaras*
	pitar	*pitar* + *au*	*pitar* + *as*

Observe—*Pitṛi* seems to be corrupted from *pātṛi*, 'a protector' (*pā*, 'to protect'). The cognate languages have preserved the root in πατήρ, *pater*, 'father,' &c. The Latin *Jupiter*, however, is literally *Dyu-piter*, or rather *Dyaush-piter*, 'father of heaven.' It is clear that bases like *dātṛi*, *pitṛi*, &c., originally ended in *ar*.

a. Observe—नप्तृ *naptṛi*, 'a grandson' (though said to be derived from *na* and *pitṛi*, 'not the father'), is declined like दातृ *dātṛi*.

b. There are a few nouns, which neither express relationship nor agency, falling under this class. नृ *nṛi*, m., 'a man,' is said to be declined like *pitṛi*: thus, N. ना *nā*, Ac. नरं, I. न्रा, D. न्रे, Ab. G. नुर्, &c. It is doubtful, however, whether the forms न्रा, न्रे, नुर् are ever used, at least, by good writers. The following forms certainly occur: N. sing. ना, Ac. नरं; N. Ac. du. नरौ, I. D. Ab. नृभ्यां, G. L. नरोः; N. pl. नरः, Ac. नॄन्, D. Ab. नृभ्यः, G. नृणां or नॄणां, L. नृषु; but in the inst. dat. gen. loc. sing., the corresponding cases of नर are generally substituted.

c. क्रोष्टृ m., 'a jackal,' *must* form its strong cases (except V. sing.) and *may* form its weak cases (p. 86) from क्रोष्टु. N. क्रोष्टा, -ष्टारौ, -ष्टारः; Ac. -ष्टारं, -ष्टारौ, -ष्टून् or -ष्टॄन्; I. -ष्ट्रा or -ष्टुना, -ष्टुभ्यां, &c.; D. -ष्ट्रे or -ष्टवे, &c.; Ab. -ष्टुर् or -ष्टोः, &c.; G. -ष्टुर् or -ष्टोः, -ष्ट्रोः or -ष्ट्वोः, -ष्टूनां or -ष्टॄणां; L. -ष्टरि or -ष्टौ, &c.; V. -ष्टो. As the last member of a compound adjective, in the neuter, क्रोष्टु alone is used.

d. Nouns like यन्तृ m. 'a charioteer,' त्वष्टृ m. 'a carpenter,' नेष्टृ m., होतृ m., पोतृ m., 'different kinds of priests,' योद्धृ m. 'a warrior,' of course, follow *dātṛi*. But सव्येष्ठृ m., 'a charioteer,' follows *pitṛi*.

129. Feminine bases in ऋ *ṛi* belong to nouns of relationship, like *mātṛi*, 'a mother' (from *mā*, 'to create,' 'the producer'); and only differ from *pitṛi* in acc. plur., which ends in *s* instead of *n*: thus, मातॄः. Compare μήτηρ, μητέρα, voc. μῆτερ.

a. स्वसृ *svasṛi*, 'a sister,' however, follows दातृ *dātṛi*; but the Ac. pl. is still स्वसॄः. The lengthening of the penultimate is probably caused by the loss of the *t* from *tṛi*, preserved in the English *sister*. So *soror* for *sostor*.

b. The feminine base of nouns of agency is formed by adding ई *ī* to the final ऋ *ṛi*: thus, दातृ + ई, दात्री *dātrī*, f., 'a giver;' and कर्तृ + ई, कर्त्री f. 'a doer.' See 80. XXVI. Their declension follows *nadī* at 106.

130. The neuter base is thus declined: N. Ac. दातृ, दातृणी, दातॄणि; V. दातर् or दातृ. The rest may conform to *vāri* at 114, or resemble the masc.: thus, I. दात्रा or दातृणा, &c. But neuter bases in ऋ *ṛi* belong generally to nouns of agency or

of relationship, when used at the end of compound adjectives, such as बहुदातृ *bahu-dātṛi*, 'giving much,' or दिव्यमातृ *divya-mātṛi*, agreeing with कुलं, i.e. 'a family having a divine mother,' or द्विमातृ 'having two mothers' (compare διμήτωρ). Their declension may resemble that of *vāri* at 114, or conform to the masc. in all cases but the N. V. Ac.; thus, N. Ac. दातृ, दातृणी, दातॄणि; V. दातृ or दातर्, &c.; I. दातृणा or दात्रा, &c.; D. दातृणे or दात्रे, &c.; Ab. G. दातृणस् or दातुर्, &c.; L. दातृणि or दातरि, &c. N. Ac. -मातृ, -मातृणी, -मातॄणि; V. -मातृ or -मातर्, &c.; I. -मातृणा or -मात्रा, &c.

Nouns ending in ऐ ai, ओ o, औ au.

131. We may notice here a few monosyllabic nouns, whose bases end in ऐ, ओ, and औ, not sufficiently numerous to form separate classes.

132. रै *rai*, m. f., 'substance,' 'wealth' (Lat. *res*): N. voc. राः, रायौ, रायस्; Ac. रायं, &c.; I. राया, राभ्यां, राभिस् (*rebus*); D. राये, राभ्यां, राभ्यस्; Ab. रायस्, &c.; G. रायस्, रायोस्, रायां; L. रायि, &c.

133. गो *go*, m. f., 'a cow' or 'ox' (*bos*, βοῦς), 'the earth:' N. voc. गौस्, गावौ, गावस्; Ac. गां, गावौ, गास्; I. गवा, गोभ्यां, गोभिस्; D. गवे, &c.; Ab. गोस्, &c.; G. गोस्, गवोस्, गवां; L. गवि (*bovi*), गवोस्, गोषु. Compare गां with γῆν.

134. नौ *nau*, f., 'a ship' (cf. *navis*, ναῦς), is declined at 94, being the most regular of all nouns. With the N. pl. *nāvas*, compare *naves*, νᾶες (νῆες). The gen. νηός for νᾱός or ναϝος = *nāvas*. Similarly may be declined ग्लौ m. 'the moon;' N. *glaus*, *glāvau*, *glāvas*, &c.

a. These nouns may occur at the end of compounds; as, बहुरै 'rich,' उपगो 'near a cow,' बहुनौ 'having many ships.' In that case the neuter is बहुरि, उपगु, and बहुनु; of which the inst. cases will be बहुरिणा or बहुराया, उपगुना or उपगवा, बहुनुना or बहुनावा; and so with the other vowel-cases: but बहुरि becomes बहुरा before all consonantal terminations, except the nom. sing.

SECTION II.

INFLECTION OF NOUNS WHOSE BASES END IN CONSONANTS, OR OF THE LAST FOUR CLASSES OF NOUNS.

135. Observe—The last four classes of nouns, though comprehending many substantives, consist chiefly of adjectives, participles, or roots used as adjectives at the end of compound words. All the nouns under these remaining classes take the memorial terminations at 91 with perfect regularity.

a. These terminations are here repeated with Bopp's division into strong, weaker, and weakest, as applicable especially to nouns ending in consonants (though not to all of these even). The strong will be denoted by the letter **S**, the weaker may be called middle and denoted by the letter M, and the weakest by the letter w.

But in those nouns which distinguish between strong and weak cases only, the weak will be indicated by both M and w.

	SINGULAR, M.F.	N.	DUAL, M.F.	N.	PLURAL, M.F.	N.
Nom. Voc.	स् *s* (S)	(Neut. M)	औ *au* (S)	(Neut. w)	अस् *as* (S)	(Neut. S)
Acc.	अम् *am* (S)	(Neut. M.)	— *au* (S)	(Neut. w)	— *as* (w)	(Neut. S)
Inst.	आ *á* (w)		भ्याम् *bhyám* (M)		भिस् *bhis* (M)	
Dat.	ए *e* (w)		— *bhyám* (M)		भ्यस् *bhyas* (M)	
Abl.	अस् *as* (w)		— *bhyám* (M)		— *bhyas* (M)	
Gen.	— *as* (w)		ओस् *os* (w)		आम् *ám* (w)	
Loc.	इ *i* (w)		— *os* (w)		सु *su* (M)	

That is, the strong cases in both masc. and fem. are the Nom. Voc. sing. du. and pl. and the Acc. sing. du. The weaker or middle cases are those of the remainder whose terminations begin with consonants, and the weakest are those whose terminations begin with vowels. In neuter nouns the N. V. Ac. sing. are middle, the N. V. Ac. du. weak, but both N. and Ac. plur. are strong. Hence it follows that the acc. pl., and in neuter nouns the inst. sing., is generally the guide to the form assumed before the remaining vowel-terminations. This division of cases has not been noticed before, because it is of no real importance for bases ending in vowels. That it applies to bases ending in *ṛi* is accounted for by the fact that these originally ended in *ar*.

b. In Pāṇini the strong terminations are called *sarva-náma-sthána* (P. I. 1, 42, 43), and the name *bha* is given to the base before the weak.

FIFTH CLASS OF NOMINAL BASES INFLECTED.

Masculine, feminine, and neuter bases in त् t *and* द् d.

This class answers to Latin words like *comes* (from a base *comit*), *eques* (from a base *equit*), *ferens* (from *ferent*); and to Greek words like χάρις (from a base χαριτ), κέρας (from κερατ), χαρίεις (from χαριεντ).

136. Masculine and feminine bases in त् *t*, declined like हरित् *harit*, m. f., 'green' (declined at p. 68), and सरित् *sarit*, f. 'a river.'

The inflective base does not differ from the crude base.

Observe—The nom. case sing. is properly *harits*, but *s* is rejected by 43. *e*. The same applies to all nouns ending in consonants. So αἰθήμων for αἰθημονς; but it is remarkable, that Latin and Greek, when the final of the base refuses to combine with the *s* of the nom., often prefer rejecting the base-final: thus, χάρις for χαριτς, *comes* for *comits*. In these languages the final consonant may frequently combine with the *s* of the nom.; as in *lex* (for *leks*), φλόξ (for φλογς).

N.V.	सरित् *sarit* *sarit + s* (*s* rejected. 43. *a*.)	सरितौ *saritau* *sarit + au*. 41. *b*.	सरितस् *saritas* *sarit + as*. 41. *b*.
Ac.	सरितम् *saritam* *sarit + am*. 41. *b*.	— *saritau*	— *saritas*
I.	सरिता *saritá* *sarit + á*	सरिद्भ्याम् *saridbhyám* *sarit + bhyám*. 41.	सरिद्भिस् *saridbhis* *sarit + bhis*. 41.
D.	सरिते *sarite* *sarit + e*	— *saridbhyám*	सरिद्भ्यस् *saridbhyas* *sarit + bhyas*
Ab.	सरितस् *saritas* *sarit + as*	— *saridbhyám*	— *saridbhyas*
G.	— *saritas*	सरितोस् *saritos* *sarit + os*	सरिताम् *saritám* *sarit + ám*
L.	सरिति *sariti* *sarit + i*	— *saritos*	सरित्सु *saritsu* *sarit + su*. 40.

137. Neuter bases in त् *t* are declined like हरित् *harit*, n., 'green.'

These only differ from the masculine and feminine in the N. du. pl., Ac. sing. du. and pl., the usual neuter terminations ई *í*, इ *i* (see 97), being required, and *n* being inserted before the final of the base in N. Ac. pl.: thus,

N. Ac. V. हरित् *harit*, हरिती *harití*, हरिन्ति *harinti*; I. हरिता *haritá*, हरिद्भ्याम् *haridbhyám*, &c.

138. Masculine and feminine bases in द् *d*, like धर्मविद् *dharma-vid*, m. f., 'knowing one's duty'—a compound composed of the substantive *dharma*, 'duty,' and the root *vid*, 'knowing.' See 84. I.

N.V.	-वित् *-vit* *-vid + s*. 42, 43. *a*.	-विदौ *-vidau* *-vid + au*	-विदस् *-vidas* *-vid + as*
Ac.	-विदम् *-vidam* *-vid + am*	— *-vidau*	— *-vidas*
I.	-विदा *-vidá* *-vid + á*	-विद्भ्याम् *-vidbhyám* *-vid + bhyám*	-विद्भिस् *-vidbhis* *-vid + bhis*
D.	-विदे *-vide* *-vid + e*	— *-vidbhyám*	-विद्भ्यस् *-vidbhyas* *-vid + bhyas*
Ab.	-विदस् *-vidas* *-vid + as*	— *-vidbhyám*	— *-vidbhyas*
G.	— *-vidas*	-विदोस् *-vidos* *-vid + os*	-विदाम् *-vidám* *-vid + ám*
L.	-विदि *-vidi* *-vid + i*	— *-vidos*	-वित्सु *-vitsu* *-vid + su*. 41.

139. Neuter bases in द् *d* are declined like धर्मविद् *dharma-vid*, n., 'knowing one's duty,' and हृद् *hṛid*, n., 'the heart.'

These differ from the masculine and feminine forms in the same cases, and in the same manner, as neuter bases in त् *t*: see 137: thus,

N. Ac. V. धर्मवित्, धर्मविदी, धर्मविन्दि. N. Ac. V. हृत्, हृदी, हृन्दि.

a. So also, कुमुद् n. 'a lotus:' N. Ac. V. कुमुत्, कुमुदी, कुमुन्दि; I. कुमुदा, &c.

Observe—All the nouns whose formation is explained at 84. I. II. III. follow the declension of हरित् and धर्मविद्.

140. Possessive adjectives formed with the affixes वत् *vat* and मत् *mat*, like धनवत् *dhanavat*, m. f. n., 'rich,' and धीमत् *dhímat*, 'wise,' are declined like *harit* for the masculine; but in the strong cases (see p. 86) *n* is inserted before the final of the base, and the preceding *a* is lengthened in N. sing.

N.	धनवान् *dhanaván* *dhanavánt* + *s*. 43. *a*.	धनवन्तौ *dhanavantau* *dhanavant* + *au*	धनवन्तः *dhanavantas* *dhanavant* + *as*
Ac.	धनवन्तम् *dhanavantam* *dhanavant* + *am*	— *dhanavantau*	धनवतः *dhanavatas* *dhanavat* + *as*

I. धनवता *dhanavatá*, &c.; V. धनवन् *dhanavan*.

The remaining cases follow हरित्; thus, I. धनवता, &c.; but the vocative singular is धनवन् *dhanavan*. Similarly, धीमत् 'wise:' N. धीमान्, धीमन्तौ, धीमन्तः; Ac. धीमन्तं, धीमन्तौ, धीमतः, &c.; V. धीमन्, &c.

a. In the same manner are declined active past participles of the form कृतवत्; thus, N. कृतवान्, कृतवन्तौ, कृतवन्तः, &c.

b. The feminine bases of adjectives like धनवत् and धीमत्, and participles like कृतवत्, are formed by adding ई *í* to the weak form of the masc. base; thus, धनवती, धीमती, कृतवती: declined after नदी at 106; thus, N. धनवती, धनवत्यौ, धनवत्यः, &c.

c. The neuter is declined like the neuter of *harit*; thus, N. Ac. V. धनवत्, धनवती, धनवन्ति.

141. Present participles like पचत् *paćat*, 'cooking' (524), and future participles like करिष्यत् *karishyat*, 'about to do,' are declined after *dhanavat* (140), excepting in the N. sing., where *a* is not lengthened before *n*: thus, N. V. sing. पचन् *paćan* (for *paćants* or *paćans*), and not पचान् *paćán*: N. du. pl. पचन्तौ, पचन्तः; Ac. पचन्तं, पचन्तौ, पचतः; I. पचता, &c. Compare the declension of Latin participles like *ferens*, *ferentis*, *ferentem*, &c.

a. Observe, however, that all reduplicated verbs, such as verbs of the 3d conjugation—a few verbs from polysyllabic roots (75. *a*)—and some few other verbs, such as जक्ष् 'to eat,' शास् 'to rule'—which reject the nasal in the 3d pl. of the

Parasmai-pada, reject it also in the declension of the pres. participle. Hence the pres. participle of such verbs is declined like *harit*, the N. case being identical with the base; thus, from *dá*, 'to give,' 3d conj., N. V. sing. du. pl. *dadat*, *dadatau*, *dadatas*; Ac. *dadatam*, &c.: from *bhṛi*, 'to bear,' 3d conj., N. V. sing. du. pl. *bibhrat*, *bibhratau*, *bibhratas*. So also, *jágrat*, 'watching' (from *jágṛi*), *ásat*, 'ruling' (from *ás*), *jakshat*, 'eating' (from *jaksh*). The rejection of the nasal is doubtless owing to the encumbrance of the syllable of reduplication.

Observe—These verbs optionally reject the nasal from the N. V. Ac. pl. neut.: thus, *dadati* or *dadanti*, *jakshati* or *jakshanti*.

b. In present participles derived from verbs of the 1st, 4th, and 10th conjugations, a nasal is inserted for the feminine base: thus, पचन्ती from पच्, 1st conj. (declined like *nadí* at 106); and this nasal is carried through all the inflections, not merely, as in the masculine, through the first five. So दीव्यन्ती from *div*, 4th conj.; and चोरयन्ती from *cur*, 10th conj. The same conjugations also insert a nasal in the N. V. Ac. dual neuter as well as the plur.: thus, पचत्, पचन्ती, पचन्ति.

In all verbs of the 6th conj., in verbs ending in *á* of the 2d, and in all participles of the 2d future, Parasmai, the insertion of the nasal in the feminine is optional; thus, *tudatí* or *tudantí* from *tud*, 6th conj.; *yátí* or *yántí* from *yá*, 2d conj.; *karishyatí* or *karishyantí* from *kṛi*. It is also optional in the N. V. Ac. du. neut., which will resemble the nom. sing. fem.: thus, *tudantí* or *tudatí*, *yántí* or *yátí*, *karishyantí* or *karishyatí*.

c. The other conjugations, viz. the 2d, 3d, 5th, 7th, 8th, and 9th, follow 140. *b.* *c*, and insert no nasal for the feminine nor for the N. Ac. V. du. neuter; although all but the 3d assume a nasal in the first five inflections of the masculine: thus, *adat* (from *ad*, 2d conj.); N. V. masc. *adan*, *adantau*, *adantas*; fem. *adatí*: *juhvat* (from *hu*, 3d conj.); N. V. masc. *juhvat*, *juhvatau*, *juhvatas*; fem. *juhvatí*: *rundhat* (from *rudh*, 7th conj.); N. V. masc. *rundhan*, *rundhantau*, *rundhantas*; fem. *rundhatí*. The neut. will be N. Ac. V. *adat*, *adatí*, *adanti*; *juhvat*, du. *juhvatí*, but pl. *juhvanti* or *juhvati* (see observation 141. *a*, line 8 above).

142. The adjective महत्, 'great,' is properly a pres. part. from the root मह् *mah*, 'to increase;' but, unlike present participles, it lengthens the *a* of *at* before *n* in the N. Ac. sing., N. V. Ac. du., N. V. pl., and in N. V. Ac. pl. neut.: thus, N. masc. महान्, महान्तौ, महान्तः; Ac. महान्तं, महान्तौ, महतः; I. महता, &c.; V. महन्, महान्तौ, &c.; N. fem. महती, &c., see 140. *a*. *b*: N. V. Ac. neut. महत्, महती, महान्ति.

a. बृहत् m. f. n. 'great,' जगत् m. f. n. 'moving,' and पृषत् m. f. 'a deer,' follow pres. participles: thus, N. V. masc. बृहन्, बृहन्तौ, बृहन्तः. Feminine बृहती. Neut. बृहत्, &c.

143. The honorific pronoun भवत् (said to be a contraction of भगवत् or else of भावत् *bhá-vat*) follows धनवत् (at 140), making the *a* of *at* long in the N. sing.: thus, भवान् 'your honour,' and not भवन्. The vocative is भवन्. The feminine is भवती, see 233. As to भवत्, present participle of भू 'to be,' it follows of course पचत् at 141.

144. यकृत् n. 'the liver' (ἧπαρ, jecur), and शकृत् n. 'ordure,' both neuter nouns,

may optionally be declined in Ac. pl. and remaining cases as if their bases were यकन् and शकन्: thus, N. V. यकृत्, यकृती, यकृन्ति; Ac. यकृत्, यकृती, यकृन्ति or यकानि; I. यकृता or यक्ना, यकृद्भ्याम् or यकभ्याम्, यकृद्भिस् or यकभिस्; D. यकृते or यक्ने, &c.

145. पाद्, 'a foot,' at the end of compounds becomes पद् in Ac. pl. and remaining weakest cases: thus, सुपाद्, 'having beautiful feet,' makes N. V. सुपाद्, सुपादौ, सुपादस्; Ac. सुपादं, -पादौ, सुपदस्; I. सुपदा, सुपाद्भ्यां, सुपाद्भिस्, &c.

SIXTH CLASS OF NOUNS INFLECTED.

Masculine, feminine, and neuter bases in अन् an *and* इन् in.

Note, that this class answers to Latin and Greek words like *sermo* (from *sermon*), *homo* (from *homin*), δαίμων (from δαιμον).

146. Masculine and feminine (151) bases in अन् *an*, preceded by *m* or *v* at the end of a conjunct consonant, declined like आत्मन् *ātman*, m., 'soul,' 'self.'

All masc. and fem. nouns, without exception, ending in *an*, lengthen the *a* in the strong cases (V. sing. excepted): and drop the *n* before all the consonantal terminations (see 57). Hence the inflective bases *ātmān*, *ātman*, *ātma*.

Observe—Latin agrees with Sanskrit in suppressing the *n* in the N. masc. and fem., but not in neut.: thus *homo* is the N. of the base *homin*, the stronger vowel *o* being substituted for *i*, just as *ā* is substituted for *a* in Sanskrit; but *nomen* is the N. of the neuter base *nomin*.

N.	आत्मा *ātmā* *ātmā* (*n* and *s* rejected. 43.a, 57.)	आत्मानौ *ātmānau* *ātmān* + *au*	आत्मानस् *ātmānas* *ātmān* + *as*
Ac.	आत्मानम् *ātmānam* *ātmān* + *am*	— *ātmānau*	आत्मनस् *ātmanas* *ātman* + *as*
I.	आत्मना *ātmanā* *ātman* + *ā*	आत्मभ्याम् *ātmabhyām* *ātma* (*n* dropped, 57) + *bhyām*	आत्मभिस् *ātmabhis* *ātma* (*n* dropped. 57) + *bhis*
D.	आत्मने *ātmane* *ātman* + *e*	— *ātmabhyām*	आत्मभ्यस् *ātmabhyas* *ātma* (*n* dropped. 57) + *bhyas*
Ab.	आत्मनस् *ātmanas* *ātman* + *as*	— *ātmabhyām*	— *ātmabhyas*
G.	— *ātmanas*	आत्मनोस् *ātmanos* *ātman* + *os*	आत्मनाम् *ātmanām* *ātman* + *ām*
L.	आत्मनि *ātmani* *ātman* + *i*	— *ātmanos*	आत्मसु *ātmasu* *ātma* (*n* dropped. 57) + *su*
V.	आत्मन् *ātman* *ātman* (*s* rejected)	आत्मानौ *ātmānau* *ātmān* + *au*	आत्मानस् *ātmānas* *ātmān* + *as*

147. Similarly यज्वन् *yajvan*, m., 'a sacrificer;' पाप्मन् *pāpman*, m., 'sin;' अश्मन् *aśman*, m., 'a stone;' ऊष्मन् *ūshman*, m., 'the hot

season;' शुष्मन् *śushman*, m., 'fire;' अध्वन् *adhvan*, m., 'a road;' दृश्वन् *driśvan*, m. f., 'a looker.' N. दृश्वा, दृश्वानौ, दृश्वानस्; Ac. दृश्वानं, दृश्वानौ, दृश्वनस्; I. दृश्वना, &c.

148. But if *an* be preceded by any other consonant, whether conjunct or not, than *m* or *v* (as in the following example *rájan*), or even by *m* or *v* if not conjunct (as in *pívan* at 150), the *a* of *an* is dropped in the Ac. plur. and before all the other *vowel*-terminations, and the remaining *n* is compounded with the preceding consonant: thus,

Masculine and feminine bases in अन् *an*, preceded by any other consonant, whether conjunct or not, than *m* or *v*, declined like राजन् *rájan*, m., 'a king;' मूर्द्धन् *múrddhan*, m., or मूर्धन् *múrdhan*, 'the head.'

N.	राजा *rájá* *rájá* (*n* and *s* rejected. 43-*a*, 57.)	राजानौ *rájánau* *ráján* + *au*	राजानस् *rájánas* (*regēs*) *ráján* + *as*
Ac.	राजानम् *rájánam* *ráján* + *am*	— *rájánau*	राज्ञस् *rájńas* *rájń* + *as*
I.	राज्ञा *rájńá* *rájń* + *á*	राजभ्याम् *rájabhyám* *rája* (*n* dropped. 57) + *bhyám*	राजभिस् *rájabhis* *rája* (*n* dropped. 57) + *bhis*
D.	राज्ञे *rájńe* *rájń* + *e*	— *rájabhyám*	राजभ्यस् *rájabhyas* *rája* (*n* dropped. 57) + *bhyas*
Ab.	राज्ञस् *rájńas* *rájń* + *as*	— *rájabhyám*	— *rájabhyas*
G.	— *rájńas*	राज्ञोस् *rájńos* *rájń* + *os*	राज्ञाम् *rájńám* *rájń* + *ám*
L.	राज्ञि *rájńi* or राजनि *rájń* + *i* or *rájan* + *i*	— *rájńos*	राजसु *rájasu* *rája* (*n* dropped. 57) + *su*
V.	राजन् *rájan* *rájan*. 92.	राजानौ *rájánau* *ráján* + *au*	राजानस् *rájánas* *ráján* + *as*

So मूर्द्धन् m., 'head;' I. मूर्द्ध्ना, &c.; L. मूर्द्ध्नि or मूर्द्धनि, &c.: तक्षन् m. 'a carpenter,' तक्ष्णा, &c.: लघिमन् m., 'lightness,' लघिम्ना, &c.

149. Observe—If न् becomes in this manner conjunct with a previous palatal it must take the palatal form; and if with a cerebral, the cerebral form; as in तक्ष्णा from तक्षन्.

150. If preceded by *m* or *v*, not conjunct, they are still like *rájan*: thus, पीवन् *pívan*, m. f., 'fat:' N. पीवा, पीवानौ, पीवानस्; Ac. पीवानं, पीवानौ, पीव्नस्; I. पीव्ना, &c.; L. पीव्नि or पीवनि, &c. So सीमन् m. 'a border;' वेमन् m. 'a loom' (85. I).

a. When a feminine base in ई *í* is formed from words like राजन्, it follows the same rule for the rejection of the *a* of *an*: thus, राज्ञी *rájńí*, 'a queen.'

151. There are no simple feminine substantives in *an*; but when masculine nouns are taken to form the last member of a compound adjective, they take a feminine and neuter form; as in *mahátman*, m. f. n., 'magnanimous.' The feminine form is declined precisely like the masculine, and the neuter follows the declension of neuter nouns, 152.

a. But when *rájan* occurs at the end of a compound, it is declined like *śiva* (103); as, N. sing. m. *mahárájas*; Ac. *mahárájam*, &c.

152. Neuter bases in अन् *an*, declined like कर्मन् 'an action,' and नामन् 'a name' (*nomen*, ὄνομα*).

Observe—The retention or rejection of *a* in *an* before the inst. c. sing. and remaining vowel-terminations, as well as optionally before the nom. acc. du., is determined by the same rule as in masculines (148). They only differ from masculine nouns in nom. voc. and acc., sing., du., pl.

N. Ac. कर्म, कर्मणी, कर्माणि; I. कर्मणा, कर्मभ्यां, &c.; D. कर्मणे, &c., like आत्मन्; but V. sing. कर्म or कर्मन्.

N. Ac. नाम, नाम्नी or नामनी, नामानि; I. नाम्ना, &c.; D. नाम्ने, &c.; Ab. G. नाम्नस्; L. नाम्नि or नामनि, &c., like राजन्; but V. sing. नाम or नामन्.

With gen. plur. *námnám* compare Latin *nominum*.

153. So also the neuter nouns जन्मन् 'birth,' वेश्मन् 'house,' वर्मन् 'armour,' वर्त्मन् 'road,' चर्मन् 'leather,' छद्मन् 'pretext,' follow the declension of *karman*; but दामन् 'string,' सामन् 'conciliation,' धामन् 'mansion,' व्योमन् 'sky,' रोमन् (*for* रोहमन् *rohman, from ruh*), 'hair,' प्रेमन् 'love,' that of *náman*.

154. Neuters in *an* composing the last member of compound adjectives, must be declined like masculines or feminines when agreeing with masculine or feminine substantives: thus, विष्णुशर्मनामा पण्डितः 'a Paṇḍit named Vishṇuśarma.'

155. There are a few anomalous nouns in *an*: श्वन् m. 'a dog' (*canis*, κύων); युवन् m. 'a youth;' मघवन् m. 'a name of Indra:' thus declined:

a. N. श्वा, श्वानौ, श्वानस्; Ac. श्वानं, श्वानौ, शुनस्; I. शुना, श्वभ्यां, श्वभिस्; D. शुने, &c.; Ab. शुनस्, &c.; G. शुनस् (κυνός), शुनोस्, शुनां; L. शुनि, शुनोस्, श्वसु; V. श्वन्, श्वानौ, &c. See 135. *a.* Fem. शुनी, &c. (like *nadí* at 106).

b. N. युवा, -वानौ, -वानस्; Ac. युवानं, -वानौ, यूनस्; I. यूना, युवभ्यां, युवभिस्; D. यूने, &c.; Ab. यूनस्, &c.; G. यूनस्, यूनोस्, यूनां; L. यूनि, यूनोस्, युवसु; V. युवन्, -वानौ, &c. See 135. *a.* Fem. यूनी (like *nadí*) or युवतिः (like *mati*). Neut. युव, यूनी, युवानि, &c.

c. N. मघवा, -वानौ, -वानस्; Ac. मघवानं, -वानौ, मघोनस्; I. मघोना, मघवभ्यां, -वभिस्; D. मघोने, मघवभ्यां, &c.; Ab. मघोनस्, &c.; G. मघोनस्, मघोनोस्, मघोनां; L. मघोनि, मघोनोस्, मघवसु; V. मघवन्, &c. Fem. मघोनी or मघवती.

---

* Greek has a tendency to prefix vowels to words beginning with consonants in the cognate languages. Compare also *nakha*, 'nail,' ὄνυξ; *laghu*, 'light,' ἐλαχύ; भ्रू 'brow,' ὀφρύ.

The last may also be declined like a noun in *vat*: N. मघवान्, -वन्तौ, &c. See 140.

156. अहन् n., 'a day,' takes its form, in the N. Ac. V. sing. and the middle cases, from an obsolete base, अहस् *ahas*: in the other cases it is like *nâman*: thus, N. Ac. V. अहः (43. *e*), अह्नी or अहनी, अहानि; I. अह्ना, अहोभ्यां, अहोभिस्; D. अह्ने, अहोभ्यां, अहोभ्यस्; Ab. अह्नस्, &c.; G. अह्नस्, अह्नोस्, अह्नां; L. अह्नि or अहनि, अह्नोस्, अहस्सु or अहःसु. At the end of compounds it may be declined as a masc.: thus, N. दीर्घाहास्, -हाणौ, -हाणस्; Ac. -हाणं, &c.; V. -हस्, &c., or sometimes becomes अह or अह्न.

a. दिवन् m., 'a day,' in those cases where the *a* of *an* is rejected, lengthens the *i*: thus, Ac. pl. दीव्नस्; I. दीव्ना, &c.

157. अर्यमन् m. 'the sun,' पूषन् m. 'the sun,' and compounds having -हन् as the last member, such as ब्रह्महन् m. 'the murderer of a Brahman,' agree in not lengthening the *a* of *an* in the N. du. pl., Ac. sing. du.: thus, N. अर्यमा, अर्यमणौ, अर्यमणस्; Ac. अर्यमणं, अर्यमणौ, अर्यम्णस्; I. अर्यम्णा, &c. Similarly, N. पूषा, पूषणौ, &c.; Ac. पूषणं, &c.; but the acc. pl., and remaining weakest cases, may be optionally formed from a base पूष; thus, Ac. pl. पूष्णस् or पूषस्.

Similarly, N. ब्रह्महा, ब्रह्महणौ, &c.; but in Ac. pl. ब्रह्मघ्नस्; I. ब्रह्मघ्ना, ब्रह्महभ्यां, &c. (*h* becoming *gh* where the *a* of *han* is dropped).

158. अर्वन् m. 'a horse,' or m. f. n. 'low,' 'vile,' is declined like nouns in *vat* at 140, excepting in N. sing.: thus, N. अर्वा, अर्वन्तौ, अर्वन्तस्; Ac. अर्वन्तं, &c.; I. अर्वता, अर्वद्भ्यां, अर्वद्भिस्; V. अर्वन्, &c. If the negative अन् precedes, अर्वन् is regular: thus, N. अनर्वा, -र्वाणौ, &c.; Ac. अनर्वाणं, &c.; I. pl. अनर्वभिस्.

159. Masculine bases in इन् *in*, declined like धनिन् *dhanin*, m., 'rich.'

N.	धनी *dhanî* *dhanî* (*n* and *s* rejected 43. *a*, 57.)	धनिनौ *dhaninau* *dhanin* + *au*	धनिनस् *dhaninas* *dhanin* + *as*
Ac.	धनिनम् *dhaninam* *dhanin* + *am*	— *dhaninau*	— *dhaninas*
I.	धनिना *dhaninâ* *dhanin* + *â*	धनिभ्याम् *dhanibhyâm* *dhani* (*n* dropped. 57) + *bhyâm*	धनिभिस् *dhanibhis* *dhani* (*n* dropped. 57) + *bhis*
D.	धनिने *dhanine* *dhanin* + *e*	— *dhanibhyâm*	धनिभ्यस् *dhanibhyas* *dhani* (*n* dropped. 57) + *bhyas*
Ab.	धनिनस् *dhaninas* *dhanin* + *as*	— *dhanibhyâm*	— *dhanibhyas*
G.	— *dhaninas*	धनिनोस् *dhaninos* *dhanin* + *os*	धनिनाम् *dhaninâm* *dhanin* + *âm*
L.	धनिनि *dhanini* *dhanin* + *i*	— *dhaninos*	धनिषु *dhanishu* *dhani* (*n* dropped. 57) + *su*. 70.
V.	धनिन् *dhanin* *dhanin*. 92.	धनिनौ *dhaninau* *dhanin* + *au*	धनिनस् *dhaninas* *dhanin* + *as*

Observe—A great many adjectives of the forms explained at 85. VI. VII. VIII. are declined like धनिन् for the masculine: thus, मेधाविन् *medhávin*, 'intellectual;' N. मेधावी, -विनौ, -विनस्, &c. Also a vast number of nouns of agency, like कारिन् 'a doer,' at 85. V: thus, N. कारी, कारिणौ (58), कारिणस्, &c.

160. Note—The feminine base of such adjectives and nouns of agency is formed by adding ई *í* to the masc. base; as, from धनिन्, धनिनी f.; from कारिन्, कारिणी f.; declined like *nadí* at 106: thus, N. धनिनी, -न्यौ, -न्यस्, &c.

161. The neuter is regular, and is like the declension of *vári* as far as the gen. plur.: thus, N. Ac. धनि, धनिनी, धनीनि. But the gen. plur. धनिनाम्, not धनीनाम्; V. sing. धनि or धनिन्.

162. पथिन् m. 'a road,' मथिन् m. 'a churning-stick,' and ऋभुक्षिन् m. 'a name of Indra,' are remarkable as exhibiting both affixes, *an* and *in*, in the same word. They form their N. V. sing. from the bases पन्थास्, मन्थास्, ऋभुक्षास्; their other strong cases, from the bases पन्थन्, मन्थन्, ऋभुक्षन्; their Ac. pl., and remaining weak cases, from the bases पथ्, मथ्, ऋभुक्ष्; in their middle cases they follow 159 regularly: thus, N. V. पन्थास् (163), पन्थानौ, पन्थानस्; Ac. पन्थानम्, पन्थानौ, पथस्; I. पथा, पथिभ्याम्, पथिभिस्; D. पथे, &c. Similarly, N. V. मन्थास्, &c.; ऋभुक्षास्, &c.: I. मथा, &c.; ऋभुक्षा, &c. Observe—The V. is the same as the N.

a. The compound सुपथिन्, 'having a good road,' is similarly declined for the masc.; the nom. fem. is सुपथी, -थ्यौ, -थ्यस्, like *nadí* at 106; the neut. is N. Ac. सुपथि, -थी, -पन्थानि, &c.; V. सुपथिन् or सुपथि; the rest as the masc.

SEVENTH CLASS OF NOUNS INFLECTED.

***Masculine, feminine, and neuter bases in* अस् as, *इस्* is, *and* उस् us.**

Note, that this class answers to Greek and Latin words like πάθος, μένος, *genus*, *scelus*, &c.

163. Masculine and feminine bases in अस् *as*, declined like चन्द्रमस् *čandramas*, m., 'the moon.'

The *a* of *as* is lengthened in N. sing. to compensate for the rejection of the termination.

N.	चन्द्रमास् *čandramás* *čandramás* (*s* rejected, 43. *a*.)	चन्द्रमसौ *čandramasau* *čandramas* + *au*	चन्द्रमसस् *čandramasas* *čandramas* + *as*
Ac.	चन्द्रमसम् *čandramasam* *čandramas* + *am*	— *čandramasau*	— *čandramasas*
I.	चन्द्रमसा *čandramasá* *čandramas* + *á*	चन्द्रमोभ्याम् *čandramobhyám* *čandramas* + *bhyám*. 64.	चन्द्रमोभिस् *čandramobhis* *čandramas* + *bhis*. 64.

D.	चन्द्रमसे *ćandramase* *ćandramas + e*	चन्द्रमोभ्याम् *ćandramobhyám*	चन्द्रमोभ्यस् *ćandramobhyas* *ćandramas + bhyas.* 64.
Ab.	चन्द्रमसस् *ćandramasas* *ćandramas + as*	— *ćandramobhyám*	— *ćandramobhyas*
G.	— *ćandramasas*	चन्द्रमसोस् *ćandramasos* *ćandramas + os*	चन्द्रमसाम् *ćandramasám* *ćandramas + ám*
L.	चन्द्रमसि *ćandramasi* *ćandramas + i*	— *ćandramasos*	चन्द्रमःसु *ćandramaḥsu* or -स्सु *ćandramas + su.* 62. a, 63.
V.	चन्द्रमस् *ćandramas* *ćandramas.* 92.	चन्द्रमसौ *ćandramasau* *ćandramas + au*	चन्द्रमसस् *ćandramasas* *ćandramas + as*

a. After the same manner is declined अप्सरस् *apsaras*, f., 'a nymph.'

164. Neuter bases in अस् *as*, declined like मनस् *manas*, n., 'the mind' (*μένος, mens*).

These differ from the masc. and fem. in the N. Ac. V. The *a* of *as* remains short in N. sing., but is lengthened in N. Ac. V. plur. before inserted Anusvára.

N. Ac. V.	मनस् *manas* *manas* (*s* rejected. 43. *a*.)	मनसी *manasí* *manas + í*	मनांसि *manáṃsi* *manáṃs + i*

I. मनसा *manasá*, &c., like the masc. and fem.

a. Observe—Nearly all simple substantives in *as* are neuter like *manas*; but when these neuters are taken to form a compound adjective, they are declinable also in the masculine and feminine like *ćandramas*. Thus, when *manas* is taken to form the compound adjective *mahá-manas*, 'magnanimous,' it makes in the nom. (masc. and fem.) *mahá-manás, mahá-manasau, mahá-manasas*. In the same way *sumanas*, 'well-intentioned,' *durmanas*, 'evil-minded' (nom. *sumanás, durmanás*, &c.); compare εὐμενής, δυσμενής, m. f., neut. εὐμενές, δυσμενές, derived from μένος.

b. Where final *as* is part of a root and not an affix, the declension will follow पिण्डग्रस् 'one who devours a mouthful:' thus, N. V. sing. m. f. पिण्डग्रस्; Ac. -ग्रसं. N. V. Ac. du. -ग्रसौ, pl. -ग्रसस्; I. -ग्रसा, -ग्रोभ्यां, &c. N. V. Ac. neut. -ग्रस्, -ग्रसी, -ग्रंसि. When a root ends in *ás*, *s* will be rejected before *bh* by 66. *a*; thus, चकास्, 'brilliant,' makes in I. du. चकाभ्यां.

165. Neuter bases in इस् *is* and उस् *us* (see 68. *a*) are declined analogously to मनस् *manas* at 164, *i* and *u* being substituted for *a* throughout, *sh* for *s* (70), *ir* or *ur* for *o* (65): thus, हविस् *havis*, n., 'ghee:' N. Ac. V. हविस्, हविषी, हवींषि; I. हविषा, हविर्भ्यां, हविर्भिस्; D. हविषे, हविर्भ्यां, हविर्भ्यस्; Ab. हविषस्, हविर्भ्यां, हविर्भ्यस्; G. हविषस्, हविषोस्, हविषां; L. हविषि, हविषोस्, हविःषु or -ष्षु.

a. Similarly, चक्षुस् *ćakshus*, n., 'the eye:' N. Ac. V. चक्षुस्, चक्षुषी, चक्षूंषि; I. चक्षुषा, चक्षुर्भ्यां, चक्षुर्भिस्; D. चक्षुषे, चक्षुर्भ्यां, चक्षुर्भ्यस्; Ab. चक्षुषस्, चक्षुर्भ्यां, चक्षुर्भ्यस्; G. चक्षुषस्, चक्षुषोस्, चक्षुषां; L. चक्षुषि, चक्षुषोस्, चक्षुःषु or -ष्षु.

166. Nouns formed with the affixes *is* and *us* are neuter, though one or two may be also masc. and fem. There are some, however, in which the final sibilant is part of the root itself, and not of an affix; such as आशिस् *âśis*, f., 'a blessing' (from the root शास्), and सजुस् m. f. 'an associate' (from जुष्). These follow the analogy of masc. and fem. nouns in *as* (163) in the N. Ac. cases; and, moreover, before the consonantal terminations, where the final sibilant is changed to *r*, unlike nouns formed with *is* and *us*, they lengthen the *i* and *u* (compare nouns ending in *r* at 180); thus, N. आशीस्, -शिषौ, -शिषस्; Ac. -शिषं, -शिषौ, -शिषस्; I. -शिषा, -शीर्भ्यां, -शीर्भिस्, &c. N. सजूस्, -जुषौ, -जुषस्; Ac. -जुषं, &c.; I. -जुषा, -जूर्भ्यां, &c.

a. Nouns formed from desiderative bases in *ish* (497), such as जिगदिष् (for *jigadish*) 'desirous of speaking,' are similarly declined: thus, N. V. m. f. जिगदीस्, -दिषौ, &c.; I. du. -दीर्भ्यां. The N. V. Ac. neut. plur. is जिगदिषि, the nasal being omitted. So चिकीर्ष्, 'desirous of doing,' makes N. V. m. f. चिकीः, -कीर्षौ, &c.

b. सुहुस् 'well-sounding,' where *us* is radical, makes N. V. sing. m. f. सुहूस्; Ac. सुहुसं; N. V. Ac. du. सुहुसौ, pl. सुहुसस्; I. सुहुसा, सुहूर्भ्यां, सुहूर्भिस्, &c. N. V. Ac. neut. सुहुस्, सुहुसी, सुहुंसि. *Âśis* at 166 is peculiar in changing its final *s*.

c. Observe—When neuter nouns in *is* or *us* are taken for the last member of compound adjectives, analogy would require them to be declined in the masc. and fem. according to *ćandramas* at 163: thus, उत्पलचक्षुस् m. f. n., 'having lotus eyes,' N. masc. and fem. उत्पलचक्षूस्, -चक्षुषौ, &c.; and सुज्योतिस् m. f. n., 'having brilliant rays,' N. masc. and fem. सुज्योतीस्, सुज्योतिषौ, &c.*; but, according to most authorities, the N. sing. does not lengthen the vowel of the last syllable.

d. दोस् *dos*, m., 'an arm,' follows the declension of nouns in *is* and *us*; but in Ac. pl., and remaining cases, optionally substitutes *doshan* for its base: thus, N. V. दोस्, -षौ, -षस्; Ac. -षं, -षौ, -षस् or -ष्णस्; I. दोषा or दोष्णा, दोर्भ्यां or दोषभ्यां, &c. As a neuter noun it makes in N. Ac. V. दोस्, दोषी, दोंषि.

167. Comparatives formed with the affix ईयस् *îyas* (192), lengthen the *a* of *as*, and insert *n*, changeable to Anusvâra before *s*, in N. sing. du. pl., V. du. pl., Ac. sing. du. masc.: thus, बलीयस् m. f. n., 'more powerful,' makes N. masc. बलीयान् (for बलीयांस्, *s* rejected by 43.*a*), -यांसौ, -यांसस्; Ac. -यांसं, -यांसौ, -यसस्; I. -यसा, -योभ्यां, &c., like *ćandramas* at 163. The V. sing. is बलीयन्; du. and pl. like the nom. The fem. बलीयसी follows *nadî* at 106. The neut. बलीयस् is like *manas* throughout.

168. Participles of the 2d preterite, formed with *vas* (see 554), are similarly declined in the strong cases (135. *b*). But in Ac. pl., and remaining weak cases, *vas* becomes *ush*, and in the middle cases *vat*; so that there are three forms of the base, viz. in *vâṅs*, *ush*, and *vat*†: thus, विविद्वस् (part. of 2d pret., from विद् 'to know'):

---

* These words are so declined in Wilson's dictionary (2d edit.). In a copy of Manu, which I received direct from Calcutta, the word *ćâru-ćakshus*, agreeing with *mahîpatiḥ* (IX. 256), has been altered by the native editor to *ćâru-ćakshuḥ*.

† *Vat* is evidently connected with the Greek οτ. Compare *tutupvat* (from *tup*) with τετυφ-(F)οτ, and *tutupvatsu* with τετυφ-ο(τ)σι.

N. विविद्वान्, विविद्वांसौ, विविद्वांसः; Ac. विविद्वांसं, विविद्वांसौ, विविदुषः; I. विविदुषा, विविद्वद्भ्यां, विविद्वद्भिः; D. विविदुषे, &c.; V. विविद्वन्, विविद्वांसौ, &c. When this participle is formed with *ivas* instead of *vas* (see 554), the vowel *i* is rejected in the cases where *vas* becomes *ush*: thus, जग्मिवस् (from *gam*, 'to go'): N. masc. जग्मिवान्, &c.; Ac. जग्मिवांसं, जग्मिवांसौ, जग्मुषः, &c.; I. जग्मुषा, &c.; V. जग्मिवन्, जग्मिवांसौ, &c. Similarly, तेनिवस् (from *tan*, 'to stretch'): N. तेनिवान्, तेनिवांसौ, &c.; Ac. तेनिवांसं, तेनिवांसौ, तेनुषः, &c.; V. तेनिवन्, -वांसौ, &c. But not when the *i* is part of the root: thus, चिचिवस् (from चि), निनीवस् (from नी), make in the Ac. pl. चिच्युषः, निन्युषः. चकृवस् (from कृ) makes, of course, चक्रुषः. The N. feminine of these participles is formed from *ush*; and the N. Ac. neuter, sing., du., and plur., from *vat*, *ush*, and *vas*, respectively: thus, N. fem. विविदुषी, &c., declined like *nadí* at 106. Similarly, from the root तुप् comes तुतुपुषी (compare τετυφυῖα). The neuter is N. विविद्वत्, -दुषी, -द्वांसि. Those formed with *ivas* do not retain *i* in the feminine: thus, *tenivas* makes N. sing. masc. fem. neut. *teniván*, *tenushí* *, *tenivat*.

a. The root विद्, 'to know,' has an irregular pres. part. विद्वस् *vidvas*, used commonly as an adjective ('learned'), and declined exactly like विविद्वस् above, leaving out the reduplicated *vi*: thus, N. masc. विद्वान्, विद्वांसौ, विद्वांसः; V. विद्वन्, &c. With reference to 308. *a*, it may be observed, that as a contracted perfect (2d pret.) of *vid* is used as a present tense, so a contracted participle of the perfect is used as a present participle.

169. पुंस् m., 'a male,' forms its V. sing. from पुमंस्, and its other strong cases (135. *b*) from पुमांस्; but Ac. pl., and remaining weakest cases, from पुंस्; and I. du., and remaining middle cases, from पुम्: thus, N. पुमान्, पुमांसौ, पुमांसः; Ac. पुमांसं, पुमांसौ, पुंसः; I. पुंसा, पुम्भ्यां, पुम्भिः; D. पुंसे, &c.; Ab. पुंसः, &c.; G. पुंसः, पुंसोः, पुंसां; L. पुंसि, पुंसोः, पुंसु; V. पुमन्, पुमांसौ, &c.

170. उशनस् m., 'a name of the regent of the planet Śukra,' forms N. sing. उशना from a base उशनन् (147). Similarly, पुरुदंशस् m. 'a name of Indra,' and अनेहस् m. 'time.' The other cases are regular: thus, N. du. उशनसौ. But उशनस् may be optionally in the vocative sing. उशनन् or उशन or उशनः.

171. जरस्, 'decay' (γῆρας), though properly a neuter noun, supplies its consonantal cases (viz. N. V. sing. I. D. Ab. du. pl. L. pl.) from the feminine जरा (at 108. *d*). Its other cases may be either from जरस् or जरा: thus, N. sing. जरा; V. जरे; Ac. जरसं † or जरां; I. जरसा and जरया, जराभ्यां, जराभिः, &c.

* There seems, however, difference of opinion as to the rejection of *i*; and some grammarians make the feminine *tenyushí*.

† Since जरसं certainly occurs, it may be inferred that the N. Ac. V. du. are जरसौ or जरे; N. Ac. V. pl. जरसः or जराः. These forms are given in the grammar of Íśvara-ćandra Vidyá-ságara, p. 51.

EIGHTH CLASS OF NOUNS INFLECTED.

Masculine, feminine, and neuter bases in any consonant, except त् t (*or* द् d), न् n, स् s.

172. This class consists principally of roots used as nouns, either alone or at the end of compounds, or preceded by prepositions and adverbial prefixes. Roots ending in त् *t* (or द् *d*), employed in this manner, are of common occurrence; but their declension falls under the fifth class at 136. Roots ending in other consonants are not very frequently found, and the only difficulty in their declension arises from their combination with the consonantal terminations.

173. Whatever change of the final consonant, however, takes place in the nominative sing. is preserved before all the consonantal terminations; remembering only, that before such terminations the rules of Sandhi come into operation.

174. Before the vowel-terminations the final consonant of the root, whatever it may be, is always preserved. If in one or two nouns there may be any peculiarity in the formation of the accus. pl., the same peculiarity runs through the remaining weakest or vowel cases. The terminations themselves undergo no change, but the *s* of the nom. sing. is of course rejected by 43. *a*. There is generally but one form of declension for both masc. and fem.; the neuter follows the analogy of other nouns ending in consonants.

175. Masculine and feminine bases in क् *k*, ख् *kh*, ग् *g*, घ् *gh*, declined like सर्वशक् *sarva-śak*, m. f., 'omnipotent' (from *sarva*, 'all,' and शक् 'to be able'), and चित्रलिख् m. 'a painter' (from चित्र 'a painting,' and लिख् 'to write'). N.V. -शक् (43. *a*), -शकौ (41. *b*), -शकः; Ac. -शकं, -शकौ, -शकः; I. -शका, -शग्भ्यां (41), -शग्भिः, &c.; L. pl. -शक्षु* (70). N.V. -लिक् (43. *b*, 43. *a*), -लिखौ (174), -लिखः; Ac. -लिखं, &c.; I. -लिखा, -लिग्भ्यां (41), -लिग्भिः, &c.; L. pl. -लिक्षु*.

a. The neuter is N. Ac. V. -शक्, -शकी, -शंकि, &c.; -लिक्, -लिखी, -लिंखि, &c.; the rest like the masc. and fem.

b. In the same way final ग्, घ् are changed to क्, and घ् to ग्; and here it may be noted that when final घ्, ढ्, ध्, भ्, ह् lose their aspirate form, the aspirate must be transferred to the initial, if that initial be ग्, द्, ड्, or ब्.

---

* Wilkins and Wilson give also -शक्ष्षु, -लिक्ष्षु for the loc. plur., but -शक्षु, -लिक्षु are the more correct forms. At 41. *b*. -लिक्सु is given as the first combination before r. 70 is applied.

c. सुवल्ग् m. f., 'jumping well,' makes N. V. सुवल्क्, सुवल्गौ, &c.; Ac. सुवल्गं, &c.; I. सुवल्गा, सुवल्ग्भ्यां, &c.; D. सुवल्गे, &c.; Ab. G. सुवल्गस्, &c.; L. सुवल्गि, सुवल्गोस्, सुवल्क्षु. Neut. N. Ac. V. -वल्क्, -वल्गी, सुवल्न्गि or (see 176. *b*) सुवल्गि.

d. Observe—The semivowel ल्, like र् and क् (see r. 70), changes a स् immediately following to ष्, but this change can rarely occur.

176. Masculine and feminine bases in च् *c*, छ् *ch*, ज् *j*, झ् *jh*, declined like वाच् *vāc*, f., 'speech' (from वच् 'to speak'); मांसभुज् *māṃsa-bhuj*, m. f., 'flesh-eater' (from मांस *māṃsa*, 'flesh,' and भुज् 'to eat'); प्राछ् *prāch*, m. f., 'an asker' (from प्रछ् 'to ask'). Final च् is changed to क् or ग्; final छ् to ट् or ड्; final ज् to क् (ग्) or ट् (ड्); and final झ्, which is rare, to क् or ग्, before the consonantal terminations (43. *d*, 92. *a*).

N. V. वाक् (for *vāks*, 43. *a*; *vox*, ὄψ), वाचौ (ὄπε), वाचस् (*voces*, ὄπες); Ac. वाचं (*vocem*), वाचौ, वाचस् (ὄπας); I. वाचा, वाग्भ्यां, वाग्भिस्; D. वाचे, वाग्भ्यां, वाग्भ्यस्; Ab. वाचस्, वाग्भ्यां, वाग्भ्यस्; G. वाचस्, वाचोस्, वाचां; L. वाचि (ὀπί), वाचोस्, वाक्षु. Compare Latin *vox*, and Greek ὄψ or ὀπ for Ϝοπ throughout.

N. V. -भुक्, -भुजौ, -भुजस्; Ac. -भुजं, &c.; I. -भुजा, -भुग्भ्यां, -भुग्भिस्, &c.

N. V. प्राट्, प्राछौ, प्राछस्; Ac. प्राछं, &c.; I. प्राछा, प्राड्भ्यां, &c.; L. pl. प्राट्सु.

The last optionally substitutes श् *ś* for its final छ् *ch* before the vowel-terminations: thus, N. du. प्राछौ or प्राशौ, &c. पयोमुच्, 'a cloud,' is declined like वाच्.

a. The neuter is N. Ac. V. -वाक्, -वाची, -वाञ्चि, &c. (as in सुवाच् 'speaking well'); भुक्, भुजी, भुञ्जि, &c.; प्राट्, प्राछी, प्राञ्छि, &c.

b. The root अञ्च् *añc*, 'to go,' preceded by certain prepositions and adverbial prefixes, forms a few irregular nouns; such as, प्राञ्च् 'eastern,' 'going before;' अवाञ्च् 'southern;' प्रत्यञ्च् 'western;' उदञ्च् 'northern;' सम्यञ्च् 'going with,' 'fit,' 'proper;' तिर्यञ्च् 'going crookedly, as an animal;' and a few others less common. It may also form a few compounds with words ending in *a*; such as, अधराञ्च् 'tending downwards,' &c. These all reject the nasal in the acc. pl. and remaining cases masculine. In nom. sing. the final च् *c* being changed to क् *k*, causes the preceding nasal to take the guttural form, and the क् is rejected by 43. *e*. In the acc. plur., and remaining weakest cases, there is a further modification of the base in all, excepting प्राञ्च् and अवाञ्च्.

N. V. masc. प्राङ्, प्राञ्चौ, प्राञ्चस्; Ac. प्राञ्चं, प्राञ्चौ, प्राचस्; I. प्राचा, प्राग्भ्यां, प्राग्भिस्; D. प्राचे, &c.; L. pl. प्राक्षु. Similarly, अवाञ्च्.

N. V. masc. प्रत्यङ्, प्रत्यञ्चौ, प्रत्यञ्चस्; Ac. प्रत्यञ्चं, प्रत्यञ्चौ, प्रतीचस्; I. प्रतीचा, प्रत्यग्भ्यां, प्रत्यग्भिस्; D. प्रतीचे, &c. Similarly, सम्यञ्च् and even उदञ्च्, which make in acc. pl., and remaining weakest cases, समीचस्, उदीचस्. So also, विष्वञ्च्, 'going every where,' makes in acc. pl., and remaining weakest cases, विषूचस्. But तिर्यञ्च् makes in acc. pl., and remaining weakest cases, तिरश्चस्.

The feminine, and the neut. dual of these nouns follow the analogy of the acc. pl.: thus, N. fem. प्राची &c., अवाची &c., प्रतीची &c., उदीची &c., समीची &c., तिरश्ची

&c., declined like मरुत्. The neuter is N. Ac. V. प्राक्, प्राची, प्राञ्चि, &c.; प्रत्यक्, प्रतीची, प्रत्यञ्चि, &c.

c. प्राञ्च्, when it signifies 'worshipping,' retains the nasal throughout; but c is rejected before the consonantal terminations, and the nasal then becomes guttural: thus, N. V. प्राङ्, प्राञ्चौ, &c.; Ac. प्राञ्चं, &c.; I. प्राञ्चा, प्राङ्भ्यां, &c. Similarly, क्रुञ्च् 'a curlew:' N. V. क्रुङ्, क्रुञ्चौ, &c.; Ac. क्रुञ्चं, &c.; I. क्रुञ्चा, क्रुङ्भ्यां, &c.; L. pl. क्रुङ्क्षु or क्रुङ्षु.

d. असृज् n., 'blood,' is regular: thus, N. Ac. V. असृक्, असृजी, असृञ्जि, &c.; but it may optionally take its Ac. pl. and other inflexions from an obsolete base, असन् asan: thus, N. V. pl. असृञ्जि; Ac. pl. असृञ्जि or असानि; I. असृजा or अस्ना, असृग्भ्यां or असभ्यां, &c.; L. असृजि or असनि or अस्नि, &c.

e. Nouns formed with the roots यज् 'to worship,' राज् 'to shine,' मृज् 'to rub,' भ्राज् 'to shine,' भ्रस्ज् 'to fry,' व्रज् 'to wander,' सृज् 'to create,' generally change the final ज् to ड् or ट् before the consonantal terminations: thus, देवेज् m. 'a worshipper of the gods' (यज् becoming इज्); N. V. sing. देवेट् or देवेड्: राज् m. 'a ruler;' N. sing. राट्, I. dual राड्भ्यां: परिमृज् 'a cleanser;' N. sing. परिमृट्: विभ्राज् m. f. 'splendid;' N. sing. विभ्राट्: परिव्राज् m. 'a religious mendicant' (व्रज् becoming व्राज्); N. sing. परिव्राट्: विश्वसृज् 'the creator of the world;' N. sing. विश्वसृट्. But विश्व when it precedes राज्, as in विश्वराज् 'a universal ruler,' becomes विश्वा wherever ज becomes ड् or ट्: thus, N. विश्वाराट्, विश्वराजौ, &c. ऋत्विज् m., 'a priest' (ऋतु + इज् for यज्), is regularly N. V. ऋत्विक्.

f. अवयाज् m., 'a kind of priest,' 'part of a sacrifice,' forms the consonantal cases from an obsolete base, अवयस्; N. V. sing. du. pl. अवयाः, -याजौ, -याजः; Ac. -याजं, &c.; I. -याजा, -योभ्यां, &c.; L. pl. अवयस्सु or अवयःसु.

g. भृज्ज्, 'one who fries,' makes N. V. भृट्, भृज्जौ, भृज्जः; Ac. भृज्जं, &c. Similarly, वृश्च्, 'one who cuts,' makes, according to some, वृट्, &c., and not वृक्, &c.

h. ऊर्ज् m. f., 'strong,' makes N. V. ऊर्क्, &c.; Ac. ऊर्जं, &c.; I. ऊर्जा, ऊर्ग्भ्यां, &c. The neuter is N. Ac. V. *ūrk*, *ūrjī*, *ūrñji*. But in these cases where a word ends in a compound consonant, the first member of which is *r* or *l*, the nasal may be optionally omitted in the plural, so that *ūrji* would be equally correct.

177. Masculine and feminine bases in थ् *th*, ध् *dh*, declined like कथ् m. f. 'one who tells,' युध् f. 'battle.' The final aspirate is changed to its unaspirated form before the consonantal terminations (43. *b*, 41), but not before the vowel (41. *b*). N. V. कत्, कथौ, कथः; Ac. कथं, &c.; I. कथा, कद्भ्यां, &c. N. V. युत्, युधौ, युधः; Ac. युधं, &c.; I. युधा, युद्भ्यां, &c. In the case of बुध् m. f., 'one who knows,' the initial ब *b* becomes भ *bh* wherever the final ध् *dh* becomes *t* or *d*, by 175. *b*. and 42. *c*: thus, N. V. भुत्, बुधौ, बुधः; Ac. बुधं, &c.; I. बुधा, भुद्भ्यां, &c.; L. pl. भुत्सु.

a. The neuter is N. Ac. V. कत्, कथी, कन्थि, &c.; युत्, युधी, युन्धि, &c.

178. Masculine and feminine bases in प् *p*, फ् *ph*, ब् *b*, भ् *bh*, declined like गुप् m. f. 'one who defends,' लभ् m. f. 'one who obtains.' N. V. गुप्, गुपौ, गुपः;

Ac. गुधं, &c.; I. गुधा, गुद्भ्यां, गुद्भिस्, &c. N.V. लप्, लभौ, लभस्; Ac. लभं, &c.; I. लभा, लब्भ्यां, लब्भिस्, &c.; L. pl. लप्सु.

a. The neuter is N. Ac. V. गुत्, गुधी, गुन्धि, &c.; लप्, लभी, लम्भि, &c.

b. अप् f. 'water,' declined generally (when not compounded) in the plural only, is irregular: thus, N.V. आपस्; Ac. अपस्; I. अद्भिस्; D. Ab. अद्भ्यस्; G. अपां; L. अप्सु.

179. Masculine and feminine bases in म् *m*, declined like शम् m. f. 'one who pacifies.' The final *m* becomes *n* before the consonantal terminations: thus, N.V. शन्, शमौ, शमस्; Ac. शमं, &c.; I. शमा, शन्भ्यां, शन्भिस्, &c.; L. pl. शन्सु.

a. Similarly, प्रशाम् m. f., 'quiet,' makes N.V. प्रशान्, -शामौ, -शामस्; Ac. प्रशामं, &c.; I. प्रशामा, प्रशान्भ्यां, &c.; L. pl. प्रशान्सु or प्रशान्त्सु. Compare 53. *b*.

b. The neuter is N. Ac. V. शन्, शमी, शंमि, &c.; प्रशान्, -शामी, -शाम्मि, &c.

180. Masculine and feminine bases in र् *r*, declined like चर् m. f. 'one who goes,' गिर् f. 'speech,' द्वार् f. 'a door.' If the vowel that precedes final *r* be *i* or *u*, it is lengthened before the consonantal terminations (compare 166); and final *r*, being a radical letter, does not become Visarga before the *s* of the loc. pl. (71. *a*). N.V. चर्, चरौ, चरस्; Ac. चरं, &c.; I. चरा, चर्भ्यां, चर्भिस्, &c.; L. pl. चर्षु. N.V. गीर्, गिरौ, गिरस्; Ac. गिरं, &c.; I. गिरा, गीर्भ्यां, गीर्भिस्, &c.; L. pl. गीर्षु. N.V. द्वार्, द्वारौ, द्वारस्, &c.

a. The neuter is N. Ac. V. चर्, चरी, चरि, &c.; गीर्, गिरी, गिरि, &c.

So also, वार् n. 'water:' N. Ac. वार्, वारी, वारि.

b. There is one irregular noun ending in the semivowel व् *v*, viz. दिव् f. 'the sky,' which forms its N.V. sing. from द्यौ, and becomes द्यु in the other consonantal cases: thus, N.V. द्यौस्, दिवौ, दिवस्; Ac. दिवं, दिवौ, दिवस्; I. दिवा, द्युभ्यां, &c.

181. Masculine and feminine bases in श् *ś* and ष् *sh*. The difficulty in these is to determine which roots change their finals to क् and which to ट् (see 43. *c*). In the roots दिश्, दृश्, स्पृश्, सृज्, and धृष् (the last forming दधृष् 'impudent') the final becomes क्, and in नश् it is optionally changed to क् or ट्. Otherwise both श् and ष् at the end of roots pass into ट्. The following will serve as examples of declension: विश् m. f. 'one who enters,' or 'a man of the mercantile and agricultural class,' दिश् f. 'a quarter of the sky,' द्विष् m. f. 'one who hates,' मृष् m. f. 'one who endures.' N.V. विट् (43. *c*), विशौ, विशस्; Ac. विशं, &c.; I. विशा, विड्भ्यां, &c. N.V. दिक् (43. *c*, 17. *b*), दिशौ, दिशस्; Ac. दिशं, &c.; I. दिशा, दिग्भ्यां, &c. N.V. द्विट् (43. *c*), द्विषौ, द्विषस्; Ac. द्विषं, &c.; I. द्विषा, द्विड्भ्यां, &c. N.V. मृट् (43. *c*), मृषौ, मृषस्; Ac. मृषं, &c.; I. मृषा, मृड्भ्यां, &c.

The neuter is N. Ac. V. विट्, विशी, विंशि, &c.; दिक्, दिशी, दिंशि, &c.; द्विट्, द्विषी, द्विंषि, &c.; मृट्, मृषी, मृंषि, &c.

a. पुरोडाश् 'a priest,' in the Veda, makes N.V. sing. पुरोडास्, and forms its other consonantal cases from an obsolete base, पुरोडस्. Compare 176. *f*.

b. सुहिंस् m. f., 'very injurious,' makes N.V. सुहिन्, सुहिंसौ, &c.; Ac. सुहिंसं, &c.; I. सुहिंसा, सुहिन्भ्यां, &c. But nouns ending in स्, preceded by vowels, fall under 163.

c. गोरक्ष्, 'a cow-keeper,' makes N.V. गोरक् or गोरट्, गोरक्षौ, &c.

182. Masculine and feminine bases in ह् *h*, declined like लिह् m. f. 'one who licks;' दुह् m. f. 'one who milks.' In roots beginning with द् *d*, the final aspirate generally becomes क् *k* or ग् *g* (see 17. *a*), in other roots ट् *ṭ* or ड् *ḍ*, before the consonantal terminations; and in roots whose initial is द् *d* or ग् *g*, the *h*, which disappears as a final, is transferred to the initial, which becomes *dh* or *gh* wherever final *h* becomes *k* or *g* or *ṭ* or *ḍ*. See 175. *b*. N. V. लिट् (43. e), लिहौ, लिहस्; Ac. लिहं, &c.; I. लिहा, लिड्भ्यां, &c.; L. pl. लिट्सु or लिट्त्सु. N. V. धुक्, दुहौ, दुहस्; Ac. दुहं, &c.; I. दुहा, धुग्भ्यां, धुग्भिस्, &c.; L. pl. धुक्षु. The neuter is N. Ac. V. लिट्, लिही, लिंहि, &c.; धुक्, दुही, दुंहि, &c.

a. But द्रुह् m. f., 'one who injures,' makes N. ध्रुक् or ध्रुट्; I. द्रुहा, ध्रुग्भ्यां or ध्रुड्भ्यां, &c.; L. pl. ध्रुक्षु or ध्रुट्सु; and मुह् m. f., 'foolish,' N. मुक् or मुट्. The same option is allowed to स्निह् 'one who loves' and स्नुह् 'one who vomits.'

b. उष्णिह् f., 'a particular kind of metre,' changes its final to *k* or *g* before the consonantal terminations, like roots beginning with *d*. N. उष्णिक्, उष्णिहौ, &c.

c. वाह्, 'bearing' (from the root वह् 'to bear'), changes वा to ऊ *ū* in the acc. plur. and remaining weakest cases (and before the ई *ī* of the fem.) if the word that precedes it in the compound ends in *a* or *ā*, this *a* or *ā* combining with *ū* into औ *au* (instead of ओ *o*, by 32): thus, भारवाह् m. f. 'one who bears a burden:' N. V. masc. भारवाट्, भारवाहौ, भारवाहस्; Ac. भारवाहं, भारवाहौ, भारौहस्; I. भारौहा, भारवाड्भ्यां, &c. N. fem. भारौही, &c. So प्रष्ठवाह् m. 'a steer' and विश्ववाह् 'all-sustaining.' Under other circumstances the change of *vāh* to *ūh* is optional: thus, शालिवाह्, 'bearing rice,' makes in Ac. pl. शाल्यूहस् or शालिवाहस्.

d. श्वेतवाह् m., 'Indra' (who is borne by white horses), may optionally retain वा in Ac. plur. &c.; and in consonantal cases is declined as if the base were श्वेतवस्: thus, N. V. श्वेतवास्, श्वेतवाहौ, श्वेतवाहस्; Ac. श्वेतवाहं, श्वेतवाहौ, श्वेतौहस् or श्वेतवाहस्; I. श्वेतौहा or श्वेतवाहा, श्वेतवोभ्यां, श्वेतवोभिस्, &c.

e. In तुराषाह्, 'a name of Indra,' the ष् is changed to स् wherever ह् becomes ट् or ड्; N. तुरासाट्, तुराषाहौ, तुराषाहस्; Ac. तुराषाहं, &c.; I. तुराषाहा, तुरासाड्भ्यां, &c.

f. अनडुह् m., 'an ox' (for अनोवाह्, from अनस् 'a cart,' and वाह् 'bearing'), forms the N. V. sing. from अनड्वस्; the other strong cases from अनड्वाह्, and the middle cases from अनडुद्: thus, N. अनड्वान्, अनड्वाहौ, अनड्वाहस्; Ac. अनड्वाहं, अनड्वाहौ, अनडुहस्; I. अनडुहा, अनडुद्भ्यां, अनडुद्भिस्, &c.; L. pl. अनडुत्सु; V. अनड्वन्. There is a feminine form अनड्वाही, but at the end of compounds this word makes fem. N. sing. अनडुही; neut. N. V. अनडुत्, अनडुही, अनड्वांहि.

183. नह्, 'binding,' 'tying,' at the end of compounds, changes the final to त् or द्, instead of ट् or ड्: thus, उपानह् f., 'a shoe,' makes N. V. उपानत्, उपानहौ, उपानहस्; Ac. उपानहं, &c.; I. उपानहा, उपानद्भ्यां, &c.; L. pl. उपानत्सु. See 306. *b*.

SECTION III.

ADJECTIVES.

184. The declension of substantives includes that of adjectives; and, as already seen, the three examples of substantives, given under

each class, serve as the model for the three genders of adjectives falling under the same class. Simple adjectives, coming immediately from roots, and not derived from substantives, are not very common. Such as do occur belong chiefly to the first, second, and third classes of nouns; 80, 81, 82.

185. Adjectives *formed from substantives* (i. e. secondary derivatives, called *taddhita*) are numerous, as may be seen at 80, 84, 85. They belong chiefly to the first, fifth, and sixth classes of nouns.

186. Compound adjectives, whether formed by using roots or substantives at the end of compounds, are most abundant under every one of the eight classes.

The following table exhibits examples of the most common kind of adjectives in the nom. case masc., fem., and neut., and indicates the class to which their declension is to be referred.

187. *Examples of simple adjectives.*

	BASE.	NOM. MASC.	NOM. FEM.	NOM. NEUT.
1ST CLASS.	प्रिय 'dear'	प्रियस्*	प्रिया	प्रियं
	शुभ 'fortunate'	शुभस्	शुभा	शुभं
	सुन्दर 'beautiful'	सुन्दरस्	सुन्दरा or सुन्दरी	सुन्दरं
2D CLASS.	शुचि 'pure'	शुचिस्	शुचिस्	शुचि
3D CLASS.	पाण्डु 'pale'	पाण्डुस्	पाण्डुस्	पाण्डु
	साधु 'good'	साधुस्	साधुस् or साध्वी 106.	साधु
	मृदु 'tender'	मृदुस्	मृद्वी	मृदु
	भीरु 'timid'	भीरुस्	भीरुस् or भीरूस् 125.	भीरु

188. *Examples of adjectives formed from substantives.*

	BASE.	NOM. MASC.	NOM. FEM.	NOM. NEUT.
1ST CLASS.	मानुष 'human'	मानुषस्	मानुषी	मानुषं
	धार्मिक 'religious'	धार्मिकस्	धार्मिकी	धार्मिकं
5TH CLASS.	बलवत् 'strong'	बलवान्	बलवती 106.	बलवत्
	श्रीमत् 'prosperous'	श्रीमान्	श्रीमती 106.	श्रीमत्
6TH CLASS.	सुखिन् 'happy'	सुखी	सुखिनी 106.	सुखि

* When it is remembered that *s* is equivalent in pronunciation to *s*, the three genders of this adjective might be written *priyas*, *priyá*, *priyam*; thus offering a perfect similarity to Latin adjectives in *us*.

189. *Examples of compound adjectives.*

	BASE.	NOM. MASC.	NOM. FEM.	NOM. NEUT.
1ST CLASS.	बहुविद्य 'very learned'	बहुविद्यः	बहुविद्या	बहुविद्यं
2D CLASS.	दुर्बुद्धि 'foolish'	दुर्बुद्धिः	दुर्बुद्धिः	दुर्बुद्धि
3D CLASS.	अल्पतनु 'small bodied'	अल्पतनुः	अल्पतनुः	अल्पतनु
4TH CLASS.	बहुदातृ 'very liberal'	बहुदाता	बहुदात्री 106.	बहुदातृ
5TH CLASS.	सर्वजित् 'all-conquering'	सर्वजित्	सर्वजित्	सर्वजित्
6TH CLASS.	सुजन्मन् 'well-born'	सुजन्मा	सुजन्मा	सुजन्म
7TH CLASS.	गतचेतस् 'deprived of sense'	गतचेताः	गतचेताः	गतचेतः
8TH CLASS.	मर्मस्पृश् 'piercing the vitals'	मर्मस्पृक्	मर्मस्पृक्	मर्मस्पृक्

190. *Examples of some other compound adjectives.*

शङ्खध्मा 'a shell-blower' (108. *a.*)	शङ्खध्माः	शङ्खध्माः	शङ्खध्मं
नष्टधी 'ruined' (123. *b.*)	नष्टधीः	नष्टधीः	नष्टधि
खलपू 'a sweeper' (126. *b.*)	खलपूः	खलपूः	खलपु
दिव्यमातृ 'having a divine mother' (130.)	दिव्यमाता	दिव्यमाता	दिव्यमातृ
बहुरै 'rich' (134. *a.*)	बहुराः	बहुराः	बहुरि
बहुगो 'having many cattle' (134. *a.*)	बहुगौः	बहुगौः	बहुगु
बहुनौ 'having many ships' (134. *a.*)	बहुनौः	बहुनौः	बहुनु

191. The degrees of comparison are formed in two ways; 1st, by adding to the base तर *tara* (nom. *-taras*, *-tará*, *-taram*, cf. Greek τερος) for the comparative; and तम *tama* (nom. *-tamas*, *-tamá*, *-tamam*, cf. Latin *timus*, Greek τατος) for the superlative: thus, पुण्य *puṇya*, 'holy,' पुण्यतर *puṇyatara*, 'more holy,' पुण्यतम *puṇyatama*, 'most holy,' declined like nouns of the first class at 103. So also, *dhanavat*, 'wealthy,' *dhanavattara*, 'more wealthy,' *dhanavattama*, 'most wealthy.' A final *n* is rejected; as, *dhanin*, 'rich,' *dhanitara*,

'more rich,' *dhanitama*, 'most rich;' but these adjectives generally take the affixes at 192 (see the examples at 193).

a. विद्वस्, 'wise,' makes विद्वत्तर, विद्वत्तम. Compare 168. *a.*

192. 2dly, by adding ईयस् *īyas* (nom. *-īyān*, *-īyasī*, *-īyas*, Greek ιων, see declension below) for the comparative; and इष्ठ *ishṭha* (nom. *-ishṭhas*, *-ishṭhā*, *-ishṭham*, declined at 103, cf. Greek ιστος) for the superlative.

a. Note, that while the base of the Sanskrit comparative affix strictly appears to end in *n* and *s* (*īyans*), the Greek has adhered to the *n* throughout (N. *īyān* = ιων, voc. *īyan* = ιον); and the Latin has taken the *s* for its neuter (*īyas* = *ius*, neuter of *ior*; *s* being changed to *r*, in the masc. and oblique cases). Compare Sanskrit *garīyas* with *gravius*.

193. In general, before *īyas* and *ishṭha*, the base disburdens itself of a final vowel, or of the more weighty affixes *in*, *vin*, *vat*, *mat*, and *tṛi*: thus, बलिन् 'strong,' बलीयस् 'more strong,' बलिष्ठ 'strongest' (declined at 103); पापिन् 'wicked,' पापीयस् 'more wicked,' पापिष्ठ 'most wicked;' लघु 'light,' लघीयस् 'lighter,' लघिष्ठ 'lightest;' मेधाविन् 'intelligent,' मेधीयस् 'more intelligent,' मेधिष्ठ 'most intelligent.' Similarly, महत् 'great,' महीयस् 'greater,' महिष्ठ 'greatest.'

a. Compare स्वादीयान् (N. of *svādīyas*) from *svādu*, 'sweet,' with ἡδίων from ἡδύς; and स्वादिष्ठ with ἥδιστος.

The declension of बलीयस् masc. is here given in full (see 167).

N.	बलीयान् *balīyān*	बलीयांसौ *balīyāṃsau*	बलीयांसस् *balīyāṃsas*
Ac.	बलीयांसम् *balīyāṃsam*	— *balīyāṃsau*	बलीयसस् *balīyasas*
I.	बलीयसा *balīyasā*	बलीयोभ्याम् *balīyobhyām*	बलीयोभिस् *balīyobhis*
D.	बलीयसे *balīyase*	— *balīyobhyām*	बलीयोभ्यस् *balīyobhyas*
Ab.	बलीयसस् *balīyasas*	— *balīyobhyām*	— *balīyobhyas*
G.	— *balīyasas*	बलीयसोस् *balīyasos*	बलीयसाम् *balīyasām*
L.	बलीयसि *balīyasi*	— *balīyasos*	बलीयःसु *balīyaḥsu*
V.	बलीयन् *balīyan*	बलीयांसौ *balīyāṃsau*	बलीयांसस् *balīyāṃsas*

The declension of the neut. and fem. is explained at 167.

194. And besides the rejection of the final, the base often undergoes considerable change, as in Greek (compare ἐχθίων, ἔχθιστος, from ἐχθρός); and its place is sometimes supplied by a substitute (compare βελτίων, βέλτιστος, from ἀγαθός). The following is a list of the substitutes:

POSITIVE.	SUBSTITUTE.	COMPARATIVE.	SUPERLATIVE.
अन्तिक *antika*, 'near'	नेद *neda*	नेदीयस्	नेदिष्ठ
अल्प *alpa*, 'little' *	कन *kana*	कनीयस्	कनिष्ठ
उरु *uru*, '*large*' (εὐρύς)	वर *vara*	वरीयस्	वरिष्ठ (ἄριστος)
ऋजु *ṛiju*, 'straight' *	ऋज *ṛija*	ऋजीयस्	ऋजिष्ठ
कृश *kṛiśa*, 'thin,' 'lean'	क्रश *kraśa*	क्रशीयस्	क्रशिष्ठ
क्षिप्र *kshipra*, 'quick'	क्षेप *kshepa*	क्षेपीयस्	क्षेपिष्ठ
क्षुद्र *kshudra*, 'small,' 'mean'	क्षोद *kshoda*	क्षोदीयस्	क्षोदिष्ठ
गुरु *guru*, 'heavy' (βαρύς)	गर *gara*	गरीयस् (*gravius*)	गरिष्ठ
तृप्र *tṛipra*, 'satisfied'	त्रप *trapa*	त्रपीयस्	त्रपिष्ठ
दीर्घ *dīrgha*, 'long'	द्राघ *drāgha*	द्राघीयस्	द्राघिष्ठ
दूर *dūra*, 'distant'	दव *dava*	दवीयस्	दविष्ठ
दृढ *dṛiḍha*, 'firm'	द्रढ *draḍha*	द्रढीयस्	द्रढिष्ठ
परिवृढ *parivṛiḍha*, 'eminent'	परिव्रढ *parivraḍha*	परिव्रढीयस्	परिव्रढिष्ठ
पृथु *pṛithu*, 'broad' (πλατύς)	प्रथ *pratha*	प्रथीयस्	प्रथिष्ठ
प्रशस्य *praśasya*, 'good'	श्र † *śra*	श्रेयस्	श्रेष्ठ
	ज्या † *jyā*	ज्यायस्	ज्येष्ठ
प्रिय *priya*, 'dear'	प्र † *pra*	प्रेयस्	प्रेष्ठ
बहु *bahu*, 'much,' 'frequent'	भू † *bhū*	भूयस्	भूयिष्ठ
बहुल *bahula*, 'much'	बंह *baṃha*	बंहीयस्	बंहिष्ठ
भृश *bhṛiśa*, 'excessive'	भ्रश *bhraśa*	भ्रशीयस्	भ्रशिष्ठ
मृदु *mṛidu*, 'soft'	म्रद *mrada*	म्रदीयस्	म्रदिष्ठ
युवन् *yuvan*, 'young' (*juvenis*)	यव *yava*	यवीयस्	यविष्ठ
वाढ *vāḍha*, 'firm,' 'thick'	साध *sādha*	साधीयस्	साधिष्ठ
वृद्ध *vṛiddha*, 'old'	वर्ष *varsha*	वर्षीयस्	वर्षिष्ठ
	ज्या † *jyā*	ज्यायस्	ज्येष्ठ
वृन्दारक *vṛindāraka*, 'excellent'	वृन्द *vṛinda*	वृन्दीयस्	वृन्दिष्ठ
स्थिर *sthira*, 'firm,' 'stable'	स्थ *stha*	स्थेयस्	स्थेष्ठ
स्थूल *sthūla*, 'gross,' 'bulky'	स्थव *sthava*	स्थवीयस्	स्थविष्ठ
स्फिर *sphira*, 'turgid'	स्फ *spha*	स्फेयस्	स्फेष्ठ
ह्रस्व *hrasva*, 'short'	ह्रस *hrasa*	ह्रसीयस्	ह्रसिष्ठ

195. *Tara* and *tama* may be added to nouns substantive; as, from राजन्, 'a king,' राजतर, &c.; from दुःख, 'pain,' दुःखतर, &c. If added to a word like सर्पिस्, 'clarified butter,' the usual euphonic changes must take place: thus,

* अल्प may be also regularly अल्पीयस्, अल्पिष्ठ; and ऋजु may be रजीयस्, &c.

† In the case of श्र and प्र the final vowel is not rejected, but combines with *īyas* and *ishṭha* agreeably to Sandhi. In ज्या and भू, *yas* is affixed in place of *īyas*.

कवितर, &c. (r. 70). They are also added to inseparable prepositions; as, उद् 'up,' उत्तर 'higher,' उत्तम 'highest.' Compare Latin *extimus*, *intimus*, &c.

196. Sometimes, but rarely, to feminine bases ending in the vowels ई *ī* and ऊ *ū*, which may either be retained before *tara* and *tama*, or be shortened: thus, from सती, 'a faithful wife,' सतीतर, सतीतम or सतितर, सतितम.

a. They are sometimes added to pronominal bases (236), and to numerals (209, 211).

197. They may even be added, in conjunction with the syllable आम् *ām*, to the inflexions of verbs; as, जल्पतितरां 'he talks more than he ought.'

a. Sometimes the two affixes *īyas* and *tara*, *ishṭha* and *tama* are combined together in the same word: thus, श्रेयस्तर, श्रेयस्तम; ज्येष्ठतम; नेदिष्ठतम, &c.; and *tara* may be even added to *ishṭha*: thus, ज्येष्ठतर.

SECTION IV.

NUMERAL ADJECTIVES.

CARDINALS.

198. The cardinals are, एक 1, १; द्वि 2, २; त्रि 3, ३; चतुर् 4, ४; पञ्चन् 5, ५; षष् 6, ६; सप्तन् 7, ७; अष्टन् 8, ८; नवन् 9, ९; दशन् 10, १०; एकादशन् 11, ११; द्वादशन् 12, १२; त्रयोदशन् 13, १३; चतुर्दशन् 14, १४; पञ्चदशन् 15, १५; षोडशन् 16, १६; सप्तदशन् 17, १७; अष्टादशन् 18, १८; नवदशन् or ऊनविंशति 19, १९; विंशति 20; एकविंशति 21; द्वाविंशति 22; त्रयोविंशति 23; चतुर्विंशति 24; पञ्चविंशति 25; षड्विंशति 26; सप्तविंशति 27; अष्टाविंशति 28; नवविंशति or ऊनत्रिंशत् 29; त्रिंशत् 30; एकत्रिंशत् 31; द्वात्रिंशत् 32; त्रयस्त्रिंशत् 33; चतुस्त्रिंशत् 34; पञ्चत्रिंशत् 35; षट्त्रिंशत् 36; सप्तत्रिंशत् 37; अष्टात्रिंशत् 38; नवत्रिंशत् or ऊनचत्वारिंशत् 39; चत्वारिंशत् 40; एकचत्वारिंशत् 41; द्विचत्वारिंशत् or द्वाचत्वारिंशत् 42; त्रिचत्वारिंशत् or त्रयश्चत्वारिंशत् 43; चतुश्चत्वारिंशत् 44; पञ्चचत्वारिंशत् 45; षट्चत्वारिंशत् 46; सप्तचत्वारिंशत् 47; अष्टाचत्वारिंशत् or अष्टचत्वारिंशत् 48; नवचत्वारिंशत् or ऊनपञ्चाशत् 49; पञ्चाशत् 50; एकपञ्चाशत् 51; द्विपञ्चाशत् or द्वापञ्चाशत् 52; त्रिपञ्चाशत् or त्रयःपञ्चाशत् 53; चतुःपञ्चाशत् 54; पञ्चपञ्चाशत् 55; षट्पञ्चाशत् 56; सप्तपञ्चाशत् 57; अष्टपञ्चाशत् or अष्टापञ्चाशत् 58; नवपञ्चाशत् or ऊनषष्टि 59; षष्टि 60; एकषष्टि 61; द्विषष्टि or द्वाषष्टि 62; त्रिषष्टि or त्रयःषष्टि* 63; चतुःषष्टि* 64; पञ्चषष्टि 65; षट्षष्टि 66; सप्तषष्टि 67; अष्टषष्टि or अष्टाषष्टि 68; नवषष्टि or ऊनसप्तति 69; सप्तति 70; एकसप्तति 71; द्विसप्तति or द्वासप्तति 72; त्रिसप्तति or त्रयःसप्तति 73; चतुःसप्तति 74; पञ्चसप्तति 75; षट्सप्तति 76; सप्तसप्तति 77; अष्टसप्तति or अष्टासप्तति 78; नवसप्तति or ऊनाशीति 79; अशीति 80; एकाशीति 81; द्व्यशीति 82; त्र्यशीति 83;

* These may also be written त्रयष्षष्टि, चतुष्षष्टि. See rules 62.*a.* and 63.

चतुरशीति 84; पञ्चाशीति 85; षडशीति 86; सप्ताशीति 87; अष्टाशीति 88; नवाशीति or ऊननवति 89; नवति 90; एकनवति 91; द्विनवति or द्वानवति 92; त्रिनवति or त्रयोनवति 93; चतुर्नवति 94; पञ्चनवति 95; षण्णवति 96 (41. *d*); सप्तनवति 97; अष्टनवति or अष्टानवति 98; नवनवति or ऊनशत n. (m) 99; शत n. (also occasionally masc.*) 100. एक may be placed before the last numeral: thus, एकं शतं or एकशतं. Similarly 200 is expressed by द्वे शते (nom. du. n.) or शते (nom. du. n.) or द्विशतं (nom. sing. n.); 300 by त्रीणि शतानि (nom. pl. n.) or त्रिशतं (nom. sing. n.); 400 by चत्वारि शतानि (nom. pl. n.) or चतुःशतं; 500 by पञ्चशतं; 600 by षट्शतं; and so on up to 1000, which is expressed by सहस्रं n. (occasionally m.) or दशशतं n. or दशशती f.; 2000 by द्वे सहस्रे or द्विसहस्रं; 3000 by त्रीणि सहस्राणि or त्रिसहस्रं; and so forth.

199. The intervening numbers between 100 and 1000, and those between 1000 and 2000, are usually expressed by compounding the adjective अधिक *adhika*, 'more,' 'plus,' with the cardinal numbers: thus 101 may be expressed by एकाधिकं शतं, i. e. 'a hundred plus one,' or more concisely एकाधिकशतं. Similarly, द्व्यधिकं शतं or द्व्यधिकशतं 102; त्र्यधिकं शतं or त्र्यधिकशतं 103; त्रिंशदधिकशतं 130; पञ्चाशदधिकशतं or सार्धशतं 150; षड्विंशत्यधिकद्विशतं 226; त्र्यशीत्यधिकत्रिशतं 383; पञ्चाशीत्यधिकचतुःशतं 485; षण्णवत्यधिकपञ्चशतं 596; षट्षष्ट्यधिकषट्शतं 666; षोडशशतं or षट्शताधिकसहस्रं 1600; षट्षष्ट्यधिकषोडशशतं 1666†.

In the same way the adjective ऊन 'less,' 'minus,' is often placed before a cardinal number, to denote one less than that number, एक 'one' being either expressed or understood: thus, ऊनविंशति or एकोनविंशति 'twenty minus one' or 'nineteen' (compare the Latin *undeviginti*, i. e. *unus de viginti*). And other cardinals, besides एक 'one,' are sometimes prefixed to ऊन, to denote that they are to be subtracted from a following number; as, पञ्चोनं शतं or पञ्चोनशतं 'a hundred less five' or 'ninety-five.'

a. The ordinals, however, are sometimes joined to the cardinals to express 111 and upwards: thus, एकादशं शतं or एकादशशतं 111; त्रिंशं शतं or त्रिंशशतं 130; विंशं सहस्रं or विंशसहस्रं 1020.

b. Single words are used for the highest numbers: thus, अयुत n. 'ten thousand;'

---

* I have found शतं शताः 'a hundred hundred' and सप्तशताः 'seven hundred' (agreeing with पाशाः) in the Mahá-bhárata.

† Similarly 2130 might be expressed by त्रिंशदधिकैकविंशतिशतं or -शतानि or by using पर; thus, त्रिंशदधिकैकशतपरे द्वे सहस्रे.

लक्ष n. or लक्षा f. 'a lac,' 'one hundred thousand;' नियुत n. (according to Amara also m.) or प्रयुत n. 'one million;' कोटि f. 'a krore,' 'ten millions;' अर्बुद m. n. 'one hundred millions;' महार्बुद n. (m.) 'one thousand millions;' वृन्द n. or अब्ज n. 'ten thousand millions;' महापद्म n. 'one hundred thousand millions;' खर्व n. 'a billion;' महाखर्व n. 'ten billions;' शङ्ख m. n. or समुद्र m. 'a hundred billions;' महाशङ्ख m. n. 'a thousand billions;' हाहा m. 'ten thousand billions;' महाहाहा m. or परार्ध m. 'one hundred thousand million;' धुन n. (धुन्न) 'one million billion;' महाधुन n. (महाधुन्न) 'ten million billion;' अक्षौहिणी f. 'one hundred million billion;' महाक्षौहिणी 'one thousand million billion.' These words are declinable according to their finals; e.g. अयुत like शिव n., and कोटि like मति f. (104, 112.)

DECLENSION OF CARDINALS.

200. एक 1, द्वि 2 (*duo*, *δύο*), त्रि 3 (*tres*, *τρεῖς*, *τρία*), चतुर् 4 (*quatuor*), are declined in three genders.

एक *eka*, 'one' (no dual), follows the declension of the pronominals at 237: nom. m. *ekas;* dat. m. *ekasmai;* nom. f. *ekā;* dat. f. *ekasyai;* nom. n. *ekam;* nom. pl. m. *eke*, 'some.' It may take the affixes *tara* and *tama:* thus, *ekatara*, 'one of two;' *ekatama*, 'one of many;' which also follow the declension of pronominals; see 236, 238.

201. द्वि *dvi*, 'two' (dual only), is declined as if the base were द्व *dva:* thus, N. Ac. V. m. द्वौ *dvau*, f. n. द्वे *dve;* I. D. Ab. m. f. n. द्वाभ्यां; G. L. द्वयोः.

202. त्रि *tri*, 'three' (plural only), is declined in the masculine like the plural of nouns whose bases end in इ *i* at 110, except in the gen.: thus, N. V. masc. त्रयः; Ac. त्रीन्; I. त्रिभिः; D. Ab. त्रिभ्यः; G. त्रयाणां; L. त्रिषु. The feminine forms its cases from a base तिसृ: thus, N. Ac. V. fem. तिस्रः; I. तिसृभिः; D. Ab. तिसृभ्यः; G. तिसृणां; L. तिसृषु. The N. Ac. neut. is त्रीणि; the rest as the masculine.

203. चतुर् *ćatur*, 'four' (plural only), is thus declined: N. V. masc. चत्वारः (*τέτταρες*, *τέσσαρες*); Ac. चतुरः; I. चतुर्भिः; D. Ab. चतुर्भ्यः; G. चतुर्णां or चतुर्ण्णां; L. चतुर्षु. N. Ac. V. fem. चतस्रः; I. चतसृभिः; D. Ab. चतसृभ्यः; G. चतसृणां; L. चतसृषु. N. Ac. V. neut. चत्वारि; the rest as the masculine.

204. पञ्चन् *pańćan*, 'five' (plural only), is the same for masc., fem., and neut. It is declined in I. D. Ab. L. after the analogy of nouns in *an* (147). The gen. lengthens the penultimate: thus, N. Ac. V. पञ्च (*πέντε*); I. पञ्चभिः; D. Ab. पञ्चभ्यः; G. पञ्चानां; L. पञ्चसु. Similarly are declined, सप्तन् 'seven' (*septem*, *ἑπτά*), नवन्

'nine' (*novem*), दशन् 'ten' (*decem*, δέκα), एकादशन् 'eleven' (*undecim*), द्वादशन् 'twelve' (*duodecim*), and all other numerals ending in *an*, excepting अष्टन् 'eight.'

205. षष् *shash*, 'six,' and अष्टन् *ashṭan*, 'eight,' are the same for masc., fem., and neut., and are thus declined: N. Ac. V. षट्; I. षड्भिस्; D. Ab. षड्भ्यस्; G. षण्णां *shaṇṇám* (41. *d*); L. षट्सु. N. Ac. V. अष्टौ or अष्ट (*octo*, ὀκτώ); I. अष्टाभिस् or अष्टभिस्; D. Ab. अष्टाभ्यस् or अष्टभ्यस्; G. अष्टानां; L. अष्टासु or अष्टसु.

a. The numerals from पञ्चन् 'five' to नवदशन् 'nineteen' have no distinction of gender, but agree in number and case with the nouns to which they are joined: thus, पञ्चभिर् नारीभिः 'by five women.'

206. All the remaining cardinal numbers, from ऊनविंशति 'nineteen' to शत 'a hundred,' सहस्र 'a thousand,' and upwards, may be declined in the singular, even when joined with masculine, feminine, or neuter nouns in the plural. Those ending in ति *ti* are feminine, and declined like मति *mati* at 112; and those in त् *t* are also feminine, and declined like सरित् *sarit* at 136: thus, विंशत्या पुरुषैः 'with twenty men;' विंशतिं पुरुषान् acc. pl. 'twenty men;' त्रिंशता पुरुषैः 'with thirty men;' त्रिंशतं पुरुषान् acc. pl. 'thirty men.' शत 'a hundred' and सहस्र 'a thousand' are declined like शिव *śiva* at 104; and all the higher numbers according to their finals: thus, शतं पितरः 'a hundred ancestors;' एकाधिकशतं पितरः 'a hundred and one ancestors;' सहस्रेण पितृभिः 'with a thousand ancestors.'

207. Although these numerals, from ऊनविंशति 'nineteen,' when joined with plural nouns, may be declined in the singular, yet they may often take a dual or plural; as, विंशती 'two twenties;' त्रिंशती 'two thirties;' त्रिंशतस् 'many thirties;' शते 'two hundred;' शतानि 'hundreds;' सहस्राणि 'many thousands;' 'sixty thousand sons,' षष्टिः पुत्रसहस्राणि; and the things numbered may be put in the genitive; thus, द्वे सहस्रे रथानां 'two thousand chariots;' सप्तशतानि नागानां 'seven hundred elephants;' एकविंशतिः शराणां 'twenty-one arrows.' See other examples in syntax at 835.

ORDINALS.

208. The ordinals are, प्रथम 'first'* (compare πρῶτος, *primus*); द्वितीय 'second' (δεύτερος); तृतीय 'third' (*tertius*); declined like *sarva* and the pronominals at 237, 238; but प्रथम may be declined like

* Other adjectives may be used to express 'first;' as, आद्यस्, -आ, -अं; आदिमस्, -आ, -अं; अग्रस्, -आ, -अं; अग्रिमस्, -आ, -अं.

śiva (103) in N.V. plur. masc. (प्रथमे or प्रथमाः); and the other two in D. Ab. G. L. sing. m. f. n.; thus, D. m. n. द्वितीयस्मै or द्वितीयाय, f. द्वितीयस्यै or द्वितीयायै. See also 239.

209. चतुर्थ 'fourth' * (τέταρτος); पञ्चम 'fifth;' षष्ठ 'sixth;' सप्तम 'seventh' (*septimus*); अष्टम 'eighth;' नवम 'ninth' (*nonus*); दशम 'tenth' (*decimus*); declined like *śiva* at 103, 104, for the masc. and neut.; and like *nadí* at 106 for the feminine: thus, Nom. m. चतुर्थस्, f. चतुर्थी. (In पञ्चम, &c., the old superlative affix *ma* may be noted.)

210. The ordinals from 'eleventh' to 'nineteenth' are formed from the cardinals by rejecting the final *n*: thus, from एकादशन् 'eleven,' एकादश 'eleventh' (Nom. m. f. n. एकादशस्, -शी, -शं, 103, 106, 104).

211. 'Twentieth,' 'thirtieth,' 'fortieth,' and 'fiftieth,' are formed either by adding the superlative affix *tama* (196. *a*) to the cardinal, or by rejecting the final syllable or letter of the cardinal; as, from विंशति 'twenty,' विंशतितम or विंश 'twentieth' (Nom. m. f. n. -तमस्, -मी, -मं; -शस्, -शी, -शं, 103, 106, 104). Similarly, त्रिंशत्तम or त्रिंश 'thirtieth,' पञ्चाशत्तम or पञ्चाश 'fiftieth,' &c. The intermediate ordinals are formed by prefixing the numeral, as in the cardinals: thus, एकविंशतितम or एकविंश 'twenty-first,' &c.

212. The other ordinals, from 'sixtieth' to 'ninetieth,' are formed by adding *tama*; also by changing *ti* to *ta* in the case of another numeral preceding, but not otherwise: thus, from षष्टि 'sixty,' षष्टितम 'sixtieth;' but षष्ट for 'sixtieth' can only be used when another numeral precedes, as एकषष्ट or एकषष्टितम 'sixty-first,' त्रिषष्ट or त्रिषष्टितम 'sixty-third:' from नवति 'ninety,' नवतितम 'ninetieth;' but नवत for 'ninetieth' can only be used when another numeral precedes.

213. 'Hundredth' and 'thousandth' are formed either by adding *tama* to शत and सहस्र, or simply by converting these ordinals into adjectives, declinable in three genders: thus, शततम or शत 'hundredth' (Nom. m. f. n. शततमस्, -मी, -मं; शतस्, -ती, -तं). Similarly, सहस्रतमस्, -मी, -मं, or सहस्रस्, -स्री, -स्रं, 'thousandth.'

214. The aggregation of two or more numbers is expressed by modifications of the ordinal numbers: thus, द्वयं 'a duad,' त्रयं 'a triad,' चतुष्टयं 'the aggregate of four.'

215. There are a few adverbial numerals; as, सकृत् 'once,' द्विस् 'twice,' त्रिस् 'thrice,' चतुस् 'four times.' कृत्वस् may be added to cardinal numbers, with a

* तुरीयस्, -या, -यं; तुर्यस्, -र्या, -र्यं — are also used for 'fourth.'

similar signification; as, पञ्चकृत्वस् 'five times.' The neuter of the ordinals may be used adverbially; as, प्रथमं 'in the first place.'

216. *Numerical symbols.*

१	२	३	४	५	६	७	८	९	१०	११	१२	
1	2	3	4	5	6	7	8	9	10	11	12	&c.

CHAPTER V.

PRONOUNS.

FORMATION OF THE BASE.

217. PRONOUNS (*sarva-nâma*) have no crude base analogous to that of nouns; that is, no state distinct from all inflexion, serving as the basis on which all the cases are constructed. The reason of this may be, that the pronouns in Sanskṛit, as in all languages, are so irregular and capricious in their formation, that no one base would be equally applicable to all the cases. Thus in the 1st personal pronoun, the base of the nom. sing. would be अह् *ah*, while that of the oblique cases sing. would be म *ma*. In the 2d, the base of the sing. is practically त्व *tva*, while that of the dual and plural is यु *yu*. The 3d would have स *sa* for the base of the nom. sing., and त *ta* for the other cases.

a. The question then arises, What form of the pronoun is to be used in the formation of compound words? In the pronouns of the first and second persons, the ablative cases, singular and plural, and in the other pronouns, the nominative and accusative cases singular neuter, are considered as expressive of the most general and comprehensive state of the pronoun. These cases, therefore, discharge the office of a crude base in respect of compound words.

DECLENSION OF THE PERSONAL PRONOUNS.

Observe.—In Sanskṛit, as in other languages, to denote the general and indefinite character of the first two personal pronouns, no distinction of gender is admitted. For the same reason, the formation of the nom. case of pronouns is made to resemble the neuter, as the most general state. This may also be the reason why the 3d pronoun *sa* drops the *s* of the nom. case before all consonants. There is no vocative case.

218. अस्मद् *asmad*, 'I.'

N.	अहम् *aham*, 'I'	आवाम् *ávám*, 'we two'	वयम् *vayam*, 'we'
Ac.	माम् *mám* or मा *má*, 'me'	— *ávám* or नौ *nau*, 'us two'	अस्मान् *asmán* or नस् *nas*, 'us'
I.	मया *mayá*	आवाभ्याम् *ávábhyám*	अस्माभिस् *asmábhis*
D.	मह्यम् *mahyam* or मे *me*	— *ávábhyám* or नौ *nau*	अस्मभ्यम् *asmabhyam* or नस् *nas*
Ab.	मत् *mat* or *mattas**	— *ávábhyám*	अस्मत् *asmat*
G.	मम *mama* or मे *me*	आवयोस् *ávayos* or नौ *nau*	अस्माकम् *asmákam* or नस् *nas*
L.	मयि *mayi*	— *ávayos*	अस्मासु *asmásu*

219. युष्मद् *yushmad*, 'thou,' 'you.'

N.	त्वम् *tvam*, 'thou'	युवाम् *yuvám*, 'you two'	यूयम् *yúyam*, 'you' or 'ye'
Ac.	त्वाम् *tvám* or त्वा *tvá*	— *yuvám* or वाम् *vám*	युष्मान् *yushmán* or वस् *vas*
I.	त्वया *tvayá*	युवाभ्याम् *yuvábhyám*	युष्माभिस् *yushmábhis*
D.	तुभ्यम् *tubhyam* or ते *te*	— *yuvábhyám* or वाम् *vám*	युष्मभ्यम् *yushmabhyam* or वस् *vas*
Ab.	त्वत् *tvat* or *tvattas**	— *yuvábhyám*	युष्मत् *yushmat*
G.	तव *tava* or ते *te*	युवयोस् *yuvayos* or वाम् *vám*	युष्माकम् *yushmákam* or वस् *vas*
L.	त्वयि *tvayi*	— *yuvayos*	युष्मासु *yushmásu*

220. तद् *tad*, 'he,' 'that.'

MASCULINE.

N.	सस् *sas* (usually स *sa*†), 'he'	तौ *tau*, 'they two'	ते *te*, 'they,' 'those'
Ac.	तम् *tam*	— *tau*	तान् *tán*
I.	तेन *tena*	ताभ्याम् *tábhyám*	तैस् *tais*
D.	तस्मै *tasmai*	— *tábhyám*	तेभ्यस् *tebhyas*
Ab.	तस्मात् *tasmát*	— *tábhyám*	— *tebhyas*
G.	तस्य *tasya*	तयोस् *tayos*	तेषाम् *teshám*
L.	तस्मिन् *tasmin*	— *tayos*	तेषु *teshu*

FEMININE.

N.	सा *sá*, 'she'	ते *te*	तास् *tás*
Ac.	ताम् *tám*	— *te*	— *tás*
I.	तया *tayá*	ताभ्याम् *tábhyám*	ताभिस् *tábhis*
D.	तस्यै *tasyai*	— *tábhyám*	ताभ्यस् *tábhyas*
Ab.	तस्यास् *tasyás*	— *tábhyám*	— *tábhyas*

---

* As *mat* is generally used in compounds, *mattas* and *tvattas* more commonly stand for the ablative; see r. 719. Similarly, the ablative plural may be *yushmattas*, *asmattas*; but these very rarely occur.

† By rule 67, स will be the usual form. सस् usually exists as सो, see 64. a.

G.	तस्यास् *tasyás*	तयोस् *tayos*	तासाम् *tásám*
L.	तस्याम् *tasyám*	— *tayos*	तासु *tásu*

NEUTER.

N. Ac. तत् *tat* or तद् *tad*, ते *te*, तानि *táni*; the rest like the masculine. Compare the Greek article with the above pronoun.

a. The above pronoun *tad* is sometimes used *emphatically* with the other pronouns, like *ille* and *ipse*: thus, सोऽहं '*ille ego*;' ते वयं '*illi nos*;' स त्वं '*ille tu*;' ते यूयं '*illi vos*;' स एषः '*ille ipse*;' तद् एतत् '*id ipsum*.'

221. There is a modification of the pronoun *tad* (rarely used), formed by combining it with the relative *ya*: thus, N. स्यस्, त्यौ, त्ये; Ac. त्यं, &c. Fem. स्या, त्ये, त्यास्, &c.

a. Observe the resemblance of the Sanskṛit personal pronouns to those of the dead and living cognate languages. *Aham* or *ah* is the Greek ἐγώ (Æolic ἐγών), Latin *ego*, German *ich*, English 'I;' *mám* or *má* (the latter being the oldest form found in the Vedas) equals ἐμέ, *me*; *mahyam* = *mihi*; *mayi* = *mei*: the *mat* of the abl. sing. and of *asmat*, *yushmat*, corresponds to the Latin *met* in *memet*, *nosmet*, &c.; *vayam* or *ve* is the English 'we;' *asmán* = *us*; *nas* = *nos*; *tvam* = *tu*, 'thou;' *tvám* or *tvá* = *te*, 'thee;' *tubhyam* = *tibi*; *tvayi* = *tui*; *yúyam* = ὑμεῖς, English 'you;' *vas* = *vos*. The 3d personal pronoun corresponds to the Greek article: thus, *tau* = τώ, *tam* = τόν; *tábhyám* = τοῖν, ταῖν, &c.

REFLEXIVE PERSONAL PRONOUN.

222. The oblique cases of आत्मन् *átman*, 'soul,' 'self' (declined at 147), are used reflexively, in place of the three personal pronouns, like the Latin *ipse*.

Thus, *átmánam* (*me ipsum*) *anáhárena hanishyámi*, 'I will kill myself by fasting;' *átmánam* (*te ipsum*) *mṛitavad darśaya*, 'show thyself as if dead;' *átmánam* (*se ipsum*) *nindati*, 'he blames himself.' It is generally used in the singular, even when it refers to a plural; as, *abudhair átmá paropakaraṇíkṛitaḥ*, 'foolish people make themselves the tools of others.'

a. The indeclinable pronoun स्वयम् *svayam* is sometimes joined, in the sense of 'self,' to the three personal pronouns: thus, अहं स्वयं 'I myself,' &c.

DEMONSTRATIVE PERSONAL PRONOUNS.

223. The third personal pronoun तद् *tad*, 'he,' declined above at 220, is constantly used in a demonstrative sense, to signify 'that' or 'this;' and by prefixing ए *e* to it, another common pronoun is formed, more proximately demonstrative: thus, एतद् *etad*, 'this.' Observe—The *t* of *etad* may optionally be changed to *n* in the Ac. sing. du. pl., I. sing., G. L. du., in all three genders: thus,

एतद् *etad*, 'this.'

MASCULINE.

N.	एषस् *eshas* (usu. एष *esha*) 70.	एतौ *etau*	एते *ete*
Ac.	एतम् *etam* or एनम् *enam*	— *etau* or एनौ *enau*	एतान् *etán* or एनान् *enán*
I.	एतेन *etena* or एनेन *enena*	एताभ्याम् *etábhyám*	एतैस् *etais*
D.	एतस्मै *etasmai*	— *etábhyám*	एतेभ्यस् *etebhyas*
Ab.	एतस्मात् *etasmát*	— *etábhyám*	— *etebhyas*
G.	एतस्य *etasya*	एतयोस् *etayos* or एनयोस् *enayos*	एतेषाम् *eteshám*
L.	एतस्मिन् *etasmin*	— *etayos* or — *enayos*	एतेषु *eteshu*

The feminine is N. एषा *eshá*, एते *ete*, एतास् *etás*; Ac. एतां or एनां, एते or एने, एतास् or एनास्; I. एतया or एनया, एताभ्यां, एताभिस्; D. एतस्यै, &c.

The neuter is N. एतत् or एतद्, एते, एतानि; Ac. एतत् or एनत्, एते or एने, एतानि or एनानि, &c.

a. Observe, that forms like एनं &c. for एतं &c. are enclitic, and ought not to be used at the beginning of a sentence.

With the above pronoun compare the Latin *iste, ista, istud*: *etam* = *istam*, *etasya* = *istius*, *etat* = *istud*.

224. There is another common demonstrative pronoun, of which इदम् *idam*, 'this,' the N. neuter, is considered to represent the most general state (compare the Latin *is, ea, id*). The true base, however, might rather be said to be the vowels अ *a* and इ *i*, the latter of which serves also as the source of certain pronominals, such as इतर, ईदृश, इयत्. See 234, 236, and 234. *b*.

MASCULINE.

N.	अयम् *ayam*, 'this'	इमौ *imau*, 'these two'	इमे *ime*, 'these'
Ac.	इमम् *imam*	— *imau*	इमान् *imán*
I.	अनेन *anena*	आभ्याम् *ábhyám*	एभिस् *ebhis**
D.	अस्मै *asmai*	— *ábhyám*	एभ्यस् *ebhyas*
Ab.	अस्मात् *asmát*	— *ábhyám*	— *ebhyas*
G.	अस्य *asya*	अनयोस् *anayos*	एषाम् *eshám*
L.	अस्मिन् *asmin*	— *anayos*	एषु *eshu*

* This is an example of the old form for the instr. pl. of masculine nouns of the first class, common in the Vedas.

FEMININE.

N. इयम् *iyam*	इमे *ime*	इमास् *imás*
Ac. इमाम् *imám*	— *ime*	— *imás*
I. अनया *anayá*	आभ्याम् *ábhyám*	आभिस् *ábhis*
D. अस्यै *asyai*	— *ábhyám*	आभ्यस् *ábhyas*
Ab. अस्यास् *asyás*	— *ábhyám*	— *ábhyas*
G. — *asyás*	अनयोस् *anayos*	आसाम् *ásám*
L. अस्याम् *asyám*	— *anayos*	आसु *ásu*

NEUTER.

N. Ac. इदम् *idam*	इमे *ime*	इमानि *imáni*

225. There is another demonstrative pronoun (rarely used, excepting in nom. sing.), of which अदस्, 'this' or 'that,' is supposed to represent the most general state, though the base is अमु *amu*, and in N. sing. असु *asu*. It is thus declined: Masc. N. असौ, अमू, अमी; Ac. अमुं, अमू, अमून्; I. अमुना, अमूभ्यां, अमीभिस्; D. अमुष्मै, अमूभ्यां, अमीभ्यस्; Ab. अमुष्मात्, अमूभ्यां, अमीभ्यस्; G. अमुष्य, अमुयोस्, अमीषां; L. अमुष्मिन्, अमुयोस्, अमीषु. Fem. N. असौ, अमू, अमूस्; Ac. अमूं, अमू, अमूस्; I. अमुया, अमूभ्यां, अमूभिस्; D. अमुष्यै, अमूभ्यां, अमूभ्यस्; Ab. अमुष्यास्, &c.; G. अमुष्यास्, अमुयोस्, अमूषां; L. अमुष्यां, अमुयोस्, अमूषु. Neut. N. Ac. अदस्, अमू, अमूनि.

RELATIVE PRONOUN.

226. The relative is formed by substituting य *y* for the initial letter of the pronoun *tad*, at 220: thus,

यद् *yad*, 'who,' 'which.'

MASCULINE.

N. यस् *yas*	यौ *yau*	ये *ye*, 'who' or 'which'
Ac. यम् *yam*	— *yau*	यान् *yán*
I. येन *yena*	याभ्याम् *yábhyám*	यैस् *yais*
D. यस्मै *yasmai*	— *yábhyám*	येभ्यस् *yebhyas*
Ab. यस्मात् *yasmát*	— *yábhyám*	— *yebhyas*
G. यस्य *yasya*	ययोस् *yayos*	येषाम् *yeshám*
L. यस्मिन् *yasmin*	— *yayos*	येषु *yeshu*

The feminine and neuter follow the fem. and neut. of *tad*, at 220. Fem. N. या *yá*, ये *ye*, यास् *yás*; Ac. याम् *yám*, &c. &c. Neut. N. Ac. यत् *yat* or यद् *yad*, ये *ye*, यानि *yáni*; the rest like the masculine.

With the above pronoun compare the Greek relative ὅς, ἥ, ὅ; the Sanskrit *y* being often represented in Greek words by the *spiritus asper*.

INTERROGATIVE PRONOUNS.

227. The interrogative differs from the relative in substituting *k* instead of *y* for the initial letter of the pronoun *tad*, at 220; and in making the N. Ac. sing. neut. किम् instead of कद्*: thus, Masc. N. कस् *kas*, कौ *kau*, के *ke*, 'who?' 'which?' 'what?' Ac. कम् *kam*, 'whom?' &c. Fem. N. का *ká*, के *ke*, कास् *kás*, &c. The N. Ac. Neut. are किम् *kim*, के *ke*, कानि *káni*. Although the real base of this pronoun is *ka*, yet *kim* is taken to represent the most general state, and occurs in a few compounds; such as किमर्थं 'on what account?' 'why?'

a. To the true base *ka* may be affixed *ti*, to form कति *kati* (*quot*), 'how many?' The same affix is added to *ta* and *ya*, the proper bases of the third personal and relative pronouns, to form *tati*, 'so many' (*tot*), and *yati*, 'as many.' These are thus declined in pl. only: N. Ac. V. कति; I. कतिभिस्; Dat. Ab. कतिभ्यस्; G. कतीनां; L. कतिषु.

Note—The Latin *quot* and *tot*, which drop the final *i*, take it again in composition; as, *quotidie*, *totidem*, &c.

INDEFINITE PRONOUNS.

228. The indeclinable affixes *ćit*, *api*, and *ćana*, affixed (in accordance with the rules of Sandhi) to the several cases of the interrogative pronouns, give them an indefinite signification; as, कश्चित् *kaśćit*, 'somebody,' 'some one,' 'any one,' 'a certain one:'

MASCULINE.

N.	कश्चित् *kaśćit* 62.	कौचित् *kaućit*	केचित् *kećit*, 'some persons'
Ac.	कञ्चित् *kańćit* 59.	— *kaućit*	कांश्चित् *kánśćit* 53.
I.	केनचित् *kenaćit*	काभ्याञ्चित् *kábhyáńćit*	कैश्चित् *kaiśćit* 62.
D.	कस्मैचित् *kasmaićit*	— *kábhyáńćit*	केभ्यश्चित् *kebhyaśćit*
Ab.	कस्माच्चित् *kasmáććit* 48.	— *kábhyáńćit*	— *kebhyaśćit*
G.	कस्यचित् *kasyaćit*	कयोश्चित् *kayośćit* 62.	केषाञ्चित् *keshánćit*
L.	कस्मिंश्चित् *kasminśćit* 53.	— *kayośćit*	केषुचित् *keshućit*

Similarly, Fem. Nom. काचित्, केचित्, काश्चित्; Ac. काञ्चित्, &c.: and Neut. Nom. Ac. किञ्चित् 'something,' 'any thing,' केचित्, कानिचित्, &c.

229. So also by affixing अपि; as, Masc. Nom. कोऽपि (64. *a*) 'some one,' 'a certain one,' कावपि, केऽपि (37, 35); Ac. कमपि, &c.; I. केनापि, &c. (31); D. कस्मा-

---

* *Kat* or *kad*, however (= Latin *quod*), was the old form, and is retained in a few words; such as *kaććit*, 'perhaps;' *kadartha*, 'useless' ('of what use?'); *kadadhvan*, 'a bad road' ('what sort of a road?').

चित्, &c. (37); Ab. कस्माच्चित्, &c.; G. कस्यचित्, &c.; L. कस्मिंश्चित्, &c. (52). Fem. Nom. काचित्, &c.; Ac. कांचित्, &c.; I. कयाचित्, &c. &c. Neut. Nom. किंचित् 'something,' 'any thing,' &c. The affix *ćana* is rarely found, except in Nom. Masc. कश्चन 'some one,' 'any one;' and in Nom. Neut. किंचन 'something.'

230. In the same way interrogative adverbs are made indefinite: thus, from *kati*, 'how many?' *katićit*, 'a few;' from *kadá*, 'when?' *kadáćit* or *kadáćana* or *kadápi*, 'at some time;' from *katham*, 'how?' *kathamćana*, 'some how;' from *kva*, 'where?' *kvaćit* or *kvápi*, 'somewhere.'

POSSESSIVE PRONOUNS.

231. These are formed by affixing *íya* (80. XV) to those forms of the personal pronouns, ending in *d*, which are used as crude bases: thus, from मद् and अस्मद् 'I,' मदीय *madíya* (45), 'mine,' and अस्मदीय *asmadíya*, 'our;' from त्वद् 'thou,' त्वदीय *tvadíya*, 'thine;' from तद् 'he,' तदीय *tadíya*, 'his.' Similarly, भवदीय 'yours' (see 233). They are declined like nouns of the first class at 103.

Observe, however, that the genitive case of the personal pronouns is more usually used for the possessive: thus, तस्य पुत्रः 'his son;' मम पुत्री 'my daughter.'

REFLEXIVE POSSESSIVE PRONOUNS.

232. स्व *sva* (*suus*) is used reflexively, in reference to all three persons, and may stand for 'my own' (*meus*), 'thy own' (*tuus*), 'his own,' 'our own,' &c. (compare σφός, σφή, σφόν). It often occupies the first place in a compound: thus, स्वगृहं गच्छति 'he goes to his own house.' The gen. case of आत्मन् *átman* at 147, or often the crude base, is used with the same signification; as, आत्मनो गृहं or आत्मगृहं गच्छति. It is used in the singular even when it refers to more than one*. In the most modern Sanskrit, निज *nija* is often used in place of स्व and आत्मन्, and from it transferred to Bengálí.

स्व, in the sense of 'own,' is declined like *sarva* at 237; as a pronominal the Ab. L. sing. masc. neut. and N. pl. masc. may optionally follow *śiva* at 103: thus, N. pl. m. *sve* or *svás* in the sense of 'own;' but in the sense of 'kinsmen' or 'property,' *sva* can only follow *śiva* (N. pl. m. *svás*).

HONORIFIC OR RESPECTFUL PRONOUN.

233. भवत् *bhavat*, 'your Honour,' requiring the 3d person of the verb, is declined like *dhanavat* at 140: thus, N. masc. भवान् *bhaván*,

---

* Prof. Lassen cites an example from the Rámáyana, in which *átman* refers to the dual: *Putram átmanaḥ spṛishṭvá nipetatuḥ*. 'They two fell down after touching their son.' Anthol. p. 171.

भवन्तौ *bhavantau*, भवन्तस् *bhavantas*; V. भवन्; N. fem. भवती *bhavatí*, भवत्यौ *bhavatyau*, भवत्यस् *bhavatyas*, &c.; V. भवति. It is constantly used, to denote 'respect,' in place of the 2d personal pronoun: thus, भवान् गृहं गच्छतु 'Let your Honour go home' for 'Go thou home.'

DERIVATIVE PRONOUNS OF QUANTITY AND SIMILITUDE.

234. Modifications of the demonstrative, relative, and interrogative pronouns may take the affix वत् *vat* to express 'quantity,' and the affix दृश *dṛiśa* or दृश् *dṛiś** to express 'similitude:' thus, तावत् *távat*, एतावत् *etávat*, 'so many,' 'so much' (*tantus*); यावत् (*quantus*) 'as many,' 'as much' (declined like *dhanavat* at 140); तादृश *tádṛiśa* or तादृश् *tádṛiś*, 'such like' (*talis*, τηλίκος); एतादृश *etádṛiśa* or एतादृश् *etádṛiś*, 'like this or that' (following *śiva*, at 103, 104, for masc. and neut.; *nadí*, at 106, for the fem. of those ending in श *śa*; and *diś*, at 181, for the masc. fem. neut. of those in श् *ś*). Similarly, यादृश or यादृश् 'as like,' 'how like!' (*qualis*, ἡλίκος); ईदृश or ईदृश् 'so like;' कीदृश or कीदृश् 'how like?' (*qualis?*).

a. Note, that the affix दृश is derived from the root *dṛiś*, 'to see,' 'appear,' and is in fact our English 'like,' *d* being interchangeable with *l*, and *ś* with *k*.

b. कियत् 'how much,' 'how many,' and इयत् 'so much,' are declined like भवत् at 233.

'WHOSOEVER,' 'WHATSOEVER.'

235. Expressed by prefixing the relative to the indefinite: thus, यः कश्चित् 'whosoever,' यत् किंचित् 'whatsoever:' or sometimes to the interrogative; as, येन केन प्रकारेण 'by any means whatsoever:' or sometimes by repeating the relative; as, यो यः, यद् यद्.

PRONOMINALS.

236. There are certain common adjectives, called *pronominals*, which partake of the nature of pronouns, and follow the declension of *tat* at 220; but may also take a vocative case.

These are, इतर 'other' (cf. Latin *iterum*); कतर 'which of the two?' (πότερος for κότερος); कतम 'which of many?' ततर 'that one of two;' ततम 'that one of many;' यतर 'who or which of two;' यतम 'who or which of many' (formed by adding the comparative and superlative affixes to the various pronominal bases, 196. *a*); अन्य 'other,' 'another;' अन्यतर 'one of two;' and एकतम 'one of many.' They are declined like तद्, and make the N. V. Ac. neut. sing. in *at*: thus, *anyat*, *itarat*, *anyatarat*, *katarat*, *katamat*, &c.; but they have a vocative, viz. V. masc. *anya*, V. fem. *anye*, V. neut. *anyat*, &c.; the V. du. and plural is like the masc.

237. There are other pronominals, which make *am* instead of *at* in the N. Ac. neuter. The model of these is सर्व *sarva*, 'all:' thus,

---

* दृक्ष *dṛiksha*, declined like *śiva* (103), is also used.

Masc. N. सर्वस् *sarvas*, सर्वौ *sarvau*, सर्वे *sarve*; Ac. सर्वं, सर्वौ, सर्वान्; I. सर्वेण, सर्वाभ्यां, सर्वैस्; D. सर्वस्मै, सर्वाभ्यां, सर्वेभ्यस्; Ab. सर्वस्मात्, सर्वाभ्यां, सर्वेभ्यस्; G. सर्वस्य, सर्वयोस्, सर्वेषां; L. सर्वस्मिन्, सर्वयोस्, सर्वेषु; V. सर्व, &c. Fem. N. सर्वा *sarvá*, सर्वे *sarve*, सर्वास् *sarvás*; Ac. सर्वां, सर्वे, सर्वास्; I. सर्वया, सर्वाभ्यां, सर्वाभिस्; D. सर्वस्यै, सर्वाभ्यां, सर्वाभ्यस्; Ab. सर्वस्यास्, &c.; V. सर्वे (see 220). Neut. N. Ac. सर्वं, सर्वे, सर्वाणि; V. सर्व.

238. Like *sarva* are declined उभय 'both;' विश्व 'all;' एकतर 'one of two' (ἑκάτερος); एकतम 'one of many;' सम meaning 'all,' but not when it signifies 'equal;' सिम 'the whole;' त्व 'other;' नेम 'half.' The N. Ac. sing. neuter of these will end in *am*, but त्व is optionally त्वद्. In N.V. pl. masc. नेम is नेमे or नेमास्.

a. अधर 'inferior,' पर 'other,' अवर 'other,' अपर 'posterior,' 'west,' उत्तर 'superior,' 'north,' दक्षिण 'south,' 'right,' पूर्व 'east,' 'prior,' अन्तर meaning either 'outer' or 'an under-garment,' स्व 'own' (232), follow *sarva*, and optionally *śiva*, at 103, in abl. loc. sing. masc. and neut., and nom. voc. pl. masc.; as, अधरस्मात् or अधरात्, &c. They can only be declined like pronominals when they denote relative position; hence *dakshiṇáḥ* (not *dakshiṇe*) *gáthakáḥ*, 'clever singers.' Moreover, the pronominal inflection is optional in certain compounds.

239. एक, 'one,' generally follows *sarva*, see 200; द्वितीय 'second,' तृतीय 'third,' follow *sarva* and optionally *śiva* in certain cases, as explained at 208; they make their feminine in *á*.

240. अल्प 'a few,' अर्ध or अर्द्ध 'half,' कतिपय 'how few?' 'few,' प्रथम 'first,' चरम 'last,' द्वितय 'twofold,' पञ्चतय 'fivefold,' properly follow *sarva* at 237; but may make their nom. voc. plur. masc. in *ás*; as, अल्पे or अल्पास् 'few,' &c.

a. उभ, 'both' (*ambo*, ἄμφω), is declined only in the dual; उभौ, उभाभ्यां, उभयोस्; though a pronominal, its declension being only dual, resembles *śiva*.

b. अन्योन्य, इतरेतर, 'one another,' 'mutual,' make their nom. acc. sing. neut. in *am*, not *at*; and voc. in *a*.

CHAPTER VI.

VERBS.

GENERAL OBSERVATIONS.

241. ALTHOUGH the Sanskrit verb (*ákhyáta*, *kriyá*) offers many striking and interesting analogies to the Greek, nevertheless so peculiar and artificial is the process by which it is formed, that it would be difficult, in treating of it, to adopt an arrangement which would be likely to fall in with the preconceived notions of the classical student.

There are ten tenses and moods (*kála*). Seven of them are of common occurrence; viz. 1. the present, 2. the imperfect (often called the first preterite), 3. the potential (or optative), 4. the imperative, 5. the perfect (often called the second preterite), 6. the first future, 7. the second future. Three are not so commonly used; viz. 8. the aorist (often called the third preterite), 9. the precative (also called the benedictive), 10. the conditional. There is also an infinitive mood, and several participles. Of these, the present, the three past tenses, and the two futures, belong to the indicative mood. As to the imperative, potential, precative, and conditional (see p. 122, l. 4), these are moods susceptible of various times; but, as there is only one form for each, it can lead to no embarrassment to arrange them indiscriminately with the tenses of the indicative, and to call them tenses with the native grammarians.

Four of the tenses, viz. the present, imperfect, potential, and imperative, are called *conjugational tenses*, and are placed first in order, because the distinctive character of the ten Sanskrit conjugations is established by the form they assume (as will be explained afterwards at 248).

a. Observe—The ancient Sanskrit of the Veda is more rich in grammatical forms than the later or classical Sanskrit. There is a Vedic subjunctive mood, technically called *Leṭ*, which comprises under it a present, imperfect, and aorist; the Vedic potential has distinct forms for the present, aorist, perfect, and future tenses; and the Vedic imperative distinct forms for the present, aorist, and perfect tenses. The Vedic infinitive, too, has ten or eleven different forms, though it is doubtful whether these are all to be assigned to different tenses.

242. Although the three past tenses are used without much distinction, yet it should be observed, that they properly express different degrees of past time. The imperfect or first preterite (*anadyatana-bhúta*) corresponds in form to the imperfect of Greek verbs, and properly has reference to an event done at some time recently past, but before the current day. It may denote action past and continuing, or it may be used like the Greek aorist. The perfect or second preterite (*paroksha-bhúta*) is said to have reference to an event completely done before the present day at some remote period, unperceived by or out of sight of the narrator: it answers in form to the Greek perfect, but may also be used like the aorist. The aorist or third preterite refers to an event done and past at some indefinite period, whether before or during the current day: it corresponds in form and sense to the Greek 1st and 2d aorist, and sometimes to the pluperfect *. Again,

* The fact is, that neither one of the three past tenses is very commonly used to represent the completeness of an action. This is generally done by employing

the two futures properly express, the first, definite, the second, indefinite futurity *: the second, however, is the most used, and answers to the Greek future. The potential may generally be rendered in English by some one of the auxiliaries, 'may,' 'can,' 'would,' 'should,' 'ought †.' The conditional (or imperfect of the future) is occasionally used after the conjunctions *yadi* and *ćet*, 'if:' it has an augment like the imperfect and aorist, and ought on that account to be classed with the tenses of the indicative. The precative or benedictive is a tense sometimes used in praying and blessing (*āśishi*). It is a modification of the potential. There is no tense exactly equivalent to the pluperfect in Sanskrit: the sense of this tense may often be expressed by the past indeclinable participle or by the past passive participle; as, *tasmin apakrānte*, 'after he had departed.' See Syntax, 840, 899. *a*.

The infinitive mood generally has an active, but is capable of a passive signification.

a. Native grammars designate the moods and tenses by the following technical words: present, *laṭ*; potential, *liṅ*; imperative, *loṭ*; imperfect or first preterite, *laṅ*; perfect or second preterite, *liṭ*; first future, *luṭ*; second future, *lṛiṭ*; third preterite, *luṅ*; precative or benedictive, *liṅ* (*āśishi*); conditional, *lṛiṅ*. The Vedic subjunctive is called *leṭ*.

243. Every tense has three numbers, singular, dual, and plural.

To each tense belong two sets of active terminations; one for the active voice (properly so called), the other for a kind of middle or reflexive voice. The former of these voices is called by Indian grammarians *Parasmai-pada* ('word ‡ directed to another'), because the action is supposed to be transitive, or to pass *parasmai*, 'to another (object)'; the latter is called *Átmane-pada* ('word ‡ directed

---

the passive participle with an instr. case; or by adding *vat* to the pass. part., and combining it with the present tense of *as*, 'to be;' as, *uktavān asmi*, 'I have said.' See Syntax, 897.

* The first future (*luṭ*) is said to be *anadyatane*, i. e. to be so far definite as to denote what will happen at a future period, not in the course of the current day (Pāṇini III. 3. 15); whereas the second future may refer to immediate futurity, as, for instance, श्वो गन्तास्मि 'to-morrow I will go,' अद्य सायंकाले श्वो वा गमिष्यामि 'this very evening or to-morrow I will go.'

† The potential is said to be capable of the following senses: 'commanding,' 'directing,' 'inviting,' 'expression of wish,' 'enquiring,' 'requesting.' Pāṇini III. 3. 161.

‡ Pada is an inflected word as distinguished from an uninflected root. Pāṇ. I. 4. 14. The term *pada* or voice has here reference to the scheme of terminations only; so that in this sense there are only two voices in Sanskrit, and they are often used indiscriminately. Although the Átmane-pada has occasionally a kind of middle signification, yet it cannot be said to correspond entirely with the Greek middle

to oneself'), because the action is supposed to be restricted *âtmane*, 'to oneself.' This distinction, however, is not always observed, and we often find both Parasmai and Átmane employed indifferently for transitive verbs. Some verbs, however, are conjugated only in the Átmane-pada, especially those which are neuter, or in which the direct fruit of the action accrues to the agent (see the distinction of *Udâttetaḥ* and *Anudâttetaḥ* at 75. *c*): thus, *mud* and *ruć* meaning 'to be pleased,' 'please oneself;' *bhuj* meaning 'to eat' (not 'to protect'); *dá*, 'to give,' with *á* prefixed, meaning 'to give to oneself,' 'to take,' are restricted to the Átmane-pada. Sometimes, when a verb takes both *padas*, the Átmane, without altering the idea expressed by the root, may be used to direct the action in some way towards the agent: thus, *paćati* means 'he cooks,' but *paćate*, 'he cooks for himself:' *yajati*, 'he sacrifices;' *yajate*, 'he sacrifices for himself;' *namati*, 'he bends;' *namate*, 'he bends himself;' *darśayati* (causal), 'he shows;' *darśayate*, 'he shows himself,' 'appears:' *kârayati*, 'he causes to make;' *kârayate*, 'he causes to be made for himself;' and *yâć*, 'to ask,' although employing both voices, is more commonly used in the Átmane, because the act of asking generally tends to the advantage of the asker.

a. Some verbs are restricted to particular *padas* when particular prepositions are used: thus the root *ram* with prep. *vi* (meaning 'to cease') is only Parasmai (P. I. 3. 83), but with prep. *upa*, is used in both voices. Again, *kṛi* with *parâ* ('to reject') and with *anu* ('to imitate') are Parasmai only. But *ji* either with prep. *vi* or *parâ* (meaning 'to conquer') is restricted to the Átmane (P. I. 3. 19). So *viś* with prep. *ni* (meaning 'to enter') and *krî* with *vi* (meaning 'to sell') and *dâ* with *â* (meaning 'to take') are Átmane only. See this subject more fully explained at 786.

b. Passive verbs are conjugated in the Átmane-pada. Indeed, in all the tenses, excepting the first four, the passive is generally undistinguishable from the Átmane-pada of the primitive verb. But in the present, imperfect, potential, and imperative (unlike the Greek, which exhibits an identity between the middle and passive voices in those tenses), the Sanskṛit passive, although still employing the Átmane-pada terminations, has a special structure of its own, common to all verbs, and distinct from the conjugational form

voice. We prefer to regard the passive as a distinct derivative from the root, using the Átmane terminations.

of the Átmane-pada. Thus the Greek ἀκούω makes for both the middle and passive of those four tenses, 1st sing. ἀκούομαι, ἠκουόμην, ἀκουοίμην, ἀκούου. But the Sanskrit *śru*, 'to hear,' makes for the conjugational form of the Átmane, शृण्वे, अशृण्वि, शृण्वीय, शृणवै; while for the passive it is श्रूये, अश्रूये, श्रूयेय, श्रूयै. Compare 253, and see Bopp's Comparative Grammar, 426, 733.

244. As in nouns the formation of an inflective base out of a root precedes the subject of declension, the root requiring some change or addition before the case-terminations can be affixed; so in verbs the formation of a verbal base out of a root must be antecedent to conjugation. Again, as in nouns every case has its own termination, so in verbs each of the three persons, in the three numbers of every tense, has a termination (*vibhakti*), one for the Parasmai-pada, and one for the Átmane-pada, which is peculiarly its own. Moreover, as in nouns, so in verbs, some of the terminations may be combined with memorial letters, which serve to aid the memory, by indicating that where they occur peculiar changes are required in the root. Thus the three terminations which belong to the 1st, 2d, and 3d persons of the present tense, Parasmai-pada, respectively, are *mi*, *si*, *ti*; and these are combined with the letter P (*mi*P, *si*P, *ti*P), to indicate that the roots of verbs of the second and third groups (see 257. *b. c.* and 293) must be modified in a particular way, before these terminations are affixed.

245. The annexed tables exhibit, 1st, the scheme of terminations for Parasmai and Átmane-pada, with the most useful of the memorial letters (indicated by capitals), in all the tenses, the four conjugational being placed first; 2dly, the same scheme without memorial letters. Observe—Since the various classes of roots require various changes in the terminations of some of the tenses, the figures, in the second table, will indicate the classes in which these changes occur.

246. *Terminations with memorial letters.*

PARASMAI-PADA. ÁTMANE-PADA.

Present tense.

PERS.	SING.	DUAL.	PLURAL.	SING.	DUAL.	PLURAL.
1.	मिप् *mi*P	वस् *vas*	मस् *mas*	ए *e*	वहे *vahe*	महे *mahe*
2.	सिप् *si*P	थस् *thas*	थ *tha*	से *se*	आथे *áthe*	ध्वे *dhve*
3.	तिप् *ti*P	तस् *tas*	अन्ति *anti*	ते *te*	आते *áte*	अन्ते *ante*

Imperfect or *first preterite* (requiring the augment *a*).

1. अम् *am* AP	व *va*	म *ma*	इ *i*	वहि *vahi*	महि *mahi*
2. सिप् *s* P	तम् *tam*	त *ta*	थास् *thás*	आथाम् *áthám*	ध्वम् *dhvam*
3. तिप् *t* P	ताम् *tám*	अन् *an*	त *ta*	आताम् *átám*	अन्त *anta*

Potential or *optative.*

1. याम् *yám*	याव *yáva*	याम *yáma*	ईय *íya*	ईवहि *ívahi*	ईमहि *ímahi*
2. यास् *yás*	यातम् *yátam*	यात *yáta*	ईथास् *íthás*	ईयाथाम् *íyáthám*	ईध्वम् *ídhvam*
3. यात् *yát*	याताम् *yátám*	युस् *yus*	ईत *íta*	ईयाताम् *íyátám*	ईरन् *íran*

Imperative.

1. आनिप् *áni* P	आवप् *áva* P	आमप् *áma* P	ऐप् *ai* P	आवहैप् *ávahai* P	आमहैप् *ámahai* P
2. हि *hi*	तम् *tam*	त *ta*	स्व *sva*	आथाम् *áthám*	ध्वम् *dhvam*
3. तुप् *tu* P	ताम् *tám*	अन्तु *antu*	ताम् *tám*	आताम् *átám*	अन्ताम् *antám*

Perfect or *second preterite.*

1. णप् *Ṇa* P	व *va*	म *ma*	ए *e*	वहे *vahe*	महे *mahe*
2. थप् *tha* P	अथुस् *athus*	अ *a*	से *se*	आथे *áthe*	ध्वे *dhve* (ढ्वे)
3. णप् *Ṇa* P	अतुस् *atus*	उस् *us*	ए *e*	आते *áte*	इरे *ire*

First future.

1. तास्मि *tásmi*	तास्वस् *tásvas*	तास्मस् *tásmas*	ताहे *táhe*	तास्वहे *tásvahe*	तास्महे *tásmahe*
2. तासि *tási*	तास्थस् *tásthas*	तास्थ *tástha*	तासे *táse*	तासाथे *tásáthe*	ताध्वे *tádhve*
3. ता *tá*	तारौ *tárau*	तारस् *táras*	ता *tá*	तारौ *tárau*	तारस् *táras*

Second future.

1. स्यामि *syámi*	स्यावस् *syávas*	स्यामस् *syámas*	स्ये *sye*	स्यावहे *syávahe*	स्यामहे *syámahe*
2. स्यसि *syasi*	स्यथस् *syathas*	स्यथ *syatha*	स्यसे *syase*	स्येथे *syethe*	स्यध्वे *syadhve*
3. स्यति *syati*	स्यतस् *syatas*	स्यन्ति *syanti*	स्यते *syate*	स्येते *syete*	स्यन्ते *syante*

Aorist or *third preterite* (requiring the augment *a*).

1. सम् *sam*	स्व *sva*	स्म *sma*	सि *si*	स्वहि *svahi*	स्महि *smahi*
2. सीस् *sís*	स्तम् *stam*	स्त *sta*	स्थास् *sthás*	साथाम् *sáthám*	ध्वम् *dhvam* (ढ्वम्)
3. सीत् *sít*	स्ताम् *stám*	सुस् *sus*	स्त *sta*	साताम् *sátám*	सत *sata*

Precative or *benedictive.*

1. यासम् *yásam*	यास्व *yásva*	यास्म *yásma*	सीय *síya*	सीवहि *sívahi*	सीमहि *símahi*
2. यास् *yás*	यास्तम् *yástam*	यास्त *yásta*	सीष्ठास् *síshṭhás*	सीयास्थाम् *síyásthám*	सीध्वम् *sídhvam*
3. यात् *yát*	यास्ताम् *yástám*	यासुस् *yásus*	सीष्ट *síshṭa*	सीयास्ताम् *síyástám*	सीरन् *síran*

Conditional (requiring the augment *a*).

1. स्यम् *syam*	स्याव *syáva*	स्याम *syáma*	स्ये *sye*	स्यावहि *syávahi*	स्यामहि *syámahi*
2. स्यस् *syas*	स्यतम् *syatam*	स्यत *syata*	स्यथास् *syathás*	स्येथाम् *syethám*	स्यध्वम् *syadhvam*
3. स्यत् *syat*	स्यताम् *syatám*	स्यन् *syan*	स्यत *syata*	स्येताम् *syetám*	स्यन्त *syanta*

a. Observe—Those terminations which are marked with P will be called the P terminations. They are as follows: *Present*, Parasmai, 1, 2, 3 sing. *Imperfect* (*First Pret.*), Parasmai, 1, 2, 3 sing. *Imperative*, Parasmai, 1, 3 sing., 1 du., 1 pl.; Átmane, 1 sing., 1 du., 1 pl. In these the P is indicatory only with reference to certain classes of roots (see 244), but in the *Perfect* (*Second Pret.*), Parasmai, the indicatory P in 1, 2, 3 sing. applies to all the classes (see 293. *a*).

b. Instead of ṆaP, *tha*P, ṆaP (which are from Vopadeva), Páṇini gives ṆaL, *tha*L, ṆaL; but the L only refers to the accent, and is of no use for practical purposes.

c. Professor Bopp calls the P forms 'strong or increased' (*auctæ*). All the others he calls 'pure or simple.' It will sometimes be convenient to adopt the same expressions, 'strong forms,' in speaking of the form assumed by the base before the P terminations. The terminations of the first four, or conjugational tenses, are called by Páṇini *sárvadhátuka*; those of the other six, *árdhadhátuka*.

247. *The same terminations, without memorial letters, but exhibiting the substitutions required in different classes.*

PARASMAI-PADA. ÁTMANE-PADA.

Present tense.

PERS. SING.	DUAL.	PLURAL.	SING.	DUAL.	PLURAL.
1. *mi*	*vas*	*mas*	*i* 1, 4, 6, 10. *e* 2, 3, 7; 5, 8, 9.	*vahe*	*mahe*
2. *si*	*thas*	*tha*	*se*	*ithe* 1, 4, 6, 10. *áthe* 2, 3, 7; 5, 8, 9.	*dhve*
3. *ti*	*tas*	*nti* 1, 4, 6, 10. *anti* 2, 7; 5, 8, 9. *ati* 3 (2).	*te*	*ite* 1, 4, 6, 10. *áte* 2, 3, 7; 5, 8, 9.	*nte* 1, 4, 6, 10. *ate* 2, 3, 7; 5, 8, 9.

An initial *s*, as in *si*, *se*, &c., is liable to become *sh* by r. 70.

Imperfect or first preterite (requiring the augment *a*).

1. *m* 1, 4, 6, 10. *am* 2, 3, 7; 5, 8, 9.	*va*	*ma*	*i*	*vahi*	*mahi*
2. *s*	*tam*	*ta*	*thás*	*ithám* 1, 4, 6, 10. *áthám* 2, 3, 7; 5, 8, 9.	*dhvam*
3. *t* or *d*	*tám*	*n* 1, 4, 6, 10. *an* 2, 7; 5, 8, 9. *us* 3 (2).	*ta*	*itám* 1, 4, 6, 10. *átám* 2, 3, 7; 5, 8, 9.	*nta* 1, 4, 6, 10. *ata* 2, 3, 7; 5, 8, 9.

Potential.

In 1, 4, 6, 10.			In all the classes.		
1. *iyam*	*iva*	*ima*	1. *íya*	*ívahi*	*ímahi*
2. *is*	*itam*	*ita*	2. *íthás*	*íyáthám*	*ídhvam*
3. *it*	*itám*	*iyus*	3. *íta*	*íyátám*	*íran*
In 2, 3, 7; 5, 8, 9.					
1. *yám*	*yáva*	*yáma*			
2. *yás*	*yátam*	*yáta*			
3. *yát*	*yátám*	*yus*			

Imperative.

1. *áni*	*áva*	*áma*	*ai*	*ávahai*	*ámahai*
2. — 1, 4, 6, 10; 5, 8. *hi* 2, 3; 5, 9. *dhi* (*ḍhi*) 2, 3, 7. — after *ána* 9.	*tam*	*ta*	*sva*	*ithám* 1, 4, 6, 10. *áthám* 2, 3, 7; 5, 8, 9.	*dhvam*
3. *tu*	*tám*	*ntu* 1, 4, 6, 10. *antu* 2, 7; 5, 8, 9. *atu* 3 (2).	*tám*	*itám* 1, 4, 6, 10. *átám* 2, 3, 7; 5, 8, 9.	*ntám* 1, 4, 6, 10. *atám* 2, 3, 7; 5, 8, 9.

In 9, *hi* is dropped after *ána*, substituted for the characteristic *ná* of the 2d sing. imperative, Parasmai, in the case of roots ending in consonants. A form तात् *tát* (cf. Latin *to*, Greek τω) may be substituted for *hi* and *tu*, and even for *ta*, to imply benediction, chiefly used in the Vedas.

Perfect or *second preterite.*

1. *a*	**iva*	**ima*	*e*	**ivahe*	**imahe*
2. *itha* or *tha*	*athus*	*a*	**ishe*	*áthe*	**idhve* or **iḍhve*
3. *a*	*atus*	*us*	*e*	*áte*	*ire*

* Only eight roots, viz. *śru*, *stu*, *dru*, *sru*, *kṛi*, *bhṛi*, *sṛi*, *vṛi*, reject the initial *i* from the terminations marked with *; and of these eight all but *vṛi* (meaning 'to cover') necessarily reject it also in the 2d sing. Parasmai. These eight roots also take *ḍhve* for *dhve* in the 2d pl. Ātmane. The option of *iḍhve* for *idhve* is allowed in other roots when a semivowel or *h* immediately precedes.

First future.

1. *tásmi*	*tásvas*	*tásmas*	*táhe*	*tásvahe*	*tásmahe*
2. *tási*	*tásthas*	*tástha*	*táse*	*tásáthe*	*tádhve*
3. *tá*	*tárau*	*táras*	*tá*	*tárau*	*táras*

Many roots prefix *i* to the above terminations: thus, 1. *itásmi*, 2. *itási*, &c. ग्रह् lengthens this *i*; वृ *vṛi* and all roots in long *ṛí* optionally do so.

Second future.

1. *syāmi*	*syāvas*	*syāmas*	*sye*	*syāvahe*	*syāmahe*
2. *syasi*	*syathas*	*syatha*	*syase*	*syethe*	*syadhve*
3. *syati*	*syatas*	*syanti*	*syate*	*syete*	*syante*

Many roots prefix i to the above terminations: thus, 1. *ishyāmi* (r. 70), 2. *ishyasi*, &c. ग्रह् lengthens this *i*; वृ and all roots in long *ṛī* optionally do so.

Aorist or *third preterite* (requiring the augment *a*).

FORM I.—Terminations of the memorial scheme.

1. *sam*	*sva*	*sma*	*si*	*svahi*	*smahi*
2. *sīs*	*stam* or *tam*	*sta* or *ta*	*sthās* or *thās*	*sāthām*	*dhvam*
3. *sīt*	*stām* or *tām*	*sus*	*sta* or *ta*	*sātām*	*sata*

ढ्वम् *ḍhvam* is used for *dhvam* after any other vowel but *a* or *ā*, or after र् *r* immediately preceding.

The same terminations with *i* prefixed, except in 2d and 3d sing., where initial *s* is rejected.

1. *isham*	*ishva*	*ishma*	*ishi*	*ishvahi*	*ishmahi*
2. *īs*	*ishṭam*	*ishṭa*	*ishṭhās*	*ishāthām*	*idhvam*
3. *īt*	*ishṭām*	*ishus*	*ishṭa*	*ishātām*	*ishata*

इढ्वम् *iḍhvam* may be used for *idhvam* when a semivowel or *h* immediately precedes. ग्रह् lengthens the *i* throughout; वृ and all roots in long *ṛī* optionally do so in Ātm.

FORM II.—Terminations resembling those of the imperfect or 1st preterite.

1. *am*	*āva* or *va*	*āma* or *ma*	*e* or *i*	*āvahi*	*āmahi*
2. *as* or *s*	*atam* or *tam*	*ata* or *ta*	*athās*	*ethām* or *āthām*	*adhvam*
3. *at* or *t*	*atām* or *tām*	*an* or *us*	*ata*	*etām* or *ātām*	*anta* or *ata*

Precative or *benedictive.*

1. *yāsam*	*yāsva*	*yāsma*	*sīya*	*sīvahi*	*sīmahi*
2. *yās*	*yāstam*	*yāsta*	*sīshṭhās*	*sīyāsthām*	*sīdhvam*
3. *yāt*	*yāstām*	*yāsus*	*sīshṭa*	*sīyāstām*	*sīran*

Many roots prefix *i* to the Ātmane, but not to the Parasmai, of the above: thus, 1. *ishīya*, &c. ग्रह् lengthens the *i* in this tense also, but no other root can do so. सीढ्वम् is used for *sīdhvam* after any other vowel but *a*, and optionally after the prefixed *i*, when immediately preceded by a semivowel or *h*.

Conditional (requiring the augment *a*).

1. *syam*	*syāva*	*syāma*	*sye*	*syāvahi*	*syāmahi*
2. *syas*	*syatam*	*syata*	*syathās*	*syethām*	*syadhvam*
3. *syat*	*syatām*	*syan*	*syata*	*syetām*	*syanta*

Many roots prefix *i* to the above terminations throughout: thus, 1. *ishyam*, 2. *ishyas*, &c. ग्रह् lengthens this *i*; वृ and all roots in long *ṛī* optionally do so.

Observe—We shall in future speak of the 1st, 2d, and 3d preterites under the name of imperfect, perfect, and aorist, respectively.

a. If we examine the terminations exhibited above, we shall find that they are composed of two distinct elements, one marking person, number, and voice; the other, mood and tense. The terminations in which the former element prevails may be called simple, and belong to the present, imperfect, imperative, perfect, and 2d form of the aorist; those which include the second may be called compound, and are peculiar to the other tenses. Thus the terminations of the potential consist of *ī* or *ī* or *yā* as characterising the mood, and of *m*, *s*, *t*, *va*, *tam*, *tām*, &c., as marking person, number, and voice. So, also, in the 2d future the syllable *sya* prefixed to all the terminations, characterises the future tense, while the *mi*, *si*, *ti*, *vas*, *thas*, *tas*, &c., mark person, number, and voice. If, then, such initial parts of every termination as mark mood or tense were left out, an examination of the remaining parts would show that the present and imperfect are the prototypes of the terminations of all the other tenses, that is to say, that the formation of the terminations of every other tense may be referred back to one or other of these two. The present tense may in this way be connected with the two futures. These three tenses agree in showing a certain fulness of form, which is wanting in most of those connected with the imperfect. The terminations of the perfect, however, partake of the character of both the present and imperfect. In the Ātmane-pada they very closely resemble the present. Many of them exhibit the same fulness as that tense, while some of the other terminations of the perfect show even more lightness than those of the imperfect *. It should be observed, too, that the terminations of the imperative, though evidently connected with the imperfect, are in some instances even more full than those of the present.

b. Although comparative grammarians have bestowed much labour on the elucidation of the origin of Sanskṛit verbal terminations, the only point which may be asserted with probability is, that they stand in a certain relationship to the pronominal bases *ma*, *tva*, *ta*. The *m* of the first persons is related to the base *ma*; the *t*, *th*, *sv*, *s*, of the second persons, to the base *tva* of the second personal pronoun; and the *t*, of the third person, to the base *ta*. We may also observe a community of character between the termination *nti* of the 3d plur. and the plural of neuter nouns like *dhanavat* (*dhanavanti*). But whether the *v* in the dual stands for *m* or relates to a pronominal base *va* occurring in *ā-vām*, *va-yam*; whether the terminations of the dual and plural are formed from those of the singular by adding *s* as a mark of the plural, or by the composition of several pronominal bases; whether the terminations of the Ātmane-pada are formed from those of the Parasmai-pada by guṇation or by composition of the latter with other bases,—these and others are questions which cannot be determined with any certainty.

c. As an aid, however, in committing the terminations to memory, the student

* Comparative grammar, however, has established that these terminations were originally as full as those of the present.

may observe that the letter *m* generally enters into the 1st sing. Parasmai; *s* into the 2d sing. Parasmai and Ātmane; and *t* into the 3d sing. du. and pl. Parasmai and Ātmane of all the tenses. Moreover, that the letter *v* occurs in the 1st dual, *m* in the 1st plural of all the tenses, and *dhe* in every 2d plural Ātmane-pada. In the imperfect and potential Ātmane, and in the perfect Parasmai, *th* is admitted, instead of *s*, into the 2d sing.; and in the 2d pl. of the last tense, *th* has been dropped, owing to the influence of the heavy reduplication. For the same reason the *m* and *t* are dropped in the 1st and 3d sing. perfect. Observe also—When the 1st dual Parasmai is *vas*, the 2d and 3d end in *as* (except the 3d du. 1st future), and the 1st plural is *mas*. When the 1st dual Parasmai is *va*, the 2d and 3d end in *tam*, *tām* (except in the perfect), and the 1st plural in *ma*. When the 1st dual Ātmane is *vahe*, the 1st plural is *mahe*, and the last letter of the remaining terminations is generally *e*. When the 1st dual Ātmane is *vahi*, the 2d and 3d end in *ām*; the 1st plural is *mahi*, and the 2d plural is *dhvam*.

d. The frequent occurrence of *m* in the 1st sing., of *s* in the 2d, of *t* in the 3d, of *mas* and *ma* in the 1st pl., of *ta* in the 2d pl., and of *nti* in the 3d pl., suggests a comparison with the Greek and Latin verb. We may remark, that *m*, the characteristic of the 1st person sing., is suppressed in the present tense active of all Greek verbs except those in μι (*asmi* = εἰμί, Dor. ἐμμί for ἐσμι, *dadāmi* = δίδωμι), and also in Latin verbs (except *sum* and *inquam*); but ω and *o* answer to the Sanskrit *ā* of *bharāmi* = φέρω, *fero*. In the Greek middle and passive, the μι, which originally belonged to all active verbs, becomes μαι; while the Sanskrit, on the other hand, here suppresses the *m*, and has *e* for *ai*; *bhare* (for *bhara-me*) = φέρομαι. In the imperfect, Greek has ν for the Sanskrit and Latin mute *m*; *atarpam* = ἔτερπον, *adadām* = ἐδίδων, *astṛiṇavam* = ἐστόρνυν, *avaham* = *vehebam*. Greek has μι in the 1st sing. optative or potential; and in verbs in μι, ν takes the place of the mute *m* of Sanskrit and Latin: thus, *bhareyam* = φέροιμι, *feram*; *dadyām* = διδοίην, *dem*; *tishṭheyam* = ἱσταίην, *stem*. In the first Greek aorist, *m* is suppressed, so that Sanskrit *adiksham* (3d pret.) = ἔδειξα; but not in the 2d aorist, so that *adām* = ἔδων. In the perfect the Sanskrit *a* = Greek α, *tutopa* = τέτυφα. In the Greek middle and passive futures, *m* is retained, but not in the active; *dāsyāmi* = δώσω, *dekshyāmi* = δείξω, *dāsye* = δώσομαι. As to the 1st person plural, the Sanskrit *mas* of the pres. is μεν (for μες) in Greek, and *mus* in Latin; *tarpā-mas* = τέρπο-μεν; *sarpā-mas* = ἕρπο-μεν, *serpi-mus*; *dad-mas* = δίδο-μεν, *da-mus*; *tishṭhā-mas* = ἵστα-μεν, *sta-mus*. The Ātmane-pada *mahe* answers to the Greek μεθα: *dad-mahe* = διδό-μεθα. As in the other tenses, in the imperfect 1st pl. *abharā-ma* = ἐφέρο-μεν, *ferēba-mus*; *avahā-ma* = *vehēba-mus*; *adad-ma* = ἐδίδο-μεν; *abharā-mahi* = ἐφερόμεθα. In the potential 1st pl. *bhare-ma* = φέροι-μες (-μεν), *fera-mus*; *dadyāma* = διδοίημες (-μεν), *demus*; *dadī-mahi* = διδοί-μεθα. In the 2d future, *dāsyā-mas* = δώσο-μεν, *dekshyā-mas* = δείξο-μεν. In the 2d pers. sing. active, the characteristic *s* has been preserved in all three languages: thus, in the present, the Sanskrit *asi* (for original *assi*) = ἐσσί, *es*; *dadā-si* = δίδως, *das*; *bhara-si* = φέρεις, *fers*; *vahasi* = *vehis*. In the Ātmane, the Sanskrit *se* (for *sai*, by 32) answers exactly to the Greek σαι of verbs in μι (*tishṭha-se* = ἵστα-σαι). In other Greek verbs, σ has been rejected, and σαι contracted into ῃ, something in the way of Sanskrit (τύπτῃ for τύπτε-σαι). In the 2d dual, *thas* = Greek τον, and in the 2d plur. *tha* = τε and *tis*; *bhara-thas* = φέρε-τον; *tishṭha-tha* = ἵστα-τε, *statis*; *bhara-tha* = φέρε-τε, *fer-tis*. In the 2d pl. Ātmane, *bhara-dhve* = φέρεσθε. As to the other tenses, in the 2d sing. imperfect, *atarpas* = ἔτερπες, *avahas* = *vehebas*, &c. So also, *tam* = τον, *adat-tam* = ἐδίδο-τον, *ta* = τε, *adat-ta* = ἐδίδο-τε. In the Ātmane, *thās* is found for *sās* in the 2d sing. of the imperfect, as well as of the potential; hence *abhara-thās* = ἐφέρε-σο, *adat-thās* = ἐδίδο-σο, *dadī-thās* = διδοῖ-(σ)ο. In the 2d sing. potential, *tishṭhes* = ἱσταίης, *stes*; *dadyās* = διδοίης, *des*; *vahes* = *vehas*; *bhares* = φέροις, *feras*. In 2d du. *bhare-tam* = φέροι-τον; in 2d pl. *tishṭheta* = ἱσταίητε, *stetis*; *dadyāta* = διδοίητε, *detis*; *bhareta* = φέροιτε, *feratis*. In the 2d sing. imperative, *hi* and *dhi* answer to Greek θι. *Dhi* was originally universal in Sanskrit (see 291), as in Greek verbs in μι; *e-dhi* = ἴσ-θι, *viddhi* = ἴσ-θι, *de-hi* = δίδο-θι. Many verbs drop the termination *hi* both in Greek and Sanskrit; as, भर = φέρε, and compare δείκνυ with *dice*, &c. In the 2d du. imp. *tam* = τον, and *ta* = τε. In the imperative Ātmane, *sva* = the old form σο; *bhara-sva* = φέρε-σο (old form of φέρου); *dat-sva* = δίδο-σο; *āthām* = εσθον, &c. In the perfect, the *tha* of the 2d sing. = Latin *sti*; *dad-itha* = *dedi-sti*, *tasthi-tha* = *steti-sti*, *tutodi-tha* = *tutudi-sti*. In the aorist, *adās* = ἔδως, *avākshīs* = *vexisti*. In the 3d pers. sing. active, Greek has dropped the characteristic *t* (except in ἐστί = Sansk. *asti*, Lat. *est*); *bharati* = φέρε(τ)ι, *fert*; *vahati* = *vehit*. Verbs in μι have changed *t* to *s*; *dadāti* = δίδωσι (for δίδωτι). In the Ātmane, *bharate* = φέρεται. In the imperfect, *avahat* = *vehebat*, *abharata* = ἐφέρετο. In the potential, *bharet* = φέροι, *dadyāt* = διδοίη. In the imperative, *bhara-tu* or *bhara-tāt* = φερέ-τω, *fer-to*. In the perfect, *tutopa* = τέτυφε. In the aorist, *avākshīt* = *vexit*, *adikshata* = ἐδείξατο. As to the 3d pl., in the above tenses, *bharanti* = φέρουσι, *ferunt*; *vahanti* = *vehunt*; *bharante* = φέρονται; *dadati* = διδόασι; *tishṭhanti* = *stant*; *bhareyus* = φέροιεν; *bharantu* = *ferunto*; *abharan* = ἔφερον; *abharanta* = ἐφέροντο; *āsan* = ἦσαν; *atarpishus* = ἔτερψαν; *dāsyante* = δώσονται.

248. The above terminations are supposed to be applicable to all verbs, whether primitive or derivative: and as in nouns, so in verbs, the theory of Indian grammarians is, that before these terminations can be affixed to roots, an inflective base must be formed out of the root. Ten different rules, therefore, are propounded for forming verbal bases out of roots in the first four tenses; while all verbs are arranged under ten classes, according to the form of the base required by one or other of these rules. In the other tenses there is one general rule for forming the base, applicable to all verbs of whatever class.

These ten classes of verbs are said to form *ten conjugations*; and the four tenses, which alone are affected by these conjugational rules (viz. the present, imperfect, potential, and imperative), are called *the conjugational tenses*. It is evident, however, that the ten classes hardly form distinct conjugations in the classical sense of the term. They are rather ten rules for forming ten classes of verbs from roots; or, in other words, for moulding and fashioning ten classes of roots into the proper form for receiving a common scheme of terminations in four of the tenses only.

249. Although it will be afterwards shown (at 257) that these ten classes may be grouped together under three general heads (I. comprising the 1st, 4th, 6th, and 10th classes; II. the 2d, 3d, and 7th; III. the 5th, 8th, and 9th), yet it will be better in the first place to give a brief summary of the ten rules for forming the base of the four conjugational tenses in the ten classes of verbs, according to the Indian order.

1st class. Guṇate the vowel of the root (unless it be अ *a*, or a long vowel *not final*, or a short vowel followed by a double consonant, 28. *b*) before *every termination of the four tenses*, and affix अ *a*—lengthened to आ *á* before initial *m* * and *v*—to the root thus guṇated.

2d class. Guṇate the vowel of the root (if capable of Guṇa, as in the last) before those terminations only which are marked with P in the scheme at 246. Before all the other terminations the original vowel of the root must be retained.

3d class. Reduplicate the initial consonant and vowel (see 331) of the root, and guṇate the radical but not the reduplicated vowel before the P terminations only, as in the 2d conjugation.

4th class. Affix य *ya*—lengthened to या *yá* before initial *m* * and *v*—to the root, the vowel of which is generally left unchanged.

5th class. Affix नु *nu* to the root, and guṇate this *nu* into *no* before the P terminations only.

6th class. Affix अ *a*—lengthened to आ *á* before initial *m* * and *v*—to the root, which in other respects generally remains unchanged.

7th class. Insert न *na* between the vowel and final consonant of the root before the P terminations, and न् *n* before the other termi-

* But not before *m* the termination of the 1st sing. imperfect Parasmai.

nations. Observe the peculiarity of this conjugation—that the conjugational *na* or *n* is inserted into the *middle* of the root, and not affixed.

8th class. Affix उ *u* to the root, and guṇate this *u* into *o* before the P terminations only. Observe—As all the roots, except one, in this class, end in *n*, the 8th conjugation will appear similar to the 5th.

9th class. Affix ना *ná* to the root before the P terminations; नी *ní* before all the others, except those beginning with vowels, where only न् *n* is affixed.

10th class. Guṇate the radical vowel (if capable of Guṇa) throughout all the persons of all the tenses, and affix अय *aya*—lengthened to अया *ayá* before initial *m* * and *v*—to the root thus guṇated.

250. It will appear, from a cursory examination of the above rules, that the object of all of them, except the 2d, 3d, and 7th, is to insert a vowel, either alone or preceded by *y* or *n*, between the modified root and the terminations; and that the 1st, 4th, 6th, and 10th, agree in requiring that the vowel, which is immediately to precede the terminations, shall be *a* or *á*. It will appear, moreover, that the 2d, 3d, and 7th, alone agree in not interposing a vowel between the final of the root and the terminations; and that the 5th, 8th, and 9th, agree in interposing either *u*, *á*, or *í*, after the letter *n*.

a. It must never, however, be forgotten, that the conjugational characteristic, whatever it may be, has reference only to the four conjugational tenses (except only in the 10th conjugation), and that in the other tenses the base is formed accordiug to one general rule for all verbs of whatever class; or, in other words, that in these tenses all verbs, of whatever class, are as if they belonged to one common conjugation.

b. It is evident, that a comparison between the difficulty of the Sanskrit and Greek verb would be greatly to the advantage of the former. The Greek verb has three voices, and about ninety tenses and moods: the Sanskrit has only two voices, and not more than twenty tenses and moods. Besides which, a far greater number of verbs are susceptible of the three voices in Greek, than of the two in Sanskrit. Moreover, in Sanskrit there are no contracted verbs, and no difficulties resulting from difference of dialect; and although there are ten conjugations, yet these have

---

* But not before *m* the termination of the 1st sing. imperfect Parasmai.

reference to four tenses only; and, under some of these conjugations, only two or three common verbs are contained.

251. Hence it appears, that conjugation in Sanskrit is really *conjugation*, i.e. a process of *Sandhi* or 'junction' of a verbal base (formed out of a root according to ten rules for four of the tenses, and one general rule for the other six) with a common scheme of terminations, and that in conjugating a verb, two things have to be done; 1st, to form the base from the root, in the manner described above; 2dly, to join the base with the terminations, according to euphonic rules.

252. Before proceeding to a detailed explanation of the formation of the verbal base of the simple or primitive verb, under the several classes, it will be worth while to specify the four other verbs deducible from roots, and to explain how they are derived.

a. It has been already shown, at 74, that there are a large number of monosyllabic sounds in Sanskrit, called *roots*, which are the source of verbs as well as nouns. These roots are in number about two thousand; and the theory of grammarians is, that each of them may serve as the rough block out of which the inflective bases of five kinds of verbs may be fashioned: 1. of a primitive, transitive or intransitive; 2. of a passive; 3. of a causal, having often a causal and often merely a transitive signification; 4. of a desiderative, giving a sense of wishing to the root; and 5. of a frequentative (or intensive), implying repetition, or heightening the idea contained in the root.

b. It will be found, however, in practice, that a great number of these two thousand roots never occur at all in the form of verbs, and not always even in the form of nouns; and that the verbs in real use are comparatively few. Of these, moreover, certain particular roots (such, for example, as कृ *kṛi*, 'to do') are made to do the work of others, and applied to the expression of the most various ideas by compounding them with prepositions and other prefixes. Nevertheless, theoretically, from every root in the language may be elicited five kinds of verbal bases.

c. The first, or primitive verb, is formed from the root, according to the ten different rules, already given, for the formation of the base in the first four tenses. The second, or passive, is formed according to the rule for the change of the root, required by the 4th class; viz. the addition of *ya* in the first four tenses. The third, or causal, is formed according to the rule for the change of the root, required by the 10th class; viz. the addition of *aya* to the root in all the tenses excepting the aorist. The fourth, or desiderative, is formed by the addition of *sa* or *isha*, the root also undergoing reduplication. The fifth, or frequentative, is formed like the passive, according to the rule required by the 4th class, and is, in fact, a reduplicated passive verb. It may also be formed analogously to the rule for the 3d class. Thus, take the root शुभ् *śubh*, conveying the idea of 'shining'—from this are elicited, 1st, the primitive verbal base, *śobha*, 'to shine;' 2dly, the passive, *śubhya*, 'to be bright;' 3dly, the causal, *śobhaya*, 'to cause to shine' or 'illuminate;' 4thly, the desiderative, *śuśobhisha*, 'to desire to shine;' 5thly, the frequentative or intensive, *śośubhya* or *śośubh*, 'to shine very brightly.'

d. Note, that as every root may be the source of five different kinds of verbs, so every noun may be the source of a class of verbs (not much used) called *nominal verbs*. An explanation of these will be found after frequentatives at 518.

253. It has already been remarked, that the passive can hardly be considered a voice, according to the classical acceptation of the term. In Greek and Latin, a verb in the passive voice corresponds in form with the same verb in the active: thus *audior* corresponds with *audio*, ἀκούομαι with ἀκούω, the terminations or system of inflection only being changed. And in Greek, a verb in the passive corresponds with the same verb in the middle voice, both in the form and in the terminations of most of its tenses. But, in Sanskrit, the form of the passive varies entirely in the conjugational tenses from that of the active verb (unless that verb belong to the 4th conjugation), whilst the terminations may sometimes be the same, viz. those of the Ātmane-pada. It is rather a distinct derivative from the root, formed on one invariable principle, without any necessary community with the conjugational structure of the active verb. Thus the root *bhid*, 'to divide,' is of the 7th class, and makes *bhinatti* or *bhinte*, 'he divides;' *dvish*, 'to hate,' is of the 2d class, and makes *dveshṭi* or *dvishṭe*, 'he hates;' but the passive of both is formed according to one invariable rule, by the simple insertion of *ya*, without reference to the conjugational form of the active: thus, *bhidyate*, 'he is divided;' *dvishyate*, 'he is hated.' See 243. *a*.

a. In fact, though it be a distinct form of the root, a passive verb is really nothing but a verb conjugated according to the rule for the 4th class restricted to the Ātmane-pada: and to say that every root may take a passive form, is to say that roots of the 1st, 2d, 3d, 5th, 6th, 7th, 8th, 9th, and 10th classes may all belong to the 4th, when they yield a passive sense: so that if a root be already of the 4th class, its passive is frequently identical in form with its own Ātmane-pada (the only difference being, that the accent in the former is on the syllable *ya*, and not, as in the Ātmane of the primitive, on the radical syllable).

b. It might even be suspected, that the occasional assumption of a neuter signification and a Parasmai-pada inflection by a passive verb, was the cause which gave rise to a 4th class as distinct from the passive. Instances are certainly found of passive verbs taking Parasmai-pada terminations, and some passive verbs (e. g. *jáyate*, 'he is born,' from the root *jan*; *púryate*, 'he is filled,' from *pṛí*; and *tapyate*, 'he is heated,' from *tap*) are regarded by native grammarians as Átmane-verbs of the 4th class *. So that it seems not unlikely, that, by making a 4th class, grammarians meant to say that the passive form of verbs, or the addition of *ya* to the root, is also the form that may be used to express a neuter or intransitive signification; the only difference requisite to be made between the two forms being that the one should take the Átmane-pada; the other, the Parasmai-pada inflection. This, at least, is clear that the Parasmai-pada form of the 4th class often yields a neuter signification; and that the Átmane-pada of the same class is identical with the form used to yield a passive sense †. Hence it arises, that many roots appear in the 4th class as neuter verbs, which also appear in some one of the other nine as transitive. For example, *yuj*, 'to join,' when used in an active sense, is conjugated either in the 7th conjugation, or in the causal; when in a neuter, in the 4th. So also, *push*, 'to nourish;' *kshubh*, 'to agitate;' *klis*, 'to vex;' *sidh*, 'to accomplish.'

254. Similarly, although causal verbs are said to be distinct derivatives from the root, they are in point of fact verbs conjugated according to the rule for the 10th class, and inflected either in Parasmai or Átmane. To say, therefore, that every root may take a causal form, is to say that roots of the first nine classes may all belong to the 10th, when they take a causal sense; and that if a root be originally of the 10th class, it can then have no distinct form for its causal, the primitive verb and the causal being in that case identical (see 289). Indeed, it might be conjectured, that the occasional employment of a causal verb in a transitive, rather than a causal sense, was the reason for creating a 10th conjugation. It would certainly simplify the subject, if this conjugation were not separated from the causal; or, in other words, if the addition of *aya* to the root were considered in all cases as the mark of a causal verb; especially as this affix is not the sign of a separate conjugation, in the way of any other conjugational syllable; for it is retained in most of the other tenses of the verb, not only in the first four, just as the desiderative *ish* is retained.

255. The subject of verbs, therefore, will divide itself into two

* That the passive does occasionally take the terminations of the Parasmai-pada is shown by Professor Bopp, who gives several instances; as, *chidyet* for *chidyeta*, 'it may be cut.' Nala xiv. 6; *mokshyasi* for *mokshyase*, 'thou shalt be liberated.' Other instances may be found in Westergaard; as, *vidyati* for *vidyate*; and अदृश्यत is used in Nala xx. 39. for 'he was seen.'

† The forms given for the aorists of such verbs as *pad*, 'to go,' *budh*, 'to know' (which are said to be Átmane-verbs of the 4th class), could only belong to passive verbs. The forms given by Westergaard are, *apádi*, *abodhi*. See 475.

heads. In the first place, the formation of the base; 1st of primitive, 2dly of passive, 3dly of causal, 4thly of desiderative, 5thly of frequentative verbs; with their respective participles. In the second place, the exhibition, at full, of the base, united to its terminations, under each of the five forms of verbs consecutively.

Under the first head will be shown, how the root has to be changed before the terminations can be affixed; while the mode of affixing the terminations to the root, thus changed, will at the same time be indicated. Under the second head, examples of the five forms of verbs beginning with primitives will appear conjugated in detail; the base, or changed root, being combined with its terminations in regular sequence.

PRIMITIVE VERBS.

FORMATION OF THE BASE OF THE FIRST FOUR TENSES, IN THE TEN CLASSES.

256. A brief summary of the formation of the base, in the ten classes of verbs, has already been given at 249; and a great peculiarity has been noted—that the special rules for forming the base in the ten classes have reference only to the first four tenses, called *conjugational*, viz. the present, imperfect, potential, and imperative.

Remember, that after passing these *four tenses* the conjugational structure of the base is forgotten; and in the formation of the bases of the six remaining tenses all roots are as if they belonged to one general conjugation. Hence the last six tenses are called *non-conjugational*. The tenth class alone retains the conjugational structure of the base throughout *most of the non-conjugational tenses*; but as this class consists chiefly of causal verbs, no confusion can arise from this apparent inconsistency. Of the 2000 roots, more than half belong to the 1st class, about 130 to the 4th, about 140 to the 6th, and all may belong to the 10th (see 289). Of the remaining roots, about 70 belong to the 2d, but not more than 20 are in common use; about 20 to the 3d, of which not half are in common use; about 24, of which hardly 6 are common, belong to the 7th; about 30, of which 10 are common, to the 5th; about 10, of which only 2 are common, to the 8th; about 52, of which 15 are common, to the 9th.

257. Primitive verbs, therefore, separate themselves into ten classes, according as they form their conjugational tenses agreeably to one or other of the ten rules given at 249; and these ten classes may be aggregated into three groups, which can be regarded as forming three distinct general conjugations, as follows:

a. GROUP I. This (like the first class of nouns whose bases end in *a* and *á*) is by far the most important and comprehensive, as comprising verbs of the 1st, 4th, 6th, and 10th classes, which agree in making their inflective bases end in *a* (liable to be lengthened to *á*). These also resemble each other in taking substitutions for some of the terminations, after the analogy of nominal bases ending in *a* and *á*. (See the substitutions indicated in the table at 249.)

b. GROUP II. This comprises verbs of the 2d, 3d, and 7th classes, which agree in affixing the regular terminations (at 246) to the final letter of the root, without the intervention of a vowel, after the analogy of the last four classes of nouns whose bases end in consonants.

c. GROUP III, comprising verbs of the 5th, 8th, and 9th classes, also affixes the regular terminations (at 246) to the root; but after the intervention of either *u*, *á*, or *í*, preceded by the consonant *n*.

It will simplify the subject to adhere to the above grouping in giving a detailed explanation of the formation of the base under each class of verbs.

258. Observe—Although, to prevent confusion, it is advisable to preserve the Indian classification of verbs into ten classes; yet it is more in unison with the classical idea of a conjugation, to arrange all verbs under three classes and three conjugations, according to the above grouping. The classical student, therefore, may consider that verbs of the 1st, 4th, 6th, and 10th classes constitute his first conjugation; verbs of the 2d, 3d, and 7th classes, his second conjugation; and verbs of the 5th, 8th, and 9th, his third conjugation.

259. In comparing Sanskrit verbs with Greek and Latin, it might be shown that group I, comprising the 1st, 4th, 6th, and 10th classes, answers to the Greek 1st conjugation in ω, the conjugational अ *a* being represented in Greek by ο or ε (*terpámas* = τέρπομεν, *terpatha* = τέρπετε); and although the Greek 1st conjugation contains more subdivisions than the first group in Sanskrit, yet the inflection of these subdivisions is similar. As to the Sanskrit 10th conjugation, however, it appears to correspond to Greek verbs in αζω and ιζω, which, like the 10th, are generally found in company with other verbs from the same root: thus, καθαρίζω, 'I make pure' (καθαίρω), στενάζω, 'I groan' (στένω), where ζ is substituted for य *y*, as in ζεά for यव 'barley.' To this class also may be referred verbs in αω, εω, and οω; thus *párayámi* = περάω, where the *y* has been dropped, and the two *a*'s combined. Latin verbs in *io*, like *audio* &c., seem to be related to the Sanskrit 4th class, as well as to the 10th: thus *cupio* answers to *kupyámi*; and the *i* of *audiebam* answers to the *aya* of the 10th, just as in Prákrit *aya* is contracted into ए *e*. The second and third groups of conjugations in Sanskrit (viz. the 2d, 3d, 7th, 5th, 8th, and 9th) answer to Greek verbs in μι: thus *emi* 2d conj. = εἶμι, *dadámi* 3d conj. = δίδωμι. The 7th conjugation, however, has no exact parallel in

Greek, but many Greek and Latin verbs resemble it in inserting a nasal into the middle of the root; see 342. *a*. The 5th and 8th conjugations answer to Greek verbs in νυ and υ; and νυ and υ are lengthened before certain terminations, just as *nu* is gunated in Sanskrit: thus *stṛiṇomi* = στόρνυμι, *stṛiṇoshi* = στόρνυς, *stṛiṇoti* = στόρνυσι, *stṛiṇumas* = στόρνυμες, &c. The 9th conjugation answers to Greek verbs in νā (νη): thus *krīṇāmi* = πέρνᾱμι (πέρνημι), *krīṇīmas* = πέρναμες. Compare also Latin forms in *ni*: thus *sternimus* = Sans. *stṛiṇīmas*, from *stṛī*, 9th conj.

THE AUGMENT अ *a*.

260. Before considering each group in succession, it should be noted that it is an universal rule in all ten classes that the augment अ *a* be prefixed to the base of the imperfect (1st preterite); and when the base begins with अ *a* or आ *á*, the augment blends with these vowels into *á*, by 31 (just as in Greek ε and ε become η in ἤγειρον, &c.).

a. But when the augment *a* is prefixed to bases beginning with the vowels इ *i*, उ *u*, and ऋ *ri*, short or long, it blends with them into ऐ *ai*, औ *au*, आर् *ár* (instead of *e*, *o*, *ar*, by 32). Thus the base इच्छ *ichha* becomes in the 3d sing. imperfect ऐच्छत् *aichhat*, the base ऊह *úha* becomes औहत *auhata*, and the base ऋध्नो *ridhno* becomes आर्ध्नोत् *árdhnot*.

b. This rule applies to two of the non-conjugational tenses also, viz. the aorist (or 3d preterite) and the conditional. Observe, that the imperfect, aorist, and conditional are the only three tenses that take the augment *a*.

GROUP I.—FORMATION OF THE BASE IN THE 1ST, 4TH, 6TH, AND 10TH CLASSES OF VERBS.

Before entering upon the formation of the base in this group, the student should turn back to the scheme at 247, and recollect that the 1st, 4th, 6th, and 10th classes of verbal bases ending in *a* and *á* take substitutions for some of the terminations (especially, in the potential Parasmai, and in the 2d and 3d dual of the present, imperfect, and imperative, Átmane-pada), just as nominal bases ending in *a* and *á* require occasional substitutions in the case-affixes. In the 2d sing. imperative they reject the termination*.

* Probably in consequence of the haste with which 'command' is generally expressed.

(GROUP I.)—*First class, containing about* 1000 *primitive verbs.*

261. Rule for the formation of the base in the four conjugational tenses. Guṇate the vowel of the root (except when debarred by 28. *b*) before *every termination of all the four tenses*, and affix the vowel अ *a* to the root so guṇated. Remember, that this vowel अ *a* is lengthened into आ *ā* before the initial *m* and *v* of a termination, but not when *m* is final, as in the 1st sing. imperfect (1st preterite).

262. Thus, from the root बुध् *budh*, 'to know,' is formed the base बोध *bodha*, lengthened into बोधा *bodhā* before *m* and *v* (Pres. 1.* *bodhā* + *mi* = बोधामि *bodhāmi*, *bodha* + *si* = बोधसि *bodhasi*, *bodha* + *ti* = बोधति *bodhati*; Du. 1. *bodhā* + *vas* = बोधावस् *bodhāvas*, &c.; Ātm. Pres. *bodha* + i = बोधे *bodhe* by 32, *bodha* + *se* = बोधसे *bodhase*, &c.). See table at 583.

263. Similarly, from जि *ji*, 'to conquer' (see 590), comes the base जय *jaya*, liable to be lengthened into जया *jayā*, as before (36. *a*); from नी *nī*, 'to lead,' the bases *naya* and *nayā*; from भू *bhū*, 'to be' (φύω, Lat. *fu*), the bases *bhava* and *bhavā* (Pres. 1. भवामि *bhavāmi*, 36. *a*; 2. भवसि *bhavasi*, φύεις, &c., see 584); from सृप् *sṛip*, 'to creep,' the bases सर्प *sarpa* and *sarpā* (see 28); from क्लृप् *klṛip*, 'to fashion,' the bases कल्प *kalpa* and *kalpā*.

a. Note, that *bhū*, 'to be' or 'to become,' is one of the commonest verbs in the language, and like *as*, 'to be,' at 584. 321, is sometimes used as an auxiliary. It is conjugated at full at 585.

264. The base of the imperfect (1st preterite) has the augment अ *a* prefixed by 260 (Impf.* 1. *abodha* + *m* = अबोधम् *abodham*, 2. *abodha* + *s* = अबोधस् *abodhas*, &c.).

265. In the potential the final *a* of the base blends with the initial *i* of the termination by 32 (Pot. 1. *bodha* + *iyam* = बोधेयम् *bodheyam*). So also in the Pres. Ātm. (बोधे &c.). See table at 583.

266. In the imperative the termination is rejected in the 2d. sing. (Impv.* 1. *bodha* + *āni* = बोधानि *bodhāni*, 2. बोध *bodha*, 3. *bodha* + *tu* = बोधतु *bodhatu*).

267. Roots like पच् 'to cook,' भिक्ष् 'to beg,' जीव् 'to live' (603), cannot change their radical vowels (see 27. *a*, 28. *b*), but, as before, affix अ *a*, liable to be lengthened to आ *ā* (Pres. 1. पचामि &c. Ātm. 1. भिक्षे &c.; Pres. 1. जीवामि &c.).

---

* 1. stands for 1st singular; Du. 1. for 1st dual; Pl. 1. for 1st plural, &c.; Impf. for imperfect; Impv. for imperative.

268. There are some roots ending in the Vṛiddhi ऐ *ai* which cannot be guṇated, but suffer the usual change of Sandhi before अ *a* and आ *á* by 37: as, from गै 'to sing,' ग्लै 'to be weary,' त्रै Átm. 'to preserve *,' ध्यै 'to meditate,' म्लै 'to fade,' are formed the bases *gáya, gláya, tráya, dhyáya, mláya*. See 595. *a*.

269. Some roots of the 1st class form their bases in the first four tenses by a change peculiar to themselves, which change is of course discarded in the other tenses: thus, from स्था 'to stand' (see 587), घ्रा *ghrá*, 'to smell' (588), पा 'to drink' (589), ध्मा 'to blow,' म्ना 'to repeat' or 'think over,' come the bases तिष्ठ *tishṭha*, जिघ्र *jighra*, पिब *piba*, धम *dhama*, मन *mana*, the final *a* being, as before, liable to be lengthened.

a. It should be noted that स्था *sthá* and घ्रा *ghrá* are properly reduplicated verbs of the 3d class at 330. The reduplicated base, by 331, would be *tasthá, jaghrá*: but as the reduplication is irregular, and the radical *á* gives way to the conjugational *a*, grammarians place these roots under the 1st class. The Greek ἵστημι, on the other hand, has not shortened its radical vowel in the singular.

270. Again, from दृश् 'to see,' गम् 'to go,' यम् 'to restrain,' ऋ 'to go,' सद् 'to sink,' शद् (Átm. in conj. tenses, Par. in others) 'to fall,' 'to perish,' are formed the bases पश्य *paśya*, गच्छ *gaććha*, यच्छ *yaććha*, ऋच्छ *ṛiććha*, सीद *sída*, शीय *śíya* (Pres. 1. पश्यामि *paśyámi*, &c.).

a. According to Páṇini (VII. 3, 78), दा 'to give' may sometimes substitute the base यच्छ *yaććha*; and सृ 'to go,' the base धाव *dháva*.

b. गुह् 'to conceal' forms गूह; ष्ठिव् 'to spit,' ष्ठीव; मृज् 'to cleanse,' मार्ज (Pres. 1. गूहामि &c.).

c. क्रम् 'to step,' क्लम् 'to tire,' चम् (with आ) 'to rinse the mouth,' lengthen their medial vowels, but the first only in Parasmai (Pres. 1. क्रामामि &c., but Átm. क्रमे).

d. दंश् 'to bite,' रञ्ज् 'to colour,' सञ्ज् 'to adhere,' स्वञ्ज् 'to embrace,' drop their nasals (Pres. 1. दशामि &c., रजामि &c.).

e. जभ् Átm. 'to yawn' makes its base जम्भ, and even लभ् Átm. 'to receive' sometimes becomes लम्भ in Epic poetry.

271. कम् Átm. 'to love' forms its base after the analogy of the 10th class (Pres. 1. कामये &c.), and some other roots add *áya*: thus, from गुप् 'to protect,' गोपाय *gopáya*; from धूप् 'to fumigate,' धूपाय; from विच्छ् 'to go,' विच्छाय; from पण् Átm. (meaning 'to praise,' not 'to wager'), पणाय; from पन् Átm. 'to praise,' पनाय.

a. कुर्द् Átm. 'to play,' like all roots containing *ir* and *ur* compounded with another consonant, lengthens the vowel (Pres. 1. कूर्दे &c.).

(GROUP I.)—*Fourth class, containing about 130 primitive verbs.*

272. Rule for the formation of the base in the four conjugational

---

* A form त्राहि, as well as त्रायस्व, is found in Epic poetry for the 2d sing. imperative of this root.

tenses. Affix य *ya* to the root. The vowel of the root is not gunated, and generally remains unchanged. Remember, that the inserted य *ya* is liable to become या *yá* before an initial *m* and *v* of the terminations of the four tenses (but not before the *m* of the 1st sing. imperfect), as in the 1st class at 261.

273. Thus, from सिध् *sidh*, 'to succeed,' is formed the base सिध्य *sidhya* (Pres. 1. *sidhyá* + *mi* = सिध्यामि *sidhyámi*, 2. सिध्यसि *sidhyasi*, &c.; Impf. *asidhya* + *m* = असिध्यम् *asidhyam*, &c.; Pot. 1. *sidhya* + *iyam* = सिध्येयम् *sidhyeyam*, 2. सिध्येस् *sidhyes*, &c.; Impv. 1. *sidhya* + *áni* = सिध्यानि *sidhyáni*, &c. Átm. Pres. 1. *sidhya* + *i* = सिध्ये *sidhye*, *sidhya* + *se* = सिध्यसे *sidhyase*, &c.). See 616.

274. Similarly, from मा *má*, 'to measure,' the base माय *máya* (Pres. 1. Átm. *máya* + *i* = माये *máye*, &c.); from क्षिप् *kship*, 'to throw,' क्षिप्य *kshipya*; from नृत् *nrit*, 'to dance,' नृत्य *nritya*; from डी 'to fly,' डीय (Pres. Átm. 1. डीये).

275. Roots ending in *am* and *iv*, and one in *ad*, lengthen the vowel; as, from दिव् *div*, 'to play,' दीव्य *dívya*; from भ्रम् *bhram* (also c. 1), 'to wander,' भ्राम्य *bhrámya*; from मद् *mad*, 'to be mad,' माद्य *mádya*. Similarly, क्रम् (also c. 1) 'to step,' क्षम् 'to endure,' क्लम् 'to grow weary,' तम् 'to be afflicted,' दम् 'to be tamed;' but *bhram* may optionally form भ्रम्य *bhramya*.

276. If a root contain a nasal it is generally rejected; as, from भ्रंश् 'to fall,' भ्रश्य *bhraśya*; from रञ्ज् 'to colour,' रज्य; जन् 'to be born' makes जाय *jáya* (Pres. 1. Átm. जाये), lengthening the vowel, to compensate for the loss of *n*.

a. Roots ending in ओ *o* drop this *o* before the conjugational *ya*: thus, सो *so*, 'to end,' makes its base *sya*. Similarly, छो 'to cut,' शो 'to sharpen,' दो 'to divide.'

277. The following are anomalous. From जॄ 'to grow old,' जीर्य *jírya*; from व्यध् 'to pierce,' विध्य *vidhya*; from मिद् 'to be viscid,' मेद्य *medya*.

Observe—Although this class includes only 130 primitive verbs (generally neuter in signification), yet every one of the 2000 roots in the language may have a passive form which follows the Átmane-pada of this class, differing from it only in the position of the accent, see 253. *a*.

(Group I.)—*Sixth class, containing about 140 primitive verbs.*

278. Rule for the formation of the base in the four conjugational tenses. Affix the vowel अ *a* to the root, which is not gunated, and in other respects generally remains unchanged. Remember, that the inserted अ *a* becomes आ *á* before an initial *m* and *v* of the terminations of the four tenses (but not before the *m* of the 1st sing. imperfect), as in the 1st and 4th conjugations at 261 and 272.

279. Thus, from क्षिप् *kship*, 'to throw,' comes the base क्षिप *kshipa* (Pres. 1. *kshipá + mi* = क्षिपामि *kshipámi*, 2. *kshipa + si* = क्षिपसि *kshipasi*; Pot. 1. *kshipa + iyam* = क्षिपेयम् *kshipeyam*, &c. Átm. Pres. 1. *kshipa + i* = क्षिपे *kshipe*; see 635); from तुद् *tud*, 'to strike,' तुद *tuda*; from दिश् *diś*, 'to point out,' दिश *diśa*.

280. Roots in इ *i*, उ *u* or ऊ *ú*, ऋ *ṛi* and ॠ *ṛí*, generally change those vowels into इय् *iy*, उव् *uv*, रिय् *riy*, and इर् *ir* respectively; as, from रि, 'to go,' comes the base रिय *riya*; from नु 'to praise,' नुव *nuva*; from धू 'to agitate,' धुव *dhuva*; from मृ 'to die,' म्रिय *mriya* (626); from कॄ *kṛí*, 'to scatter,' किर *kira* (627).

a. गॄ 'to swallow' makes either गिर or गिल.

281. A considerable number of roots of the sixth class, ending in consonants, insert a nasal before the final consonant in the four tenses; as, from मुच्, 'to let go,' comes the base मुञ्च *muńća*; from लिप् 'to anoint,' लिम्प *limpa*; from कृत् 'to cut,' कृन्त *kṛinta*; from सिच् 'to sprinkle,' सिञ्च *sińća*; from लुप् 'to break,' लुम्प *lumpa*. Similarly, पिश् 'to form,' 'organize,' विद् 'to find,' खिद् 'to trouble.'

282. The following are anomalous. From इष्, 'to wish,' comes the base इच्छ *iććha*; from प्रच्छ् 'to ask,' पृच्छ *pṛiććha*; from भ्रस्ज् 'to fry,' भृज्ज *bhṛijja*; from व्यच् 'to deceive,' विच *vića*; from व्रश्च् 'to cut,' वृश्च *vṛiśća*; from तृंह् 'to kill,' तृह *tṛiha*.

a. The roots सद् and शद् are sometimes regarded as falling under this class; see their bases at 270.

(Group I.)—*Tenth class, containing a few primitive verbs and all causals.*

283. Rule for forming the base in the four conjugational tenses. Guṇate the vowel of the root throughout every person of all the four tenses (except when debarred by 28. *b*), and affix अय *aya* to the root so guṇated. This अय *aya* becomes अया *ayá* before initial *m* and *v* of the terminations of the four tenses, but not before *m* of the 1st sing. imperfect.

284. Thus, from चुर् *ćur*, 'to steal,' is formed the base चोरय *ćoraya* (Pres. 1. *ćorayá + mi* = चोरयामि *ćorayámi*, 2. *ćoraya + si* = चोरयसि *ćorayasi*, &c.; Impf. 1. *aćoraya + m* = अचोरयम् *aćorayam*, &c., see 638; Pot. 1. *ćoraya + íyam* = चोरयेयम् *ćorayeyam*; Impv. 1. *ćoraya + áni* = चोरयाणि *ćorayáṇi*, &c., see 58).

285. Roots ending in vowels generally take Vṛiddhi instead of Guṇa; as, from प्री 'to please,' प्रायय *práyaya* (see 485. *a*); from धृ 'to hold,' धारय *dháraya*. But वृ 'to choose' makes वरय *varaya*. This last, however, is generally regarded as a causal.

286. Roots containing the vowel अ *a* before a single consonant generally lengthen this vowel; as, from ग्रस् 'to swallow,' ग्रासय *grāsaya*: but from अङ्क् 'to mark,' अङ्कय; from दण्ड् 'to punish,' दण्डय.

a. The following, however, do not lengthen the medial *a*, though followed by a single consonant: कथ् 'to say' (कथय); गण् 'to count;' अघ् 'to sin;' यम् 'to tie;' रच् 'to arrange;' वर् Ātm. in the sense of 'to surround;' रट् 'to scream;' व्रण् 'to wound;' श्रथ् and श्लथ् in the sense of 'to be lax or weak;' रह् 'to quit;' पद् Ātm. 'to go;' गद् 'to sound;' स्वन्, स्तन्, ध्वन्, 'to sound;' कल् 'to count' (also lengthened in Epic poetry); व्यय् 'to spend;' and others less common.

287. कॄत्, 'to celebrate,' 'to praise,' makes कीर्तय *kīrtaya* (Pres. कीर्तयामि).

288. A few roots with a medial ऋ *ṛi* retain that vowel unchanged; as, from स्पृह् 'to desire,' स्पृहय; मृग् 'to search,' मृगय; मृष् 'to bear,' मृषय (more commonly मर्षय); गृह् Ātm. 'to take,' गृहय (also ग्राहय); कृप् 'to pity,' कृपय; but मृज् 'to wipe' takes Vṛiddhi (मार्जय). Some of these may be regarded as nominals.

a. The following also do not gunate their medial vowels: सुख् 'to make happy,' कुह् 'to bind,' स्फुट् 'to become manifest,' कुण् or गुण् 'to consult.'

b. There are a few roots of more than one syllable (see 75. *a*) said to belong to the 10th class, viz. सभाज् 'to worship,' अवधीर् 'to despise,' संग्राम् 'to fight,' कुमार् or कुमाल् 'to play,' गवेष् 'to search,' विडम्ब् 'to imitate,' निवास् 'to put on,' संकेत् 'to invite,' आन्दोल्, हिन्दोल्, हिल्लोल्, प्रेङ्खोल्, 'to swing,' पल्पूल् or वल्पूल् or पल्यूल् 'to cut off.' These and a few monosyllabic roots of the 10th class, such as अंश् 'to divide,' अर्थ् 'to ask,' मिश्र् 'to mix,' लक्ष् 'to mark,' मूत्र् 'to make water,' सूत्र् 'to thread,' वीज् 'to fan,' छिद्र् 'to perforate,' शब्द् 'to sound,' and others less common, can, according to some grammarians, form their bases optionally with *āpaya*: thus, अंश् may make in Pres. 1. अंशापयामि or अंशयामि.

289. It has been shown that every root may have a causal form, which follows the rule of conjugation of the 10th class; and it has already been remarked at 254. that it may be owing to the fact that there are a number of active primitive verbs not causal in their signification, but conjugated like causals, that a 10th class has arisen as distinct from the causal. In verbs of this class the causal form will generally be identical with the primitive. Again, as some verbs which are really causal in their signification are regarded as belonging to the 10th class, there will often be a difficulty in determining whether a verb be a primitive verb of the 10th conjugation, or a causal verb. Hence the consideration of the 10th conjugation must to a great extent be mixed up with that of the causal form of the root. See the special changes applicable to causals at 483—488.

a. Observe, that all verbs, whether primitive or causal, which belong to the 10th class, have this great peculiarity, viz. that the conjugational *aya* is carried throughout all the tenses of the verb, non-conjugational as well as conjugational, except only the aorist and the precative, Parasmai-pada (compare 254). For this reason the formation of the base of the non-conjugational tenses of verbs of the 10th conjugation will not be explained under the general head of the non-conjugational tenses (at 363), but will fall under causal verbs.

b. According to some grammarians all verbs of the 10th class may also belong to the 1st. It has been already pointed out that many verbs of the 10th are also conjugated in other classes; and many may be regarded as nominals.

FORMATION OF THE BASE IN GROUPS II AND III, COMPRISING THE 2D, 3D, 7TH, 5TH, 8TH, AND 9TH CLASSES OF VERBS.

290. Before entering upon the formation of the base in the remaining two groups, the student should turn back to the table at 247, and observe that they take the regular terminations of the memorial scheme, with few substitutions, except in the 3d plur. present and imperative, Átmane-pada, where the nasal is rejected in all six classes.

a. The 3d class, however, owing to the burden occasioned by reduplication, rejects the nasal from the 3d plur. of the Parasmai-pada, as well as from the Átmane-pada, in these two tenses, and takes *us* for *an* in the 3d pl. imperfect.

b. Two roots, moreover, in the 2d class (जक्ष् 'to eat' and शास् 'to rule')*, and roots of more than one syllable (as, दरिद्रा 'to be poor,' चकास् 'to shine,' जागृ 'to be awake,' all formed by reduplication), resemble the 3d class in rejecting the nasal from the 3d pl. Parasmai, and taking *us* for *an* in the imperfect.

c. Some roots ending in *á*, as या, वा, and a few others of the 2d class, as विद्, द्विष्, &c., also optionally take *us* for *an* in the imperfect, before which a final *á* is dropped.

291. Observe also, that roots *ending in consonants*, of the 2d and 3d, and all roots of the 7th, and the root हु *hu* of the 3d class, take *dhi* (the Greek θι) for *hi* in the 2d sing. imperative† (see 247); and that roots *ending in vowels*, of the 5th, and all roots of the 8th, and roots ending in consonants of the 9th class, resemble the first group of classes at 259, in rejecting this termination *hi* altogether.

292. Again, roots ending in consonants will reject the terminations *s* and *t* of the 2d and 3d sing. imperfect by 43. *a*, changing the final of the root, if a soft consonant, to an unaspirated hard, by 42. *a*; and in other respects changing a final consonant, as indicated at 43. *b*, *c*, *d*, *e*. In roots ending in द्, ध्, स्, ष्, the 3d person rejects the termination *t* regularly, and ends therefore in simple द्; the 2d person optionally rejects either the termination *s*, and ends therefore in *t*, or the

---

* *Śás* probably follows the analogy of reduplicated verbs, on account of its double sibilant. It may have been a contraction of शशस्. So जक्ष् may be a corruption of जघस्.

† *Dhi* was originally the only form. Hence in the Veda श्रुधि (κλῦθι); and in the Mahá-bhárata चकृधि. *Dhi* then passed into *hi*, as *dhita* passed into *hita*, and *bhúmi* into the Latin *humus*.

final dental of the root, and ends then in *s*; ex. gr. *vid*—3d person *avet*, 2d person *avet* or *aves*.

a. If a root end in स् *s*, this *s* must be changed to त् *t* in the 3d person; and may be optionally so changed in the 2d person, see 304. *a*.

b. If a root end in ह् *h*, this final *h* becomes क् *k* in the 2d and 3d sing. imperfect of roots beginning with द् *d*; in all other roots the final ह् *h* becomes ट् *ṭ* (cf. 305). In both cases the aspiration is thrown back on the first consonant of the root, if this is allowed by the general rule (42. *c*, 306. *a*).

293. Although comparatively few verbs fall under the last two groups of classes, yet some of these are among the most useful in the language. Their formation presents more difficulties than that of the 1st group, containing the 1st, 4th, 6th, and 10th classes. In these latter the verbal base, although varying slightly in each, preserves the form assumed in the singular before all the terminations of every conjugational tense; but in the last two groups the base is liable to variation in the various persons and numbers of most of the tenses, such variation being denoted by the letter P and other indicatory letters of the memorial scheme at 246, which, be it remembered, are significant only in reference to the second and third groups, and not to the first.

a. In the perfect (2d preterite), however, being a non-conjugational tense, the P is equally significant for verbs of all conjugations. Observe—This P, which usually indicates that in those persons of the tense where it occurs, the verbal base must be guṇated, is generally to be found after light terminations. The 1st, 2d, and 3d sing. Parasmai of the present, imperfect, and perfect are manifestly light terminations. The 3d sing. Parasmai of the imperative is also clearly light. The object, therefore, of the P in these forms is to show, that fulness of form or weight is to be imparted to the root or base before these light terminations, and these only: thus इ *i*, 2d conj., 'to go,' is in the pres. sing. *emi*, *eshi*, *eti*; in du. *ivas*, *ithas*, *itas*; in pl. *imas*, &c.: just as in Greek εἶμι, εἶς, εἶσι; ἴτον, ἴτον; ἴμεν, &c.: compare also φημί (for φᾶμι), φής, φησί, φατόν, φατόν, φαμέν, φατέ, φασί. So again, *stṛi*, 'to strew,' is in pres. sing. *stṛiṇomi*, *stṛiṇoshi*, *stṛiṇoti*; in du. *stṛiṇuvas*, *stṛiṇuthas*, *stṛiṇutas*; in pl. *stṛiṇumas*, &c.: just as in Greek στόρνῡμι, στόρνῡς, στόρνῡσι, στόρνυτον, στόρνυτον, στόρνυμες, &c. Similarly, *krī*, 'to buy,' is in pres. sing. *krīṇāmi*, *krīṇāsi*, *krīṇāti*; in du. &c. *krīṇīvas*, *krīṇīthas*, *krīṇītas*, *krīṇīmas*, &c., the *ā* being heavier than *ī*. Compare Greek πέρνᾱμι (πέρνημι), πέρνᾱς, πέρνᾱτι, πέρνατον, πέρνατον, &c. The P stands after the terminations of the first six persons of the imperative, Parasmai and Ātmane, to indicate that even before these heavy terminations the base must be full. Perhaps the reason of this may be that these six forms agree more with the Vedic mood called *Leṭ* than with the other forms of the imperative. See Bopp's Comp. Gr. 722. When a root ending in a consonant is long by nature or position, no additional weight is necessary, and no Guṇa is then possible (see 28. *b*); but in place of Guṇa, the root or base sometimes remains unmutilated before the light terminations, while mutilation takes place before the heavy. The same holds good in roots ending in *á*: thus *dá* and *dhá* suppress their final vowels before the heavy terminations, and preserve them before the light; see 335, 336. Similarly, *as*, 'to be,' which by 28. *b*. cannot be guṇated, drops its initial vowel before the heavy terminations, retaining it before the light; see 322, and compare 320.

294. Another source of difficulty is, that in the second group (viz. the 2d, 3d, and 7th) the verbal base will generally end in a consonant, as most of the roots in these classes end in consonants, and there is no provision for the interposition of a vowel between the root and the terminations. This group of verbal bases, therefore, will resemble the last four classes of nominal bases; and the combination of the final consonant of a base with the initial *t*, *th*, *dh*, or *s*, of a termination in the conjugational tenses of these three classes requires a knowledge of the laws of Sandhi already propounded, as well as of the following additional rules.

a. Remember, that as regards the initial *m*, *v*, *y*, or vowel of a termination, a hard consonant at the end of a root is not made soft before these letters, but remains unchanged: thus, *vać* + *mi* = *vaćmi*, *ćekship* + *vas* = *ćekshipvas*, and *vać* + *yám* = *vaćyám*. See r. 41. c.

295. Observe—The following rules will also apply in forming the conjugational tenses of the Parasmai-frequentative (see 514), and in forming the base of the non-conjugational tenses of *all* the class except the 10th, and in some of the participles; for although in most roots ending in consonants provision is made for the insertion of the vowel इ *i* (see 391) before the terminations of these tenses, yet there is a large class of common roots which reject this inserted vowel, leaving the final of the base to coalesce with the initial consonant of the termination. It will be convenient, therefore, in the following pages to introduce by anticipation examples from the non-conjugational tenses and participles.

Combination of final च् ć, छ ćh, ज् j, झ jh, *with* त t, थ th, ध dh, स s.

296. Final च् *ć* and ज् *j*, before त *t*, थ *th*, ध *dh*, and स *s*, are changed to क् *k* (compare 43. *d*), the क *k* blending with *s* into क्ष् *ksh* by 70, and becoming ग् *g* before *dh*: thus, *vać* + *ti* = *vakti*; *vać* + *thas* = *vakthas*; *vać* + *si* = *vakshi*; *moć* + *syámi* = *mokshyámi*; *muć* + *ta* = *mukta*;

tyaj + *ta* = *tyakta*; *tyaj* + *syámi* = *tyakshyámi*. The same applies to final झ् *jh*, but this is not likely to occur.

a. Similarly, final छ् *ćh* before *s*; as, *praćh* + *syámi* = *prakshyámi*.

297. But a final छ् *ćh* and ज् *j* are sometimes changed to ष् *sh* before त् *t*, थ् *th*; and त् *t*, थ् *th*, then become ट, ठ: thus, मार्ज् + *ti* = मार्ष्टि; मृज् + *thas* = मृष्ठस्; मृज् + *ta* = मृष्ट; प्रच्छ् + *tá* = प्रष्टा.

a. Similarly, a final ज् *j* may be changed to ड् *ḍ* before ध् *dh*, which then becomes ढ् *ḍh*.

b. भ्रस्ज् 'to fry,' मस्ज् 'to be immersed,' and व्रश्च् 'to cut,' reject their last consonant, and the first two are treated as if ending in ष्, the last as if ending in श्. See 632, 633, 630.

Combination of final ध् dh, भ् bh, *with* त् t, थ् th, स् s.

298. Final ध् *dh* and भ् *bh*, before त् *t* and थ् *th*, are changed, the one to द् *d*, the other to ब् *b*, and both *t* and *th* then become ध् *dh*: thus, *rundh* with *tas* or *thas* becomes equally रुन्द्धस् *runddhas*; *labh* + *táhe* = लब्धाहे *labdháhe*; *bodh* + *táhe* = बोद्धाहे.

Note—A similar rule applies to final घ् *gh*, which must be changed to ग् *g*, but this can rarely occur.

a. Observe—When final ध् *dh* is preceded by a conjunct न् *n*, as in *rundh*, then the final *dh*, which has become *d* (before *t* and *th* changed to *dh*), may optionally be rejected; so that *rundh* + *tas* = रुन्द्धस् or रुन्धस्; *rundh* + *tam* = रुन्द्धं or रुन्धं.

299. Final ध् *dh* and भ् *bh*, before स् *s*, are changed by 42, the one to त् *t*, the other to प् *p*: thus, रुणध् *ruṇadh* + सि *si* becomes रुणत्सि *ruṇatsi*; *sedh* + *syámi* = *setsyámi*; *labh* + *sye* = *lapsye*.

a. If the initial of the syllable containing the final aspirate be *g*, *d*, *b*, or *ḍ*, then the aspirate, which has been rejected in the final, is thrown back on the initial; as, बोध् *bodh* + स्ये *sye* = भोत्स्ये *bhotsye*; दध् *dadh* + *sva* = *dhatsva*: and in the case of दध् the same applies before *t* and *th*, against 298. See 336, 664. Cf. θρέψω from τρέφω.

b. The aspirate is also thrown back on the initial, when final *dh* is changed to *d*, before the terminations *dhve* and *dhvam*. See 336, 664.

Combination of final श् ś, ष् sh, ह् h, *with* त् t, थ् th, स् s, ध् dh.

300. Final श् *ś*, before त् *t* and थ् *th*, is changed to ष् *sh*: and the *t*, *th*, take the cerebral form ट, ठ: thus, ईश् + *te* = ईष्टे; and ईश् + *thás* = ईष्ठास्.

301. Similarly, final ष् *sh*, before त् *t* and थ् *th*, requires the change of *t*, *th*, to ट्, ठ्: thus, द्वेष् + *ti* = द्वेष्टि; and द्विष् + *thas* = द्विष्ठः.

302. Final श् *ś* or ष् *sh*, before स् *s*, is changed to क् *k* by 43.*c*, the स् *s* then becoming ष् *sh* by 70: thus, वश् + *si* = वक्षि; द्वेष् + *si* = द्वेक्षि; दृश् + *syámi* = द्रक्ष्यामि.

a. Final क्ष् *ksh* is also changed to क् *k*; as, चक्ष् + षे = चक्षे.

303. Final श् *ś* or ष् *sh*, before ध् *dh*, is changed to ड् *ḍ*, the ध् *dh* becoming ढ् *ḍh* by 51: thus, द्विष् + *dhi* = द्विड्ढि. Similarly, द्विष् + *dhvam* = द्विड्ढ्वं. A final ज् *j* may also follow this rule; see 632, 651.

a. Final क्ष् *ksh* also becomes ड्, *k* being dropped; as, चक्ष् + ध्वे = चड्ढ्वे.

304. Final स् *s*, before ध् *dh*, is either dropped or changed to द् *d*: thus, *ćakás* + *dhi* = either चकाधि *ćakádhi* or चकाद्धि *ćakáddhi*; शास् + *dhi* = शाधि; घिंस् + *dhi* = घिन्धि or घिन्द्धि, see 658, 673.

a. Before स् *s* it is changed to त् *t*; as, *vas* + *syámi* = *vatsyámi*. So optionally in 2d sing. impf. of शास्, *aśás* + *s* = *aśáts* = *aśát* (or *aśás*).

Combination of final ह् h *with* त् t, थ् th, स् s, ध् dh.

305. In roots beginning with द् *d*, like दुह् *duh*, 'to milk,' final ह् *h* is treated as if it were घ् *gh*, and is changed to ग् *g* before त् *t* and थ् *th*, and both *t* and *th* then become ध् *dh*: thus, दुह् *duh* + *tas* or *thas* becomes equally दुग्धः *dugdhas*; दह् *dah* + *tásmi* = *dagdhásmi*.

Note—In the root नह् the final *h* is treated as if it were ध् *dh*, and becomes द् *d*, after which *t* and *th* both become *dh*. See 624.

a. But if a root begin with any other letter than द् *d* or न् *n*, then its final ह् *h* is dropped, and both the त् *t* and थ् *th* of the termination become ढ् *ḍh*. Moreover, to compensate for the rejection of the final *h*, a radical vowel (except *ṛi*), if not guṇated, is lengthened, and in the roots सह् *sah* and वह् *vah*, 'to bear,' changed to *o*; as, गुह् + *ta* = गूढ; रुह् + *ta* = रूढ; लेह् *leh* + *ti* = लेढि *leḍhi*; रोह् + *tásmi* = रोढास्मि; *sah* + *tá* = सोढा; *vah* + *tá* = वोढा. But तृह् + त = तृढ (Páṇ. VI. 3, 111).

b. द्रुह् 'to injure,' मुह् 'to be foolish,' स्निह् 'to love,' स्नुह् 'to vomit,' optionally follow either 305 or 305. *a*.

306. Final ह् *h*, before स् *s*, follows the analogy of final श् *ś* and ष् *sh*, and is changed to क् *k*, which blends with स् *s* into क्ष् *ksh*: thus, लेह् *leh* with *si* becomes लेक्षि; रोह् + *syámi* = रोक्ष्यामि. Similarly, in Latin, final *h* becomes *k* before *s*; as, *vehsit* (*vexit*) from *veho*.

a. And if the initial of the syllable ending in ह् *h* be द् *d*, ग् *g*, ब् *b*, or ड् ḍ (the two latter, however, are not likely to occur), then the final ह् h is still changed to क् k before s; but the initial द् d and ग् g are aspirated according to the analogy of 42. c; thus, दोह् doh + si = धोक्षि; दह् dah + syāmi = धक्ष्यामि; अगुह् aguh + sam = अघुक्षं.

b. In the root नह् nah final ह् h is treated as if it were dh, and becomes त् t before स् s. Compare 182. e, and see 624.

c. In roots beginning with द् d, like दुह् duh and दिह् dih, final ह् h becomes ग् g before dh; i. e. before the dhi of the 2d sing. imperative, and before the terminations dhve and dhvam (see d. below): thus, दुह् duh + dhi = दुग्धि dugdhi. And in a root beginning with n, like नह् nah, final h becomes d before these terminations.

But if the root begin with any other letter than द् d or न् n, then final ह् h is dropped, and the ध dh of the termination becomes ढ ḍh, the radical vowel (except ऋ ṛi) being lengthened: thus, लिह् lih + dhi = लीढि; lih + dhvam = लीढ्वं. An option, however, is allowed in the case of the roots at 305. b.

d. And 306. a. applies before dhve and dhvam, when final ह् h becomes ग् g or is dropped, although not before dhi of the imperative: thus, duh + dhve = धुग्ध्वे dhugdhve; and aguh + dhvam = अघूढ्वम् aghūḍhvam.

(Group II.)—*Second class, containing 70 primitive verbs.*

(See rr. 290, 291, 292.)

307. Rule for forming the base in the four conjugational tenses. Guṇate the vowel of the root (except when debarred by 28. b) in the *strong forms*, or before those terminations only which are marked with P in the memorial scheme at 246. Before all the other terminations the original vowel of the root must be retained by 293. a.

Remember, that no vowel is interposed between the root and the terminations. Compare Greek verbs like εἶμι, φημί, &c. See 258. a, 294.

308. Thus, from विद् vid, 'to know' (Greek εἴδω, ἴδον, Lat. video), is formed the base of the singular present ved (1. ved + mi = वेद्मि vedmi, &c.), and the base of the dual and plural vid (Du. 1. vid + vas = विद्वस् vidvas, &c.; Pl. 1. vid + mas = विद्मस् vidmas, &c.). So also the base of the imperfect aved and avid (1. aved + am = avedam, 2. aved + s = avet or aves by 43. a. and 292); the base of the potential vid (1. vid + yām = विद्याम् vidyām, &c.); and the base of the imperative

ved and *vid* (1. *ved* + *āni* = *vedāni*, 2. *vid* + *dhi* = *viddhi* 291, *ved* + *tu* = *vettu*; Du. 1. *ved* + *āva* = *vedāva*, &c.*). See the table at 583.

a. A contracted form of the perfect of *vid* (365) is sometimes used for the present: thus, Sing. *veda*, *vettha*, *veda*; Du. *vidva*, *vidathus*, *vidatus*; Pl. *vidma*, *vida*, *vidus*; see 168. *a.* Compare the Greek οἶδα or Ϝοῖδα from the root Ϝιδ (εἴδω), also used with a present signification; and the Latin *vidi*, *vidisti*, &c. Cf. also the present *vidmas* with ἴδμεν (ἴσμεν), *vittha* with ἴστε, and *viddhi* with ἴσθι. Compare also the old English verb 'to wit.'

309. Similarly, from द्विष्, 'to hate,' come the bases *dvesh* and *dvish* (Pres. 1. द्वेष्मि; Du. 1. द्विष्वस्, &c.; see 657).

310. So also, from इ i, 'to go,' come the bases *e* and *i* (Pres. 1. एमि *emi*, cf. εἶμι, 2. एषि by 70, 3. एति; Pl. 1. इमस्, ἴμεν, see 645).

a. जागृ 'to awake' makes, in the same way, *jāgar* and *jāgṛi* (Pres. 1. जागर्मि, &c.; Du. 1. जागृवस्; Pl. 3. जाग्रति; Impf. 2, 3. अजागर् or अजागः; Du. 3. अजागृतां; Pl. 3. अजागरुस्; Pot. 1. जागृयां; Impv. 3. जागर्तु; Pl. 3. जाग्रतु 290. *b*).

311. The preposition अधि *adhi*, 'over,' prefixed to the root इ *i*, 'to go,' gives the sense of 'to read' (Ātmane-pada only): इ then becomes *iy* (compare 123) and blends with *adhi* into अधीय् *adhīy* before the vowel-terminations of the pres., impf., and pot. Before the consonantal terminations it becomes अधी *adhī*. (Hence the Pres. 1. अधीये, 2. अधीषे, 3. अधीते; Du. 1. अधीवहे, &c.; Pl. 3. अधीयते; Impf. 1. *adhi*+*a*+*iy*+*i* = अध्यैयि by 260. *a*, 2. अध्यैथास्, 3. अध्यैत; Du. 1. अध्यैवहि, 2. अध्यैयाथां, &c.; Pot. 1. अधीयीय, अधीयीथास्, &c.; Impv. 1. *adhi*+*e*+*ai* = अध्ययै by 36. *a*, 2. अधीष्व, &c.)

a. The preposition आ *ā* is prefixed to the root इ *i*, according to the usual rules of Sandhi, and gives the sense of 'to come:' thus, Pres. एमि, एषि, एति; एवस्, &c.; Impf. आयं, ऐस्, &c.; Pot. इयां, इयास्, &c.; Impv. आयानि, इहि, एतु, &c. Again, the prep. अप *apa* prefixed gives the sense of 'to go away;' thus, Pres. अपैमि, &c.; and the prep. अव gives the sense of 'to know;' as, Pres. अवैमि.

312. So also other roots in ई *ī* and उ *u* or ऊ *ū* change these vowels to *iy* and *uv* (compare 123 and 125. *a*) before the vowel-terminations; as, from वी *vī*, 'to go,' come *ve*, *vī*, and *viy* (Pres. 1. वेमि, &c.; Du. 1. वीवस्; Pl. 3. वियन्ति)†. Similarly, सू 'to bring forth' (Ātmane only), makes in Pres. S. Du. Pl. 3. सूते, सुवाते, सुवते; and in Impv. S. Du. Pl. 1. सुवै, सुवावहै, सुवामहै, Guṇa being suppressed.

---

* The imperative of *vid* is optionally formed with the syllable *ām* and the auxiliary verb *kṛi* (compare 384): thus, S. 3. विदांकरोतु or विदाङ्करोतु. Pāṇini III. 1, 41. And this root may optionally insert *r* in the 3d pl. Ātm. of the pres., impf., and impv.: thus, विद्रते or विदते, अविद्रत or अविदत, विद्रतां or विदतां.

† According to some the 3d pl. impf. of वी is अवयन् as well as अवियन्.

313. स्तु *stu* and नु *nu*, 'to praise;' यु *yu*, 'to join,' 'to mix;' and रु *ru*, 'to sound'—follow 312, but take Vṛiddhi instead of Guṇa before the consonantal P terminations*. Hence the bases स्तौ *stau*, स्तु *stu*, and स्तुव् *stuv*; see 648. Before the vowel P terminations both Vṛiddhi and Guṇa are generally (but not always) suppressed, and *uv* substituted, as in यु at 312. Note, that these roots may optionally insert an ई *í* before the consonantal P terminations; and before this vowel Guṇa, not Vṛiddhi, is required. According to some authorities, however, *í* is inserted before *all* the consonantal-terminations; and, according to others, before all the consonants, except *y*, *v*, or *m*, not followed by an indicatory P.

314. ब्रू, 'to speak,' can never take Vṛiddhi, like the roots at 313; but inserts an ई *í* after Guṇa in the places where those roots optionally insert it, viz. before the consonantal P terminations. Hence the bases *bravī*, *brū*, *bruv*. See 649.

a. Before the vowel P terminations Guṇa is not suppressed, excepting in the 1st sing. impf., which may be either अब्रवं or अब्रुवं.

315. शी, 'to lie down,' 'to sleep' (Ātmane only), guṇates the radical vowel before *all* the terminations, and inserts *r* in the 3d pl. pres., impf., and imperative, after the analogy of the 3d pl. potential. See 646.

316. ऊर्णु, 'to cover', takes either Vṛiddhi or Guṇa of the final *u* before the consonantal P terminations, except before the 2d and 3d sing. of the impf., where Guṇa only is admissible. Before the vowel-terminations it follows 312, but Guṇa is retained before the vowel P terminations, excepting in the 1st sing. impf. Hence the bases *ūrṇau*, *ūrṇo*, *ūrṇu*, and *ūrṇuv* (Pres. Par. 1. ऊर्णौमि or ऊर्णोमि; Du. 1. ऊर्णुवस्; Pl. 3. ऊर्णुवन्ति, see 290. *b*; Impf. 1. और्णवं or और्णुवं by 260. *a*, 2. और्णोस्, &c.; Pot. 1. ऊर्णुयां; Impv. S. 1. ऊर्णवानि, 3. ऊर्णौतु or ऊर्णोतु. Pres. Ātm. 3. ऊर्णुते, ऊर्णुवाते, ऊर्णुवते).

317. या 'to go,' पा 'to protect,' अद् 'to eat' (*edo*), आस् 'to sit,' Ātm., and other roots having *a* or *ā* for their vowels, cannot be changed, but are themselves the inflective bases (Pres. 1. या *yā*+*mi*=*yāmi*, see 644; अद् *ad*+*mi*=*admi*, 2. *ad*+*si*=*atsi*, 3. *ad*+*ti*=*atti*; Du. 3. *ad*+*tas*=*attas*, &c., see 652). With *atti* compare Lat. *edit*.

a. आस् 'to sit' is similar; thus *ās*+*e*=*āse*, *ās*+*se*=*āsse*, *ās*+*te*=*āste*. The final of *ās* is dropped before *dh*, hence Pl. 2. आध्वे *ādhve*, &c.

b. अद् 'to eat,' before the terminations of the 2d and 3d sing. imperfect, inserts the vowel अ *a* by special rule, see 652; and some other roots of this class require peculiar changes, as follows:—

318. दरिद्रा *daridrā*, 'to be poor,' follows 290. *b*, making its base *daridri* before the consonantal terminations not marked with P, and *daridr* before *ati*, *us*, *atu* (Pres. S. Du. Pl. 3. दरिद्राति, दरिद्रितस्, दरिद्रति; Impf. 1. अदरिद्रां; Pl. 3. अदरिद्रुस्; Pot. 3. दरिद्रियात्; Impv. 1. दरिद्राणि; Du. 1. दरिद्राव; Pl. 3. दरिद्रतु).

319. दीधी *dīdhī*, 'to shine' (Ātm.), and वेवी 'to go' (Ātm.), change their final to *y*, and not to *iy*, before the vowel-terminations (compare 312); but in the poten-

* That is, the terminations marked with P, which begin with consonants.

tial the final *ś* coalesces with the *s* of the terminations (Pres. Sing. 1. ईशे; वेशे; Pl. 3. ईशते; वेशते; Pot. 1. ईशीय, &c.).

320. वच् *vac*, 'to speak,' changes its final palatal to a guttural before all the hard consonantal terminations, in conformity with 176; but not before the soft (except *dh*), by 294. a. It is defective in the 3d pl. present and imperative, where its place must be supplied by ब्रू at 314, 649. Hence the bases *vac* and *vak*. See 650.

321. मृज् *mṛj*, 'to cleanse,' is vṛiddhied in strong forms, and optionally before the vowel-terminations having no P. Hence the bases *mārj* and *mṛj*. See 651.

322. रुद् *rud*, 'to weep,' besides the usual Guṇa change before the P terminations, inserts the vowel इ *i* before all the consonantal terminations except *y*, and optionally *a* or ई *ī* in the 2d and 3d sing. impf. Hence *rodi*, *rudi*, *rud*. See 653.

a. स्वप् 'to sleep,' श्वस् and अन् 'to breathe,' and जक्ष् 'to eat,' are similar, but without Guṇa. The last obeys 290. *b*. In the Epic poems, forms like स्वपामि are found as well as स्वपिमि, while in the Veda other roots besides the above five insert *i* (as क्रोशिति, वमिति, वसिति, स्तनिहि, &c.).

323. हन् *han*, 'to kill,' makes its base ह *ha* before *t* or *th* (by 57. *a*); घ्न् *ghn* before *anti*, *an*, *antu*; and ज *ja* before हि. The last change is to avoid the proximity of two aspirates. See 654, and compare 331. *b*.

324. वश् *vaś*, 'to desire,' 'to choose,' suppresses the *a*, and changes *v* to *u* before the terminations which have no P (see 293. *a*); and उश् *uś* becomes उष् *uṣ* before *t* and *th* by 300. See 656.

325. ईश् *īś*, 'to rule' (Ātmane only), and ईड् *īḍ*, 'to praise' (Ātm.), not guṇated by 28. *b*, insert the vowel इ *i* between the root and the terminations of the 2d person से, स्व, ध्वे, and ध्वम् (ईड्—Pres. 1. ईडे, 2. ईडिषे, 3. ईट्टे (see 48. *b*); Du. 1. ईड्वहे; Pl. 2. ईडिध्वे; Impf. 3. ऐट्ट, &c.; Pot. 1. ईडीय, &c.; Impv. 1. ईडै, 2. ईडिष्व, 3. ईट्टाम्; Pl. 2. ईडिध्वम्. ईश्—Pres. 1. ईशे, 2. ईशिषे, 3. ईष्टे by 302; Impf. 3. ऐष्ट, &c.; Impv. 3. ईष्टाम्, &c.).

326. चक्ष् *cakṣ*, 'to speak' (Ātm.), drops the penultimate *k* before all consonantal terminations, except those beginning with *m* or *v* (Pres. 1. चक्षे, 2. चक्ष् + से = चक्षे, 3. चष्टे, &c., see 302. *a*, 303. *a*; Impf. 3. अचष्ट; Pot. 3. चक्षीत). Kátyáyana considers चक्षा the original root, whence is formed ख्या; the latter being substituted for चक्ष् in the non-conjugational tenses.

327. अस् *as*, 'to be' (Parasmai-pada only), a very useful auxiliary verb, follows 293. *a*, and rejects its initial *a*, except before the P terminations. The 2d pers. sing. of the pres. is असि for अस्सि. The impf. has the character of an aorist, and retains the initial *a* throughout, and inserts ई *ī* before the *s* and *t* of the 2d and 3d sing.; see 584. The 2d sing. imperative substitutes *e* for *as*, and takes the termination *dhi*. This root is found in the Ātmane-pada, with the prepositions *vi* and *ati*, when the Present is Sing. व्यतिहे, -से, -स्ते; Du. -स्वहे, -साथे, -साते, -स्महे, -ध्वे, -सते; Pot. S. 1. व्यतिषीय, &c. (Pāṇ. VIII. 3. 87). See 584.

328. शास् *śās*, 'to rule,' in Parasmai (but not in Ātmane), changes its vowel to इ *i* before the consonantal terminations having no P, except that of the 2d sing.

Impv. Before that and all vowel-terminations, as well as in the strong forms, the vowel of the root remains unchanged; and, after *i*, स् becomes ष् by 70. Hence the bases शास् and शिष्. See 658.

a. चकास्, 'to shine,' is Pres. 1. चकास्मि, 2. चकास्सि, 3. चकास्ति; Du. 1. चकास्वस्; Pl. 3. चकासति (290. *b*); Impf. 1. अचकासम्, 2. अचकास् or अचकात् (292. *a*), 3. अचकात्; Du. 1. अचकास्व; Pl. 3. अचकासुस्; Pot. 1. चकास्याम्; Impv. 1. चकासानि, 2. चकाधि or चकाद्धि (304), 3. चकास्तु; Du. 1. चकासाव, 2. चकास्तम्; Pl. 3. चकासतु.

329. दुह् *duh*, 'to milk,' and लिह् *lih*, 'to lick,' form their bases as explained at 305, 306. They are conjugated at 660, 661.

(Group II.)—*Third class, containing about* 20 *primitive verbs.*

RULES OF REDUPLICATION.

Applicable to the 3d class and to all reduplicated forms, such as the perfect (or 2d pret.), aorist (or 3d pret.), desiderative, and frequentative.

330. In doubling a root the initial consonant and first vowel are generally repeated, as *lilip* from *lip*, but there are special rules;

331. 1st, As to consonants. A corresponding unaspirated letter is substituted for an aspirate: thus, द् *d* for ध् *dh*. So in Greek τ is repeated for θ; as, θύω, τέθυκα, &c.

a. The palatal च् *ć* is substituted for the gutturals क् *k* or ख् *kh*; and the palatal ज् *j* for the gutturals ग् *g*, घ् *gh*, or ह् *h*.

b. Note—हन्, 'to kill,' and हि, 'to go,' substitute घ् *gh* for ह् when reduplicated.

c. If a root begin with a double consonant, the first consonant only, or its substitute, is repeated; but if with a double consonant, whose first is a sibilant and whose second is hard, the second, or its substitute, is reduplicated: thus, च् *ć* for क्ष् *ksh*; स् *s* for स्य् *sy*; ज् *j* for ह्र् *hr*; त् *t* for स्थ् *sth*; च् *ć* for स्क् *sk*; प् *p* for स्प् *sp*.

d. 2dly, As to vowels. A short vowel is repeated for a long, and diphthongal sounds are represented by their second element: thus, अ *a* is reduplicated for आ *á*; इ *i* for ई *í*, ऋ *ri*, ॠ *rí*, ए *e*, and ऐ *ai*; उ *u* for ऊ *ú*, ओ *o*, and औ *au*. In certain cases इ *i* is also repeated for *a* and *á*, as being a lighter vowel.

e. Note—द्युत्, 'to shine,' makes *didyut* for *dudyut*.

f. Observe—As a general rule, the reduplicated syllable has a tendency to lighten the weight of the radical syllable.

g. Observe also, that when a form has once been reduplicated, it is never reduplicated again in forming other derivatives from it (see 517. *e*), and that when roots which have to be reduplicated have any changed form, this modified form is taken in the reduplication rather than the original root: thus स्मृ, 'to remember,' being changed to स्मूर् in the desiderative, the vowel of the root does not appear in the reduplication (सुस्मूर्).

Formation of the base.

332. Rule for forming the base in the four conjugational tenses. Reduplicate the initial consonant and vowel of the root, and guṇate the vowel of the *radical syllable* before the P terminations only, as in the 2d conjugation, by 293. *a.*

Observe—This class resembles the 2d in interposing no vowel between the root and terminations. It is the only class that necessarily rejects the nasal in 3d plur. Parasmai-pada, by 290. *a*, and takes *us* for *an* in 3d plur. imperfect Parasmai, before which *us* Guṇa is generally required. See 290, 291, 292.

Thus, from भृ *bhṛi*, 'to bear' (φέρω, *fero*), is formed the base of the present singular बिभर् *bibhar* (1. *bibhar* + *mi* = बिभर्मि), and the base of the dual and plural बिभृ *bibhṛi* (Du. 1. *bibhṛi* + *vas* = बिभृवस्; Pl. 1. *bibhṛi* + *mas* = बिभृमस्; Pl. 3. *bibhṛi* + *ati* = बिभ्रति by 34 and 290). See the table at 583.

a. Note, that *bibharti* bears the same relation to *bibhṛimas* that *fert* does to *ferimus*, and *vult* to *volumus*.

333. Similarly, from भी *bhí*, 'to fear,' come the two bases *bibhe* and *bibhí*; from हु *hu*, 'to sacrifice,' the two bases *juho* and *juhu*. The former of these roots may optionally shorten the radical vowel before a consonant, when not guṇated. See 666. The latter may optionally reject its final before *vas* and *mas*, and is the only root ending in a vowel which takes *dhi* for *hi* in the 2d sing. imperative. See 662.

a. ह्री, 'to be ashamed,' is like भी, but changes its final ई to इय् *iy* before the vowel-terminations, in conformity with 123. *a.* See 666. *a.*

334. ऋ *ṛi*, 'to go,' is the only verb in this class that begins with a vowel. It substitutes *iy* for *ṛi* in the reduplication, and makes its bases इयर् *iyar* and इयृ *iyṛi* (Pres. S. Du. Pl. 3. इयर्ति, इयृतस्, इय्रति; Impf. 1. ऐयरं, 2. ऐयर्, 3. ऐयर्; Du. 3. ऐयृतां; Pot. 3. इयृयात्; Impv. 1. इयराणि).

335. दा *dá*, 'to give' (δίδωμι, *do*), drops its final *á* before all excepting the P terminations. Hence the bases *dadá* and *dad*. It becomes दे *de* before the *hi* of the imperative. See 663.

336. धा *dhá*, 'to place' (τίθημι), is similar. Hence the bases *dadhá* and *dadh*; but *dadh* becomes धत् before *t*, *th*, and *s*; and *dhad* before *dhve* and *dhvam* by 299. *a*, *b*; and *dhe* before the *hi* of the imperative. See 664.

337. हा *há*, 'to abandon,' changes its final *á* to ई *í* before the consonantal

terminations not marked with P, and drops the final altogether before the vowel-terminations, and before *y* of the potential. Hence the bases *jahí*, *jahi*, *jah*. Before *hi* of the imperative the base is optionally *jahá*, *jahí*, or *jahi*. According to some authorities, जही may be shortened into जहि in the present, imperfect, and imperative. See 665.

338. मा *má*, 'to measure' (Átm.), and हा *há*, 'to go' (Átm.), make their bases मिमी *mimí* and जिही *jihí* before the consonantal terminations not marked with P. Before the vowel-terminations their bases are *mim* and *jih* (Sing. Du. Pl. 3. जिहीते, जिहाते, जिहते; Impf. 3. अजिहीत; Impv. 3. जिहीतां). See मा at 664. *a*.

339. जन् *jan*, 'to produce' (Parasmai-pada), rejects the final nasal (see 57. *a*), and lengthens the radical *a* before *t* and *th* and *hi*, and optionally before *y*. Before consonantal terminations beginning with *m* or *v* the radical *jan* remains, but before vowel-terminations not marked with P the medial *a* is dropped, and the nasal combining with *j* becomes palatal (compare the declension of *rájan* at 149). Hence the three bases *jajan*, *jajá*, and *jajñ*. See 666. *b*.

340. भस् *bhas*, 'to eat,' 'to shine,' like *jan*, rejects the radical *a* before the vowel-terminations not marked with P; and *bh* coalescing with *s* becomes *p* by 42 (Pres. S. Du. Pl. 3. बभस्ति, बब्धस्, बप्सति). The same contraction takes place before terminations beginning with त, थ, but the final *s* is then dropped, and the usual rules of Sandhi applied: thus, बभस्+तां = बब्धां by 298.

341. निज् 'to purify,' विज् 'to separate,' and विष् 'to pervade,' 'to penetrate,' guṇate the reduplicated syllable before *all* the terminations, and forbid the usual Guṇa of the radical syllable before terminations beginning with vowels, as in the 1st sing. impf. and the 1st sing. du. pl. impv. (Pres. 1. नेनेज्मि, 2. नेनेक्षि, 3. नेनेक्ति; Du. 1. नेनिज्वस्, &c.; Pl. 1. नेनिज्मस्, 3. नेनिजति; Impf. 1. अनेनिजम्, 2. अनेनेक्, &c.; Pl. 3. अनेनिजुस्, &c.; Impv. 1. नेनिजानि; Du. 1. नेनिजाव; Pl. 1. नेनिजाम.

(Group II.)—*Seventh class, containing about 24 primitive verbs.*

342. Rule for forming the base in the four conjugational tenses. Insert न *na* (changeable to ण *ṇa* after *ṛi* &c. by 58) *between* the vowel and final consonant* of the root before the P terminations, and न् *n* (changeable to ङ्, ञ्, ण्, न्, or Anusvára †, according to the consonant immediately succeeding) before all the other terminations.

Observe—This class resembles the 2d and 3d in interposing no vowel between the final consonant of the root and the terminations.

a. Similarly, *n* is inserted in certain Greek and Latin roots; as, *μαθ*, *μανθάνω*; *λαβ*, *λαμβάνω*; *θιγ*, *θιγγάνω*; *scid*, *scindo*; *fid*, *findo*; *tag*, *tango*; *liq*, *linquo*, &c. See 258. *a*.

---

* All the roots in this class end in consonants.

† The change to Anusvára will take place before sibilants and ह्. See 6. *b*.

343. Thus, from भिद् *bhid*, 'to divide,' 'to break,' is formed the base of the present tense singular भिनद् *bhinad*, and the base of the dual and plural भिन्द् *bhind*, changeable to *bhinat* and *bhint* by 46 (1. *bhinad* + *mi* = भिनद्मि, 3. *bhinad* + *ti* = भिनत्ति; Du. 1. *bhind* + *vas* = भिन्द्वस्, 3. *bhind* + *tas* = भिन्त्तस् or भिन्तस्; Pl. 3. *bhind* + *anti* = भिन्दन्ति). See the table at 583.

344. Similarly, from रुध् *rudh*, 'to hinder,' the two bases रुणध् *ruṇadh* and रुन्ध् *rundh*, changeable to *ruṇat*, *ruṇad*, and *rund* (1. *ruṇadh* + *mi* = रुणध्मि, 2. *ruṇadh* + *si* = रुणत्सि, 3. *ruṇadh* + *ti* = रुणद्धि; Du. 3. *rundh* + *tas* = रुन्द्धस्); see 671. So also, from पिष्, 'to grind,' the two bases पिनष् and पिंष् (Pres. 3. पिनष् + ति = पिनष्टि; Impv. 2. पिंष् + हि = पिण्ड्ढि or पिण्ढि).

345. Observe—Roots ending in त् *t* and द् *d* may reject these letters before *th*, *t*, and *dhi*, when *n* immediately precedes: hence भिन्तस् may be written for भिन्त्तस्; भिन्धि for भिन्द्धि. Similarly, रुन्धस् may be written for रुन्द्धस्, see 298. a; and on the same principle तृण्ढस् is written for तृण्ढ्ढस् from तृह्, see 674.

346. भुज् 'to eat,' युज् 'to join,' विच् 'to distinguish,' conform to 296. Hence, from *bhuj* come *bhunaj* and *bhuñj*, changeable to *bhunak* and *bhuṅ-k*, see 668. a.

347. भञ्ज् 'to break,' अञ्ज् 'to anoint,' उन्द् 'to moisten,' इन्ध् 'to kindle,' हिंस् 'to injure,' तञ्च् or तञ्ज् 'to contract,' fall under this class; but the nasal belonging to the root takes the place of the conjugational nasal, and becomes न *na* in the strong forms. Hence, from *bhañj* come the two bases *bhanaj* and *bhañj*, changeable to *bhanak* and *bhaṅ-k*; from *und* come *unad* and *und* (Pres. 3. *unatti*, *untas*, *undanti*; Impf. 1. *aunadam*, 2. *aunas*, 3. *aunat*; Du. 3. *auntām*, &c.). See 669, 668, 673. Similarly, from इन्ध्, Pres. 1. *indhe*, 2. *intse*, 3. *inddhe*; Pl. 3. *indhate*; Impf. 2. *ainddhās*, 3. *ainddha*; Impv. 1. *inadhai*, &c.

348. तृह् 'to strike,' 'to kill,' inserts ने instead of न before all the P terminations, except in 1st sing. impf. and 1st sing. du. pl. imperative. See 674.

GROUP III.—FORMATION OF THE BASE IN THE 5TH, 8TH, AND 9TH CLASSES OF VERBS.

(Group III.)—*Fifth class, containing about* 30 *primitive verbs.*

349. Rule for forming the base in the four conjugational tenses. Add नु *nu* (changeable to णु by 58) to the root, which must be guṇated into नो *no* (changeable to णो) before the P terminations (293. a). Roots ending in consonants add *nuv*, instead of *nu*, to the root before the vowel-terminations. Roots ending in *vowels* may drop the *u* of *nu* before initial *v* and *m* (not marked with P), and always reject the termination *hi* of the imperative. See 291.

a. This change of *nu* to *no* is supplied in the corresponding Greek affix νυ, by lengthening the *v*, as in ζεύγνῡμι, ζεύγνυμεν; δείκνῡμι, δείκνυμεν. See 258. *a.*

350. Thus, from चि *ći*, 'to gather,' are formed the bases *ćino* and *ćinu* (Pres. 1. *ćino* + *mi* = चिनोमि, *ćino* + *si* = चिनोषि by 70; Du. 1. *ćinu* + *vas* = चिनुवस् or चिन्वस्; Pl. 1. *ćinu* + *mas* = चिनुमस् or चिन्मस्, 3. *ćinu* + *anti* = चिन्वन्ति by 34; Impv. 1. *ćino* + *āni* = चिनवानि by 36. *b*, 2. *ćinu* by 291). See the table at 583.

351. Similarly, from आप् *āp*, 'to obtain,' come *āpno*, *āpnu*, and *āpnuv*. See 681.

352. श्रु *śru*, 'to hear' (sometimes placed under the 1st class), substitutes शृ *śri* for the root, and makes its bases *śriṇo* and *śriṇu*. See 677.

a. दम्भ् 'to deceive,' स्कम्भ् and स्तम्भ् 'to support,' स्कुम्भ् 'to stop,' and स्तुम्भ् 'to astonish,' reject their nasals in favour of the conjugational *nu*: thus, *dabhnu*, *skabhnu*, &c.

(Group III.)—*Eighth class, containing* 10 *primitive verbs.*

353. Rule for forming the base in the four conjugational tenses. Add उ *u* to the root, which must be guṇated into ओ *o* before the P terminations by 293. *a.*

a. Observe—Only ten roots are generally enumerated in this conjugation, and nine of these end either in न् *n* or ण् *ṇ*: hence the addition of *u* and *o* will have the same apparent effect as the addition of *nu* and *no* in the 5th class.

354. The termination of the 2d sing. imperative is rejected: thus, from तन् *tan*, 'to stretch,' 'to extend,' are formed the bases *tano* and *tanu* (Pres. 1. *tano* + *mi* = तनोमि, 2. *tano* + *si* = तनोषि by 70; Du. 1. *tanu* + *vas* = तनुवस् or तन्वस्; Pl. 1. *tanu* + *mas* = तनुमस् or तन्मस्; Impv. 1. *tano* + *āni* = तनवानि by 36. *b*, 2. तनु *tanu*). Compare the Greek τάνυμι, τάνυμεν.

a. The root सन् *san*, 'to give,' optionally rejects its *n*, and lengthens the radical *a* before the *y* of the potential: thus, सन्याम् *sanyām* or सायाम् *sāyām*, &c.

b. When the vowel of a root is capable of Guṇa, it may optionally take it: thus the base of ऋण् 'to go' may be either ऋणु or अर्णु (1. अर्णोमि or ऋणोमि).

355. One root in this class, कृ *kri*, 'to do,' 'to make,' is by far the most common and useful in the language. This root guṇates the radical vowel *ri*, as well as the conjugational *u*, before the P terminations. Before the other terminations it changes the radical *ri* to *ur*. The rejection of the conjugational *u* before initial *m* (not marked with P) and *v*, which is allowable in the 5th class, is in this

verb compulsory, and is, moreover, required before initial *y*. Hence the three bases *karo*, *kuru*, and *kur*. See 682.

(GROUP III.)—*Ninth class, containing about 52 primitive verbs.*

356. Rule for forming the base in the four conjugational tenses. Add ना *nā* to the root before the P terminations; नी *nī* before all the others, except those beginning with vowels, where only न् *n* is added, by 293. *a.* Observe—ना, नी, and न्, are changeable to णा, णी, and ण्, by 58.

357. Thus, from यु *yu*, 'to join,' are formed the three bases *yunā*, *yunī*, and *yun* (Pres. 1. *yunā* + *mi* = युनामि; Du. 1. *yunī* + *vas* = युनीवस्; Pl. 1. *yunī* + *mas* = युनीमस्, 3. *yun* + *anti* = युनन्ति. Pres. Ātm. 1. *yun* + *e* = युने; Impv. 1. *yunā* + *ni* = युनानि, 2. *yunī* + *hi* = युनीहि, &c.).

a. Observe—Roots ending in consonants substitute *āna* for their conjugational sign in the 2d sing. imperative, and reject the termination *hi*: so, अशान 'eat thou,' from अश् 'to eat;' पुषाण 'nourish thou,' from पुष्; क्षुभाण 'shake thou,' from क्षुभ्, &c. See 696, 698, 694.

358. री 'to go,' व्ली 'to go,' प्ली 'to go,' 'to choose,' व्री 'to choose,' ली 'to adhere,' भ्री 'to fear,' 'to bear,' क्षी 'to destroy,' धू 'to shake,' पू 'to purify' (583), लू 'to cut' (691), ॠ 'to go,' कॄ 'to hurt,' गॄ 'to sound,' जॄ 'to grow old,' दॄ 'to split,' नॄ 'to lead,' पॄ 'to fill,' भॄ 'to bear,' 'to blame,' मॄ 'to kill,' वॄ or वॄ 'to choose,' शॄ 'to injure,' स्तॄ 'to spread,' कॄ or गॄ or स्तॄ or मॄ 'to hurt,' shorten the radical vowel in forming their bases: thus, from पू 'to purify' come the bases *punā*, *punī*, and *pun*: see the table at 683.

a. क्री 'to buy,' प्री 'to love,' श्री 'to cook,' क्नु or क्नू* 'to sound,' वृ 'to hurt,' do not shorten their vowels. See 689, 690.

359. ग्रह्, 'to take,' becomes गृह्, and makes its bases गृह्णा, गृह्णी, and गृह्ण्. See 699.

a. ज्या, 'to grow old,' becomes जि, and makes its bases *jinā*, *jinī*, and *jin*.

360. बन्ध्, ग्रन्थ्, मन्थ्, श्रन्थ्, कुन्थ्, and स्कम्भ्, reject the radical nasal in favour of the conjugational: thus, from *bandh* are formed the three bases *badhnā*, *badhnī*, and *badhn*. See 692, 693, 695.

361. ज्ञा 'to know,' in the same way, rejects its nasal in favour of the conjugational, and makes its bases *jānā*, *jānī*, and *jān*. See 688.

362. खव्, 'to appear as a spectre,' changes *v* to *u*, and makes its bases *khaunā*, *khaunī*, and *khaun*.

---

* क्नू, however, may optionally shorten it.

PRIMITIVE VERBS OF THE FIRST NINE CLASSES IN THE SIX NON-CONJUGATIONAL TENSES.

363. Observe—The general rules for the formation of the base in the perfect (or 2d preterite), 1st and 2d futures, aorist (or 3d preterite), precative (or benedictive), and conditional, apply to all verbs of the first nine classes indiscriminately; see 250. *a*. The 10th class alone carries its conjugational characteristic into most of the non-conjugational tenses; and for this reason the consideration of its last tenses falls most conveniently under causal verbs. Compare 289. *a*.

Reduplicated perfect (*second preterite*).

Terminations repeated from page 127.

Parasmai.			Átmane.		
a (*au*)	**iva*	**ima*	*e*	**ivahe*	**imahe*
itha or *tha*	*athus*	*a*	**ishe*	*áthe*	**idhve* or **iḍhve*
a (*au*)	*atus*	*us*	*e*	*áte*	*ire*

364. Rule for forming the base in verbs of the first nine classes. In the first place, if a root begin with a consonant, reduplicate the initial consonant, with its vowel, according to the rules given at 330 (but *a* is reduplicated for a radical *a*, *á*, *ri*, *rí*, *lri* (and even for radical *e*, *ai*, *o*, if final); *i* for *i*, *í*, *e*; *u* for *u*, *ú*, *o*): thus, from पच् *pać*, 'to cook,' *papać*; from याच् *yáć*, 'to ask,' *yayáć*; from कृ *kri*, 'to do,' *ćakri*; from नृत् *nrit*, 'to dance,' *nanrit*; from तॄ *trí*, 'to cross,' *tatrí*; from क्लृप् *klrip*, 'to be able,' *ćaklrip*; from मे *me*, 'to change,' *mame*; from गै *gai*, 'to sing,' *jagai*; from सो *so*, 'to finish,' *saso*; from सिध् *sidh*, 'to accomplish,' *sishidh* (70); from जीव् *jív*, 'to live,' *jijív*; from सेव् *sev*, 'to serve,' *sishev*; from द्रु *dru*, 'to run,' *dudru*; from पू *pú*, 'to purify,' *pupú*; from बुध् *budh*, 'to know,' *bubudh*; from लोक् *lok*, 'to see,' *lulok*; from स्मि *smi*, 'to smile,' *sishmi*; from स्था *sthá*, 'to stand,' *tasthá*.

a. And if it begin with a vowel, double the initial vowel: thus, from अस् *as*, 'to be,' comes *a as* = आस् *ás* by 31; from आप् *áp*, 'to obtain,' *a áp* = *áp*; from इष् *ish*, 'to wish,' *i ish* = *ísh* (see 31).

b. In the second place, if the root end in a consonant, gunate † the vowel of the radical syllable, if capable of Guṇa (see 28. *b*), in

---

† The gunation of the vowel is indicated by the P of णल्, थल्, णल्, in the singular terminations. See scheme at 246.

1st, 2d, and 3d *singular*, Parasmai-pada; but leave the vowel unchanged before all other terminations, both Parasmai and Ātmane-pada. See 293. *a*.

c. If the root end in a simple consonant, preceded by short *a*, this *a* is lengthened optionally in 1st and necessarily in 3d sing.; and before the other terminations it is either left unchanged, or is liable to become *e* (see 375. *a*).

d. If the root end in a vowel, vṛiddhi the vowel of the radical syllable in 1st and 3d *singular*, Parasmai *, and guṇate it in 2d *sing.* (optionally in 1st sing.). Before all other terminations, Parasmai and Ātmane, the root must revert to its original form, but the terminations must be affixed according to euphonic rules.

e. Greek affords many examples of verbs which suffer a kind of Guṇa or Vṛiddhi change in the perfect; but this change is not confined to the singular, as in Sanskṛit. Compare λέλοιπα (from λείπω, ἔλιπον), πέποιθα (from πείθω, ἔπιθον), τέτροφα (from τρέφω), τέθεικα (from τίθημι), &c.

365. Thus, from बुध् *budh*, 1st c., comes the base of the singular Parasm. बुबोध् *bubodh*, and the base of the rest of the tense बुबुध् *bubudh* (1. *bubodh* + *a* = *bubodha*, 2. *bubodh* + *itha* = *bubodhitha*, 3. *bubodh* + *a* = *bubodha*; Du. 1. *bubudh* + *iva* = *bubudhiva*, 2. *bubudh* + *athus* = *bubudhathus*, &c. Ātm. 1. *bubudh* + *e* = *bubudhe*, &c.). Similarly, from विद् *vid*, 2d c., 'to know,' come the two bases विवेद् *vived* and विविद् *vivid*; from पच्, 'to cook,' the two bases पपाच् *papāć* and पपच् *papać* (1. 3. *viveda*; Du. 1. *vividiva*; Pl. 1. *vividima*, &c.: 1. *papāća* or *papaća*, 3. *papāća*, &c.).

a. There is one Greek root which agrees very remarkably with the Sanskṛit in restricting Guṇa to the singular, viz. ϝιδ (εἴδω), 'to know,' answering to the Sanskṛit *vid* above: thus, οἶδα, οἶσθα, οἶδε; ἴστον, ἴστον; ἴσμεν, ἴστε, ἴσασι. The root *vid* has a contracted form of its perfect used for the present, which agrees exactly with οἶδα: thus, *veda*, *vettha*, &c. See 308. *a*.

366. Again, from कृ *kṛi*, 'to do' (see 684), comes the base of the 1st and 3d singular Parasm. चकार् *ćakār* (331. *a*), the base of the 2d sing. चकर् *ćakar* (which is optionally the base of the 1st sing. also), and the base of the rest of the tense चकृ *ćakṛi* (1. *ćakār* + *a* = *ćakāra* (or *ćakara*), 2. *ćakar* + *tha* = *ćakartha*, 3. *ćakār* + *a* = *ćakāra*: Du. 1. *ćakṛi* + *va* = *ćakṛiva* (369), 2. *ćakṛi* + *athus* = *ćakrathus* by 34. Ātm. 1. *ćakṛi* + *e* = *ćakre*; Pl. 2. *ćakṛi* + *ḍhve* = चकृढ्वे. See 684).

---

* Vṛiddhi is indicated by the ण् of णप् ṇaP. See scheme at 246.

a. Observe—The roots enumerated at 390. *a.* reject Guṇa in the 2d sing.; thus, भिद् makes 1. 3. बिभेद, but 2. बिभेदिथ. So कु or कू 'to cry' makes 1. चुकाव or चुकव, 2. चुकुविथ.

367. We have seen at 364. *a.* that if a root, ending in a single consonant, begin with a vowel, this vowel is repeated, and the two similar vowels blend into one long one by 31. But when an initial *i* or *u* is guṇated in the sing. Parasmai, then the reduplicated *i* becomes *iy* before *e*, and the reduplicated *u* becomes *uv* before *o*: thus, from इष् *ish*, 'to wish,' come the two bases *iyesh* and *īsh* (1. 3. इयेष; Du. 1. ईषिव; see 637); and from उख् *ukh*, 'to move,' *uvokh* and *ūkh* (1. 3. उवोख; Du. 1. ऊखिव).

a. The same holds good in the root इ *i*, 'to go,' which makes the reduplicated syllable *iy* before the Vṛiddhi and Guṇa of the sing. In the remainder of the tense the base becomes *iy* (compare 375. *e*), which is reduplicated into *īy* (1. 3. इयाय, 2. इययिथ or इयेथ; Du. 1. ईयिव). But when the prep. *adhi* is prefixed, the perfect is formed as if from *gā*, Ātmane only (Sing. Du. Pl. 3. *adhijage*, *-jagāte*, *-jagire*).

b. And if a root begin with अ *a*, and end in a *double* consonant, or begin with ऋ *ṛi* and end in a single consonant, the reduplicated syllable is आन् *ān*: thus, from अर्च् *arć*, 'to worship,' comes the base आनर्च् *ānarć* (1. 3. आनर्च); from ऋध् *ṛidh*, 'to flourish,' comes आनर्ध् *ānardh* (1. 3. आनर्ध; Du. 1. आनृधिव, &c.).

c. अश् Ātm. 'to pervade,' although ending in a *single* consonant श्, follows the last rule (1. 3. आनशे).

368. Observe—In the perfect (or 2d preterite) the 1st and 3d sing. Parasmai and Ātmane have the same termination, and are generally identical in form; but when Vṛiddhi of a final vowel is required in both, then there is optionally Guṇa in the first; and when a medial *a* is lengthened, this *a* may optionally remain unchanged in the first: thus कृ 'to do' may be in 1st sing. either चकार or चकर, and पच् 'to cook' may be either पपाच or पपच in 1st sing.; but in 3d sing. these roots can only make चकार and पपाच.

369. By referring back to the scheme at pp. 160, 127, it will be seen that all the terminations of this tense (except optionally the 2d sing. Parasmai) begin with vowels. Those which begin with *i* are all (except the 3d pl. Ātmane) distinguished by the mark *, because

eight roots only in the language (viz. कृ 'to do*,' भृ 'to bear,' सृ 'to go,' वृ 'to surround,' श्रु 'to hear,' स्तु 'to praise,' द्रु 'to run,' स्रु *sru*, 'to flow') *necessarily* reject the *i* from these terminations.

Rejection of i *from* itha (*2d sing. perfect, Parasmai*).

370. The above eight roots (except वृ *vri* when it means 'to cover,' and except कृ *kri*, 'to do,' when compounded with the prep. *sam**) also reject *i* from the 2d sing. Parasmai.

a. Moreover, the 2d sing. Parasmai is formed with *tha* instead of *itha* after roots ending in ऋ *ri* (except after the root ऋ *ri* itself, and वृ *vri* and जागृ *jágri*, which only allow *itha*: thus, *áritha*, *vavaritha*, *jágaritha*; and except स्वृ at *b*);

b. and optionally with *tha* or *itha* after the root स्वृ *svri*, 'to sound' (*sasvartha* or *sasvaritha*);

c. and optionally with *tha* or *itha* after roots ending in आ *á*, ए *e* (except व्ये *vye*, which allows only *itha*), and after roots in ऐ *ai*, ओ *o*, इ *i*, ई *í*, उ *u*, and the root धू 'to shake' (except those indicated at 397, 398, as necessarily inserting *i* in the futures &c.; e. g. श्रि, which makes *śiśrayitha* only, and so also most roots in ऊ *ú*);

d. and optionally with *tha* or *itha* after those roots enumerated at 400—414, which have a medial *a*, and which reject *i* either necessarily or optionally from the futures &c. (e. g. शक्, *śekitha* or *śaśaktha*; क्षम्, *ćakshamitha* or *ćakshantha*, &c.); but not अद् and घस्, which can only make *áditha*, *jaghasitha*;

e. and optionally with *tha* or *itha* after most of the roots enumerated at 415, as optionally inserting *i* in the futures &c.:

f. but all other roots, which necessarily take *i*, and even most of those (*having no medial a*) at 400—414 which necessarily reject *i* in the futures &c., must take *itha* only in the 2d sing. of the perfect: thus तुद् is तोत्तासि *tottási* in the 2d sing. 1st future, but तुतोदिथ *tutoditha* in the 2d sing. perfect (Du. 1. *tutudiva*). Some few of these, however, are allowed the alternative of *tha*, as सृज् 'to create' makes ससर्जिथ or सस्रष्ठ; दृश् 'to see,' ददर्शिथ or दद्रष्ठ; both these roots requiring the radical *ri* to be changed to र *ra*, instead of guṇated, when *tha* is used.

g. मस्ज् 'to dip' and नश् 'to perish,' which belong to 370. *d*, insert a nasal when *tha* is used: thus, ममज्जिथ or ममंक्थ, नेशिथ or ननंष्ठ.

* But कृ 'to do,' if स् is inserted after a preposition, as in संस्कृ, does not reject *i*, and follows 375. *k*: thus, 2. संचस्करिथ.

b. तृप् 'to be satisfied' and दृप् 'to be proud,' which belong to 370. *e*, either gunate the radical *ṛi* or change it to र *ra* when *tha* is used (ततर्प्थ or तत्रप्थ or ततर्पिथ).

Observe—When *tha* is affixed to roots ending in consonants, the rules of Sandhi, propounded at 296, &c., must be applied.

Optional rejection of i, *in certain cases, from the dual and remaining terminations (of the perfect, Parasmai and Ātmane, marked with* *).

371. The roots enumerated at 415, as optionally rejecting or inserting *i* in the futures &c., may optionally reject it also from the dual and remaining terminations of the perfect marked with * in the table at p. 160: thus क्षम् makes चक्षमिव or चक्षण्व, चक्षंसे or चक्षमिषे, चक्षमिध्वे or चक्षन्ध्वे; but the forms with the inserted *i* are the most usual, and all other roots, even those which necessarily reject *i* from the futures &c. (except the eight enumerated at 369), must take *i* in the dual and remaining terminations of the perfect marked with *.

Observe—The *i* is never rejected from the 3d plur. Ātmane, except in the Veda.

Substitution of ढ्वे *for* ध्वे *(2d plur. perfect, Ātmane).*

372. ढ्वे is used instead of ध्वे by the eight roots at 369, also in certain cases by the roots mentioned at 371. The usual rules of Sandhi must then be observed, as in चकृढ्वे from कृ.

a. इढ्वे for इध्वे may be optionally used by other roots when a semivowel or *h* immediately precedes, as लुलुविध्वे or -विढ्वे from लू, शिश्रियिध्वे or -यिढ्वे from श्रि.

Anomalies in forming the base of the perfect (second preterite).

373. Roots ending in आ *ā* (as दा *dā*, 'to give;' धा *dhā*, 'to place;' या *yā*, 'to go;' स्था *sthā*, 'to stand') drop the *ā* before all the terminations except the *tha* of the 2d sing., and substitute औ *au* for the terminations of the 1st and 3d sing. Parasmai. Hence, from दा *dā* comes the base दद् *dad* (1. 3. ददौ, 2. ददिथ or ददाथ; Du. 1. ददिव. Ātm. 1. 3. ददे, 2. ददिषे, &c. See 663).

a. दरिद्रा 'to be poor' makes 1. 3. ददरिद्रौ; Du. 3. ददरिद्रतुस्; Pl. 3. ददरिद्रुस्; or more properly takes the periphrastic form of perfect. See 385.

b. ज्या 'to grow old' has a reduplicated base जिज्या (1. 3. जिज्यौ, 2. जिज्याथ or जिज्यिथ; Du. 1. जिज्यिव). Similarly, an uncommon root व्ये Ātm. 'to instruct' makes 1. 3. विव्ये.

c. क्षि 'to throw,' क्षी 'to destroy,' 'to perish,' *must* be treated in the sing. as if they ended in *á*; and ली 9th c., 'to obtain,' may optionally be so treated: thus, Sing. 1. ममौ, 2. ममाथ or ममिथ, 3. ममौ; Du. 1. मिम्यिव. But ली is 1. ललौ or लिलाय, 2. ललाथ or ललिथ or लिलेथ or लिलयिथ; Du. 1. लिलियिव.

d. Most roots ending in the diphthongs ए *e* (except ह्वे, दे, व्ये, वे, &c., see next rules), ऐ *ai*, ओ *o*, follow 373, and form their perfect as if they ended in *á*: thus, धे 1st c. 'to drink,' 1st and 3d sing. दधौ, 2. दधिथ or दधाथ, Du. 1. दधिव; गै 1st c. 'to sing,' 1. 3. जगौ, 2. जगिथ or जगाथ; म्लै 1st c. 'to fade,' 1. 3. मम्लौ; शो 4th c. 'to sharpen,' 1. 3. शशौ.

e. But ह्वे 'to call' forms its base as if from हु, see 595 (1. 3. जुहाव, &c.).

f. दे Átm. 'to pity,' 'to protect,' makes its base *digi* (1. 3. दिग्ये, 2. दिग्यिषे, &c.).

g. व्ये 'to cover' makes *vivyáy*, *vivyay*, and *vivy* (1. 3. विव्याय, 2. विव्ययिथ; Du. 1. विव्ययिव or विव्यिव, &c.).

h. वे 'to weave' forms its bases as if from *vá* or *vav* or *uy* (1. 3. ववौ or उवाय, 2. वविथ or ववाथ or उवयिथ; Du. 1. वविव or ऊविव or ऊयिव, &c. Átm. 1. 3. ववे or ऊवे or ऊये, &c.).

i. प्यै Átm. 'to be fat' makes regularly पप्ये, पप्यिषे, &c.; but the root प्याय्, meaning the same, and often identified with प्यै, makes पिप्ये, पिप्यिषे, &c.

374. If a root end in इ *i* or ई *í*, this vowel does not blend with the initial *i* of the terminations in du. pl. Parasmai, sing. du. pl. Átmane, but is changed to *y*, in opposition to 31: thus, from चि *ći*, 5th c. 'to collect,' come the bases *ćićai*, *ćiće*, and *ćići*, changeable to *ćićáy*, *ćićay*, and *ćićy* (1. 3. *ćićáya*, 2. *ćićayitha* or *ćićetha*; Du. 1. चिच्यिव *ćićyiva*, 2. *ćićyathus* by 34. Átm. 1. 3. *ćićye*. See the table at 583). Observe—चि may also substitute चिकाय for चिचाय and चिक्ये for चिच्ये.

a. Similarly, नी *ní*, 'to lead' (1. 3. *nináya*; Du. 1. *ninyiva*. Átm. 1. *ninye*, &c.).

b. जि *ji*, 'to conquer,' makes its base जिगि, as if from *gi* (1. 3. जिगाय; Du. 1. जिग्यिव, &c. See 590).

c. हि *hi*, 'to go,' 'to send,' makes जिघि, as if from *ghi* (1. 3. जिघाय).

d. दी Átm. 'to sink,' 'to decay,' makes its base दिदीय् throughout: thus, 1. 3. दिदीये, 2. दिदीयिषे, &c.

e. But roots ending in इ *i* or ई *í*, and having a double initial consonant, change *i* or *í* to इय् *iy* before all terminations, except those of the sing. Parasmai; hence, from श्रि 1st c., 'to have recourse,' come the three bases *śiśrai*, *śiśre*, and *śiśriy* (1. 3. शिश्राय, 2. शिश्रयिथ; Du. 1. शिश्रियिव, &c.). So क्री 9th c. 'to buy' (1. 3. चिक्राय, 2. चिक्रयिथ or चिक्रेथ; Du. 1. चिक्रियिव, &c. See 689).

f. श्वि *śvi*, 'to swell,' like ह्वे at 373. *e*, forms its base as if from शु, but only optionally: thus, 1. 3. शिश्वाय or शुशाव, 2. शिश्वेथ or शिश्वयिथ or शुशोथ or शुशविथ.

g. And *all roots* ending in उ *u* or ऊ *ú* change *u* or *ú* to उव् *uv* before the terminations of the du. and plur. Parasmai and the whole Átmane (except of course श्रु, स्तु, द्रु, स्रु, in the persons marked with * at p. 127; and except भू 'to be,' see next rule but one): thus, from धू *dhú*, 'to shake,' come the bases *dudhau*, *dudho*, and *dudhuv* (1. 3. दुधाव, 2. दुधविथ or दुधोथ; Du. 1. दुधुविव. Átm. 1. 3. दुधुवे). Similarly, उ *u*, Átm. 'to sound,' makes 1. 3. ऊवे, 2. ऊविषे.

h. But शु makes 1. 3. शुशाव, 2. शुशोथ; Du. 1. शुशुव, 2. शुशुवथुः. Ātm. 1. 3. शुशुवे; and similarly, स्नु, द्रु, and स्रु *sru*.

i. भू 'to be' is anomalous, and makes its base बभूव् throughout; see 585, 586. So सू 'to bring forth' makes in the Veda ससूव.

j. ऊर्णु 'to cover' (although properly requiring the periphrastic form of perfect, see 385) is reduplicated into ऊर्णुनु. In the 2d sing. it may reject Guṇa: thus, ऊर्णुनविथ or ऊर्णुनुविथ, 3d sing. ऊर्णुनाव; Du. 1. ऊर्णुनुविव, 3. ऊर्णुनुवतुः; Pl. 3. ऊर्णुनुवुः.

k. Roots ending in the vowel ऋ *ṛi*, *preceded by a double consonant*, and most roots in long ॠ *ṛī*, instead of retaining this vowel and changing it to *r* by 364. *d*, guṇate it into *ar* in the 2d sing., and throughout the whole tense, except the 1st and 3d sing. (and even in the 1st there may be optionally Guṇa by 368): thus, from स्मृ *smṛi*, 'to remember,' 1. *sasmára* or *sasmara*, 2. *sasmartha*, 3. *sasmára*; Du. 1. *sasmariva*, &c. Ātm. 1. 3. *sasmare*.

l. But धृ *dhṛi*, 'to hold,' not being preceded by a double consonant, makes regularly 1. Sing. Du. Pl. दधार, दध्रिव, दध्रिम.

m. पॄ 'to fill,' शॄ 'to injure,' and दॄ 'to rend,' may *optionally* retain *ṛi*, changeable to *r*: thus, Du. पपरिव or पप्रिव.

n. ऋ *ṛi*, 'to go,' takes Vṛiddhi, and makes its base आर् *ár* throughout: thus, 1. 3. आर, 2. आरिथ; Du. 1. आरिव.

o. मृ Ātm. 'to die,' although properly Ātmane, is Parasmai in perfect: thus 1. 3. ममार, 2. ममर्थ.

p. जागृ 'to awake,' which properly takes the periphrastic form of perfect (जागरांचकार, see 385), may also take the reduplicated form, and may optionally drop the reduplicated syllable: thus, 1. 3. जजागार or जागार, 2. जजागरिथ or जागरिथ (370. *a*).

q. गॄ 'to swallow' may optionally change र् to ल्: thus, जगार or जगाल.

r. त्रॄ 'to pass' follows 375. *a*, as if it were तर्: thus, 1. 3. ततार, 2. तेरिथ; Du. 1. तेरिव.

s. जॄ 'to grow old' optionally follows 375. *a* (3. जजार, 2. जजरिथ or जेरिथ; Du. 3. जजरतुः or जेरतुः).

375. We have already seen, at 364, that roots beginning with any consonant and ending with a single consonant, and enclosing short अ *a*, lengthen this vowel in the 3d sing. and optionally in the 1st; as, from पच् *pach*, 'to cook,' पपाच् *papách*; from *tyaj*, 'to quit,' *tatyáj* (1. 3. *tatyája*, 2. *tatyajitha* or *tatyaktha*; Du. 1. *tatyajiva*, &c.).

a. Moreover, before *itha* and in the dual and plur. Parasmai, and all the persons of the Ātmane, if the initial as well as the final consonant of the root be single, and if the root does not begin with व् *v*, and does not require a substituted consonant in the reduplication, the reduplication is suppressed, and, to compensate for this, the अ a is changed to ए e*: thus, from pać come the bases पपाच् papáć, papać, and पेच् peć (1. papáća or papaća, 2. pećitha or papaktha, 3. papáća 296; Du. 1. pećiva. Átm. 1. 3. peće, &c.). Similarly, from लभ् labh, 1st c. Átm., 'to obtain' (cf. λαμβάνω, ἔλαβον), the base लेभ् lebh throughout (lebhe, lebhishe, lebhe, lebhimahe, &c.). So नह् nah, 'to bind,' makes 1. nanáha or nanaha, 2. nehitha or nanaddha, 3. nanáha by 305; Du. 1. nehiva, &c. Átm. nehe, &c.

Similarly, नश् naś, 'to perish,' 1. nanáśa or nanaśa, 2. neśitha or nanaṃshṭha (ननंष्ठ), 3. nanáśa, &c.: see 620, 370. g.

b. Roots that require a substituted consonant in the reduplication are excepted from 375. a (but not भज् bhaj and फल् phal, see g. below): thus, भण् 'to speak' makes 1. 3. बभाण; Du. 1. बभणिव.

c. वच् 'to speak,' वद् 'to say,' वप् 'to sow,' वश् 'to wish,' वस् 'to dwell,' वह् 'to carry,' beginning with v, are also excepted. These require that the reduplicated syllable be उ u, or the corresponding vowel of the semivowel, and also change va of the root to उ u before every termination, except those of the sing. Parasmai, the two u's blending into one long ऊ ú: thus, from वच् vać, 'to speak,' come the two bases उवाच् uváć and ऊच् úć (1. uváća or uvaća, 2. uvaćitha or uvaktha, 3. uváća; Du. 3. úćatus; Pl. 3. úćus).

वह् vah, 'to carry,' changes the radical vowel to ओ o before tha (see 305. a), optionally substituted for itha (1. 3. उवाह, 2. उवहिथ or उवोढ). Compare 424.

d. Observe—वम् vam, 'to vomit,' is excepted from 375. c (thus, 3. vavāma, vavamatus, vavamus, Páṇ. VI. 4, 126); it may also, according to Vopadeva, follow 375. a (3. vavāma, vematus, vemus).

e. यज् yaj, 'to sacrifice,' is excepted from 375. a, and follows the analogy of 375. c (1. 3. iyája; Du. 3. íjatus; Pl. 3. íjus): the 2d sing. is इयजिथ or इयष्ठ by 297; Átmane 1. 3. ईजे, 2. ईजिषे, see 597. Yej is allowed optionally in the weak forms, and optionally in 2d sing., especially in the Veda.

f. शस् 'to injure' and दद् Átm. 'to give' are excepted from 375. a (शशास, शशसिथ, दददिषे).

g. भज् 'to honour,' फल् 'to loosen,' त्रप् 'to be ashamed,' फल् 'to bear fruit,' necessarily conform to 375. a, although properly excepted (thus, भेजिव, भेजिम, &c.). The following conform to 375. a. optionally: फण् 'to go,' स्वन् 'to sound,' (according to some) ध्वन् 'to sound,' भ्रम् 'to wander,' वम् 'to vomit,' and (according to some) स्वन् and स्यम् 'to sound,' त्रस् 'to tremble' (thus, पफणिव or फेणिव, तत्रसिव or त्रेसिव, &c.).

h. The following also conform optionally to 375. a: ग्रन्थ् 'to tie,' श्रन्थ् 'to loosen,' दम्भ् 'to deceive;' and, when they do so, drop their nasals (thus, जग्रन्थिव or ग्रेथिव, ददम्भुम or देभुम).

i. The following, although their radical vowel is long, also conform optionally

* Bopp deduces forms like pećima, from papaćima, by supposing that the second p is suppressed, the two a's combined into á, and á weakened into e.

to 375. *a*: राज्, भ्राज् Âtm., भ्राश्, and भ्लाश्, all meaning 'to shine' (रराजिथ or रेजिथ, &c.).

f. राध्, when it signifies 'to injure,' necessarily conforms to 375. *a* (2. रेधिथ; Du. 1. रेधिव, 3. रेधतुस्; Pl. 3. रेधुस्).

h. तॄ 'to pass' follows 375. *a*, and जॄ 'to grow old' may do so. See 374. *r*, *s*.

376. गम् *gam*, 'to go,' जन् *jan*, 'to be born,' खन् *khan*, 'to dig,' and हन् *han*, 'to kill' (which last forms its perfect as if from घन् *ghan*), drop the medial *a* before all the terminations, except those of the sing. Parasm. (compare the declension of *rájan* at 149). Hence, *gam* makes in sing. du. pl. 3. *jagáma*, *jagmatus*, *jagmus*; *jan* makes *jajána*, *jajnatus*, *jajnus*; *khan* makes *čakhána*, *čakhnatus*, *čakhnus*; and *han* makes 1. 3. *jaghána*, *jaghnatus*, *jaghnus*, 2. *jaghanitha* or *jaghantha*.

377. घस् *ghas*, 'to eat,' is analogous, making *jaghása*, *jakshatus*, *jakshus*; Du. 1. *jakshiva*. See 42 and 70. And in the Veda some other roots follow this analogy: thus, पत् 'to fall' (पप्तिम &c.); तन् 'to stretch' (तत्निषे &c.); भस् 'to eat' (बप्सिम &c.).

378. सञ्ज् 'to adhere,' स्वञ्ज् 'to embrace,' and दंश् 'to bite,' can optionally drop their nasals in du. pl. Parasmai and all the Âtmane: thus, ससञ्जिव or ससजिव, सस्वञ्जे or सस्वजे.

379. रध् 'to perish' and जभ् Âtm. 'to yawn' may insert a nasal before vowel-terminations (ररन्ध, ररन्धिथ or ररद्ध; Du. 1. ररन्धिव or रेध्व, see 371: 1. 3. जजम्भे).

380. मृज् 'to clean' makes its base ममार्ज् in sing. Parasmai, and may do so before the remaining terminations (1. 3. ममार्ज, 2. ममार्जिथ or ममार्ष्ठ; Du. 1. ममार्जिव or ममृजिव or ममृज्व, see 651).

381. प्रछ् *pračh*, 'to ask,' makes its base पप्रछ्* throughout; see 631. भ्रस्ज् *bhrajj*, 6th c., 'to fry,' makes either बभर्ज् or बभ्रज्ज् throughout. See 632.

a. ऋछ् or ऋच्छ् 'to go' gunates the radical vowel throughout: thus, 1. 3. आनर्छ, 2. आनर्छिथ; Du. 1. आनर्छिव.

382. स्वप् *svap*, 'to sleep,' makes its bases सुष्वाप् and सुषुप्. See 655.

a. ष्ठिव् or ष्टिव् 'to spit' may substitute त् *t* for ट् *ṭ* in the reduplication: thus, 1. 3. टिष्ठेव or तिष्ठेव, टिष्टेव or तिष्टेव.

383. व्यध् 'to pierce,' व्यच् 'to encompass,' 'to deceive,' व्यथ् Âtm. 'to be pained,' make their reduplicated syllable *vi*; and the first two roots change *vya* to *vi* before all the terminations, except the sing. Parasmai: thus, from *vyadh* comes sing. du. pl. 3. विव्याध, विविधतुस्, विविधुस्; Âtm. विविधे, &c.: from *vyač*, विव्याच, विविचतुस्, विविचुस्: from *vyath*, विव्यथे, विव्यथाते, विव्यथिरे. See 615 and 629.

a. द्युत् 1st c. Âtm., 'to shine,' makes its reduplicated syllable *di* (1. 3. *didyute*).

384. ग्रह् *grah*, 9th c., 'to take,' makes its base जग्राह् and जगृह् (S. Du. Pl. 3. जग्राह, जगृहतुस्, जगृहुस्). But sing. 2. जग्रहिथ. See 699.

a. गुह् 'to conceal' lengthens its radical vowel instead of gunating it in the sing. Paras. जुगूह, जुगूहिथ, &c.

---

* This rests on Siddhánta Kaum. 134. Some grammarians make the base in du. and pl. &c. पपृछ्.

b. अह् *ah*, 'to say,' is only used in the perfect. It is defective in sing. du. pl. 1. and pl. 2, and forms 2d sing. from आत् (2. आत्थ, 3. आह; Du. 2. आहथुस्, 3. आहतुस्; Pl. 3. आहुस्).

c. ब्रू 'to say' has no perfect of its own, but substitutes either that of वच् (375. *e*) or the above forms from अह्. Again, अद् 'to eat' has a perfect of its own, but may substitute that of घस् 378. Similarly, अज् 'to drive' (*ago*) may substitute that of वी.

Periphrastic perfect.

385. Roots which begin with a vowel, long by nature or position (*except the vowel á, as in* आप् *'to obtain,'* 364. *a, and in* आछ् *'to stretch;' and except* ऋच्छ् *'to go,'* 381. *a; and roots having an initial a before two consonants,* 371), and all roots of more than one syllable (*except* ऊर्णु *'to cover,'* 375. *j; and except optionally* जागृ *'to awake,'* 375. *p, and* दरिद्रा *'to be poor,'* 373. *a*), form their perfects by adding आम् *ám* to the root or base (which generally guṇates its last vowel if ending in *i*, *u*, *ṛi*, short or long), and affixing the perfect of some one of the auxiliary verbs, अस् *as*, 'to be;' भू *bhú*, 'to be;' कृ *kṛi*, 'to do.'

a. Observe—This *ám* may be regarded as the accus. case of an abstract noun formed from the verbal base. With कार it becomes आंचकार or आञ्चकार by 59. Thus, from ईश्, 'to rule,' comes 1st and 3d sing. ईशामास or ईशांबभूव or ईशांचकार; the last might be translated 'he made ruling,' and in the former cases the accusative may be taken adverbially. So also, from चकास्, 'to shine,' comes चकासांचकार 'he made shining.'

b. When the Átmane-pada inflection has to be employed, कृ only is used: thus, ईड् Átm., 'to praise,' makes 1st and 3d sing. ईडांचक्रे 'he made praising or praised.'

c. Roots of the 10th class also form their perfect in this way, the syllable *ám* blending with the final *a* of the base: thus, from चुर् *ćur*, 10th c., 'to steal,' *ćorayámása*, 'I have or he has stolen.'

d. Also all derivative verbs, such as causals, desideratives, and frequentatives. See 490, 505, 513, 516.

e. Also the roots अय् *ay*, 'to go;' दय् *day*, Átm., 'to pity;' आस् *ás*, Átm., 'to sit;' कास् *kás*, 'to cough,' 'to shine' (कासांचक्रे &c.)*.

And optionally the roots भी *bhí*, 3d c., 'to fear' (बिभाय or बिभयांचकार); ह्री *hrí*, 3d c., 'to be ashamed' (जिह्राय or जिह्रयांचकार); भृ *bhṛi*, 3d c., 'to bear' (बभार or

* Páṇini III. 1. 37, 35.

बिभराञ्चकार); हु *hu*, 3d c., 'to sacrifice' (जुहाव or जुहवाञ्चकार); विद् *vid*, 2d c., 'to know' (विवेद or विदाञ्चकार); उष् *ush*, 1st c., 'to burn' (उवोष or ओषाञ्चकार).

f. The roots कम् Átm., गुप्, धूप्, विछ्, पण्, पन्, whose peculiarity of conjugational form is explained at 271, and ऋत् Átm. 'to blame,' may optionally employ a periphrastic perfect, not derived from the root, but from the conjugational base: thus, चकमे or कामयाञ्चक्रे, जुगोप or गोपायाञ्चकार, दुधूप or धूपायाञ्चकार, विविछ or विच्छायाञ्चकार, पेणे or पणायाञ्चकार, पेने or पनायाञ्चकार, आनर्ते or ऋतीयाञ्चक्रे.

g. Observe—Bases ending in *i*, *u*, or *ṛi*, short or long, are generally gunated before *ám*; but दीधी 'to shine' and वेवी 'to go' make दीध्याञ्चक्रे, वेव्याञ्चक्रे, &c.

386. *First and second future.*

Terminations of first future repeated from page 127.

Parasmai.			Átmane.		
tásmi	*tásvas*	*tásmas*	*táhe*	*tásvahe*	*tásmahe*
tási	*tásthas*	*tástha*	*táse*	*tásáthe*	*tádhve*
tá	*tárau*	*táras*	*tá*	*tárau*	*táras*

Terminations of second future repeated from page 128.

syámi	*syávas*	*syámas*	*sye*	*syávahe*	*syámahe*
syasi	*syathas*	*syatha*	*syase*	*syethe*	*syadhve*
syati	*syatas*	*syanti*	*syate*	*syete*	*syante*

a. Observe—The first future results from the union of the nom. case of the noun of agency (formed with the affix तृ *tṛi*, see 83. I) with the present tense of the verb अस् *as*, 'to be:' thus, taking दातृ *dátṛi*, 'a giver' (declined at 127), and combining its nom. case with अस्मि *asmi* and हे *he*, we have *dátásmi* and *dátáhe*, 'I am a giver,' identical with the 1st pers. sing. Parasmai and Átmane of the 1st fut., 'I will give.' So also *dátási* and *dátáse*, 'thou art a giver,' or 'thou wilt give.' In the 1st and 2d persons dual and plur. the sing. of the noun is joined with the dual and plur. of the auxiliary. In the 3d person the auxiliary is omitted, and the 3d sing. dual and plur. of the 1st future in both voices is then identical with the nom. case sing. dual and plur. of the noun of agency: thus, *dátá*, 'a giver,' or 'he will give;' *dátárau*, 'two givers,' or 'they two will give,' &c.*

387. The terminations of the second future appear also to be derived from the verb अस् joined, as in forming the passive and 4th conjugational class, with the *y* of the root या 'to go,' just as in English we often express the future tense by the phrase 'I am going.'

388. Rule for forming the base in verbs of the first nine classes. Gunate the vowel of the root (except as debarred at 28. *b*, and ex-

* The future signification inherent in the noun of agency *dátá*, seems implied in Latin by the relation of *dator* to *daturus*.

cept in certain roots of the 6th class, noted at 390, 390. a) throughout all the persons of both first and second future; and in all roots ending in consonants (except those enumerated at 400—414), and in a few ending in vowels (enumerated at 392), insert the vowel इ *i* between the root so guṇated, and the terminations.

389. Thus, from जि *ji*, 1st c., 'to conquer,' comes the base जे *je* (1st Fut. *je* + *tásmi* = जेतास्मि, &c.; Ātm. *je* + *táhe* = जेताहे. 2d Fut. *je* + *syámi* = जेष्यामि, &c.; Ātm. *je* + *sye* = जेष्ये, by 70). Similarly, from श्रु *śru*, 5th c., 'to hear,' comes the base श्रो *śro* (1st Fut. *śro* + *tásmi* = श्रोतास्मि, &c.; 2d Fut. *śro* + *syámi* = श्रोष्यामि, &c., by 70).

a. So also, from बुध् *budh*, 1st c., 'to know,' comes the base बोधि *bodhi* (1st Fut. *bodhi* + *tásmi* = बोधितास्मि, &c.; Ātm. *bodhi* + *táhe* = बोधिताहे. 2d Fut. *bodhi* + *syámi* = बोधिष्यामि, &c.; Ātm. *bodhi* + *sye* = बोधिष्ये).

390. The roots ending in उ *u* and ऊ *ū* of the 6th class, forbidding Guṇa, are कु or कू 'to call out,' गु or गू 'to void excrement,' ध्रु or ध्रू 'to be firm,' नु or नू 'to praise,' धू 'to shake.' These generally change their final *ū* to *uv*: thus, कुविताहे &c. from कू, but कुताहे &c. from कु; गुवितास्मि &c. from गू, but गुतास्मि &c. from गु.

a. The roots ending in consonants of the 6th class, not *guṇated*, are कुच् 'to contract,' गुज् 'to sound,' कुट् 'to make crooked,' पुट् 'to resist,' 'to oppose,' छुट् or त्रुट् 'to cut,' तुट् 'to quarrel,' लुट् 'to break,' पुट् 'to embrace,' 'to enclose,' तुड् or थुड् or स्थुड् 'to pound,' 'to break in pieces,' स्फुट् 'to burst in pieces,' घुट् 'to revolve,' 'to roll,' कुड् 'to play,' ब्रुड् or त्रुड् 'to be immersed,' चुड्, पुड्, थुड्, लुड्, कुड्, चुड्, हुड्, व्रुड्, स्थुड्, स्फुड्, all meaning 'to cover,' गुड् 'to guard,' तुड् 'to hinder,' चुट् 'to bind,' तुड् 'to strike,' छुट् 'to let out,' 'to emit,' लुट् 'to adhere,' कुड् 'to collect,' क्षिप् 'to throw,' गुर् Ātm. 'to make effort,' छुर् 'to cut,' स्फुर् or स्फुल् 'to glitter,' 'to quiver,' ध्रुव् 'to be firm,' 'to go,' कुड् 'to eat,'—nearly all uncommon as verbs. To these must be added विज् 7th c. 'to tremble.'

b. ऊर्णु 'to cover' may either guṇate its final or change it to *uv* (ऊर्णवितास्मि or ऊर्णुवितास्मि, ऊर्णविष्यामि or ऊर्णुविष्यामि).

c. दीधी Ātm. 'to shine,' वेवी Ātm. 'to go,' drop their finals before the inserted *i* (दीधिताहे &c.). Similarly, दरिद्रा 'to be poor' (दरिद्रितास्मि &c., दरिद्रिष्यामि &c.).

d. Roots in ए *e*, ऐ *ai*, ओ *o*, change their finals to *á*: thus, ह्वे 'to call' (ह्वातास्मि, ह्वास्यामि).

e. मि 'to throw,' मी 'to perish,' and दी Ātm. 'to decay,' *must* change, and ली 'to obtain' may optionally change their finals to *á* (मातास्मि, मास्यामि, &c.; दाताहे, &c.; लेतास्मि or लातास्मि, &c.; लेष्यामि or लास्यामि, &c.). Compare 373. e.

f. Roots containing the vowel *ṛi*, as सृप् 'to creep,' मृश् 'to handle,' स्पृश् 'to touch,' कृष् 'to draw,' are generally guṇated, but may optionally change the vowel ṛi to र ra: thus, कर्ष्टास्मि or क्रष्टास्मि &c., कर्क्ष्यामि or क्रक्ष्यामि &c.

g. Reversing this principle, भ्रस्ज् 'to fry' may make either भ्रष्टास्मि or भर्ष्टास्मि &c., भ्रक्ष्यामि or भर्क्ष्यामि &c.

h. The alternative is not allowed when *i* is inserted: thus, तृप् 'to be satisfied' makes तर्प्तास्मि or त्रप्तास्मि, but only तर्पितास्मि. Similarly, दृप् 'to be proud.'

i. सृज् 'to let go,' 'to create,' and दृश् 'to see,' necessarily change ṛi to *ra*: thus, स्रष्टास्मि, स्रक्ष्यामि, &c.; द्रष्टास्मि, द्रक्ष्यामि, &c.

j. मृज् 'to rub', 'to clean,' takes Vṛiddhi instead of Guṇa (मार्जितास्मि or मार्ष्टास्मि).

k. मस्ज् 'to be immersed,' and नश् 'to perish' when it rejects *i*, insert a nasal: thus, मंक्तास्मि, मंक्ष्यामि, &c.; नंष्टास्मि, नंक्ष्यामि, &c.; but नशितास्मि &c., नशिष्यामि &c.

l. कम् Ātm., गुप्, धूप्, विछ्, पण्, पन्, ऋत्, at 385. *f*, may optionally carry their peculiar conjugational form into the futures (कमिताहे or कामयिताहे, गोप्तास्मि or गोपितास्मि or गोपायितास्मि, विच्छितास्मि or विच्छायितास्मि, ऋतिताहे or ऋतीयिताहे, &c.).

m. गुह् 'to conceal' lengthens its vowel when *i* is inserted. See 415. *m*.

n. अस् 'to be,' ब्रू 'to say,' and चक्ष् 'to speak,' have no futures of their own, and substitute those of भू, वच्, and ख्या respectively; अद् 'to eat' may optionally substitute the futures of घस्, and अज् 'to drive' of वी (अजितास्मि or वेतास्मि &c.). Compare 384. *c*.

o. The rules at 296—306 must, of course, be applied to the two futures: thus, नह् 'to tie' makes नत्स्यामि &c. See 306. *b*.

Observe—The above rules apply generally to the aorist, precative (Ātmane), and conditional, as well as to the two futures.

391. It will be necessary here to give the rules for the insertion or rejection of the vowel इ *i*.

RULES FOR INSERTION OR REJECTION OF THE VOWEL इ *i*, IN FORMING THE LAST FIVE TENSES AND DESIDERATIVE.

a. Observe—These rules do not apply to form II of the aorist at 435, or to the Parasmai of the precative (benedictive) at 442, which can never insert *i*.

b. The manifest object of the inserted *i* is to take the place of the conjugational vowel, and prevent the coalition of consonants. Hence it is evident that roots ending in vowels do not properly require the inserted *i*. Nevertheless, even these roots often insert it; and if it were always inserted after roots ending in consonants, there would be no difficulty in forming the last five tenses of the Sanskṛit verb.

Unfortunately, however, its insertion is forbidden in about one hundred roots ending in consonants, and the combination of the final radical consonant with the initial *t* and *s* of the terminations will require an acquaintance with the rules already laid down at 296, &c.

We now proceed to enumerate, 1st, the roots which insert *i*; 2dly, those which reject it; 3dly, those which optionally insert or reject it.

Observe—In the following lists of roots the 3d sing. will sometimes be given between brackets, and the roots will be arranged in the order of their vowels.

It is of the utmost importance that the attention of the student be directed to this subject, as the assumption or rejection of this inserted vowel is not confined to the two futures, but extends to many other parts of the verb; insomuch, that if the first future reject इ *i*, it is generally rejected in form I of the aorist, in the *Átmane-pada* of the benedictive, in the conditional, infinitive mood, passive past participle, indeclinable past participle, future participle formed with the affix *tavya*, and noun of agency formed with the affix *tri*; and often (though not invariably) decides the formation of the desiderative form of the root by *s* instead of *ish*. So that the learner, if he know the first future, will pass on with greater ease to the formation of these other parts of the verb, and may always look to this tense as his guide. For example, taking the root *kship*, 'to throw,' and finding the 1st future to be *ksheptásmi*, he knows that *i* is rejected. Therefore he understands why it is that the 2d future is *kshepsyámi*; the aorist, *akshaipsam*; the *Átmane* of the benedictive, *kshipsíya*; the conditional, *akshepsyam*; the infinitive, *ksheptum*; the passive past participle, *kshipta*; the indeclinable participle, *kshiptvá*; the future participle, *ksheptavya*; the noun of agency, *ksheptri*; the desiderative, *ćikshipsámi*. On the other hand, taking the root *yáć*, 'to ask,' and finding the 1st future to be *yáćitá*, he knows that *i* is inserted, and therefore the same parts of the verb will be *yáćishyámi*, *ayáćisham*, *yáćishíya*, *ayáćishyam*, *yáćitum*, *yáćita*, *yáćitvá*, *yáćitavya*, *yáćitri*, *yiyáćishámi*, respectively.

Roots ending in vowels inserting इ *i* (*except as indicated at* 391. *a*).

As before remarked, it is evident that roots ending in vowels do not properly require the insertion of another vowel. The following, however, take *i*:

392. Five of those in इ *i* and ई *í*, viz. श्रि 'to have recourse' (श्रयति, अशिश्रियत्), श्वि 'to swell,' डी 'to fly,' शी 'to lie down,' स्मि 'to smile' (in desid. alone).

a. Six of those in उ *u*, viz. क्षु 'to sneeze,' क्ष्णु 'to sharpen,' नु 'to praise,' यु 'to join,' रु 'to sound,' 'to roar,' स्नु *snu* 'to ooze' (the last only when Parasmai *).

* If स्नु is inflected in the *Átmane*, it may reject *i*.

b. All in ऊ *ú*, as भू 'to be' (भविता, भविष्यति), except सू and धू (which optionally reject *i*), and except in the desiderative. See 395, 395. *a.*

c. All in short ऋ *ṛi*, in the 2d future and conditional, &c., but not in the 1st future, as कृ 'to do' (करिष्यति, but कर्ता).

d. Two in short ऋ *ṛi* (viz. वृ 'to choose' and जागृ 'to awake') also in 1st future (वरिता, वरिष्यति, जागरिता, &c.).

e. All in long ॠ *ṛí*, as तॄ 'to pass' (तरिता, तरिष्यति).

393. Observe—वृ 'to choose,' and all roots in long ॠ *ṛí*, may optionally lengthen the inserted i, except in aorist Parasmai and precative Átmane (वरिता or वरीता, वरिष्यति or वरीष्यति, तरिता or तरीता, &c.).

Roots ending in vowels rejecting इ i.

394. All in आ *á*, as दा 'to give' (दाता, दास्यति).

a. Nearly all in इ *i* and ई *í*, as जि 'to conquer,' नी 'to lead' (नेता, नेष्यति, &c.).

b. Nearly all in short उ *u*, as श्रु 'to hear' (श्रोता, श्रोष्यति).

c. Those in long ऊ *ú* generally in the desiderative only.

d. All in short ऋ *ṛi* (except वृ) in the 1st future only, as कृ 'to do' (कर्ता, but करिष्यति). See 392. *c.*

e. All in ए *e*, ऐ *ai*, ओ *o*. See 390. *d.*

Roots ending in vowels optionally *inserting or rejecting* इ i, *either in all the last five tenses and desiderative, or in certain of these forms only.*

395. सू or सु 2d and 4th c. Átm. 'to bring forth' (सोता or सविता, सोष्यते or सविष्यते).

a. धू 'to shake' (धविता or धोता, धविष्यति or धोष्यति, &c., but *i* must be inserted in aorist Parasmai, see 430), पू 'to purify,' optionally in desiderative only (पुपूष, पिपविष Átm.).

b. प्यै Átm. 'to grow fat' (प्याता and प्यायिता, प्यास्यते and प्यायिष्यते; but necessarily inserts *i* in desid.).

c. ऋ 'to go,' वृ or वॄ 'to spread,' 'to cover,' and स्वृ 'to sound,' all in 1st fut., and the latter two optionally in desiderative also (अर्ता, वरिता or (ī) वरीता; वर्ता, वरिता or वरीता; स्वर्ता or स्वरिता; विवरीषति or विवरिषति or विवरीषति; सिस्वरिषति or सुस्वूर्षति).

396. दरिद्रा 'to be poor' optionally in the desiderative (दिदरिद्रास् or दिदरिद्रिष्).

397. All roots in long ॠ ṝ optionally in the desiderative, as तॄ makes तितरिषति or तितीर्षति.

398. स्मि, पू, ऋ, वृ, optionally in desiderative. Compare 392.

Roots ending in consonants inserting इ i.

399. As a general rule, all roots ending in ख् *kh*, ग् *g*, घ् *gh*, झ् *jh*, ट् *ṭ*, ठ् *ṭh*, ड् *ḍ*, ढ् *ḍh*, ण् *ṇ*, त् *t*, थ् *th*, फ् *ph*, ब् *b*, य् *y*, र् *r*, ल् *l*, व् *v*: thus, लिख् 'to write' makes लेखिता, लेखिष्यति, &c.; वल्ग् 'to leap' makes वल्गिता, वल्गिष्यति.

a. ग्रह् 'to take' lengthens the inserted *i* in all the last five tenses, except the precative Parasmai (ग्रहीता, ग्रहीष्यति), see 699. It rejects *i* in the desiderative.

Roots ending in consonants rejecting इ i.

Observe—The rules at 296—306 must in all cases be applied. When a number is given after a root, it indicates that the root only rejects *i* if conjugated in the class to which the number refers. When a number is given between brackets, this refers to the rule under which the root is conjugated.

400. One in क् *k*.—शक् 5. *to be able* (शक्ता, शक्ष्यति 679).

401. Six in च् *c*.—पच् *to cook* (पक्ता, पक्ष्यति); वच् *to speak* (650); रिच् 7. *to make empty* (रेक्ता, रेक्ष्यति); विच् 7. 3. *to separate*; सिच् *to moisten, to sprinkle*; मुच् *to loosen* (628).

402. One in छ् *ch*.—प्रछ्* *to ask* (प्रष्टा, प्रक्ष्यति 631).

403. Fifteen in ज् *j*.—त्यज् *to quit* (596); भज् *to honour*; यज् *to sacrifice* (597); भ्रस्ज्† 6. *to fry* (632); मस्ज् *to be immersed* (633); भञ्ज् *to break* (669); रञ्ज् *to colour, to be attached*; सञ्ज् *to adhere* (597. *a*); स्वञ्ज् *to embrace*; निज् *to cleanse* (नेक्ता, नेक्ष्यति); विज्‡ 3. *to tremble* (वेक्ता, &c.); भुज् 6. *to bend*, 7. *to enjoy* (668. *a*); युज् *to join* (670); रुज् *to break* (रोक्ता, &c.); सृज् *to create, to let go* (625).

404. One in त् *t*.—वृत् *to be, to turn*, but only in 2d fut. Par., cond. Par., aor. Par., desid. Par. (This root is generally Ātm. and inserts *i*, 598.)

405. Fourteen in द् *d*.—अद् *to eat* (652); पद् *to go* (पत्ता, पत्स्यते); शद् *to fall, to perish*; सद् *to sink*; स्कन्द् 1. Parasmai, *to mount, to leap*; हद् *to void excrement*; खिद् *to be troubled* (खेत्ता, &c.); भिद् *to*

---

* प्रछ् inserts *i* in the desiderative.

† भ्रस्ज् optionally inserts *i* in the desiderative.

‡ When विज् belongs to the 7th c., it takes *i*: thus, विजिता, विजिष्यति. See 390. *a*.

cut (667); भिद् *to break* (583); विद् 7. *to recognise*, 4. *to be, to exist*, 6. *to find*; स्विद् 4. *to sweat*; क्षुद् *to pound, to crush* (क्षोत्ता, क्षोत्स्यति); तुद् *to strike* (634); नुद् *to impel*.

406. Thirteen in ध् *dh*.—बन्ध् *to bind* (692); व्यध् *to pierce* (615); राध् *to accomplish* (राद्धा, रात्स्यति); साध् 5. *to accomplish*; सिध् 4. *to be accomplished* (616); क्रुध् *to be angry* (क्रोद्धा, क्रोत्स्यति); क्षुध् *to be hungry*; बुध् 4. Átm. *to be aware* (614)*; युध् Átm. *to fight*; रुध् *to obstruct* (671); शुध् *to be pure*; वृध् *to increase*, only in 2d fut. Par., cond. Par., aor. Par.; शृध् *to break wind*, only in 2d fut. Par., cond. Par., aor. Par. (both these last insert *i* throughout the Átmane).

407. Two in न् *n*.—मन् 4. Átm. *to think* (617); हन् *to kill* (654), but the last takes *i* in 2d fut. and conditional.

408. Eleven in प् *p*.—तप् *to burn* (तप्ता, तप्स्यति); वप् *to sow*; शप् *to curse*; स्वप् *to sleep* (655); आप् *to obtain* (681); क्षिप् *to throw* (635); तिप् Átm. *to distil*; लिप् *to anoint*; छुप् *to touch* (छोप्ता, छोप्स्यति); लुप् 6. *to break* (लोप्ता, लोप्स्यति); सृप् *to creep* (390. *f*).

409. Three in भ् *bh*.—यभ् *to lie with carnally* (यब्धा, यप्स्यति); रभ् Átm. *to long after* (with आ *to begin*, 601. *a*); लभ् Átm. *to obtain* (601).

410. Five in म् *m*.—गम् *to go* (602), but takes *i* in 2d fut. and cond.; नम् *to bend* (नन्ता, नंस्यति); यम् *to restrain*; रम् Átm. *to sport*; क्रम् 'to walk' in the Átmane (क्रन्ता, क्रंस्यते).

411. Ten in श् *ś*.—दंश् *to bite* (दंष्टा, दंक्ष्यति); दिश् 6. *to point out* (583); विश् *to enter* (वेष्टा, वेक्ष्यति); रिश् *to hurt*; लिश् *to become small*; क्रुश् *to cry out* (क्रोष्टा, क्रोक्ष्यति); रुश् 6. *to hurt*; दृश् 1. *to see* (390. i, 604, द्रष्टा, द्रक्ष्यति); मृश् *to handle* (390. *f*); स्पृश् 6. *to touch* (390. *f*, 636, स्प्रष्टा, स्प्रक्ष्यति).

412. Eleven in ष् *sh*.—त्विष् *to shine* (त्वेष्टा, त्वेक्ष्यति); द्विष् *to hate* (657); पिष् 7. *to crush, to pound*; विष् *to pervade, to sprinkle*, &c.; शिष् 7. *to distinguish* (672); श्लिष् 4. *to embrace* (301, 302); तुष् 4. *to be satisfied* (तोष्टा, तोक्ष्यति); दुष् 4. *to be sinful*; पुष् 4. *to be nourished* † (पोष्टा, पोक्ष्यति); शुष् 4. *to become dry* (शोष्टा, शोक्ष्यति); कृष् *to draw* (390. *f*, 606).

413. Two in स् *s*.—घस् *to eat* (घस्ता, घत्स्यति); वस् 1. *to dwell* (607) ‡.

* When बुध् belongs to the 1st c., it inserts *i*.

† When पुष् belongs to the 9th c., it takes *i* (पोषितुं, पोषिष्यति).

‡ वस् c. 2. Átm. 'to put on,' 'to wear,' inserts *i* (वसितुं, वसिष्यते).

414. Eight in ह् h.—दह् *to burn* (610); नह् *to tie, to string together* (624); वह् *to carry* (611); दिह् *to anoint* (659); मिह् *to make water* (मेढा 305. a, मेक्ष्यति); लिह् 2. *to lick* (661); दुह् 2. *to milk* (660) *; रुह् *to ascend* (रोढा, रोक्ष्यति).

Roots ending in consonants* optionally *inserting or rejecting* इ i, *either in all the last five tenses and desiderative, or in certain of these forms only.

Observe—When no tenses are specified, the option applies to all except to form II of the aorist and the Parasmai of the precative (benedictive), which can never insert *i*.

415. Two in च् *č*.—तञ्च् or तच् 7. *to contract;* व्रश्च् *to cut* (630).

a. Three in ज् *j*.—अञ्ज् 7. *to anoint* (668, but necessarily inserts *i* in desid.); मृज् *to rub, to clean* (390. *j*, 651); भ्रस्ज् *to fry* (optionally in desid. only, necessarily rejects *i* in other forms).

b. Four in त् *t*.—पत् *to fall* (optionally in desid. only; necessarily inserts *i* in futures and cond., and rejects it in aor.); कृत् 6. *to cut* (optionally in 2d fut., cond., and desid.; necessarily inserts *i* in 1st fut. and aor.); चृत् *to kill* (optionally in 2d fut., cond., and desid.; necessarily inserts *i* in 1st fut. and aor.); नृत् *to dance* (optionally in 2d fut. and desid., necessarily inserts *i* in 1st fut. and aor.).

c. Four in द् *d*.—स्यन्द् *to flow* (optionally in all forms except 2d fut. and cond. Parasmai, and desid. Parasmai, where *i* is necessarily rejected); क्लिद् *to be wet,* छृद् *to shine,* and तृद् *to kill, to injure* (the last two optionally in all forms except 1st fut., which necessarily inserts *i*).

d. Three in ध् *dh*.—रध् *to perish;* सिध् 1. *to rule, to restrain, to keep off;* ऋध् *to prosper* (the last optionally in desid. only, necessarily inserts *i* in other forms, see 680).

e. Two in न् *n*.—तन् *to stretch* and सन् *to honour, to give* (both optionally in desid. only, necessarily insert *i* in other forms, see 583).

f. Five in प् *p*.—त्रप् *to be ashamed;* गुप् 1. *to defend;* तृप् 4. *to be satisfied* (618); दृप् 4. *to be proud;* कृप् *to be capable* (when it rejects *i*, it is Parasmai only).

g. Two in भ् *bh*.—लुभ् 4. *to desire* (optionally in 1st fut., necessarily

* दुह् c. 1, 'to afflict,' inserts *i* (दोहिता, &c.).

inserts *i* in other forms*); दम्भ् *to deceive* (optionally in desid. only, दिदम्भिषति or धिप्सति or धीप्सति, necessarily inserts *i* in other forms).

h. One in म् *m.*—क्षम् 1. 4. *to bear* (क्षमिता or क्षन्ता, क्षमिष्यते, -ति, or क्षंस्यते, -ति).

i. All in इव् *iv* (optionally in desid. only); as, दिव् *to play*, ष्ठिव् *to spit*, सिव् *to sew*.

j. Two in य् *y.*—चाय् *to honour*; प्याय or स्फाय् *to be fat* (but both necessarily insert *i* in desid., compare 395. *b*).

k. Three in श् *ś.*—अश् 5. Ātm. *to pervade*† (but necessarily inserts *i* in desid., see 681. *a*); नश् 4. *to perish* (see 390. *k*, and 620); क्लिश् 9. *to torment* (697).

l. Seven in ष् *sh.*—अक्ष् *to pervade*; तक्ष् *to cut in pieces, to carve* (तक्षिता or तष्टा, तक्षिष्यति or तक्ष्यति, &c.); त्वक्ष् *to cut, to carve*; कुष् with निर् *to extract* (otherwise necessarily inserts *i*); इष् 6. *to wish* (637); रिष् *to injure, to kill*; रुष् 1. *to injure* (the last three optionally in 1st fut., but necessarily insert *i* in other forms).

m. Twelve in ह् *h.*—सह् Ātm. *to bear* (optionally in 1st fut. only, necessarily inserts *i* in other forms, see 611. *a*); गृह् *to take* (गृहिता or गृढा, &c.); गाह् *to penetrate*; बाह् *to measure* (बाहिता or बाढा, &c.); स्निह् snih, *to love* (स्नेहिता or स्नेग्धा or स्नेढा, &c.); स्नुह् snuh, *to love, to vomit*; मुह् *to be perplexed* (612); गुह् *to conceal* (गूहिता or गोढा, गूहिष्यति or घोक्ष्यति, see 306. *a*, 390. *m*); द्रुह् *to bear malice, to seek to injure* (623); तृह् 6. 7. or तृंह् 6. *to kill* (674); वृह् or बृह् *to extol, to raise*; स्तृह् or स्तृंह् 6. *to kill*.

Aorist (third preterite).

This complex and multiform tense, the most troublesome and intricate in the whole Sanskṛit verb, but fortunately less used in classical Sanskṛit than the other past tenses, is not so much one tense, as an aggregation of several, all more or less allied to each other, all bearing a manifest resemblance to the imperfect or first preterite, but none of them exactly assignable to that tense, and none of them so distinct in its character or so universal in its application as to admit of segregation from the general group, under a separate title.

416. Grammarians assert that there are seven different varieties of

---

* Except the aorist, following form II at p. 184.

† अश् 9, 'to eat,' inserts *i*.

the Sanskrit aorist, four of which correspond more or less to the Greek 1st aorist, and three to the 2d aorist, but we shall endeavour to show that all these varieties may be included under two distinct forms of terminations given in the table at p. 128, and again below, and at p. 184.

417. Form I is sub-divided like the terminations of all the last five tenses into (A) those which reject *i*, and (B) those which assume it; A belongs to many of those roots at 394, 400—414, which reject *i*; B to most of those at 392, 399, which insert it: but in the latter case the initial *s* becomes *sh* by 70, and in the 2d and 3d sing. the initial *s* is rejected, the *i* blending with the *í*, which then becomes the initial of those terminations. Moreover, in the case of roots which insert *i* the base is formed according to rules different to those which apply in the case of roots which reject *i*.

a. Form II at p. 184 resembles the terminations of the imperfect or first preterite, and belongs, in the first place, to some of those roots rejecting *i*, whose bases in the imperfect present some important variation from the root (see 436); in the second, to certain of the roots rejecting *i*, which end in श् *ś*, ष् *sh*, or ह् *h*, and which have i u, or *ṛi*, for their radical vowel (see 439); in the third, to verbs of the 10th class and causals.

Form I.

418. The terminations are here repeated from 247, p. 128.

A. *Terminations without* इ i.

	Parasmai.		Átmane.		
1. *sam*	*sva*	*sma*	*si*	*svahi*	*smahi*
2. *sís*	*stam* [*tam*]	*sta* [*ta*]	*sthás* [*thás*]	*sáthám*	*dhvam* or *ḍhvam*
3. *sít*	*stám* [*tám*]	*sus*	*sta* [*ta*]	*sátám*	*sata*

B. *Terminations with* इ i.

	Parasmai.		Átmane.		
1. *isham*	*ishva*	*ishma*	*ishi*	*ishvahi*	*ishmahi*
2. *ís*	*ishṭam*	*ishṭa*	*ishṭhás*	*isháthám*	*idhvam* or *iḍhvam*
3. *ít*	*ishṭám*	*ishus*	*ishṭa*	*ishátám*	*ishata*

419. Observe—The brackets in the A terminations indicate the rejection of initial *s* from those terminations in which it is compounded with *t* and *th*, if the base ends in any consonant except a nasal or semivowel, or in any *short* vowel such as *a*, *i*, *u*,

or *ṛí*. Observe also, that initial *s* is liable to become *sh* by r. 70, in which case a following *t* or *th* is cerebralized. The substitution of *ḍhvam* for *dhvam* and *iḍhvam* for *idhvam*, in certain cases, is explained in the table at p. 128.

420. General rule for forming the base for those verbs of the first nine classes which reject इ *i* and so take the A terminations.

In Parasmai, if a root end in either a vowel or a consonant, vṛiddhi the radical vowel before *all* the terminations.

In Átmane, if a root end in इ *i*, ई *í*, उ *u*, or ऊ *ú*, guṇate the radical vowel; if in ऋ *ṛi* or any consonant, leave the vowel unchanged before *all* the terminations. Final consonants must be joined to the A terminations according to the rules propounded at 296—306.

Observe—The augment अ *a* must always be prefixed, as in the imperfect; but it will be shown in the Syntax at 889, that when the aorist is used as a prohibitive imperative, the particle *má* or *má sma* being prefixed, the augment is then rejected.

a. When a root begins with the vowels इ *i*, उ *u*, or ऋ *ṛi*, short or long, the augment is prefixed in accordance with 260. *a*, *b*.

b. Thus, from नी 'to lead' come the two bases *anai* for Parasmai and *ane* for Átmane (*anai* + *sam* = अनैषम् by 70; Átm. *ane* + *si* = अनेषि, *ane* + *sthás* = अनेष्ठास्, &c.); and from कृ 8th c., 'to make,' come the two bases *akár* for Parasmai and *akṛi* for Átmane (*akár* + *sam* = अकार्षम् by 70, &c.; Átm. *akṛi* + *si* = अकृषि by 70, *akṛi* + *thás* = अकृथास् by 419, *akṛi* + *ta* = अकृत, &c.). See 682. Similarly, भृ 3d c., 'to bear.' See the table at 583.

c. So, from युज् 'to join' come the two bases *ayauj* for Parasmai and *ayuj* for Átmane (Parasmai *ayauj* + *sam* = अयौक्षम् by 296, *ayauj* + *sva* = अयौक्ष्व, *ayauj* + *tam* = अयौक्तम् by 419; Átm. *ayuj* + *si* = अयुक्षि by 296, *ayuj* + *thás* = अयुक्थास्, *ayuj* + *ta* = अयुक्त); and from रुध् 7th c., 'to hinder,' the bases *araudh* and *arudh* (Parasmai *araudh* + *sam* = अरौत्सम् by 299, Du. *araudh* + *sva* = अरौत्स्व, *araudh* + *tam* = अरौद्धम्; Átm. *arudh* + *si* = अरुत्सि, *arudh* + *thás* = अरुद्धास्, &c.).

d. Similarly, from पच् 'to cook' come the bases *apáć* and *apać* (*apáć* + *sam* = अपाक्षम् by 296; Átm. *apać* + *si* = अपक्षि, *apać* + *thás* = अपक्थास्, &c.); and from दह् 'to burn' (610), the bases *adáh* and *adah* (*adáh* + *sam* = अधाक्षम् by 306. *a*, *adáh* + *tam* = अदाग्धम् by 305; Átm. *adah* + *si* = अधक्षि by 306. *a*, *adah* + *thás* = अदग्धास्, &c.).

421. By referring to 391. *b*. it will be easy to understand that most roots in *i*, *í*,

short *u*, and short *ṛi*, take the A terminations. Most of those in *á*, *e*, *ai*, *o*, do so *in the Átmane*, and a few of those in *á* also in the Parasmai.

a. स्तृ or स्तॄ 'to spread' takes either A or B; and in Átmane when it takes A, changes *ṛí* to *ír*. See 678.

b. वृ or वॄ 'to choose,' 'to cover,' changes its vowel to *ûr*, under the same circumstances. See 675.

c. Roots in *e*, *ai*, *o*, change these vowels to *á* as in the other non-conjugational tenses: thus, from व्ये 'to cover,' अव्यासिषं &c. (see 433), अव्यासीत् &c. Similarly, मि, मी, दी, and optionally ली, see 390. *e* (अमासिषं &c., अमासीत् &c.).

d. दा 'to give' (see 663), धा 'to place' (see 664), स्था 'to stand' (see 587), दे 'to protect,' 'to pity,' धे 'to drink' (if in Átm.), दो or दा 'to cut' (if in Átm.), change their finals in the Átmane to *i* (अदिषि, अदिथास् 419, अदित, अदिष्वहि; 2d pl. अदिढ्वं). In Parasmai they follow 438.

e. गा used for इ 'to go,' with अधि prefixed, signifying 'to go over,' 'to read' (Átmane only), changes its final to *í* (अध्यगीषि, -गीष्ठास्, -गीष्ट, &c.).

f. कु Átm. 'to cry out,' गु 'to void excrement,' and धु 'to be firm,' all of the 6th class, preserve their vowels unchanged (अकुषि, &c.; अकुष्ठास्, अकुष्ट, &c.; अगुषं, &c.); धु may also make अधौषं, and गु may also make अगुविषं, but the latter root is then generally regarded as गू.

422. The following roots of those rejecting *i*, enumerated at 400—414, take the A terminations only, both for Par. or Átm.: पच्; शक्; मुच्, रिच्, वच्, सिच्, मस्ज्, यज्, रञ्ज्, सञ्ज्, स्वञ्ज् Átm., भुज्, रुज्, युज्; पद् Átm., खिद् Átm., छिद्, तुद्, नुद्; क्रुध्, क्षुध्, राध्, साध्, बुध् 4. Átm., युध्; मन् 4. Átm.; आप्, तप्, वप्, शप्, क्षिप्, लिप् Átm., लुप्; गम्, रम्, नम्; दंश्; वस्; दह्, नह्, वह्.

a. The following take in the Parasmai either the A terminations of form I or optionally form II; but in the Átmane usually the A form of I, sometimes form II: रिच्, विच् 3, निज्, विज् 3, स्कन्द्, भिद्, छिद्, क्षुद्, रुध्, दृश्, युज्, सृज्, कृप्.

b. The following take in the Parasmai only form II; but in the Átmane the A form of I, or sometimes the B form of I: श्वि (Átmane doubtful), सिच्, मुच्, विद् 6. 'to find' (Átmane doubtful), 4. 7. (only Átmane), शद्, सद्, क्लिद्, स्विद् 4, रुष्, सिध् 4, क्षुध्, शुष्, दृश् (see 424. *b*; घस् with the B terminations is generally used for Parasmai, but अघसत् occurs in Epic po.), आप्, लिप्, लुप्, तृप्, गम्, वस्.

423. The following of those inserting or rejecting *i*, enumerated at 415, take either the A or B terminations: स्पृश् or मृश्, कृष्, तृप्, स्यन्द् generally Átm. only, क्लिश्, अश् Átm., गुप्, क्षुभ् Átm., दृप्, तृप् (the last three in Parasmai take also form II), वृत् generally Átm. (may also follow form II in Parasmai), त्रास् (or त्रै) Átm., बाह्, वह्, गुह्, गाह्, नाह्, तृंह्.

424. The rules at 296—306 must in all cases be applied, as well as the special rules applicable to certain roots in forming the futures at 390 and 390. *a*—*o*: thus, भज् makes अभाक्षं by 297. *b* (see 630); मस्ज् makes अमाङ्क्षं by 390. *k* (see 633); गाह् in Átm., अगाहि or अगाहिषि; वस्, अवात्सं or अवात्सीं, अवात्सि or अवात्सिं by 390. *g*; नृत्, अनर्तिषं by 390. *j* (also अनर्तिषि); वह्, अवाक्षं by 306. *b*.

a. पद् *Átm.* 'to go,' बुध् *Átm.* 'to be aroused,' जन् *Átm.* 'to be born,' may form their 3d sing. as if they were passive verbs (see 475): thus, अपादि, Du. 3. अपत्साताम्; अबोधि (or optionally अबुद्ध), Du. 3. अभुत्साताम्; अजनि (or optionally अजनिष्ट).

b. Roots ending in म् and न् must change these letters to Anusvára before *s*, and म् becomes न् before स्त: thus, मन् makes अमंसि, अमंस्थास्, अमंस्त (or if in class 8. अमनिष्ट, or by *c.* below अमत); यम् makes अयंसि &c., Du. 2. अयंसाथाम्.

हन् (generally Parasmai) drops its nasal before the *Átmane* terminations (अहसि, अहसाताम्, &c.; initial *s* being rejected according to 419).

गम् does so optionally (अगंसि or अगसि, अगंस्थाम् or अगसाताम्, &c.).

c. Roots in न् and ण् of the 8th class, which properly take the B terminations, are allowed an option of dropping the nasal in the 2d and 3d sing. *Átmane*, in which case initial *s* is rejected according to 419: thus, तन् makes 3. अतनिष्ट or अतत (Páṇ. II. 4. 79).

d. Similarly, सन् makes 3. असनिष्ट or असत; and क्षण्, अक्षणिष्ट or अक्षत.

e. सन् 'to give' is allowed the option of lengthening the *a*, when *n* is dropped: thus, Sing. 2. असाथास् or असनिष्ठास्, 3. असात or असनिष्ट. Compare 354. *a.* 339 (Páṇ. II. 4. 79).

f. The nasal of दंश् 'to bite' becomes ङ् before क् and ञ् before ष्: thus, अदांक्षम्, Du. 2. अदांष्टम्; *Átm.* 1. अदंक्षि, Du. 2. अदंक्षाथाम्. See 303.

425. वह् 'to carry' (see 611) changes its radical vowel to ओ *o* before those terminations which reject an initial *s* by 305. *a*: thus, *avákshan*, *avákshís*, *avákshít* (Lat. *vexit*), *avákshva*, *avoḍham*, &c.; *Átm.* *avakshi* (Lat. *vexi*), *avoḍhás*, *avoḍha*.

a. सह् *Átm.*, 'to bear,' generally takes the B terminations (*asahishi*, &c.), though the form असोढ is also given for the 3d sing.

426. नह् 'to tie,' 'to fasten,' makes *anátsam*, *anátsís*, *anátsít*, *anátsva*, *anáddham*, &c.; and *Átm.* *anatsi*, *anaddhás*, &c., by 306. *b* (compare 183).

a. वस् 'to dwell' (see 607) makes *avátsam*, &c., by 304. *a.*

427. Verbs which assume *i*, and so take the B terminations at 418, require a different rule for the formation of their base, as follows:—

a. If a root end in the vowels इ *i*, ई *í*, उ *u*, ऊ *ú*, ऋ *ṛi*, ॠ *ṛí*, vṛiddhi those vowels in the Parasmai before *all* the terminations, and guṇate them in the *Átmane*.

Thus, from पू 'to purify' come the two bases *apau* for Parasmai and *apo* for *Átmane* (*apau* + *i* + *sam* = अपाविषम् by 37, *apau* + *i* + *ís* = अपावीस्, *apau* + *i* + *ít* = अपावीत्, &c.; *Átm.* *apo* + *i* + *si* = अपविषि, &c., by 36), see 583; and from तॄ 1st c., 'to cross,' comes the base *atár* for Parasmai (*atár* + *i* + *sam* = अतारिषम् &c.).

So, from शी 'to lie down' comes अशयिषि, अशयिष्ठास्, &c.; but roots ending in any other vowel than *ú* and long *ṛí* more frequently take the A terminations, as they generally reject *i*.

b. If a root end in a single consonant, guṇate the radical vowel in both Parasmai and Ātmane (except as debarred at 28. *b*, and except in the roots enumerated at 390. *a*).

Thus, बुध् *budh*, 1st c., 'to know,' makes its base *abodh* (*abodhisham*, &c.), see 583; and वृत् *vṛit*, 'to be,' *avart* (*avartishi*, &c.); and एध् *edh*, 'to increase,' *aidh* (*aidhishi*, &c., 260. *b*), see 600.

428. A medial *a* in roots ending in र् and ल् is lengthened in the Parasmai, but not in Ātmane: thus, चर् 'to go' makes अचारिषं; ज्वल् 'to blaze,' अज्वालिषं. The roots वद् 'to speak' and व्रज् 'to go' also lengthen the *a* in Parasmai (अवादिषं; but not in Ātmane अवदिषि &c.).

a. But those in ह्, म्, य् never lengthen the *a* in Parasmai: thus, स्यम् 'to sound' makes अस्यमिषं. The following roots also are debarred from lengthening the *a*: कख्, क्नथ्, रग्, लग्, कग्, स्थग्, ह्रग्, ह्लग्, चट्, कम्, चर्, क्षप्, पथ्, मथ्, चह्, चष्, चल्, हस्. One or two do so optionally; as, कण् and रण् 'to sound.'

429. Observe, that as the majority of Sanskrit verbs assume *i*, it follows that rule 427. *a*, *b*, will be more universally applicable than rule 420, especially as the former applies to the aorist of intensives, desideratives, and nominals, as well as to that of simple verbs.

430. The special rules for the two futures at 390. *a*—*o* will of course hold good for the aorist; thus the roots enumerated at 390 and 390. *a* (कुट् &c.) forbid Guṇa; and गु, ध्रु, नू, कू generally change their finals to *uv* (अनुविषं &c., अगुविषं &c.); but when गू is written गु it makes अगुषं &c., see 421. *f*, and नू may also make अनाविषं, and धू, अधाविषं.

a. ऊर्णु makes और्णाविषं or और्णविषं or और्णुविषं &c., and in Ātmane और्णविषि or और्णुविषि.

b. According to 390. *c*. दीधी, वेवी, and दरिद्रा drop their finals (अदीधिषि, अदरिद्रिषं, &c.; see also 433).

431. In the Ātmane, वृ 'to choose,' 'to cover,' and all roots in long ॠ *ṝ*, such as स्तॄ 'to spread,' may optionally lengthen the inserted *i*: thus, अवरिषि or अवरीषि &c., अस्तरिषि or अस्तरीषि; but in Parasmai only अवारिषं, अस्तारिषं.

432. श्वि 'to swell' and जागृ 'to awake' take Guṇa instead of Vṛiddhi (अश्वयिषं &c., see also 440. *a*; अजागरिषं &c.).

a. ग्रह् according to 399. *a*. makes अग्रहीषं, and by 390. *m*. गुह् makes अगूहिषं. The latter also conforms to 439 and 439. *b*. See 609.

b. हन् 'to kill' forms its aorist from वध् (अवधिषं &c.), but see 422. *b*.

433. Many roots in आ *á*, ए *e*, ओ *o*, and ऐ *ai*, with three in म् *m*, viz. यम् *yam*, रम् *ram*, नम् *nam*, assume *i*, but *in the Parasmai* insert *s* before it; final *e*, *o*, and *ai*, being changed to आ *á*: thus, from या 'to go' comes अयासिषं, &c. (see 644); from शो 'to sharpen,' अशासिषं, &c.; from यम् 'to restrain,' अयंसिषं, &c.

दरिद्रा 'to be poor' makes *adaridrisham* or *adaridrásisham*, &c.

434. In the Átmane these roots reject the *i* and the *s* which precedes it, and follow 418: thus, from मा 'to measure' comes अमासि, &c. (see 664. *a*); from व्ये 'to cover,' अव्यासि (see 431. *c*); from रम् 'to sport,' अरंसि, अरंस्वहि, अरंस्त, &c.

Form II.

435. Resembling the imperfect or first preterite.

	Parasmai.			Átmane.	
1. *am*	*áva* [*va*]	*áma* [*ma*]	*e* [*i*]	*ávahi*	*ámahi*
2. *as* [*s*]	*atam* [*tam*]	*ata* [*ta*]	*athás*	*ethám* [*áthám*]	*adhvam*
3. *at* [*t*]	*atám* [*tám*]	*an* [*us*]	*ata*	*etám* [*átám*]	*anta*

436. Observe—No confusion arises from the similarity which this form bears to the imperfect or 1st preterite, as in all cases where the above terminations are used for the aorist, the imperfect presents some difference in the form of its base: thus, गम् 'to go' make *agaććham* for its imperfect, *agamam* for its aorist (see 602); भिद् 'to break' makes *abhinadam* for its imperfect, *abhidam* for its aorist (see 583). So again, the sixth conjugation, which alone can show a perfect identity of root and base, never makes use of this form for its aorist, unless by some special rule the base of its imperfect is made to differ from the root: thus, लिप् 'to smear' (cf. ἀλείφω), which makes *alipam* in its aorist, is *alimpam* in its imperfect (281). So in Greek, compare the imperfect ἔλειπον with the 2d aor. ἔλιπον; ἐλάμβανον with ἔλαβον; ἐδάμνην with ἔδαμον, &c.

a. Note—This form of the Sanskrit aorist corresponds to the Greek 2d aorist (compare *asthám*, *asthás*, *asthát*, with ἔστην, ἔστης, ἔστη), and the first form is more or less analogous to the 1st aorist. The substitution of *i* for *e*, and *áthám*, *átám*, for *ethám*, *etám*, in the Átmane of form II, is confined to a class of roots mentioned at 439.

437. Rule for forming the base in verbs of the first nine classes. In general the terminations are attached directly to the root; as in *agamam*, &c., *abhidam*, &c., at 436. So also, नश् 'to perish' makes अनशं (also अनेशं, see 441, 424).

a. Observe, however, that most of the roots which follow this form in the Parasmai, follow form I at 418 in the Átmane: thus, भिद् 'to break' makes *abhitsi*, &c., in Átmane; see the table at 583: similarly, छिद् 'to cut,' see 667. And a few roots, which are properly restricted to the Átmane, have a Parasmai aorist of this 2d form:

thus, रुच् Átm. 'to shine,' 'to be pleasing,' makes Parasmai *arućam*, as well as Átmane *aroćishi*.

b. One or two roots in आ *á*, इ *i*, and ए *e* reject their finals; and one or two in ऋ *ṛi* and ॠ *ṝí* guṇate these vowels before the above terminations: thus, ख्या 'to tell' makes अख्यं &c., अख्ये &c.; श्वि 'to swell,' अश्वं; ह्वे 'to call' makes अह्वं (see 595); सृ 'to go,' असरं; ऋ 'to go,' आरं; जॄ 'to grow old,' अजरं.

c. दृश् 'to see' guṇates its vowel (अदर्शं, see 604).

d. Penultimate nasals are generally dropped: thus, स्तम्भ् 'to stop' makes अस्तभं; स्यन्द् 'to distil,' अस्यदं; स्कन्द् 'to mount,' अस्कदं; भ्रंश् 'to fall,' अभ्रशं.

e. A form अक्षं occurs in the Veda, from घस् 'to eat,' the medial *a* being dropped.

438. In the Parasmai certain roots ending in long आ *á* and ए *e* conform still more closely to the terminations of the imperfect, rejecting the initial vowel, as indicated by the brackets in the table at 435. In the 3d plur. they take *us* for *an*: thus, दा 3d c., 'to give,' makes *adám*, *adás*, *adát*, *adáva*, &c., 3d pl. *adus*, see 663. So also, धा 3d c., 'to place,' makes *adhám*, &c., 664; and स्था 1st c., 'to stand,' makes *asthám*, &c., 587.

a. Similarly, भू 1st c., 'to be,' except 1st sing. and 3d pl. (अभूवं, अभूः, अभूत्, अभूव, &c.; but 3d pl. अभूवन्, see 585).

b. Observe, however, that some roots in *á*, like *yá*, 'to go,' follow 433.

c. And some roots in ए *e* and ओ *o*, which follow 433, optionally follow 438; in which case *e* and *o* are changed as before to *á*: thus, धे *dhe*, 1st c., 'to drink,' makes either *adhásisham* &c., or *adhám* &c., also *adadham*, see 440. *a*; सो *so*, 4th c., 'to come to an end,' makes either *asásisham* or *asám*, see 613.

d. In the Átmane-pada, roots like दा, धा, स्था, दे, धे, दो, follow 421. *d*.

e. इ 'to go' makes its aorist from a root गा: thus, *agám*, *agás*, &c.

Note—*Adadám*, the imperfect of the root *dá*, 'to give,' bears the same relation to its aorist *adám* that ἐδίδων does to ἔδων. So also the relation of *adhám* (aorist of *dhá*, 'to place') to *adadhám* (imperfect or 1st pret.) corresponds to that of ἔθην to ἐτίθην. Compare also *abhavas* and *abhús* with ἔφυες and ἔφυς.

439. Certain roots ending in श् *ś*, ष् *sh*, ह् *h*, enclosing a medial *i*, *u*, or *ṛi*, form their aorists according to form II at 435; but whenever confusion is likely to arise between the imperfect and aorist, *s* is prefixed to the terminations, before which sibilant the final of the root becomes *k* by 302 and 306.

Thus, दिश् 'to point out,' the imperfect of which is अदिशं, makes अदिक्षं &c. in aorist (compare the Greek 1st aorist ἔδειξα). Similarly, द्विष् 2d c., 'to hate,' makes *adviksham* &c. 657; दुह् 2d c., 'to milk,' makes अधुक्षं *adhuksham* &c. by 306. *a*. See 660.

a. This class of roots substitutes *i* for *e*, and *áthám*, *átám*, for *ethám*, *etám*, in the *Á*tmane terminations: thus, *adikshi*, *adikshathás*, *adikshata*, *adikshávahi*, *adiksháthám*, &c.; 3d pl. *adikshanta*.

b. A few roots in ह् *h* (viz. लिह्, दिह्, गुह्, दुह्) optionally in the *Á*tmane reject the initial *a* from the terminations of the 2d and 3d sing., 1st du., and 2d pl.: thus, लिह् may make अलिक्षि, अलीढास्, अलीढ; Du. 1. अलिह्वहि; Pl. 2. अलीढ्वं, 661; and दुह् 'to milk,' अदुग्धि, अदुग्धास्, &c. See 661, 659, 609, 660.

c. According to some authorities, a few roots (e. g. तृप्, दृप्, सृप्) which generally follow form I, A, in *Á*tmane, may optionally conform to form II, taking the terminations *i*, *áthám*, *átám*, rejecting initial *a* and *á* from the other terminations, and taking *ata* for *anta*: thus, *atripi*, *atripthás*, *atripta*, *atripvahi*, &c.

440. Causal verbs and verbs of the 10th class make use of form II, but the base assumes both reduplication and augment (as in the Greek pluperfect): thus, बुध् 1st c., 'to know,' makes in the causal aorist अबूबुधं, &c. This will be explained at 492.

a. A few primitive verbs besides those of the 10th class take a reduplicated base, analogous to causals (see 492): thus, श्रि 'to have recourse' makes अशिश्रियं &c.; श्वि 'to swell' makes अशिश्वियं (also अश्वं and अश्वयिषं, see 432, 437. *b*); द्रु 1st c., 'to run,' अदुद्रुवं; स्रु 'to flow,' असुस्रुवं; धे 'to drink,' अदधं; कम् 'to love,' अचकमे, &c. This last is defective when it belongs to the 1st c., having no conjugational tenses; but when it belongs to the 10th c. (Pres. कामये, &c.) its aorist is अचीकमे.

441. The following primitive verbs take a contracted form of reduplicated base: वच् 2d c., 'to speak,' makes अवोचम् *avočam* (from अववचं for अववचं 650); पत् 1st c., 'to fall,' अपप्तं (from अपपतं; compare Greek ἔπεπτον); शास् 2d c., 'to rule,' अशिषं (from अशिशसं, but the *Á*tmane follows 427; see 658); अस् 4th c., 'to throw,' आस्थं (from आससं, contracted into आस्सं for आस्तं 304. *a*, whence by transposition आस्थं); नश् 4th c., 'to perish,' अनेशं (from अननशं for अननिशं 620, 436).

Precative or benedictive.

Terminations of precative or benedictive repeated from page 128.

Parasmai.			Átmane.		
yásam	*yásva*	*yásma*	*síya*	*sívahi*	*símahi*
yás	*yástam*	*yásta*	*síshṭhás*	*síyásthám*	*sídhvam* or *síḍhvam*
yát	*yástám*	*yásus*	*síshṭa*	*síyástám*	*síran*

Síḍhvam is used for *sídhvam* when immediately preceded by any other vowel but *a* or *á*, and optionally *ishíḍhvam* for *ishídhvam* when immediately preceded by a semivowel or *h*.

442. Observe, that the terminations of this tense resemble those of the potential in the memorial scheme at p. 125. In the 2d and 3d singular they are identical. In the other persons of the Parasmai a sibilant is inserted, and in some of the Átmane, both prefixed and inserted. The only difference between the potential and precative of verbs of the 2d and 3d groups, at 290, will often be that the potential will have the conjugational characteristic: thus, *bhid*, 7th c., 'to break,' will be *bhindyát* in the potential, and *bhidyát* in the precative. Compare the optative of the Greek aorist δοίην with the optative of the present διδοίην.

443. Rule for forming the base in verbs of the first nine classes. In the Parasmai, as a general rule, either leave the root unchanged before the *y* of the terminations, or make such changes as are required in the passive (see 465—472), or by the conjugational rule of the 4th class, and never insert *i*.

In Átmane, as a general rule, prefix *i* to the terminations in those roots ending in consonants or vowels which take *i* in the futures (see 392, 399), and before this *i* guṇate the radical vowel. Guṇate it also in the Átmane in some roots ending in vowels which reject *i*: but if a root end in a *consonant*, and *reject i*, the radical vowel is generally left unchanged in the Átmane, as well as Parasmai.

444. Thus, from भू 1st c., 'to be,' come the base of the Parasmai *bhú*, and the base of the Átmane *bhavi*, by 36. *a* (*bhú* + *yásam* = भूयासं &c., *bhavi* + *shya* = भविषीय by 70).

445. Frequently, as already observed, before the *y* of the Parasmai terminations, the root is liable to changes analogous to those which take place before the *y* of the 4th conjugational class at 272, and the *y* of passive verbs at 465; and not unfrequently it undergoes changes similar to those of the perfect at 373, &c., as follows:—

446. A final आ *á* is changed to ए *e* in the Parasmai, but remains unchanged in the Átmane, as before the *s* of the 2d future terminations: thus, दा 3d c., 'to give,' makes देयासं &c. for Parasmai, but दासीय &c. for Átmane-pada; पा 'to drink' makes पेयासं &c.

a. But ज्या 'to become old' makes जीयासं &c., and दरिद्रा 'to be poor' drops its final even in Parasmai (दरिद्र्यासं, दरिद्रिषीय, &c. Compare 390. *e*).

447. Final इ *i* and उ *u* are lengthened in Parasmai, as before the *y* of passives, and guṇated in Átmane, as before the *s* of the 2d future: thus, चि 'to gather' makes चीयासं &c., चेषीय &c.; and हु 'to sacrifice' makes हूयासं &c., होषीय &c.

a. When इ 'to go' is preceded by a preposition, it is not lengthened (इयात् &c.; otherwise ईयात्).

b. दीधी and वेवी drop their finals as at 390. *c* (दीधिषीय &c.).

448. Final ऋ *ṛi* is changed to रि *ri* in Parasmai, but retained in Ātmane: thus, कृ 'to do' makes क्रियात् &c., and कृषीय &c. After a double consonant *ṛi* is guṇated in Parasmai, as well as before inserted *i*: thus, स्तृ 'to spread' makes स्तर्यात् &c., स्तृषीय &c., or स्तरिषीय &c.

a. It is also guṇated in ऋ *ṛi*, 'to go,' and जागृ 'to awake' (अर्यात्, जागर्यात्, &c.).

b. वृ 'to cover,' 'to choose,' makes either व्रियात् or वूर्यात्, वृषीय or वरिषीय or वूर्षीय.

449. Final ॠ *ṝi* is changed to ईर् *īr* in both voices, but is guṇated before inserted *i* in Ātmane: thus, तॄ 1st c., 'to cross,' makes तीर्यात् &c., तीर्षीय &c., or तरिषीय &c., or तरीषीय &c.

a. One root, पॄ 10th c., 'to fill,' makes पूर्यात् &c. Compare 448. *a.*

450. Of roots in ए *e*, धे 'to drink' makes धेयात् &c. (which is also the precative of धा 'to hold'); दे 'to protect,' देयात्.

a. But ह्वे 'to call' makes हूयात् &c., and ह्वासीय &c.; व्ये 'to cover' makes वीयात् &c., and व्यासीय &c.; and वे 'to weave' makes ऊयात् &c., and वासीय &c. Compare 465. *c.*

451. Final ऐ *ai* and ओ *o* are often treated like final *ā* at 446: thus गै 'to sing' makes गेयात् &c.; सै 'to waste' and सो 'to destroy' make सेयात्; दो 'to cut,' like दा 'to give,' and दे 'to protect' make देयात्. But sometimes they are changed to *ā*: thus, त्रै 'to preserve' makes त्रासीय &c.; दै 'to purify' makes दायात्; ध्यै 'to think' either ध्यायात् or ध्येयात्; ग्लै 'to be weary' either ग्लायात् or ग्लेयात्.

452. As already stated, if a root end in a consonant, there is no change in Parasmai, except the usual changes before *y*; moreover, unlike the 2d future, there is no Guṇa in Ātmane, *unless the root take i*; the other changes in Ātmane are similar to those applicable before the *s* of the 2d future terminations (390. *a*): thus, दुह् 'to milk' makes दुह्यात् &c., and धुक्षीय &c., by 306. *a*; द्विष् 'to hate' makes द्विष्यात् &c., and द्विक्षीय &c., by 302; and बुध् 'to know' makes बुध्यात् &c., and बोधिषीय &c. See 443.

a. Roots of the 10th class, however, retain Guṇa in the Parasmai, as well as in the Ātmane, rejecting the conjugational *aya* in the Parasmai only; see under Causals (495).

453. According to the usual changes in the 4th class and in passives, roots ending in a double consonant, of which the first member is a nasal, generally reject the nasal: thus, भञ्ज् *bhañj*, 7th c., makes *bhajyāsam*, &c. Compare 469.

a. So again, according to 472, ग्रह् 'to take' makes in Parasmai गृह्यात् &c.; प्रच्छ् 'to ask,' पृच्छ्यात् &c.; भ्रस्ज् 'to fry,' भृज्ज्यात् (632); व्रश्च् 'to cut,' वृश्च्यात् (636); व्यध् 'to pierce,' विध्यात्; व्यच् 'to deceive,' विच्यात्; शास् 'to teach,' शिष्यात् &c. In the Ātmane they are regular.

b. So again, इ *i* and उ *u* before *r* and *v* are lengthened: thus, कुर् 'to sound' makes कूर्यात्; and दिव् 'to play,' दीव्यात्. Compare 446.

454. वच् 'to speak,' वद् 'to say,' वप् 'to sow,' वश् 'to wish,' वस् 'to

dwell,' वह् 'to carry,' and स्वप् 'to sleep,' substitute उ u for व va in the Parasmai, and यज् 'to sacrifice' substitutes i for ya: thus, उष्यासं, सुप्यासं, इज्यासं, &c. In the Ātmane they are regular; as, वक्षीय from वह्; यक्षीय from यज्.

a. जन्, सन्, and खन् conform to 470: thus, जायासं or जन्यासं &c.; compare 424. c.

Observe—In addition to these rules, the other special changes which take place before the s of the 2d future terminations, noted at 390 and 390. a–o, will apply to the Ātmane of the precative: thus, वृ or वॄ at 390 makes वृषीय or वरिषीय; भ्रस्ज् at 390. g. makes भ्रक्षीय or भर्क्षीय; कम् at 390. l. makes कामयिषीय or कमिषीय; and गुप् may be गुप्यासं or गोपाय्यासं even in Parasmai.

Conditional.

Terminations of conditional repeated from page 128.

Parasmai.			Ātmane.		
syam	*syáva*	*syáma*	*sye*	*syávahi*	*syámahi*
syas	*syatam*	*syata*	*syathás*	*syethám*	*syadhvam*
syat	*syatám*	*syan*	*syata*	*syetám*	*syanta*

455. Observe, that this tense bears the same relation to the 2d future that the imperfect does to the present. In its formation it lies half-way between the imperfect or first preterite and the second future. It resembles the imperfect in prefixing the augment अ a to the base (see 260), and in the latter part of its terminations: it resembles the second future in the first part of its terminations in gunating the radical vowel, in inserting इ i in exactly those roots in which the future inserts i, and in the other changes of the base.

456. The rule for the formation of the base in verbs of the first nine classes after prefixing the augment अ a, according to the usual rules, will be the same as for the 2d future at 388. Gunate the radical vowel, except as debarred by 28. b. &c., and insert i before the terminations if the futures insert i. When i is rejected, the rules of Sandhi must of course be observed, and all other changes as in the 2d future, see 388—415.

457. Thus, बुध् 1st c., 'to know,' makes अबोधिष्यं &c.; दुह् 'to milk' makes अधोक्ष्यं &c. (see 414 and 306. a); द्विष् 'to hate,' अद्वेक्ष्यं &c. (see 412); गुह् 'to conceal,' अगूहिष्यं or अघोक्ष्यं (415. m); मज्ज् 'to be immersed,' अमंक्ष्यं (390. k).

a. The augment will be prefixed to roots beginning with vowels according to the rules for the imperfect: thus, ऊर्णु 'to cover' makes और्णुविष्यं or और्णविष्यं, see r. 260. a, b, and compare 390. b.

b. इ 'to go,' with अधि prefixed (meaning 'to read'), may optionally form its conditional from the root गा (अध्यैष्ये or अध्यगीष्ये, see 421. c).

Infinitive.

458. The termination of the infinitive is तुम् *tum*, like the *tum* of the Latin *supine*.

Observe—The affix *tum* is probably the accusative of an affix *tu*, of which the affix *tvá* of the indeclinable participle (see 555. *a*) is the instrumental case, and of which other cases are used as infinitives in the Veda.

459. Rule for forming the base in verbs of the ten classes. The base of the infinitive is identical with the base of the first future, and where one inserts इ *i*, the other does also: thus, *budh*, 1st c., 'to know,' makes बोधितुम् *bodhitum*; क्षिप् *kship*, 6th c., 'to throw,' makes क्षेप्तुम् *ksheptum*. Moreover, all the rules for the change of the root before the *t* of the future terminations apply equally before the *t* of the infinitive. Hence, by substituting *um* for the final *á* of the 3d pers. sing. of the 1st future, the infinitive is at once obtained: thus, त्यक्ता, त्यक्तुं; यष्टा, यष्टुं; भोक्ता, भोक्तुं; जनिता, जनितुं. So also, दुह् makes दोग्धुं; द्रुह्, द्रोग्धुं or द्रोढुं or द्रोहितुं; कुष्, कुषितुं. See 388—415.

a. In the Veda, infinitives may be formed by any of the affixes, असे, अध्यै, तोस्, ध्यै, से, तवे, तवै, अम्, ए, ऐ, तवम्.

b. The following examples will show how remarkably the Sanskrit infinitive answers to the Latin *supine*. S. स्थातुं 'to stand,' L. *statum*; S. दातुं 'to give,' L. *datum*; S. पातुं 'to drink,' L. *potum*; S. एतुं 'to go,' L. *itum*; S. स्तर्तुं 'to strew,' L. *stratum*; S. अंक्तुं 'to anoint,' L. *unctum*; S. जनितुं 'to beget,' L. *genitum*; S. स्वनितुं 'to sound,' L. *sonitum*; S. सर्प्तुं 'to go,' L. *serptum*; S. वमितुं 'to vomit,' L. *vomitum*.

DERIVATIVE VERBS.

460. Having explained the formation of the verbal base in the ten classes of primitive verbs, we come next to the four kinds of derivative verbs, viz. passives, causals, desideratives, and frequentatives.

PASSIVE VERBS.

461. Every root in every one of the ten classes may take a passive form (see 253, and 253. *a*, *b*), which is conjugated as an *Átmane-pada* verb of the 4th class, the only difference being in the accent *.

a. There will be three kinds of passive verbs: 1st, The passive, properly so called; as, from तुद्, तुद्यते 'be is struck' (i.e. 'by another'), where the verb

* The accent in passives is on the characteristic *ya*, whereas in the *Átmane-pada* of primitive verbs of the 4th class, it falls on the radical syllable. There are occasional instances in the Mahá-bhárata of passive verbs conjugated in the Parasmai.

implies that the person or thing spoken of suffers some action from another person or thing.

b. 2dly, An impersonal passive, generally formed from a neuter verb, and only occurring in the 3d singular; as, from गम् 'to go,' गम्यते 'it is gone;' from नृत् 'to dance,' नृत्यते 'it is danced,' where the verb itself implies neither person nor thing as either acting or suffering, but simply expresses a state or condition. This impersonal form is commonly used in classical Sanskṛit, with an instrumental case, in place of the active verb: thus गम्यते मया 'it is gone by me' is equivalent to गच्छामि 'I go;' and तेन गम्यतां 'let it be gone by him' is idiomatically used for स गच्छतु 'let him go.'

c. 3dly, A reflexive passive, where there is no object as distinct from the subject of the verb, or, in other words, where the subject is both agent and sufferer, as in पच्यते 'it is ripened' (i. e. 'becomes ripe of itself'); जायते 'he is born,' &c. In these latter, if a vowel immediately precedes the characteristic *y*, the accent may fall on the radical syllable, as in the 4th class. They may also, in some cases, make use of the Ātmane-pada of the active, and drop the *y* altogether: thus to express 'he is adorned by himself,' it would be right to use भूषते 'he adorns himself.'

462. Observe—Passive verbs take the regular Ātmane-pada terminations at 247, making use of the substitutions required in the 4th class. In the aorist (or 3d preterite) they take either the A or B terminations of form I at 418, according as the root may admit the inserted इ *i* or not; but they require that in the 3d singular of both forms the termination be इ *i* in place of *sta* and *ishṭa*.

Conjugational tenses.

463. Rule for the formation of the base in the four conjugational tenses, Ātmane-pada, of roots of the first nine classes. The rule is the same as in the 4th class at 272, viz. affix य *ya*—lengthened to या *yā* before initial *m* and *v*—to the root, the vowel of which is not guṇated, and often remains unchanged.

Observe—This *ya* is probably derived from *yā*, 'to go,' just as the causal *aya* is derived from *i*, 'to go.' It is certain that in Bengālī and Hindī the passive is formed with the root *yā*. Compare the Latin *amatum iri*, &c. See 481.

464. Thus, from भू 1st c., 'to be,' comes the base भूय *bhūya* (Pres. *bhūya* + *i* = भूये, *bhūya* + *se* = भूयसे, &c.; Impf. *abhūya* + *i* = अभूये, &c.; Pot. *bhūya* + *īya* = भूयेय, &c.; Impv. *bhūya* + *ai* = भूयै, &c.); from तुद् 6th c., 'to strike,' comes *tudya* (Pres. *tudya* + *i* = तुद्ये, &c.).

465. The root, however, often undergoes changes, which are generally analogous to those of the 4th class and the precative Parasmai-pada (see 275 and 445); but a final *ā* is not changed to *e* as in the precative.

Six roots in आ á, and one or two in ए e, ऐ ai, and ओ o, change their final vowels to ई í: thus, दा 'to give,' दे 'to protect,' and दो 'to cut,' make Pres. दीये, दीयसे, दीयते, &c. So also, धा 'to place,' स्था 'to stand,' मा 'to measure,' पा 'to drink,' and हा 'to quit' (हीये); धे 'to drink' (3d sing. धीयते, &c.); गै 'to sing' (गीयते); सो 'to destroy' (सीयते).

a. But other roots in आ á remain unchanged; and most others in ai and e are changed to á: thus, ख्या 'to tell' makes 3d sing. ख्यायते; and ज्ञा 'to know,' ज्ञायते; पा 'to protect,' पायते; ध्यै 'to meditate,' ध्यायते; शो 'to sharpen,' शायते.

b. दरिद्रा, दीधी, and वेवी, drop their finals as at 390. c (दरिद्र्यते, दीध्यते, &c.); and ज्या 'to become old' makes 1. जीये 446. e.

c. ह्वे 'to call,' व्ये 'to cover,' वे 'to weave,' make their bases húya, víya, and úya (3d sing. हूयते). Compare 450. a.

466. Final इ i or उ u are lengthened, as also a medial i or u before v or r: thus, from चि, श्रु, दिव्, कुर्, come चीय, श्रूय, दीव्य, कूर्य. See 447 and 453. b.

a. But श्वि 'to swell' makes 3d sing. शूयते; and शी 'to sleep,' शय्यते.

467. Final ऋ ṛi becomes रि ri, but if preceded by a double consonant is gunated: thus, कृ makes 3. क्रियते; हृ, ह्रियते; but स्मृ, स्मर्यते.

a. The roots ऋ and जागृ are also gunated (अर्यते, &c.). See 448 and 448. a.

468. Final ॠ ṛí becomes ईर् ír: thus, कॄ 'to scatter' makes 3. कीर्यते; but पॄ 'to fill,' पूर्यते. See 449 and 449. a.

469. Roots ending in a double consonant, of which the first is a nasal, usually reject the nasal; as, from बन्ध्, स्रंस्, मन्थ्, come the bases badhya, &c. (बध्यते, &c.).

a. The roots at 390. l. carry their peculiarities into the passive (ऋत्यते or ऋतीयते, गुप्यते or गोपाय्यते, विच्छ्यते or विच्छाय्यते, धूप्यते or धूपाय्यते).

470. जन् 'to produce,' खन् 'to dig,' तन् 'to stretch,' सन् 'to give,' optionally reject the final nasal, and lengthen the preceding a: thus, जायते or जन्यते, &c.

471. वच् 'to speak,' वद् 'to say,' वप् 'to sow,' वश् 'to wish,' वस् 'to dwell,' वह् 'to bear,' स्वप् 'to sleep,' यज् 'to sacrifice,' make their bases उच्य, उद्य, उप्य, उश्य, उष्य, उह्य, सुप्य, इज्य respectively, (उच्यते, &c.)

472. ग्रह् 'to take,' प्रच्छ् 'to ask,' भ्रस्ज् 'to fry,' वञ्च् 'to deceive,' व्यध् 'to pierce,' व्रश्च् 'to cut,' शास् 'to rule,' make their bases गृह्य, पृच्छ्य, भृज्ज्य, विच्य, विध्य, वृश्च्य, शिष्य respectively, (गृह्यते, &c.)

a. ऊह् 'to reason' shortens its vowel after prepositions (उह्यते; otherwise ऊह्यते).

b. अज् forms its passive from वी; अद् from घस्; अस् from भू; ब्रू from वच्; and चक्ष् from ख्या.

Non-conjugational tenses.—Perfect (or *second preterite*) *of passives.*

473. The base of this tense in the passive verb is identical with that of all primitive verbs, in all ten conjugations. The bases, therefore, as formed at 364—384, will serve equally well for the perfect of the passive, provided only that they be restricted to the Átmane-pada inflection: thus, बुबुधे, बेभे, &c.

a. When the periphrastic perfect has to be employed (see 385) the auxiliaries अस् and भू may be used in the Átmane, as well as कृ. Compare 385. b.

First and second future of passives.

474. In these and the remaining tenses no variation generally occurs from the bases of the same tenses in the primitive, Ātmane-pada, unless the root end in a vowel. In that case the insertion of इ *i* may take place in the passive, although prohibited in the primitive, provided the final vowel of the root be first vriddhied: thus, from चि *ći*, 5th c., 'to gather,' may come the base of the 1st and 2d fut. pass. *ćāyi* (*ćāyitāhe* &c., *ćāyishye* &c.), although the base of the same tenses in the primitive is *će* (*ćetāhe* &c., *ćeshye* &c.). Similarly, from हु *hu* and हृ *hṛi* may come *hāvi* and *hāri* (*hāvitāhe*, *hāritāhe*), although the bases in the primitive are *ho* and *har*.

a. In like manner इ *i* may be inserted when the root ends in long आ *ā*, or in ए *e*, ऐ *ai*, ओ *o*, changeable to आ *ā*, provided that, instead of Vriddhi (which is impossible), *y* be interposed between the final *ā* and inserted *i*: thus, from दा *dā*, 'to give,' may come the base of the fut. pass. *dāyi* (*dāyitāhe* &c.), although the base of the same tenses in the primitive is *dā* (*dātāhe* &c.); from ह्वे *hve*, 'to call,' may come *hvāyi* (ह्वायिताहे &c.), although the base in the primitive is *hvā*. But in all these cases it is permitted to take the base of the primitive for that of the passive, so that *ćetāhe* or *ćāyitāhe* may equally stand for the 1st fut. pass.; and similarly with the others.

b. In the case of roots ending in consonants, the base of the two futures in the passive will be identical with that of the same tenses in the primitive verb, the inflection being that of the Ātmane. दृश् 'to see,' however, in the passive, may be दर्शिताहे, दर्शिष्ये, as well as द्रष्टाहे, द्रक्ष्ये; and हन् 'to kill' may be घानिताहे, घानिष्ये, as well as हन्ताहे, हनिष्ये; and ग्रह् 'to take' may be ग्राहिताहे, ग्राहिष्ये, as well as ग्रहीताहे, ग्रहीष्ये.

c. In verbs of the 10th class and causals, deviation from the Ātmane form of the primitive may take place in these and the succeeding tenses. See 496.

Aorist (or *third preterite*) *of passives.*

475. In this tense, also, variation from the primitive may occur when the root ends in a *vowel*. For in that case the insertion of इ *i* may take place, although forbidden in the primitive verb, provided the final of the root be vriddhied: thus, from चि *ći* may come the base of the aorist pass. *aćāyi* (*aćāyishi* &c., 427), although the base in the Ātmane of the primitive is *aće* (*aćeshi* &c., 420). So also, from हु *hu* and हृ *hṛi* may come *ahāvi* and *ahāri* (*ahāvishi*, *ahārishi*, 427), although the bases in the Ātmane of the primitive are *aho* and *ahṛi* (*ahoshi*, *ahṛishi*, 420). Again, *i* may be inserted when the root ends in long आ *ā*, or in ए *e*, ऐ *ai*, ओ *o*, changeable to आ *ā*, provided that *y* be interposed between final *ā* and inserted *i*: thus, from दा 'to give,' त्रै 'to protect,' दै 'to purify,' दो 'to cut,' may come *adāyi* (*adāyishi* &c.), although the bases in the Ātmane of the primitives are different (as *adishi* &c.). But in all these cases it is permitted to take the base of the primitive for that of the passive (so that the passive of *ći* may be either *aćāyishi* or *aćeshi*), except in the

3d pers. sing., where the terminations *ishṭa* and *sta* being rejected, the base, as formed by Vṛiddhi and the inserted *i*, must stand alone: thus, *achāyi*, 'it was gathered;' *ahāvi*, 'it was sacrificed;' *akāri*, 'it was done;' *adāyi*, 'it was given,' 'protected,' 'purified,' 'cut.'

a. Sometimes the usual form of the aorist Ātmane is employed throughout (see 461. *c*). This is the case whenever the sense is that of a reflexive passive, not of the real passive: thus, चक्षा 'to tell' in the aorist passive 3d sing. is अचक्षायि, but in the sense of a reflexive passive अचक्षत; श्रि 'to have recourse' makes passive aorist 1st sing. अश्रयिषि, but reflexive अशिश्रियि; and कम् 'to love' makes 3d sing. passive अकमि or अकामि, but reflexive अचकमे.

b. If the root end in a *consonant*, the base of the aorist pass. will always be identical with that of the Ātmane of the primitive, except in the 3d sing., where इ *i* being substituted for the terminations *ishṭa* and *sta* of form I at p. 179, generally requires before it the lengthening of a medial *a* (if not already long by position), and the Guṇa of any other short medial vowel *. Hence, from *tan*, 'to stretch,' 1st, 2d, and 3d sing. *atanishi*, *atanishṭhās*, *atāni*; from *kship*, 'to throw,' *akshipsi*, *akshipthās*, *akshepi*; from *vid*, 'to know,' *avedishi*, *avedishṭhās*, *avedi*, &c.

c. The lengthening of a medial *a*, however, is by no means universal; and there are other exceptions in the 3d sing., as follows:—Nearly all roots in *am* forbid the lengthening of the vowel in the 3d sing.: thus, अक्रमि from क्रम् 'to walk;' अक्षमि from क्षम् 'to bear;' अशमि from शम् 'to be calm' (but in the sense of 'to observe,' अशामि).

d. Similarly, अवधि from वध् and अजनि from जन्. The former may optionally substitute अघानि from हन्.

e. कुष् and गुह् lengthen their vowels (अकूषि, अगूहि).

f. The roots at 390. *l.* will have two forms, अघटि or अघाटि, अगोपि or अगोपायि, अविच्छि or अविच्छायि, &c.

g. रध् 'to perish,' जभ् 'to yawn,' रभ् 'to desire,' insert nasals (अरन्धि, अजम्भि, अरम्भि). Similarly, लभ् 'to receive,' when it has a preposition (e. g. प्रालम्भि), and optionally when it has none (अलम्भि or अलाभि, Pāṇ. VII. 1, 69).

h. भञ्ज् 'to break' may drop its nasal, in which case the medial *a* is lengthened (अभञ्जि or अभाजि).

i. वेष्ट् 'to clothe' may either retain the *e* or change it to *í* or *i* (अवेष्टि or अविष्टि or अवीष्टि).

j. इ 'to go' substitutes गा, and optionally does so when *adhi* is prefixed in the sense of 'to read' (अध्यगायि or अध्यायि).

k. चाय् 'to blame' makes अचायि or अचारि.

Precative (or *benedictive*) *and conditional of passives.*

476. In these tenses the same variation is permitted in the case of roots ending in vowels as in the last; that is, the insertion of इ *i* is allowed, provided that,

---

* A medial vowel, long by nature or position, remains unchanged (by 28. *b*), and in one or two cases a short; as, *adami* for *adámi*.

before it, Vṛiddhi take place in a final vowel capable of such a change, and *y* be interposed after final *á*: thus, from चि *ći* may come the bases *ćáyi* and *aćáyi* (*ćáyishíya*, *aćáyishye*); from हु *hu*, *hávi* and *ahávi*; from कृ *kṛi*, *kári* and *akári*; from दा *dá*, *dáyi* and *adáyi*. But *ćeshíya*, *aćeshye*, *hoshíya*, *ahoshye*, &c., the forms belonging to the Átmane of the primitive verb, are equally admissible in the passive.

Passive infinitive mood.

477. There is no passive infinitive mood in Sanskrit distinct in form from the active. The affix *tum*, however, is capable of a passive sense, when joined with certain verbs, especially with the passive of शक् *śak*, 'to be able.' It is also used passively, in connection with the participles *árabdha*, *nirúpita*, *yukta*, &c. See Syntax, 869.

Passive verbs from roots of the 10th class.

478. In forming a passive verb from roots of the 10th class, although the conjugational अय is rejected in the first four tenses, yet the other conjugational changes of the root are retained before the affix *ya*: thus, from चुर् 10th c., 'to steal,' comes the base *ćorya* (चोर्यते). In the perfect अय is retained (see 473. *a*), and in the other non-conjugational tenses the base may deviate from the Átmane form of the primitive by the optional rejection or assumption of अय, especially in the aorist. See Causal Passives at 496.

CAUSAL VERBS.

479. Every root in every one of the ten classes may take a causal form, which is conjugated as a verb of the 10th class; and which is not only employed to give a causal sense to a primitive verb, but also an active sense to a neuter verb; see 289, 254: thus the primitive verb *bodhati*, 'he knows' (from the root *budh*, 1st c.), becomes in the causal बोधयति *bodhayati*, 'he causes to know,' 'he informs;' and the neuter verb *kshubhyati*, 'he shakes,' 'is shaken' (from *kshubh*, 4th c.), becomes क्षोभयति 'he shakes' (actively).

a. This form may rarely imply other analogous senses: thus, *hárayati*, 'he allows to take;' *náśayati*, 'he suffers to perish;' *abhishećayati*, 'he permits himself to be inaugurated;' *kshamayati*, 'he asks to be forgiven;' अभिषेचय आत्मानं 'allow yourself to be inaugurated.'

480. As to the terminations of causal verbs, they are the same as those of the scheme at 247, p. 126; and the same substitutions are required in the first four tenses as in the 1st, 4th, 6th, and 10th classes.

Conjugational tenses.

481. General rule for forming the base in the four conjugational tenses of roots of the ten classes. If a root end in a vowel, vṛiddhi that vowel; if in a consonant, guṇate the radical vowel before *all* the terminations, and affix अय *aya* * (changeable to *ayā* before initial *m* and *v*, but not before simple *m*) to the root so vṛiddhied or guṇated.

482. Thus, from नी 'to lead' comes the base नायय by 37 (Pres. *nāyayā* + *mi* = नाययामि, *nāyaya* + *si* = नाययसि &c.; Impf. *anāyaya* + *m* = अनाययं &c.; Pot. *nāyaya* + *iyam* = नाययेयं &c.; Impv. *nāyaya* + *āni* = नाययानि &c. Ātm. Pres. *nāyaya* + *i* = नायये &c. In Epic poetry a doubtful form नाययामि is found). Similarly, from शी 'to lie down' comes शायय *śāyaya* (शाययामि &c.); from भू *bhū*, 'to be,' comes भावय *bhāvaya* (भावयामि &c.); and from कृ 'to do' and कॄ 'to scatter' the base कारय *kāraya*.

But from बुध् 'to know' comes the guṇated बोधय *bodhaya* (बोधयामि); and from सृप् 1st c., 'to creep,' the guṇated सर्पय *sarpaya*.

Observe—कृत् 'to celebrate,' and other verbs of the 10th class, will take the changes already explained at 285—289.

483. Roots ending in आ *ā*, or in ए *e*, ऐ *ai*, ओ *o*, changeable to आ *ā*, cannot be vṛiddhied, but frequently insert प् *p* between the root and the affix *aya*: thus, दा 'to give,' दे 'to love,' and दो 'to cut,' all make दापयामि *dāpayāmi*, &c.; धे 'to drink,' धापयामि *dhāpayāmi*, &c.; गै 'to sing,' गापयामि *gāpayāmi*, &c. See 484.

a. So also other roots in *ā* insert *p*, except पा 1st c., 'to drink,' which inserts य् *y* (पाययामि &c.); and पा 2d c., 'to preserve,' which inserts ल् *l* (पालयामि &c.); and वा 2d c., in the sense of 'to agitate,' which inserts ज (वाजयामि &c.).

b. So also other roots in *ai* insert *p*, but most others in *e* and *o* insert *y*: thus, ह्वे 'to call' makes ह्वाययामि &c. Similarly, वे 'to weave,' व्ये 'to put on.' शो 'to sharpen' makes शाययामि &c. Similarly, छो 'to cut,' सो 'to destroy.'

484. ज्ञा 'to know,' श्रा or श्रै 'to stew,' स्ना 'to bathe,' and ग्लै 'to languish,' may optionally shorten the *ā*, the last two only when not joined with prepositions: thus, ज्ञापयामि &c., or ज्ञपयामि &c.; ग्लापयामि &c., or ग्लपयामि &c. (but with परि only, परिग्लापयामि). क्षै 'to waste away' makes only क्षपयामि.

485. Some roots in *i*, *ī*, *ṛi*, also insert *p*, after changing the final vowel to *ā*: thus, जि 'to conquer' makes जापयामि &c. Similarly, क्षि 'to throw,' मी 'to perish,' क्री 'to buy' (मापयामि, क्रापयामि, &c.).

a. स्मि 'to smile' makes स्मापयामि &c., and स्मापये &c.

---

* This may be derived from the root इ *i*, 'to go,' just as the passive *ya* is supposed to be derived from *yā*. See 463.

b. चि 'to collect' has four forms; 1. चापयामि &c., 2. चपयामि &c., 3. चाययामि &c., 4. चययामि &c.

c. भी 3d c., 'to fear,' has three forms; 1. भाययामि &c., 2. भापये &c., Âtm. only, 3. भीषये &c., Âtm. only.

d. इ 2d c., 'to go,' makes आययामि &c., especially with the preposition अधि 'over,' अध्यापयामि 'I cause to go over,' 'I teach.'

e. Three roots insert *n*: ली 4th c., 'to embrace,' 'to adhere,' making (with prep. वि in the sense of 'to dissolve') -लीनयामि &c., as well as -लापयामि, -लाययामि, and -लालयामि &c.; in some senses, however, लापयामि only can be used: प्री 9th c., 'to please,' makes प्रीणयामि (also प्राययामि); and धू 5th and 9th c., 'to shake,' धूनयामि.

486. ह्री 3d c., 'to be ashamed,' री 'to flow,' व्री 'to choose,' and ऋ 1st c., 'to go,' insert *p* after guṇation: thus, ह्रेपयामि &c., अर्पयामि &c.

a. दीधी and वेवी and दरिद्रा (see 390. *e*) drop their finals (दीधयामि, वेवयामि, दरिद्रयामि, &c.).

b. जागृ 'to awake,' स्मृ in sense of 'to long for,' जॄ 4th c., 'to grow old,' दॄ in sense of 'to fear,' नॄ 'to lead,' take Guṇa (जागरयामि). But दॄ 'to tear,' दारयामि.

c. गॄ 'to swallow' makes गारयामि or गालयामि.

487. Roots ending in single consonants, enclosing a medial अ *a*, generally lengthen the *a*: thus, पच् 1st c., 'to cook,' makes पाचयामि &c. There are, however, many exceptions: thus, चट् 'to be sick,' त्वर् 'to hasten,' &c., do not lengthen the vowel. In ज्वल् 'to blaze,' and some others, the lengthening is optional.

a. Few roots in *m* lengthen the *a*: thus, गम् 1st c., 'to go,' makes गमयामि &c.; क्लम् 'to be weary,' क्लमयामि &c. Some, however, optionally do so; as, नम् 'to bend,' &c. One or two always lengthen the *a*: as, कम् 'to love' makes कामयामि.

b. The roots रध्, जभ्, रभ्, and लभ् (see 475. *e*) insert nasals (रन्धयामि &c.).

488. Other anomalies.—रुह् 'to grow' makes रोहयामि or रोपयामि; क्नूय् or क्नू 'to sound,' क्नोपयामि; दुष् 'to be corrupt,' दूषयामि; हन् 'to kill,' घातयामि; शद् 'to fall,' 'to perish,' शातयामि; स्फुर् 'to quiver,' स्फारयामि or स्फोरयामि; स्फाय् 'to increase,' स्फावयामि; क्ष्माय् 'to shake' as the earth, क्ष्मापयामि &c.; मृज् 'to rub,' मार्जयामि (390. *i*); गुह् 'to conceal,' गूहयामि (390. *m*).

a. The roots गुप्, विछ्, धूप्, पण्, पन्, ऋत्, at 390. *l*, will have two forms (गोपयामि or गोपाययामि &c., see 390. *l*).

b. सिध् 'to be finished' makes its causal either साधयामि or, with reference to sacred rites, सेधयामि; भ्रस्ज् 'to fry' either भ्रज्जयामि or भर्जयामि; but the last form may be from भृज्.

c. हेड् 'to clothe' makes हिडयामि; रञ्ज् in the sense of 'to hunt,' रजयामि.

Observe—The causal of verbs of the 10th class will be identical with the primitive; see 289. The causals of causals will also be identical with the causals themselves.

Non-conjugational tenses.

489. The changes of the root required to form the base of the conjugational tenses are continued in the non-conjugational. Moreover, *aya* is retained in all these tenses, except the aorist and except the benedictive, Parasmai; but the last *a* of *aya* is dropped before the inserted इ i, which is invariably assumed in all other conjugational tenses.

Perfect (second preterite) of causals.

490. This tense must be of the periphrastic form, as explained at 385; that is, आम् *ám* added to the causal base is prefixed to the perfect of one of the three auxiliary verbs, अस् 'to be,' भू 'to be,' or कृ 'to do:' thus, बुध् 'to know' makes in causal perfect बोधयाञ्चकार or बोधयामास or बोधयाम्बभूव*.

First and second future of causals.

491. In these tenses the inserted इ *i* is invariably assumed between the base, as formed in the conjugational tenses, and the usual terminations: thus, बुध् makes बोधयितास्मि &c., बोधयिष्यामि &c.

Aorist (third preterite) of causals and verbs of the 10th class.

492. The terminations are those of form II at 435. In the formation of the base of this tense, the affix *ay* is rejected; but any other change that may take place in the conjugational tenses, such as the insertion of *p* or *y*, is preserved. The base is a reduplicated form of this change, and to this reduplication the augment अ *a* is prefixed: thus, taking the bases *bodhay* and *jápay* (causal bases of *budh*, 'to know,' and *ji*, 'to conquer'), and rejecting *ay*, we have *bodh* and *jáp*; and from these are formed the bases of the aorist *abúbudh* and *ajíjap* (अबूबुधम् *abúbudham* &c., अबूबुधे *abúbudhe* &c., अजीजपम् *ajíjapam* &c., अजीजपे *ajíjape* &c., cf. the Greek pluperfect).

493. The rule for this reduplication is as follows:—The initial consonant of the root, with its vowel, is reduplicated, and the reduplicated consonant follows the rules given at 331; but the reduplication of the vowel is peculiar.

Reduplication of the vowel of the initial consonant in the causal aorist.

a. Causal bases, after rejecting *ay*, will generally end in *áy*, *ár*, *ár*, or a consonant

---

* It may be questioned whether अस् is found added to causals.

preceded by *a*, *á*, *e*, *o*, or *ar*. The usual reduplicated vowel for all these, except *o*, is इ *i*. But उ *u* is reduplicated for *o*, and sometimes also for *ár*. The rule is, that either the reduplicated or base syllable must be long either by nature or position; and in general the reduplicated vowel *i* or *u* is made long, and, to compensate for this, the long vowel of the causal base shortened, or, if it be Guṇa, changed to its cognate short vowel: thus, the causal base *náy* (from नी, rejecting *ay*) makes the base of the aorist *anínay* (अनीनयम् *anínayam* &c.); the causal base *bháv* (from भू) makes *abíbhav* (अबीभवं &c.); the causal base *kár* (from कृ), *aćíkar*; *gam* (from गम्), *ajígam*; *páṭ* (from पट्), *apípaṭ*; *pál* (from पा), *apípal*; *ved* (from विद्), *avívid*. But *bodh* (from बुध्), *abúbudh*; and *sáv* (from सु), *asúshav*.

b. Sometimes the reduplicated vowel is only long by position before two consonants, the radical vowel being still made short; as, *śráv* (from श्रु) makes *aśiśrav* or *aśuśrav*; *dráv* (from द्रु), *adudrav* or *adidrav*; भ्राज्, *abibhraj* (also *ababhráj*).

c. Sometimes the reduplicated vowel remains short, whilst the vowel of the causal base, which must be long either by nature or position, remains unchanged: thus, the causal base *jív* (from जीव्) may make अजिजीवं (also अजीजिवं); *ćint*, *aćićint*; *kalp*, *aćikalp*. In such cases *a* is generally reduplicated for *a* or *á*; as, *laksh* makes *alalaksh*; *yáć*, *ayayáć*; *vart* (from *vṛit*), *avavart*, &c.

d. Observe—If the base has *ar*, *ár*, *ír*, *al* (from radical *ṛi*, *ṝí*, or *ḷṛi*), these are either left unchanged or *ar*, *ár*, *ír* may be changed to ऋ *ṛi*, and *al* to ऌ *ḷṛi*: thus, *vart* (from वृत्) may make *avívṛit* as well as *avavart*; *kírt* (from कृत्) either *aćíkírt* or *aćíkṛit*, &c.

e. The following are other examples, some of which are anomalous: from *páy* (causal of *pá*, 'to drink'), अपीप्यं &c.; from *sthāp* (caus. of *sthá*, 'to stand'), अतिष्ठिपं &c.; from *ghráp* (caus. of *ghrá*, 'to smell'), अजिघ्रिपं &c., and अजिघ्रपं &c.; from *adhyáp* (caus. of *i*, 'to go,' with *adhi*), अध्यजीगपं &c.; from *ćeshṭ* (caus. of *ćeshṭ*, 'to make effort'), अचचेष्टं or अचिचेष्टं; from *hváy* (caus. of *hve*, 'to call'), अजुहावं or अजूहवं; from *tvar* (caus. of *tvar*, 'to hasten'), अतत्वरं; from *stár* (caus. of *stṛi* or *stṝí*, 'to spread'), अतस्तरं or अतिस्तरं; from *dár* (caus. of *dṝí*, 'to tear'), अददरं; from *dyot* (caus. of *dyut*, 'to shine'), अदिद्युतं; from *śváy* (caus. of *śvi*, 'to swell'), अशूशवं or अशिश्वयं; from *smár* (caus. of *smṛi*, 'to remember'), असस्मरं; from *sváp* (caus. of स्वप् 'to sleep'), असूषुपं; from *kath* (10th c. 'to tell'), अचकथं or अचीकथं; from गण् (10th c. 'to count'), अजगणं or अजीगणं; from *prath* (caus. of प्रथ् 'to spread'), अपप्रथं.

Reduplication of an initial vowel in the causal aorist.

494. Roots beginning with vowels, and ending with single consonants, form their causal aorists by a peculiar reduplication of the root (after rejecting अय्). The rule is that not only the initial vowel, as in the perfect (2d pret.) at 364. *a*, but the final consonant also be reduplicated. In fact, the whole root is doubled, as it would be if it began with a consonant, and ended with a vowel; the consonant is reduplicated according to the rules at 331, but the second vowel is generally इ *i*. This *i* (which probably results from a weakening of *a*) takes the place of the base

vowel, which then becomes the initial of the reduplicated syllable, and combines with the augment अ *a*, according to 260. *a*: thus, ऊह् 'to infer' makes the base of its causal aorist ऊजिह् *újih*; and with अ prefixed, औजिहम् (औजिहं 'I caused to infer'). So also, आप् 5th c., 'to obtain,' makes आपिपं 'I caused to obtain;' ईड् 2d c., 'to praise,' makes ऐडिडं 'I caused to praise.' Compare the Greek 2d aorist ἤγαγον from ἄγω, and ὤρορον from ὄρνυμι.

a. If a root end in a compound consonant, the first member of which is a nasal or *r*, this nasal or *r* is rejected from the final, but not from the reduplicated letter: thus, अर्ह् 'to be worthy' makes आर्जिहं 'I caused to be worthy,' 'I honoured;' so अर्द्धि, causal base from ऋध् 'to prosper,' makes आर्दिधं 'I caused to prosper;' and उन्द् 'to moisten' makes औन्दिदं 'I caused to moisten.'

b. But when the first member of the compound is any other letter, then the corresponding consonant to this first member of the compound is reduplicated by 331. *c*: thus, ईक्ष् 'to see' makes ऐचिक्षम् *aichiksham*, 'I caused to see;' अट्ट् 'to go' makes आटिटं 'I caused to go.'

c. Roots consisting of a single vowel, form their causal aorists from the causal base (after rejecting *aya*): thus, the root ऋ 'to go' makes its causal base *arp*, 'to deliver over;' and its causal aorist आर्पिपं 'I caused to deliver.'

d. ऊर्णु 'to cover' makes its causal aorist और्णुनुवं; अन्ध् 10th c. 'to be blind,' आन्दधं; and ऊन् 10th c. 'to diminish,' औननं.

e. When the consonant which follows the initial vowel has another vowel after it, this vowel must appear in the reduplication: thus, from अवधीर् 10th c., 'to despise,' comes the aorist आववधीरं.

Benedictive and conditional of causals.

495. The base of the causal benedictive Átmane, and of the causal conditional in both voices, does not differ from that of the non-conjugational tenses; but the last *a* of *aya* is dropped before the inserted इ *i*, which is always assumed. In the benedictive Parasmai both *aya* and *i* are rejected, but any other change of the root is retained: thus, बुध् 'to know' makes in causal benedictive *bodhyásam* &c., *bodhayishíya* &c.; in conditional, *abodhayishyam* &c., *abodhayishye* &c.

Infinitive of causals.

a. The infinitive is formed regularly from the 3d sing. 1st future, as explained at 459: thus, from बुध् comes बोधयिता 'he will cause to know,' बोधयितुं 'to cause to know.'

Passive of causals.

496. In forming a passive verb from a causal base, the causal

affix अय is rejected, but the other causal changes of the root are retained before the passive affix *ya:* thus, from the causal base पातय *pátaya* (from पत् 'to fall') comes the passive पात्य *pátya*, making 1st sing. पात्ये 'I am made to fall,' 3d sing. पात्यते 'he is made to fall.' Similarly, स्था 'to stand' makes स्थापयति 'he causes to stand,' स्थाप्यते 'he is caused to stand;' and ज्ञा 'to know' makes ज्ञपयति 'he causes to know,' and ज्ञप्यते 'he is caused to know,' 'he is informed.'

a. In the non-conjugational tenses, the base of all the tenses, excepting the perfect, may vary from the Átmane form by the optional rejection of the conjugational अय. But in the perfect (2d preterite), the Átmane of the usual form with *ám* and the auxiliaries (490, 385) is admitted for the passive. In the aorist (3d preterite), the usual reduplicated form (492) gives place to the Átmane form which belongs to those verbs of the first nine classes which assume *i:* thus, from भावय, the causal base of भू 'to be,' come the passive perfect भावयाञ्चक्रे or भावयामासे or भावयाम्बभूवे; 1st fut. भावयिताहे or भाविताहे; 2d fut. भावयिष्ये or भाविष्ये; aorist अभावयिषि or अभाविषि, 3d sing. अभावि; bened. भावयिषीय or भाविषीय; cond. अभावयिष्ये or अभाविष्ये. Similarly, from बोधय, causal base of बुध् 'to know,' come passive perfect बोधयाञ्चक्रे &c. 'I have been caused to know;' 1st fut. बोधयिताहे or बोधिताहे &c. 'I shall be caused to know;' 2d fut. बोधयिष्ये or बोधिष्ये &c.; aorist अबोधयिषि or अबोधिषि, 2. अबोधयिष्ठाः or अबोधिष्ठाः, 3. अबोधि 'I have been caused to know,' &c. So also, from शमय, causal base of शम् 'to cease,' come the passive perfect शमयाञ्चक्रे or शमयामासे &c. 'I have been caused to cease,' &c.; 1st fut. शमयिताहे or शमिताहे; 2d fut. शमयिष्ये or शमिष्ये; aorist अशमयिषि or अशमिषि, 3d sing. अशमि; bened. शमयिषीय &c.: and the radical *a* may be optionally lengthened; thus, 1st fut. शमयिताहे or शामयिताहे &c.

b. So also, अह्वयि or अह्वायि, 3d sing. aorist, from causal of ह्वे.

Even रच्, कथ्, गण्, and some other roots which end in a double consonant, may optionally lengthen the medial *a:* thus, aorist 3d sing. अरचि or अराचि.

Desiderative of causals.

497. When causals and verbs of the 10th class take a desiderative form (see 498), they retain *ay*, and are all formed with *isha:* thus, चुर् makes *chichorayishámi*, 'I desire to cause to steal,' &c.; पातयति

'I cause to fall' makes पिपातयिषामि 'I desire to cause to fall;' स्वापयामि 'I cause to sleep' makes सुष्वापयिषामि 'I desire to cause to sleep.'

a. The desiderative base of the causal of अधी, 'to go over,' is either अध्यापिपयिष or अधिजिगापयिष; of the causal of ह्वे 'to call,' जुहावयिष (as if from हावय); of the causal of ज्ञा 'to know,' ज्ञीप्स (or regularly जिज्ञापयिष or जिज्ञपयिष); of the causal of श्वि 'to swell,' शुशावयिष (or regularly शिश्वाययिष).

DESIDERATIVE VERBS.

498. Every root in the ten classes may take a desiderative form.

a. Although this form of the root is not often used, in classical composition, in its character of a verb, yet nouns and participles derived from the desiderative base are not uncommon (see 80. XXII, and 82. III). Moreover, there are certain primitive roots which take a desiderative form, without yielding a desiderative sense; and these, as equivalent to primitive verbs (amongst which they are generally classed), may occur in classical Sanskrit. For example, *jugups*, 'to blame,' from गुप् *gup*; *ćikits*, 'to cure,' from कित् *kit*; *titiksh*, 'to bear,' from तिज् *tij*; मीमांस् *mímáns*, 'to reason,' from मन् *man*; *bíbhats*, 'to abhor,' from बाध् or बध्.

499. Desideratives take the terminations of the scheme at 247, with the substitutions required in the 1st, 4th, 6th, and 10th classes; and their inflection, either in the Parasmai or Átmane, is generally, though not invariably, determined by the practice of the primitive verb: thus, the root बुध् *budh*, 1st c., 'to know,' taking both inflections in the primitive, may take both in the desiderative (*bubodhishámi* &c., or *bubodhishe* &c., 'I desire to know'); and लभ् *labh*, 'to obtain,' taking only the Átmane in the primitive, may take only the Átmane in the desiderative (*lipse* &c., 'I desire to obtain').

500. Rule for forming the base in the four conjugational tenses. Reduplicate the initial consonant and vowel of the root, and generally, though not invariably, if the primitive verb inserts इ *i* (see 392—415), affix इष् *ish* or in a few roots ईष् (see 393); if it rejects *i*, then simply स *s*, changeable to ष् *sh* (by 70)*, to the root so reduplicated. The vowel *a* is then added, as in the 1st, 4th, 6th, and 10th classes; and, agreeably to the rule in those classes, this *a* becomes *á* before terminations beginning with *m* and *v* (but not before simple *m*).

* See, however, 500. *f.*

a. Thus, from क्षिप् *kship*, 'to throw,' comes the base *ćikshipsa* (*ćikshipsā* + *mi* = चिक्षिप्सामि *ćikshipsāmi* &c., 'I desire to throw'); but from विद् *vid*, 'to know,' taking inserted *i*, comes *vividisha* (*vividishā* + *mi* = विविदिषामि *vividishāmi* &c. In Ātm. *vivitsa*).

b. Some roots, however, which reject the inserted *i* in other forms, assume it in the desiderative, and *vice versa*. Some, again, allow an option: thus, भृ 'to be' makes बिभरिषे &c. or बिभूर्षामि &c. See the lists at 392—415.

c. The reduplication of the consonant is in conformity with the rules at 331; that of the vowel belonging to the initial consonant follows the analogy of causal aorists at 493; that is, the vowel इ *i* is reduplicated for *a*, *ā*, *i*, *ī*, *ri*, *rī*, *lri*, *e*, or *ai*; but the vowel उ *u* for *u*, *ū*, and *o*; and also for the *a* of *av* or *āv* preceded by any consonant except *j*, a labial or a semivowel: thus, from पच् 'to cook' comes the base *pipaksha* by 296; from याच् 'to ask' comes *yiyāćisha*; from जीव् 'to live,' *jijīvisha*; from दृश् 'to see,' *didṛiksha*; from सेव् 'to serve,' *sisevisha*; from गै 'to sing,' *jigāsa*; from ज्ञा 'to know,' *jijnāsa* (γιγνώσκω): but from युज् 'to join' comes *yuyuksha*; from पू 'to purify,' *pupūsha*; from बुध् 4th c., 'to know,' बुभुत्स *bubhutsa*, see 299. *a*; from नावय, causal base of नु 'to praise,' *nunāvayisha*; from पावय, causal base of *pū*, 'to purify,' *pipāvayisha*.

d. And if the root begin with a vowel the reduplication still follows the analogy of the same tense at 494: thus, from अश् comes आशिशम्; and with *isha* added, अशिशिषिष. Similarly, from अर्ह् comes *arjihisha*; from ऊह्, *ūjihisha*; from ईक्ष्, *īćikshisha*; from उन्द्, *undidisha*: see 494.

Observe—In reduplication the vowel *i* takes the place of *a*, as being lighter: see 331. *d.* It is probably the result of a weakening of *a*.

e. In desiderative bases formed from the causals of च्यु 'to fall,' द्रु 'to run,' प्रु 'to go,' प्लु 'to leap,' श्रु 'to hear,' स्रु 'to distil,' and स्रु 'to flow,' *a* or *ā* may be represented by either *u* or *i*: thus, the causal of च्यु makes चिच्यावयिष or चुच्यावयिष.

f. Observe—When the inserted *s* becomes *sh* by r. 70, the initial स् of a root will not be affected by the vowel of the reduplicated syllable: thus, *sić* makes *sisiksha*, not *sishiksha*; and *sev* makes *sisevisha*. Except, however, स्तु, which makes तुष्टूष; and except the desid. of causals, as सिषेवयिष from causal of सिव्.

501. When a root takes the inserted *i* or *ī* (393), and forms its desiderative with *isha* or *īsha*, then final ॠ *rī* is guṇated: thus, तॄ 'to cross' makes *titarisha* or *titarīsha* (also *titīrsha*, see 502).

a. Moreover, initial and medial *i*, *u*, *ṛi* are often, but not always, guṇated if followed by a single consonant: thus, उख् 'to go' makes *oćikhisha*; इष् 'to wish,' *eshishisha*; दिव् 'to play,' *didevisha*; नृत् 'to dance,' *ninartisha*: but विद् 'to know,' *vividisha*.

b. An option, as to Guṇa, is however generally allowed to medial *i* and *u*: thus, मुद् 'to rejoice' makes either *mumudisha* or *mumodisha*; क्लिद् 'to become moist' either *ciklidisha* or *cikledisha*; but roots in *iv* (e. g. *siv*) are peculiar, see 502. *b*.

c. इ 'to go' and उ 'to sound,' having no consonant, reduplicate the characteristic letter of the desiderative with *i*: thus, इषिष (used with the prepositions *adhi* and *prati*), so उपिष.

502. When a root rejects *i* and forms its desiderative with स *sa*, this *sa* if affixed to roots ending in vowels, has the effect of lengthening a final इ *i* or उ *u*; of changing ए *e*, ऐ *ai*, ओ *o*, to आ *á*; ऋ *ṛi* or ॠ *ṛí* to ईर् *ír*, or after a labial to ऊर् *úr*: thus, from चि comes *ćićísha*; from श्रु, *śuśrúsha*; from कृ, *ćikírsha*; from गै, *jigása*; from तॄ, *titírsha*; from पॄ, *pupúrsha*; from भृ, *bubhúrsha*; from मृ, *mumúrsha*.

a. When it is affixed to roots ending in consonants, the radical vowel generally remains unchanged, but the final consonant combines with the initial sibilant, in accordance with the rules laid down at 296; as, from युध् comes *yuyutsa* (299); from दह् comes *didhaksha* (306. *a*); from दुह्, *dudhuksha*; from भुज्, *bubhuksha*.

b. A medial long *ṛí* becomes *ír*, and final *iv* becomes *yú* or is guṇated: thus, from कॄत् comes *ćikírtayisha*; from सिव्, *susyúsha* or *sisevisha*.

c. Many of the special rules for forming the base in the last five tenses at 390. *a*—*o* apply to the desiderative: thus the roots at 390. *a*. generally forbid Guṇa (*ćukućisha* &c.).

d. So भ्रस्ज् makes *bibhraksha* or *bibharksha* or *bibhrajjisha* or *bibharjisha* (390. *g*); मस्ज् and नश्, *mimaṅksha* and *ninaṅksha* (390. *k*); नह्, *ninatsa* (390. *o*); दरिद्रा, *didaridrisha* (390. *c*, but makes also *didaridrása*); कम्, *ćikamisha* or *ćikámayisha*; गुप्, *jugopisha* or *jugopáyisha* or *jugupsa* (390. *l*).

503. The following is an alphabetical list of other desiderative bases, some of them anomalous: अटिटिष from अट् 'to wander;' अंहिहिष from अंह् 'to transgress;' अरिरिष from ऋ 'to go;' ईप्स from आप् 'to obtain;' ईर्त्स (or regularly अर्दिधिष) from ऋध् 'to prosper;' ईर्ष्यिषिष or ईर्ष्यियिष from ईर्ष्य् 'to envy;' ऊर्णुनूष or ऊर्णुनविष or ऊर्णुनुविष (390. *b*) from ऊर्णु 'to cover;' चिचीष (or regularly चिचयिष) from चि 'to collect;' जिगांस (or regularly जिगमिष) from गम् 'to go;' जिगरिष (or regularly जिगलिष) from गॄ 'to swallow' (cf. 375. *g*); जिगीष from जि 'to conquer;' जिघत्स from अद् 'to eat' (used as desid. of अद्); जिघांस from हन् 'to kill;' जिघीष from हि 'to send;' जिघृक्ष from ग्रह् 'to take;' जुहूष from ह्वे 'to call;' तितांस (or regularly तितनिष) from तन् 'to stretch;' तितृक्ष from तृह् 'to kill;' दित्स from दा 'to give,' दे 'to love,' and दो 'to cut;' दिदरिष from दृ 'to respect;' दिदरिष or दिदरीष or दिदीर्ष from दॄ 'to tear;' दिद्युतिष or दिद्योतिष from

द्युत् 'to shine;' दिधरिष from धृ 'to hold;' दुद्यूष (or regularly दिदेविष) from दिव् 'to play;' धित्स from धा 'to place' and धे 'to drink;' धिप्स or धीप्स (or दिदम्भिष) from दम्भ् 'to deceive;' पित्स (or पिपतिष) from पत् 'to fall' and पद् 'to go;' पिपविष or पुपूष from पू 'to purify;' पिपृच्छिष from प्रच्छ् 'to ask;' बिभरिष or बुभूर्ष from भृ 'to bear;' मित्स from मा 'to measure,' मि 'to throw,' मी 'to perish,' and मे 'to change;' मिमार्जिष or मिमृक्ष from मृज् 'to rub;' मोक्ष from मुच् (in the sense of 'desiring release from mundane existence,' otherwise मुमुक्ष); यियविष or युयूष from यु 'to join;' रित्स from राध् 'to accomplish;' रिप्स from रभ् 'to begin;' लिप्स from लभ् 'to obtain;' विवरिष or विवरीष or वुवूर्ष from वृ 'to choose;' विव्रक्ष from व्रश्च् 'to cut;' शिक्ष from शक् 'to be able;' शिश्रयिष (or शिश्रीष) from श्रि 'to have recourse;' सिषास (or सिसनिष) from सन् 'to obtain,' 'to give;' सिस्मयिष from स्मि 'to smile;' सिस्वरिष (or सुस्वूर्ष) from स्वृ 'to sound;' सुषुप्स from स्वप् 'to sleep.'

Non-conjugational tenses of desideratives.

504. The perfect must be of the periphrastic form as explained at 385; that is, आम् *ám* added to the desiderative base, as already formed, with *sa*, *isha*, or *íshe* (500), is prefixed to the perfect of one of the auxiliaries *kṛi*, *as*, or *bhú* (see 385): thus, from *pipaksha* (root *pac*, 'to cook') comes the perfect *pipaksháḿ cakára*, 'I wished to cook;' from *bubodhisha* (root *budh*, 'to know') comes *bubodhisháḿ cakára*, *bubodhishám ása*, *bubodhishám babhúva*, 'he wished to know.'

a. In all the remaining tenses it is an universal rule, that inserted *i* be assumed after the desiderative base, whether formed by *sa* or *isha*, except in the precative (bened.) Parasmai: thus, from *pac* comes 1st fut. 1st sing. *pipakshitásmi* &c.; 2d fut. *pipakshishyámi* &c.; aorist *apipakshisham* &c. (form I, B, at 418); precative Parasmai *pipakshyásam* &c.; Átmane *pipakshishíya* &c.; cond. *apipakshishyam* &c. So also, taking *vividish* (formed with *isha* from *vid*, 'to know'), the 1st fut. is *vividishitásmi*; 2d fut. *vividishishyámi*; aorist *avividishisham* &c. Similarly, from *bubodhisha*, 1st fut. *bubodhishitásmi* &c.; 2d fut. *bubodhishishyámi*; aorist *abubodhishisham* &c.

b. The infinitive is formed regularly from the 1st future: thus, from *bubodhishitá*, 'he will wish to know,' comes *bubodhishitum*, 'to wish to know.'

Passive of desideratives.

505. Desideratives may take a passive form by adding *ya* to the desiderative base after rejecting final *a*: thus, from *bubodhisha* comes *bubodhishye*, 'I am wished to know,' &c. The non-conjugational tenses will not vary from the active Átmanepada form of desiderative except in the aorist 3d sing., which will be *abubodhishi* instead of *abubodhishishṭa*.

Causal of desideratives.

506. Desiderative verbs may take a causal form: thus, *dudyúshámi*, 'I desire to play' (from *div*, 'to play'), makes in causal *dudyúshayámi*, 'I cause to desire to play,' &c.

FREQUENTATIVE OR INTENSIVE VERBS.

507. Every one of the roots in nine of the classes may take a frequentative form.

a. Nevertheless this form is even less common in classical composition than the desiderative. In the present participle, however, and in nouns, it not unfrequently appears (see 80. XXII). It either expresses repetition or gives intensity to the radical idea: thus, from दीप् 'to shine' comes the frequentative base *dedípya* (Pres. 3d sing. *dedípyate*, 'it shines brightly'), and the present participle *dedípyamána*, 'shining brightly:' so also, from शुभ् 'to be beautiful' comes *śośubhya* and *śośubhyamána*; from रुद् 'to weep,' *rorudya* and *rorudyamána*.

b. Observe—There is no frequentative form for roots of the 10th class, or for polysyllabic roots (ऊर्णु 'to cover' excepted, which has for its first frequentative form ऊर्णोनूय, and for its second ऊर्णोनु), or for most roots beginning with vowels. Some few roots, however, beginning with vowels take the Átmane form of frequentative; see examples at 511. *a*, *b*, 681. *a*.

508. There are two kinds of frequentative verb, the one a reduplicated Átmane-pada verb, with *ya* affixed, conforming, like neuter and passive verbs, to the conjugation of the 4th class, and usually, though not always, yielding a neuter signification; the other a reduplicated Parasmai-pada verb, following the conjugation of the 3d class of verbs. The latter is less common in classical Sanskrit than the former, and will therefore be considered last *.

a. The terminations for the first form of frequentative will be those of the Átmane at 247, with the usual substitutions required for the 4th class of verbs. For the second form they will be the regular Parasmai-pada terminations of the memorial scheme at 246.

ÁTMANE-PADA FREQUENTATIVES, FORMED BY REDUPLICATION AND AFFIX *ya*.

509. Rule for forming the base in the four conjugational tenses. Reduplicate the initial consonant and vowel of the passive base according to the rules for reduplicating consonants at 331, and guṇate the reduplicated vowel (if capable of Guṇa), *whether it be a long or short vowel*: thus, from the passive base दीय (of *dá*, 'to give') comes

* Intensive or frequentative forms are found in Greek, such as παιπάλλω, δαιδάλλω, μαιμάζω or μαιμάω, παμφαίνω, ἀλαλάζω.

the frequentative base *dedīya* (Pres. 1. *dedīya* + *i* = देदीये, 2. *dedīya* + *se* = देदीयसे &c.); from हीय (passive of *hā*, 'to quit') comes *jehīya* (*jehīye* &c.); from स्तीर्य (of स्तृ 'to spread') comes *testīrya* (also *tā-starya*); from पूय (of पू 'to purify'), *popūya*; from विद्य (of विद् 'to know'), *vevidya*; from बुध्य (of बुध् 'to know'), *bobudhya* (Pres. बोबुध्ये, बोबुध्यसे, बोबुध्यते, &c.). The conjugation of all four tenses corresponds exactly with that of the passive.

510. As to the reduplication of the vowel, if the passive base contain a medial अ *a*, long *ā* is substituted: thus, *pāpacya* from *pacya*; *sāsmarya* from *smarya*.

a. If it contain a medial आ *ā*, ए *e*, or ओ *o*, the same are reduplicated; as, *yāyācya* from *yācya*; *sesevya* from *sevya*; *loloḍya* from *loḍya*.

b. If it contain a medial ऋ *ṛi*, then अरी *arī* * is substituted in the reduplication; as, दरीदृश्य from *dṛiśya*; परीस्पृश्य from *spṛiśya*, &c.; परीपृच्छ्य from प्रच्छ्; बरीभृज्ज्य from भ्रस्ज्. Similarly, *alī* is substituted for ऌ *ḷi*, in कॢप् making चलीकॢप्य.

511. If a passive base has रि *ri* before *ya*, this रि *ri* becomes री *rī* in the frequentative base; as, चेक्रीय from क्रिय (passive of कृ 'to do').

a. If the base begin with अ *a*, as in अट्य *aṭya* (from अट् 'to wander'), the initial *aṭ* is repeated, and the radical *a* lengthened: thus, अटाट्य *aṭāṭya* (3d sing. अटाट्यते). Similarly, अशाश्य from अश् 'to pervade.'

b. ऋ *ṛi*, 'to go,' makes its base अरार्य *arārya*.

512. If the passive base contain a nasal after short *a*, this nasal generally appears in the reduplicated syllable, and is treated as final म् *m*; thus, from गम् 'to go' comes जङ्गम्य 'to walk crookedly;' from भ्रम् 'to wander,' बम्भ्रम्य; from हन् 'to kill,' जङ्घन्य.

a. The passive bases जप्य, जभ्य, दह्य, and some others formed from roots containing nasals (as दंश्य, भंज्य), may insert nasals, instead of lengthening the vowel in the reduplication: thus, जञ्जप्य, जञ्जभ्य, दन्दह्य, &c.

b. Anomalous forms.—पद् 'to go' (making पद्य) inserts नी *nī*: thus, पनीपद्य. Similarly, पत् 'to fall,' कस् or कष् 'to go,' भ्रंश् 'to fall,' स्रंस् 'to drop,' ध्वंस् 'to fall,' स्कन्द् 'to go,' वञ्च् 'to deceive' (बनीभ्रश्य, पनीपत्य, चनीकस्य, सनीस्रस्य, दनीध्वस्य, चनीस्कद्य, &c.). चर् 'to go' makes चञ्चूर्य.

c. हन् 'to kill' makes जेघ्नीय; घ्रा 'to smell,' जेघ्रीय; ध्मा 'to blow,' देध्मीय (देध्मीये &c.); गॄ 'to swallow,' जेगिल्य.

Non-conjugational tenses of Ātmane-pada frequentatives.

513. In these tenses frequentatives follow the analogy of passives, and reject the affix य *ya*. Since, however, the base of the perfect is formed by affixing आम् *ām* (as usual in all polysyllabic forms, see 385), and since, in all the other tenses, inserted *i* is assumed, a coalition of vowels might arise were it not allowed to retain *y* in all

* This seems to support the idea that the original Guṇa of *ṛi* is *ari*. See 29. *b*.

cases in which a vowel immediately precedes that letter*: thus, from देदीप्य is formed the perfect (or 2d pret.) 1st sing. देदीपाञ्चक्रे &c., rejecting *ya*; but from देदीय comes देदीयाञ्चक्रे &c., retaining *y*. Similarly in the other tenses: 1st fut. *dedípitáhe*, *dedíyitáhe*, &c.; 2d fut. *dedípishye*, *dedíyishye*, &c.; aorist *adedípishi*, *adedíyishi*, &c.; precative (or bened.) *dedípishíya*, *dedíyishíya*, &c.; cond. *adedípishye*, *adedíyishye*, &c. In the 3d sing. of the aorist (or 3d preterite) इ *i* is not allowed to take the place of the regular terminations, as in the passive form.

a. The infinitive, as formed in the usual manner from the 3d sing. 1st future, will be *dedípitum* &c.

PARASMAI-PADA FREQUENTATIVES.

514. Rule for forming the base in the four conjugational tenses. The base is here also formed by a reduplication similar to that of Átmane-pada frequentatives; not, however, from the passive, but from the root: thus, from the root पच् *pać* comes *pápać*; from विद् *vid* comes *vevid*; from दृश् comes *darídṛiś*; from कृ comes *ćaríkṛi*.

a. But in the Parasmai form of frequentative, अरि *ari* and अर् *ar* as well as अरी *arí* may be reduplicated for the vowel ऋ *ṛi*; so that दृश् may make दरीदृश् or दरिदृश् or दर्दृश्; and कृ, चरीकृ or चरिकृ or चर्कृ. Similarly, क्लृप् may make चलीक्लृप् or चलिक्लृप् or चल्क्लृप्.

b. Again, in roots ending in long ॠ *ṛí*, *á* is reduplicated for ॠ *ṛí*, and this *á* is retained even when *ṛí* becomes *ir*: thus, कॄ 'to scatter' makes 1. *ćákarmi*; Pl. 3. *ćákirati*. Similarly, from तॄ 'to cross' come *tátarmi* and *tátirati*.

c. In accordance with the rules for the 2d and 3d class (307, 332), the radical vowel is gunated before the P terminations of the scheme at 246. Hence, from *vid* come the two bases *veved* and *vevid* (Pres. *vevedmi*, *vevetsi*, *vevetti*; Du. *vevidvas*, &c.; Impf. *avevedam*, *avevet*, *avevet*, *avevidva*, &c.; Pot. *vevidyám*, &c.; Impv. *vevedáni*, *veviddhi*, *vevettu*, *vevedáva*, *vevittam*, &c.).

d. Again, the base will vary in accordance with the rules of combination at 296—306, as in बुध् *budh* (Pres. *bobodhmi*, *bobhotsi*, *boboddhi*, *bobudhvas*, &c.; see 298). So also, वह् *vah* makes in 3d sing. वावोढि *vávoḍhi* (see 305. *a*); दुह् makes दोदोग्धि (305); नह् makes नानद्धि (305 note); द्रुह् makes दोद्रोढि or दोद्रोग्धि; and स्निह्, सेस्नेढि or सेस्नेग्धि (305. *b*).

e. And in further analogy to the 2d class (313, 314) long *í* is often optionally inserted before the consonantal P terminations (Pres. *vevedími*, *vevedíshi*, *vevedíti*; Du. *vevidvas*, &c.; Impf. *avevedam*, *avevedís*, *avevedít*, *avevidva*, &c.; Impv. *vevedáni*, *veviddhi*, *vevedítu*).

515. Lastly, when the root ends in a vowel, the usual changes take place of *i* and *í* to *y* or *iy*; of *u* and *ú* to *uv*; and of *ṛi* to *r* (see 312): as in the roots भी *bhí*,

---

* In passives this coalition of vowels is avoided by the change of a final vowel to Vṛiddhi, as of *ći* to *ćáy*, of *hu* to *háv*, and of *kṛi* to *kár*; and by the change of final *á* to *áy*, as of *dá* to *dáy*; see 474.

भू *bhú*, कृ *kri* (Pres. 1st sing. *bobhomi*, *bobhavími*, *ćarkarmi*; 3d plur. *bobhuvati*, *bobhu-vati*, *ćarkrati*).

a. Observe—Many of the anomalous formations explained under Átmane-pada frequentatives must be understood as belonging also to the Parasmai-pada: thus, पत् (512. *b*) makes in Parasmai पनीपत्मि, पनीपतीमि, पनीपतिम, &c.; and so with the other roots at 512. *b*.

b. हन् 'to kill,' गॄ 'to swallow' (512. *c*), and some others have a separate Parasmai-pada form (जङ्घन्मि, जागर्मि; the last identical with pres. of जागृ).

Non-conjugational tenses of Parasmai-pada frequentatives.

516. The perfect (or second preterite) follows the usual rule for polysyllabic bases (385), and affixes आम् *ám* with the auxiliaries: thus, from बुध् *budh*, 'to know,' comes *bobudhámása*, *bobudhámbabhúva*, *bobudháńćakára*; from विद् *vid*, 'to know,' comes *vevidámása*. Guṇa of a final and sometimes of a penultimate vowel is required before *ám*: thus, *bobhú* (from भू) becomes *bobhavámása*. So also, वृत् makes *varvartámása*. In the other tenses, excepting the benedictive, inserted *i* is invariably assumed; and before this inserted *i* some roots are said to forbid the usual Guṇa change of the radical vowel in the 1st future &c.: thus, *budh* is said to make *bobudhitásmi*; *bhí*, 'to fear,' *bebhyitásmi*, &c. (374); 2d fut. *bobudhi-shyámi*, *bebhyishyámi*, &c.; aorist *abobudhisham*, *abebhyisham*, &c.; prec. or bened. *bobudhyásam*, *bebhíyásam*, &c.; cond. *abobudhishyam*, *abebhyishyam*, &c. The rejection of Guṇa from the radical syllable, however, admits of question: thus, *bhú*, 'to be,' makes, according to the best authorities, *bobhavitásmi*, &c. The infinitive will be formed in the usual way from the 1st future, see 513. *e*.

Passive, causal, desiderative, and desiderative causal form of frequentatives.

517. Frequentatives are capable of all these forms. The passive, when the root ends in a consonant, will be identical with the Átmane-pada frequentative formed by reduplication and the affix *ya*: thus, from the frequentative base *totud*, 'to strike often,' comes *totudye*, 'I am struck often;' but from *loláya* (*lú*, 'to cut'), *loláyye*, &c. Again, from *totud* comes *totudayámi*, 'I cause to strike often;' *totudishámi*, 'I desire to strike often;' *totudayishámi*, 'I desire to cause to strike often.'

a. The *ya* of the Átmane-pada frequentative if preceded by a consonant is rejected; but not if preceded by a vowel: thus, *loláya*, frequentative base of *lú*, 'to cut,' makes *loláyishámi*, 'I desire to cut often.' See 331. *g*.

NOMINAL VERBS, OR VERBS DERIVED FROM NOUNS.

518. These are formed by adding certain affixes to the crude base of nouns. They are not in very common use, but, theoretically, there is no limit to their formation. They might be classed according to their meaning; viz. 1st, transitive nominals, yielding the

sense of performing, practising, making or using the thing or quality expressed by the noun; 2d, intransitive nominals, giving a sense of behaving like, becoming like, acting like the person or thing expressed by the noun; 3d, desiderative nominals, yielding the sense of wishing for the thing expressed by the noun. It will be more convenient, however, to arrange them under five heads, according to the affixes by which they are formed, as follows:—

519. 1st, Those formed by affixing अ *a* (changeable to *á* before a syllable beginning with *m* and *v*) to a nominal base, after Guṇa of its final vowel (if capable of Guṇa). When the base ends in *a*, this vowel takes the place of the affix *a*. A final *á* absorbs the affix.

Observe—The terminations of nominals will be those of the scheme at 247, making use of the substitutions required by the 1st, 4th, 6th, and 10th classes.

a. Thus, from कृष्ण 'Krishṇa,' Pres. 1. कृष्णामि 'I act like Krishṇa,' 2. कृष्णसि, 3. कृष्णति, &c. So, from कवि 'a poet,' Pres. 1. कवयामि 'I act the poet,' 2. कवयसि, &c.; and from पितृ 'a father,' Pres. 1. पितरामि 'I act like a father,' 2. पितरसि, 3. पितरति; Átm. Pres. 1. पितरे, &c.: from माला 'a garland,' Pres. 1. मालामि, 2. मालासि, 3. मालाति; Impf. 1. अमालाम्, 2. अमालाः, &c.; Pot. मालेयम्, &c.: from स्व 'own,' Pres. 3. स्वति 'he acts like himself.' Sometimes a final *i* or *u* is not guṇated; as, from चञ्चु 'a beak,' Pres. चञ्च्वामि, चञ्च्वसि, चञ्च्वति, 'he uses his beak,' 'he pecks;' from कवि 'a poet,' कव्यामि, कव्यसि, &c. Words ending in nasals preserve the nasals, and lengthen the preceding vowels; as, राजानति 'he acts like a king,' पथीनति 'it serves as a road,' इदामति 'he acts like this.'

520. 2dly, Those formed by affixing य *ya* to a nominal base.

a. If a word end in a consonant, *ya* is generally affixed without change; as, from वाच् 'a word,' वाच्यति 'he wishes for words;' from दिव् 'heaven,' दिव्यति 'he wishes for heaven' (or, according to some, दीव्यति); from तपस् 'penance,' तपस्यति 'he does penance;' from नमस् 'reverence,' नमस्यति 'he does reverence.' Final *n* is dropped, and the next rule then applied: thus, from राजन् 'a king,' Pres. राजीयामि, Pot. राजीयेयं; from धनिन् 'rich,' धनीयामि, &c.

b. A final अ *a* or आ *á* is generally changed to ई *í*; final इ *i* or उ *u* lengthened; final ऋ *ri* changed to री *rí*; ओ *o* to *av*; औ *au* to *áv*.

Thus, from पुत्र 'a son,' Pres. 1. पुत्रीयामि 'I desire a son,' 2. पुत्रीयसि, &c.; from पति 'a husband,' Pres. 1. पतीयामि 'I desire a husband,' &c. So also, from मातृ 'a mother' comes मात्रीयामि, &c.

c. This form of nominal has not always a desiderative meaning. The following are examples of other meanings, some of which properly belong to the next form: प्रासादीयति 'he fancies himself in a palace;' कवीयति 'he acts like a poet;' कण्डूयति or -ते 'he scratches;' मन्तूयति or -ते 'he sins' or 'he is angry;' मित्रीयते 'he acts the part of a friend;' पुत्रीयति छात्रं 'he treats the pupil as a son;' विष्णूयति द्विजं

'he treats the Brahman as if he were Vishṇu;' तिरस्यति 'he vanishes;' गव्यति 'he seeks cows' (from गो 'a cow').

d. In the sense of 'behaving like,' 'acting like,' 'doing like,' a final अ *a* is generally lengthened, a final आ *ā* retained, and a final स् *s*, न् *n*, or त् *t*, dropped: thus, from पण्डित 'a wise man,' Pres. 1. पण्डिताये 'I act the part of a wise man,' 2. पण्डितायसे, 3. पण्डितायते, &c.; from द्रुम 'a tree,' Pres. 1. द्रुमाये, &c.; from शब्द 'a noise,' शब्दाये 'I am noisy;' from राजन् 'a king,' Pres. 1. राजाये, &c.; from उन्मनस् 'sorrowful,' Pres. उन्मनाये, &c.; from बृहत् 'great,' Pres. बृहाये, &c.

e. This nominal is sometimes found with an active sense, especially when derived from nouns expressive of colour; as, from कृष्ण 'black,' कृष्णायते or -ति 'he blackens:' and sometimes in the Parasmai with a neuter sense; as, from जिह्म 'crooked,' जिह्मायति 'it is crooked;' from दास 'a slave,' दासायति 'he is a slave.' It corresponds to Greek desiderative denominatives in ιάω, as θανατιάω &c.

521. 3dly, Those formed by affixing अय *aya* to a nominal base. This form is similar to that of causals and verbs of the 10th class, with which it is sometimes confounded. Like them it has generally an active sense. A final vowel must be dropped before *aya;* and if the nominal base have more than one syllable, and end in a consonant, both the consonant and its preceding vowel must be dropped.

a. Thus, from वस्त्र 'cloth,' Pres. 1. वस्त्रयामि 'I clothe,' 2. वस्त्रयसि, 3. वस्त्रयति, &c.; from वर्मन् 'armour,' Pres. 1. वर्मयामि 'I put on armour,' &c.; from प्रमाण 'authority,' प्रमाणयामि 'I propose as authority;' from स्रज् 'a garland,' स्रजयामि 'I crown;' from घट 'a jar,' घटयामि 'I make a jar' or 'I call it a jar,' &c.

b. In further analogy to causals, a प् *p* is sometimes inserted between the base and *aya*, especially if the noun be monosyllabic, and end in *a*. Before this प् *p*, Vṛiddhi is required: thus, from स्व 'own,' Pres. स्वापयामि 'I make my own.' There are one or two examples of dissyllabic nouns: thus, from सत्य 'true,' सत्यापयामि, &c.; and from अर्थ 'substance,' अर्थापयामि, &c.

c. If the base be monosyllabic, and end in a consonant, Guṇa may take place; as, from क्षुध् 'hunger,' क्षोधयामि.

d. Whatever modifications adjectives undergo before the affixes *īyas* and *ishṭha* at 194, the same generally take place before *aya*: thus, from दीर्घ 'long,' द्राघयामि 'I lengthen;' from अन्तिक 'near,' नेदयामि 'I make near,' &c.

e. This form of nominal is sometimes neuter, as चिरयति 'he delays' (from चिर 'long'). According to Prof. Bopp, Greek denominatives in αω, εω, οω, ιζω, correspond to this form; as, πολεμ-όω, γυναικ-ίζω.

522. 4thly, Those formed by affixing स्य *sya* or अस्य *asya* to a nominal base, giving it the form of a future tense, generally with the sense of 'desiring,' 'longing for.'

a. Thus, from क्षीर 'milk,' Pres. 1. क्षीरस्यामि 'I desire milk,' 2. क्षीरस्यसि, &c.;

from वृष 'a bull,' वृषस्यति '(the cow) desires the bull;' from दधि 'curds,' दधस्यामि 'I desire curds,' &c. Compare Greek desideratives in *σείω*.

523. 5thly, Those formed by affixing काम्य *kámya* (derived from *kam*, 'to desire') to a nominal base; as, from पुत्र 'a son,' Pres. 1. पुत्रकाम्यामि 'I desire a son,' 2. पुत्रकाम्यसि, 3. पुत्रकाम्यति, &c.; from यशस् 'fame,' यशस्काम्यामि 'I desire fame.'

a. The non-conjugational tenses of these nominals will generally be formed analogously to those of other verbs: thus, from स्वामि 'I act like self' comes the perfect सस्वौ; from कुमारयामि 'I play like a boy' comes the aorist अचुकुमारं, &c. A long vowel in the base generally remains unchanged, and is not shortened: thus, मालयामि (from माला 'a garland') makes अममालत्. So also, समिधिष्यति 'he will wish for fuel' (Guṇa being omitted), पुत्रीयिष्यति 'he will wish for a son.'

b. Nominal verbs may take passive, causal, desiderative, and frequentative forms. The causal of those formed with *aya* will be identical with the primitive nominal: thus, वर्मयामि 'I put on armour' or 'I cause to put on armour.' In reduplicating for the desiderative or frequentative, sometimes the last syllable is repeated, sometimes the first: thus, कण्डूय 'to scratch' makes its desiderative base कण्डूयियिष्, and पुत्रीय 'to treat as a son' makes पुपुत्रीयिष् or पुत्रीयियिष्. According to some, the middle syllable may be reduplicated: thus, पुतित्रीयिष्.

PARTICIPLES.

PRESENT PARTICIPLES; PARASMAI-PADA.—FORMATION OF THE BASE.

524. These are the only participles the formation of which is connected with the conjugational class of the verb. The base in the Parasmai is formed by substituting त् *t* for *nti*, and अत् *at* for *anti* and *ati*, the terminations of the 3d plural present: thus, from पचन्ति *paćanti*, 'they cook' (3d pl. pres. of पच्, 1st c.), comes पचत् *paćat*, 'cooking;' from घ्नन्ति *ghnanti*, 'they kill' (3d pl. of *han*, 2d c.), comes घ्नत् *ghnat*, 'killing;' from सन्ति *santi*, 'they are' (3d pl. of *as*, 2d c., 'to be'), comes सत् *sat*, 'being;' from यन्ति *yanti*, 'they go' (3d pl. of इ, 2d c.), यत् *yat*, 'going;' from यान्ति *yánti*, 'they go' (3d pl. of या, 2d c.), यात् *yát*; from जुह्वति *juhvati*, 'they sacrifice' (3d pl. of *hu*, 3d c.), जुह्वत् *juhvat*; from नृत्यन्ति *nrityanti*, 'they dance,' 4th c., नृत्यत् *nrityat*; from चिन्वन्ति *ćinvanti*, 'they gather,' 5th c., चिन्वत् *ćinvat*;

from आप्नुवन्ति *āpnuvanti*, 'they obtain,' 5th c., आप्नुवत् *āpnuvat*; from तुदन्ति *tudanti*, 'they strike,' 6th c., *tudat*; from रुन्धन्ति *rundhanti*, 'they hinder,' 7th c., *rundhat*; from कुर्वन्ति *kurvanti*, 'they do,' 8th c., *kurvat*; from पुनन्ति *punanti*, 'they purify,' 9th c., *punat*.

525. The same holds good in derivative verbs: thus, from the causal बोधयन्ति, 'they cause to know' (479), comes बोधयत् 'causing to know;' from the desiderative बुबोधिषन्ति, 'they desire to know' (499), comes बुबोधिषत् 'desiring to know;' from दित्सन्ति, 'they desire to give' (503), comes दित्सत् 'desiring to give;' from the frequentative चेक्षिपति, 'they throw frequently,' comes चेक्षिपत् 'throwing frequently.'

a. Nominals form their present participles in the same way: thus, from कृष्णन्ति 'they act like Kṛishṇa,' कृष्णत् 'acting like Kṛishṇa;' from तपस्यन्ति 'they do penance,' तपस्यत् 'doing penance.'

b. In corroboration of the remark made at 253. *b*, that the passive verb appears in a few rare instances to assume a Parasmai-pada inflection, and that many of the neuter verbs placed under the 4th conjugation might be regarded (except for the accent) as examples of this form of the passive, it is certain that a Parasmai-pada present participle derivable from a passive base is occasionally found: thus, दृश्यत् 'being seen,' from the passive base दृश्य *dṛiśya*; चीयत् 'being gathered,' from चीय *chīya* (passive base of *chi*).

c. The inflection of Parasmai-pada present participles is explained at 141. The first five inflections of this participle in nine conjugational classes insert a nasal, proving that the base in all the classes, except the third, and a few other verbs (141. *a*), properly ends in *ant*. The Parasmai-pada frequentative, as conforming to the conjugational rule for the 3d class, also rejects the nasal. In the cognate languages the *n* is preserved throughout.

d. Thus, compare Sanskrit *bharan*, *bharantam* (from *bhṛi*), with φέρων, φέροντα, *ferentem*; also, *bharantau* (Ved. *bharantā*) with φέροντε; *bharantas* with φέροντες, *ferentes*; *bharatas* with φέροντας; gen. sing. *bharatas* with φέροντος, *ferentis*. So also, Sanskrit *vahan*, *vahantam*, with *vehens*, *vehentem*; and *san*, *santam* (from *as*, 'to be'), with the *sens* of *ab-sens*, *præ-sens*. Compare also the base *stṛiṇvant* with στορνυντ.

PRESENT PARTICIPLES; ÁTMANE-PADA.—FORMATION OF THE BASE.

526. The base is formed by substituting मान *māna* for न्ते *nte*, the termination of the 3d plur. pres. of verbs of the 1st, 4th, and 6th

classes, and passives; and by substituting आन *ána* for अते *ate*, the termination of the 3d plur. pres. of verbs of the other classes; see 247, p. 126 thus, from पचन्ते *pacante* (1st c.) comes पचमान *pacamána*, 'cooking;' from तिष्ठन्ते (*sthá*, 1st c.), तिष्ठमान 'standing;' from नह्यन्ते (4th c.), नह्यमान; from लिम्पन्ते (*lip*, 6th c.), लिम्पमान.

a. But from ब्रुवते *bruvate* (ब्रू 2d c.), ब्रुवाण *bruváṇa* (see 58); from निघ्नते (हन् with नि 2d c.), निघ्नान; from दधते (*dhá*, 3d c.), दधान; from चिन्वते (5th c.), चिन्वान; from युञ्जते (7th c.), युञ्जान; from कुर्वते (8th c.), कुर्वाण; from युनते (9th c.), युनान. The root आस् 2d c., 'to sit,' makes आसीन for आसान; and शी 2d c. is शेरते in 3d pl. (see 315), but शयान in the pres. participle.

b. Observe—The real affix for the Ātmane-pada pres. participle is *mána*, of which *ána* is probably an abbreviation. Compare the Greek μενος भरमाण (58) = φερόμενος.

527. Verbs of the 10th class and causals may substitute either मान *mána* or आन *ána*: thus, from बोधयन्ते *bodhayante* comes बोधयमान *bodhayamána* and बोधयान *bodhayána*; from दर्शयन्ते, दर्शयान; from वेदयन्ते, वेदयान, &c.

528. Passives and all derivative verbs substitute मान *mána* for the Ātmane: thus, from क्रियन्ते 'they are made' comes क्रियमाण 'being made' (58); from दीयन्ते 'they are given,' दीयमान 'being given;' from the desiderative दित्सन्ते 'they desire to give,' दित्समान 'desiring to give;' from जिघांसन्ते 'they desire to kill,' जिघांसमान 'desiring to kill;' from the frequentative बोबुध्यन्ते 'they know repeatedly,' बोबुध्यमान 'knowing repeatedly.'

529. The inflection of Ātmane-pada pres. participles follows that of the 1st class of nouns at 103: thus, N. masc. sing. पचमानः; fem. पचमाना; neut. पचमानं.

PAST PARTICIPLES.

PAST PASSIVE PARTICIPLES.—FORMATION OF THE BASE.

530. This is the most common and useful of all participles. In general the base is formed by adding त *ta* directly to roots ending in vowels, and to most roots ending in consonants; as, from या *yá*, 'to go,' यात *yáta*, 'gone;' from जि 'to conquer,' जित 'conquered;'

from नी 'to lead,' नीत 'led;' from क्षिप् *kship*, 'to throw,' क्षिप्त *kshipta*, 'thrown.'

a. But if the root end in ॠ *ṛí*, by adding न *na*, changeable to ण *ṇa* by 58; as, from कॄ *kṛí*, 'to scatter,' कीर्ण *kírṇa*, 'scattered,' see 534.

531. Some roots in आ *á*, ई *í*, and ऊ *ú*, some in ऐ *ai* preceded by two consonants, with some of those in द् *d*, र् *r*, ज् *j*, one in ग् *g* (लग्), and one or two in च् *ch*, श् *śh* (see 541, 544), also take *na* instead of *ta*; see 532, 536, 540, &c.

532. Roots ending in vowels do not generally admit inserted इ *i* in this participle, even when they admit it in the futures (392, 395, &c.), but attach *ta* or *na* directly to the root; as, from पा 'to protect,' पात; from श्रि 'to have recourse,' श्रित; from श्रु 'to hear,' श्रुत; भू 'to become,' भूत; कृ 'to do,' कृत; घ्रा 'to smell,' घ्राण (58); डी 'to fly,' डीन; दी 'to decay,' दीन; मी 'to perish,' मीन; ली 'to embrace,' लीन; ह्री 'to be ashamed,' ह्रीण; लू 'to cut,' लून; दू 'to be afflicted,' दून; श्वि 'to swell,' शून.

a. But when they do retain i, guṇation of the final vowel is required as in the future: thus, शी 'to lie down' makes शयित; and पू 'to purify,' पवित (also पूत); and जागृ 'to awake,' जागरित.

533. In certain cases the final vowel of the root is changed: thus, some roots in आ *á* change *á* to *i* before *ta*; as, from स्था *sthá*, 'to stand,' स्थित *sthita*; from मा 'to measure,' मित; from दरिद्रा 'to be poor,' दरिद्रित.

a. धा 'to place' becomes हित; दा 'to give,' दत्त.

Observe—When prepositions are prefixed to *datta*, the initial *da* may be rejected: thus, *átta* for *ádatta*, 'taken;' *prátta* for *pradatta*, 'bestowed;' *vyátta* for *vyádatta*, 'expanded;' *nítta* for *nidatta*, 'given away;' *parítta* for *paridatta*, 'delivered over;' *sútta* for *sudatta*, 'well given,' the *i* and *u* being lengthened.

b. पा 'to drink' makes पीत; but हा 'to quit,' हीन; and ज्या 'to grow old,' जीन; हा 'to go,' हान.

c. Some roots in *á* take both *na* and *ta*; as, from घ्रा 'to smell,' घ्राण and घ्रात; from वा 'to blow,' with the preposition निर्, निर्वाण and निर्वात; from श्रा (or श्रै) 'to cook,' श्राण or शृत.

534. Roots in ॠ *ṛí* change *ṛí* to *ír* before *na*, which passes into ण *ṇa* by 58; as, from तॄ 'to pass,' तीर्ण 'passed.' But when a labial precedes, *ṛí* becomes *úr*; as, from पॄ or पूर्, पूर्ण or पूर्त 'full,' 'filled.'

535. The root धे *dhe*, 'to suck,' becomes धीत; ह्वे *hve*, 'to call,' हूत; वे *ve*, 'to weave,' उत; व्ये *vye*, 'to cover,' वीत; मे 'to barter,' मित.

536. Roots in ऐ *ai* generally change *ai* to *á* before *na* or *ta*; as, from म्लै *mlai*, 'to fade,' म्लान *mlána*; from ध्यै 'to meditate,' ध्यात (in the Veda धीत); from दै 'to purify,' दात; from त्रै 'to rescue,' त्राण or त्रात; from प्यै 'to grow fat,' प्यान, &c.

a. But from गै 'to sing,' गीत; from क्षै 'to waste,' क्षीत; from क्षै 'to waste,' क्षाम, see 548; from श्यै 'to coagulate,' शीत or शीन or श्यान; from स्त्यै 'to accumulate,' स्त्यान (with प्र), स्तीत or स्तीम.

537. Of the four or five roots in ओ *o*, सो 'to destroy' makes सित (same as from सि 'to bind'); शो 'to sharpen,' शित or शात; दो 'to tie,' दित; छो 'to cut,' छात and छित; ज्यो 'to instruct,' जीत.

538. Those roots ending in consonants which take the inserted *i* in the last five tenses (399), generally take this vowel also in the past passive participle, but not invariably (see 542); and when *i* is assumed, *ta* is generally affixed, and not *na*; as, from पत् *pat*, 'to fall,' पतित *patita*, 'fallen.'

a. इ *i*, उ *u*, or ऋ *ṛi* preceding the final consonant of a root may occasionally take Guṇa, especially if the participle be used impersonally or actively; as, from स्विद् 'to sweat,' स्वेदित or स्विन्न; from स्निह् 'to be unctuous,' स्नेहित or स्निग्ध; from द्युत् 'to shine,' द्योतित or द्युतित; from धृष् 'to bear,' धर्षित and धृष्ट. See Syntax, 895.

b. ग्रह् 'to take' lengthens the inserted *i*, making गृहीत. See 399. *a.*

539. Roots ending in consonants which reject the inserted *i* in the last five tenses (400—415), generally reject it in the past passive participle. They must be combined with *ta*, agreeably to the rules of Sandhi at 296, &c. Whatever change, therefore, the final consonant undergoes before the termination *tá* of the 1st future (see 400—415), the same will often be preserved before the *ta* of the past participle; so that, in many cases, the form of this participle resembles that of the 3d sing. 1st future, provided the final *á* be shortened, and the vowel of the root preserved unaltered: thus, taking some of the roots at 400—415; शक् (शक्ता), शक्त; सिच् (सेक्ता), सिक्त; मुच् (मोक्ता), मुक्त; त्यज्, त्यक्त; युज्, युक्त; सृज्, सृष्ट; मृज् and मृज्, मृष्ट; सिध्, सिद्ध; युध्, युद्ध; बुध्, बुद्ध; क्षिप्, क्षिप्त; लुप्, लुप्त; तृप्, तृप्त; दृप्, दृप्त; लभ्, लब्ध; लुभ्, लुब्ध; विश्, विष्ट; दृश्, दृष्ट; मृश्, मृष्ट; शिष्, शिष्ट; तुष्, तुष्ट; कृष्, कृष्ट; इष्, इष्ट; दह्, दग्ध; वह्, ऊढ (415. *m*); नह्, नद्ध (414); गाह्, गाढ (415. *m*); लिह्, लीढ; दिह्, दिग्ध; स्निह्, स्निग्ध; रुह्, रूढ; मुह्, मूढ or मुग्ध (415. *m*); दुह्, दुग्ध; गुह्, गूढ (415. *m*).

540. Most roots ending in द् *d*, forbidding the inserted इ *i* (405), take *na* instead of *ta*, and are combined with *na*, agreeably to 47; as, from पद् 'to go,' पन्न; from विद् 'to find,' विन्न (also वित्त); from नुद् 'to impel,' नुन्न (also नुत्त); from

भिद् 'to break,' भिन्न; from सद् 'to sit,' 'to sink,' सन्न, with नि, निषण्ण (70, 58); from क्षुद् 'to pound,' क्षुण्ण; from छृद् 'to play,' 'to vomit,' छृण्ण; from अद् 'to eat,' अन्न (unless जग्ध be substituted). ह्लाद् 'to rejoice' makes ह्लन्न.

541. Roots ending in च् *c* or ज् *j* of course change these letters to *k* before *ta*; see examples at 539. Similarly, those which take *na*, change *c* and *j* to *g* before *na*; as, from नज् 'to be ashamed,' नग्न 'naked;' from विज् 'to tremble,' विग्न; from रुज् 'to break,' रुग्ण or रुग्न; from स्फूर्ज् 'to thunder,' स्फूर्ग्ण; from अञ्च् 'to move' (in some senses), अक्ण. So, from मस्ज् 'to be immersed,' rejecting one *j*, मग्न; from लस्ज् 'to be ashamed,' लग्न (as well as लज्जित). लग् 'to adhere' also makes लग्न. But स्फुर्छ् 'to forget,' स्फूर्ण; हुर्छ् 'to be crooked,' हूर्ण.

542. Some roots which admit *i* necessarily or optionally in one or both of the futures, reject it in this participle: thus, धृष् 'to be bold' makes धृष्ट; अर्द् 'to move' makes अर्ण (with prep.) also आर्त (आर्त 'pained'); दृंह् 'to make firm,' दृढ; वृह् 'to extol,' वृढ; मद् 'to be mad,' मत्त; दीप् 'to shine,' दीप्त; नश् 'to perish,' नष्ट; मुर्छ् 'to faint,' मूर्त as well as मूर्छित; म्लेछ् 'to speak barbarously,' म्लिष्ट as well as म्लेछित; नृत् 'to dance,' नृत्त.

543. If in forming the passive base (471), or in the reduplicated perfect (2d preterite, 375. *c*), the *v* or *y* contained in a root is changed to its semivowel *u* or *i*, the same change takes place in the past passive participle: thus, from वच् *vac*, 'to say,' उक्त *ukta*; from वद् 'to speak,' उदित; from वश् 'to wish,' उशित; from वस् 'to dwell,' उषित; from वप् 'to sow,' उप्त; from वह् 'to carry,' ऊढ (with प्र, प्रौढ); from स्वप् 'to sleep,' सुप्त; from यज् 'to sacrifice,' इष्ट.

a. Similarly, दिव् 'to play,' द्यून or द्यूत; त्वर् 'to hasten,' तूर्ण (also त्वरित).

544. Some other changes which take place in forming the passive base (472) are preserved before *ta*: thus, from शास् 'to rule,' शिष्ट; from व्यध् 'to pierce,' विद्ध; from व्यच् 'to deceive,' विचित; from भ्रस्ज् 'to fry,' भृष्ट; from प्रछ् 'to ask,' पृष्ट; from व्रश्च् 'to cut,' वृक्ण or वृक्त (58).

a. When a root ends in a conjunct consonant, of which the first is a nasal, this nasal is generally rejected before *ta*; as, from बन्ध् 'to bind,' बद्ध; from संस् 'to fall,' सस्त; from ध्वंस् 'to fall,' ध्वस्त; from अञ्च् 'to move' and अञ्ज् 'to anoint,' अक्त; from सञ्ज् 'to adhere,' सक्त; from रञ्ज् 'to colour,' रक्त; from इन्ध् 'to kindle,' इद्ध; from उन्द् 'to be wet,' उत्त or उन्न; from स्यन्द् 'to ooze,' स्यन्न; from स्कन्द् 'to ascend,' स्कन्न; from स्तम्भ् 'to stop,' स्तब्ध; from स्कम्भ् 'to stop,' स्कब्ध; from दम्भ् 'to deceive,' दब्ध; from भञ्ज् 'to break,' भग्न; from दंश् 'to bite,' दष्ट; from तञ्च् 'to contract,' तक्त.

b. But not if इ *i* is inserted; as, from खण्ड् 'to break,' खण्डित; from नन्द्, नन्दित (except मन्थ् 'to churn,' making मथित; and ग्रन्थ् 'to tie,' ग्रथित).

545. Many roots ending in म् *m*, न् *n*, or ण् *ṇ* reject these nasals before *ta* if *i* is not inserted; as, गम् *gam*, 'to go,' गत *gata*; यम् *yam*, 'to restrain,' यत *yata*; रम् 'to sport,' रत; तन् 'to stretch,' तत; हन् 'to kill,' हत; नम् 'to bend,' नत; मन् 'to think,' मत; क्षण् 'to hurt,' क्षत: but अन् 'to breathe' and अम् 'to go' make आन्त (the latter also अमित); and स्वन् 'to sound,' स्वनित (also स्वान्त with prep.).

a. जन् 'to be born' makes जात; and खन् 'to dig,' खात; सन् 'to give,' सात; medial *a* being lengthened.

546. Those roots ending in म् *m*, of the 4th conjugation, which lengthen a medial *a* before the conjugational affix *ya*, also lengthen it before *ta*, changing *m* to *n* as in the futures: thus, from क्रम् 'to step,' क्रान्त; from भ्रम् 'to wander,' भ्रान्त; from शम् 'to be appeased,' शान्त; from दम् 'to tame,' दान्त (also दमित); from क्षम् 'to be patient,' क्षान्त; from क्लम् 'to be sad,' क्लान्त.

a. Similarly, वम् 'to vomit,' वान्त; कम् 'to love,' कान्त; चम् 'to eat,' चान्त.

547. From स्फाय् 'to swell' is formed स्फीत; from क्ष्माय् 'to shake,' क्ष्मात; from पूय् 'to be putrid,' पूत; from वे 'to weave,' ऊत; from प्याय् 'to be fat,' पीन (with आ, आपान); from क्नूय् 'to stink,' क्नूत.

a. गुर् or गूर् 'to make effort' forms गूर्ण; तुर्व् 'to kill,' like त्वर् 'to hasten,' तूर्ण; मुर्व् 'to bind or tie' makes मूर्ण; ष्ठिव् or ष्ठीव् 'to spit,' ष्ठ्यूत; क्षिव् or क्षीव् 'to spit,' क्ष्यूत; दिव् 'to play,' द्यूत or द्यून; सिव् 'to sew,' स्यूत; धाव् 'to wash,' धौत.

b. फल् 'to bear fruit' makes फुल्ल; and चर् 'to eat,' चर्ण.

548. The following are quite anomalous: पच् *pac*, 'to cook,' पक्व; शुष् 'to dry,' शुष्क; क्षीव् 'to be drunk,' क्षीब; कृश् 'to grow thin,' कृश; क्षै 'to waste,' क्षाम.

c. From the above examples it appears that sometimes two or three roots have the same form of passive participle. The following may also be noted: पूय् 'to stink' and पू 'to purify' both make पूत; मा 'to measure' and मे 'to barter,' मित; मृज् 'to wipe,' मृश् 'to touch,' and मृष् 'to bear,' all make मृष्ट; शंस् 'to tell' and शस् 'to kill,' शस्त; शास् 'to rule' and शिष् 'to distinguish,' शिष्ट; सो 'to destroy' and सि 'to tie,' सित. On the other hand, भुज् 'to enjoy' makes भुक्त; but भुज् 'to bend,' भुग्न.

549. In forming the past passive participles of causals, the causal affix अय *aya* is rejected, but the inserted इ *i* is always assumed: thus, from कारय, causal of कृ 'to make,' comes कारित *kárita*, 'caused to be made;' from स्थापय, causal of स्था 'to stand,' comes स्थापित *sthápita*, 'placed.'

550. In adding त *ta* to a desiderative or frequentative base, the inserted इ *i* is assumed, final *a* of the base being dropped; and in the case of roots ending in consonants, final *ya* being dropped; as, from पिपास 'to desire to drink' comes पिपासित; from चिकीर्ष 'to desire to do,' चिकीर्षित; from ईप्स 'to desire to obtain,' ईप्सित, &c.; from लोलूय 'to cut often,' लोलूयित; from बेभिद्य 'to break frequently,' बेभिदित.

551. त *ta* with *i* is added to nominal bases, final *a* being dropped: thus, from शिथिल 'loose,' शिथिलित 'loosened;' from जिह्म 'crooked,' जिह्मित 'curved.' These may be regarded as the passive participles of the transitive nominal verbs शिथिलयति, जिह्मयति (521). So again, from नमस्य 'to do reverence' comes नमस्यित or नमसित.

a. Moreover, as *na* sometimes takes the place of *ta*, so *ina* is added to some nouns instead of *ita*: thus, *malina*, 'soiled,' from *mala*, 'dirt;' शृङ्गिण 'horned,' from शृङ्ग 'a horn.'

b. Corresponding forms in Latin are *barbatus*, *alatus*, *cordatus*, *turritus*, &c.; and in Greek, ὀμφαλωτός, κροκωτός, αὐλωτός, &c.

552. The inflection of past passive participles follows that of the first class of nouns at 103; thus exhibiting a perfect similarity to the declension of Latin participles in *tus*: thus, कृत *kṛita*, nom. sing. masc. fem. neut. कृतस्, कृता, कृतं.

c. The resemblance between Sanskṛit passive participles in *ta*, Latin participles in *tu-s*, and Greek verbals in το-ς, will be evident from the following examples: Sanskṛit *jñātas* = (*g*)*notus* (*ignotus*), γνωτός; *dattas* = *datus*, δοτός; *śrutas* = *clutus*, κλυτός; *bhūtas* = φυτός; *yuktas* = *junctus*, ζευκτός; *labdhas* = ληπτός; *pītas* = πότος; *bhṛitas* = *fertus*, φερτός; *dishṭas* = *dictus*, δεικτός. And, like Sanskṛit, Latin often inserts an *i*, as in *domitus* (= Sanskṛit *damitas*), *monitus*, &c. This is not the case in Greek, but ε is inserted in forms like μενετός, ἑρπετός. There are also examples of Latin and Greek formations in *nu-s* and νο-ς, corresponding to the Sanskṛit participle in *na*: thus, *plenus* (= *pūrṇa*), *magnus* (from Sanskṛit root *mah*), *dignus* (from Sanskṛit *diś*, *dik*, Greek δεικ); and στυγνό-ς, στεγνό-ς, σεμνό-ς, &c.

PAST ACTIVE PARTICIPLES.

These are of two kinds: 1st, those derived from the past passive participle; 2dly, those belonging to the perfect. These later rarely occur. The former are much used to supply the place of a perfect tense active.

PAST ACTIVE PARTICIPLES DERIVED FROM PAST PASSIVE PARTICIPLES.—FORMATION OF THE BASE.

553. The base of these participles is easily formed by adding वत् *vat* to that of the past passive participle: thus, from कृत 'made,' कृतवत् 'having made or who or what has made;' from दग्ध 'burnt,' दग्धवत् 'having burnt;' from उक्त 'said,' उक्तवत् 'having said;' from भिन्न 'broken,' भिन्नवत् 'having broken;' from स्थापित 'placed,' स्थापितवत् 'having placed,' &c.

a. For the declension of these participles see 140. *a*, *b*, *c*.

Participles of the reduplicated perfect (*2d preterite*).

554. In these participles, either वस् *vas* or इवस् *ivas* is added to the base of the reduplicated perfect, as formed in the dual and plural. *Vas* is added when the

base in the dual and plural (as it appears in its unchanged form before the terminations are added) consists of more than one syllable: thus, from *ćakṛi* (root *kṛi*, 'to do'), *ćakṛivas*; from *vivid* (365), *vividvas*; from *ćići* (374), *ćićivas*; from *sasṛit* (364. compare 45. *e*), *sasṛitvas*; from *sasmar* (374. *k*), *sasmarvas*.

a. And *ivas* is added when the base in the dual and plural consists of one syllable only; as, from *ten* (375. *a*), *tenivas*; from *jagm* (376), *jagmivas*; from *jaksh* (377), *jakshivas*.

b. When *vas* is affixed, it will be necessary to restore to its original state, the final of a root ending in *i*, *í*, *u*, *ú*, or *ṛi*, if changed before the terminations of the du. and plur. to *y*, *v*, *r*, *iy*, *uv*, or *úv*: thus, श्रि *śri*, changed by 374. *e*. to *śiśriy*, becomes शिश्रिवस्; क्री, changed to *ćikriy*, becomes चिक्रीवस् *ćikrívas*; धू, changed by 374. *g*. to *dudhuv*, becomes दुधूवस् *dudhúvas*; भू, changed by 374. *l*. to *babhúv*, becomes बभूवस् *babhúvas*. In declension, the 3d pers. plur. with its termination *us* is the form of the base in the weakest cases (135. *a*), the final *s* becoming *sh* by 70: thus, from *jagmus*, I. *jagmushá*; from *tenus*, I. *tenushá*, &c. See 168.

c. Roots which take the periphrastic perfect (see 385) form the participles of this tense by adding the perfect participles of *kṛi*, *bhú*, and *as*, to *ám*: thus, from *ćur*, 10th c., *ćorayámbabhúvas*, *ćorayáńćakṛivas*, *ćorayámásivas*.

d. There is an Átmane-pada participle of the reduplicated perfect formed by changing *ire*, the termination of the 3d plur., into *ána*: thus, *vividána*, *ćićyána*, *jagmána*. See 526. *a*; and compare the Greek perfect participle in μενο: तुतुपान = τετυμμένος.

e. The Parasmai-pada form of these participles is inflected at 168. Those of the Átmane-pada follow the inflection of the first class of nouns at 103.

PAST INDECLINABLE PARTICIPLES.

555. These fall under two heads: 1st, as formed by affixing त्वा *tvá* to *uncompounded* roots; as, from भू *bhú*, 'to be,' भूत्वा *bhútvá*, 'having been:' 2dly, as formed by affixing य *ya* to roots *compounded* with prepositions or other adverbial prefixes; thus, from अनुभू *anubhú*, 'to perceive,' अनुभूय *anubhúya*, 'having perceived;' from सज्जीभू *sajjíbhú*, 'to become ready,' सज्जीभूय *sajjíbhúya*, 'having become ready.' The sense involved in them is generally expressed by the English 'when,' 'after,' 'having,' or 'by:' thus, तत् कृत्वा *tat kṛitvá*, 'when he had done that,' 'after he had done that,' 'having done that,' 'by doing that.' They are capable also of a passive sense, though this is rare. See Syntax.

a. The affix *tvá* of this participle is thought by some to be the instrumental case of an affix *tu*, of which the infinitive affix *tum* is the accusative. The indeclinable participle has certainly much of the character of an instrumental case (see Syntax, 901); but the form of its base often varies considerably from that of the infinitive:

thus, *vaktum*, *uktvá*, from *vach*; *yashṭum*, *ishṭvá*, from *yaj*, &c. त्वाय, त्वानं, त्वीनं or त्वी are sometimes used for त्वा in the Veda.

Indeclinable participles formed with tvá from uncompounded roots.

556. When the root stands alone and uncompounded, the indeclinable participle is formed with त्वा *tvá*.

This affix is closely allied to the त *ta* of the past passive participle at 531, so that the rules for the affixing of त *ta* to the root generally apply also to the indeclinable affix त्वा *tvá*, and the formation of one participle then involves that of the other: thus, from क्षिप्त *kshipta*, 'thrown,' क्षिप्त्वा *kshiptvá*, 'having thrown;' from कृत 'done' (root कृ), कृत्वा 'having done;' from स्थित (root स्था), स्थित्वा; from युक्त (root युज्), युक्त्वा; from दत्त (root दा), दत्त्वा; from पीत (root पा), पीत्वा; from क्रान्त (root क्रम्), क्रान्त्वा; from गृहीत (root ग्रह्), गृहीत्वा; from उषित (root वस्), उषित्वा; from उक्त (root वच्), उक्त्वा; from बुद्ध (root बुध्), बुद्ध्वा; from ऊढ (root वह्), ऊढ्वा; from हित (root धा), हित्वा; from त्यक्त (root त्यज्), त्यक्त्वा; from गत (root गम् 545), गत्वा.

a. Where *i* is inserted, there is generally guṇation of final *i*, *í*, *u*, *ú*, and of final ॠ *ṛí* and of medial ऋ *ṛi*; and optional guṇation of medial *i*, *u* (except as debarred by 28. *b*): thus, शयित्वा from शी; पवित्वा (also पूत्वा) from पू; तरित्वा or तरीत्वा from तॄ; लिखित्वा or लेखित्वा from लिख्; द्युतित्वा or द्योतित्वा from द्युत्; वर्षित्वा from वृष्; मृषित्वा or मर्षित्वा from मृष्.

b. But from दिव्, देवित्वा and द्यूत्वा; from सिव्, सेवित्वा and स्यूत्वा. So सिध् &c. The root जागृ makes जागरित्वा (532. *a*); and initial *i*, *u*, before single consonants, must be guṇated; as, इष् makes एषित्वा.

c. The roots in the list at 390. *a.* do not admit Guṇa: thus, विज् can make only विजित्वा.

d. When there are two forms of the passive participle, there is often only one of the indeclinable: thus, गुह् makes गूढ and गूहित, but only गूहित्वा; लग्, लग्न and लगित, but only लगित्वा; and, *vice versa*, वस् (543) only उषित, but उषित्वा and उष्ट्वा; सह्, सोढ, but सहित्वा and सोढ्वा; गुप्, गुप्त, but गोपित्वा and गुप्त्वा. So, some roots in nasals optionally insert *i*: तन्, तत्वा or तनित्वा; खन्, खात्वा or खनित्वा; क्रम्, क्रान्त्वा or क्रमित्वा; भ्रम्, भ्रान्त्वा or भ्रन्त्वा or भ्रमित्वा; शम्, शान्त्वा or शमित्वा.

e. The penultimate nasal, which is rejected before *ta* (544. *a*), is optionally so rejected before *tvá* in रञ्ज्, भञ्ज्, स्रंस्, दंश् or भ्रंश्, and वञ्च्: thus, from रञ्ज् comes रक्त, but रंक्त्वा or रक्त्वा; from वञ्च्, वञ्चित्वा, वंक्त्वा or वक्त्वा.

f. मस्ज् and नश् optionally insert nasals; मक्त्वा or मंक्त्वा, नष्ट्वा or नंष्ट्वा, 390. *k*.

g. Some few roots necessarily retain their nasals: thus, स्कन्द् makes स्कन्त्वा; and स्यन्द्, स्यन्त्वा or स्यन्दित्वा.

557. The only important variation from the passive participle occurs in those roots, at 531. *a*, which take *na* for *ta*. The change of *ṛí* to *ír* and *úr* (534) is preserved (unless *i* be inserted), but *tvá* never becomes *rṇá*: thus, कॄ, कीर्णे, but करित्वा (or करीत्वा); from गॄ, गीर्णे, but गरित्वा; from पॄ, पूर्णे, but पूर्त्वा; from छिद्, छिन्न, but छित्वा; from भञ्ज्, भग्न, but भंक्त्वा or भक्त्वा (556. *e*); from हन्, हत, but हत्वा; from हा, हीन, but हित्वा 'having quitted' (not distinguishable in form from हित्वा 'having placed,' root धा).

558. Observe, moreover, that verbs of the 10th class and causals, which reject the characteristic *aya* before the *ita* of the past passive participle, retain *ay* before *itvá*; thus, स्थापित 'made to stand' (from the causal base स्थापय), but स्थापयित्वा 'having made to stand;' चिन्तित 'thought' (from चिन्त् 10th c., 'to think'), but चिन्तयित्वा 'having thought.'

a. All derivative verbs of course assume *i*, and form their indeclinable participles analogously to causals: thus, बुबोधिषित्वा (from desid. of बुध्), and बोबुधित्वा (from freq. of बुध्). In regard to the Átmane frequentatives, लोलूयित्वा is formed from लोलूय, and देदीपित्वा from देदीप्य (*ya* in the latter being preceded by a consonant).

b. There are one or two instances of compounded roots formed with *tvá*: thus, अनुध्यात्वा (from ध्यै), Rámáyaṇa I. 2, 20; also [illegible] Rámáy. I. 74, 23. Especially in the case of causals; as, निवर्तयित्वा.

c. When अ *a*, 'not,' is prefixed, *tvá* is always used; as, अकृत्वा 'not having done,' 'without having done;' अदत्त्वा 'not having given.'

Indeclinable participles formed with ya from compounded roots.

559. When a root is compounded with a preposition or any indeclinable prefix (except अ *a*, 'not,' see 558. *c*), the indeclinable participle is formed by affixing य *ya*, and the rules for annexing it to the root are some of them analogous to those which prevail in other cases in which *ya* is affixed; see the rules for forming the conjugational tenses in the fourth class at 272, for passives at 461, and for the precative or benedictive at 443.

560. But if a root end in a short vowel, instead of lengthening this vowel, त् *t* is interposed; as, from आश्रि *áśri*, 'to take refuge' (root श्रि with आ), आश्रित्य *áśritya*, 'having taken refuge;' from निश्चि (root चि with निस्), निश्चित्य; from उद्धृ, उद्धृत्य; from संस्कृ (root कृ with सं), संस्कृत्य; from निःसृ, निःसृत्य. The lengthening of the radical vowel by coalition does not prevent this rule; as, from अती *atí* (root इ with अति), अतीत्य *atítya*.

a. जागृ 'to awake' gunates its final as in प्रजागर्य and क्षि 'to destroy,' 'to waste;' lengthens its final as in प्रक्षीय. उपक्षीय.

561. If a root end in long आ *á*, ई *í*, or ऊ *ú*, no change generally takes place; as, from विधा, विधाय; from उपक्री, उपक्रीय; from विभू, विभूय.

a. If it end in long ॠ *ṛí*, this vowel becomes *ír*, and after labial letters, *úr*: thus, from अवकॄ, अवकीर्य 'having scattered;' from आपॄ (root पॄ 'to fill'), आपूर्य (compare 534).

562. Final diphthongs pass into आ *á*; as, from परिध्यै, परिध्याय (also परिधीय); from अभिध्यै, अभिध्याय; from अवसो, अवसाय.

a. But ह्वे with आ makes आहूय. In Epic poetry, सो with अव makes अवस्य.

b. मि 'to throw,' मी 'to kill,' मा 'to measure,' and मे 'to barter,' all -माय. Similarly, दी 'to decay,' -दाय; but ली 'to adhere,' -लाय or -लीय (see 390. *e*). ज्या and श्वि conform to the rule for the passive (-जीय, -शूय).

563. A penultimate nasal is generally rejected, as in passives (see 469): thus, from समासञ्ज् *samásañj*, समासज्य *samásajya*; from प्रमन्थ्, प्रमथ्य (used adverbially in the sense 'violently').

a. Some few roots retain the nasal: thus, आशङ्क् makes आशङ्क्य; and आलिङ्ग्, आलिङ्ग्य.

b. लभ् 'to acquire' may insert a nasal after the prepositions आ and उप: thus, आलम्भ्य &c. (otherwise -लभ्य).

564. If a root end in a consonant the general rule is, that no change takes place; as, from निक्षिप् *nikship*, निक्षिप्य *nikshipya*; from प्राप् (root आप् with प्र), प्राप्य; from वीक्ष् (root ईक्ष् with वि), वीक्ष्य.

a. But roots in र् or व्, preceded by *i* or *u*, lengthen these vowels, as in प्रतिदीव्य from दिव्, विस्फूर्य from स्फुर्.

b. Four roots in अम् (गम्, नम्, यम्, रम्) optionally reject the nasal, and interpose *t* between the final *a* and *ya*; as, from निगम्, निगत्य or निगम्य. The roots हन्, मन्, तन्, वन्, क्षण्, क्षिण्, ऋण्, तृण्, घृण् always reject the nasal; as, from निहन्, निहत्य.

c. जन्, सन्, and खन् optionally reject the न्; but instead of interposing *t*, lengthen the final *a*, as in passives (see 470): thus, from उत्खन्, उत्खाय (or उत्खन्य).

565. The changes which take place in certain roots before the *ya* of the passive (471, 472) are preserved before *ya*; as, from निवप्, उप्य; from विवस्, उष्य; from प्रवच्, प्रोच्य; from अनुवद्, अनूद्य; from विग्रह्, विगृह्य; from आप्रच्छ्, आपृच्छ्य; from आव्यध्, आविध्य; and so with all the roots at 471, 472.

a. The roots at 390. *l.* have two forms: thus, from गुप् comes -गोपाय्य and -गुप्य, &c.

b. There are one or two instances in which an uncompounded root takes य; as, अर्च्य 'having reverenced.' Manu VII. 145. I. 4. Mahá-bhárata 3. 8017. उष्य 'having resided,' Nala V. 42 (from वस्); गृह्य 'having taken,' Astra-śikshá 21.

566. In affixing य *ya* to the bases of causal verbs of the 10th class, and the 3d class of nominals (see 521), the characteristic अय is generally rejected; as, from प्रबोधय *prabodhaya*, प्रबोध्य *prabodhya*; from प्रचारय, प्रचार्य; from सन्दर्शय, सन्दर्श्य; from विचारय, विचार्य.

a. It is, however, retained when the root ends in a single consonant and encloses short *a*: thus, विगणय्य 'having calculated' (गण with वि); आकलय्य 'having imagined' (कल् with आ); संकथय्य 'having narrated' (कथ् with सं).

b. The final *a* of frequentative bases is of course dropped, and the final *ya* of both frequentatives and nominals, if preceded by a consonant; as, from लोलूय comes -लोलूय; from बोभूय, -बोभूय; from नमस्य, -नमस्य.

Adverbial indeclinable participle.

567. There is another indeclinable participle yielding the same sense as those formed with *tvá* and *ya*, but of rare occurrence. It is equivalent to the accusative case of a noun derived from a root, used adverbially; and is formed by adding अम् *am* to the root, before which affix changes of the radical vowel take place, similar to those required before the causal affix अय (481) or before the 3d sing. aorist passive (see 475): thus, from नी *ní*, 'to lead,' नायम् *náyam*, 'having led;' from पा 'to drink,' पायं 'having drunk;' from ह्वे, ह्वायं; from पच्, पाचं; from छिद्, छेदं; from हन् 'to kill,' घातं. It often occupies the last place in a compound; as in the expression समूलघातं 'having totally exterminated;' and in the following passage from Bhaṭṭi:

लतानुपातं कुसुमान्यगृह्णात् स नद्यवस्कन्दमुपास्पृशच्च ।
कुतूहलाच्चारुशिलोपवेशं काकुत्स्थ ईषत्स्मयमान आस्त ॥

'The descendant of Kakutstha, smiling softly, repeatedly bending down the creepers, would pluck the blossoms; descending to the streams, would sip (the waters); seating himself on some variegated rock, would recline in admiration (of the scene).' Compare also the passage at the end of Act V. of Śakuntalá; बाहूत्क्षेपं क्रन्दितुं प्रवृत्ता 'repeatedly throwing up her arms she began to weep.'

c. These participles generally imply repetition of the action, as in the passage above, and in this sense are themselves often repeated; as, *dáyam*, *dáyam*, 'having repeatedly given.'

FUTURE PASSIVE PARTICIPLES.

568. These are amongst the most common and useful of all participles, and may be classed under three heads: 1st, as formed with the affix तव्य *tavya*; 2dly, as formed with अनीय *aníya*; 3dly, as formed with य *ya*. These affixes yield a sense corresponding to the Latin future passive participle in *dus*, and the English *able* and *ible*, and most commonly denote 'obligation' or 'propriety' and 'fitness.'

a. Although these participles agree in signification with the Latin participles in *dus*, yet Prof. Bopp considers that the affix *tavya* corresponds in form to the Latin *tivus*, and in sense as well as form to the Greek τεος. In some of the Latin formations with *tivus*, the passive sense is preserved, as in *captivus*, *nativus*, *coctivus*. Compare Sanskrit *dátavya* with *dativus* (*dandus*), δοτέος; *yoktavya* with (*con*)*junctivus* (*jungendus*); *janitavya* with *genitivus* (*gignendus*); *dhátavya* with θετέος, &c.

Future passive participles formed with तव्य tavya.

569. These are formed by substituting तव्य *tavya* for ता *tā*, the termination of the 3d pers. sing. of the 1st future: thus, from क्षेप्ता *kshep्tā*, 'he will throw,' क्षेप्तव्य *kshep्tavya*, 'to be thrown;' कर्ता 'he will do,' कर्तव्य 'to be done;' from भविता 'he will be,' भवितव्य 'about to be;' from कुचिता, कुचितव्य (see 390. *a*); from विजिता, विजितव्य. And in the case of those roots ending in consonants which reject *i*, whatever changes take place before *tā*, the same take place before *tavya*, and all the special rules at 390. *a*—*o*. will equally apply to this affix: thus, त्यक्ता, त्यक्तव्य (*relinquendus*); मन्ता, मन्तव्य; द्रष्टा, द्रष्टव्य; योद्धा, योद्धव्य; दग्धा, दग्धव्य; सोढा, सोढव्य; कमिता or कामयिता, कमितव्य or कामयितव्य; दीपिता, दीपितव्य; मार्ष्टा or मार्जिता, मार्ष्टव्य or मार्जितव्य; and from the causal कारयिता, कारयितव्य; from the desiderative बुबोधिषिता, बुबोधिषितव्य; from the frequentative बोबुधिता, बोबुधितव्य; from बोभविता, बोभवितव्य. See the rules at 388, 390, 491, 505, 513, 516.

Future passive participles formed with अनीय anīya.

570. This affix is added directly to the root, and generally without other change than guṇation (if Guṇa is admissible): thus, from चि *ći*, 'to gather,' चयनीय *ćayanīya*, 'to be gathered;' from भू, भवनीय; from कृ, करणीय (58); from लिख्, लेखनीय; from मुच्, मोचनीय; from स्पृश्, स्पर्शनीय; from कृष्, कर्षणीय; from चुर् (10th c.), चोरणीय: but मृज्, मार्जनीय; गुह्, गूहनीय; दीधी, दीध्यनीय; कम्, कमनीय and कामनीय: गुप्, गोपनीय and गोपायनीय, &c. See 390. *j*, *l*, *m*.

a. A final diphthong is changed to आ *ā*, which blends with the initial *a* of *anīya*; as, from ध्यै, ध्यानीय; from गै, गानीय.

b. The roots at 390, 390. *a*. of course forbid Guṇa: thus, कुचनीय from कुच्; गुवनीय from गु, &c.

c. As to derivative verbs, *aya* is rejected from a causal base, and *a* from the bases of other derivative verbs, and *ya*, if a consonant precedes: thus, बोधनीय from the causal base बोधय; बुबोधिषणीय from the desiderative बुबोधिष; also बोबुधनीय, चेक्षिपणीय, from the frequentatives बोबुध, चेक्षिप्य; and तपस्यनीय or तपसनीय from the nominal तपस्य.

Future passive participles formed with य ya.

571. Before this affix, as before all others beginning with *y*, certain changes of final vowels become necessary.

a. If a root end in आ *á*, or in ए *e*, ऐ *ai*, ओ *o*, changeable to आ *á*, this vowel becomes ए *e* (compare 446); as, from मा *má*, 'to measure,' मेय *meya*, 'to be measured,' 'measurable;' from हा *há*, 'to quit,' हेय *heya*; from ध्यै *dhyai*, 'to meditate,' ध्येय *dhyeya*; from ग्लै 'to be weary,' ग्लेय; from दा 'to give,' दे 'to pity,' and दो 'to cut,' देय.

b. If in इ *i*, ई *í*, उ *u*, or ऊ *ú*, these vowels are guṇated; as, from चि *ći*, चेय *ćeya* (in the Veda चाय्य with अप); but नी with उद्, -नीय.

But the Guṇa ओ *o* is changed to *av*, and sometimes ए *e* to *ay*, before *ya* (as if before a vowel): thus, from भू, भव्य; from जि 'to conquer,' जय्य; from क्री 'to buy,' क्रय्य; from क्षि 'to destroy,' क्षय्य.

And the Guṇa ओ *o* passes into *áv* before *y*, especially when it is intended to lay emphasis on the meaning; as, from लू, लाव्य; from श्रु, श्राव्य; from भू, भाव्य. But धू 'to shake' makes धूय.

c. If in ऋ *ṛi* or ॠ *ṛí*, these vowels are vṛiddhied; as, from कृ 'to do,' कार्य; from भृ 'to support,' भार्य (also भृत्य, see 572); from वृ 'to choose,' वार्य (also वृत्य).

d. The roots at 390. *c.* drop their finals (दरिद्र्य, दरिद्राय्य).

572. Sometimes if a root end in a short vowel no change takes place, but *t* is interposed, after the analogy of the indeclinable participle formed with *ya* at 560; so that the crude base of the future participle is often not distinguishable from the indeclinable: thus, from जि *ji*, 'to conquer,' जित्य *jitya* (also *jeya*), 'conquerable;' from स्तु *stu*, 'to praise,' स्तुत्य *stutya*, 'laudable;' from कृ *kṛi*, 'to do,' कृत्य *kṛitya* (as well as कार्य), 'practicable;' from इ 'to go,' इत्य 'to be gone;' from आदृ 'to honour,' आदृत्य 'to be honoured.'

573. If a root end in a single consonant with a medial *a*, the latter may be vṛiddhied; as, from ग्रह् *grah*, 'to take,' ग्राह्य *gráhya*; from त्रप् 'to be ashamed,' त्राप्य; from कम् 'to love,' काम्य: but not always; as, from शक्, शक्य; from सह्, सह्य; from वध्, वध्य; from यज्, यज्य: and not if the final is a labial (except लप्, रप्, दभ्); as, from गम्, गम्य; from शप्, शप्य; from लभ् 'to receive,' लभ्य (and लम्भ्य). The root मद् 'to be mad' makes माद्य after prepositions, but otherwise मद्य. Similarly, गद् and चर्. The root भज् 'to serve' makes भज्य and भाग्य (see 574).

a. If with a medial इ *i* or उ *u*, these are generally guṇated; as, from भुज्, भोज्य; from लिह्, लेह्य; but युज्, युज्य: and sometimes only optionally; as, गुह् makes गुह्य as well as गोह्य; and दुह्, दुह्य and दोह्य.

b. If with a medial ऋ *ṛi*, no change generally takes place; as, from स्पृश्, स्पृश्य; from दृश्, दृश्य; from मृज्, मृज्य (after परि and अप, मार्ग्य); from वृष्, वृष्य (also वर्ष्य); but from वृध्, वृध्य or वर्ध्य.

c. The roots at 390, 390. *a.* are, as usual, debarred from Guṇa: thus, कुच्य, &c.

574. A final च् *c* may sometimes be changed to क् *k*, and final ज् *j* to ग् *g*, when the past passive participle rejects *i*; as, from पच् *pac*, पाक्य *pákya* and पाच्य *pácya*; from युज्, योग्य or युज्य. When the final is unchanged, as in *pácya*, the obligation implied is said to be more absolute; but the two forms may have distinct meanings: thus, *bhojya* (from *bhuj*) means 'to be eaten,' but *bhogya*, 'to be enjoyed;' *vácya* (from *vac*) means 'proper to be said,' but *vákya*, 'that which is actually to be said.'

a. Again, भाज्य (from भज्) is used after the prepositions नि and प्र, otherwise भाग्य. Similarly, योज्य (from युज्) after नि and प्र, and वाच्य or वाक्य (from वच्) after the same prepositions.

b. Other anomalous changes may take place, some of which are similar to those before the *ya* of passives: thus, from ग्रह्, गृह्य as well as ग्राह्य (472); from वह्, उह्य (471, also वाह्य); from यज्, इज्य (471); from शास्, शिष्य (472); from खन् 'to dig,' खेय; from शंस् 'to praise,' शस्य or शंस्य; from भ्रस्ज् 'to fry,' भर्ज्य or भृज्य; from हन्, वध्य or घात्य.

c. The roots beginning with गुप् at 390. *l.* have two forms: thus, गोप्य or गोपाय्य.

575. Many of these participles are used as substantives: thus, वाक्य n. 'speech;' भोज्य n. 'food;' भोग्या f. 'a harlot;' इज्या f. 'sacrifice;' खेय n. 'a ditch;' भार्या f. 'a wife,' from भृ 'to support,' &c.

576. The affix *ya* may be added to desiderative, frequentative, and nominal bases in the same way as *cáyya*: thus, बुभोधिष्य, बोभूय्य, चेक्रिय्य, नमस्य. So also, from मुसल 'a pestle,' मुसल्य 'to be pounded with a pestle.'

a. अ *a* added to a root after guṇation (if Guṇa is possible) gives the sense of a future passive participle when in composition with सु, दुस्, and ईषत्; as, सुकर 'easy to be done,' दुष्कर 'difficult to be done,' दुस्तर 'difficult to be crossed.'

b. Again, an affix एलिम added to a few roots has the same force as the affixes of the future passive participle; e. g. पचेलिम 'fit to ripen' or 'to be cooked,' भिदेलिम 'to be broken.'

577. The inflection of future passive participles follows that of the first class of nouns at 103: thus, कर्तव्य 'to be done;' N. sing. m. f. n. *kartavyas*, *kartavyá*, *kartavyam*. Similarly, *karaṇíyas*, *karaṇíyá*, *karaṇíyam*; and *káryas*, *káryá*, *káryam*.

PARTICIPLES OF THE SECOND FUTURE.—FORMATION OF THE BASE.

578. These are not common. They are of two kinds, either Parasmai-pada or Átmane-pada; and are formed, like present participles, by changing अन्ति *anti*, the termination of the 3d plur. of the 2d future, into अत् *at*, for the Parasmai-pada; and by changing अन्ते *ante* into अमान *amána*, for the Átmane: thus, from करिष्यन्ति *karishyanti* and करिष्यन्ते *karishyante*, 'they will do,' come करिष्यत् *karishyat* and करिष्यमाण *karishyamáṇa* (58), 'about to do;' from the passive 2d fut. वक्ष्यन्ते 'they will be said' comes वक्ष्यमाण 'about to be said.'

a. In their inflection, as well as their formation, they resemble present participles; see 524 and 526.

b. Observe—The future participle in *mána* may be compared with the Greek in μενο: *dásyamána* = δωσόμενος.

PARTICIPIAL NOUNS OF AGENCY.

579. These have been already incidentally noticed at 80, 83, 84, 85, 87. As, however, they partake of the nature of participles, and are often used as participles (see Syntax, 909—911), a fuller explanation of them is here given. They may be classed under three heads: 1st, as formed from the root; 2dly, as formed from the 1st future; 3dly, as formed from the root by changes similar to those which form the causal base.

580. The base of the first class is often identical with the root itself; that is, the unchanged root is frequently used at the end of compounds as a noun of agency, *t* being added if it ends in a short vowel; see the examples at 84. I. and 87.

a. Another common noun of agency is formed from the root by affixing अ *a* (as in the first group of conjugational classes at 257. *a*), before which *a*, Guṇa, and rarely Vṛiddhi, of a final vowel is required; as, from जि *ji*, 'to conquer,' जय *jaya*, 'conquering.' Medial vowels are generally unchanged; as, from वद् *vad*, 'to say,' वद *vada*, 'saying;' from तुद् *tud*, 'to vex,' तुद *tuda*, 'vexing.'

b. And final आ *á*, अम् *am*, or अन् *an*, are dropped; as, from दा *dá*, 'to give,' द *da*, 'giving;' from गम् *gam*, 'to go,' ग *ga*, 'going;' from जन् *jan*, 'to be born,' ज *ja*, 'being born.' Their declension follows the first class of nouns at 103.

581. The base of the second class (see 83) is formed from the 3d pers. sing. of the 1st future of primitive verbs, by substituting the vowel ऋ *ṛi* for the final vowel *á*, the nominative case being therefore *identical* with the 3d pers. sing. of that tense (see 386): thus, from भोक्ता *bhoktá*, 'he will eat,' भोक्तृ *bhoktṛi*, 'an eater;' from योद्धा 'he will fight,' योद्धृ 'a fighter;' from याचिता 'he will ask,' याचितृ 'an asker;' from वोढा 'he will bear,' वोढृ 'a bearer,' &c. They are inflected at 127.

582. The base of the third class is formed in three ways.

a. By adding इन् *in* to the root (see 85. V), before which affix changes take place similar to those required before the causal affix *aya* (481, 482, 483); as, from कृ, कारिन् *kárin*, 'a doer;' from हन् (488), घातिन् *ghátin*, 'a killer;' from शी, शायिन् 'a sleeper:' *y* being inserted after roots in *á* (483); as, from पा, पायिन् 'a drinker;' from दा, दायिन् *dáyin*, 'a giver.' They are inflected at 159.

b. By adding अक *aka* to the root (see 80. IV), before which affix changes take place analogous to those before the causal *aya* (481, 482, 483); as, from कृ, कारक *káraka*, 'a doer,' 'doing;' from नी, नायक *náyaka*, 'a leader,' 'leading;' from ग्रह्, ग्राहक *gráhaka*; from छिद्, छेदक; from हन्, घातक; from दुष्, दूषक; from जन्, जनक; from नन्द्, नन्दक; from स्था, स्थापक.

c. By adding अन *ana* to some few roots ending in consonants (see 80. V), after changes similar to those required before the causal affix; as, from नन्द्, नन्दन *nandana*, 'rejoicing;' from दुष्, दूषण 'vitiating;' from शुध्, शोधन 'cleansing.'

Observe—The inflection of the last two follows that of the first class of nouns at 103.

EXAMPLES OF PRIMITIVE VERBS IN THE TEN CLASSES, AND OF DERIVATIVE VERBS INFLECTED AT FULL.

583. We begin by giving a synopsis of the inflection of the primitive forms of the ten roots: बुध् *budh*, 'to know,' 1st c.; नृत् *nrit*, 'to dance,' 4th c.; दिश् *diś*, 'to point out,' 6th c.; युज् *yuj*, 'to unite,' 10th c.; विद् *vid*, 'to know,' 2d c.; भृ *bhri*, 'to bear,' 3d c.; भिद् *bhid*, 'to break,' 7th c.; चि *ći*, 'to gather,' 5th c.; तन् *tan*, 'to stretch,' 8th c.; पू *pú*, 'to purify,' 9th c.: grouping together, first, the 1st, 4th, 6th, and 10th classes; then the 2d, 3d, and 7th; and lastly, the 5th, 7th, and 9th, for the reasons stated at 257. In the next place, the passive forms of these ten roots will be synoptically exhibited, followed by the present tense of the causal, desiderative, and frequentative forms, and the participles. Examples will then be given of primitive verbs of all the ten classes (according to the same grouping), *inflected at full;* and under every verb the derivative forms and participles will be indicated. Lastly, a full example will be given of each of the four kinds of derivative verbs, passives, causals, desideratives, and frequentatives.

INFLECTION OF THE BASE OF PRIMITIVE VERBS OF THE TEN CLASSES OR CONJUGATIONS.

PRESENT.

	Parasmai-pada.									Ātmane-pada.								
ROOT.	SING.			DUAL.			PLURAL.			SING.			DUAL.			PLURAL.		
1. Budh	bodhá	bodha	bodha	bodhá	bodha	bodha	bodhá	bodha	bodha	bodha	bodha	bodha	bodhá	bodha	bodha	bodhá	bodha	bodha
4. Nṛit	nṛityá	nṛitya	nṛitya	nṛityá	nṛitya	nṛitya	nṛityá	nṛitya	nṛitya	nṛitya	nṛitya	nṛitya	nṛityá	nṛitya	nṛitya	nṛityá	nṛitya	nṛitya
6. Diś	diśá	diśa	diśa	diśá	diśa	diśa	diśá	diśa	diśa	diśa	diśa	diśa	diśá	diśa	diśa	diśá	diśa	diśa
10. Yuj	yojayá	yojaya	yojaya	yojayá	yojaya	yojaya	yojayá	yojaya	yojaya	yojaya	yojaya	yojaya	yojayá	yojaya	yojaya	yojayá	yojaya	yojaya
2. Vid	ved	vet *	vet	vid	vit	vit	vid	vit	vid	vid	vit *	vit	vid	vid	vid	vid	vid	vid
3. Bhṛi	bibhar	bibhar	bibhar	bibhṛi	bibhṛi	bibhṛi	bibhṛi	bibhṛi	bibhr *	bibhr	bibhṛi	bibhṛi	bibhṛi	bibhr	bibhr	bibhṛi	bibhṛi	bibhr
7. Bhid	bhinad	bhinat *	bhinat	bhind	bhint	bhint	bhind	bhint	bhind	bhind	bhint *	bhint	bhind	bhind	bhind	bhind	bhind	bhind
5. Ći	ćino	ćino	ćino	ćinu	ćinu	ćinu	ćinu	ćinu	ćinv	ćinv	ćinu	ćinu	ćinu	ćinv	ćinv	ćinu	ćinu	ćinv
8. Tan	tano	tano	tano	tanu	tanu	tanu	tanu	tanu	tanv	tanv	tanu	tanu	tanu	tanv	tanv	tanu	tanu	tanv
9. Pū	punā	punā *	punā	punī	punī	punī	punī	punī	pun	pun	punī	punī	punī	pun	pun	punī	punī	pun
1. 4. 6. 10.		* si							nti	i	* se			ithe	ite			nte
—	mi		ti	vas	thas	tas	mas	tha				te	vahe			mahe	dhve	
2. 3. 7. 5. 8. 9.		si							anti * ati	e	se			āthe	āte			ate

Observe.—The base is to be united with the terminations: thus, 1st sing. Pres. Parasmai, bodhā+mi=bodhāmi, 2d sing. bodha+si=bodhasi, 3d sing. bodha+ti=bodhati; 1st dual, bodhā+vas=bodhāvas, &c. Ātmane, bodha+i=bodhe, bodha+se=bodhase, &c. Whenever the terminations of the 1st, 4th, 6th, and 10th classes differ from those of the others, they are placed in the upper line. As to the optional dropping of the u of ćinu and tanu, see 349.

IMPERFECT or FIRST PRETERITE.

Roots.	Parasmai-pada. Sing.			Dual.			Plural.			Ātmane-pada. Sing.			Dual.			Plural.		
1. Budh	abodha	abodha	abodha	abodhā	abodha	abodha	abodhā	abodha	abodha	abodha	abodha	abodha	abodhā	abodha	abodha	abodhā	abodha	abodha
4. Nṛit	anṛitya	anṛitya	anṛitya	anṛityā	anṛitya	anṛitya	anṛityā	anṛitya	anṛitya	anṛitya	anṛitya	anṛitya	anṛityā	anṛitya	anṛitya	anṛityā	anṛitya	anṛitya
6. Diś	adiśa	adiśa	adiśa	adiśā	adiśa	adiśa	adiśā	adiśa	adiśa	adiśa	adiśa	adiśa	adiśā	adiśa	adiśa	adiśā	adiśa	adiśa
10. Yuj	ayojaya	ayojaya	ayojaya	ayojayā	ayojaya	ayojaya	ayojayā	ayojaya	ayojaya	ayojaya	ayojaya	ayojaya	ayojayā	ayojaya	ayojaya	ayojayā	ayojaya	ayojaya
2. Vid	aved	avet	avet	avid	avit	avit	avid	avit	avid*	avid	avit	avit	avid	avid	avid	avid	avid	avid
3. Bhṛi	abibhar	abibhar	abibhar	abibhṛi	abibhṛi	abibhṛi	abibhṛi	abibhṛi	abibhar*	abibhr	abibhṛi	abibhṛi	abibhṛi	abibhr	abibhr	abibhṛi	abibhṛi	abibhr
7. Bhid	abhinad	abhinat	abhinat	abhind	abhint	abhint	abhind	abhint	abhind	abhind	abhint	abhint	abhind	abhind	abhind	abhind	abhind	abhind
5. Ći	aćinav	aćino	aćino	aćinu	aćinu	aćinu	aćinu	aćinu	aćinv	aćinv	aćinu	aćinu	aćinu	aćinv	aćinv	aćinu	aćinu	aćinv
8. Tan	atanav	atano	atano	atanu	atanu	atanu	atanu	atanu	atanv	atanv	atanu	atanu	atanu	atanv	atanv	atanu	atanu	atanv
9. Pū	apunā	apunā	apunā	apunī	apunī	apunī	apunī	apunī	apun	apun	apunī	apunī	apunī	apun	apun	apunī	apunī	apun
1. 4. 6. 10. }	am								n					ithām	itām			nta
		s	t	va	tam	tām	ma	ta		i	thās	ta	vahi			mahi	dhvam	
2. 3. 7. 5. 8. 9. }	am								an *us					āthām	ātām			ata

Observe.—In the 2d and 3d sing., Parasmai, the roots of the 2d group reject the terminations by 293: thus, 2d and 3d sing., avet, abibhar, abhinat. In the Ātmane the final a of the bases of the roots of the 1st group will blend with the initial i of a termination into e by 32. As to the optional dropping of the u of aćinu and atanu, see 349.

POTENTIAL.

ROOT.	Parasmai-pada. Sing.			Dual.			Plural.			Átmane-pada. Sing.			Dual.			Plural.		
1. *Budh*	bodha	bodha	bodha	bodha	bodha	bodha	bodha	bodha	bodha	bodha	bodha	bodha	bodha	bodha	bodha	bodha	bodha	bodha
4. *Nrit*	nritya	nritya	nritya	nritya	nritya	nritya	nritya	nritya	nritya	nritya	nritya	nritya	nritya	nritya	nritya	nritya	nritya	nritya
6. *Diś*	diśa	diśa	diśa	diśa	diśa	diśa	diśa	diśa	diśa	diśa	diśa	diśa	diśa	diśa	diśa	diśa	diśa	diśa
10. *Yuj*	yojaya	yojaya	yojaya	yojaya	yojaya	yojaya	yojaya	yojaya	yojaya	yojaya	yojaya	yojaya	yojaya	yojaya	yojaya	yojaya	yojaya	yojaya
2. *Vid*	vid	vid	vid	vid	vid	vid	vid	vid	vid	vid	vid	vid	vid	vid	vid	vid	vid	vid
3. *Bhṛi*	bibhṛi	bibhṛi	bibhṛi	bibhṛi	bibhṛi	bibhṛi	bibhṛi	bibhṛi	bibhṛi	bibhr	bibhr	bibhr	bibhr	bibhr	bibhr	bibhr	bibhr	bibhr
7. *Bhid*	bhind	bhind	bhind	bhind	bhind	bhind	bhind	bhind	bhind	bhind	bhind	bhind	bhind	bhind	bhind	bhind	bhind	bhind
5. *Ći*	ćinu	ćinu	ćinu	ćinu	ćinu	ćinu	ćinu	ćinu	ćinu	ćinv	ćinv	ćinv	ćinv	ćinv	ćinv	ćinv	ćinv	ćinv
8. *Tan*	tanu	tanu	tanu	tanu	tanu	tanu	tanu	tanu	tanu	tanv	tanv	tanv	tanv	tanv	tanv	tanv	tanv	tanv
9. *Pú*	puní	puní	puní	puní	puní	puní	puní	puní	puní	pun	pun	pun	pun	pun	pun	pun	pun	pun
1. 4. 6. 10.	iyam	is	it	iva	itam	itám	ima	ita	iyus	íya	íthás	íta	ívahi	íyáthám	íyátám	ímahi	ídhvam	íran
2. 3. 7. 5. 8. 9.	yám	yás	yát	yáva	yátam	yátám	yáma	yáta	yus									

Observe—As the base in the 1st group of conjugations ends in *a*, and the terminations begin with *i*, these two vowels will blend into *e* by 32: thus, *bodha + iyam = bodheyam*, *bodha + is = bodhes*, &c.; Átmane, *bodha + íya = bodheya*.

IMPERATIVE.

Root.	Parasmai-pada. Sing.			Dual.			Plural.			Âtmane-pada. Sing.			Dual.			Plural.		
1. Budh	bodha	bodha	bodha	bodha	bodha	bodha	bodha	bodha	bodha	bodha	bodha	bodha	bodha	bodha	bodha	bodha	bodha	bodha
4. Nṛit	nṛitya	nṛitya	nṛitya	nṛitya	nṛitya	nṛitya	nṛitya	nṛitya	nṛitya	nṛitya	nṛitya	nṛitya	nṛitya	nṛitya	nṛitya	nṛitya	nṛitya	nṛitya
6. Diś	diśa	diśa	diśa	diśa	diśa	diśa	diśa	diśa	diśa	diśa	diśa	diśa	diśa	diśa	diśa	diśa	diśa	diśa
10. Yuj	yojaya	yojaya	yojaya	yojaya	yojaya	yojaya	yojaya	yojaya	yojaya	yojaya	yojaya	yojaya	yojaya	yojaya	yojaya	yojaya	yojaya	yojaya
2. Vid	ved	vid †	vet	ved	vit	vit	ved	vit	vid	ved	vit *	vit	ved	vid	vid	ved	vid	vid
3. Bhṛi	bibhar	bibhṛi	bibhar	bibhar	bibhṛi	bibhṛi	bibhar	bibhṛi	bibhṛ *	bibhar	bibhṛi	bibhṛi	bibhar	bibhr	bibhr	bibhar	bibhṛi	bibhr
7. Bhid	bhinad	bhind †	bhinat	bhinad	bhint	bhint	bhinad	bhint	bhind	bhinad	bhint *	bhint	bhinad	bhind	bhind	bhinad	bhind	bhind
5. Ći	ćinav	ćinu *	ćino	ćinav	ćinu	ćinu	ćinav	ćinu	ćinv	ćinav	ćinu	ćinu	ćinav	ćinv	ćinv	ćinav	ćinu	ćinv
8. Tan	tanav	tanu *	tano	tanav	tanu	tanu	tanav	tanu	tanv	tanav	tanu	tanu	tanav	tanv	tanv	tanav	tanu	tanv
9. Pú	punā	punī	punā	punā	punī	punī	punā	punī	pun	punā	punī	punī	punā	pun	pun	punā	punī	pun
1. 4. 6. 10.	āni	* —	tu	āva	tam	tām	āma	ta	ntu	ai	* sva	tām	āvahai	ithām	itām	āmahai	dhvam	ntām
2. 3. 7. 5. 8. 9.		hi † dhi							antu * atu		shva			āthām	ātām			atām

Observe—In the 2d sing., Parasmai, the roots of the 5th and 8th conj. are like those of the 1st group, and make ćinu, tanu, rejecting the termination. The 2d and 7th take dhi for hi by 291, and make viddhi, bhinddhi. Bhṛi makes bibhratu for bibhrantu in 3d pl. by 290. a. In the Âtmane, bodha + ai = bodhai and punā + ai = punai by 33, bodha + ithām = bodhethām by 32.

PERFECT or SECOND PRETERITE.

Parasmai-pada.

Root.	Sing.			Dual.			Plural.		
1. Budh	bubodh	bubodh	bubodh	bubudh	bubudh	bubudh	bubudh	bubudh	bubudh
4. Nṛit	nanart	nanart	nanart	nanṛit	nanṛit	nanṛit	nanṛit	nanṛit	nanṛit
6. Diś	dideś	dideś	dideś	didiś	didiś	didiś	didiś	didiś	didiś
10. Yuj	yojay†	yojay†	yojay†	yojay†	yojay†	yojay†	yojay†	yojay†	yojay†
2. Vid	vived	vived	vived	vivid	vivid	vivid	vivid	vivid	vivid
3. Bhṛi*	babhār	babhar*	babhār	babhṛi*	babhr	babhr	babhṛi*	babhr	babhr
7. Bhid	bibhed	bibhed	bibhed	bibhid	bibhid	bibhid	bibhid	bibhid	bibhid
5. Ći	ćikāy	ćikay	ćikāy	ćiky	ćiky	ćiky	ćiky	ćiky	ćiky
8. Tan	tatān	ten	tatān	ten	ten	ten	ten	ten	ten
9. Pā	papāu	papau	papāu	pap	pap	pap	pap	pap	pap
	a	itha *tha	a	iva *va	athus	atus	ima *ma	a	us

Ātmane-pada.

Root.	Sing.			Dual.			Plural.		
1. Budh	bubudh	bubudh	bubudh	bubudh	bubudh	bubudh	bubudh	bubudh	bubudh
4. Nṛit	nanṛit	nanṛit	nanṛit	nanṛit	nanṛit	nanṛit	nanṛit	nanṛit	nanṛit
6. Diś	didiś	didiś	didiś	didiś	didiś	didiś	didiś	didiś	didiś
10. Yuj	yojay†	yojay†	yojay†	yojay†	yojay†	yojay†	yojay†	yojay†	yojay†
2. Vid	vivid	vivid	vivid	vivid	vivid	vivid	vivid	vivid	vivid
3. Bhṛi*	babhr	babhṛi*	babhr	babhṛi*	babhr	babhr	babhṛi*	babhṛi*	babhr
7. Bhid	bibhid	bibhid	bibhid	bibhid	bibhid	bibhid	bibhid	bibhid	bibhid
5. Ći	ćiky	ćiky	ćiky	ćiky	ćiky	ćiky	ćiky	ćiky	ćiky
8. Tan	ten	ten	ten	ten	ten	ten	ten	ten	ten
9. Pā	pap	pap	pap	pap	pap	pap	pap	pap	pap
	e	ishe *she	e	ivahe *vahe	āthe	āte	imahe *mahe	idhve *dhve	ire

† The syllable ām must be added to yojay throughout; and the base of the second preterites of as, bhū, or kṛi, must be affixed to yojayām: thus, 1st sing. yojayāmāsa + a or yojayāmbabhūv + a or yojayāmćakār + a; see 385. a. Ći may optionally take tha as well as itha in the 2d sing.: thus, ćikayitha or ćiketha; but bhṛi makes only babhartha, see pp. 127 and 163. As to the alternative ćikay, tatan, papau, in the bases of 1st sing., see 368. As to idhve, see 372. a.

FIRST FUTURE.

ROOT.	BASE.	PAR. TERM.	ĀTM. TERM.
1. *Budh*	*bodhi* *	*tāsmi*	*tāhe*
4. *Nṛit*	*narti*	*tāsi*	*tāse*
6. *Diś*	*deś*	*tā*	*tā*
10. *Yuj*	*yojayi*		
		tāsvas	*tāsvahe*
2. *Vid*	*vedi*	*tāsthas*	*tāsāthe*
3. *Bhṛi*	*bhar*	*tārau*	*tārau*
7. *Bhid*	*bhet*		
		tāsmas	*tāsmahe*
5. *Ći*	*će*	*tāstha*	*tādhve*
8. *Tan*	*tani*	*tāras*	*tāras*
9. *Pū*	*pavi*		

* Note, that *budh* also forms *boddhāhe* &c. in Ātm. by 406. After *deś* the *t* of the terminations will become *ṭ* by 300.

SECOND FUTURE.

ROOT.	BASE.	PAR. TERM.	ĀTM. TERM.
1. *Budh*	*bodhi* *	*shyāmi*	*shye*
4. *Nṛit*	*narti*	*shyasi*	*shyase*
6. *Diś*	*dek*	*shyati*	*shyate*
10. *Yuj*	*yojayi*		
		shyāvas	*shyāvahe*
2. *Vid*	*vedi*	*shyathas*	*shyethe*
3. *Bhṛi*	*bhari*	*shyatas*	*shyete*
7. *Bhid*	*bhet* *		
		shyāmas	*shyāmahe*
5. *Ći*	*će*	*shyatha*	*shyadhve*
8. *Tan*	*tani*	*shyanti*	*shyante*
9. *Pū*	*pavi*		

* Note, that *budh* also forms *bhotsye* &c. in Ātm. by 406; and that after *bhet* the terminations will be *syāmi* &c.

AORIST or THIRD PRETERITE.

Form I.

ROOT.	BASE.	PAR. TERM.	ÁTM. TERM.
1. *Budh*	*abodhi* †	*sham*	*si*
		sís or † *ís*	*sthás* or *thás*
4. *Nṛit*	*anarti* †	*sít* or † *ít*	*sta* or *ta*
		sva	*svahi*
2. *Vid*	*avedi* †	*stam*	*sáthám*
		stám	*sátám*
3. *Bhṛi*	Par. *abhár* / Átm. *abhṛi* *	*sma*	*smahi*
5. *Ći*	Par. *aćai* / Átm. *aće* *	*sta*	*dhvam* or * *ḍhvam*
		sus	*sata*
8. *Tan*	Par. *atáni* † / Átm. *atani*		
9. *Pú*	Par. *apávi* † / Átm. *apavi* *		

Note, that *bhṛi* makes *abhṛithás*, *abhṛita*. *Bhid*, 7th c., follows this form in Átm., and makes *abhitsi*, *abhitthás*, *abhitta*, &c., by 419. *Tan* may make *atathás*, *atata*, as well as *atanishṭhás*, &c., by 426. c.

Form II.

ROOT.	BASE.	PAR. TERM.	ÁTM. TERM.
6. *Diś*	*adiksh*	*am*	*i* or * *e*
		as	*athás*
10. *Yuj*	*ayúyuj* *	*at*	*ata*
7. *Bhid* follows this form in Parasmai, but not in Átmane; see note under form I.	*abhid*	*áva*	*ávahi*
		atam	*áthám* or * *ethám*
		atám	*átám* or * *etám*
		áma	*ámahi*
		ata	*adhvam*
		an	*anta*

PRECATIVE OR BENEDICTIVE.

ROOT.	BASE.	PAR. TERM.	BASE.	ÁTM. TERM.
1. *Budh*	*budh*	*yásam*	*bodhi*	*shíya*
4. *Nṛit*	*nṛit*	*yás*	*narti*	*shíshṭhás*
6. *Diś*	*diś*	*yát*	*dik*	*shíshṭa*
10. *Yuj*	*yuj*	*yásva*	*yojayi*	*shívahi*
		yástam		*shíyásthám*
2. *Vid*	*vid*	*yástám*	*vedi*	*shíyástám*
3. *Bhṛi*	*bhṛi*		*bhṛi*	*shímahi*
7. *Bhid*	*bhid*	*yásma*	*bhit* *	*shídhvam*
		yásta		*shíran*
5. *Ċi*	*ći*	*yásus*	*će*	
8. *Tan*	*tan*		*tani*	
9. *Pú*	*pú*		*pavi*	

* Note, that after *bhit* the terminations will be *síya* &c. As to *shídhvam*, see p. 187.

CONDITIONAL.

ROOT.	BASE.	PAR. TERM.	ÁTM. TERM.
1. *Budh*	*abodhi*	*shyam*	*shye*
4. *Nṛit*	*anarti*	*shyas*	*shyathás*
6. *Diś*	*adek*	*shyat*	*shyata*
10. *Yuj*	*ayojayi*	*shyáva*	*shyávahi*
		shyatam	*shyethám*
2. *Vid*	*avedi*	*shyatám*	*shyetám*
3. *Bhṛi*	*abhari*		
7. *Bhid*	*abhet* *	*shyáma*	*shyámahi*
		shyata	*shyadhvam*
5. *Ċi*	*aće*	*shyan*	*shyanta*
8. *Tan*	*atani*		
9. *Pú*	*apavi*		

* Note, that after *abhet* the terminations will be *syam* &c.

INFINITIVE.

ROOT.	BASE.	TERM.
1. *Budh*	*bodhi*	
4. *Nṛit*	*narti*	
6. *Diś*	*desh* *	
10. *Yuj*	*yojayi*	
		tum
2. *Vid*	*vedi*	or * *ṭum*
3. *Bhṛi*	*bhar*	after *desh*
7. *Bhid*	*bhet*	by 320.
5. *Ċi*	*će*	
8. *Tan*	*tani*	
9. *Pú*	*pavi*	

INFLECTION OF THE BASE OF PASSIVE VERBS FROM THE SAME TEN ROOTS.

PRESENT.

ROOT.	BASE.	TERM.
1. *Budh*	*budhya* / *budhyá* *	*i*
4. *Nrit*	*nritya* / *nrityá* *	*se*
6. *Diś*	*diśya* / *diśyá* *	*te*
10. *Yuj*	*yojya* / *yojyá* *	* *vahe*
2. *Vid*	*vidya* / *vidyá* *	*ithe*
3. *Bhri*	*bhriya* / *bhriyá* *	*ite*
7. *Bhid*	*bhidya* / *bhidyá* *	* *mahe*
5. *Ći*	*ćíya* / *ćíyá* *	*dhwe*
8. *Tan*	*tanya* / *tanyá* *	*nte*
9. *Pú*	*púya* / *púyá* *	

IMPERFECT.

ROOT.	BASE.	TERM.
1. *Budh*	*abudhya* / *abudhyá* *	*i*
4. *Nrit*	*anritya* / *anrityá* *	*thás*
6. *Diś*	*adiśya* / *adiśyá* *	*ta*
10. *Yuj*	*ayojya* / *ayojyá* *	* *vahi*
2. *Vid*	*avidya* / *avidyá* *	*ithám*
3. *Bhri*	*abhriya* / *abhriyá* *	*itám*
7. *Bhid*	*abhidya* / *abhidyá* *	* *mahi*
5. *Ći*	*aćíya* / *aćíyá* *	*dhwam*
8. *Tan*	*atanya* / *atanyá* *	*nta*
9. *Pú*	*apúya* / *apúyá* *	

POTENTIAL.

ROOT.	BASE.	TERM.
1. *Budh*	*budhya*	*íya*
4. *Nrit*	*nritya*	*íthás*
6. *Diś*	*diśya*	*íta*
10. *Yuj*	*yojya*	*ívahi*
2. *Vid*	*vidya*	*íyáthám*
3. *Bhri*	*bhriya*	*íyátám*
7. *Bhid*	*bhidya*	*ímahi*
5. *Ći*	*ćíya*	*ídhwam*
8. *Tan*	*tanya*	*íran*
9. *Pú*	*púya*	

IMPERATIVE.

ROOT.	BASE.	TERM.
1. *Budh*	*budhya*	*ai*
4. *Nrit*	*nritya*	*swa*
6. *Diś*	*diśya*	*tám*
10. *Yuj*	*yojya*	*ávahai*
2. *Vid*	*vidya*	*ithám*
3. *Bhri*	*bhriya*	*itám*
7. *Bhid*	*bhidya*	*ámahai*
5. *Ći*	*ćíya*	*dhwam*
8. *Tan*	*tanya*	*ntám*
9. *Pú*	*púya*	

PERFECT.

ROOT.	BASE.	TERM.
1. *Budh*	*bubudh*	*e*
4. *Nṛit*	*nanṛit*	* *ishe*
6. *Diś*	*didiś*	*e*
10. *Yuj*	*yojayáńćakṛ*	* *ivahe*
2. *Vid*	*vivid*	*áthe*
3. *Bhṛi*	*babhr* / *babhṛ* *	*áte*
7. *Bhid*	*bibhid*	
5. *Ći*	*ćićy*	* *imahe*
8. *Tan*	*ten*	* *idhve*, 372.a.
9. *Pú*	*pupuv*	*ire*

FIRST FUTURE.

ROOT.	BASE.	TERM.
1. *Budh*	*bodhi*	*táhe*
4. *Nṛit*	*narti*	*táse*
6. *Diś*	*dash (300)*	*tá*
10. *Yuj*	*yojayi* or *yoji*	*tásvahe*
2. *Vid*	*vedi*	*tásáthe*
3. *Bhṛi*	*bhári* or *bhar*	*tárau*
7. *Bhid*	*bhet*	
5. *Ći*	*ćáyi* or *će*	*tásmahe*
8. *Tan*	*tani*	*tádhve*
9. *Pú*	*pávi* or *pavi*	*táras*

SECOND FUTURE.

ROOT.	BASE.	TERM.
1. *Budh*	*bodhi*	*shye*
4. *Nṛit*	*narti*	*shyase*
6. *Diś*	*dek (302)*	*shyate*
10. *Yuj*	*yojayi* or *yoji*	*shyávahe*
2. *Vid*	*vedi*	*shyethe*
3. *Bhṛi*	*bhári* or *bhari*	*shyete*
7. *Bhid*	*bhet*	
5. *Ći*	*ćáyi* or *će*	*shyámahe*
8. *Tan*	*tani*	*shyadhve*
9. *Pú*	*pávi* or *pavi*	*shyante*

AORIST.

ROOT.	BASE.	TERM.	BASE OF 3D SING.	TERM.	
1. *Budh*	*abodhi*	*shi*	*abudh*	*i*	* Observe—After *abhit* the initial *sh* of the termination takes the dental form *s*, in this and the following tenses. Again *adik* and *abhit* reject the sibilant from *shṭhās*, and become *adig* and *abhid* before *ḍhvam*; thus, *adikshi*, *adikthās*, *adishṭa*, *adikshvahi*, *adikshāthām*, *adikshātām*, *adikshmahi*, *adigḍhvam*, *adikshata*. So, *abhitsi*, *abhitthās*, *abhitta*, *abhitsvahi*, &c. See also 419, 475. *b*.
4. *Nṛit*	*anarti*	*shṭhās*	*anart*		
6. *Diś*	*adik* *		*adiś*		
10. *Yuj*	*ayojayi* (496. *a*) or *ayoji*	— *shvahi*	*ayoj*		
2. *Vid*	*avedi*	*shāthām*	*aved*		
3. *Bhṛi*	*abhāri* or *abhṛi* (475)	*shātām*	*abhṛ*		
7. *Bhid*	*abhit* *	—	*abhed*		
5. *Ći*	*aćāyi* or *aće*	*shmahi* *ḍhvam*	*aćāy*		
8. *Tan*	*atani*	*shata*	*atān*		
9. *Pū*	*apāvi* or *apavi*		*apāv*		

PRECATIVE.

ROOT.	BASE.	TERM.
1. *Budh*	*bodhi*	*shīya*
4. *Nṛit*	*narti*	*shīshṭhās*
6. *Diś*	*dik*	*shīshṭa*
10. *Yuj*	*yojayi* or *yoji*	— *shīvahi*
2. *Vid*	*vedi*	*shīyāsthām*
3. *Bhṛi*	*bhāri* or *bhṛi*	*shīyāstām*
7. *Bhid*	*bhit*	— *shīmahi*
5. *Ći*	*ćāyi* or *će*	*shīḍhvam*, p. 187.
8. *Tan*	*tani*	*shīran*
9. *Pū*	*pāvi* or *pavi*	

CONDITIONAL.

ROOT.	BASE.	TERM.
1. *Budh*	*abodhi*	*shye*
4. *Nṛit*	*anarti*	*shyathās*
6. *Diś*	*adek*	*shyata*
10. *Yuj*	*ayojayi* or *ayoji*	— *shyāvahi*
2. *Vid*	*avedi*	*shyethām*
3. *Bhṛi*	*abhāri* or *abhari*	*shyetām*
7. *Bhid*	*abhet*	— *shyāmahi*
5. *Ći*	*aćāyi* or *aće*	*shyadhvam*
8. *Tan*	*atani*	*shyanta*
9. *Pū*	*apāvi* or *apavi*	

CAUSAL FORM.
PRESENT TENSE.

ROOT.	BASE.	PAR. TERM.	ÁTM. TERM.
1. *Budh*	*bodhaya* / *bodhayá* *	*mi	*i*
4. *Nṛit*	*nartaya* / *nartayá* *	*si*	*se*
6. *Diś*	*deśaya* / *deśayá* *	*ti*	*te*
10. *Yuj*	*yojaya* / *yojayá* *	*vas	*vahe
2. *Vid*	*vedaya* / *vedayá* *	*thas*	*ithe*
3. *Bhṛi*	*bhāraya* / *bhārayá* *	*tas*	*ite*
7. *Bhid*	*bhedaya* / *bhedayá* *	*mas	*mahe
5. *Ći*	*ćāyaya* / *ćāyayá* *	*tha*	*dhve*
8. *Tan*	*tānaya* / *tānayá* *	*nti*	*nte*
9. *Pū*	*pāvaya* / *pāvayá* *		

Note—*Ći* also makes *ćāpaya*, &c. See 485. *b*.

DESIDERATIVE FORM.
PRESENT TENSE.

ROOT.	BASE.	PAR. TERM.	ÁTM. TERM.
1. *Budh*	*bubodhisha* / *bubodhishá* *	*mi	*i*
4. *Nṛit*	*ninartisha* / *ninartishá* *	*si*	*se*
6. *Diś*	*didiksha* / *didikshá* *	*ti*	*te*
10. *Yuj*	*yuyojayisha* / *yuyojayishá* *	*vas	*vahe
2. *Vid*	*vividisha* / *vividishá* *	*thas*	*ithe*
3. *Bhṛi*	*bibharisha* / *bibharishá* *	*tas*	*ite*
7. *Bhid*	*bibhitsa* / *bibhitsá* *	*mas	*mahe
5. *Ći*	*ćićisha* / *ćićishá* *	*tha*	*dhve*
8. *Tan*	*titanisha* / *titanishá* *	*nti*	*nte*
9. *Pū*	*pipavisha* / *pipavishá* *		

Observe—*Nṛit* also makes its base *ninṛitsa*; *bhṛi*, *bubhūrsha*; *ći*, *ćikīsha*; *tan*, *titaṃsa* or *titāṃsa*; *pū*, *pupūsha*—in both Átmane and Parasmai; and *budh* and *vid* may respectively make their bases *bubhutsa* (299. *a*) and *vivitsa*, but in Átmane only.

FREQUENTATIVE FORM.
PRESENT ÁTMANE.

ROOT.	BASE.	TERM.
1. *Budh*	*bobudhya* / *bobudhyá* *	*e*
4. *Nṛit*	*narīnṛitya* / *narīnṛityá* *	*se*
6. *Diś*	*dediśya* / *dediśyá* *	*te*
10. *Yuj* †		*vahe
2. *Vid*	*vevidya* / *vevidyá* *	*ithe*
3. *Bhṛi*	*bebhrīya* / *bebhrīyá* *	*ite*
7. *Bhid*	*bebhidya* / *bebhidyá* *	*mahe
5. *Ći*	*ćećīya* / *ćećīyá* *	*dhve*
8. *Tan*	*tantanya* / *tantanyá* *	*nte*
9. *Pū*	*popūya* / *popūyá* *	

† Observe—The 10th class has no frequentative form.

PARTICIPLES.

ROOT.	PRES. PARASM.	PRES. ÁTMANE.	PRES. PASSIVE.	PAST PASSIVE.	PAST ACTIVE.	PERFECT PARASMAI.	PERFECT ÁTMANE.	PAST INDECL.	FUTURE PASS. 1.	FUTURE PASS. 2.	FUTURE PASS. 3.	2D FUT. PARASMAI.	2D FUT. ÁTMANE OR PASSIVE.
1. Budh	budhat	budhamána	budhyamána	buddha	buddhavat	bubudhvas	bubudhána	buddhvá	boddhavya	bodhaníya	bodhya	bodhishyat	bodhishyamáṇa
4. Nrit	nrityat	nrityamána	nrityamána	nritta or nartita	nrittavat or nartitavat	nanritvas	nanritána	nartitvá	nartitavya	nartaníya	nritya	nartishyat	nartishyamáṇa
6. Diś	diśat	diśamána	diśyamána	dishṭa	dishṭavat	didiśvas	didiśána	dishṭvá	deshṭavya	deśaníya	dṛiśya	dekshyat	dekshyamáṇa
10. Yuj	yojayat	yojayána	yojyamána	yojita	yojitavat	yojayáṃ †	yojayáṃ †	yojayitvá	yojayitavya	yojaníya	yojya	yojayishyat	yojayishyamáṇa
2. Vid	vidat	vidána	vidyamána	vidita	viditavat	vividvas	vividána	viditvá	veditavya	vedaníya	vedya	vedishyat	vedishyamáṇa
3. Bhṛi	bibhrat	bibhráṇa	bhriyamáṇa	bhṛita	bhṛitavat	babhṛivas	babhráṇa	bhṛitvá	bhartavya	bharaṇíya	bhárya	bharishyat	bharishyamáṇa
7. Bhid	bhindat	bhindána	bhidyamána	bhinna	bhinnavat	bibhidvas	bibhidána	bhittvá	bhettavya	bhedaníya	bhedya	bhetsyat	bhetsyamána
5. Či	činvat	činvána	číyamána	čita	čitavat	čičivas	čičyána	čitvá	četavya	čayaníya	čeya	češyat	češyamáṇa
8. Tan	tanvat	tanvána	tanyamána	tata	tatavat	tenivas	tenána	tanitvá	tanitavya	tananíya	tánya	tanishyat	tanishyamáṇa
[illegible]	[illegible]	[illegible]	púyamána	púta	pútavat	pupúvas	pupuvána	pútvá	pavitavya	pavaníya	pávya	pavishyat	pavishyamáṇa

† Čakṛivas is added to yojayáṃ for the participle of the perfect Parasmai, and čakráṇa for that of the perfect Átmane.

PARASMAI-PADA (see 327).

584. Note, that although this root belongs to the 2d class, its inflection is exhibited here, both because it is sometimes used as an auxiliary, and because it is desirable that the student should study its inflection at the same time with that of the other substantive verb भू *bhú*, 'to be,' which will follow at 585, and which supplies many of the defective tenses of अस्. Two other roots in Sanskrit are sometimes employed as substantive verbs, with the sense 'to be,' viz. स्था 1st c. 'to stand' (see 269, 587), and आस् 2d c. 'to sit' (see 317. *a*). Indeed, the root अस् *as*, here inflected, is probably only an abbreviation of आस् *ás*.

All the cognate languages have two roots similar to the Sanskrit for the substantive verb 'to be.' Compare φυ and ἐσ (ἐσ) in Greek, *es* (*sum*) and *fu* (*fui*) in Latin; and observe how the different parts of the Sanskrit verbs correspond to the Greek and Latin: thus, *asmi, asi, asti*; ἐμμί, ἐσσί, ἐστί; *sum, es, est*. Compare also *santi* with *sunt*; *ástam, ástám*, with ἦστον, ἤστην; *ásma, ásta*, with ἦσμεν, ἦστε, &c.

Present, 'I am.'			*Potential*, 'I may be,' &c.		
PERS. SING.	DUAL.	PLURAL.	SING.	DUAL.	PLURAL.
1st, अस्मि *asmi*	स्वः *svas*	स्मः *smas*	स्याम् *syám*	स्याव *syáva*	स्याम *syáma*
2d, असि *asi*	स्थः *sthas*	स्थ *stha*	स्याः *syás*	स्यातम् *syátam*	स्यात *syáta*
3d, अस्ति *asti*	स्तः *stas*	सन्ति *santi*	स्यात् *syát*	स्याताम् *syátám*	स्युः *syus*

Imperfect or *first preterite*, 'I was.'			*Imperative*, 'Let me be.'		
आसम् *ásam*	आस्व *ásva*	आस्म *ásma*	असानि *asáni*	असाव *asáva*	असाम *asáma*
आसीः *ásís*	आस्तम् *ástam*	आस्त *ásta*	एधि *edhi*	स्तम् *stam*	स्त *sta*
आसीत् *ását*	आस्ताम् *ástám*	आसन् *ásan*	अस्तु *astu*	स्ताम् *stám*	सन्तु *santu*

Perfect or *second preterite* *, 'I was,' &c.

PARASMAI.			ÁTMANE.		
आस *ása*	आसिव *ásiva*	आसिम *ásima*	आसे *áse*	आसिवहे *ásivahe*	आसिमहे *ásimahe*
आसिथ *ásitha*	आसथुः *ásathus*	आस *ása*	आसिषे *ásishe*	आसाथे *ásáthe*	आसिध्वे *ásidhve*
आस *ása*	आसतुः *ásatus*	आसुः *ásus*	आसे *áse*	आसाते *ásáte*	आसिरे *ásire*

Observe—The root *as*, 'to be,' has no derivative forms, and only two participles, viz. those of the present, Parasmai and Átmane, सत् *sat*, सान *sána* (see 524, 526). The conjugational tenses have an Átmane-pada, which is not used unless the root is compounded with prepositions. In this Pada ह् *h* is substituted for the root in 1st sing. pres., and स् *s* is dropped before *dh* in 2d plur.: thus, Pres. *he, se, ste; svahe, sáthe, sáte; smahe, dhve, sate*: Impf. *ási, ásthás, ásta; ásvahi, ásáthám, ásátám; ásmahi, ádhvam, ásata*: Pot. *síya, síthás, síta; sívahi, síyáthám, síyátám; símahi, sídhvam, síran*: Impv. *asai, sva, stám; asávahai, sáthám, sátám; asámahai, dhvam, satám*: see 327.

* The perfect of *as* is not used by itself, but is employed in forming the perfect of causals and some other verbs, see 385. 490; in which case the Átmane may be used. The other tenses of *as* are wanting, and are supplied from *bhú* at 585.

GROUP I. CLASS I.

EXAMPLES OF PRIMITIVE VERBS OF THE FIRST CONJUGATIONAL CLASS, EXPLAINED AT 261.

585. Root भू *bhú*. Infin. भवितुम् *bhavitum*, 'to be' or 'become.'

PARASMAI-PADA. *Present tense*, 'I am' or 'I become.'

PERS.	SING.	DUAL.	PLURAL.
1st,	भवामि *bhavámi*	भवावः *bhavávas*	भवामः *bhavámas*
2d,	भवसि *bhavasi*	भवथः *bhavathas*	भवथ *bhavatha*
3d.	भवति *bhavati*	भवतः *bhavatas*	भवन्ति *bhavanti*

Imperfect or first preterite, 'I was.'

अभवम् *abhavam*	अभवाव *abhaváva*	अभवाम *abhaváma*
अभवः *abhavas*	अभवतम् *abhavatam*	अभवत *abhavata*
अभवत् *abhavat*	अभवताम् *abhavatám*	अभवन् *abhavan*

Potential, 'I may be.'

भवेयम् *bhaveyam*	भवेव *bhaveva*	भवेम *bhavema*
भवेः *bhaves*	भवेतम् *bhavetam*	भवेत *bhaveta*
भवेत् *bhavet*	भवेताम् *bhavetám*	भवेयुः *bhaveyus*

Imperative, 'Let me be.'

भवानि *bhaváni*	भवाव *bhaváva*	भवाम *bhaváma*
भव *bhava*	भवतम् *bhavatam*	भवत *bhavata*
भवतु *bhavatu*	भवताम् *bhavatám*	भवन्तु *bhavantu*

Perfect or second preterite, 'I was.'

बभूव *babhúva*	बभूविव *babhúviva*	बभूविम *babhúvima*
बभूविथ *babhúvitha*	बभूवथुः *babhúvathus*	बभूव *babhúva*
बभूव *babhúva*	बभूवतुः *babhúvatus*	बभूवुः *babhúvus*

First future, 'I will be.'

भवितास्मि *bhavitásmi*	भवितास्वः *bhavitásvas*	भवितास्मः *bhavitásmas*
भवितासि *bhavitási*	भवितास्थः *bhavitásthas*	भवितास्थ *bhavitástha*
भविता *bhavitá*	भवितारौ *bhavitárau*	भवितारः *bhavitáras*

Second future, 'I shall be.'

भविष्यामि *bhavishyámi*	भविष्यावः *bhavishyávas*	भविष्यामः *bhavishyámas*
भविष्यसि *bhavishyasi*	भविष्यथः *bhavishyathas*	भविष्यथ *bhavishyatha*
भविष्यति *bhavishyati*	भविष्यतः *bhavishyatas*	भविष्यन्ति *bhavishyanti*

Aorist or third preterite, 'I was' or 'had been,' &c.

अभूवम् *abhúvam*	अभूव *abhúva*	अभूम *abhúma*
अभूस् *abhús*	अभूतम् *abhútam*	अभूत *abhúta*
अभूत् *abhút*	अभूताम् *abhútám*	अभूवन् *abhúvan*

Precative or benedictive, 'May I be.'

भूयासम् *bhúyásam*	भूयास्व *bhúyásva*	भूयास्म *bhúyásma*
भूयास् *bhúyás*	भूयास्तम् *bhúyástam*	भूयास्त *bhúyásta*
भूयात् *bhúyát*	भूयास्ताम् *bhúyástám*	भूयासुस् *bhúyásus*

Conditional, (If) 'I should be.'

अभविष्यम् *abhavishyam*	अभविष्याव *abhavishyáva*	अभविष्याम *abhavishyáma*
अभविष्यस् *abhavishyas*	अभविष्यतम् *abhavishyatam*	अभविष्यत *abhavishyata*
अभविष्यत् *abhavishyat*	अभविष्यताम् *abhavishyatám*	अभविष्यन् *abhavishyan*

586. Átmane-pada. *Present tense*, 'I am,' &c.

भवे *bhave*	भवावहे *bhavávahe*	भवामहे *bhavámahe*
भवसे *bhavase*	भवेथे *bhavethe*	भवध्वे *bhavadhve*
भवते *bhavate*	भवेते *bhavete*	भवन्ते *bhavante*

Imperfect or first preterite, 'I was.'

अभवे *abhave*	अभवावहि *abhavávahi*	अभवामहि *abhavámahi*
अभवथास् *abhavathás*	अभवेथाम् *abhavethám*	अभवध्वम् *abhavadhvam*
अभवत *abhavata*	अभवेताम् *abhavetám*	अभवन्त *abhavanta*

Potential, 'I may be,' &c.

भवेय *bhaveya*	भवेवहि *bhavevahi*	भवेमहि *bhavemahi*
भवेथास् *bhavethás*	भवेयाथाम् *bhaveyáthám*	भवेध्वम् *bhavedhvam*
भवेत *bhaveta*	भवेयाताम् *bhaveyátám*	भवेरन् *bhaveran*

Imperative, 'Let me be.'

भवै *bhavai*	भवावहै *bhavávahai*	भवामहै *bhavámahai*
भवस्व *bhavasva*	भवेथाम् *bhavethám*	भवध्वम् *bhavadhvam*
भवताम् *bhavatám*	भवेताम् *bhavetám*	भवन्ताम् *bhavantám*

Perfect or second preterite, 'I was,' &c.

बभूवे *babhúve*	बभूविवहे *babhúvivahe*	बभूविमहे *babhúvimahe*
बभूविषे *babhúvishe*	बभूवाथे *babhúváthe*	बभूविढ्वे (ध्वे) *babhúvidhve*
बभूवे *babhúve*	बभूवाते *babhúváte*	बभूविरे *babhúvire*

First future, 'I will be,' &c.

भविताहे *bhavitáhe*	भवितास्वहे *bhavitásvahe*	भवितास्महे *bhavitásmahe*
भवितासे *bhavitáse*	भवितासाथे *bhavitásáthe*	भविताध्वे *bhavitádhve*
भविता *bhavitá*	भवितारौ *bhavitárau*	भवितारस् *bhavitáras*

Second future, 'I shall be,' &c.

भविष्ये *bhavishye*	भविष्यावहे *bhavishyávahe*	भविष्यामहे *bhavishyámahe*
भविष्यसे *bhavishyase*	भविष्येथे *bhavishyethe*	भविष्यध्वे *bhavishyadhve*
भविष्यते *bhavishyate*	भविष्येते *bhavishyete*	भविष्यन्ते *bhavishyante*

Aorist or *third preterite*, 'I was' or 'had been,' &c.

अभविषि *abhavishi*	अभविष्वहि *abhavishvahi*	अभविष्महि *abhavishmahi*
अभविष्ठास् *abhavishṭhás*	अभविषाथाम् *abhavishátham*	अभविढ्वम् (ध्वम्) *abhavidhvam*
अभविष्ट *abhavishṭa*	अभविषाताम् *abhavishátám*	अभविषत *abhavishata*

Precative or *benedictive*, 'I wish I may be.'

भविषीय *bhavishíya*	भविषीवहि *bhavishívahi*	भविषीमहि *bhavishímahi*
भविषीष्ठास् *bhavishíshṭhás*	भविषीयास्थाम् *bhavishíyásthám*	भविषीढ्वम् (ध्वम्) *bhavishídhvam*
भविषीष्ट *bhavishíshṭa*	भविषीयास्ताम् *bhavishíyástám*	भविषीरन् *bhavishíran*

Conditional, (If) 'I should be,' &c.

अभविष्ये *abhavishye*	अभविष्यावहि *abhavishyávahi*	अभविष्यामहि *abhavishyámahi*
अभविष्यथास् *abhavishyathás*	अभविष्येथाम् *abhavishyethám*	अभविष्यध्वम् *abhavishyadhvam*
अभविष्यत *abhavishyata*	अभविष्येताम् *abhavishyetám*	अभविष्यन्त *abhavishyanta*

Passive (461), *Pres.* भूये, भूयसे, &c.; *Aor.* 3*d sing.* (475) अभावि. Causal (479), *Pres.* भावयामि, भावयसि, &c.; *Aor.* (492) अबीभवं, &c. Desiderative (498), *Pres.* बुभूषामि, बुभूषसि, &c. *Desiderative form of Causal* (497) बिभावयिषामि, &c. Frequentative (507), *Pres.* बोभूये, बोभोमि or बोभवीमि*. Participles, *Pres.* भवत् (524); *Past pass.* भूत (531); *Past indecl.* भूत्वा (556), -भूय (559); *Fut. pass.* भवितव्य (569), भवनीय (570), भाव्य or भव्य (571).

EXAMPLES OF OTHER VERBS OF THE FIRST CLASS IN THE ORDER OF THEIR FINAL LETTERS.

Par. stands for Parasmai; Átm. for Átmane; Impf. for Imperfect; Impv. for Imperative.

587. Root स्था. *Inf.* स्थातुं 'to stand' (269, 269. *a*). Par. and Átm. *Pres.* तिष्ठामि, तिष्ठसि, तिष्ठति; तिष्ठावस्, तिष्ठथस्, तिष्ठतस्; तिष्ठामस्, तिष्ठथ,

* These derivative verbs will be inflected at full at 703, 705, 706, 707.

तिष्ठन्ति. Ātm. तिष्ठे, तिष्ठसे, तिष्ठते; तिष्ठावहे, तिष्ठेथे, तिष्ठेते; तिष्ठामहे, तिष्ठध्वे, तिष्ठन्ते. *Impf.* अतिष्ठं, अतिष्ठः, &c. Ātm. अतिष्ठे, &c. *Pot.* तिष्ठेयं, तिष्ठेः, तिष्ठेत्; तिष्ठेव, &c. Ātm. तिष्ठेय, तिष्ठेथाः, तिष्ठेत; तिष्ठेवहि, तिष्ठेयाथां, &c. *Impv.* तिष्ठानि, तिष्ठ, तिष्ठतु; तिष्ठाव, &c. Ātm. तिष्ठै, तिष्ठस्व, तिष्ठतां; तिष्ठावहै, &c. *Perf.* तस्थौ (373), तस्थिथ or तस्थाथ, तस्थौ; तस्थिव, तस्थथुः, तस्थतुः; तस्थिम, तस्थ, तस्थुः. Ātm. तस्थे, तस्थिषे, तस्थे; तस्थिवहे, तस्थाथे, तस्थाते; तस्थिमहे, तस्थिध्वे, तस्थिरे. *1st Fut.* स्थातास्मि, स्थातासि, &c. Ātm. स्थाताहे, स्थातासे, &c. *2d Fut.* स्थास्यामि, स्थास्यसि, स्थास्यति, &c. Ātm. स्थास्ये, स्थास्यसे, स्थास्यते, &c. *Aor.* (438) अस्थां, अस्थाः, अस्थात्; अस्थाव, अस्थातं, अस्थातां; अस्थाम, अस्थात, अस्थुः. Ātm. (438. *d*, 421. *d*) अस्थिषि, अस्थिथाः, अस्थित; अस्थिष्वहि, अस्थिषाथां, -षातां; अस्थिष्महि, अस्थिढ्वं, अस्थिषत. *Prec.* स्थेयासं, स्थेयाः, &c. Ātm. स्थासीय, स्थासीष्ठाः, &c. *Cond.* अस्थास्यं, अस्थास्यः, &c. Ātm. अस्थास्ये, अस्थास्यथाः, &c. Pass., *Pres.* स्थीयते (465); *Aor. 3d sing.* अस्थायि. Caus., *Pres.* स्थापयामि, -ये; *Aor.* अतिष्ठिपं, अतिष्ठिपे. Des. तिष्ठासामि, &c. Freq. तेष्ठीये or तास्थेमि or तास्थामि. Part., *Pres.* तिष्ठत्; *Past pass.* स्थित; *Past indecl.* स्थित्वा, -स्थाय, -ष्ठाय; *Fut. pass.* स्थातव्य, स्थानीय, स्थेय.

588. Root घ्रा. *Inf.* घ्रातुं 'to smell' (269). Par. *Pres.* जिघ्रामि, जिघ्रसि, &c. *Impf.* अजिघ्रं, अजिघ्रः, &c. *Pot.* जिघ्रेयं, जिघ्रेः, &c. *Impv.* जिघ्राणि (58), जिघ्र, &c. *Perf.* जघ्रौ (373), जघ्रिथ or जघ्राथ, जघ्रौ; जघ्रिव, जघ्रथुः, जघ्रतुः; जघ्रिम, जघ्र, जघ्रुः. *1st Fut.* घ्रातास्मि, घ्रातासि, &c. *2d Fut.* घ्रास्यामि, घ्रास्यसि, &c. *Aor.* (438) अघ्रां, अघ्राः, अघ्रात्; अघ्राव, अघ्रातं, अघ्रातां; अघ्राम, अघ्रात, अघ्रुः. Or by 433, अघ्रासिषं, अघ्रासीः, अघ्रासीत्; अघ्रासिष्व, अघ्रासिष्टं, -ष्टां; अघ्रासिष्म, -ष्ट, -षुः. *Prec.* घ्रायासं, घ्रायाः, &c. Or घ्रेयासं, &c. *Cond.* अघ्रास्यं, अघ्रास्यः, &c. Pass., *Pres.* घ्रायते (465. *a*); *Aor. 3d sing.* अघ्रायि. Caus., *Pres.* घ्रापयामि; *Aor.* अजिघ्रपं or अजिघ्रिपं. Des. जिघ्रासामि. Freq. जेघ्रीये, जाघ्रामि or जाघ्रेमि. Part., *Pres.* जिघ्रत्; *Past pass.* घ्रात or घ्राण; *Past indecl.* घ्रात्वा, -घ्राय; *Fut. pass.* घ्रातव्य, घ्राणीय, घ्रेय.

589. Root पा. *Inf.* पातुं 'to drink' (269). Par. *Pres.* पिबामि, पिबसि, &c. *Impf.* अपिबं, अपिबः, &c. *Pot.* पिबेयं, पिबेः, &c. *Impv.* पिबानि, पिब, &c. *Perf.* (373) पपौ, पपिथ or पपाथ, पपौ; पपिव, पपथुः, पपतुः; पपिम, पप, पपुः. *1st Fut.* पातास्मि, पातासि, &c. *2d Fut.* पास्यामि, पास्यसि, &c. *Aor.* (438) अपां, अपाः, अपात्; अपाव, अपातं, अपातां; अपाम, अपात, अपुः. *Prec.* पेयासं, पेयाः, &c. *Cond.* अपास्यं, अपास्यः, &c. Pass., *Pres.* पीयते (465); *Aor. 3d sing.* अपायि (475). Caus., *Pres.* पाययामि, -ये; *Aor.* अपीप्यं (493. *e*). Des. पिपासामि. Freq. पेपीये, पापेमि or पापामि.

Part., *Pres.* पिबत्; *Past pass.* पीत (533. *b*); *Past indecl.* पीत्वा, -पाय; *Fut. pass.* पातव्य, पानीय, पेय.

590. Root जि. *Inf.* जेतुं 'to conquer.' Par.* *Pres.* जयामि, जयसि, जयति; जयावः, जयथः, जयतः; जयामः, जयथ, जयन्ति. *Impf.* अजयं, अजयः, अजयत्; अजयाव, अजयतं, अजयतां; अजयाम, अजयत, अजयन्. *Pot.* जयेयं, जयेः, जयेत्; जयेव, जयेतं, जयेतां; जयेम, जयेत, जयेयुः. *Impv.* जयानि, जय, जयतु; जयाव, जयतं, जयतां; जयाम, जयत, जयन्तु. *Perf.* जिगाय (368, 374. *b*), जिगयिथ or जिगेथ, जिगाय; जिग्यिव (374), जिग्यथुः, जिग्यतुः; जिग्यिम, जिग्य, जिग्युः. *1st Fut.* जेतास्मि, जेतासि, जेता; जेतास्वः, जेतास्थः, जेतारौ; जेतास्मः, जेतास्थ, जेतारः. *2d Fut.* जेष्यामि, जेष्यसि, जेष्यति; जेष्यावः, जेष्यथः, जेष्यतः; जेष्यामः, जेष्यथ, जेष्यन्ति. *Aor.* अजैषं (420. *b*), अजैषीः, अजैषीत्; अजैष्व, अजैष्टं, अजैष्टां; अजैष्म, अजैष्ट, अजैषुः. *Prec.* जीयासं, जीयाः, जीयात्; जीयास्व, जीयास्तं, जीयास्तां; जीयास्म, जीयास्त, जीयासुः. *Cond.* अजेष्यं, अजेष्यः, अजेष्यत्; अजेष्याव, अजेष्यतं, अजेष्यतां; अजेष्याम, अजेष्यत, अजेष्यन्. Pass., *Pres.* जीये, &c.; *Aor. 3d sing.* अजायि. Caus., *Pres.* जापयामि; *Aor.* अजीजपं. Des. जिगीषामि. Freq. जेजीये, जेजेमि or जेजयीमि. Part., *Pres.* जयत्; *Past pass.* जित; *Past indecl.* जित्वा, -जित्य; *Fut. pass.* जेतव्य, जयनीय, जेय or जित्य or जय्य (571, 572).

a. Like जि may be conjugated नी. *Inf.* नेतुं 'to lead.' But the Causal is नाययामि; Caus., *Aor.* अनीनयं; Des. निनीषामि. In Epic poetry the *Perfect* is sometimes नयामास for निनाय, and the 2d *Fut.* नयिष्यामि for नेष्यामि (especially when preceded by the prep. आ).

591. Root स्मि. *Inf.* स्मेतुं 'to smile.' Âtm. *Pres.* स्मये, स्मयसे, &c. *Impf.* अस्मये, अस्मयथास्, &c. *Pot.* स्मयेय, स्मयेथास्, &c. *Impv.* स्मयै, स्मयस्व, &c. *Perf.* (374. *e*) सिष्मिये†, सिष्मियिषे, सिष्मिये; सिष्मियिवहे, सिष्मियाथे, सिष्मियाते; सिष्मियिमहे, सिष्मियिढ्वे or -ध्वे, सिष्मियिरे. *1st Fut.* स्मेताहे, स्मेतासे, &c. *2d Fut.* स्मेष्ये, स्मेष्यसे, &c. *Aor.* अस्मेषि, अस्मेष्ठास्, अस्मेष्ट; अस्मेष्वहि, अस्मेषाथां, -षातां; अस्मेष्महि, अस्मेढ्वं, अस्मेषत. *Prec.* स्मेषीय, &c. *Cond.* अस्मेष्ये, &c. Pass., स्मीये, &c.; *Aor. 3d sing.* अस्मायि. Caus., *Pres.* स्माययामि or स्मापयामि; *Aor.* असिस्मयं or असिस्मपं. Des. सिस्मयिषे. Freq. सेष्मीये, सेष्मेमि or सेष्मयीमि. Part., *Pres.* स्मयमान; *Past pass.* स्मित; *Past indecl.* स्मित्वा, -स्मित्य; *Fut. pass.* स्मेतव्य, स्मयनीय, स्मेय.

592. Root द्रु. *Inf.* द्रोतुं 'to run.' Par. *Pres.* द्रवामि, द्रवसि, द्रवति; द्रवावः, द्रवथः, द्रवतः; द्रवामः, द्रवथ, द्रवन्ति. *Impf.* अद्रवं, अद्रवः, &c.

* जि is not generally used in the Âtmane, excepting with the prepositions *vi* or *parâ*. See 243. *a*.

† When वि is prefixed, the perfect is विसिस्मिये against r. 70.

Pot. द्रवेयं, द्रवेस्, &c. *Impv.* द्रवाणि (58), द्रव, &c. *Perf.* दुद्राव, दुद्रोथ, दुद्राव; दुद्रुव (369), दुद्रुवथुस् (374. g), दुद्रुवतुस्; दुद्रुम, दुद्रुव, दुद्रुवुस्. *1st Fut.* द्रोतास्मि. *2d Fut.* द्रोष्यामि, द्रोष्यसि, &c. *Aor.* अदुद्रुवं (440. a), अदुद्रुवस्, अदुद्रुवत्; अदुद्रुवाव, अदुद्रुवतं, अदुद्रुवतां; अदुद्रुवाम, अदुद्रुवत, अदुद्रुवन्. *Prec.* द्रूयासं, द्रूयास्, &c. *Cond.* अद्रोष्यं. Pass., *Pres.* द्रूये; *Aor. 3d sing.* अद्रावि. Caus., *Pres.* द्रावयामि; *Aor.* अदुद्रुवं or अदिद्रवं. Des. दुद्रूषामि. Freq. दोद्रूये, दोद्रोमि or दोद्रवीमि. Part., *Pres.* द्रवत्; *Past pass.* द्रुत; *Past indecl.* द्रुत्वा, -द्रुत्य; *Fut. pass.* द्रोतव्य, द्रवणीय, द्राव्य or द्रव्य.

a. Like द्रु may be conjugated स्रु (sometimes written श्रु). *Inf.* स्रोतुं 'to flow.'

593. Root हृ. *Inf.* हर्तुं 'to seize,' 'to take.' Par. and Ātm. *Pres.* हरामि. Ātm. हरे, हरसे, हरते; हरावहे, &c. *Impf.* अहरं, अहरस्, अहरत्; अहराव, &c. Ātm. अहरे, अहरथास्, अहरत; अहरावहि, &c. *Pot.* हरेयं. Ātm. हरेय, हरेथास्, &c. *Impv.* हराणि (58), हर, &c. Ātm. हरै, हरस्व, &c. *Perf.* जहार, जहर्थ (370. a), जहार; जहृव, जह्रथुस्, जह्रतुस्; जहृम, जह्र, जह्रुस्. Ātm. जह्रे, जहृषे, जह्रे; जहृवहे, जह्राथे, जह्राते; जहृमहे, जहृढ्वे or जहृध्वे, जह्रिरे. *1st Fut.* हर्तास्मि. Ātm. हर्ताहे, हर्तासे, &c. *2d Fut.* हरिष्यामि. Ātm. हरिष्ये, हरिष्यसे, &c. *Aor.* अहार्षं, अहार्षीस्, अहार्षीत्; अहार्ष्व, अहार्ष्टं, अहार्ष्टां; अहार्ष्म, अहार्ष्ट, अहार्षुस्. Ātm. अहृषि, अहृथास्, अहृत; अहृष्वहि, अहृषाथां, अहृषातां; अहृष्महि, अहृढ्वं, अहृषत. *Prec.* ह्रियासं. Ātm. हृषीय, हृषीष्ठास्, &c. *Cond.* अहरिष्यं. Ātm. अहरिष्ये, अहरिष्यथास्, &c. Pass., *Pres.* ह्रिये; *Aor. 3d sing.* अहारि. Caus., *Pres.* हारयामि, -ये; *Aor.* अजीहरं. Des. जिहीर्षामि, -र्षे. Freq. जेह्रीये, जर्हर्मि or जर्हरीमि or जरिहरीमि or जरीहर्मि or जरि- or जरीहर्मि. Part., *Pres.* हरत्; *Pass.* ह्रियमाण; *Past pass.* हृत; *Past indecl.* हृत्वा, -हृत्य; *Fut. pass.* हर्तव्य, हरणीय, हार्य.

594. Root स्मृ. *Inf.* स्मर्तुं 'to remember.' Par. and Ātm. *Pres.* स्मरामि. Ātm. स्मरे. *Impf.* अस्मरं, अस्मरस्, &c. Ātm. अस्मरे. *Pot.* स्मरेयं. Ātm. स्मरेय, &c. *Impv.* स्मराणि (58). Ātm. स्मरै, &c. *Perf.* (367 c) सस्मार, सस्मर्थ (370. a), सस्मार; सस्मरिव, सस्मरथुस्, सस्मरतुस्; सस्मरिम, सस्मर, सस्मरुस्. Ātm. सस्मरे, सस्मरिषे, सस्मरे; सस्मरिवहे, सस्मराथे, सस्मराते; सस्मरिमहे, सस्मरिध्वे or -रिढ्वे, सस्मरिरे. *1st Fut.* स्मर्तास्मि. Ātm. स्मर्ताहे. *2d Fut.* स्मरिष्यामि. Ātm. स्मरिष्ये. *Aor.* अस्मार्षं, &c. (see हृ at 593). Ātm. अस्मृषि, अस्मृथास् (see हृ at 593). *Prec.* स्मर्यासं. Ātm. स्मृषीय or स्मरिषीय. *Cond.* अस्मरिष्यं. Ātm. अस्मरिष्ये. Pass., *Pres.* स्मर्ये; *Aor. 3d sing.* अस्मारि. Caus., *Pres.* स्मारयामि, -ये; *Aor.* असस्मरं. Des. सुस्मूर्षे. Freq.

सास्नाये, सास्नाति or सास्नातीति. Part., Pres. स्नात्; Past pass. स्नात; Past indecl. स्नात्वा, -स्नाय; Fut. pass. स्नातव्य, स्नानीय, स्नेय.

595. Root ह्वे. Inf. ह्वातुं 'to call.' Par. and Ātm. Pres. ह्वयामि. Ātm. ह्वये. Impf. अह्वयं, &c. Ātm. अह्वये. Pot. ह्वयेयं. Ātm. ह्वयेय. Impv. ह्वयानि. Ātm. ह्वयै. Perf. (373. e) जुहाव, जुहविथ or जुहोथ, जुहाव; जुहुविव, जुहुवथुः, जुहुवतुः; जुहुविम, जुहुव, जुहुवुः. Ātm. जुहुवे, जुहुविषे, जुहुवे; जुहुविवहे, जुहुवाथे, जुहुवाते; जुहुविमहे, जुहुविढ्वे or -विध्वे, जुहुविरे. 1st Fut. ह्वातास्मि. Ātm. ह्वाताहे. 2d Fut. ह्वास्यामि. Ātm. ह्वास्ये. Aor. (438. c) अह्वं, अह्वः, अह्वत्; अह्वाव, अह्वतं, अह्वतां; अह्वाम, अह्वत, अह्वन्. Ātm. अह्वे, अह्वथाः, अह्वत; अह्वावहि, अह्वेथां, अह्वेतां; अह्वामहि, अह्वध्वं, अह्वन्त. Or अह्वासि (433. a), अह्वास्थाः, अह्वास्त; अह्वास्वहि, अह्वासाथां, अह्वासातां; अह्वास्महि, अह्वाध्वं, अह्वासत. Prec. हूयासं. Ātm. ह्वासीय. Cond. अह्वास्यं. Ātm. अह्वास्ये. Pass. हूये (465. b); Aor. 3d sing. अह्वायि or अह्वायिष्ट or अह्वत or अह्वास्त. 2d Fut. ह्वास्यते or ह्वायिष्यते (474. a). Caus., Pres. ह्वाययामि (483); Aor. अजूहवं. Des. जुहूषामि, जुहूषे. Freq. जोहूये, जोहोमि or जोहवीमि. Part., Pres. ह्वयत्; Pass. हूयमान; Past pass. हूत; Past indecl. हूत्वा, -हूय; Fut. pass. ह्वातव्य, ह्वानीय, ह्वेय.

a. गै (268), Inf. गातुं 'to sing,' follows the analogy of ह्वे, the final diphthong being changed to ā before all terminations beginning with t or s. Pres. गायामि. Impf. अगायं, &c. Pot. गायेयं. Impv. गायानि. Perf. (373. d) जगौ, जगिथ or जगाथ, जगौ; जगिव, जगथुः, जगतुः; जगिम, जग, जगुः. 1st Fut. गातास्मि. 2d Fut. गास्यामि. Aor. (433) अगासिषं, अगासीः, अगासीत्; अगासिष्व, अगासिष्टं, अगासिष्टां; अगासिष्म, अगासिष्ट, अगासिषुः. Prec. गेयासं (451). Cond. अगास्यं. Pass. गीये (465); Aor. 3d sing. अगायि. Caus., Pres. गापयामि (483); Aor. अजीगपं. Des. जिगासामि. Freq. जेगीये, जागेमि or जागामि. Part., Pres. गायत्; Pass. गीयमान; Past pass. गीत; Past indecl. गीत्वा, -गाय; Fut. pass. गातव्य, गानीय, गेय.

b. Like गै may be conjugated ग्लै 'to be weary;' ध्यै 'to meditate;' म्लै 'to fade;' and all other roots in ai.

c. Root पच्. Inf. पक्तुम् 'to cook.' Par. and Ātm. Pres. पचामि. Ātm. पचे. Impf. अपचं, अपचत्, &c. Ātm. अपचे. Pot. पचेयं, पचेत्, &c. Ātm. पचेय. Impv. पचानि, पच, &c. Ātm. पचै. Perf. पपाच or पपच, पपक्थ or पेचिथ (370. d), पपाच; पेचिव, पेचथुः, पेचतुः; पेचिम, पेच, पेचुः. Ātm. पेचे, पेचिषे, पेचे; पेचिवहे, पेचाथे, पेचाते; पेचिमहे, पेचिध्वे, पेचिरे. 1st Fut. पक्तास्मि. Ātm. पक्ताहे. 2d Fut. पक्ष्यामि. Ātm. पक्ष्ये. Aor. (420. d) अपाक्षं, अपाक्षीः, अपाक्षीत्; अपाक्ष्व, अपाक्तं, अपाक्तां;

अयाक्ष्म, अयाष्ट, अयाक्षुः. Ātm. अयक्षि, अयष्ठाः, अयष्ट; अयक्ष्वहि, अयक्षाथां, अयक्षातां; अयक्ष्महि, अयड्ढ्वं, अयक्षत. *Prec.* इज्यासं. Ātm. यक्षीय. *Cond.* अयक्ष्यं. Ātm. अयक्ष्ये. Pass., *Pres.* इज्ये; *Impf.* ऐज्ये; *Aor.* 3d *sing.* अयाजि. Caus., *Pres.* याजयामि, याजये; *Aor.* अयीयजं. Des. यियक्षामि, यियक्षे. Freq. यायज्ये, यायज्मि or यायजीमि. Part., *Pres.* यजत्; Ātm. यजमान; *Pass.* इज्यमान; *Past pass.* इष्ट; *Past indecl.* इष्ट्वा, -इज्य; *Fut. pass.* यष्टव्य, यजनीय, याज्य or यज्य.

d. Root याच्. *Inf.* याचितुं 'to ask.' Par. and Ātm. *Pres.* याचामि. Ātm. याचे. *Impf.* अयाचं, अयाचत्, &c. Ātm. अयाचे. *Pot.* याचेयं, याचेत्, &c. Ātm. याचेय. *Impv.* याचानि, याच, &c. Ātm. याचै. *Perf.* ययाच, ययाचिथ, ययाच; ययाचिव, ययाचथुः, ययाचतुः; ययाचिम, ययाच, ययाचुः. Ātm. ययाचे, ययाचिषे, ययाचे; ययाचिवहे, ययाचाथे, ययाचाते; ययाचिमहे, ययाचिध्वे (372. *a*), ययाचिरे. *1st Fut.* याचितास्मि. Ātm. याचिताहे. *2d Fut.* याचिष्यामि. Ātm. याचिष्ये. *Aor.* (427) अयाचिषं, अयाचीः, अयाचीत्; अयाचिष्व, अयाचिष्टं, -ष्टां; अयाचिष्म, -चिष्ट, -चिषुः. Ātm. अयाचिषि, अयाचिष्ठाः, अयाचिष्ट; अयाचिष्वहि, अयाचिषाथां, -षातां; अयाचिष्महि, अयाचिढ्वं, अयाचिषत. *Prec.* याच्यासं. Ātm. याचिषीय. *Cond.* अयाचिष्यं. Pass., *Pres.* याच्ये. Caus., *Pres.* याचयामि; *Aor.* अययाचं. Des. यियाचिषामि, -षे. Freq. यायाच्ये, यायाच्मि; 3d *sing.* यायाक्ति. Part., *Pres.* याचत्; Ātm. याचमान; *Past pass.* याचित; *Past indecl.* याचित्वा; *Fut. pass.* याचितव्य, याचनीय, याच्य.

e. Root शुच्. *Inf.* शोचितुं 'to grieve.' Par. (Ep. rarely Ātm.). *Pres.* शोचामि. *Impf.* अशोचं, अशोचत्, &c. *Pot.* शोचेयं, शोचेत्, &c. *Impv.* शोचानि, शोच, &c. *Perf.* शुशोच, शुशोचिथ, शुशोच; शुशुचिव, शुशुचथुः, शुशुचतुः; शुशुचिम, शुशुच, शुशुचुः. *1st Fut.* शोचितास्मि. *2d Fut.* शोचिष्यामि. *Aor.* (427. *b*) अशोचिषं, अशोचीः, अशोचीत्; अशोचिष्व, अशोचिष्टं, अशोचिष्टां; अशोचिष्म, अशोचिष्ट, अशोचिषुः. *Prec.* शुच्यासं. *Cond.* अशोचिष्यं. Pass., *Pres.* शुच्ये; *Aor.* 3d *sing.* अशोचि. Caus., *Pres.* शोचयामि; *Aor.* अशूशुचं. Des. शुशुचिषामि or शुशोचिषामि. Freq. शोशुच्ये, शोशोच्मि; 3d *sing.* शोशोक्ति. Part., *Pres.* शोचत्; *Pass.* शुच्यमान; *Past pass.* शुचित and शोचित; *Past indecl.* शुचित्वा or शोचित्वा, -शुच्य; *Fut. pass.* शोचितव्य, शोचनीय, शोच्य.

596. Root त्यज्. *Inf.* त्यक्तुं 'to abandon,' 'to quit.' Par. *Pres.* त्यजामि. *Impf.* अत्यजं, अत्यजत्, &c. *Pot.* त्यजेयं. *Impv.* त्यजानि, त्यज, &c. *Perf.* तत्याज, तत्यजिथ or तत्यक्थ (370. *d*), तत्याज; तत्यजिव, तत्यजथुः, तत्यजतुः; तत्यजिम, तत्यज, तत्यजुः. *1st Fut.* त्यक्तास्मि. *2d Fut.* त्यक्ष्यामि. *Aor.* (423, 296) अत्याक्षं, अत्याक्षीः, अत्याक्षीत्; अत्याक्ष्व, अत्याक्तं, अत्याक्तां; अत्याक्ष्म, अत्याक्त,

अत्याक्षुः. *Prec.* त्यज्यासं. *Cond.* अत्यक्ष्यं, &c. Pass., *Pres.* त्यज्ये; *Aor. 3d sing.* अत्याजि. Caus., *Pres.* त्याजयामि; *Aor.* अतित्यजं. Des. तित्यक्षामि. Freq. तात्यज्ये, तात्यज्मि or तात्यजीमि. Part., *Pres.* त्यजत्; *Past pass.* त्यक्त; *Past indecl.* त्यक्त्वा, -त्यज्य; *Fut. pass.* त्यक्तव्य, त्यजनीय, त्याज्य (573).

597. Root यज्. *Inf.* यष्टुं 'to sacrifice,' 'to worship.' Par. and Ātm. *Pres.* यजामि. Ātm. यजे. *Impf.* अयजं, अयजत्, &c. Ātm. अयजे. *Pot.* यजेयं. Ātm. यजेय. *Impr.* यजानि, यज, &c. Ātm. यजै. *Perf.* (375. *e*) इयाज, इयजिथ or येजिथ or इयष्ठ (297), इयाज; ईजिव, ईजथुः, ईजतुः; ईजिम, ईज, ईजुः. Ātm. ईजे, ईजिषे, ईजे; ईजिवहे, ईजाथे, ईजाते; ईजिमहे, ईजिध्वे, ईजिरे. *1st Fut.* यष्टास्मि (403). Ātm. यष्टाहे. *2d Fut.* यक्ष्यामि (403). Ātm. यक्ष्ये. *Aor.* (422) अयाक्षं, अयाक्षीत्, अयाक्षीत्; अयाक्ष्व, अयाष्टं, अयाष्टां; अयाक्ष्म, अयाष्ट, अयाक्षुः. Ātm. अयक्षि, अयष्ठाः, अयष्ट; अयक्ष्वहि, अयक्षाथां, अयक्षातां; अयक्ष्महि, अयड्ढ्वं, अयक्षत. *Prec.* इज्यासं. Ātm. यक्षीय. *Cond.* अयक्ष्यं. Ātm. अयक्ष्ये. Pass., *Pres.* इज्ये (471); *Impf.* ऐज्ये (260. *a*); *Aor. 3d sing.* अयाजि. Caus., *Pres.* याजयामि, -ये; *Aor.* अयीयजं. Des. यियक्षामि, -क्षे. Freq. यायज्ये, यायज्मि or यायजीमि. Part., *Pres.* यजत्; Ātm. यजमान; *Pass.* इज्यमान; *Past pass.* इष्ट; *Past indecl.* इष्ट्वा, -इज्य; *Fut. pass.* यष्टव्य, यजनीय, याज्य or यज्य.

a. Root सञ्ज् (270. *d*). *Inf.* संक्तुं 'to adhere,' 'to embrace.' Par. *Pres.* सजामि*. *Impf.* असजं. *Pot.* सजेयं. *Impv.* सजानि. *Perf.* ससञ्ज, ससञ्जिथ or ससंक्थ, ससञ्ज; ससञ्जिव, ससञ्जथुः, ससञ्जतुः; ससञ्जिम, ससञ्ज, ससञ्जुः. *1st Fut.* संक्तास्मि, &c. *2d Fut.* संक्ष्यामि, &c. *Aor.* असांक्षं, -क्षीत्, -क्षीत्; असांक्ष्व, असांक्तं, -क्तां; असांक्ष्म, असांक्त, असांक्षुः. *Prec.* सज्यासं, &c. *Cond.* असंक्ष्यं, &c. Pass., *Pres.* सज्ये. Caus., *Pres.* सञ्जयामि; *Aor.* अससञ्जं. Des. सिसंक्षामि, &c. Freq. सासज्ये, सासंक्मि. Part., *Pres.* सजत्; *Pass.* सज्यमान; *Past pass.* सक्त; *Past indecl.* सक्त्वा or संक्त्वा, -सज्य; *Fut. pass.* संक्तव्य, सञ्जनीय, संग्य or संज्य.

b. Root द्युत्. *Inf.* द्योतितुं 'to shine.' Ātm. (and Par. in *Aor.*). *Pres.* द्योते. *Impf.* अद्योते. *Pot.* द्योतेय. *Impr.* द्योतै. *Perf.* दिद्युते (383. *a*), दिद्युतिषे, दिद्युते; दिद्युतिवहे, दिद्युताथे, दिद्युताते; दिद्युतिमहे, दिद्युतिध्वे, दिद्युतिरे. *1st Fut.* द्योतिताहे. *2d Fut.* द्योतिष्ये. *Aor.* अद्योतिषि, अद्योतिष्ठाः, अद्योतिष्ट; अद्योतिष्वहि, -तिषाथां, -तिषातां; -तिष्महि, -तिढ्वं, -तिषत. *Par.* अद्युतं, -तः, -तत्; -ताव, -तं, -तां; -ताम, -त, -तन्. *Prec.* द्योतिषीय. *Cond.* अद्योतिष्ये. Pass., *Pres.* द्युत्ये; *Aor. 3d sing.* अद्योति. Caus., *Pres.* द्योतयामि; *Aor.* अदिद्युतं.

* The final *j* is sometimes incorrectly doubled (Pres. सज्जामि, सज्जसि, सज्जति, &c.); but the root must not, therefore, be confounded with an uncommon root सज्ज् or सस्ज्, meaning 'to go,' 'to move,' also 1st c., and making सज्जामि &c.

Des. दिद्युतिषे or दिद्योतिषे. Freq. देद्युते, देद्योत्मि or देद्युतीमि. Part., *Pres.* द्योतमान; *Past pass.* द्युतित or द्योतित; *Past indecl.* द्युतित्वा or द्योतित्वा, -द्युत्य; *Fut. pass.* द्योतितव्य, द्योतनीय, द्योत्य.

c. Root पत्. *Inf.* पतितुं 'to fall.' Par. *Pres.* पतामि. *Impf.* अपतं. *Pot.* पतेयं. *Impv.* पतानि. *Perf.* पपात or पपत (370. *f*), पेतिथ, पपात; पेतिव, पेतथुस्, पेततुस्; पेतिम, पेत, पेतुस्. *1st Fut.* पतितास्मि. *2d Fut.* पतिष्यामि. *Aor.* अपप्तं (441), अपप्तस्, अपप्तत्; अपप्ताव, अपप्ततं, अपप्ततां; अपप्ताम, अपप्तत, अपप्तन्. *Prec.* पत्यासं. *Cond.* अपतिष्यं. Pass., *Pres.* पत्ये; *Impf.* अपत्ये; *Aor. 3d sing.* अपाति. Caus., *Pres.* पातयामि, पातये and पतयामि, पतये; *Aor.* अपीपतं. Des. पिपतिषामि or पित्सामि. Freq. पनीपत्ये, पनीपत्मि or पनीपतीमि. Part., *Pres.* पतत्; *Pass.* पत्यमान; *Past pass.* पतित; *Past indecl.* पतित्वा, -पत्य; *Fut. pass.* पतितव्य, पतनीय, पात्य or पत्य.

598. Root वृत्. *Inf.* वर्तितुं or वर्त्तितुं (73) 'to be,' 'to exist.' Ātm. (and optionally Par. in *2d Fut.*, *Aor.*, and *Cond.*, when it rejects *i*). *Pres.* वर्ते. *Impf.* अवर्ते. *Pot.* वर्तेय. *Impv.* वर्तै. *Perf.* ववृते, ववृतिषे, ववृते; ववृतिवहे, ववृताथे, ववृताते; ववृतिमहे, ववृतिध्वे, ववृतिरे. *1st Fut.* वर्तिताहे. *2d Fut.* वर्तिष्ये. *Aor.* अवर्तिषि, अवर्तिष्ठास्, अवर्तिष्ट; अवर्तिष्वहि, -तिषाथां, -तिषातां; -तिष्महि, -तिढ्वं, -तिषत. Par. अवृतं, -तस्, -तत्; -ताव, -ततं, -ततां; -ताम, -तत, -तन्. *Prec.* वर्तिषीय. *Cond.* अवर्तिष्ये or अवर्त्स्यं. Pass., *Pres.* वृत्ये. Caus., *Pres.* वर्तयामि; *Aor.* अवीवृतं or अववर्तं. Des. विवर्तिषे or विवृत्सामि. Freq. वरीवृत्ये, वरीवर्त्मि or वरीवृतीमि. Part., *Pres.* वर्तमान; *Past pass.* वृत्त; *Past indecl.* वर्तित्वा or वृत्त्वा, -वृत्य; *Fut. pass.* वर्तितव्य, वर्तनीय, वृत्य.

599. Root वद्. *Inf.* वदितुं 'to speak.' Par. *Pres.* वदामि. *Impf.* अवदं, अवदस्, &c. *Pot.* वदेयं. *Impv.* वदानि. *Perf.* (375. *c*) उवाद, उवदिथ, उवाद; ऊदिव, ऊदथुस्, ऊदतुस्; ऊदिम, ऊद, ऊदुस्. *1st Fut.* वदितास्मि, वदितासि, &c. *2d Fut.* वदिष्यामि, वदिष्यसि, &c. *Aor.* (428) अवादिषं, अवादीस्, अवादीत्; अवादिष्व, अवादिष्टं, अवादिष्टां; अवादिष्म, अवादिष्ट, अवादिषुस्. *Prec.* उद्यासं, उद्यास्, &c. *Cond.* अवदिष्यं, अवदिष्यस्, &c. Pass., *Pres.* उद्ये (471); *Aor. 3d sing.* अवादि. Caus., *Pres.* वादयामि; *Aor.* अवीवदं. Des. विवदिषामि, -षे. Freq. वावद्ये, वावद्मि or वावदीमि. Part., *Pres.* वदत्; *Pass.* उद्यमान; *Past pass.* उदित (543); *Past indecl.* उदित्वा, -उद्य; *Fut. pass.* वदितव्य, वदनीय, वाद्य or उद्य.

a. Root सद् (270). *Inf.* सत्तुं 'to sink.' Par. *Pres.* सीदामि. *Impf.* असीदं. *Pot.* सीदेयं. *Impv.* सीदानि. *Perf.* ससाद, सेदिथ (375. *a*) or ससत्थ, ससाद; सेदिव, सेदथुस्, सेदतुस्; सेदिम, सेद, सेदुस्. *1st Fut.* सत्तास्मि. *2d Fut.* सत्स्यामि. *Aor.* असदं (436, 437), असदस्, असदत्; असदाव, असदतं, असदतां; असदाम, असदत, असदन्. *Prec.* सद्यासं. *Cond.* असत्स्यं. Pass., *Pres.* सद्ये; *Aor. 3d sing.* असादि. Caus., *Pres.* सादयामि; *Aor.* असीषदं. Des. सिष-

त्सामि. Freq. सासद्ये, सासत्ति or सासदीति. Part., *Pres.* सीदत्; *Past pass.* सन्न (540); *Past indecl.* सत्त्वा, -सद्य; *Fut. pass.* सत्तव्य, सदनीय, साद्य.

b. Root वृध्. *Inf.* वर्धितुं 'to increase.' Ātm. (and Par. in *Fut.*, *Cond.*, and *Aor.*). *Pres.* वर्धे. *Impf.* अवर्धे, अवर्धेथास्, &c. *Pot.* वर्धेय. *Impv.* वर्धै, वर्धस्व, &c. *Perf.* ववृधे, ववृधिषे, ववृधे; ववृधिवहे, ववृधाथे, ववृधाते; ववृधिमहे, ववृधिध्वे (372. *a*), ववृधिरे. 1*st Fut.* वर्धिताहे. Par. वर्धितास्मि. 2*d Fut.* वर्धिष्ये. Par. वर्त्स्यामि. *Aor.* अवर्धिषि, अवर्धिष्ठास्, अवर्धिष्ट; अवर्धिष्वहि, अवर्धिषाथां, अवर्धिषातां; अवर्धिष्महि, अवर्धिढ्वं, अवर्धिषत. Par. अवृधं, अवृधस्, अवृधत्; अवृधाव, अवृधतं, अवृधतां; अवृधाम, अवृधत, अवृधन्. *Prec.* वर्धिषीय. *Cond.* अवर्धिष्ये. Par. अवर्त्स्यं, अवर्त्स्यस्, &c. Pass., *Pres.* वृध्ये; *Impf.* अवृध्ये; *Aor.* 3*d sing.* अवर्धि. Caus., *Pres.* वर्धयामि; *Aor.* अवीवृधं and अववर्धं. Des. विवर्धिषे, विवृत्सामि. Freq. वरीवृध्ये, वरीवर्धि or वरीवृधीमि. Part., *Pres.* वर्धमान; *Pass.* वृध्यमान; *Past pass.* वृद्ध; *Past indecl.* वर्धित्वा, वृद्ध्वा, -वृध्य. *Fut.* वर्धनीय, वर्धितव्य, वृध्य.

600. Root एध्. *Inf.* एधितुं 'to increase,' 'to flourish.' Ātm. *Pres.* एधे, एधसे, &c. *Impf.* ऐधे (260), ऐधथास्, &c. *Pot.* एधेय. *Impv.* एधै, एधस्व, &c. *Perf.* (385) एधांचक्रे, एधांचकृषे, एधांचक्रे; एधांचकृवहे, एधांचक्राथे, एधांचक्राते; एधांचकृमहे, एधांचकृढ्वे, एधांचक्रिरे. 1*st Fut.* एधिताहे. 2*d Fut.* एधिष्ये. *Aor.* ऐधिषि (427. *b*, 260. *b*), ऐधिष्ठास्, ऐधिष्ट; ऐधिष्वहि, ऐधिषाथां, ऐधिषातां; ऐधिष्महि, ऐधिढ्वं, ऐधिषत. *Prec.* एधिषीय. *Cond.* ऐधिष्ये (260. *b*). Pass. एध्ये; *Aor.* 3*d sing.* ऐधि. Caus., *Pres.* एधयामि; *Aor.* ऐदिधे (494). Des. एदिधिषे (500. *b*). Part., *Pres.* एधमान; *Past pass.* एधित; *Past indecl.* एधित्वा, -एध्य; *Fut. pass.* एधितव्य, एधनीय, एध्य.

a. Root तप्. *Inf.* तप्तुं 'to burn.' Par. and Ātm. *Pres.* तपामि. Ātm. तपे. *Impf.* अतपं. Ātm. अतपे. *Pot.* तपेयं. Ātm. तपेय. *Impv.* तपानि, तप, &c. Ātm. तपै. *Perf.* तताप or ततप, ततप्थ or तेपिथ, तताप; तेपिव, तेपथुस्, तेपतुस्; तेपिम, तेप, तेपुस्. Ātm. तेपे, तेपिषे, तेपे; तेपिवहे, तेपाथे, तेपाते; तेपिमहे, तेपिध्वे, तेपिरे. 1*st Fut.* तप्तास्मि, &c. Ātm. तप्ताहे, &c. 2*d Fut.* तप्स्यामि (Ep. also तपिष्यामि). Ātm. तप्स्ये. *Aor.* अताप्सं, अताप्सीस्, अताप्सीत्; अताप्स्व, अताप्तं, अताप्तां; अताप्स्म, अताप्त, अताप्सुस्. Ātm. अतप्सि, अतप्थास्, अतप्त; अतप्स्वहि, अतप्साथां, अतप्सातां; अतप्स्महि, अतब्ध्वं, अतप्सत. *Prec.* तप्यासं. Ātm. तप्सीय. *Cond.* अतप्स्यं. Ātm. अतप्स्ये. Pass., *Pres.* तप्ये; *Impf.* अतप्ये; *Aor.* 3*d sing.* अतापि. Caus., *Pres.* तापयामि, तापये; *Aor.* अतीतपं, अतीतपे. Des. तितप्सामि, तितप्से. Freq. तातप्ये, तातप्मि or तातपीमि. Part., *Pres.* तपत्; Ātm. तपमान; *Pass.* तप्यमान; *Past pass.* तप्त; *Past indecl.* तप्त्वा, -तप्य; *Fut.* तप्तव्य, तपनीय, ताप्य or तप्य.

601. Root लभ्. *Inf.* लब्धुं 'to take.' Ātm. *Pres.* लभे, लभसे, लभते; लभावहे, लभेथे, लभेते; लभामहे, लभध्वे, लभन्ते. *Impf.* अलभे, अलभथास्,

अलभत ; अलभावहि, अलभेथां, अलभेतां ; अलभामहि, अलभध्वं, अलभन्त. *Pot.* लभेय, लभेथास्, लभेत ; लभेवहि, लभेयाथां, लभेयातां ; लभेमहि, लभेध्वं, लभेरन्. *Impv.* लभै, लभस्व, लभतां ; लभावहै, लभेथां, लभेतां ; लभामहै, लभध्वं, लभन्तां. *Perf.* लेभे (375. *a*), लेभिषे, लेभे ; लेभिवहे, लेभाथे, लेभाते ; लेभिमहे, लेभिध्वे, लेभिरे. *1st Fut.* लब्धाहे (409), लब्धासे, लब्धा, &c. *2d Fut.* लप्स्ये (299), लप्स्यसे, &c. *Aor.* अलप्सि (420, 299), अलब्धास् (298), अलब्ध ; अलप्स्वहि, अलप्साथां, अलप्सातां ; अलप्स्महि, अलब्ध्वं, अलप्सत. *Prec.* लप्सीय, लप्सीष्ठास्, लप्सीष्ट, &c. *Cond.* अलप्स्ये, &c. Pass., *Pres.* लभ्ये ; *Aor.* अलप्सि, अलब्धास्, अलाभि (475) or अलम्भि, &c. Caus., *Pres.* लम्भयामि, &c. ; *Aor.* अललम्भं. Des. लिप्से (503). Freq. लालभ्ये, लालम्भीमि. Part., *Pres.* लभमान ; *Past pass.* लब्ध ; *Past indecl.* लब्ध्वा, -लभ्य ; *Fut. pass.* लब्धव्य, लभनीय, लभ्य.

a. Like लभ् is conjugated रभ् (with prep. आ ā), आरब्धुं 'to begin.'

602. Root गम् (270). *Inf.* गन्तुं 'to go.' Par. *Pres.* गच्छामि, गच्छसि, गच्छति ; गच्छावस्, गच्छथस्, गच्छतस् ; गच्छामस्, गच्छथ, गच्छन्ति. *Impf.* अगच्छं, अगच्छस्, &c. *Pot.* गच्छेयं, गच्छेस्, &c. *Impv.* गच्छानि, गच्छ, &c. *Perf.* (376) जगाम, जगमिथ or जगन्थ, जगाम ; जग्मिव, जग्मथुस्, जग्मतुस् ; जग्मिम, जग्म, जग्मुस्. *1st Fut.* गन्तास्मि. *2d Fut.* गमिष्यामि, गमिष्यसि, गमिष्यति, &c. *Aor.* (436) अगमं, अगमस्, अगमत् ; अगमाव, अगमतं, अगमतां ; अगमाम, अगमत, अगमन्. *Prec.* गम्यासं. *Cond.* अगमिष्यं. Pass., *Pres.* गम्ये ; *Aor. 3d sing.* अगामि. Caus., *Pres.* गमयामि ; *Aor.* अजीगमं. Des. जिगमिषामि. Freq. जङ्गम्ये, जङ्गन्मि or जङ्गमीमि ; see 709. Part., *Pres.* गच्छत् ; *Past pass.* गत ; *Past indecl.* गत्वा, -गम्य, -गत्य (563. *a*, 560) ; *Fut. pass.* गन्तव्य, गमनीय, गम्य.

a. Root नम्. *Inf.* नन्तुं 'to bend.' Par. and Ātm. ('to bow oneself'). *Pres.* नमामि. Ātm. नमे. *Impf.* अनमं. Ātm. अनमे. *Pot.* नमेयं. Ātm. नमेय. *Impv.* नमानि. Ātm. नमै. *Perf.* (375. *a*) ननाम or ननम, ननन्थ or नेमिथ, ननाम ; नेमिव, नेमथुस्, नेमतुस् ; नेमिम, नेम, नेमुस्. Ātm. नेमे, नेमिषे, नेमे ; नेमिवहे, नेमाथे, नेमाते ; नेमिमहे, नेमिध्वे (372. *a*), नेमिरे. *1st Fut.* नन्तास्मि. Ātm. नन्ताहे. *2d Fut.* नंस्यामि. Ātm. नंस्ये. *Aor.* अनंसिषं, अनंसीस्, अनंसीत् ; अनंसिष्व, अनंसिष्टं, अनंसिष्टां ; अनंसिष्म, अनंसिष्ट, अनंसिषुस्. Ātm. अनंसि, अनंस्थास्, अनंस्त ; अनंस्वहि, अनंसाथां, अनंसातां ; अनंस्महि, अनन्ध्वं, अनंसत. *Prec.* नम्यासं. Ātm. नंसीय. *Cond.* अनंस्यं. Ātm. अनंस्ये. Pass., *Pres.* नम्ये ; *Impf.* अनम्ये ; *Aor. 3d sing.* अनामि or अनमि. Caus. नमयामि or नामयामि ; *Aor.* अनेनमं or अनीनमं. Des. निनंसामि. Freq. नंनम्ये, नंनमीमि or नंनन्मि. Part., *Pres.* नमत् ; Ātm. नममान ; *Pass.* नम्यमान ; *Past pass.* नत ; *Past indecl.* नत्वा, -नम्य or -नत्य ; *Fut. pass.* नन्तव्य, नमनीय, नाम्य or नम्य.

b. Root चल्. *Inf.* चलितुं 'to move.' Par. *Pres.* चलामि. *Impf.*

अचलत्. *Pot.* चलेयं. *Impv.* चलानि, चल, &c. *Perf.* चचाल or चचल, चेलिथ, चचाल; चेलिव, चेलथुस्, चेलतुस्; चेलिम, चेल, चेलुस्. *1st Fut.* चलितास्मि. *2d Fut.* चलिष्यामि. *Aor.* अचालिषं, अचालीस्, अचालीत्; अचालिष्व, अचालिष्टं, -ष्टां; अचालिष्म, -लिष्ट, -लिषुस्. *Prec.* चल्यासं. *Cond.* अचलिष्यं. Pass., *Pres.* चल्यते. Caus., *Pres.* चलयामि or चालयामि. Des. चिचलिषामि. Freq. चाचल्यते, चाचल्मि. Part., *Pres.* चलत्; *Past pass.* चलित; *Past indecl.* चलित्वा, -चल्य; *Fut. pass.* चलितव्य, चलनीय, चल्य or चाल्य.

603. Root जीव्. *Inf.* जीवितुं 'to live.' Par. *Pres.* जीवामि. *Impf.* अजीवं. *Pot.* जीवेयं. *Impv.* जीवानि, जीव, &c. *Perf.* जिजीव, जिजीविथ, जिजीव; जिजीविव, जिजीवथुस्, जिजीवतुस्; जिजीविम, जिजीव, जिजीवुस्. *1st Fut.* जीवितास्मि. *2d Fut.* जीविष्यामि. *Aor.* अजीविषं, अजीवीस्, अजीवीत्; अजीविष्व, अजीविष्टं, अजीविष्टां; अजीविष्म, अजीविष्ट, अजीविषुस्. *Prec.* जीव्यासं. *Cond.* अजीविष्यं. Pass., *Pres.* जीव्यते; *Aor. 3d sing.* अजीवि. Caus., *Pres.* जीवयामि; *Aor.* अजिजीवं or अजीजिवं. Des. जिजीविषामि. Freq. जेजीव्यते. Part., *Pres.* जीवत्; *Past pass.* जीवित; *Past indecl.* जीवित्वा, -जीव्य; *Fut. pass.* जीवितव्य, जीवनीय, जीव्य.

a. Root धाव्. *Inf.* धावितुं 'to run,' 'to wash.' Par. and Ātm. *Pres.* धावामि. Ātm. धावे. *Impf.* अधावं. Ātm. अधावे. *Pot.* धावेयं. Ātm. धावेय. *Impv.* धावानि. Ātm. धावै. *Perf.* दधाव, दधाविथ, दधाव; दधाविव, दधावथुस्, -वतुस्; दधाविम, दधाव, दधावुस्. *1st Fut.* धावितास्मि. Ātm. धाविताहे. *2d Fut.* धाविष्यामि. Ātm. धाविष्ये. *Aor.* अधाविषं, अधावीस्, अधावीत्; अधाविष्व, -विष्टं, -विष्टां; अधाविष्म, -विष्ट, -विषुस्. Ātm. अधाविषि, -विष्ठास्, -विष्ट; अधाविष्वहि, &c. *Prec.* धाव्यासं. Ātm. धाविषीय. *Cond.* अधाविष्यं. Ātm. अधाविष्ये. Pass., *Pres.* धाव्यते. Caus., *Pres.* धावयामि; *Aor.* अदीधवं. Des. दिधाविषामि, -षे. Freq. दाधाव्यते. Part., *Pres.* धावत्, धावमान; *Past pass.* धावित, धौत ('washed'); *Past indecl.* धावित्वा or धौत्वा; *Fut. pass.* धावितव्य, धावनीय, धाव्य.

604. Root दृश् (270). *Inf.* द्रष्टुं 'to see.' Par. *Pres.* पश्यामि, पश्यसि, पश्यति; पश्यावस्, पश्यथस्, पश्यतस्; पश्यामस्, पश्यथ, पश्यन्ति. *Impf.* अपश्यं, अपश्यस्, अपश्यत्; अपश्याव, &c. *Pot.* पश्येयं, पश्येस्, पश्येत्; पश्येव, &c. *Impv.* पश्यानि, पश्य, पश्यतु; पश्याव, &c. *Perf.* ददर्श, ददर्शिथ or दद्रष्ठ (370. *f*), ददर्श; ददृशिव, ददृशथुस्, ददृशतुस्; ददृशिम, ददृश, ददृशुस्. *1st Fut.* द्रष्टास्मि. *2d Fut.* द्रक्ष्यामि. *Aor.* (437. *c*) अदर्शं, अदर्शस्, अदर्शत्; अदर्शाव, अदर्शतं, अदर्शतां; अदर्शाम, अदर्शत, अदर्शन्. Or अद्राक्षं (420, 390. *f*), अद्राक्षीस्, अद्राक्षीत्; अद्राक्ष्व, अद्राष्टं, अद्राष्टां; अद्राक्ष्म, अद्राष्ट, अद्राक्षुस्. *Prec.* दृश्यासं. *Cond.* अद्रक्ष्यं. Pass., *Pres.* दृश्यते; *Aor. 3d sing.* अदर्शि. Caus., *Pres.* दर्शयामि; *Aor.* अदीदृशं or अददर्शं; see 703. Des. दिदृक्षे.

Freq. दरीदृश्ये, दरी-, दरि-, दर्दर्शि or -दृशीमि. Part., *Pres.* पश्यत्; *Past pass.* दृष्ट; *Past indecl.* दृष्ट्वा, -दृश्य; *Fut. pass.* द्रष्टव्य, दर्शनीय, दृश्य.

605. Root ईक्ष्. *Inf.* ईक्षितुं 'to see.' Ātm. *Pres.* ईक्षे. *Impf.* ऐक्षे (260. *a*). *Pot.* ईक्षेय. *Impv.* ईक्षै. *Perf.* ईक्षाञ्चक्रे, &c. (385. and compare इन्ध् at 600). *1st Fut.* ईक्षिताहे. *2d Fut.* ईक्षिष्ये. *Aor.* ऐक्षिषि (260. *b*), ऐक्षिष्ठास्, ऐक्षिष्ट; ऐक्षिष्वहि, ऐक्षिषाथां, ऐक्षिषातां; ऐक्षिष्महि, ऐक्षिढ्वं, ऐक्षिषत. *Prec.* ईक्षिषीय, &c. *Cond.* ऐक्षिष्ये. Pass. ईक्ष्ये; *Aor. 3d sing.* ऐक्षि. Caus., *Pres.* ईक्षयामि; *Aor.* ऐचिक्षं (494). Des. ईचिक्षिषे (500. *b*). Part., *Pres.* ईक्षमाण; *Past pass.* ईक्षित; *Past indecl.* ईक्षित्वा, -ईक्ष्य; *Fut. pass.* ईक्षितव्य, ईक्षणीय, ईक्ष्य.

606. Root कृष्*. *Inf.* कर्ष्टुं or क्रष्टुं 'to draw,' 'to drag.' Par. and Ātm. *Pres.* कर्षामि. Ātm. कर्षे. *Impf.* अकर्षं. Ātm. अकर्षे. *Pot.* कर्षेयं. Ātm. कर्षेय. *Impv.* कर्षाणि. Ātm. कर्षै. *Perf.* चकर्ष, चकर्षिथ, चकर्ष; चकृषिव, चकृषथुस्, चकृषतुस्; चकृषिम, चकृष, चकृषुस्. Ātm. चकृषे, चकृषिषे, चकृषे; चकृषिवहे, चकृषाथे, चकृषाते; चकृषिमहे, चकृषिढ्वे, चकृषिरे. *1st Fut.* कर्ष्टास्मि. Ātm. कर्ष्टाहे or क्रष्टाहे. *2d Fut.* कर्क्ष्यामि or क्रक्ष्यामि. Ātm. कर्क्ष्ये or क्रक्ष्ये. *Aor.* अकार्क्षं, अकार्क्षीस्, अकार्क्षीत्; अकार्क्ष्व, अकार्ष्टं, अकार्ष्टां; अकार्क्ष्म, अकार्ष्ट, अकार्क्षुस्. Or अक्राक्षं, अक्राक्षीस्, &c. Or अकृक्षं, अकृक्षस्, अकृक्षत्; अकृक्षाव, अकृक्षतं, अकृक्षतां; अकृक्षाम, अकृक्षत, अकृक्षन्. Ātm. अकृक्षि, अकृक्षथास् or अकृष्ठास्, अकृक्षत or अकृष्ट; अकृक्षावहि or अकृक्ष्वहि, अकृक्षाथां, अकृक्षातां; अकृक्षामहि or अकृक्ष्महि, अकृक्षध्वं or अकृड्ढ्वं, अकृक्षन्त or अकृक्षत. *Prec.* कृष्यासं. Ātm. कृक्षीय. *Cond.* अकर्क्ष्यं or अक्रक्ष्यं. Ātm. अकर्क्ष्ये or अक्रक्ष्ये. Pass., *Pres.* कृष्ये; *Aor. 3d sing.* अकर्षि. Caus., *Pres.* कर्षयामि; *Aor.* अचकर्षं or अचीकृषं. Des. चिकृक्षामि, -क्षे. Freq. चरीकृष्ये, चरीकर्ष्मि or चरीकर्षिम. Part., *Pres.* कर्षत्; *Past pass.* कृष्ट; *Past indecl.* कृष्ट्वा, -कृष्य; *Fut. pass.* कर्ष्टव्य or क्रष्टव्य, कर्षणीय, कृष्य.

a. Root भाष्. *Inf.* भाषितुं 'to speak.' Ātm. *Pres.* भाषे. *Impf.* अभाषे. *Pot.* भाषेय. *Impv.* भाषै. *Perf.* बभाषे, बभाषिषे, बभाषे; बभाषिवहे, -षाथे, -षाते; बभाषिमहे, -षिढ्वे, -षिरे. *1st Fut.* भाषिताहे. *2d Fut.* भाषिष्ये. *Aor.* अभाषिषि, -षिष्ठास्, -षिष्ट; अभाषिष्वहि, -षिषाथां, -षिषातां; अभाषिष्महि, -षिढ्वं, -षिषत. *Prec.* भाषिषीय. *Cond.* अभाषिष्ये. Pass., *Pres.* भाष्ये; *Aor. 3d sing.* अभाषि. Caus. भाषयामि; *Aor.* अबभाषं and अबीभषं. Des. बिभाषिषे. Freq. बाभाष्ये, बाभाष्मि; *3d sing.* बाभाष्टि. Part., *Pres.* भाषमाण; *Past pass.* भाषित; *Past indecl.* भाषित्वा, -भाष्य; *Fut. pass.* भाषितव्य, भाषणीय, भाष्य.

b. Root रक्ष्. *Inf.* रक्षितुं 'to preserve,' 'to defend.' Par. *Pres.* रक्षामि.

---

* This root is also conjugated in the 6th conj.: Pres. कृषामि, &c.; Pot. कृषेयं, &c.

Impf. अरक्षं. *Pot.* रक्षेयं. *Impv.* रक्षाणि (58), रक्ष, &c. *Perf.* ररक्ष, ररक्षिथ, ररक्ष; ररक्षिव, ररक्षथुस्, ररक्षतुस्; ररक्षिम, ररक्ष, ररक्षुस्. *1st Fut.* रक्षितास्मि. *2d Fut.* रक्षिष्यामि. *Aor.* अरक्षिषं, अरक्षीस्, अरक्षीत्; अरक्षिष्व, अरक्षिष्टं, अरक्षिष्टां; अरक्षिष्म, अरक्षिष्ट, अरक्षिषुस्. *Prec.* रक्ष्यासं. *Cond.* अरक्षिष्यं. Pass., *Pres.* रक्ष्ये. Caus., *Pres.* रक्षयामि, &c.; *Aor.* अररक्षं. Des. रिरक्षिषामि, &c. Freq. रारक्ष्ये, &c., रारक्ष्मि. Part., *Pres.* रक्षत्; *Past pass.* रक्षित; *Past indecl.* रक्षित्वा, -रक्ष्य; *Fut. pass.* रक्षितव्य, रक्षणीय, रक्ष्य.

607. Root वस्. *Inf.* वस्तुं 'to dwell.' Par. *Pres.* वसामि. *Impf.* अवसं. *Pot.* वसेयं. *Impv.* वसानि, वस, &c. *Perf.* उवास (368), उवसिथ or उवस्थ, उवास; ऊषिव, ऊषथुस्, ऊषतुस्; ऊषिम, ऊष, ऊषुस्. *1st Fut.* वस्तास्मि. *2d Fut.* वत्स्यामि (304. *a*). *Aor.* अवात्सं (304. *a*, 426. *a*), अवात्सीस्, अवात्सीत्; अवात्स्व, अवात्तं, अवात्तां; अवात्स्म, अवात्त, अवात्सुस्. *Prec.* उष्यासं. *Cond.* अवत्स्यं (304. *a*). Pass., *Pres.* उष्ये (471); *Aor. 3d sing.* अवासि. Caus., *Pres.* वासयामि, -ये; *Aor.* अवीवसं. Des. विवत्सामि (304. *a*). Freq. वावस्ये, वावस्मि or वावसीमि. Part., *Pres.* वसत्; *Past pass.* उषित (with नि, वस); *Past indecl.* उषित्वा, -उष्य (565); *Fut. pass.* वस्तव्य, वसनीय, वास्य.

608. Root अर्ह्. *Inf.* अर्हितुं 'to deserve.' Par. *Pres.* अर्हामि. *Impf.* आर्हं. *Pot.* अर्हेयं. *Impv.* अर्हाणि (58). *Perf.* (367. *b*) आनर्ह, आनर्हिथ, आनर्ह; आनर्हिव, आनर्हथुस्, आनर्हतुस्; आनर्हिम, आनर्ह, आनर्हुस्. *1st Fut.* अर्हितास्मि. *2d Fut.* अर्हिष्यामि. *Aor.* आर्हिषं, आर्हीस्, आर्हीत्; आर्हिष्व, आर्हिष्टं, आर्हिष्टां; आर्हिष्म, आर्हिष्ट, आर्हिषुस्. *Prec.* अर्ह्यासं. *Cond.* आर्हिष्यं. Pass. अर्ह्ये; *Aor. 3d sing.* आर्हि. Caus., *Pres.* अर्हयामि, -ये; *Aor.* आर्जिहं (494). Des. अर्जिहिषामि, &c. (500. *d*). Part., *Pres.* अर्हत्; *Past pass.* अर्हित; *Past indecl.* अर्हित्वा, -अर्ह्य; *Fut. pass.* अर्हितव्य, अर्हणीय, अर्ह्य.

609. Root गुह् (270. *b*). *Inf.* गूहितुं or गोढुं 'to hide.' Par. and Ātm. *Pres.* गूहामि. Ātm. गूहे. *Impf.* अगूहं. Ātm. अगूहे. *Pot.* गूहेयं. Ātm. गूहेय. *Impv.* गूहानि. Ātm. गूहै. *Perf.* जुगूह (384. *a*), जुगूहिथ or जुगोढ (305. *a*), जुगूह; जुगुहिव or जुगुह्व (372), जुगुहथुस्, जुगुहतुस्; जुगुहिम or जुगुह्म, जुगुह, जुगुहुस्. Ātm. जुगुहे, जुगुहिषे, जुगुहे, &c. *1st Fut.* (415. *m*) गूहितास्मि or गोढास्मि (305. *a*). Ātm. गूहिताहे or गोढाहे. *2d Fut.* गूहिष्यामि or घोक्ष्यामि. Ātm. गूहिष्ये or घोक्ष्ये. *Aor.* अगूहिषं, अगूहीस्, अगूहीत्; अगूहिष्व, अगूहिष्टं, अगूहिष्टां; अगूहिष्म, अगूहिष्ट, अगूहिषुस्. Or अघुक्षं (306. *a*), अघुक्षस्, अघुक्षत्; अघुक्षाव, अघुक्षतं, अघुक्षतां; अघुक्षाम, अघुक्षत, अघुक्षन्. Ātm. अगूहिषि, अगूहिष्ठास्, अगूहिष्ट, &c. Or अघुक्षि (439), अघुक्षथास् or अगूढास्, अघुक्षत or अगूढ; अघुक्षावहि or अगुह्वहि, अघुक्षाथां, अघुक्षातां; अघुक्षामहि, अघुक्षध्वं or अघूढ्वं, अघुक्षन्त. *Prec.* गुह्यासं.

Ātm. गूहिषीष्ट or घुक्षीष्ट (306. a). *Cond.* अगूहिष्यं or अघोक्ष्यं, अगूहिष्ये or अघोक्ष्ये. Pass., *Pres.* गुह्ये; *Aor. 3d sing.* अगूहि. Caus., *Pres.* गूहयामि; *Aor.* अजूगुहं. Des. जुघुक्षामि, -क्षे. Freq. जोगुह्ये, जोगोह्मि (*3d sing.* जोगोढि) or जोगुहीमि. Part., *Pres.* गूहत्; *Past pass.* गूढ (305. a); *Past indecl.* गूहित्वा or गूढ्वा or गुहित्वा, -गुह्य; *Fut. pass.* गूहितव्य or गोढव्य, गूहनीय, गुह्य or गोह्य.

610. Root दह्. *Inf.* दग्धुं 'to burn.' Par. *Pres.* दहामि. *Impf.* अदहं. *Pot.* दहेयं, &c. *Impv.* दहानि, दह, &c. *Perf.* ददाह, देहिथ (375. a) or ददग्ध (305), ददाह; देहिव, देहथुः, देहतुः; देहिम, देह, देहुः. *1st Fut.* दग्धास्मि. *2d Fut.* धक्ष्यामि (306. a). *Aor.* अधाक्षं (422), अधाक्षीः, अधाक्षीत्; अधाक्ष्व, अदाग्धं, अदाग्धां; अधाक्ष्म, अदाग्ध, अधाक्षुः. *Prec.* दह्यासं. *Cond.* अधक्ष्यं. Pass., *Pres.* दह्ये; *Aor. 3d sing.* अदाहि. Caus., *Pres.* दाहयामि, -ये; *Aor.* अदीदहं. Des. दिधक्षामि (502. a). Freq. दन्दह्ये, दन्दह्मि or दन्दहीमि; *3d sing.* दन्दग्धि or दन्दहीति. Part., *Pres.* दहत्; *Past pass.* दग्ध; *Past indecl.* दग्ध्वा, -दह्य; *Fut. pass.* दग्धव्य, दहनीय, दाह्य.

611. Root वह्. *Inf.* वोढुं 'to carry.' Par. and Ātm. *Pres.* वहामि. Ātm. वहे. *Impf.* अवहं. Ātm. अवहे. *Pot.* वहेयं. Ātm. वहेय. *Impv.* वहानि, वह, &c. Ātm. वहै. *Perf.* (375. c) उवाह (368), उवहिथ or उवोढ, उवाह; ऊहिव, ऊहथुः, ऊहतुः; ऊहिम, ऊह, ऊहुः. Ātm. ऊहे, ऊहिषे, ऊहे; ऊहिवहे, ऊहाथे, ऊहाते; ऊहिमहे, ऊहिध्वे or ऊहिढ्वे, ऊहिरे. *1st Fut.* वोढास्मि. Ātm. वोढाहे. *2d Fut.* वक्ष्यामि. Ātm. वक्ष्ये. *Aor.* (425) अवाक्षं, अवाक्षीः, अवाक्षीत्; अवाक्ष्व, अवोढं, अवोढां; अवाक्ष्म, अवोढ, अवाक्षुः. Ātm. अवक्षि, अवोढाः, अवोढ; अवक्ष्वहि, अवक्षाथां, अवक्षातां; अवक्ष्महि, अवोढ्वं, अवक्षत. *Prec.* उह्यासं. Ātm. वक्षीय. *Cond.* अवक्ष्यं. Ātm. अवक्ष्ये. Pass., *Pres.* (471) उह्ये; *Impf.* औह्ये (260. a); *Aor. 3d sing.* अवाहि. Caus., *Pres.* वाहयामि, -ये; *Aor.* अवीवहं. Des. विवक्षामि, -क्षे. Freq. वावह्ये, वावह्मि; *3d sing.* वावोढि (compare 425). Part., *Pres.* वहत्; Ātm. वहमान; *Pass.* उह्यमान; *Past pass.* ऊढ; *Past indecl.* ऊढ्वा, -उह्य (565); *Fut. pass.* वोढव्य, वहनीय, वाह्य.

a. सह्, *Inf.* सोढुं 'to bear,' is Ātm. only, and follows *vah* in making सोढाहे &c. in *1st Fut.*: but in this tense optionally, and in the other non-conjugational tenses necessarily inserts *i*; thus, *1st Fut.* सहिताहे; *2d Fut.* सहिष्ये; *Aor.* असहिषि; *Prec.* सहिषीय; *Cond.* असहिष्ये. The *Perf.* is सेहे (375. a), सेहिषे, सेहे; सेहिवहे, &c. The other tenses are like the Ātm. of *vah*; thus, *Pres.* सहे, &c.

EXAMPLES OF PRIMITIVE VERBS OF THE FOURTH CONJUGATIONAL CLASS, EXPLAINED AT 272.

612. Root मुह् *muh.* Infin. मोहितुम् *mohitum*, 'to be troubled.'

PARASMAI-PADA. *Present tense*, 'I am troubled.'

मुह्यामि *muhyāmi*	मुह्यावः *muhyāvas*	मुह्यामः *muhyāmas*
मुह्यसि *muhyasi*	मुह्यथः *muhyathas*	मुह्यथ *muhyatha*
मुह्यति *muhyati*	मुह्यतः *muhyatas*	मुह्यन्ति *muhyanti*

Imperfect or first preterite, 'I was troubled.'

अमुह्यम् *amuhyam*	अमुह्याव *amuhyāva*	अमुह्याम *amuhyāma*
अमुह्यः *amuhyas*	अमुह्यतम् *amuhyatam*	अमुह्यत *amuhyata*
अमुह्यत् *amuhyat*	अमुह्यताम् *amuhyatām*	अमुह्यन् *amuhyan*

Potential, 'I may be troubled.'

मुह्येयम् *muhyeyam*	मुह्येव *muhyeva*	मुह्येम *muhyema*
मुह्येः *muhyes*	मुह्येतम् *muhyetam*	मुह्येत *muhyeta*
मुह्येत् *muhyet*	मुह्येताम् *muhyetām*	मुह्येयुः *muhyeyus*

Imperative, 'Let me be troubled.'

मुह्यानि *muhyāni*	मुह्याव *muhyāva*	मुह्याम *muhyāma*
मुह्य *muhya*	मुह्यतम् *muhyatam*	मुह्यत *muhyata*
मुह्यतु *muhyatu*	मुह्यताम् *muhyatām*	मुह्यन्तु *muhyantu*

Perfect or second preterite, 'I became troubled.'

मुमोह *mumoha*	मुमुहिव *mumuhiva*	मुमुहिम *mumuhima*
मुमोहिथ *mumohitha* *	मुमुहथुः *mumuhathus*	मुमुह *mumuha*
मुमोह *mumoha*	मुमुहतुः *mumuhatus*	मुमुहुः *mumuhus*

First future †, 'I will be troubled.'

मोहितास्मि *mohitāsmi*	मोहितास्वः *mohitāsvas*	मोहितास्मः *mohitāsmas*
मोहितासि *mohitāsi*	मोहितास्थः *mohitāsthas*	मोहितास्थ *mohitāstha*
मोहिता *mohitā*	मोहितारौ *mohitārau*	मोहितारः *mohitāras*

Second future †, 'I shall be troubled.'

मोहिष्यामि *mohishyāmi*	मोहिष्यावः *mohishyāvas*	मोहिष्यामः *mohishyāmas*
मोहिष्यसि *mohishyasi*	मोहिष्यथः *mohishyathas*	मोहिष्यथ *mohishyatha*
मोहिष्यति *mohishyati*	मोहिष्यतः *mohishyatas*	मोहिष्यन्ति *mohishyanti*

---

* Or मुमोढ (305. *a*) or मुमोग्ध (305).

† The 1st and 2d futures may optionally reject the inserted *i*; see under 412.

Aorist or *third preterite* (435), 'I became troubled.'

अमुहम् *amuham*	अमुहाव *amuhāva*	अमुहाम *amuhāma*
अमुहः *amuhas*	अमुहतम् *amuhatam*	अमुहत *amuhata*
अमुहत् *amuhat*	अमुहताम् *amuhatām*	अमुहन् *amuhan*

Precative or *benedictive*, 'May I be troubled.'

मुह्यासम् *muhyāsam*	मुह्यास्व *muhyāsva*	मुह्यास्म *muhyāsma*
मुह्याः *muhyās*	मुह्यास्तम् *muhyāstam*	मुह्यास्त *muhyāsta*
मुह्यात् *muhyāt*	मुह्यास्ताम् *muhyāstām*	मुह्यासुः *muhyāsus*

Conditional, 'I should be troubled.'

अमोहिष्यम् *amohishyam*	अमोहिष्याव *amohishyāva*	अमोहिष्याम *amohishyāma*
अमोहिष्यः *amohishyas*	अमोहिष्यतम् *amohishyatam*	अमोहिष्यत *amohishyata*
अमोहिष्यत् *amohishyat*	अमोहिष्यताम् *amohishyatām*	अमोहिष्यन् *amohishyan*

Pass., *Pres.* मुह्ये; *Aor. 3d sing.* अमोहि. Caus., *Pres.* मोहयामि; *Aor.* अमूमुहं. Des. मुमोहिषामि or मुमुहिषामि or मुमुक्षामि. Freq. मोमुह्ये, मोमोह्मि; *3d sing.* मोमोढि or मोमोग्धि (305). Part., *Pres.* मुह्यत्; *Past pass.* मूढ (305) or मुग्ध; *Past indecl.* मोहित्वा or मुहित्वा or मुग्ध्वा or मूढ्वा, -मुह्य; *Fut. pass.* मोहितव्य or मोग्धव्य, मोहनीय, मोह्य.

EXAMPLES OF OTHER VERBS OF THE FOURTH CONJUGATIONAL CLASS IN THE ORDER OF THEIR FINAL LETTERS.

613. Root सो (276. a). *Inf.* सातुं 'to destroy' (with prepositions *vi* and *ava*, 'to determine,' 'to strive'). Par. *Pres.* स्यामि. *Impf.* अस्यं. *Pot.* स्येयं. *Impv.* स्यानि. *Perf.* (373. d) ससौ, ससिथ or ससाथ, ससौ; ससिव, ससथुस्, ससतुस्; ससिम, सस, ससुस्. *1st Fut.* सातास्मि. *2d Fut.* सास्यामि. *Aor.* (438. c) असां, असास्, असात्; असाव, असातं, असातां; असाम, असात, असुस्. Or असासिषं (433), असासीस्, असासीत्; असासिष्व, असासिष्टं, असासिष्टां; असासिष्म, असासिष्ट, असासिषुस्. *Prec.* सेयासं. *Cond.* असास्यं. Pass., *Pres.* सीये; *Aor. 3d sing.* असायि. Caus. साययामि; *Aor.* असीषयं. Des. सिषासामि. Freq. सेषीये, सासेमि, सासामि. Part., *Pres.* स्यत्; *Past pass.* सित; *Past indecl.* सित्वा, -साय; *Fut. pass.* सातव्य, सानीय, सेय.

614. Root बुध्. *Inf.* बोद्धुं 'to know'*. Ātm. *Pres.* बुध्ये. *Impf.* अबुध्ये. *Pot.* बुध्येय. *Impv.* बुध्यै. *Perf.* बुबुधे; see the tables at 583. *1st Fut.* बोद्धाहे. *2d Fut.* भोत्स्ये (299. a). *Aor.* (420, 299. a) अभुत्सि, अबुद्धास्, अबुद्ध or अबोधि (424. a); अभुत्स्वहि, अभुत्साथां, अभुत्सातां; अभुत्स्महि,

* This verb is also of the 1st conjugation. See the tables at 583.

अयुद्ध्वं, अयुत्सत. *Prec.* युत्सीय. *Cond.* अयोत्स्यत. For the other forms, see युध् at 583.

615. Root व्यध् (277). *Inf.* व्यद्धुं 'to pierce.' Par. *Pres.* विध्यामि. *Impf.* अविध्यं. *Pot.* विध्येयं. *Impv.* विध्यानि. *Perf.* (383) विव्याध, विव्यधिथ or विव्यद्ध, विव्याध; विविधिव, विविधथुस्, विविधतुस्; विविधिम, विविध, विविधुस्. *1st Fut.* व्यद्धास्मि (298). *2d Fut.* व्यत्स्यामि (299). *Aor.* (420) अव्यात्सं, अव्यात्सीस्, अव्यात्सीत्; अव्यात्स्व, अव्याद्धं (419), अव्याद्धां; अव्यात्स्म, अव्याद्ध, अव्यात्सुस्. *Prec.* विध्यासं. *Cond.* अव्यत्स्यं. Pass., *Pres.* विध्ये; *Aor. 3d sing.* अव्याधि. Caus. व्याधयामि; *Aor.* अविव्यधं. Des. विव्यत्सामि. Freq. वेविध्ये, वाव्यध्मि. Part., *Pres.* विध्यत्; *Past pass.* विद्ध; *Past indecl.* विद्ध्वा, -विध्य; *Fut. pass.* व्यद्धव्य, व्यधनीय, वेध्य or व्याध्य.

616. Root सिध् (273). *Inf.* सेद्धुं 'to succeed.' Par. *Pres.* सिध्यामि. *Impf.* असिध्यं. *Pot.* सिध्येयं. *Impv.* सिध्यानि. *Perf.* सिषेध, सिषेधिथ or सिषेद्ध, सिषेध; सिषिधिव, सिषिधथुस्, सिषिधतुस्; सिषिधिम, सिषिध, सिषिधुस्. *1st Fut.* सेद्धास्मि (298)*. *2d Fut.* सेत्स्यामि (299)*. *Aor.* असिधं*, असिधस्, असिधत्; असिधाव, असिधतं, असिधतां; असिधाम, असिधत, असिधन्. *Prec.* सिध्यासं. *Cond.* असेत्स्यं. Pass. सिध्ये; *Aor. 3d sing.* असेधि. Caus., *Pres.* सेधयामि or साधयामि; *Aor.* असीषिधं. Des. सिषित्सामि. Freq. सेषिध्ये, सेषेद्धि. Part., *Pres.* सिध्यत्; *Past pass.* सिद्ध; *Past indecl.* सिद्ध्वा or सेधित्वा or सिधित्वा, -सिध्य; *Fut. pass.* सेद्धव्य, सेधनीय, सेध्य.

617. Root मन्†. *Inf.* मन्तुं 'to think,' 'to imagine.' Ātm. *Pres.* मन्ये. *Impf.* अमन्ये. *Pot.* मन्येय. *Impv.* मन्यै. *Perf.* मेने (375. a), मेनिषे, मेने; मेनिवहे, मेनाथे, मेनाते; मेनिमहे, मेनिध्वे, मेनिरे. *1st Fut.* मन्ताहे. *2d Fut.* मंस्ये. *Aor.* (424. b) अमंसि†, अमंस्थास्, अमंस्त; अमंस्वहि, अमंसाथां, अमंसातां; अमंस्महि, अमन्ध्वं, अमंसत. *Prec.* मंसीय. *Cond.* अमंस्ये. Pass., *Pres.* मन्ये; *Aor. 3d sing.* अमानि. Caus., *Pres.* मानयामि; *Aor.* अमीमनं. Des. मिमंसे or मीमांसे or मिमनिषे. Freq. मन्मन्ये, मन्मन्मि. Part., *Pres.* मन्यमान; *Past pass.* मत; *Past indecl.* मत्वा or मनित्वा, -मत्य; *Fut. pass.* मन्तव्य, मननीय, मान्य.

a. जन्, *Inf.* जनितुं 'to be born,' makes *Pres.* जाये; *Impf.* अजाये, &c.; *Pot.* जायेय; *Impv.* जायै. But these may be regarded as coming from Passive of *jan*, 3d conj. See 667.

618. Root तृप्. *Inf.* तर्प्तुं or त्रप्तुं or तर्पितुं 'to be satisfied.' Par. *Pres.*

---

* When सिध् is of the 1st c., it optionally inserts इ *i*: सेद्धास्मि or सेधितास्मि, सेत्स्यामि or सेधिष्यामि, असेधिषं or असैत्सं.

† The root मन् is rarely conjugated in the 8th c. Ātmane (see 684), when the aorist is अमनिषि, अमनिष्ठास् or अमथास्, अमनिष्ट or अमत, &c. See 424. b.

तृप्यामि. *Impf.* अतृप्यं. *Pot.* तृप्येयं. *Impo.* तृप्याणि. *Perf.* ततर्प, ततर्पिथ or तत्रप्थ or ततर्प्थ, ततर्प; ततृपिव or ततृप्व, ततृपथुस्, ततृपतुस्; ततृपिम or ततृप्म, ततृप, ततृपुस्. *1st Fut.* (390. *f*) तर्पितास्मि or तर्प्तास्मि or त्रप्तास्मि, &c. *2d Fut.* तर्प्स्यामि or त्रप्स्यामि or तर्पिष्यामि, &c. *Aor.* (420) अतार्प्सं, अतार्प्सीस्, अतार्प्सीत्; अतार्प्स्व, अतार्प्तं, अतार्प्तां; अतार्प्स्म, अतार्प्त, अतार्प्सुस्. Or अत्राप्सं, अत्राप्सीस्, अत्राप्सीत् (388. *c*), &c. Or अतर्पिषं, अतर्पीस्, अतर्पीत्, &c. Or अतृपं, अतृपस्, अतृपत्; अतृपाव, अतृपतं, अतृपतां; अतृपाम, अतृपत, अतृपन्. *Prec.* तृप्यासं. *Cond.* अतर्प्स्यं or अत्रप्स्यं or अतर्पिष्यं. Pass., *Pres.* तृप्ये; *Aor.* 3d *sing.* अतर्पि. Caus., *Pres.* तर्पयामि; *Aor.* अतीतृपं or अततर्पं. Des. तितृप्सामि or तित्रप्सामि or तितर्पिषामि. Freq. तरीतृप्ये, तरीतर्प्मि or तरीतृपीमि. Part., *Pres.* तृप्यत्; *Past pass.* तृप्त; *Past indecl.* तृप्त्वा, -तृप्य; *Fut. pass.* तर्पितव्य, तर्पणीय, तृप्य.

619. Root शम् (275). *Inf.* शमितुं 'to be appeased.' Par. *Pres.* शाम्यामि. *Impf.* अशाम्यं. *Pot.* शाम्येयं. *Impo.* शाम्यानि. *Perf.* शशाम (368), शेमिथ (375. *a*), शशाम; शेमिव, शेमथुस्, शेमतुस्; शेमिम, शेम, शेमुस्. *1st Fut.* शमितास्मि. *2d Fut.* शमिष्यामि. *Aor.* अशमं, अशमस्, अशमत्; अशमाव, अशमतं, अशमतां; अशमाम, अशमत, अशमन्. Or अशमिषं, अशमीस्, अशमीत्; अशमिष्व, &c. *Prec.* शम्यासं. *Cond.* अशमिष्यं. Pass., *Pres.* शम्ये. *Aor.* 3d *sing.* अशमि. Caus., *Pres.* शमयामि; *Aor.* अशीशमं, &c. Des. शिशमिषामि. Freq. शंशम्ये, शंशमि; 3d *sing.* शंशन्ति. Part., *Pres.* शाम्यत्; *Past pass.* शान्त; *Past indecl.* शान्त्वा or शमित्वा, -शम्य; *Fut. pass.* शमितव्य, शमनीय, शम्य.

620. Root नश्. *Inf.* नशितुं or नंष्टुं 'to perish.' Par. *Pres.* नश्यामि. *Impf.* अनश्यं. *Pot.* नश्येयं. *Impo.* नश्यानि. *Perf.* (375. *a*) ननाश or ननश, नेशिथ or ननंष्ठ (375. *a*), ननाश; नेशिव or नेश्व, नेशथुस्, नेशतुस्; नेशिम or नेश्म, नेश, नेशुस्. *1st Fut.* नशितास्मि or नंष्टास्मि (390. *k*). *2d Fut.* नशिष्यामि or नंक्ष्यामि. *Aor.* (437) अनशं, अनशस्, अनशत्; अनशाव, अनशतं, अनशतां; अनशाम, अनशत, अनशन्. Or अनेशं, &c. (437, 441). *Prec.* नश्यासं. *Cond.* अनशिष्यं &c. or अनंक्ष्यं. Pass., *Pres.* नश्ये; *Aor.* 3d *sing.* अनाशि. Caus., *Pres.* नाशयामि; *Aor.* अनीनशं. Des. निनशिषामि, निनंक्षामि. Freq. नानश्ये, नानंशिम; 3d *sing.* नानष्टि or नानंष्टि. Part., *Pres.* नश्यत्; *Past pass.* नष्ट; *Past indecl.* नष्ट्वा or नंष्ट्वा, -नश्य; *Fut. pass.* नशितव्य, नशनीय, नाश्य.

621. Root पुष्*. *Inf.* पोष्टुं 'to be nourished,' 'to grow fat.' Par. *Pres.* पुष्यामि. *Impf.* अपुष्यं. *Pot.* पुष्येयं. *Impo.* पुष्याणि. *Perf.* पुपोष, पुपोषिथ, पुपोष; पुपुषिव, पुपुषथुस्, पुपुषतुस्; पुपुषिम, पुपुष, पुपुषुस्. *1st Fut.* पोष्टास्मि. *2d Fut.* पोक्ष्यामि. *Aor.* (436) अपुषं, अपुषस्, अपुषत्; अपुषाव,

* This root is also conjugated in the 9th conj. See 698.

अपुषतं, अपुषतां; अपुषाम, अपुषत, अपुषन्. *Prec.* पुष्यासं. *Cond.* अपोक्ष्यं. Pass., *Pres.* पुष्ये; *Aor. 3d sing.* अपोषि. Caus., *Pres.* पोषयामि; *Aor.* अपूपुषं. Des. पुपोषिषामि or पुपुषिषामि or पुपुक्षामि. Freq. पोपुष्ये, पोपोष्मि. Part., *Pres.* पुष्यत्; *Past pass.* पुष्ट; *Past indecl.* पुष्ट्वा, -पुष्य; *Fut. pass.* पोष्टव्य, पोषणीय, पोष्य.

622. Root अस्. *Inf.* असितुं 'to throw.' Par. *Pres.* अस्यामि, &c. *Impf.* आस्यं. *Pot.* अस्येयं. *Impv.* अस्यानि. *Perf.* आस, आसिथ, आस; आसिव, आसथुस्, आसतुस्; आसिम, आस, आसुस्. *1st Fut.* असितास्मि. *2d Fut.* असिष्यामि. *Aor.* (441) आस्थं, आस्थस्, आस्थत्; आस्थाव, आस्थतं, आस्थतां; आस्थाम, आस्थत, आस्थन्. *Prec.* अस्यासं. *Cond.* आसिष्यं. Pass., *Pres.* अस्ये; *Aor. 3d sing.* आसि. Caus., *Pres.* आसयामि; *Aor.* आसिसं. Des. असिसिषामि. Part., *Pres.* अस्यत्; *Past pass.* अस्त; *Past indecl.* असित्वा or अस्त्वा, -अस्य; *Fut. pass.* असितव्य, असनीय, आस्य.

623. Root द्रुह्. *Inf.* द्रोग्धुं or द्रोहितुं 'to injure,' 'to bear malice.' Par. *Pres.* द्रुह्यामि. *Impf.* अद्रुह्यं. *Pot.* द्रुह्येयं. *Impv.* द्रुह्याणि. *Perf.* दुद्रोह, दुद्रोहिथ or दुद्रोग्ध or दुद्रोढ, दुद्रोह; दुद्रुहिव, दुद्रुहथुस्, दुद्रुहतुस्; दुद्रुहिम, दुद्रुह, दुद्रुहुस्. *1st Fut.* (415. m) द्रोग्धास्मि or द्रोढास्मि or द्रोहितास्मि, &c. *2d Fut.* ध्रोक्ष्यामि (306. a) or द्रोहिष्यामि. *Aor.* अद्रुहं, अद्रुहस्, अद्रुहत्; अद्रुहाव, अद्रुहतं, अद्रुहतां; अद्रुहाम, अद्रुहत, अद्रुहन्. *Prec.* द्रुह्यासं, &c. *Cond.* अध्रोक्ष्यं (306. a) or अद्रोहिष्यं. Pass., *Pres.* द्रुह्ये; *Aor. 3d sing.* अद्रोहि. Caus., *Pres.* द्रोहयामि; *Aor.* अदुद्रुहं. Des. दुद्रोहिषामि or दुद्रुहिषामि or दुध्रुक्षामि (306. a). Freq. दोद्रुह्ये, दोद्रोह्मि (3d *sing.* दोद्रोग्धि or दोद्रोढि 514. d). Part., *Pres.* द्रुह्यत्; *Past pass.* द्रुग्ध or द्रूढ; *Past indecl.* द्रुग्ध्वा or द्रुहित्वा or द्रोहित्वा, -द्रुह्य; *Fut. pass.* द्रोग्धव्य, द्रोहणीय, द्रोह्य.

624. Root नह्. *Inf.* नद्धुं 'to tie,' 'to bind,' 'to fasten.' Par. and Ātm. *Pres.* नह्यामि. Ātm. नह्ये. *Impf.* अनह्यं. Ātm. अनह्ये. *Pot.* नह्येयं. Ātm. नह्येय. *Impv.* नह्यानि. Ātm. नह्यै. *Perf.* ननाह or ननह, नेहिथ or ननद्ध, ननाह; नेहिव, नेहथुस्, नेहतुस्; नेहिम, नेह, नेहुस्. Ātm. नेहे, नेहिषे, नेहे; नेहिवहे, नेहाथे, नेहाते; नेहिमहे, नेहिध्वे, -ढ्वे, नेहिरे. *1st Fut.* नद्धास्मि. Ātm. नद्धाहे. *2d Fut.* (306. b) नत्स्यामि. Ātm. नत्स्ये. *Aor.* (426) अनात्सं, अनात्सीस्, अनात्सीत्; अनात्स्व, अनाद्धं, अनाद्धां; अनात्स्म, अनाद्ध, अनात्सुस्. Ātm. अनत्सि, अनद्धास्, अनद्ध; अनत्स्वहि, अनत्साथां, अनत्सातां; अनत्स्महि, अनद्ध्वं, अनत्सत. *Prec.* नह्यासं. Ātm. नत्सीय. *Cond.* अनत्स्यं. Ātm. अनत्स्ये. Pass., *Pres.* नह्ये; *Aor. 3d sing.* अनाहि. Caus. नाहयामि; *Aor.* अनीनहं. Des. निनत्सामि, -त्से. Freq. नानह्ये, नानह्मि (3d *sing.* नानद्धि). Part., *Pres.* नह्यत्; *Past pass.* नद्ध; *Past indecl.* नद्ध्वा, -नह्य; *Fut. pass.* नद्धव्य, नहनीय, नाह्य.

EXAMPLES OF PRIMITIVE VERBS OF THE SIXTH CONJUGATIONAL CLASS, EXPLAINED AT 278.

625. Root सृज् *sṛij.* Infin. स्रष्टुम् *srashṭum*, 'to create,' 'to let go.'

PARASMAI-PADA only.

Present tense, 'I create.'

सृजामि *sṛijámi*	सृजावस् *sṛijávas*	सृजामस् *sṛijámas*
सृजसि *sṛijasi*	सृजथस् *sṛijathas*	सृजथ *sṛijatha*
सृजति *sṛijati*	सृजतस् *sṛijatas*	सृजन्ति *sṛijanti*

Imperfect or *first preterite*, 'I was creating,' or 'I created.'

असृजम् *asṛijam*	असृजाव *asṛijáva*	असृजाम *asṛijáma*
असृजस् *asṛijas*	असृजतम् *asṛijatam*	असृजत *asṛijata*
असृजत् *asṛijat*	असृजताम् *asṛijatám*	असृजन् *asṛijan*

Potential, 'I may create.'

सृजेयम् *sṛijeyam*	सृजेव *sṛijeva*	सृजेम *sṛijema*
सृजेस् *sṛijes*	सृजेतम् *sṛijetam*	सृजेत *sṛijeta*
सृजेत् *sṛijet*	सृजेताम् *sṛijetám*	सृजेयुस् *sṛijeyus*

Imperative, 'Let me create.'

सृजानि *sṛijáni*	सृजाव *sṛijáva*	सृजाम *sṛijáma*
सृज *sṛija*	सृजतम् *sṛijatam*	सृजत *sṛijata*
सृजतु *sṛijatu*	सृजताम् *sṛijatám*	सृजन्तु *sṛijantu*

Perfect or *second preterite*, 'I created,' or 'I have created.'

ससर्ज *sasarja*	ससृजिव *sasṛijiva*	ससृजिम *sasṛijima*
ससर्जिथ *sasarjitha* or सस्रष्ठ *	ससृजथुस् *sasṛijathus*	ससृज *sasṛija*
ससर्ज *sasarja*	ससृजतुस् *sasṛijatus*	ससृजुस् *sasṛijus*

First future, 'I will create.'

स्रष्टास्मि *srashṭásmi* (388. e)	स्रष्टास्वस् *srashṭásvas*	स्रष्टास्मस् *srashṭásmas*
स्रष्टासि *srashṭási*	स्रष्टास्थस् *srashṭásthas*	स्रष्टास्थ *srashṭástha*
स्रष्टा *srashṭá*	स्रष्टारौ *srashṭárau*	स्रष्टारस् *srashṭáras*

Second future, 'I shall create.'

स्रक्ष्यामि *srakshyámi*	स्रक्ष्यावस् *srakshyávas*	स्रक्ष्यामस् *srakshyámas*
स्रक्ष्यसि *srakshyasi*	स्रक्ष्यथस् *srakshyathas*	स्रक्ष्यथ *srakshyatha*
स्रक्ष्यति *srakshyati*	स्रक्ष्यतस् *srakshyatas*	स्रक्ष्यन्ति *srakshyanti*

* As to *sasrashṭha*, see 370. f.

Impf. अरक्षं. *Pot.* रक्षेयं. *Impv.* रक्षाणि (58), रक्ष, &c. *Perf.* ररक्ष, ररक्षिथ, ररक्ष; ररक्षिव, ररक्षथुस्, ररक्षतुस्; ररक्षिम, ररक्ष, ररक्षुस्. *1st Fut.* रक्षितास्मि. *2d Fut.* रक्षिष्यामि. *Aor.* अरक्षिषं, अरक्षीस्, अरक्षीत्; अरक्षिष्व, अरक्षिष्टं, अरक्षिष्टां; अरक्षिष्म, अरक्षिष्ट, अरक्षिषुस्. *Prec.* रक्ष्यासं. *Cond.* अरक्षिष्यं. Pass., *Pres.* रक्ष्ये. Caus., *Pres.* रक्षयामि, &c.; *Aor.* अररक्षं. Des. रिरक्षिषामि, &c. Freq. रारक्ष्ये, &c., रारक्ष्मि. Part., *Pres.* रक्षत्; *Past pass.* रक्षित; *Past indecl.* रक्षित्वा, -रक्ष्य; *Fut. pass.* रक्षितव्य, रक्षणीय, रक्ष्य.

607. Root वस्. *Inf.* वस्तुं 'to dwell.' Par. *Pres.* वसामि. *Impf.* अवसं. *Pot.* वसेयं. *Impv.* वसानि, वस, &c. *Perf.* उवास (368), उवसिथ or उवस्थ, उवास; ऊषिव, ऊषथुस्, ऊषतुस्; ऊषिम, ऊष, ऊषुस्. *1st Fut.* वस्तास्मि. *2d Fut.* वत्स्यामि (304. *a*). *Aor.* अवात्सं (304. *a*, 426. *a*), अवात्सीस्, अवात्सीत्; अवात्स्व, अवात्तं, अवात्तां; अवात्स्म, अवात्त, अवात्सुस्. *Prec.* उष्यासं. *Cond.* अवत्स्यं (304. *a*). Pass., *Pres.* उष्ये (471); *Aor. 3d sing.* अवासि. Caus., *Pres.* वासयामि, -ये; *Aor.* अवीवसं. Des. विवत्सामि (304. *a*). Freq. वावस्ये, वावस्मि or वावसीमि. Part., *Pres.* वसत्; *Past pass.* उषित (with नि, उष्ट); *Past indecl.* उषित्वा, -उष्य (565); *Fut. pass.* वस्तव्य, वसनीय, वास्य.

608. Root अर्ह्. *Inf.* अर्हितुं 'to deserve.' Par. *Pres.* अर्हामि. *Impf.* आर्हं. *Pot.* अर्हेयं. *Impv.* अर्हाणि (58). *Perf.* (367. *b*) आनर्ह, आनर्हिथ, आनर्ह; आनर्हिव, आनर्हथुस्, आनर्हतुस्; आनर्हिम, आनर्ह, आनर्हुस्. *1st Fut.* अर्हितास्मि. *2d Fut.* अर्हिष्यामि. *Aor.* आर्हिषं, आर्हीस्, आर्हीत्; आर्हिष्व, आर्हिष्टं, आर्हिष्टां; आर्हिष्म, आर्हिष्ट, आर्हिषुस्. *Prec.* अर्ह्यासं. *Cond.* आर्हिष्यं. Pass. अर्ह्ये; *Aor. 3d sing.* आर्हि. Caus., *Pres.* अर्हयामि, -ये; *Aor.* आर्जिहं (494). Des. अर्जिहिषामि, &c. (500. *d*). Part., *Pres.* अर्हत्; *Past pass.* अर्हित; *Past indecl.* अर्हित्वा, -अर्ह्य; *Fut. pass.* अर्हितव्य, अर्हणीय, अर्ह्य.

609. Root गुह् (270. *b*). *Inf.* गूहितुं or गोढुं 'to hide.' Par. and Ātm. *Pres.* गूहामि. Ātm. गूहे. *Impf.* अगूहं. Ātm. अगूहे. *Pot.* गूहेयं. Ātm. गूहेय. *Impv.* गूहानि. Ātm. गूहै. *Perf.* जुगूह (384. *a*), जुगूहिथ or जुगोढ (305. *a*), जुगूह; जुगुहिव or जुगुह्व (371), जुगुहथुस्, जुगुहतुस्; जुगुहिम or जुगुह्म, जुगुह, जुगुहुस्. Ātm. जुगुहे, जुगुहिषे, जुगुहे, &c. *1st Fut.* (415. *m*) गूहितास्मि or गोढास्मि (305. *a*). Ātm. गूहिताहे or गोढाहे. *2d Fut.* गूहिष्यामि or घोक्ष्यामि. Ātm. गूहिष्ये or घोक्ष्ये. *Aor.* अगूहिषं, अगूहीस्, अगूहीत्; अगूहिष्व, अगूहिष्टं, अगूहिष्टां; अगूहिष्म, अगूहिष्ट, अगूहिषुस्. Or अघुक्षं (306. *a*), अघुक्षस्, अघुक्षत्; अघुक्षाव, अघुक्षतं, अघुक्षतां; अघुक्षाम, अघुक्षत, अघुक्षन्. Ātm. अगूहिषि, अगूहिष्ठास्, अगूहिष्ट, &c. Or अघुक्षि (439), अघुक्षथास् or अगूढास्, अघुक्षत or अगूढ; अघुक्षावहि or अगुह्वहि, अघुक्षाथां, अघुक्षातां; अघुक्षामहि, अघुक्षध्वं or अघूढ्वं, अघुक्षन्त. *Prec.* गुह्यासं.

Ātm. गूहिषीष्ट or घुक्षीष्ट (306. *a*). *Cond.* अगूहिष्यं or अघोक्ष्यं, अगूहिष्ये or अघोक्ष्ये. Pass., *Pres.* गुह्ये; *Aor.* 3*d sing.* अगूहि. Caus., *Pres.* गूहयामि; *Aor.* अजूगुहं. Des. जुघुक्षामि, -क्षे. Freq. जोगुह्ये, जोगोह्मि (3*d sing.* जोगोढि) or जोगुहीमि. Part., *Pres.* गूहत्; *Past pass.* गूढ (305. *a*); *Past indecl.* गूहित्वा or गूढ्वा or गुहित्वा, -गुह्य; *Fut. pass.* गूहितव्य or गोढव्य, गूहनीय, गुह्य or गोह्य.

610. Root दह्. *Inf.* दग्धुं 'to burn.' Par. *Pres.* दहामि. *Impf.* अदहं. *Pot.* दहेयं, &c. *Impv.* दहानि, दह, &c. *Perf.* ददाह, देहिथ (375. *a*) or ददग्ध (305), ददाह; देहिव, देहथुस्, देहतुस्; देहिम, देह, देहुस्. 1*st Fut.* दग्धास्मि. 2*d Fut.* धक्ष्यामि (306. *a*). *Aor.* अधाक्षं (422), अधाक्षीस्, अधाक्षीत्; अधाक्ष्व, अदाग्धं, अदाग्धां; अधाक्ष्म, अदाग्ध, अधाक्षुस्. *Prec.* दह्यासं. *Cond.* अधक्ष्यं. Pass., *Pres.* दह्ये; *Aor.* 3*d sing.* अदाहि. Caus., *Pres.* दाहयामि, -ये; *Aor.* अदीदहं. Des. दिधक्षामि (502. *a*). Freq. दन्दह्ये, दन्दह्मि or दन्दहीमि; 3*d sing.* दन्दग्धि or दन्दहीति. Part., *Pres.* दहत्; *Past pass.* दग्ध; *Past indecl.* दग्ध्वा, -दह्य; *Fut. pass.* दग्धव्य, दहनीय, दाह्य.

611. Root वह्. *Inf.* वोढुं 'to carry.' Par. and Ātm. *Pres.* वहामि. Ātm. वहे. *Impf.* अवहं. Ātm. अवहे. *Pot.* वहेयं. Ātm. वहेय. *Impv.* वहानि, वह, &c. Ātm. वहै. *Perf.* (375. *c*) उवाह (368), उवहिथ or उवोढ, उवाह; ऊहिव, ऊहथुस्, ऊहतुस्; ऊहिम, ऊह, ऊहुस्. Ātm. ऊहे, ऊहिषे, ऊहे; ऊहिवहे, ऊहाथे, ऊहाते; ऊहिमहे, ऊहिध्वे or ऊहिढ्वे, ऊहिरे. 1*st Fut.* वोढास्मि. Ātm. वोढाहे. 2*d Fut.* वक्ष्यामि. Ātm. वक्ष्ये. *Aor.* (425) अवाक्षं, अवाक्षीस्, अवाक्षीत्; अवाक्ष्व, अवोढं, अवोढां; अवाक्ष्म, अवोढ, अवाक्षुस्. Ātm. अवक्षि, अवोढास्, अवोढ; अवक्ष्वहि, अवक्षाथां, अवक्षातां; अवक्ष्महि, अवोढ्वं, अवक्षत. *Prec.* उह्यासं. Ātm. वक्षीय. *Cond.* अवक्ष्यं. Ātm. अवक्ष्ये. Pass., *Pres.* (471) उह्ये; *Impf.* औह्ये (260. *a*); *Aor.* 3*d sing.* अवाहि. Caus., *Pres.* वाहयामि, -ये; *Aor.* अवीवहं. Des. विवक्षामि, -क्षे. Freq. वावह्ये, वावह्मि; 3*d sing.* वावोढि (compare 425). Part., *Pres.* वहत्; Ātm. वहमान; *Pass.* उह्यमान; *Past pass.* ऊढ; *Past indecl.* ऊढ्वा, -उह्य (565); *Fut. pass.* वोढव्य, वहनीय, वाह्य.

a. सह्, *Inf.* सोढुं 'to bear,' is Ātm. only, and follows *vah* in making सोढाहे &c. in 1*st Fut.*: but in this tense optionally, and in the other non-conjugational tenses necessarily inserts *i*; thus, 1*st Fut.* सहिताहे; 2*d Fut.* सहिष्ये; *Aor.* असहिषि; *Prec.* सहिषीय; *Cond.* असहिष्ये. The *Perf.* is सेहे (375. *a*), सेहिषे, सेहे; सेहिवहे, &c. The other tenses are like the Ātm. of *vah*; thus, *Pres.* सहे, &c.

Impf. अरक्षं. *Pot.* रक्षेयं. *Impv.* रक्षाणि (58), रक्ष, &c. *Perf.* ररक्ष, ररक्षिथ, ररक्ष; ररक्षिव, ररक्षथुस्, ररक्षतुस्; ररक्षिम, ररक्ष, ररक्षुस्. *1st Fut.* रक्षितास्मि. *2d Fut.* रक्षिष्यामि. *Aor.* अरक्षिषं, अरक्षीस्, अरक्षीत्; अरक्षिष्व, अरक्षिष्टं, अरक्षिष्टां; अरक्षिष्म, अरक्षिष्ट, अरक्षिषुस्. *Prec.* रक्ष्यासं. *Cond.* अरक्षिष्यं. Pass., *Pres.* रक्ष्ये. Caus., *Pres.* रक्षयामि, &c.; *Aor.* अररक्षं. Des. रिरक्षिषामि, &c. Freq. रारक्ष्ये, &c., रारक्ष्मि. Part., *Pres.* रक्षत्; *Past pass.* रक्षित; *Past indecl.* रक्षित्वा, -रक्ष्य; *Fut. pass.* रक्षितव्य, रक्षणीय, रक्ष्य.

607. Root वस्. *Inf.* वस्तुं 'to dwell.' Par. *Pres.* वसामि. *Impf.* अवसं. *Pot.* वसेयं. *Impv.* वसानि, वस, &c. *Perf.* उवास (368), उवसिथ or उवस्थ, उवास; ऊषिव, ऊषथुस्, ऊषतुस्; ऊषिम, ऊष, ऊषुस्. *1st Fut.* वस्तास्मि. *2d Fut.* वत्स्यामि (304. *a*). *Aor.* अवात्सं (304. *a*, 426. *a*), अवात्सीस्, अवात्सीत्; अवात्स्व, अवात्तं, अवात्तां; अवात्स्म, अवात्त, अवात्सुस्. *Prec.* उष्यासं. *Cond.* अवत्स्यं (304. *a*). Pass., *Pres.* उष्ये (471); *Aor. 3d sing.* अवासि. Caus., *Pres.* वासयामि, -ये; *Aor.* अवीवसं. Des. विवत्सामि (304. *a*). Freq. वावस्ये, वावस्मि or वावसीमि. Part., *Pres.* वसत्; *Past pass.* उषित (with नि, उष्ट); *Past indecl.* उषित्वा, -उष्य (565); *Fut. pass.* वस्तव्य, वसनीय, वास्य.

608. Root अर्ह्. *Inf.* अर्हितुं 'to deserve.' Par. *Pres.* अर्हामि. *Impf.* आर्हं. *Pot.* अर्हेयं. *Impv.* अर्हाणि (58). *Perf.* (367. *b*) आनर्ह, आनर्हिथ, आनर्ह; आनर्हिव, आनर्हथुस्, आनर्हतुस्; आनर्हिम, आनर्ह, आनर्हुस्. *1st Fut.* अर्हितास्मि. *2d Fut.* अर्हिष्यामि. *Aor.* आर्हिषं, आर्हीस्, आर्हीत्; आर्हिष्व, आर्हिष्टं, आर्हिष्टां; आर्हिष्म, आर्हिष्ट, आर्हिषुस्. *Prec.* अर्ह्यासं. *Cond.* आर्हिष्यं. Pass. अर्ह्ये; *Aor. 3d sing.* आर्हि. Caus., *Pres.* अर्हयामि, -ये; *Aor.* आर्जिहं (494). Des. अर्जिहिषामि, &c. (500. *d*). Part., *Pres.* अर्हत्; *Past pass.* अर्हित; *Past indecl.* अर्हित्वा, -अर्ह्य; *Fut. pass.* अर्हितव्य, अर्हणीय, अर्ह्य.

609. Root गुह् (270. *b*). *Inf.* गूहितुं or गोढुं 'to hide.' Par. and Ātm. *Pres.* गूहामि. Ātm. गूहे. *Impf.* अगूहं. Ātm. अगूहे. *Pot.* गूहेयं. Ātm. गूहेय. *Impv.* गूहानि. Ātm. गूहै. *Perf.* जुगूह (384. *a*), जुगूहिथ or जुगोढ (305. *a*), जुगूह; जुगुहिव or जुगुह्व (371), जुगुहथुस्, जुगुहतुस्; जुगुहिम or जुगुह्म, जुगुह, जुगुहुस्. Ātm. जुगुहे, जुगुहिषे, जुगुहे, &c. *1st Fut.* (415. *m*) गूहितास्मि or गोढास्मि (305. *a*). Ātm. गूहिताहे or गोढाहे. *2d Fut.* गूहिष्यामि or घोक्ष्यामि. Ātm. गूहिष्ये or घोक्ष्ये. *Aor.* अगूहिषं, अगूहीस्, अगूहीत्; अगूहिष्व, अगूहिष्टं, अगूहिष्टां; अगूहिष्म, अगूहिष्ट, अगूहिषुस्. Or अघुक्षं (306. *a*), अघुक्षस्, अघुक्षत्; अघुक्षाव, अघुक्षतं, अघुक्षतां; अघुक्षाम, अघुक्षत, अघुक्षन्. Ātm. अगूहिषि, अगूहिष्ठास्, अगूहिष्ट, &c. Or अघुक्षि (439), अघुक्षथास् or अगूढास्, अघुक्षत or अगूढ; अघुक्षावहि or अगुह्वहि, अघुक्षाथां, अघुक्षातां; अघुक्षामहि, अघुक्षध्वं or अघूढ्वं, अघुक्षन्त. *Prec.* गुह्यासं.

Ātm. गुहिषीय or घुक्षीय (306. a). *Cond.* अगूहिष्यं or अघोक्ष्यं, अगूहिष्ये or अघोक्ष्ये. Pass., *Pres.* गुह्ये; *Aor. 3d sing.* अगूहि. Caus., *Pres.* गूहयामि; *Aor.* अजूगुहं. Des. जुघुक्षामि, -क्षे. Freq. जोगुह्ये, जोगोह्मि (*3d sing.* जोगोढि) or जोगुहीमि. Part., *Pres.* गूहत्; *Past pass.* गूढ (305. a); *Past indecl.* गूहित्वा or गूढ्वा or गुहित्वा, -गुह्य; *Fut. pass.* गूहितव्य or गोढव्य, गूहनीय, गुह्य or गोह्य.

610. Root दह्. *Inf.* दग्धुं 'to burn.' Par. *Pres.* दहामि. *Impf.* अदहं. *Pot.* दहेयं, &c. *Impv.* दहानि, दह, &c. *Perf.* ददाह, देहिथ (375. a) or ददग्ध (305), ददाह; देहिव, देहथुस्, देहतुस्; देहिम, देह, देहुस्. *1st Fut.* दग्धास्मि. *2d Fut.* धक्ष्यामि (306. a). *Aor.* अधाक्षं (422), अधाक्षीस्, अधाक्षीत्; अधाक्ष्व, अदाग्धं, अदाग्धां; अधाक्ष्म, अदाग्ध, अधाक्षुस्. *Prec.* दह्यासं. *Cond.* अधक्ष्यं. Pass., *Pres.* दह्ये; *Aor. 3d sing.* अदाहि. Caus., *Pres.* दाहयामि, -ये; *Aor.* अदीदहं. Des. दिधक्षामि (502. a). Freq. दन्दह्ये, दन्दह्मि or दन्दहीमि; *3d sing.* दन्दग्धि or दन्दहीति. Part., *Pres.* दहत्; *Past pass.* दग्ध; *Past indecl.* दग्ध्वा, -दह्य; *Fut. pass.* दग्धव्य, दहनीय, दाह्य.

611. Root वह्. *Inf.* वोढुं 'to carry.' Par. and Ātm. *Pres.* वहामि. Ātm. वहे. *Impf.* अवहं. Ātm. अवहे. *Pot.* वहेयं. Ātm. वहेय. *Impv.* वहानि, वह, &c. Ātm. वहै. *Perf.* (375. c) उवाह (368), उवहिथ or उवोढ, उवाह; ऊहिव, ऊहथुस्, ऊहतुस्; ऊहिम, ऊह, ऊहुस्. Ātm. ऊहे, ऊहिषे, ऊहे; ऊहिवहे, ऊहाथे, ऊहाते; ऊहिमहे, ऊहिध्वे or ऊहिढ्वे, ऊहिरे. *1st Fut.* वोढास्मि. Ātm. वोढाहे. *2d Fut.* वक्ष्यामि. Ātm. वक्ष्ये. *Aor.* (425) अवाक्षं, अवाक्षीस्, अवाक्षीत्; अवाक्ष्व, अवोढं, अवोढां; अवाक्ष्म, अवोढ, अवाक्षुस्. Ātm. अवक्षि, अवोढास्, अवोढ; अवक्ष्वहि, अवक्षाथां, अवक्षातां; अवक्ष्महि, अवोढ्वं, अवक्षत. *Prec.* उह्यासं. Ātm. वक्षीय. *Cond.* अवक्ष्यं. Ātm. अवक्ष्ये. Pass., *Pres.* (471) उह्ये; *Impf.* औह्ये (260. a); *Aor. 3d sing.* अवाहि. Caus., *Pres.* वाहयामि, -ये; *Aor.* अवीवहं. Des. विवक्षामि, -क्षे. Freq. वावह्ये, वावह्मि; *3d sing.* वावोढि (compare 425). Part., *Pres.* वहत्; Ātm. वहमान; *Pass.* उह्यमान; *Past pass.* ऊढ; *Past indecl.* ऊढ्वा, -उह्य (565); *Fut. pass.* वोढव्य, वहनीय, वाह्य.

a. सह्, *Inf.* सोढुं 'to bear,' is Ātm. only, and follows *vah* in making सोढाहे &c. in *1st Fut.*: but in this tense optionally, and in the other non-conjugational tenses necessarily inserts *i*; thus, *1st Fut.* सहिताहे; *2d Fut.* सहिष्ये; *Aor.* असहिषि; *Prec.* सहिषीय; *Cond.* असहिष्ये. The *Perf.* is सेहे (375. a), सेहिषे, सेहे; सेहिवहे, &c. The other tenses are like the Ātm. of *vah*; thus, *Pres.* सहे, &c.

EXAMPLES OF PRIMITIVE VERBS OF THE FOURTH CONJUGATIONAL CLASS, EXPLAINED AT 272.

612. Root मुह् *muh.* Infin. मोहितुम् *mohitum*, 'to be troubled.'

PARASMAI-PADA. *Present tense*, 'I am troubled.'

मुह्यामि *muhyāmi*	मुह्यावस् *muhyāvas*	मुह्यामस् *muhyāmas*
मुह्यसि *muhyasi*	मुह्यथस् *muhyathas*	मुह्यथ *muhyatha*
मुह्यति *muhyati*	मुह्यतस् *muhyatas*	मुह्यन्ति *muhyanti*

Imperfect or *first preterite*, 'I was troubled.'

अमुह्यम् *amuhyam*	अमुह्याव *amuhyāva*	अमुह्याम *amuhyāma*
अमुह्यस् *amuhyas*	अमुह्यतम् *amuhyatam*	अमुह्यत *amuhyata*
अमुह्यत् *amuhyat*	अमुह्यताम् *amuhyatām*	अमुह्यन् *amuhyan*

Potential, 'I may be troubled.'

मुह्येयम् *muhyeyam*	मुह्येव *muhyeva*	मुह्येम *muhyema*
मुह्येस् *muhyes*	मुह्येतम् *muhyetam*	मुह्येत *muhyeta*
मुह्येत् *muhyet*	मुह्येताम् *muhyetām*	मुह्येयुस् *muhyeyus*

Imperative, 'Let me be troubled.'

मुह्यानि *muhyāni*	मुह्याव *muhyāva*	मुह्याम *muhyāma*
मुह्य *muhya*	मुह्यतम् *muhyatam*	मुह्यत *muhyata*
मुह्यतु *muhyatu*	मुह्यताम् *muhyatām*	मुह्यन्तु *muhyantu*

Perfect or *second preterite*, 'I became troubled.'

मुमोह *mumoha*	मुमुहिव *mumuhiva*	मुमुहिम *mumuhima*
मुमोहिथ *mumohitha* *	मुमुहथुस् *mumuhathus*	मुमुह *mumuha*
मुमोह *mumoha*	मुमुहतुस् *mumuhatus*	मुमुहुस् *mumuhus*

First future †, 'I will be troubled.'

मोहितास्मि *mohitāsmi*	मोहितास्वस् *mohitāsvas*	मोहितास्मस् *mohitāsmas*
मोहितासि *mohitāsi*	मोहितास्थस् *mohitāsthas*	मोहितास्थ *mohitāstha*
मोहिता *mohitā*	मोहितारौ *mohitārau*	मोहितारस् *mohitāras*

Second future †, 'I shall be troubled.'

मोहिष्यामि *mohishyāmi*	मोहिष्यावस् *mohishyāvas*	मोहिष्यामस् *mohishyāmas*
मोहिष्यसि *mohishyasi*	मोहिष्यथस् *mohishyathas*	मोहिष्यथ *mohishyatha*
मोहिष्यति *mohishyati*	मोहिष्यतस् *mohishyatas*	मोहिष्यन्ति *mohishyanti*

* Or मुमोढ (305. a) or मुमोग्ध (306).

† The 1st and 2d futures may optionally reject the inserted *i*; see under 412.

Aorist or third preterite (435), 'I became troubled.'

अमुहम् *amuham*	अमुहाव *amuhâva*	अमुहाम *amuhâma*
अमुहस् *amuhas*	अमुहतम् *amuhatam*	अमुहत *amuhata*
अमुहत् *amuhat*	अमुहताम् *amuhatâm*	अमुहन् *amuhan*

Precative or benedictive, 'May I be troubled.'

मुह्यासम् *muhyâsam*	मुह्यास्व *muhyâsva*	मुह्यास्म *muhyâsma*
मुह्यास् *muhyâs*	मुह्यास्तम् *muhyâstam*	मुह्यास्त *muhyâsta*
मुह्यात् *muhyât*	मुह्यास्ताम् *muhyâstâm*	मुह्यासुस् *muhyâsus*

Conditional, 'I should be troubled.'

अमोहिष्यम् *amohishyam*	अमोहिष्याव *amohishyâva*	अमोहिष्याम *amohishyâma*
अमोहिष्यस् *amohishyas*	अमोहिष्यतम् *amohishyatam*	अमोहिष्यत *amohishyata*
अमोहिष्यत् *amohishyat*	अमोहिष्यताम् *amohishyatâm*	अमोहिष्यन् *amohishyan*

Pass., *Pres.* मुह्ये; *Aor. 3d sing.* अमोहि. Caus., *Pres.* मोहयामि; *Aor.* अमूमुहं. Des. मुमोहिषामि or मुमुहिषामि or मुमुक्षामि. Freq. मोमुह्ये, मोमोह्मि; *3d sing.* मोमोढि or मोमोग्धि (305). Part., *Pres.* मुह्यत्; *Past pass.* मूढ (305) or मुग्ध; *Past indecl.* मोहित्वा or मुहित्वा or मुग्ध्वा or मूढ्वा, -मुह्य; *Fut. pass.* मोहितव्य or मोग्धव्य, मोहनीय, मोह्य.

EXAMPLES OF OTHER VERBS OF THE FOURTH CONJUGATIONAL CLASS IN THE ORDER OF THEIR FINAL LETTERS.

613. Root सो (276. a). *Inf.* सातुं 'to destroy' (with prepositions *vi* and *ava*, 'to determine,' 'to strive'). Par. *Pres.* स्यामि. *Impf.* अस्यं. *Pot.* स्येयं. *Impv.* स्यानि. *Perf.* (373. d) ससौ, ससिथ or ससाथ, ससौ; ससिव, ससथुस्, ससतुस्; ससिम, सस, ससुस्. *1st Fut.* सातास्मि. *2d Fut.* सास्यामि. *Aor.* (438. c) असां, असास्, असात्; असाव, असातं, असातां; असाम, असात, असुस्. Or असासिषं (433), असासीस्, असासीत्; असासिष्व, असासिष्टं, असासिष्टां; असासिष्म, असासिष्ट, असासिषुस्. *Prec.* सेयासं. *Cond.* असास्यं. Pass., *Pres.* सीये; *Aor. 3d sing.* असायि. Caus. साययामि; *Aor.* असीषयं. Des. सिषासामि. Freq. सेषीये, सासेमि, सासामि. Part., *Pres.* स्यत्; *Past pass.* सित; *Past indecl.* सित्वा, -साय; *Fut. pass.* सातव्य, सानीय, सेय.

614. Root बुध्. *Inf.* बोद्धुं 'to know'*. Âtm. *Pres.* बुध्ये. *Impf.* अबुध्ये. *Pot.* बुध्येय. *Impv.* बुध्यै. *Perf.* बुबुधे; see the tables at 583. *1st Fut.* बोद्धाहे. *2d Fut.* भोत्स्ये (299. a). *Aor.* (420, 299. a) अभुत्सि, अबुद्धास्, अबुद्ध or अबोधि (424. a); अभुत्स्वहि, अभुत्साथां, अभुत्सातां; अभुत्स्महि,

* This verb is also of the 1st conjugation. See the tables at 583.

अयुग्ध्वं, अयुक्षत. *Prec.* युक्षीय. *Cond.* अयोक्ष्ये. For the other forms, see युज् at 583.

615. Root व्यध् (277). *Inf.* व्यद्धुं 'to pierce.' Par. *Pres.* विध्यामि. *Impf.* अविध्यं. *Pot.* विध्येयं. *Impv.* विध्यानि. *Perf.* (383) विव्याध, विव्यधिथ or विव्यद्ध, विव्याध; विविधिव, विविधथुस्, विविधतुस्; विविधिम, विविध, विविधुस्. *1st Fut.* व्यद्धास्मि (298). *2d Fut.* व्यत्स्यामि (299). *Aor.* (420) अव्यात्सं, अव्यात्सीस्, अव्यात्सीत्; अव्यात्स्व, अव्यात्तं (419), अव्यात्तां; अव्यात्स्म, अव्यात्त, अव्यात्सुस्. *Prec.* विध्यासं. *Cond.* अव्यत्स्यं. Pass., *Pres.* विध्ये; *Aor. 3d sing.* अव्याधि. Caus. व्याधयामि; *Aor.* अविव्यधं. Des. विव्यत्सामि. Freq. वेविध्ये, वाव्यध्मि. Part., *Pres.* विध्यत्; *Past pass.* विद्ध; *Past indecl.* विद्ध्वा, -विध्य; *Fut. pass.* व्यद्धव्य, व्यधनीय, वेध्य or व्याध्य.

616. Root सिध् (273). *Inf.* सेद्धुं 'to succeed.' Par. *Pres.* सिध्यामि. *Impf.* असिध्यं. *Pot.* सिध्येयं. *Impv.* सिध्यानि. *Perf.* सिषेध, सिषेधिथ or सिषेद्ध, सिषेध; सिषिधिव, सिषिधथुस्, सिषिधतुस्; सिषिधिम, सिषिध, सिषिधुस्. *1st Fut.* सेद्धास्मि (298)*. *2d Fut.* सेत्स्यामि (299)*. *Aor.* असिधं*, असिधस्, असिधत्; असिधाव, असिधतं, असिधतां; असिधाम, असिधत, असिधन्. *Prec.* सिध्यासं. *Cond.* असेत्स्यं. Pass. सिध्ये; *Aor. 3d sing.* असेधि. Caus., *Pres.* सेधयामि or साधयामि; *Aor.* असीषिधं. Des. सिषित्सामि. Freq. सेषिध्ये, सेषेध्मि. Part., *Pres.* सिध्यत्; *Past pass.* सिद्ध; *Past indecl.* सिद्ध्वा or सेधित्वा or सिधित्वा, -सिध्य; *Fut. pass.* सेद्धव्य, सेधनीय, सेध्य.

617. Root मन्†. *Inf.* मन्तुं 'to think,' 'to imagine.' Ātm. *Pres.* मन्ये. *Impf.* अमन्ये. *Pot.* मन्येय. *Impv.* मन्यै. *Perf.* मेने (375. *a*), मेनिषे, मेने; मेनिवहे, मेनाथे, मेनाते; मेनिमहे, मेनिध्वे, मेनिरे. *1st Fut.* मन्ताहे. *2d Fut.* मंस्ये. *Aor.* (424. *b*) अमंसि†, अमंस्थास्, अमंस्त; अमंस्वहि, अमंसाथां, अमंसातां; अमंस्महि, अमन्ध्वं, अमंसत. *Prec.* मंसीय. *Cond.* अमंस्ये. Pass., *Pres.* मन्ये; *Aor. 3d sing.* अमानि. Caus., *Pres.* मानयामि; *Aor.* अमीमनं. Des. मिमंसे or मीमांसे or मिमनिषे. Freq. मन्मन्ये, मन्मन्मि. Part., *Pres.* मन्यमान; *Past pass.* मत; *Past indecl.* मत्वा or मनित्वा, -मत्य; *Fut. pass.* मन्तव्य, मननीय, मान्य.

a. जन्, *Inf.* जनितुं 'to be born,' makes *Pres.* जाये; *Impf.* अजाये, &c.; *Pot.* जायेय; *Impv.* जायै. But these may be regarded as coming from Passive of *jan*, 3d conj. See 667.

618. Root तृप्. *Inf.* तर्प्तुं or त्रप्तुं or तर्पितुं 'to be satisfied.' Par. *Pres.*

---

* When सिध् is of the 1st c., it optionally inserts इ *i*; सेद्धास्मि or सेधितास्मि, सेत्स्यामि or सेधिष्यामि, असेधिषं or असैत्सं.

† The root मन् is rarely conjugated in the 8th c. Ātmane (see 684), when the aorist is अमनिषि, अमनिष्ठास् or अमथास्, अमनिष्ट or अमत, &c. See 424. *b*.

तृप्यामि. *Impf.* अतृप्यं. *Pot.* तृप्येयं. *Impv.* तृप्याणि. *Perf.* ततर्प, ततर्पिथ or तत्रप्थ or ततर्प्थ, ततर्प; ततृपिव or ततृप्व, ततृपथुस्, ततृपतुस्; ततृपिम or ततृप्म, ततृप, ततृपुस्. *1st Fut.* (390. *f*) तर्पितास्मि or त्रप्तास्मि or तर्प्तास्मि, &c. *2d Fut.* तर्प्स्यामि or त्रप्स्यामि or तर्पिष्यामि, &c. *Aor.* (420) अताप्सं, अताप्सीस्, अताप्सीत्; अताप्स्व, अताप्तं, अताप्तां; अताप्स्म, अताप्त, अताप्सुस्. Or अत्राप्सं, अत्राप्सीस्, अत्राप्सीत् (388. *c*), &c. Or अतर्पिषं, अतर्पीस्, अतर्पीत्, &c. Or अतृपं, अतृपस्, अतृपत्; अतृपाव, अतृपतं, अतृपतां; अतृपाम, अतृपत, अतृपन्. *Prec.* तृप्यासं. *Cond.* अतर्प्स्यं or अत्रप्स्यं or अतर्पिष्यं. Pass., *Pres.* तृप्ये; *Aor.* 3d *sing.* अतर्पि. Caus., *Pres.* तर्पयामि; *Aor.* अतीतृपं or अततर्पं. Des. तितृप्सामि or तित्रप्सामि or तितर्पिषामि. Freq. तरीतृप्ये, तरीतर्प्मि or तरीतर्पीमि. Part., *Pres.* तृप्यत्; *Past pass.* तृप्त; *Past indecl.* तृप्त्वा, -तृप्य; *Fut. pass.* तर्पितव्य, तर्पणीय, तृप्य.

619. Root शम् (275). *Inf.* शमितुं 'to be appeased.' Par. *Pres.* शाम्यामि. *Impf.* अशाम्यं. *Pot.* शाम्येयं. *Impv.* शाम्यानि. *Perf.* शशाम (368), शेमिथ (375. *a*), शशाम; शेमिव, शेमथुस्, शेमतुस्; शेमिम, शेम, शेमुस्. *1st Fut.* शमितास्मि. *2d Fut.* शमिष्यामि. *Aor.* अशमं, अशमस्, अशमत्; अशमाव, अशमतं, अशमतां; अशमाम, अशमत, अशमन्. Or अशमिषं, अशमीस्, अशमीत्; अशमिष्व, &c. *Prec.* शम्यासं. *Cond.* अशमिष्यं. Pass., *Pres.* शम्ये. *Aor.* 3d *sing.* अशमि. Caus., *Pres.* शमयामि; *Aor.* अशीशमं, &c. Des. शिशमिषामि. Freq. शंशम्ये, शंशमि; 3d *sing.* शंशन्ति. Part., *Pres.* शाम्यत्; *Past pass.* शान्त; *Past indecl.* शान्त्वा or शमित्वा, -शम्य; *Fut. pass.* शमितव्य, शमनीय, शम्य.

620. Root नश्. *Inf.* नशितुं or नंष्टुं 'to perish.' Par. *Pres.* नश्यामि. *Impf.* अनश्यं. *Pot.* नश्येयं. *Impv.* नश्यानि. *Perf.* (375. *a*) ननाश or ननश, नेशिथ or ननंष्ठ (375. *a*), ननाश; नेशिव or नेश्व, नेशथुस्, नेशतुस्; नेशिम or नेश्म, नेश, नेशुस्. *1st Fut.* नशितास्मि or नंष्टास्मि (390. *k*). *2d Fut.* नशिष्यामि or नंक्ष्यामि. *Aor.* (437) अनशं, अनशस्, अनशत्; अनशाव, अनशतं, अनशतां; अनशाम, अनशत, अनशन्. Or अनेशं, &c. (437, 441). *Prec.* नश्यासं. *Cond.* अनशिष्यं &c. or अनंक्ष्यं. Pass., *Pres.* नश्ये; *Aor.* 3d *sing.* अनाशि. Caus., *Pres.* नाशयामि; *Aor.* अनीनशं. Des. निनशिषामि, निनंक्षामि. Freq. नानश्ये, नानश्मि; 3d *sing.* नानष्टि or नानंष्टि. Part., *Pres.* नश्यत्; *Past pass.* नष्ट; *Past indecl.* नष्ट्वा or नंष्ट्वा, -नश्य; *Fut. pass.* नशितव्य, नशनीय, नाश्य.

621. Root पुष्*. *Inf.* पोष्टुं 'to be nourished,' 'to grow fat.' Par. *Pres.* पुष्यामि. *Impf.* अपुष्यं. *Pot.* पुष्येयं. *Impv.* पुष्याणि. *Perf.* पुपोष, पुपोषिथ, पुपोष; पुपुषिव, पुपुषथुस्, पुपुषतुस्; पुपुषिम, पुपुष, पुपुषुस्. *1st Fut.* पोष्टास्मि. *2d Fut.* पोक्ष्यामि. *Aor.* (436) अपुषं, अपुषस्, अपुषत्; अपुषाव,

---

* This root is also conjugated in the 9th conj. See 698.

अपुषतं, अपुषतां; अपुषाम, अपुषत, अपुषन्. *Prec.* पुष्यासं. *Cond.* अपोक्ष्यं. Pass., *Pres.* पुष्ये; *Aor. 3d sing.* अपोषि. Caus., *Pres.* पोषयामि; *Aor.* अपूपुषं. Des. पुपोषिषामि or पुपुषिषामि or पुपुक्षामि. Freq. पोपुष्ये, पोपोष्मि. Part., *Pres.* पुष्यत्; *Past pass.* पुष्ट; *Past indecl.* पुष्ट्वा, -पुष्य; *Fut. pass.* पोष्टव्य, पोषणीय, पोष्य.

622. Root अस्. *Inf.* असितुं 'to throw.' Par. *Pres.* अस्यामि, &c. *Impf.* आस्यं. *Pot.* अस्येयं. *Impv.* अस्यानि. *Perf.* आस, आसिथ, आस; आसिव, आसथुस्, आसतुस्; आसिम, आस, आसुस्. *1st Fut.* असितास्मि. *2d Fut.* असिष्यामि. *Aor.* (441) आस्थं, आस्थस्, आस्थत्; आस्थाव, आस्थतं, आस्थतां; आस्थाम, आस्थत, आस्थन्. *Prec.* अस्यासं. *Cond.* आसिष्यं. Pass., *Pres.* अस्ये; *Aor. 3d sing.* आसि. Caus., *Pres.* आसयामि; *Aor.* आसिसं. Des. असिसिषामि. Part., *Pres.* अस्यत्; *Past pass.* अस्त; *Past indecl.* असित्वा or अस्त्वा, -अस्य; *Fut. pass.* असितव्य, असनीय, आस्य.

623. Root द्रुह्. *Inf.* द्रोग्धुं or द्रोहितुं 'to injure,' 'to bear malice.' Par. *Pres.* द्रुह्यामि. *Impf.* अद्रुह्यं. *Pot.* द्रुह्येयं. *Impv.* द्रुह्याणि. *Perf.* दुद्रोह, दुद्रोहिथ or दुद्रोग्ध or दुद्रोढ, दुद्रोह; दुद्रुहिव, दुद्रुहथुस्, दुद्रुहतुस्; दुद्रुहिम, दुद्रुह, दुद्रुहुस्. *1st Fut.* (415. m) द्रोग्धास्मि or द्रोढास्मि or द्रोहितास्मि, &c. *2d Fut.* ध्रोक्ष्यामि (306. a) or द्रोहिष्यामि. *Aor.* अद्रुहं, अद्रुहस्, अद्रुहत्; अद्रुहाव, अद्रुहतं, अद्रुहतां; अद्रुहाम, अद्रुहत, अद्रुहन्. *Prec.* द्रुह्यासं, &c. *Cond.* अध्रोक्ष्यं (306. a) or अद्रोहिष्यं. Pass., *Pres.* द्रुह्ये; *Aor. 3d sing.* अद्रोहि. Caus., *Pres.* द्रोहयामि; *Aor.* अदुद्रुहं. Des. दुद्रोहिषामि or दुद्रुहिषामि or दुध्रुक्षामि (306. a). Freq. दोद्रुह्ये, दोद्रोह्मि (*3d sing.* दोद्रोग्धि or दोद्रोढि 514. d). Part., *Pres.* द्रुह्यत्; *Past pass.* द्रुग्ध or द्रूढ; *Past indecl.* द्रुग्ध्वा or द्रुहित्वा or द्रोहित्वा, -द्रुह्य; *Fut. pass.* द्रोग्धव्य, द्रोहणीय, द्रोह्य.

624. Root नह्. *Inf.* नद्धुं 'to tie,' 'to bind,' 'to fasten.' Par. and Ātm. *Pres.* नह्यामि. Ātm. नह्ये. *Impf.* अनह्यं. Ātm. अनह्ये. *Pot.* नह्येयं. Ātm. नह्येय. *Impv.* नह्यानि. Ātm. नह्यै. *Perf.* ननाह or ननह, नेहिथ or ननद्ध, ननाह; नेहिव, नेहथुस्, नेहतुस्; नेहिम, नेह, नेहुस्. Ātm. नेहे, नेहिषे, नेहे; नेहिवहे, नेहाथे, नेहाते; नेहिमहे, नेहिध्वे, -ढ्वे, नेहिरे. *1st Fut.* नद्धास्मि. Ātm. नद्धाहे. *2d Fut.* (306. b) नत्स्यामि. Ātm. नत्स्ये. *Aor.* (426) अनात्सं, अनात्सीस्, अनात्सीत्; अनात्स्व, अनाद्धं, अनाद्धां; अनात्स्म, अनाद्ध, अनात्सुस्. Ātm. अनत्सि, अनद्धास्, अनद्ध; अनत्स्वहि, अनत्साथां, अनत्सातां; अनत्स्महि, अनद्ध्वं, अनत्सत. *Prec.* नह्यासं. Ātm. नत्सीय. *Cond.* अनत्स्यं. Ātm. अनत्स्ये. Pass., *Pres.* नह्ये; *Aor. 3d sing.* अनाहि. Caus. नाहयामि; *Aor.* अनीनहं. Des. निनत्सामि, -त्से. Freq. नानह्ये, नानह्मि (*3d sing.* नानद्धि). Part., *Pres.* नह्यत्; *Past pass.* नद्ध; *Past indecl.* नद्ध्वा, -नह्य; *Fut. pass.* नद्धव्य, नहनीय, नाह्य.

EXAMPLES OF PRIMITIVE VERBS OF THE SIXTH CONJUGATIONAL CLASS, EXPLAINED AT 278.

625. Root सृज् *sṛij*. Infin. स्रष्टुम् *srashṭum*, 'to create,' 'to let go.'

PARASMAI-PADA only.

Present tense, 'I create.'

सृजामि *sṛijāmi*	सृजावस् *sṛijāvas*	सृजामस् *sṛijāmas*
सृजसि *sṛijasi*	सृजथस् *sṛijathas*	सृजथ *sṛijatha*
सृजति *sṛijati*	सृजतस् *sṛijatas*	सृजन्ति *sṛijanti*

Imperfect or *first preterite*, 'I was creating,' or 'I created.'

असृजम् *asṛijam*	असृजाव *asṛijāva*	असृजाम *asṛijāma*
असृजस् *asṛijas*	असृजतम् *asṛijatam*	असृजत *asṛijata*
असृजत् *asṛijat*	असृजताम् *asṛijatām*	असृजन् *asṛijan*

Potential, 'I may create.'

सृजेयम् *sṛijeyam*	सृजेव *sṛijeva*	सृजेम *sṛijema*
सृजेस् *sṛijes*	सृजेतम् *sṛijetam*	सृजेत *sṛijeta*
सृजेत् *sṛijet*	सृजेताम् *sṛijetām*	सृजेयुस् *sṛijeyus*

Imperative, 'Let me create.'

सृजानि *sṛijāni*	सृजाव *sṛijāva*	सृजाम *sṛijāma*
सृज *sṛija*	सृजतम् *sṛijatam*	सृजत *sṛijata*
सृजतु *sṛijatu*	सृजताम् *sṛijatām*	सृजन्तु *sṛijantu*

Perfect or *second preterite*, 'I created,' or 'I have created.'

ससर्ज *sasarja*	ससृजिव *sasṛijiva*	ससृजिम *sasṛijima*
ससर्जिथ *sasarjitha* or ससष्ठ *	ससृजथुस् *sasṛijathus*	ससृज *sasṛija*
ससर्ज *sasarja*	ससृजतुस् *sasṛijatus*	ससृजुस् *sasṛijus*

First future, 'I will create.'

स्रष्टास्मि *srashṭāsmi* (388. e)	स्रष्टास्वस् *srashṭāsvas*	स्रष्टास्मस् *srashṭāsmas*
स्रष्टासि *srashṭāsi*	स्रष्टास्थस् *srashṭāsthas*	स्रष्टास्थ *srashṭāstha*
स्रष्टा *srashṭā*	स्रष्टारौ *srashṭārau*	स्रष्टारस् *srashṭāras*

Second future, 'I shall create.'

स्रक्ष्यामि *srakshyāmi*	स्रक्ष्यावस् *srakshyāvas*	स्रक्ष्यामस् *srakshyāmas*
स्रक्ष्यसि *srakshyasi*	स्रक्ष्यथस् *srakshyathas*	स्रक्ष्यथ *srakshyatha*
स्रक्ष्यति *srakshyati*	स्रक्ष्यतस् *srakshyatas*	स्रक्ष्यन्ति *srakshyanti*

* As to *sasrashṭha*, see 370. f.

Aorist or third preterite, 'I created.'

अस्राक्षम् *asrāksham*	अस्राक्ष्व *asrākshwa*	अस्राक्ष्म *asrākshma*
अस्राक्षीः *asrākshīs*	अस्राष्टम् *asrāshṭam*	अस्राष्ट *asrāshṭa*
अस्राक्षीत् *asrākshīt*	अस्राष्टाम् *asrāshṭām*	अस्राक्षुः *asrākshus*

Precative or benedictive, 'May I create.'

सृज्यासम् *sṛijyāsam*	सृज्यास्व *sṛijyāswa*	सृज्यास्म *sṛijyāsma*
सृज्याः *sṛijyās*	सृज्यास्तम् *sṛijyāstam*	सृज्यास्त *sṛijyāsta*
सृज्यात् *sṛijyāt*	सृज्यास्ताम् *sṛijyāstām*	सृज्यासुः *sṛijyāsus*

Conditional, 'I should create.'

अस्रक्ष्यम् *asrakshyam*	अस्रक्ष्याव *asrakshyāva*	अस्रक्ष्याम *asrakshyāma*
अस्रक्ष्यः *asrakshyas*	अस्रक्ष्यतम् *asrakshyatam*	अस्रक्ष्यत *asrakshyata*
अस्रक्ष्यत् *asrakshyat*	अस्रक्ष्यताम् *asrakshyatām*	अस्रक्ष्यन् *asrakshyan*

Pass., *Pres.* सृज्ये; *Aor. 3d sing.* असर्जि. Caus., *Pres.* सर्जयामि; *Aor.* अससर्जं or असीसृजं. Des. सिसृक्षामि, -क्षे. Freq. सरीसृज्ये. Part., *Pres.* सृजत्; *Past pass.* सृष्ट; *Past indecl.* सृष्ट्वा, -सृज्य; *Fut. pass.* स्रष्टव्य, सर्जनीय, सृज्य.

EXAMPLES OF OTHER VERBS OF THE SIXTH CONJUGATIONAL CLASS IN THE ORDER OF THEIR FINAL LETTERS.

626. Root मृ (280). *Inf.* मर्तुं 'to die.' Ātm. in conj. tenses *Aor.* and *Prec.* Par. in others. *Pres.* म्रिये. *Impf.* अम्रिये. *Pot.* म्रियेय. *Impv.* म्रियै. *Perf.* ममार, ममर्थ, ममार; मम्रिव, मम्रथुस्, मम्रतुस्; मम्रिम, मम्र, मम्रुस्. Ātm. मम्रे, मम्रिषे, मम्रे; मम्रिवहे, मम्राथे, मम्राते; मम्रिमहे, मम्रिढ्वे, -ध्वे, मम्रिरे. *1st Fut.* मर्तास्मि. *2d Fut.* मरिष्यामि. *Aor.* अमृषि, अमृथाः, अमृत; अमृष्वहि, अमृषाथां, अमृषातां; अमृष्महि, अमृढ्वं, अमृषत. *Prec.* मृषीय. *Cond.* अमरिष्यं. Pass., *Pres.* म्रिये; *Aor. 3d sing.* अमारि. Caus., *Pres.* मारयामि; *Aor.* अमीमरं. Des. मुमूर्षामि (502). Freq. मेम्रीये, मर्मर्- or मरी- or मर्मर्मि. Part., *Pres.* म्रियमाण; *Past pass.* मृत; *Past indecl.* मृत्वा, -मृत्य; *Fut. pass.* मर्तव्य, मरणीय, मार्य.

627. Root कॄ (280). *Inf.* करितुं or करीतुं 'to scatter.' Par. *Pres.* किरामि. *Impf.* अकिरं. *Pot.* किरेयं. *Impv.* किराणि. *Perf.* (374. k) चकार, चकरिथ, चकार; चकरिव, चकरथुस्, चकरतुस्; चकरिम, चकर, चकरुस्. *1st Fut.* (393) करितास्मि or करीतास्मि. *2d Fut.* (393) करिष्यामि or करीष्यामि, &c. *Aor.* अकारिषं, अकारीस्, अकारीत्; अकारिष्व, अकारिष्टं, अकारिष्टां; अकारिष्म, अकारिष्ट, अकारिषुस्. *Prec.* कीर्यासं. *Cond.* अकरिष्यं or अकरीष्यं. Pass., *Pres.* कीर्ये; *Aor. 3d sing.* अकारि. Caus., *Pres.* कारयामि; *Aor.* अचीकरं. Des. चिकरिषामि*. Freq. चेकीर्ये, चाकर्मि. Part., *Pres.* किरत्; *Past pass.*

* With regard to 393, 501, कॄ and गॄ are not allowed the option of *iṭa*.

कीर्ण (531. a); *Past indecl.* कीर्त्वा, -कीर्य; *Fut. pass.* करितव्य or करीतव्य, करणीय, कार्य.

628. Root मुच् (281). *Inf.* मोक्तुं 'to loose,' 'to let go.' Par. and Âtm. *Pres.* मुञ्चामि. Âtm. मुञ्चे. *Impf.* अमुञ्चं. Âtm. अमुञ्चे. *Pot.* मुञ्चेयं. Âtm. मुञ्चेय. *Impv.* मुञ्चानि. Âtm. मुञ्चै. *Perf.* मुमोच, मुमोचिथ, मुमोच; मुमुचिव, मुमुचथुस्, मुमुचतुस्; मुमुचिम, मुमुच, मुमुचुस्. Âtm. मुमुचे, मुमुचिषे, मुमुचे; मुमुचिवहे, मुमुचाथे, मुमुचाते; मुमुचिमहे, मुमुचिध्वे, मुमुचिरे. *1st Fut.* मोक्तास्मि. Âtm. मोक्ताहे. *2d Fut.* मोक्ष्यामि. Âtm. मोक्ष्ये. *Aor.* (436) अमुचं, अमुचस्, अमुचत्; अमुचाव, अमुचतं, अमुचतां; अमुचाम, अमुचत, अमुचन्. Âtm. अमुक्षि, अमुक्थास्, अमुक्त; अमुक्ष्वहि, अमुक्षाथां, अमुक्षातां; अमुक्ष्महि, अमुग्ध्वं, अमुक्षत. *Prec.* मुच्यासं. Âtm. मुक्षीय (452). *Cond.* अमोक्ष्यं. Âtm. अमोक्ष्ये. Pass., *Pres.* मुच्ये; *Aor. 3d sing.* अमोचि. Caus., *Pres.* मोचयामि; *Aor.* अमूमुचं. Des. मुमुक्षामि, -क्षे. Freq. मोमुच्ये, मोमोच्मि (*3d sing.* मोमोक्ति). Part., *Pres.* मुञ्चत्; *Past pass.* मुक्त; *Past indecl.* मुक्त्वा, -मुच्य; *Fut. pass.* मोक्तव्य, मोचनीय, मोच्य.

629. Root व्यच् (282). *Inf.* व्यचितुं 'to deceive.' Par. *Pres.* विचामि. *Impf.* अविचं. *Pot.* विचेयं. *Impv.* विचानि. *Perf.* (383) विव्याच, विव्यचिथ, विव्याच; विविचिव, विविचथुस्, विविचतुस्; विविचिम, विविच, विविचुस्. *1st Fut.* व्यचितास्मि. *2d Fut.* व्यचिष्यामि. *Aor.* (428) अव्यचिषं, अव्यचीस्, &c., or अव्याचिषं, &c. *Prec.* विच्यासं. *Cond.* अव्यचिष्यं. Pass., *Pres.* विच्ये; *Aor. 3d sing.* अव्याचि. Caus., *Pres.* व्याचयामि; *Aor.* अविव्यचं. Des. विव्यचिषामि. Freq. वेविच्ये, वाव्यच्मि or वाव्यचीमि. Part., *Pres.* विचत्; *Past pass.* विचित; *Past indecl.* विचित्वा, -विच्य; *Fut. pass.* व्यचितव्य, व्यचनीय, व्याच्य.

630. Root व्रश्च् (282). *Inf.* व्रश्चितुं 'to cut.' Par. *Pres.* वृश्चामि. *Impf.* अवृश्चं. *Pot.* वृश्चेयं. *Impv.* वृश्चानि. *Perf.* वव्रश्च, वव्रश्चिथ or वव्रष्ठ, वव्रश्च; वव्रश्चिव or वव्रश्च्व (371), वव्रश्चथुस्, वव्रश्चतुस्; वव्रश्चिम or वव्रश्च्म, वव्रश्च, वव्रश्चुस्. *1st Fut.* (415) व्रश्चितास्मि or व्रष्टास्मि. *2d Fut.* व्रश्चिष्यामि or व्रक्ष्यामि. *Aor.* अव्रश्चिषं, अव्रश्चीस्, अव्रश्चीत्; अव्रश्चिष्व, &c., see 427. Or अव्राक्षं (423), अव्राक्षीस्, अव्राक्षीत्; अव्राक्ष्व, अव्राष्टं (297), अव्राष्टां; अव्राक्ष्म, अव्राष्ट, अव्राक्षुस्. *Prec.* वृश्च्यासं. *Cond.* अव्रश्चिष्यं or अव्रक्ष्यं. Pass., *Pres.* वृश्च्ये (472); *Aor. 3d sing.* अव्रश्चि (475. b). Caus., *Pres.* व्रश्चयामि; *Aor.* अवव्रश्चं. Des. विव्रश्चिषामि or विव्रक्षामि. Freq. वरीवृश्च्ये, वरीवृश्चीमि. Part., *Pres.* वृश्चत्; *Past pass.* वृक्ण or वृक्त (541, 58. a); *Past indecl.* व्रश्चित्वा, -वृश्च्य (565); *Fut. pass.* व्रश्चितव्य or व्रष्टव्य, व्रश्चनीय, व्रश्च्य.

a. Root सिच् (281). *Inf.* सेक्तुं 'to sprinkle.' Par. and Âtm. *Pres.* सिञ्चामि. Âtm. सिञ्चे. *Impf.* असिञ्चं. Âtm. असिञ्चे. *Pol.* सिञ्चेयं. Âtm. सिञ्चेय. *Impv.* सिञ्चानि. Âtm. सिञ्चै. *Perf.* सिषेच, सिषेचिथ, सिषेच;

सिषिचिव, सिषिचथुस्, -चतुस्; सिषिचिम, सिषिच, सिषिचुस्. *Átm.* सिषिचे, सि-षिचिषे, सिषिचे; सिषिचिवहे, &c. *1st Fut.* सेक्तास्मि, सेक्तासि, &c. *Átm.* सेक्ताहे. *2d Fut.* सेक्ष्यामि. *Átm.* सेक्ष्ये. *Aor.* असिचं, -चस्, -चत्; असिचाव, -चतं, -चतां; असिचाम, -चत, -चन्. *Átm.* असिचे, -चथास्, -चत; असिचा-वहि, -चेथां, -चेतां; असिचामहि, -चध्वं, -चन्त, or असिक्षि, असिक्थास्, असिक्त; असिक्ष्वहि, -क्षाथां, -क्षातां; असिक्ष्महि, असिग्ध्वं, असिक्षत. *Prec.* सिच्यासं. *Átm.* सिक्षीय. *Cond.* असेक्ष्यं. *Átm.* असेक्ष्ये. Pass., *Pres.* सिच्ये. Caus. सेचयामि; *Aor.* असीषिचं. Des. सिसिक्षामि, -क्षे. Freq. सेसिच्ये, सेसेक्मि. Part., *Pres.* सिञ्चत्, सिञ्चमान; *Past pass.* सिक्त; *Past indecl.* सिक्त्वा, -सिच्य; *Fut. pass.* सेक्तव्य, सेचनीय, सेच्य.

631. Root प्रछ् or प्रच्छ् (282). *Inf.* प्रष्टुं 'to ask.' Par. *Pres.* पृच्छामि. *Impf.* अपृच्छं. *Pot.* पृच्छेयं. *Impv.* पृच्छानि. *Perf.* (381) पप्रच्छ, पप्रच्छिथ or पप्रष्ठ, पप्रच्छ; पप्रच्छिव, पप्रच्छथुस्, पप्रच्छतुस्; पप्रच्छिम, पप्रच्छ, पप्रच्छुस्. *1st Fut.* प्रष्टास्मि. *2d Fut.* प्रक्ष्यामि. *Aor.* अप्राक्षं, अप्राक्षीस्, अप्राक्षीत्; अप्राक्ष्व, अप्राष्टं, अप्राष्टां; अप्राक्ष्म, अप्राष्ट, अप्राक्षुस्. *Prec.* पृच्छ्यासं. *Cond.* अप्रक्ष्यं. Pass., *Pres.* पृच्छ्ये (472); *Aor. 3d sing.* अप्रच्छि. Caus. प्रच्छ-यामि; *Aor.* अपप्रच्छं. Des. पिपृच्छिषामि. Freq. परीपृच्छ्ये, पाप्रच्छ्मि or पा-प्रष्टि. Part., *Pres.* पृच्छत्; *Past pass.* पृष्ट; *Past indecl.* पृष्ट्वा, -पृच्छ्य (565); *Fut. pass.* प्रष्टव्य, प्रच्छनीय, प्रच्छ्य.

632. Root भ्रस्ज् or भ्रज्ज्. *Inf.* भ्रष्टुं or भर्ष्टुं 'to fry.' Par. and Átm. *Pres.* भृज्जामि. *Átm.* भृज्जे. *Impf.* अभृज्जं. *Átm.* अभृज्जे. *Pot.* भृज्जेयं. *Átm.* भृज्जेय. *Impv.* भृज्जानि. *Átm.* भृज्जै. *Perf.* (381) बभ्रज्ज, बभ्रज्जिथ or बभ्रष्ठ, बभ्रज्ज; बभ्रज्जिव, बभ्रज्जथुस्, बभ्रज्जतुस्; बभ्रज्जिम, बभ्रज्ज, बभ्रज्जुस्. Or बभर्ज, बभर्जिथ or बभर्ष्ठ, बभर्ज; बभर्जिव, &c. *Átm.* बभ्रज्जे, बभ्रज्जिषे, &c. Or बभर्जे, बभर्जिषे, &c. *1st Fut.* भ्रष्टास्मि or भर्ष्टास्मि. *Átm.* भ्रष्टाहे or भर्ष्टाहे. *2d Fut.* भ्रक्ष्यामि or भर्क्ष्यामि &c., भ्रक्ष्ये or भर्क्ष्ये. *Aor.* अभ्राक्षं, अभ्राक्षीस्, अभ्राक्षीत्; अभ्राक्ष्व, अभ्राष्टं, अभ्राष्टां; अभ्राक्ष्म, अभ्राष्ट, अभ्राक्षुस्. Or अभार्क्षं. *Átm.* अभ्रक्षि, अभ्रष्ठास्, अभ्रष्ट; अभ्रक्ष्वहि, अभ्रक्षाथां, अभ्रक्षातां; अभ्रक्ष्महि, अभ्रड्ढ्वं, अभ्रक्षत. Or अभर्क्षि, अभर्ष्ठास्, अभर्ष्ट; अभर्क्ष्वहि, अभर्क्षाथां, अभर्क्षातां; अभर्क्ष्महि, अभर्ड्ढ्वं, अभर्क्षत. *Prec.* भृज्ज्यासं. *Átm.* भ्रक्षीय or भर्क्षीय. *Cond.* अभ्रक्ष्यं or अभर्क्ष्यं. *Átm.* अभ्रक्ष्ये or अभर्क्ष्ये. Pass., *Pres.* भृज्ज्ये (472). Caus., *Pres.* भ्रज्जयामि; *Aor.* अबभ्रज्जं or अबभर्जं. Des. बिभ्रक्षामि, -क्षे, or बिभर्क्षामि, -क्षे; or बिभ्रज्जिषामि, -षे, or बिभर्जिषामि, -षे, &c. Freq. बरीभृज्ज्ये, बाभर्ज्मि (3d sing. बाभर्ष्टि). Part., *Pres.* भृज्जत्; *Past pass.* भृष्ट; *Past indecl.* भृष्ट्वा, -भृज्ज्य; *Fut. pass.* भ्रष्टव्य or भर्ष्टव्य, भ्रज्जनीय or भर्जनीय, भ्रज्ज्य or भर्ज्य.

633. Root मस्ज् or मज्ज्. *Inf.* मंक्तुं 'to be immersed,' 'to sink.' Par. *Pres.* मज्जामि. *Impf.* अमज्जं. *Pot.* मज्जेयं. *Impv.* मज्जानि. *Perf.* ममज्ज, ममज्जिथ or ममंक्थ, ममज्ज; ममज्जिव, ममज्जथुस्, ममज्जतुस्; ममज्जिम, ममज्ज,

ममज्जुस्. *1st Fut.* मंक्तास्मि. *2d Fut.* मंक्ष्यामि. *Aor.* (424) अमांक्षं, अमांक्षीस्, अमांक्षीत्; अमांक्ष्व, अमांक्तं, अमांक्तां; अमांक्ष्म, अमांक्त, अमांक्षुस्. *Prec.* मज्ज्यासं. *Cond.* अमंक्ष्यं. Pass., *Pres.* मज्ज्यते. Caus., *Pres.* मज्जयामि; *Aor.* अममज्जं. Des. मिमंक्षामि. Freq. मामज्ज्यते, मामज्मि (*3d sing.* मामंक्ति). Part., *Pres.* मज्जत्; *Past pass.* मग्न; *Past indecl.* मंक्त्वा, मक्त्वा, -मज्ज्य; *Fut. pass.* मंक्तव्य, मज्जनीय, मज्ज्य.

634. Root तुद्. *Inf.* तोत्तुं 'to strike,' 'to hurt.' Par. and Ātm. *Pres.* तुदामि. Ātm. तुदे. *Impf.* अतुदं. Ātm. अतुदे. *Pot.* तुदेयं. Ātm. तुदेय. *Impv.* तुदानि. Ātm. तुदै. *Perf.* तुतोद, तुतोदिथ, तुतोद; तुतुदिव, तुतुदथुस्, तुतुदतुस्; तुतुदिम, तुतुद, तुतुदुस्. Ātm. तुतुदे, तुतुदिषे, तुतुदे; तुतुदिवहे, तुतुदाथे, तुतुदाते; तुतुदिमहे, तुतुदिध्वे, तुतुदिरे. *1st Fut.* तोत्तास्मि. Ātm. तोत्ताहे. *2d Fut.* तोत्स्यामि. Ātm. तोत्स्ये. *Aor.* अतौत्सं, अतौत्सीस्, अतौत्सीत्; अतौत्स्व, अतौत्तं, अतौत्तां; अतौत्स्म, अतौत्त, अतौत्सुस्. Ātm. अतुत्सि, अतुत्थास्, अतुत्त; अतुत्स्वहि, अतुत्साथां, अतुत्सातां; अतुत्स्महि, अतुद्ध्वं, अतुत्सत. *Prec.* तुद्यासं. Ātm. तुत्सीय (452). *Cond.* अतोत्स्यं. Ātm. अतोत्स्ये. Pass., *Pres.* तुद्ये; *Aor. 3d sing.* अतोदि. Caus., *Pres.* तोदयामि; *Aor.* अतूतुदं. Des. तुतुत्सामि, -त्से. Freq. तोतुद्ये, तोतोद्मि (*3d sing.* तोतोत्ति). Part., *Pres.* तुदत्; *Past pass.* तुन्न; *Past indecl.* तुत्त्वा, -तुद्य; *Fut. pass.* तोत्तव्य, तोदनीय, तोद्य.

635. Root क्षिप्. *Inf.* क्षेप्तुं 'to throw.' Par. and Ātm. *Pres.* क्षिपामि. Ātm. क्षिपे. *Impf.* अक्षिपं. Ātm. अक्षिपे. *Pot.* क्षिपेयं. Ātm. क्षिपेय. *Impv.* क्षिपाणि. Ātm. क्षिपै. *Perf.* चिक्षेप, चिक्षेपिथ, चिक्षेप; चिक्षिपिव, चिक्षिपथुस्, चिक्षिपतुस्; चिक्षिपिम, चिक्षिप, चिक्षिपुस्. Ātm. चिक्षिपे, चिक्षिपिषे, चिक्षिपे; चिक्षिपिवहे, चिक्षिपाथे, चिक्षिपाते; चिक्षिपिमहे, चिक्षिपिध्वे, चिक्षिपिरे. *1st Fut.* क्षेप्तास्मि. Ātm. क्षेप्ताहे. *2d Fut.* क्षेप्स्यामि. Ātm. क्षेप्स्ये. *Aor.* अक्षैप्सं, अक्षैप्सीस्, अक्षैप्सीत्; अक्षैप्स्व, अक्षैप्तं, अक्षैप्तां; अक्षैप्स्म, अक्षैप्त, अक्षैप्सुस्. Ātm. अक्षिप्सि, अक्षिप्थास्, अक्षिप्त; अक्षिप्स्वहि, अक्षिप्साथां, अक्षिप्सातां; अक्षिप्स्महि, अक्षिब्ध्वं, अक्षिप्सत. *Prec.* क्षिप्यासं, &c. Ātm. क्षिप्सीय. *Cond.* अक्षेप्स्यं. Ātm. अक्षेप्स्ये. Pass. क्षिप्ये; *Aor. 3d sing.* अक्षेपि. Caus., *Pres.* क्षेपयामि; *Aor.* अचिक्षिपं. Des. चिक्षिप्सामि, -प्से. Freq. चेक्षिप्ये, चेक्षेप्मि (710, 294. *a*). Part., *Pres.* क्षिपत्; *Past pass.* क्षिप्त; *Past indecl.* क्षिप्त्वा, -क्षिप्य; *Fut. pass.* क्षेप्तव्य, क्षेपणीय, क्षेप्य.

a. Root विश्. *Inf.* वेष्टुं 'to enter.' Par. *Pres.* विशामि, विशसि, &c. *Impf.* अविशं, अविशस्, &c. *Pot.* विशेयं, विशेस्, &c. *Impv.* विशानि, विश, &c. *Perf.* विवेश, विवेशिथ, विवेश; विविशिव, विविशथुस्, विविशतुस्; विविशिम, विविश, विविशुस्. *1st Fut.* वेष्टास्मि. *2d Fut.* वेक्ष्यामि. *Aor.* अविक्षं, -क्षस्, -क्षत्; अविक्षाव, -क्षतं, -क्षतां; अविक्षाम, -क्षत, -क्षन्. *Prec.* विश्यासं. *Cond.* अवेक्ष्यं. Pass., *Pres.* विश्ये; *Aor. 3d sing.* अवेशि. Caus.,

अपुषतं, अपुषतां; अपुषाम, अपुषत, अपुषन्. *Prec.* पुष्यासं. *Cond.* अपोक्ष्यं. Pass., *Pres.* पुष्ये; *Aor. 3d sing.* अपोषि. Caus., *Pres.* पोषयामि; *Aor.* अपूपुषं. Des. पुपोषिषामि or पुपुषिषामि or पुपुक्षामि. Freq. पोपुष्ये, पोपोष्मि. Part., *Pres.* पुष्यत्; *Past pass.* पुष्ट; *Past indecl.* पुष्ट्वा, -पुष्य; *Fut. pass.* पोष्टव्य, पोषणीय, पोष्य.

622. Root अस्. *Inf.* असितुं 'to throw.' Par. *Pres.* अस्यामि, &c. *Impf.* आस्यं. *Pot.* अस्येयं. *Impv.* अस्यानि. *Perf.* आस, आसिथ, आस; आसिव, आसथुस्, आसतुस्; आसिम, आस, आसुस्. *1st Fut.* असितास्मि. *2d Fut.* असिष्यामि. *Aor.* (441) आस्थं, आस्थस्, आस्थत्; आस्थाव, आस्थतं, आस्थतां; आस्थाम, आस्थत, आस्थन्. *Prec.* अस्यासं. *Cond.* आसिष्यं. Pass., *Pres.* अस्ये; *Aor. 3d sing.* आसि. Caus., *Pres.* आसयामि; *Aor.* आसिसं. Des. असिसिषामि. Part., *Pres.* अस्यत्; *Past pass.* अस्त; *Past indecl.* असित्वा or अस्त्वा, -अस्य; *Fut. pass.* असितव्य, असनीय, आस्य.

623. Root द्रुह्. *Inf.* द्रोग्धुं or द्रोहितुं 'to injure,' 'to bear malice.' Par. *Pres.* द्रुह्यामि. *Impf.* अद्रुह्यं. *Pot.* द्रुह्येयं. *Impv.* द्रुह्याणि. *Perf.* दुद्रोह, दुद्रोहिथ or दुद्रोग्ध or दुद्रोढ, दुद्रोह; दुद्रुहिव, दुद्रुहथुस्, दुद्रुहतुस्; दुद्रुहिम, दुद्रुह, दुद्रुहुस्. *1st Fut.* (415. m) द्रोग्धास्मि or द्रोढास्मि or द्रोहितास्मि, &c. *2d Fut.* ध्रोक्ष्यामि (306. a) or द्रोहिष्यामि. *Aor.* अद्रुहं, अद्रुहस्, अद्रुहत्; अद्रुहाव, अद्रुहतं, अद्रुहतां; अद्रुहाम, अद्रुहत, अद्रुहन्. *Prec.* द्रुह्यासं, &c. *Cond.* अध्रोक्ष्यं (306. a) or अद्रोहिष्यं. Pass., *Pres.* द्रुह्ये; *Aor. 3d sing.* अद्रोहि. Caus., *Pres.* द्रोहयामि; *Aor.* अदुद्रुहं. Des. दुद्रोहिषामि or दुद्रुहिषामि or दुध्रुक्षामि (306. a). Freq. दोद्रुह्ये, दोद्रोह्मि (*3d sing.* दोद्रोहीति or दोद्रोग्धि 514. d). Part., *Pres.* द्रुह्यत्; *Past pass.* द्रुग्ध or द्रूढ; *Past indecl.* द्रुग्ध्वा or द्रुहित्वा or द्रोहित्वा, -द्रुह्य; *Fut. pass.* द्रोग्धव्य, द्रोहणीय, द्रोह्य.

624. Root नह्. *Inf.* नद्धुं 'to tie,' 'to bind,' 'to fasten.' Par. and Ātm. *Pres.* नह्यामि. Ātm. नह्ये. *Impf.* अनह्यं. Ātm. अनह्ये. *Pot.* नह्येयं. Ātm. नह्येय. *Impv.* नह्यानि. Ātm. नह्यै. *Perf.* ननाह or ननह, नेहिथ or ननद्ध, ननाह; नेहिव, नेहथुस्, नेहतुस्; नेहिम, नेह, नेहुस्. Ātm. नेहे, नेहिषे, नेहे; नेहिवहे, नेहाथे, नेहाते; नेहिमहे, नेहिध्वे, -ढ्वे, नेहिरे. *1st Fut.* नद्धास्मि. Ātm. नद्धाहे. *2d Fut.* (306. b) नत्स्यामि. Ātm. नत्स्ये. *Aor.* (426) अनात्सं, अनात्सीस्, अनात्सीत्; अनात्स्व, अनाद्धं, अनाद्धां; अनात्स्म, अनाद्ध, अनात्सुस्. Ātm. अनत्सि, अनद्धास्, अनद्ध; अनत्स्वहि, अनत्साथां, अनत्सातां; अनत्स्महि, अनद्ध्वं, अनत्सत. *Prec.* नह्यासं. Ātm. नत्सीय. *Cond.* अनत्स्यं. Ātm. अनत्स्ये. Pass., *Pres.* नह्ये; *Aor. 3d sing.* अनाहि. Caus. नाहयामि; *Aor.* अनीनहं. Des. निनत्सामि, -त्से. Freq. नानह्ये, नानह्मि (*3d sing.* नानद्धि). Part., *Pres.* नह्यत्; *Past pass.* नद्ध; *Past indecl.* नद्ध्वा, -नह्य; *Fut. pass.* नद्धव्य, नहनीय, नाह्य.

EXAMPLES OF PRIMITIVE VERBS OF THE SIXTH CONJUGATIONAL CLASS, EXPLAINED AT 278.

615. Root सृज् *sṛij*. Infin. स्रष्टुम् *srashṭum*, 'to create,' 'to let go.'

PARASMAI-PADA only.

Present tense, 'I create.'

सृजामि *sṛijāmi*	सृजावस् *sṛijāvas*	सृजामस् *sṛijāmas*
सृजसि *sṛijasi*	सृजथस् *sṛijathas*	सृजथ *sṛijatha*
सृजति *sṛijati*	सृजतस् *sṛijatas*	सृजन्ति *sṛijanti*

Imperfect or *first preterite*, 'I was creating,' or 'I created.'

असृजम् *asṛijam*	असृजाव *asṛijāva*	असृजाम *asṛijāma*
असृजस् *asṛijas*	असृजतम् *asṛijatam*	असृजत *asṛijata*
असृजत् *asṛijat*	असृजताम् *asṛijatām*	असृजन् *asṛijan*

Potential, 'I may create.'

सृजेयम् *sṛijeyam*	सृजेव *sṛijeva*	सृजेम *sṛijema*
सृजेस् *sṛijes*	सृजेतम् *sṛijetam*	सृजेत *sṛijeta*
सृजेत् *sṛijet*	सृजेताम् *sṛijetām*	सृजेयुस् *sṛijeyus*

Imperative, 'Let me create.'

सृजानि *sṛijāni*	सृजाव *sṛijāva*	सृजाम *sṛijāma*
सृज *sṛija*	सृजतम् *sṛijatam*	सृजत *sṛijata*
सृजतु *sṛijatu*	सृजताम् *sṛijatām*	सृजन्तु *sṛijantu*

Perfect or *second preterite*, 'I created,' or 'I have created.'

ससर्ज *sasarja*	ससृजिव *sasṛijiva*	ससृजिम *sasṛijima*
ससर्जिथ *sasarjitha* or सस्रष्ठ *	ससृजथुस् *sasṛijathus*	ससृज *sasṛija*
ससर्ज *sasarja*	ससृजतुस् *sasṛijatus*	ससृजुस् *sasṛijus*

First future, 'I will create.'

स्रष्टास्मि *srashṭāsmi* (388. e)	स्रष्टास्वस् *srashṭāsvas*	स्रष्टास्मस् *srashṭāsmas*
स्रष्टासि *srashṭāsi*	स्रष्टास्थस् *srashṭāsthas*	स्रष्टास्थ *srashṭāstha*
स्रष्टा *srashṭā*	स्रष्टारौ *srashṭārau*	स्रष्टारस् *srashṭāras*

Second future, 'I shall create.'

स्रक्ष्यामि *srakshyāmi*	स्रक्ष्यावस् *srakshyāvas*	स्रक्ष्यामस् *srakshyāmas*
स्रक्ष्यसि *srakshyasi*	स्रक्ष्यथस् *srakshyathas*	स्रक्ष्यथ *srakshyatha*
स्रक्ष्यति *srakshyati*	स्रक्ष्यतस् *srakshyatas*	स्रक्ष्यन्ति *srakshyanti*

* As to *sasrashṭha*, see 370. *f*.

Aorist or third preterite, 'I created.'

असृक्षम् *asrāksham*	अस्राक्ष्व *asrākshwa*	अस्राक्ष्म *asrākshma*
अस्राक्षीः *asrākshīs*	अस्राष्टम् *asrāshṭam*	अस्राष्ट *asrāshṭa*
अस्राक्षीत् *asrākshīt*	अस्राष्टाम् *asrāshṭām*	अस्राक्षुः *asrākshus*

Precative or benedictive, 'May I create.'

सृज्यासम् *sṛijyāsam*	सृज्यास्व *sṛijyāswa*	सृज्यास्म *sṛijyāsma*
सृज्याः *sṛijyās*	सृज्यास्तम् *sṛijyāstam*	सृज्यास्त *sṛijyāsta*
सृज्यात् *sṛijyāt*	सृज्यास्ताम् *sṛijyāstām*	सृज्यासुः *sṛijyāsus*

Conditional, 'I should create.'

अस्रक्ष्यम् *asrakshyam*	अस्रक्ष्याव *asrakshyāva*	अस्रक्ष्याम *asrakshyāma*
अस्रक्ष्यः *asrakshyas*	अस्रक्ष्यतम् *asrakshyatam*	अस्रक्ष्यत *asrakshyata*
अस्रक्ष्यत् *asrakshyat*	अस्रक्ष्यताम् *asrakshyatām*	अस्रक्ष्यन् *asrakshyan*

Pass., *Pres.* सृज्ये; *Aor. 3d sing.* असर्जि. Caus., *Pres.* सर्जयामि; *Aor.* अससर्जं or असीसृजं. Des. सिसृक्षामि, -क्षे. Freq. सरीसृज्ये. Part., *Pres.* सृजत्; *Past pass.* सृष्ट; *Past indecl.* सृष्ट्वा, -सृज्य; *Fut. pass.* स्रष्टव्य, सर्जनीय, सृज्य.

EXAMPLES OF OTHER VERBS OF THE SIXTH CONJUGATIONAL CLASS IN THE ORDER OF THEIR FINAL LETTERS.

626. Root मृ (280). *Inf.* मर्तुं 'to die.' Ātm. in conj. tenses *Aor.* and *Prec.* Par. in others. *Pres.* म्रिये. *Impf.* अम्रिये. *Pot.* म्रियेय. *Impv.* म्रियै. *Perf.* ममार, ममर्थ, ममार; मम्रिव, मम्रथुः, मम्रतुः; मम्रिम, मम्र, मम्रुः. Ātm. मम्रे, मम्रिषे, मम्रे; मम्रिवहे, मम्राथे, मम्राते; मम्रिमहे, मम्रिढ्वे, -ध्वे, मम्रिरे. *1st Fut.* मर्तास्मि. *2d Fut.* मरिष्यामि. *Aor.* अमृषि, अमृथाः, अमृत; अमृष्वहि, अमृषाथां, अमृषातां; अमृष्महि, अमृढ्वं, अमृषत. *Prec.* मृषीय. *Cond.* अमरिष्यं. Pass., *Pres.* म्रिये; *Aor. 3d sing.* अमारि. Caus., *Pres.* मारयामि; *Aor.* अमीमरं. Des. मुमूर्षामि (502). Freq. मेम्रीये, मर्मर्मि or मरिमर्मि or मरीमर्मि. Part., *Pres.* म्रियमाण; *Past pass.* मृत; *Past indecl.* मृत्वा, -मृत्य; *Fut. pass.* मर्तव्य, मरणीय, मार्य.

627. Root कॄ (280). *Inf.* करितुं or करीतुं 'to scatter.' Par. *Pres.* किरामि. *Impf.* अकिरं. *Pot.* किरेयं. *Impv.* किराणि. *Perf.* (374. *k*) चकार, चकरिथ, चकार; चकरिव, चकरथुः, चकरतुः; चकरिम, चकर, चकरुः. *1st Fut.* (393) करितास्मि or करीतास्मि. *2d Fut.* (393) करिष्यामि or करीष्यामि, &c. *Aor.* अकारिषं, अकारीः, अकारीत्; अकारिष्व, अकारिष्टं, अकारिष्टां; अकारिष्म, अकारिष्ट, अकारिषुः. *Prec.* कीर्षीयं. *Cond.* अकरिष्यं or अकरीष्यं. Pass., *Pres.* कीर्ये; *Aor. 3d sing.* अकारि. Caus., *Pres.* कारयामि; *Aor.* अचीकरं. Des. चिकरिषामि*. Freq. चेकीर्ये, चाकर्मि. Part., *Pres.* किरत्; *Past pass.*

* With regard to 393. 501, कॄ and गॄ are not allowed the option of *īṭa*.

कीर्ण (531. a); *Past indecl.* कीर्त्वा, -कीर्य; *Fut. pass.* करितव्य or करीतव्य, करणीय, कार्य.

628. Root मुच् (281). *Inf.* मोक्तुं 'to loose,' 'to let go.' Par. and Ātm. *Pres.* मुञ्चामि. Ātm. मुञ्चे. *Impf.* अमुञ्चं. Ātm. अमुञ्चे. *Pot.* मुञ्चेयं. Ātm. मुञ्चेय. *Impv.* मुञ्चानि. Ātm. मुञ्चै. *Perf.* मुमोच, मुमोचिथ, मुमोच; मुमुचिव, मुमुचथुस्, मुमुचतुस्; मुमुचिम, मुमुच, मुमुचुस्. Ātm. मुमुचे, मुमुचिषे, मुमुचे; मुमुचिवहे, मुमुचाथे, मुमुचाते; मुमुचिमहे, मुमुचिध्वे, मुमुचिरे. *1st Fut.* मोक्तास्मि. Ātm. मोक्ताहे. *2d Fut.* मोक्ष्यामि. Ātm. मोक्ष्ये. *Aor.* (436) अमुचं, अमुचस्, अमुचत्; अमुचाव, अमुचतं, अमुचतां; अमुचाम, अमुचत, अमुचन्. Ātm. अमुक्षि, अमुक्थास्, अमुक्त; अमुक्ष्वहि, अमुक्षाथां, अमुक्षातां; अमुक्ष्महि, अमुग्ध्वं, अमुक्षत. *Prec.* मुच्यासं. Ātm. मुक्षीय (452). *Cond.* अमोक्ष्यं. Ātm. अमोक्ष्ये. Pass., *Pres.* मुच्ये; *Aor. 3d sing.* अमोचि. Caus., *Pres.* मोचयामि; *Aor.* अमूमुचं. Des. मुमुक्षामि, -क्षे. Freq. मोमुच्ये, मोमोच्मि (*3d sing.* मोमोक्ति). Part., *Pres.* मुञ्चत्; *Past pass.* मुक्त; *Past indecl.* मुक्त्वा, -मुच्य; *Fut. pass.* मोक्तव्य, मोचनीय, मोच्य.

629. Root व्यच् (282). *Inf.* व्यचितुं 'to deceive.' Par. *Pres.* विचामि. *Impf.* अविचं. *Pot.* विचेयं. *Impv.* विचानि. *Perf.* (383) विव्याच, विव्यचिथ, विव्याच; विविचिव, विविचथुस्, विविचतुस्; विविचिम, विविच, विविचुस्. *1st Fut.* व्यचितास्मि. *2d Fut.* व्यचिष्यामि. *Aor.* (428) अव्यचिषं, अव्यचीस्, &c., or अव्याचिषं, &c. *Prec.* विच्यासं. *Cond.* अव्यचिष्यं. Pass., *Pres.* विच्ये; *Aor. 3d sing.* अव्याचि. Caus., *Pres.* व्याचयामि; *Aor.* अविव्यचं. Des. विव्यचिषामि. Freq. वेविच्ये, वाव्यच्मि or वाव्यचीमि. Part., *Pres.* विचत्; *Past pass.* विचित; *Past indecl.* विचित्वा, -विच्य; *Fut. pass.* व्यचितव्य, व्यचनीय, व्याच्य.

630. Root व्रश्च् (282). *Inf.* व्रश्चितुं 'to cut.' Par. *Pres.* वृश्चामि. *Impf.* अवृश्चं. *Pot.* वृश्चेयं. *Impv.* वृश्चानि. *Perf.* वव्रश्च, वव्रश्चिथ or वव्रष्ठ, वव्रश्च; वव्रश्चिव or वव्रश्च्व (371), वव्रश्चथुस्, वव्रश्चतुस्; वव्रश्चिम or वव्रश्च्म, वव्रश्च, वव्रश्चुस्. *1st Fut.* (415) व्रश्चितास्मि or व्रष्टास्मि. *2d Fut.* व्रश्चिष्यामि or व्रक्ष्यामि. *Aor.* अव्रश्चिषं, अव्रश्चीस्, अव्रश्चीत्; अव्रश्चिष्व, &c., see 427. Or अव्राक्षं (423), अव्राक्षीस्, अव्राक्षीत्; अव्राक्ष्व, अव्राष्टं (297), अव्राष्टां; अव्राक्ष्म, अव्राष्ट, अव्राक्षुस्. *Prec.* वृश्च्यासं. *Cond.* अव्रश्चिष्यं or अव्रक्ष्यं. Pass., *Pres.* वृश्च्ये (472); *Aor. 3d sing.* अव्रश्चि (475. b). Caus., *Pres.* व्रश्चयामि; *Aor.* अवव्रश्चं. Des. विव्रश्चिषामि or विव्रक्षामि. Freq. वरीवृश्च्ये, वरीवृश्चीमि. Part., *Pres.* वृश्चत्; *Past pass.* वृक्ण or वृक्त (541, 58. a); *Past indecl.* व्रश्चित्वा, -वृश्च्य (565); *Fut. pass.* व्रश्चितव्य or व्रष्टव्य, व्रश्चनीय, व्रश्च्य.

a. Root सिच् (281). *Inf.* सेक्तुं 'to sprinkle.' Par. and Ātm. *Pres.* सिञ्चामि. Ātm. सिञ्चे. *Impf.* असिञ्चं. Ātm. असिञ्चे. *Pot.* सिञ्चेयं. Ātm. सिञ्चेय. *Impv.* सिञ्चानि. Ātm. सिञ्चै. *Perf.* सिषेच, सिषेचिथ, सिषेच;

चिक्षेपिथ, चिक्षिपिव, चिक्षिपथुः, -पतुः; चिक्षिपिम, चिक्षिप, चिक्षिपुः. *Ātm.* चिक्षिपे, चिक्षिपिषे, चिक्षिपे; चिक्षिपिवहे, &c. *1st Fut.* क्षेप्तास्मि, क्षेप्तासि, &c. *Ātm.* क्षेप्ताहे. *2d Fut.* क्षेप्स्यामि. *Ātm.* क्षेप्स्ये. *Aor.* अक्षैप्सं, -प्सीः, -प्सीत्; अक्षैप्स्व, -प्तं, -प्तां; अक्षैप्स्म, -प्त, -प्सुः. *Ātm.* अक्षिप्सि, -प्थाः, -प्त; अक्षिप्स्वहि, -प्साथां, -प्सातां; अक्षिप्स्महि, अक्षिब्ध्वं, अक्षिप्सत. *Prec.* क्षिप्यासं. *Ātm.* क्षिप्सीय. *Cond.* अक्षेप्स्यं. *Ātm.* अक्षेप्स्ये. Pass., *Pres.* क्षिप्ये. Caus. क्षेपयामि; *Aor.* अचिक्षिपं. Des. चिक्षिप्सामि, -प्से. Freq. चेक्षिप्ये, चेक्षेप्मि. Part., *Pres.* क्षिपत्, क्षिपमाण; *Past pass.* क्षिप्त; *Past indecl.* क्षिप्त्वा, -क्षिप्य; *Fut. pass.* क्षेप्तव्य, क्षेपणीय, क्षेप्य.

631. Root प्रछ् or प्रच्छ् (282). *Inf.* प्रष्टुं 'to ask.' Par. *Pres.* पृच्छामि. *Impf.* अपृच्छं. *Pot.* पृच्छेयं. *Impv.* पृच्छानि. *Perf.* (381) पप्रच्छ, पप्रच्छिथ or पप्रष्ठ, पप्रच्छ; पप्रच्छिव, पप्रच्छथुः, पप्रच्छतुः; पप्रच्छिम, पप्रच्छ, पप्रच्छुः. *1st Fut.* प्रष्टास्मि. *2d Fut.* प्रक्ष्यामि. *Aor.* अप्राक्षं, अप्राक्षीः, अप्राक्षीत्; अप्राक्ष्व, अप्राष्टं, अप्राष्टां; अप्राक्ष्म, अप्राष्ट, अप्राक्षुः. *Prec.* पृच्छ्यासं. *Cond.* अप्रक्ष्यं. Pass., *Pres.* पृच्छ्ये (472); *Aor. 3d sing.* अप्रच्छि. Caus. प्रच्छयामि; *Aor.* अपप्रच्छं. Des. पिपृच्छिषामि. Freq. परीपृच्छ्ये, पाप्रच्छ्मि or पाप्रष्टि. Part., *Pres.* पृच्छत्; *Past pass.* पृष्ट; *Past indecl.* पृष्ट्वा, -पृच्छ्य (565); *Fut. pass.* प्रष्टव्य, प्रच्छनीय, प्रच्छ्य.

632. Root भ्रस्ज् or भ्रज्ज्. *Inf.* भ्रष्टुं or भर्ष्टुं 'to fry.' Par. and Ātm. *Pres.* भृज्जामि. Ātm. भृज्जे. *Impf.* अभृज्जं. Ātm. अभृज्जे. *Pot.* भृज्जेयं. Ātm. भृज्जेय. *Impv.* भृज्जानि. Ātm. भृज्जै. *Perf.* (381) बभ्रज्ज, बभ्रज्जिथ or बभ्रष्ठ, बभ्रज्ज; बभ्रज्जिव, बभ्रज्जथुः, बभ्रज्जतुः; बभ्रज्जिम, बभ्रज्ज, बभ्रज्जुः. Or बभर्ज, बभर्जिथ or बभर्ष्ठ, बभर्ज; बभर्जिव, &c. Ātm. बभ्रज्जे, बभ्रज्जिषे, &c. Or बभर्जे, बभर्जिषे, &c. *1st Fut.* भ्रष्टास्मि or भर्ष्टास्मि. Ātm. भ्रष्टाहे or भर्ष्टाहे. *2d Fut.* भ्रक्ष्यामि or भर्क्ष्यामि &c., भ्रक्ष्ये or भर्क्ष्ये. *Aor.* अभ्राक्षं, अभ्राक्षीः, अभ्राक्षीत्; अभ्राक्ष्व, अभ्राष्टं, अभ्राष्टां; अभ्राक्ष्म, अभ्राष्ट, अभ्राक्षुः. Or अभार्क्षं. Ātm. अभ्रक्षि, अभ्रष्ठाः, अभ्रष्ट; अभ्रक्ष्वहि, अभ्रक्षाथां, अभ्रक्षातां; अभ्रक्ष्महि, अभ्रड्ढ्वं, अभ्रक्षत. Or अभर्क्षि, अभर्ष्ठाः, अभर्ष्ट; अभर्क्ष्वहि, अभर्क्षाथां, अभर्क्षातां; अभर्क्ष्महि, अभर्ड्ढ्वं, अभर्क्षत. *Prec.* भृज्ज्यासं. Ātm. भ्रक्षीय or भर्क्षीय. *Cond.* अभ्रक्ष्यं or अभर्क्ष्यं. Ātm. अभ्रक्ष्ये or अभर्क्ष्ये. Pass., *Pres.* भृज्ज्ये (472). Caus., *Pres.* भ्रज्जयामि; *Aor.* अबभ्रज्जं or अबभर्जं. Des. बिभ्रक्षामि, -क्षे, or बिभर्क्षामि, -क्षे; or बिभ्रज्जिषामि, -षे, or बिभर्जिषामि, -षे, &c. Freq. बरीभृज्ज्ये, बाभर्ज्मि (*3d sing.* बाभर्ष्टि). Part., *Pres.* भृज्जत्; *Past pass.* भृष्ट; *Past indecl.* भृष्ट्वा, -भृज्ज्य; *Fut. pass.* भ्रष्टव्य or भर्ष्टव्य, भ्रज्जनीय or भर्जनीय, भृज्ज्य or भर्ज्य.

633. Root मस्ज् or मज्ज्. *Inf.* मंक्तुं 'to be immersed,' 'to sink.' Par. *Pres.* मज्जामि. *Impf.* अमज्जं. *Pot.* मज्जेयं. *Impv.* मज्जानि. *Perf.* ममज्ज, ममज्जिथ or ममंक्थ, ममज्ज; ममज्जिव, ममज्जथुः, ममज्जतुः; ममज्जिम, ममज्ज,

ममज्जुस्. *1st Fut.* मंक्तास्मि. *2d Fut.* मंक्ष्यामि. *Aor.* (424) अमांक्षं, अमांक्षीस्, अमांक्षीत्; अमांक्ष्व, अमांक्तं, अमांक्तां; अमांक्ष्म, अमांक्त, अमांक्षुस्. *Prec.* मज्ज्यासं. *Cond.* अमंक्ष्यं. Pass., *Pres.* मज्ज्ये. Caus., *Pres.* मज्जयामि; *Aor.* अममज्जं. Des. मिमंक्षामि. Freq. मामज्ज्ये, मामज्जिम (*3d sing.* मामंक्ति). Part., *Pres.* मज्जत्; *Past pass.* मग्न; *Past indecl.* मंक्त्वा, मक्त्वा, -मज्ज्य; *Fut. pass.* मंक्तव्य, मज्जनीय, मज्ज्य.

634. Root तुद्. *Inf.* तोत्तुं 'to strike,' 'to hurt.' Par. and Ātm. *Pres.* तुदामि. Ātm. तुदे. *Impf.* अतुदं. Ātm. अतुदे. *Pot.* तुदेयं. Ātm. तुदेय. *Impv.* तुदानि. Ātm. तुदै. *Perf.* तुतोद, तुतोदिथ, तुतोद; तुतुदिव, तुतुदथुस्, तुतुदतुस्; तुतुदिम, तुतुद, तुतुदुस्. Ātm. तुतुदे, तुतुदिषे, तुतुदे; तुतुदिवहे, तुतुदाथे, तुतुदाते; तुतुदिमहे, तुतुदिध्वे, तुतुदिरे. *1st Fut.* तोत्तास्मि. Ātm. तोत्ताहे. *2d Fut.* तोत्स्यामि. Ātm. तोत्स्ये. *Aor.* अतौत्सं, अतौत्सीस्, अतौत्सीत्; अतौत्स्व, अतौत्तं, अतौत्तां; अतौत्स्म, अतौत्त, अतौत्सुस्. Ātm. अतुत्सि, अतुत्थास्, अतुत्त; अतुत्स्वहि, अतुत्साथां, अतुत्सातां; अतुत्स्महि, अतुद्ध्वं, अतुत्सत. *Prec.* तुद्यासं. Ātm. तुत्सीय (452). *Cond.* अतोत्स्यं. Ātm. अतोत्स्ये. Pass., *Pres.* तुद्ये; *Aor. 3d sing.* अतोदि. Caus., *Pres.* तोदयामि; *Aor.* अतूतुदं. Des. तुतुत्सामि, -त्से. Freq. तोतुद्ये, तोतोद्मि (*3d sing.* तोतोत्ति). Part., *Pres.* तुदत्; *Past pass.* तुन्न; *Past indecl.* तुत्त्वा, -तुद्य; *Fut. pass.* तोत्तव्य, तोदनीय, तोद्य.

635. Root क्षिप्. *Inf.* क्षेप्तुं 'to throw.' Par. and Ātm. *Pres.* क्षिपामि. Ātm. क्षिपे. *Impf.* अक्षिपं. Ātm. अक्षिपे. *Pot.* क्षिपेयं. Ātm. क्षिपेय. *Impv.* क्षिपाणि. Ātm. क्षिपै. *Perf.* चिक्षेप, चिक्षेपिथ, चिक्षेप; चिक्षिपिव, चिक्षिपथुस्, चिक्षिपतुस्; चिक्षिपिम, चिक्षिप, चिक्षिपुस्. Ātm. चिक्षिपे, चिक्षिपिषे, चिक्षिपे; चिक्षिपिवहे, चिक्षिपाथे, चिक्षिपाते; चिक्षिपिमहे, चिक्षिपिध्वे, चिक्षिपिरे. *1st Fut.* क्षेप्तास्मि. Ātm. क्षेप्ताहे. *2d Fut.* क्षेप्स्यामि. Ātm. क्षेप्स्ये. *Aor.* अक्षैप्सं, अक्षैप्सीस्, अक्षैप्सीत्; अक्षैप्स्व, अक्षैप्तं, अक्षैप्तां; अक्षैप्स्म, अक्षैप्त, अक्षैप्सुस्. Ātm. अक्षिप्सि, अक्षिप्थास्, अक्षिप्त; अक्षिप्स्वहि, अक्षिप्साथां, अक्षिप्सातां; अक्षिप्स्महि, अक्षिब्ध्वं, अक्षिप्सत. *Prec.* क्षिप्यासं, &c. Ātm. क्षिप्सीय. *Cond.* अक्षेप्स्यं. Ātm. अक्षेप्स्ये. Pass. क्षिप्ये; *Aor. 3d sing.* अक्षेपि. Caus., *Pres.* क्षेपयामि; *Aor.* अचिक्षिपं. Des. चिक्षिप्सामि, -प्से. Freq. चेक्षिप्ये, चेक्षेप्मि (710, 294. *a*). Part., *Pres.* क्षिपत्; *Past pass.* क्षिप्त; *Past indecl.* क्षिप्त्वा, -क्षिप्य; *Fut. pass.* क्षेप्तव्य, क्षेपणीय, क्षेप्य.

a. Root विश्. *Inf.* वेष्टुं 'to enter.' Par. *Pres.* विशामि, विशसि, &c. *Impf.* अविशं, अविशस्, &c. *Pot.* विशेयं, विशेस्, &c. *Impv.* विशानि, विश, &c. *Perf.* विवेश, विवेशिथ, विवेश; विविशिव, विविशथुस्, विविशतुस्; विविशिम, विविश, विविशुस्. *1st Fut.* वेष्टास्मि. *2d Fut.* वेक्ष्यामि. *Aor.* अविक्षं, -क्षस्, -क्षत्; अविक्षाव, -क्षतं, -क्षतां; अविक्षाम, -क्षत, -क्षन्. *Prec.* विश्यासं. *Cond.* अवेक्ष्यं. Pass., *Pres.* विश्ये; *Aor. 3d sing.* अवेशि. Caus.,

Pres. वेशयामि; *Aor.* अवीविशत्. Des. विविक्षामि. Freq. वेविश्यते, वेवेश्मि (3d *sing.* वेवेष्टि). Part., *Pres.* विशत्; *Past pass.* विष्ट; *Past indecl.* विष्ट्वा, -विश्य; *Fut. pass.* वेष्टव्य, वेशनीय, वेश्य.

636. Root स्पृश्. *Inf.* स्प्रष्टुम् or स्पर्ष्टुम् 'to touch.' Par. *Pres.* स्पृशामि. *Impf.* अस्पृशम्. *Pot.* स्पृशेयम्. *Impv.* स्पृशानि. *Perf.* पस्पर्श, पस्पर्शिथ, पस्पर्श; पस्पृशिव, पस्पृशथुस्, पस्पृशतुस्; पस्पृशिम, पस्पृश, पस्पृशुस्. 1*st Fut.* स्प्रष्टास्मि or स्पर्ष्टास्मि. 2*d Fut.* स्प्रक्ष्यामि or स्पर्क्ष्यामि. *Aor.* अस्प्राक्षम्, अस्प्राक्षीस्, अस्प्राक्षीत्; अस्प्राक्ष्व, अस्प्राष्टम्, अस्प्राष्टाम्; अस्प्राक्ष्म, अस्प्राष्ट, अस्प्राक्षुस्. Or अस्पार्क्षम्, अस्पार्क्षीस्, &c. Or अस्पृक्षम्, अस्पृक्षस्, अस्पृक्षत्; अस्पृक्षाव, अस्पृक्षतम्, अस्पृक्षताम्; अस्पृक्षाम, अस्पृक्षत, अस्पृक्षन्. *Prec.* स्पृश्यासम्. *Cond.* अस्प्रक्ष्यम् or अस्पर्क्ष्यम्. Pass., *Pres.* स्पृश्ये; *Aor.* 3*d sing.* अस्पर्शि. Caus., *Pres.* स्पर्शयामि; *Aor.* अपस्पर्शम् or अपिस्पृशम्. Des. पिस्पृक्षामि. Freq. परीस्पृश्ये, परीस्पर्शिम or परीस्पर्ष्मि. Part., *Pres.* स्पृशत्; *Past pass.* स्पृष्ट; *Past indecl.* स्पृष्ट्वा, -स्पृश्य; *Fut. pass.* स्पर्ष्टव्य or स्प्रष्टव्य, स्पर्शनीय, स्पृश्य.

637. Root इष् (282). *Inf.* एषितुम् or एष्टुम् 'to wish.' Par. *Pres.* इच्छामि. *Impf.* ऐच्छम्. *Pot.* इच्छेयम्. *Impv.* इच्छानि. *Perf.* (367), इयेष, इयेषिथ, इयेष; ईषिव, ईषथुस्, ईषतुस्; ईषिम, ईष, ईषुस्. 1*st Fut.* एषितास्मि or एष्टास्मि. 2*d Fut.* एषिष्यामि. *Aor.* ऐषिषम्, ऐषीस्, ऐषीत्; ऐषिष्व, ऐषिष्टम्, ऐषिष्टाम्; ऐषिष्म, ऐषिष्ट, ऐषिषुस्. *Prec.* इष्यासम्. *Cond.* ऐषिष्यम्. Pass., *Pres.* इष्ये; *Aor.* 3*d sing.* ऐषि. Caus., *Pres.* एषयामि; *Aor.* ऐषिषम्. Des. एषिषिषामि. Part., *Pres.* इच्छत्; *Past pass.* इष्ट; *Past indecl.* इष्ट्वा or एषित्वा, -इष्य; *Fut. pass.* एष्टव्य or एषितव्य, एषणीय, इष्य.

EXAMPLES OF PRIMITIVE VERBS OF THE TENTH CONJUGATIONAL CLASS, EXPLAINED AT 283.

638. Root चुर् *ćur*. Infin. चोरयितुम् *ćorayitum*, 'to steal.'

PARASMAI-PADA. ĀTMANE-PADA.

Present tense, 'I steal.'

चोरयामि	चोरयावस्	चोरयामस्	चोरये	चोरयावहे	चोरयामहे
चोरयसि	चोरयथस्	चोरयथ	चोरयसे	चोरयेथे	चोरयध्वे
चोरयति	चोरयतस्	चोरयन्ति	चोरयते	चोरयेते	चोरयन्ते

Imperfect or *first preterite*, 'I was stealing,' or 'I stole.'

अचोरयम्	अचोरयाव	अचोरयाम	अचोरये	अचोरयावहि	अचोरयामहि
अचोरयस्	अचोरयतम्	अचोरयत	अचोरयथास्	अचोरयेथाम्	अचोरयध्वम्
अचोरयत्	अचोरयताम्	अचोरयन्	अचोरयत	अचोरयेताम्	अचोरयन्त

Potential, 'I may steal.'

चोरयेयम्	चोरयेव	चोरयेम	चोरयेय	चोरयेवहि	चोरयेमहि
चोरयेस्	चोरयेतं	चोरयेत	चोरयेथास्	चोरयेयाथां	चोरयेध्वं
चोरयेत्	चोरयेतां	चोरयेयुस्	चोरयेत	चोरयेयातां	चोरयेरन्

Imperative, 'Let me steal.'

चोरयाणि	चोरयाव	चोरयाम	चोरयै	चोरयावहै	चोरयामहै
चोरय	चोरयतं	चोरयत	चोरयस्व	चोरयेथां	चोरयध्वं
चोरयतु	चोरयतां	चोरयन्तु	चोरयतां	चोरयेतां	चोरयन्तां

Perfect or *second preterite*, 'I stole,' or 'I have stolen.'

चोरयामास	चोरयामासिव	चोरयामासिम	चोरयाञ्चक्रे	-चकृवहे	-चकृमहे
चोरयामासिथ	चोरयामासथुस्	चोरयामास	चोरयाञ्चकृषे	-चक्राथे	-चकृढ्वे
चोरयामास	चोरयामासतुस्	चोरयामासुस्	चोरयाञ्चक्रे	-चक्राते	-चक्रिरे

First future, 'I will steal.'

चोरयितास्मि	चोरयितास्वस्	चोरयितास्मस्	चोरयिताहे	चोरयितास्वहे	चोरयितास्महे
चोरयितासि	चोरयितास्थस्	चोरयितास्थ	चोरयितासे	चोरयितासाथे	चोरयिताध्वे
चोरयिता	चोरयितारौ	चोरयितारस्	चोरयिता	चोरयितारौ	चोरयितारस्

Second future, 'I shall steal.'

चोरयिष्यामि	चोरयिष्यावस्	चोरयिष्यामस्	चोरयिष्ये	चोरयिष्यावहे	चोरयिष्यामहे
चोरयिष्यसि	चोरयिष्यथस्	चोरयिष्यथ	चोरयिष्यसे	चोरयिष्येथे	चोरयिष्यध्वे
चोरयिष्यति	चोरयिष्यतस्	चोरयिष्यन्ति	चोरयिष्यते	चोरयिष्येते	चोरयिष्यन्ते

Aorist or *third preterite*, 'I stole.'

अचूचुरम्	अचूचुराव	अचूचुराम	अचूचुरे	अचूचुरावहि	अचूचुरामहि
अचूचुरस्	अचूचुरतं	अचूचुरत	अचूचुरथास्	अचूचुरेथां	अचूचुरध्वं
अचूचुरत्	अचूचुरतां	अचूचुरन्	अचूचुरत	अचूचुरेतां	अचूचुरन्त

Precative or *benedictive*, 'May I steal.'

चोर्यासं	चोर्यास्व	चोर्यास्म	चोरयिषीय	-यिषीवहि	-यिषीमहि
चोर्यास्	चोर्यास्तं	चोर्यास्त	चोरयिषीष्ठास्	-यिषीयास्थां	-यिषीढ्वं
चोर्यात्	चोर्यास्तां	चोर्यासुस्	चोरयिषीष्ट	-यिषीयास्तां	-यिषीरन्

Conditional, 'I should steal.'

अचोरयिष्यं	अचोरयिष्याव	अचोरयिष्याम	अचोरयिष्ये	-यिष्यावहि	-यिष्यामहि
अचोरयिष्यस्	अचोरयिष्यतं	अचोरयिष्यत	अचोरयिष्यथास्	-यिष्येथां	-यिष्यध्वं
अचोरयिष्यत्	अचोरयिष्यतां	अचोरयिष्यन्	अचोरयिष्यत	-यिष्येतां	-यिष्यन्त

639. Pass., *Pres.* चोर्ये; *Aor.* 3*d sing.* अचोरि. Caus. same as the Primitive verb. Des. चुचोरयिषामि. Part., *Pres.* चोरयत्; *Past pass.* चुरित or चोरित; *Past indecl.* चोरयित्वा; *Fut. pass.* चोरयितव्य, चोरणीय, चोर्य.

EXAMPLES OF OTHER VERBS OF THE TENTH CONJUGATIONAL CLASS IN THE ORDER OF THEIR FINAL LETTERS.

640. Root पॄ or पूर्. *Inf.* पूरयितुं 'to fill*.' Par. *Pres.* पूरयामि. *Impf.* अपूरयम्. *Pot.* पूरयेयम्. *Impv.* पूरयाणि. *Perf.* पूरयामास. 1*st Fut.* पूरयितास्मि. 2*d Fut.* पूरयिष्यामि. *Aor.* अपूपुरम्. *Prec.* पूर्यासम्. *Cond.* अपूरयिष्यम्. Pass., *Pres.* पूर्ये; *Aor.* 3*d sing.* अपूरि or अपूरयि. Caus. like the Primitive. Des. पुपूरयिषामि. Part., *Pres.* पूरयत्; *Past pass.* पूर्ण or पूरित or पूर्त; *Past indecl.* पूरयित्वा or पूर्त्वा, -पूर्य; *Fut. pass.* पूरयितव्य, पूरणीय, पूर्य.

641. Root चिन्त्. *Inf.* चिन्तयितुं 'to think.' Par. *Pres.* चिन्तयामि. *Impf.* अचिन्तयम्. *Pot.* चिन्तयेयम्. *Impv.* चिन्तयानि. *Perf.* चिन्तयामास. 1*st Fut.* चिन्तयितास्मि. 2*d Fut.* चिन्तयिष्यामि. *Aor.* अचिचिन्तम्. *Prec.* चिन्त्यासम्. *Cond.* अचिन्तयिष्यम्. Pass., *Pres.* चिन्त्ये. Caus. like the Primitive. Des. चिचिन्तयिषामि. Part., *Pres.* चिन्तयत्; Ātm. चिन्तयान (527); *Past pass.* चिन्तित; *Past indecl.* चिन्तयित्वा, -चिन्त्य; *Fut. pass.* चिन्तयितव्य, चिन्तनीय, चिन्त्य.

642. Root अर्थ्. *Inf.* अर्थयितुं (with prep. प्र, प्रार्थ्, प्रार्थयितुं) 'to ask,' 'to seek.' Ātm. *Pres.* अर्थये. *Impf.* आर्थये. *Pot.* अर्थयेय. *Impv.* अर्थयै. *Perf.* अर्थयाञ्चक्रे. 1*st Fut.* अर्थयिताहे. 2*d Fut.* अर्थयिष्ये. *Aor.* आर्तिथे, आर्तिथावहि, &c. *Prec.* अर्थयिषीय. *Cond.* आर्थयिष्ये. Pass., *Pres.* अर्थ्ये. Caus. like the Primitive. Des. अर्तिथयिषामि, -षे. Part., *Pres.* अर्थयान (527); *Past pass.* अर्थित; *Past indecl.* अर्थयित्वा, -अर्थ्य; *Fut. pass.* अर्थयितव्य, अर्थनीय, अर्थ्य.

643. Root कथ्. *Inf.* कथयितुं 'to say,' 'to tell.' Par. *Pres.* कथयामि. *Impf.* अकथयम्. *Pot.* कथयेयम्. *Impv.* कथयानि. *Perf.* कथयामास. 1*st Fut.* कथयितास्मि. 2*d Fut.* कथयिष्यामि. *Aor.* अचकथम् or अचीकथम्. *Prec.* कथ्यासम्. *Cond.* अकथयिष्यम्. Pass. कथ्ये, &c. Caus. like the Primitive. Des. चिकथयिषामि. Part., *Pres.* कथयत्; *Past pass.* कथित; *Past indecl.* कथयित्वा, -कथय्य (566. *a*); *Fut pass.* कथयितव्य, कथनीय, कथ्य.

a. Root घुष्. *Inf.* घोषयितुं 'to proclaim.' Par. *Pres.* घोषयामि. *Impf.* अघोषयम्. *Pot.* घोषयेयम्. *Impv.* घोषयाणि (58). *Perf.* घोषयामास.

* This root forms its base पारय *pāraya* from पॄ, and पूरय *pūraya* from पूर्; but the meaning of पारयामि is rather 'to fulfil,' 'to accomplish,' 'to get through.'

1st *Fut.* बोधयितास्मि. 2d *Fut.* बोधयिष्यामि. *Aor.* अबूबुधं. *Prec.* बोध्यासं. *Cond.* अबोधयिष्यं. Pass., *Pres.* बोध्ये; *Aor.* 3d *sing.* अबोधि. Caus. like the Primitive. Des. बुबोधयिषामि. Part., *Pres.* बोधयत्; *Past pass.* बोधित; *Past indecl.* बोधयित्वा, -बोध्य; *Fut. pass.* बोधयितव्य, बोधनीय, बोध्य.

b. Root भक्ष्. *Inf.* भक्षयितुं 'to eat,' 'to devour.' Par. *Pres.* भक्षयामि. *Impf.* अभक्षयं. *Pot.* भक्षयेयं. *Impv.* भक्षयाणि. *Perf.* भक्षयामास. 1st *Fut.* भक्षयितास्मि. 2d *Fut.* भक्षयिष्यामि. *Aor.* अबभक्षं. *Prec.* भक्ष्यासं. *Cond.* अभक्षयिष्यं. Pass. भक्ष्ये. Des. बिभक्षयिषामि. Part., *Pres.* भक्षयत्; *Past pass.* भक्षित; *Past indecl.* भक्षयित्वा, -भक्ष्य; *Fut. pass.* भक्षयितव्य, भक्षणीय, भक्ष्य.

EXAMPLES OF PRIMITIVE VERBS OF THE SECOND CONJUGATIONAL CLASS, EXPLAINED AT 307.

644. Root या *yā*. Infin. यातुम् *yātum*, 'to go.'

PARASMAI-PADA only.

Present, 'I go.'

यामि *yāmi*	यावस् *yāvas*	यामस् *yāmas*
यासि *yāsi*	याथस् *yāthas*	याथ *yātha*
याति *yāti*	यातस् *yātas*	यान्ति *yānti*

Imperfect or first preterite, 'I was going,' or 'I went.'

अयाम् *ayām*	अयाव *ayāva*	अयाम *ayāma*
अयास् *ayās*	अयातम् *ayātam*	अयात *ayāta*
अयात् *ayāt*	अयाताम् *ayātām*	अयान् *ayān* *

Potential, 'I may go.'

यायाम् *yāyām*	यायाव *yāyāva*	यायाम *yāyāma*
यायास् *yāyās*	यायातम् *yāyātam*	यायात *yāyāta*
यायात् *yāyāt*	यायाताम् *yāyātām*	यायुस् *yāyus*

Imperative, 'Let me go.'

यानि *yāni*	याव *yāva*	याम *yāma*
याहि *yāhi*	यातम् *yātam*	यात *yāta*
यातु *yātu*	याताम् *yātām*	यान्तु *yāntu*

645. Root इ *i* (310). Infin. एतुम् *etum*, 'to go.'

For इ with *adhi*, *ā*, &c., see 311.

Present, 'I go.'

एमि *emi* †	इवस् *ivas*	इमस् *imas*
एषि *eshi*	इथस् *ithas*	इथ *itha*
एति *eti*	इतस् *itas*	यन्ति *yanti* (34)

Imperfect or first preterite, 'I was going,' or 'I went.'

आयम् *āyam* (37)	ऐव *aiva* (260. *a*)	ऐम *aima*
ऐस् *ais* (33)	ऐतम् *aitam*	ऐत *aita*
ऐत् *ait*	ऐताम् *aitām*	आयन् *āyan* ‡

Potential, 'I may go.'

इयाम् *iyām*	इयाव *iyāva*	इयाम *iyāma*
इयास् *iyās*	इयातम् *iyātam*	इयात *iyāta*
इयात् *iyāt*	इयाताम् *iyātām*	इयुस् *iyus*

Imperative, 'Let me go.'

अयानि *ayāni*	अयाव *ayāva*	अयाम *ayāma*
इहि *ihi*	इतम् *itam*	इत *ita*
एतु *etu*	इताम् *itām*	यन्तु *yantu*

* Or अयुस् *ayus* by 290. *c*.

† This root is also of the 1st class, making अयामि, अयसि, &c., in Pres. tense.

‡ Foster gives आयन्. See Pāṇini (VI. 4. 81), and compare Lagh. Kaum. 604.

Perf. ययौ (373), ययाथ or ययिथ, ययौ; ययिव, ययथुस्, ययतुस्; ययिम, यय, ययुस्. *1st Fut.* यातास्मि, यातासि, याता, &c. *2d Fut.* यास्यामि, यास्यसि, यास्यति; यास्यावस्, &c. *Aor.* अयासिषम् (433), अयासीस्, अयासीत्; अयासिष्व, अयासिष्टं, अयासिष्टां; अयासिष्म, अयासिष्ट, अयासिषुस्. *Prec.* यायासं, यायास्, यायात्; यायास्व, &c. *Cond.* अयास्यं, अयास्यस्, अयास्यत्, &c. Pass., *Pres.* यायते, &c.; *Aor. 3d sing.* अयायि. Caus., *Pres.* यापयामि, &c.; *Aor.* अयीयपं, &c. Des. यियासामि. Freq. यायाये, यायामि or यायेमि (3d sing. यायाति or यायेति). Part., *Pres.* यात् (*Nom. case* यान्); *Past pass.* यात; *Past indecl.* यात्वा, -याय; *Fut. pass.* यातव्य, यानीय, येय.

Perf. इयाय (373), इययिथ or इयेथ, इयाय; ईयिव, ईयथुस्, ईयतुस्; ईयिम, ईय, ईयुस्. *1st Fut.* एतास्मि, &c. *2d Fut.* एष्यामि, &c. *Aor.* (438. *e*) अगां, अगास्, अगात्; अगाव, अगातं, अगातां; अगाम, अगात, अगुस्. *Prec.* ईयासं, &c. (see 447. *a*). *Cond.* ऐष्यं (260. *a*). Pass., *Pres.* ईये; *1st Fut.* एताहे or आयिताहे (474); *2d Fut.* एष्ये or आयिष्ये; *Aor. 3d sing.* अगायि or अगायत or आयिषत. Caus. गमयामि (from गम् at 602) or आया-यामि or आययामि; *Aor.* अजीगमं or आयियं or आपिपं (with *adhi* prefixed, अध्यजीगपं 493. *e*). Des. जिगमिषामि (from गम् at 602) or ईषिषामि, -षे. Part., *Pres.* यत् (*Nom.* यन्); *Past pass.* इत; *Past indecl.* इत्वा, -इत्य; *Fut. pass.* एतव्य, अयनीय, इत्य or एय.

a. Like या may be conjugated भा 'to shine:' *Pres.* भामि; *Perf.* बभौ; *1st Fut.* भातास्मि; *Aor.* अभासिषं, &c.

EXAMPLES OF OTHER VERBS OF THE SECOND CONJUGATIONAL CLASS IN THE ORDER OF THEIR FINAL LETTERS.

646. Root शी (315). *Inf.* शयितुं 'to lie down,' 'to sleep.' *Âtm.* *Pres.* शये, शेषे, शेते (κεῖται); शेवहे, शयाथे, शयाते; शेमहे (κείμεθα), शेध्वे, शेरते. *Impf.* अशयि, अशेथास्, अशेत; अशेवहि, अशयाथां, अशयातां; अशेमहि, अशेध्वं, अशेरत. *Pot.* शयीय, शयीथास्, शयीत; शयीवहि, शयीयाथां, शयीयातां; शयीमहि, शयीध्वं, शयीरन्. *Impv.* शयै, शेष्व, शेतां; शयावहै, शयाथां, शयातां; शयामहै, शेध्वं, शेरतां. *Perf.* शिश्ये, शिश्यिषे, शिश्ये; शिश्यिवहे, शिश्याथे, शिश्याते; शिश्यिमहे, शिश्यिध्वे or -ढ्वे, शिश्यिरे. *1st Fut.* शयिताहे. *2d Fut.* शयिष्ये. *Aor.* अशयिषि, अशयिष्ठास्, अशयिष्ट; अशयिष्वहि, अशयिषाथां, अशयिषातां; अशयिष्महि, अशयिध्वं or -ढ्वं, अशयिषत. *Prec.* शयिषीय. *Cond.* अशयिष्ये. Pass., *Pres.* शय्ये; *Aor. 3d sing.* अशायि. Caus., *Pres.* शाययामि; *Aor.* अशीशयं. Des. शिशयिषे. Freq. शाशय्ये, शेशेमि or शेशयीमि. Part., *Pres.* शयान (526. *a*); *Past pass.* शयित; *Past indecl.* शयित्वा, -शय्य; *Fut. pass.* शयितव्य, शयनीय, शेय.

647. Root सू or षू (312). *Inf.* सोतुं or सवितुं 'to bring forth.' *Âtm.* *Pres.* सुवे, सूषे, सूते; सूवहे, सुवाथे, सुवाते; सूमहे, सूध्वे, सुवते. *Impf.*

असुवि, असूथास्, असूत; असूवहि, असुवाथां, असुवातां; असूमहि, असूध्वं, असुवत. *Pot.* सुवीय. *Impv.* सुवै (Pāṇini VII. 3, 88), सूष्व, सूतां; सुवावहै, सुवाथां, सुवातां; सुवामहै, सूध्वं, सुवतां. *Perf.* सुषुवे, सुषुविषे, सुषुवे; सुषुविवहे, सुषुवाथे, सुषुवाते; सुषुविमहे, सुषुविध्वे or -ढ्वे, सुषुविरे. *1st Fut.* सोताहे or सविताहे. *2d Fut.* सोष्ये or सविष्ये. *Aor.* असविषि, असविष्ठास्, असविष्ट; असविष्वहि, असविषाथां, असविषातां; असविष्महि, असविढ्वं or -ध्वं, असविषत. Or असोषि, असोष्ठास्, असोष्ट; असोष्वहि, असोषाथां, असोषातां; असोष्महि, असोढ्वं, असोषत. *Prec.* सोषीय or सविषीय. *Cond.* असोष्ये or असविष्ये. Pass., *Pres.* सूये; *Aor. 3d sing.* असावि. Caus., *Pres.* सावयामि; *Aor.* असूषवं. Des. सुसूषामि, -षे. Freq. सोषूये, सोषोमि or सोषवीमि. Part., *Pres.* सुवान; *Past pass.* सुत or सूत or सून; *Past indecl.* सूत्वा or सुत्वा, -सूय; *Fut. pass.* सोतव्य or सवितव्य, सवनीय, साव्य or सव्य.

648. Root स्तु (313). *Inf.* स्तोतुं 'to praise.' Par. and Ātm. *Pres.* स्तौमि or स्तवीमि, स्तौषि or स्तवीषि, स्तौति or स्तवीति; स्तुवस् or स्तुवीवस्*, स्तुथस् or स्तुवीथस्*, स्तुतस् or स्तुवीतस्*; स्तुमस् or स्तुवीमस्*, स्तुथ or स्तुवीथ*, स्तुवन्ति. Ātm. स्तुवे, स्तुषे or स्तुवीषे*, स्तुते or स्तुवीते*; स्तुवहे or स्तुवीवहे*, स्तुवाथे, स्तुवाते; स्तुमहे or स्तुवीमहे*, स्तुध्वे or स्तुवीध्वे*, स्तुवते. *Impf.* अस्तुवं or अस्तवं, अस्तौस् or अस्तवीस्, अस्तौत् or अस्तवीत्; अस्तुव or अस्तुवीव*, अस्तुतं or अस्तुवीतं, अस्तुतां or अस्तुवीतां; अस्तुम or अस्तुवीम*, अस्तुत or अस्तुवीत, अस्तुवन्. Ātm. अस्तुवि, अस्तुथास् or अस्तुवीथास्, अस्तुत or अस्तुवीत; अस्तुवहि or अस्तुवीवहि*, अस्तुवाथां, अस्तुवातां; अस्तुमहि or अस्तुवीमहि*, अस्तुध्वं or अस्तुवीध्वं*, अस्तुवत. *Pot.* स्तुयां or स्तुवीयां*. Ātm. स्तुवीय. *Impv.* स्तुवानि or स्तवानि, स्तुहि or स्तुवीहि*, स्तौतु or स्तवीतु; स्तवाव, स्तुतं or स्तुवीतं, स्तुतां or स्तुवीतां; स्तवाम, स्तुत or स्तुवीत, स्तुवन्तु. Ātm. स्तवै, स्तुष्व or स्तुवीष्व*, स्तुतां or स्तुवीतां; स्तवावहै, स्तुवाथां, स्तुवातां; स्तवामहै, स्तुध्वं or स्तुवीध्वं*, स्तुवतां. *Perf.* (369) तुष्टाव, तुष्टोथ, तुष्टाव; तुष्टुव, तुष्टुवथुस्, तुष्टुवतुस्; तुष्टुम, तुष्टुव, तुष्टुवुस्. Ātm. तुष्टुवे, तुष्टुषे, तुष्टुवे; तुष्टुवहे, तुष्टुवाथे, तुष्टुवाते; तुष्टुमहे, तुष्टुढ्वे (372), तुष्टुविरे. *1st Fut.* स्तोतास्मि. Ātm. स्तोताहे. *2d Fut.* स्तोष्यामि. Ātm. स्तोष्ये. *Aor.* (427. *a*) अस्ताविषं, अस्तावीस्, अस्तावीत्; अस्ताविष्व, अस्ताविष्टं, अस्ताविष्टां; अस्ताविष्म, अस्ताविष्ट, अस्ताविषुस्. Ātm. अस्तोषि, अस्तोष्ठास्, अस्तोष्ट; अस्तोष्वहि, अस्तोषाथां, अस्तोषातां; अस्तोष्महि, अस्तोढ्वं, अस्तोषत. *Prec.* स्तूयासं. Ātm. स्तोषीय. *Cond.* अस्तोष्यं. Ātm. अस्तोष्ये. Pass., *Pres.* स्तूये; *Aor. 3d sing.* अस्तावि. Caus., *Pres.* स्तावयामि; *Aor.* अतुष्टवं. Des. तुष्टूषामि, -षे. Freq. तोष्टूये, तोष्टोमि. Part., *Pres.* स्तुवत्; *Past pass.* स्तुत; *Past indecl.* स्तुत्वा, -स्तुत्य; *Fut. pass.* स्तोतव्य, स्तवनीय, स्तुत्य or स्ताव्य or स्तव्य.

649. Root ब्रू (314). *Inf.* वक्तुं (borrowed from वच् at 650) 'to say,'

* Some authorities reject these forms.

'to speak.' Par. and Ātm. *Pres.* ब्रवीमि, ब्रवीषि*, ब्रवीति*; ब्रूवः, ब्रूथः*, ब्रूतः*; ब्रूमः, ब्रूथ, ब्रुवन्ति*. Ātm. ब्रुवे, ब्रूषे, ब्रूते; ब्रूवहे, ब्रुवाथे, ब्रुवाते; ब्रूमहे, ब्रूध्वे, ब्रुवते. *Impf.* अब्रवं or अब्रुवं (314. *a*), अब्रवीः, अब्रवीत्; अब्रूव, अब्रूतं, अब्रूतां; अब्रूम, अब्रूत, अब्रुवन्. Ātm. अब्रुवि, अब्रूथाः, अब्रूत; अब्रूवहि, अब्रुवाथां, अब्रुवातां; अब्रूमहि, अब्रूध्वं, अब्रुवत. *Pot.* ब्रूयां, ब्रूयाः, &c. Ātm. ब्रुवीय, ब्रुवीथाः, &c. *Impv.* ब्रवाणि (58), ब्रूहि, ब्रवीतु; ब्रवाव, ब्रूतं, ब्रूतां; ब्रवाम, ब्रूत, ब्रुवन्तु. Ātm. ब्रवै, ब्रूष्व, ब्रूतां; ब्रवावहै, ब्रुवाथां, ब्रुवातां; ब्रवामहै, ब्रूध्वं, ब्रुवतां. The other tenses and forms are borrowed from वच्; as, *Perf.* उवाच, &c.; *1st Fut.* वक्तास्मि, &c.; see वच् at 650. But the *Pres.* participles are ब्रुवत् and ब्रुवाण.

650. Root वच् (320). *Inf.* वक्तुं 'to say,' 'to speak.' Par. In the non-conjugational tenses Ātm. also. *Pres.* वच्मि, वक्षि, वक्ति; वच्वः, वक्थः, वक्तः; वच्मः, वक्थ, ब्रुवन्ति (borrowed from ब्रू at 649). *Impf.* अवचं, अवक् or अवग् (292), अवक् or अवग् (292); अवच्व, अवक्तं, अवक्तां; अवच्म, अवक्त, अवचन्†. *Pot.* वच्यां, वच्याः, &c. *Impv.* वचानि, वग्धि, वक्तु; वचाव, वक्तं, वक्तां; वचाम, वक्त, ब्रुवन्तु (borrowed from ब्रू). *Perf.* (375. *c*) उवाच, उवचिथ or उवक्थ, उवाच; ऊचिव, ऊचथुः, ऊचतुः; ऊचिम, ऊच, ऊचुः. Ātm. ऊचे, ऊचिषे, ऊचे; ऊचिवहे, ऊचाथे, ऊचाते; ऊचिमहे, ऊचिध्वे, ऊचिरे. *1st Fut.* वक्तास्मि. Ātm. वक्ताहे. *2d Fut.* वक्ष्यामि. Ātm. वक्ष्ये. *Aor.* (441) अवोचं, अवोचः, अवोचत्; अवोचाव, अवोचतं, अवोचतां; अवोचाम, अवोचत, अवोचन्. Ātm. अवोचे, अवोचथाः, अवोचत; अवोचावहि, अवोचेथां, अवोचेतां; अवोचामहि, अवोचध्वं, अवोचन्त. *Prec.* उच्यासं. Ātm. वक्षीय. *Cond.* अवक्ष्यं. Ātm. अवक्ष्ये. Pass., *Pres.* उच्ये (471); *Aor. 3d sing.* अवाचि. Caus., *Pres.* वाचयामि; *Aor.* अवीवचं. Des. विवक्षामि, -क्षे. Freq. वावच्ये, वावच्मि. Part., *Pres.* ब्रुवत्; Ātm. ब्रुवाण (borrowed from ब्रू at 649); *Past pass.* उक्त; *Past indecl.* उक्त्वा, -उच्य; *Fut. pass.* वक्तव्य, वचनीय, वाच्य or वाक्य.

651. Root मृज् (321). *Inf.* मार्ष्टुं or मार्जितुं 'to wipe,' 'to rub,' 'to clean.' Par. *Pres.* मार्ज्मि, मार्क्षि (296), मार्ष्टि (297); मृज्वः, मृष्ठः, मृष्टः; मृज्मः, मृष्ठ, मार्जन्ति or मृजन्ति. *Impf.* अमार्जं, अमार्ट् or अमार्ड् (292), अमार्ट् or अमार्ड्; अमृज्व, अमृष्टं, अमृष्टां; अमृज्म, अमृष्ट, अमार्जन् or अमृजन्. *Pot.* मृज्यां. *Impv.* मार्जानि, मृड्ढि (303), मार्ष्टु; मार्जाव, मृष्टं, मृष्टां; मार्जाम, मृष्ट, मार्जन्तु or मृजन्तु. *Perf.* ममार्ज, ममार्जिथ or ममार्ष्ठ (370. *e*), ममार्ज; ममृजिव or ममार्जिव, ममृजथुः or ममार्जथुः, ममृजतुः or ममार्जतुः; ममृजिम or ममार्जिम, ममृज or ममार्ज,

* For these forms are sometimes substituted 2d sing. आत्थ, 3d sing. आह; 2d du. आहथुः, 3d du. आहतुः; 3d pl. आहुः; all from the perfect of a defective root अह्, with a present signification.

† According to some, the 3d pl. of the imperfect is also wanting.

ममृजुस् or ममार्जुस्. *1st Fut.* मार्ष्टास्मि or मार्जितास्मि (415. *a*). *2d Fut.* मार्क्ष्यामि or मार्जिष्यामि. *Aor.* अमार्क्षं, अमार्क्षीस्, अमार्क्षीत्; अमार्क्ष्व, अमार्ष्टं, अमार्ष्टां; अमार्क्ष्म, अमार्ष्ट, अमार्क्षुस्. Or अमार्जिषं, अमार्जीस्, अमार्जीत्; अमार्जिष्व, &c. *Prec.* मृज्यासं. *Cond.* अमार्क्ष्यं or अमार्जिष्यं. Pass., *Pres.* मृज्ये; *Aor. 3d sing.* अमार्जि. Caus., *Pres.* मार्जयामि; *Aor.* अममार्जं or अमीमृजं. Des. मिमार्क्षामि or मिमृक्षामि or मिमार्जिषामि. Freq. मरीमृज्ये, मरी-, मरि-, मर्मार्ज्मि (*3d sing.* -मार्ष्टि). Part., *Pres.* मार्जत्; *Past pass.* मृष्ट; *Past indecl.* मृष्ट्वा or मार्जित्वा, -मृज्य; *Fut. pass.* मार्ष्टव्य or मार्जितव्य, मार्जनीय, मार्ग्य or मृज्य.

652. Root अद् (317). *Inf.* अत्तुं 'to eat.' Par. *Pres.* अद्मि, अत्सि, अत्ति; अद्वस्, अत्थस्, अत्तस्; अद्मस्, अत्थ, अदन्ति. *Impf.* आदं, आदस्, (317. *b*), आदत् (317. *b*); आद्व, आत्तं, आत्तां; आद्म, आत्त, आदन्. *Pot.* अद्यां. *Impv.* अदानि, अद्धि, अत्तु; अदाव, अत्तं, अत्तां; अदाम, अत्त, अदन्तु. *Perf.* आद, आदिथ, आद; आदिव, आदथुस्, आदतुस्; आदिम, आद, आदुस्. *1st Fut.* अत्तास्मि. *2d Fut.* अत्स्यामि. *Aor.* अघसं (borrowed from root घस्), अघसस्, अघसत्; अघसाव, अघसतं, अघसतां; अघसाम, अघसत, अघसन्. *Prec.* अद्यासं. *Cond.* आत्स्यं. Pass., *Pres.* अद्ये; *Aor. 3d sing.* आदि. Caus., *Pres.* आदयामि; *Aor.* आदिदं. Des. जिघत्सामि (borrowed from घस्). Part., *Pres.* अदत्; *Past pass.* जग्ध; *Past indecl.* जग्ध्वा; *Fut. pass.* अत्तव्य, अदनीय, आद्य.

653. Root रुद् (322). *Inf.* रोदितुं 'to weep.' Par. *Pres.* रोदिमि, रोदिषि, रोदिति; रुदिवस्, रुदिथस्, रुदितस्; रुदिमस्, रुदिथ, रुदन्ति. *Impf.* अरोदं, अरोदस् or अरोदीस्, अरोदत् or अरोदीत् (Páṇini VII. 3. 98, 99); अरुदिव, अरुदितं, अरुदितां; अरुदिम, अरुदित, अरुदन्. *Pot.* रुद्यां. *Impv.* रोदानि, रुदिहि, रोदितु; रोदाव, रुदितं, रुदितां; रोदाम, रुदित, रुदन्तु. *Perf.* रुरोद, रुरोदिथ, रुरोद; रुरुदिव, रुरुदथुस्, रुरुदतुस्; रुरुदिम, रुरुद, रुरुदुस्. *1st Fut.* रोदितास्मि. *2d Fut.* रोदिष्यामि. *Aor.* अरुदं, अरुदस्, अरुदत्; अरुदाव, अरुदतं, अरुदतां; अरुदाम, अरुदत, अरुदन्. Or अरोदिषं, अरोदीस्, अरोदीत्; अरोदिष्व, अरोदिष्टं, अरोदिष्टां; अरोदिष्म, अरोदिष्ट, अरोदिषुस्. *Prec.* रुद्यासं. *Cond.* अरोदिष्यं. Pass., *Pres.* रुद्ये; *Aor. 3d sing.* अरोदि. Caus., *Pres.* रोदयामि; *Aor.* अरूरुदं. Des. रुरुदिषामि. Freq. रोरुद्ये, रोरोद्मि (*3d sing.* रोरोत्ति) or रोरुदीमि. Part., *Pres.* रुदत्; *Past pass.* रुदित; *Past indecl.* रुदित्वा, -रुद्य; *Fut. pass.* रोदितव्य, रोदनीय, रोद्य.

654. Root हन् (323)*. *Inf.* हन्तुं 'to kill,' 'to strike.' Par. *Pres.* हन्मि, हंसि, हन्ति*; हन्वस्, हथस्, हतस्; हन्मस्, हथ, घ्नन्ति. *Impf.* अहनं, अहन्,

* It must be borne in mind (with reference to 323) that *han* only loses its nasal before *t* and *th*, *if not marked with P.* When the prep. आ *á* is prefixed, this root may take the Átmane, in which case the 3d sing. Pres. will be आहते.

अहन् (292); अहन्व, अहतं, अहतां; अहन्म, अहत, अघ्नन्. *Pot.* हन्यां, &c. *Impv.* हनानि, जहि, हन्तु*; हनाव, हतं, हतां; हनाम, हत, घ्नन्तु. *Perf.* जघान (376), जघनिथ or जघन्थ, जघान; जघ्निव, जघ्नथुस्, जघ्नतुस्; जघ्निम, जघ्न, जघ्नुस्. *1st Fut.* हन्तास्मि. *2d Fut.* हनिष्यामि. *Aor.* (432. *b*) अवधिषं, अवधीस्, अवधीत्; अवधिष्व, अवधिष्टं, अवधिष्टां; अवधिष्म, अवधिष्ट, अवधिषुस्. *Prec.* वध्यासं. *Cond.* अहनिष्यं. Pass., *Pres.* हन्ये; *Perf.* जघ्ने (473); *Aor. 3d sing.* अघानि (or अवधि, borrowed from वध); *1st Fut.* हन्ताहे or घानिताहे; *2d Fut.* हनिष्ये or घानिष्ये. Caus., *Pres.* घातयामि; *Aor.* अजीघतं. Des. जिघांसामि. Freq. जेघ्नीये or जङ्घन्ये, जङ्घन्मि or जेघ्नीमि or जङ्घनीमि; see 708. Part., *Pres.* घ्नत्; *Past pass.* हत; *Past indecl.* हत्वा, -हत्य; *Fut. pass.* हन्तव्य, हननीय, घात्य.

655. Root स्वप् (322. *a*). *Inf.* स्वप्तुं 'to sleep.' Par. *Pres.* स्वपिमि, स्वपिषि, स्वपिति; स्वपिवस्, स्वपिथस्, स्वपितस्; स्वपिमस्, स्वपिथ, स्वपन्ति. *Impf.* अस्वपं, अस्वपस् or अस्वपीस्, अस्वपत् or अस्वपीत्; अस्वपिव, &c.; see रुद् at 653. *Pot.* स्वप्यां. *Impv.* स्वपानि, स्वपिहि, स्वपितु; स्वपाव, स्वपितं, स्वपितां; स्वपाम, स्वपित, स्वपन्तु. *Perf.* (382) सुष्वाप, सुष्वपिथ or सुष्वप्थ, सुष्वाप; सुषुपिव, सुषुपथुस्, सुषुपतुस्; सुषुपिम, सुषुप, सुषुपुस्. *1st Fut.* स्वप्तास्मि. *2d Fut.* स्वप्स्यामि. *Aor.* अस्वाप्सं, अस्वाप्सीस्, अस्वाप्सीत्; अस्वाप्स्व, अस्वाप्तं, अस्वाप्तां; अस्वाप्स्म, अस्वाप्त, अस्वाप्सुस्. *Prec.* सुप्यासं. *Cond.* अस्वप्स्यं. Pass., *Pres.* सुप्ये (471); *Aor. 3d sing.* अस्वापि. Caus., *Pres.* स्वापयामि; *Aor.* असूषुपं, &c. Des. सुषुप्सामि. Freq. सोषुप्ये, सास्वप्मि or सास्वपीमि. Part., *Pres.* स्वपत्; *Past pass.* सुप्त; *Past indecl.* सुप्त्वा, -सुप्य; *Fut. pass.* स्वप्तव्य, स्वपनीय, स्वाप्य.

656. Root वश् (324). *Inf.* वशितुं 'to desire,' 'to wish.' Par. *Pres.* वश्मि, वक्षि (302), वष्टि (300); उश्वस्, उष्ठस्, उष्टस्; उश्मस्, उष्ठ, उशन्ति. *Impf.* अवशं, अवट् or अवड् (292), अवट् or अवड्; औश्व (260. *a*), औष्टं, औष्टां; औश्म, औष्ट, औशन्. *Pot.* उश्यां. *Impv.* वशानि, उड्ढि (303), वष्टु; वशाव, उष्टं, उष्टां; वशाम, उष्ट, उशन्तु. *Perf.* (375. *c*) उवाश, उवशिथ, उवाश; ऊशिव, ऊशथुस्, ऊशतुस्; ऊशिम, ऊश, ऊशुस्. *1st Fut.* वशितास्मि. *2d Fut.* वशिष्यामि. *Aor.* अवाशिषं, अवाशीस्, अवाशीत्, &c.; or अवशिषं, -शीस्, -शीत्, &c.; see 427. *Prec.* उश्यासं. *Cond.* अवशिष्यं. Pass. उश्ये (471); *Aor. 3d sing.* अवाशि or अवशि. Caus., *Pres.* वाशयामि; *Aor.* अवीवशं. Des. विवशिषामि. Freq. वावश्ये, वावष्मि or वावशीमि. Part., *Pres.* उशत्; *Past pass.* उशित; *Past indecl.* वशित्वा, -उश्य; *Fut. pass.* वशितव्य, वशनीय, वाश्य.

---

* It must be borne in mind (with reference to 323) that *han* only loses its nasal before *t* and *th*, *if not marked with P.*

657. Root द्विष् (309). *Inf.* द्वेष्टुं 'to hate.' Par. and Ātm. *Pres.* द्वेष्मि, द्वेक्षि (302), द्वेष्टि (301); द्विष्वस्, द्विष्ठस्, द्विष्टस्; द्विष्मस्, द्विष्ठ, द्विषन्ति. Ātm. द्विषे, द्विक्षे, द्विष्टे; द्विष्वहे, द्विषाथे, द्विषाते; द्विष्महे, द्विड्ढ्वे, द्विषते. *Impf.* अद्वेषं, अद्वेट् (292), अद्वेट्; अद्विष्व, अद्विष्टं, अद्विष्टां; अद्विष्म, अद्विष्ट, अद्विषन् or अद्विषुस्. Ātm. अद्विषि, अद्विष्ठास्, अद्विष्ट; अद्विष्वहि, अद्विषाथां, अद्विषातां; अद्विष्महि, अद्विड्ढ्वं, अद्विषत. *Pot.* द्विष्यां. Ātm. द्विषीय. *Impv.* द्वेषाणि, द्विड्ढि, द्वेष्टु; द्वेषाव, द्विष्टं, द्विष्टां; द्वेषाम, द्विष्ट, द्विषन्तु. Ātm. द्वेषै, द्विक्ष्व, द्विष्टां; द्वेषावहै, द्विषाथां, द्विषातां; द्वेषामहै, द्विड्ढ्वं, द्विषतां. *Perf.* दिद्वेष, दिद्वेषिथ, दिद्वेष; दिद्विषिव, दिद्विषथुस्, दिद्विषतुस्; दिद्विषिम, दिद्विष, दिद्विषुस्. Ātm. दिद्विषे, दिद्विषिषे, दिद्विषे; दिद्विषिवहे, दिद्विषाथे, दिद्विषाते; दिद्विषिमहे, दिद्विषिध्वे, दिद्विषिरे. *1st Fut.* द्वेष्टास्मि. Ātm. द्वेष्टाहे. *2d Fut.* द्वेक्ष्यामि. Ātm. द्वेक्ष्ये. *Aor.* (439) अद्विक्षं, -क्षस्, -क्षत्; -क्षाव, -क्षतं, -क्षतां; -क्षाम, -क्षत, -क्षन्. Ātm. (439. *a*) अद्विक्षि, -क्षथास्, -क्षत; -क्षावहि, -क्षाथां, -क्षातां; -क्षामहि, -क्षध्वं, -क्षन्त. *Prec.* द्विष्यासं. Ātm. द्विक्षीय. *Cond.* अद्वेक्ष्यं. Ātm. अद्वेक्ष्ये. Pass., *Pres.* द्विष्ये, &c.; *Aor. 3d sing.* अद्वेषि. Caus., *Pres.* द्वेषयामि; *Aor.* अदिद्विषं. Des. दिद्विक्षामि, -क्षे. Freq. देद्विष्ये, देद्वेष्मि or देद्विषीमि. Part., *Pres.* द्विषत्; *Past pass.* द्विष्ट; *Past indecl.* द्विष्ट्वा, -द्विष्य; *Fut. pass.* द्वेष्टव्य, द्वेषणीय, द्वेष्य.

a. Root वस्. *Inf.* वसितुं 'to wear,' 'to put on (as clothes, &c.).' Ātm. *Pres.* वसे, वस्से (62. *b*), वस्ते; वस्वहे, वसाथे, वसाते; वस्महे, वद्ध्वे or वध्वे, वसते. *Impf.* अवसि, अवस्थास्, अवस्त; अवस्वहि, अवसाथां, अवसातां; अवस्महि, अवद्ध्वं or अवध्वं, अवसत. *Pot.* वसीय. *Impv.* वसै. *Perf.* ववसे, ववसिषे, &c. *1st Fut.* वसिताहे. *2d Fut.* वसिष्ये. *Aor.* अवसिषि, अवसिष्ठास्, अवसिष्ट; अवसिष्वहि, अवसिषाथां, अवसिषातां, &c. *Prec.* वसिषीय. *Cond.* अवसिष्ये. Pass., *Pres.* वस्ये. Caus., *Pres.* वासयामि or -ये. Des. विवसिषे. Freq. वावस्ये, वावस्मि. Part., *Pres.* वसान; *Past pass.* वसित; *Past indecl.* वसित्वा, -वस्य; *Fut. pass.* वसितव्य, वसनीय, वस्य or वास्य.

658. Root शास् (328). *Inf.* शासितुं 'to rule,' 'to punish.' Par. (With आ 'to bless,' Ātm.) *Pres.* शास्मि, शास्सि, शास्ति; शिष्वस्, शिष्ठस्, शिष्टस्; शिष्मस्, शिष्ठ, शासति (290. *b*). Ātm. शासे, शास्से (62. *b*), शास्ते; शास्वहे, शासाथे, शासाते; शास्महे, शाद्ध्वे or शाध्वे (304), शासते. *Impf.* अशासं, अशात् or अशास् (292, 304. *a*), अशात्; अशिष्व, अशिष्टं, अशिष्टां; अशिष्म, अशिष्ट, अशासुस्. Ātm. अशासि, &c. *Pot.* शिष्यां. Ātm. शासीय. *Impv.* शासानि, शाधि (304), शास्तु; शासाव, शिष्टं, शिष्टां; शासाम, शिष्ट, शासतु. Ātm. शासै. *Perf.* शशास, शशासिथ, शशास; शशासिव, शशासथुस्, शशासतुस्; शशासिम, शशास, शशासुस्. Ātm. शशासे, शशासिषे, &c. *1st Fut.* शासितास्मि. Ātm. शासिताहे. *2d Fut.* शासिष्यामि. Ātm. शासिष्ये. *Aor.* (441) अशिषं, अशिषस्, अशिषत्; अशिषाव, अशिषतं, अशिषतां; अशिषाम, अशिषत,

अक्ष्णाविषुस्. Ātm. अक्ष्णविषि, अक्ष्णविष्ठास्, अक्ष्णविष्ट; अक्ष्णविष्वहि, अक्ष्णविषाथां, अक्ष्णविषातां; अक्ष्णविष्महि, अक्ष्णविढ्वं, अक्ष्णविषत. *Prec.* क्ष्णूयासं. Ātm. क्ष्णविषीय. *Cond.* अक्ष्णविष्यं. Ātm. अक्ष्णविष्ये. Pass., *Pres.* क्ष्णूयते; *Aor.* 3d *sing.* अक्ष्णावि. Caus. क्ष्णावयति; *Aor.* अचुक्ष्णवं. Des. चिक्ष्णविषति. Freq. चोक्ष्णूयते, चोक्ष्णोमि or चोक्ष्णवीमि. Part., *Pres.* क्ष्णुवत् (141. a); *Past pass.* क्ष्णुत; *Past indecl.* क्ष्णवित्वा or क्ष्णुत्वा, -क्ष्णुत्य; *Fut. pass.* क्ष्णवितव्य, क्ष्णवनीय, क्ष्णव्य.

659. Root दिह्. *Inf.* देग्धुं 'to anoint,' 'to smear.' Par. and Ātm. *Pres.* देह्मि, धेक्षि (306. a), देग्धि (305); दिह्वस्, दिग्धस्, दिग्धस्; दिह्मस्, दिग्ध, दिहन्ति. Ātm. दिहे, धिक्षे, दिग्धे; दिह्वहे, दिहाथे, दिहाते; दिह्महे, धिग्ध्वे (306. d), दिहते. *Impf.* अदेहं, अधेक् or अधेट् (292. a), अधेक् or अधेट्; अदिह्व, अदिग्धं, अदिग्धां; अदिह्म, अदिग्ध, अदिहन्. Ātm. अदिहि, अदिग्धास्, अदिग्ध; अदिह्वहि, अदिहाथां, अदिहातां; अदिह्महि, अधिग्ध्वं, अदिहत. *Pot.* दिह्यां. Ātm. दिहीय. *Impv.* देहानि, दिग्धि, देग्धु; देहाव, दिग्धं, दिग्धां; देहाम, दिग्ध, दिहन्तु. Ātm. देहै, धिक्ष्व, दिग्धां; देहावहै, दिहाथां, दिहातां; देहामहै, धिग्ध्वं, दिहतां. *Perf.* दिदेह, दिदेहिथ, दिदेह; दिदिहिव, दिदिहथुस्, दिदिहतुस्; दिदिहिम, दिदिह, दिदिहुस्. Ātm. दिदिहे, दिदिहिषे, दिदिहे; दिदिहिवहे, दिदिहाथे, दिदिहाते; दिदिहिमहे, दिदिहिध्वे or -ढ्वे, दिदिहिरे. *1st Fut.* देग्धास्मि. Ātm. देग्धाहे. *2d Fut.* धेक्ष्यामि. Ātm. धेक्ष्ये. *Aor.* (439) अधिक्षं, अधिक्षस्, अधिक्षत्; अधिक्षाव, अधिक्षतं, अधिक्षतां; अधिक्षाम, अधिक्षत, अधिक्षन्. Ātm. (439. b) अधिक्षि, अधिक्षथास् or अदिग्धास्, अधिक्षत or अदिग्ध; अधिक्षावहि or अदिह्वहि, अधिक्षाथां, अधिक्षातां; अधिक्षामहि, अधिक्षध्वं or अधिग्ध्वं, अधिक्षन्त. *Prec.* दिह्यासं. Ātm. धिक्षीय. *Cond.* अधेक्ष्यं. Ātm. अधेक्ष्ये. Pass., *Pres.* दिह्यते; *Aor.* 3d *sing.* अदेहि. Caus., *Pres.* देहयामि; *Aor.* अदीदिहं. Des. दिधिक्षामि, -क्षे. Freq. देदिह्ये, देदेह्मि (3d *sing.* देदेग्धि). Part., *Pres.* दिहत्; Ātm. दिहान; *Past pass.* दिग्ध; *Past indecl.* दिग्ध्वा, -दिह्य; *Fut. pass.* देग्धव्य, देहनीय, देह्य.

660. Root दुह्. *Inf.* दोग्धुं 'to milk.' Par. and Ātm. *Pres.* दोह्मि, धोक्षि (306. a), दोग्धि (305); दुह्वस्, दुग्धस्, दुग्धस्; दुह्मस्, दुग्ध, दुहन्ति. Ātm. दुहे, धुक्षे, दुग्धे; दुह्वहे, दुहाथे, दुहाते; दुह्महे, धुग्ध्वे (306. d), दुहते. *Impf.* अदोहं, अधोक् or अधोट् (292. a), अधोक् or अधोट्; अदुह्व, अदुग्धं, अदुग्धां; अदुह्म, अदुग्ध, अदुहन्. Ātm. अदुहि, अदुग्धास्, अदुग्ध; अदुह्वहि, अदुहाथां, अदुहातां; अदुह्महि, अधुग्ध्वं, अदुहत. *Pot.* दुह्यां. Ātm. दुहीय. *Impv.* दोहानि, दुग्धि (306. c), दोग्धु; दोहाव, दुग्धं, दुग्धां; दोहाम, दुग्ध, दुहन्तु. Ātm. दोहै, धुक्ष्व, दुग्धां; दोहावहै, दुहाथां, दुहातां; दोहामहै, धुग्ध्वं (306. d), दुहतां. *Perf.* दुदोह, दुदोहिथ, दुदोह; दुदुहिव, दुदुहथुस्, दुदुहतुस्; दुदुहिम, दुदुह, दुदुहुस्. Ātm. दुदुहे, दुदुहिषे, दुदुहे; दुदुहिवहे, दुदुहाथे, दुदुहाते; दुदुहिमहे, दुदुहिध्वे or -ढ्वे, दुदुहिरे. *1st Fut.* दोग्धास्मि. Ātm. दोग्धाहे. *2d Fut.* धोक्ष्यामि. Ātm.

धोक्ष्ये. *Aor.* (439) अधुक्षं, अधुक्षस्, अधुक्षत्; अधुक्षाव, अधुक्षतं, अधुक्षतां; अधुक्षाम, अधुक्षत, अधुक्षन्. Átm. (439. *b*) अधुक्षि, अधुक्षथास् or अदुग्धास्, अधुक्षत or अदुग्ध; अधुक्षावहि or अदुह्वहि, अधुक्षाथां, अधुक्षातां; अधुक्षामहि, अधुक्षध्वं or अधुग्ध्वं, अधुक्षन्त. *Prec.* दुह्यासं. Átm. धुक्षीय. *Cond.* अधोक्ष्यं. Átm. अधोक्ष्ये. Pass., *Pres.* दुह्ये; *Aor.* 3*d sing.* अदोहि. Caus., *Pres.* दोहयामि; *Aor.* अदूदुहं. Des. दुधुक्षामि, -क्षे. Freq. दोदुह्ये, दोदोह्मि (3*d sing.* दोदोग्धि). Part., *Pres.* दुहत्, दुहान; *Past pass.* दुग्ध; *Past indecl.* दुग्ध्वा, -दुह्य; *Fut. pass.* दोग्धव्य, दोहनीय, दोह्य.

661. Root लिह्. *Inf.* लेढुं 'to lick.' Par. and Átm. *Pres.* (329) लेह्मि, लेक्षि (306), लेढि (305. *a*); लिह्वस्, लीढस् (305. *a*), लीढस्; लिह्मस्, लीढ, लिहन्ति. Átm. लिहे, लिक्षे, लीढे; लिह्वहे, लिहाथे, लिहाते; लिह्महे, लीढ्वे, लिहते. *Impf.* अलेहं, अलेट् or अलेड् (292. *a*), अलेट् or अलेड्; अलिह्व, अलीढं, अलीढां; अलिह्म, अलीढ, अलिहन्. Átm. अलिहि, अलीढास्, अलीढ; अलिह्वहि, अलिहाथां, अलिहातां; अलिह्महि, अलीढ्वं, अलिहत. *Pot.* लिह्यां. Átm. लिहीय. *Impv.* लेहानि, लीढि (306. *c*), लेढु; लेहाव, लीढं, लीढां; लेहाम, लीढ, लिहन्तु. Átm. लेहै, लिक्ष्व, लीढां; लेहावहै, लिहाथां, लिहातां; लेहामहै, लीढ्वं (306. *c*), लिहतां. *Perf.* लिलेह, लिलेहिथ, लिलेह; लिलिहिव, लिलिहथुस्, लिलिहतुस्; लिलिहिम, लिलिह, लिलिहुस्. Átm. लिलिहे, लिलिहिषे, &c. 1*st Fut.* लेढास्मि. Átm. लेढाहे. 2*d Fut.* लेक्ष्यामि. Átm. लेक्ष्ये. *Aor.* (439) अलिक्षं, -क्षस्, -क्षत्; -क्षाव, -क्षतं, -क्षतां; -क्षाम, -क्षत, -क्षन्. Átm. (439. *b*) अलिक्षि, अलिक्षथास् or अलीढास्, अलिक्षत or अलीढ; अलिक्षावहि or अलिह्वहि, -क्षाथां, -क्षातां; अलिक्षामहि, अलिक्षध्वं or अलीढ्वं, अलिक्षन्त. *Prec.* लिह्यासं. Átm. लिक्षीय, &c. *Cond.* अलेक्ष्यं. Átm. अलेक्ष्ये, &c. Pass., *Pres.* लिह्ये; *Aor.* 3*d sing.* अलेहि. Caus., *Pres.* लेहयामि; *Aor.* अलीलिहं. Des. लिलिक्षामि, -क्षे. Freq. लेलिह्ये, लेलेह्मि (3*d sing.* लेलेढि). Part., *Pres.* लिहत्; Átm. लिहान; *Past pass.* लीढ; *Past indecl.* लीढ्वा, -लिह्य; *Fut. pass.* लेढव्य, लेहनीय, लेह्य.

EXAMPLES OF PRIMITIVE VERBS OF THE THIRD CONJUGATIONAL CLASS, EXPLAINED AT 330.

662. Root हु *hu*. Infin. होतुम् *hotum*, 'to sacrifice.'

PARASMAI-PADA. *Present tense*, 'I sacrifice.'

जुहोमि *juhomi*	जुहुवस् *juhuvas* or जुह्वस्	जुहुमस् *juhumas* or जुह्मस्
जुहोषि *juhoshi*	जुहुथस् *juhuthas*	जुहुथ *juhutha*
जुहोति *juhoti*	जुहुतस् *juhutas*	जुह्वति *juhvati*

Imperfect or first preterite, 'I was sacrificing.'

अजुहवम् *ajuhavam*	अजुहुव *ajuhuva*	अजुहुम *ajuhuma*
अजुहोस् *ajuhos*	अजुहुतम् *ajuhutam*	अजुहुत *ajuhuta*
अजुहोत् *ajuhot*	अजुहुताम् *ajuhutám*	अजुहवुस् *ajuhavus* (330)

Potential, 'I may sacrifice.'

जुहुयाम् *juhuyám*	जुहुयाव *juhuyáva*	जुहुयाम *juhuyáma*
जुहुयास् *juhuyás*	जुहुयातम् *juhuyátam*	जुहुयात *juhuyáta*
जुहुयात् *juhuyát*	जुहुयाताम् *juhuyátám*	जुहुयुस् *juhuyus*

Imperative, 'Let me sacrifice.'

जुहवानि *juhaváni*	जुहवाव *juhaváva*	जुहवाम *juhaváma*
जुहुधि *juhudhi* (291)	जुहुतम् *juhutam*	जुहुत *juhuta*
जुहोतु *juhotu*	जुहुताम् *juhutám*	जुह्वतु *juhvatu*

Perf. (374. *g*) जुहाव, जुहविथ or जुहोथ, जुहाव; जुहुविव, जुहुवथुस्, जुहुवतुस्; जुहुविम, जुहुव, जुहुवुस्. Or जुहवाञ्चकार, &c.; see 385. *e.* *1st Fut.* होतास्मि. *2d Fut.* होष्यामि. *Aor.* अहौषं, अहौषीस्, अहौषीत्; अहौष्व, अहौष्टं, अहौष्टां; अहौष्म, अहौष्ट, अहौषुस्. *Prec.* हूयासं. *Cond.* अहोष्यं. Pass., *Pres.* हूये; *Aor. 3d sing.* अहावि. Caus., *Pres.* हावयामि; *Aor.* अजूहवं. Des. जुहूषामि. Freq. जोहूये, जोहोमि or जोहवीमि. Part., *Pres.* जुह्वत्; *Past pass.* हुत; *Past indecl.* हुत्वा, -हुत्य; *Fut. pass.* होतव्य, हवनीय, हव्य or हाव्य.

EXAMPLES OF OTHER VERBS OF THE THIRD CONJUGATIONAL CLASS IN THE ORDER OF THEIR FINAL LETTERS.

663. Root दा (335). *Inf.* दातुं 'to give.' Par. and Átm. *Pres.* ददामि, ददासि, ददाति; दद्वस्, दत्थस्, दत्तस्; दद्मस्, दत्थ, ददति. Átm. ददे, दत्से, दत्ते; दद्वहे, ददाथे, ददाते; दद्महे, दद्ध्वे, ददते. *Impf.* अददां, अददास्, अददात्; अदद्व, अदत्तं, अदत्तां; अदद्म, अदत्त, अददुस् (332). Átm. अददि, अदत्थास्, अदत्त; अदद्वहि, अददाथां, अददातां; अदद्महि, अदद्ध्वं, अददत. *Pot.* दद्यां. Átm. ददीय. *Impv.* ददानि, देहि, ददातु; ददाव, दत्तं, दत्तां; ददाम, दत्त, ददतु. Átm. ददै, दत्स्व, दत्तां; ददावहै, ददाथां, ददातां; ददामहै, दद्ध्वं, ददतां. *Perf.* (373) ददौ, ददिथ or ददाथ, ददौ; ददिव, ददथुस्, ददतुस्; ददिम, दद, ददुस्. Átm. ददे, ददिषे, ददे; ददिवहे, ददाथे, ददाते; ददिमहे, ददिध्वे, ददिरे. *1st Fut.* दातास्मि. Átm. दाताहे. *2d Fut.* दास्यामि. Átm. दास्ये. *Aor.* (438) अदां, अदास्, अदात्; अदाव, अदातं, अदातां; अदाम, अदात, अदुस्. Átm. (438. *d*) अदिषि, अदिथास्, अदित; अदिष्वहि, अदिषाथां, अदिषातां; अदिष्महि, अदिढ्वं, अदिषत. *Prec.* देयासं. Átm. दासीय. *Cond.* अदास्यं. Átm. अदास्ये. Pass., *Pres.* दीये; *Aor. 3d sing.* अदायि, see 700. Caus., *Pres.* दापयामि (483); *Aor.* अदीदपं.

Des. (503) दित्सति, दित्सते. Freq. देदीयते, दादाति or दादेति. Part., *Pres.* ददत् (141. *a*); Ātm. ददान; *Past pass.* दत्त; *Past indecl.* दत्त्वा, -दाय; *Fut. pass.* दातव्य, दानीय, देय.

664. Root धा (336). *Inf.* धातुं 'to place.' Par. and Ātm. *Pres.* दधामि, दधासि, दधाति; दध्वस्, धत्थस् (299. *a*), धत्तस् (299. *a*); दध्मस्, धत्थ, दधति. Ātm. दधे, धत्से, धत्ते; दध्वहे, दधाथे, दधाते; दध्महे, धद्ध्वे (299. *b*), दधते. *Impf.* अदधां, अदधास्, अदधात्; अदध्व, अधत्तं, अधत्तां; अदध्म, अधत्त, अदधुस्. Ātm. अदधि, अधत्थास्, अधत्त; अदध्वहि, अदधाथां, अदधातां; अदध्महि, अधद्ध्वं (229. *b*), अदधत. *Pot.* दध्यां. Ātm. दधीय. *Impv.* दधानि, धेहि, दधातु; दधाव, धत्तं, धत्तां; दधाम, धत्त, दधतु. Ātm. दधै, धत्स्व, धत्तां; दधावहै, दधाथां, दधातां; दधामहै, धद्ध्वं, दधतां. *Perf.* (373) दधौ, दधिथ or दधाथ, दधौ; दधिव, दधथुस्, दधतुस्; दधिम, दध, दधुस्. Ātm. दधे, दधिषे, &c. *1st Fut.* धातास्मि. Ātm. धाताहे, &c. *2d Fut.* धास्यामि. Ātm. धास्ये. *Aor.* (438) अधां, अधास्, अधात्; अधाव, अधातं, अधातां; अधाम, अधात, अधुस्. Ātm. (438. *d*) अधिषि, अधिथास्, अधित; अधिष्वहि, अधिषाथां, अधिषातां; अधिष्महि, अधिढ्वं, अधिषत. *Prec.* धेयासं. Ātm. धासीय. *Cond.* अधास्यं. Ātm. अधास्ये. Pass., *Pres.* धीये; *1st Fut.* धायिताहे or धाताहे; *Aor. 3d sing.* अधायि. Caus. धापयामि; *Aor.* अदीधपं. Des. धित्सामि (503). Freq. देधीये, दाधामि or दाधेमि. Part., *Pres.* दधत् (141. *a*); Ātm. दधान; *Past pass.* हित; *Past indecl.* हित्वा, -धाय; *Fut. pass.* धातव्य, धानीय, धेय.

a. Root मा (338). *Inf.* मातुं 'to measure.' Ātm. *Pres.* मिमे, मिमीषे, मिमीते; मिमीवहे, मिमाथे, मिमाते; मिमीमहे, मिमीध्वे, मिमते. *Impf.* अमिमि, अमिमीथास्, अमिमीत; अमिमीवहि, अमिमाथां, अमिमातां; अमिमीमहि, अमिमीध्वं, अमिमत. *Pot.* मिमीय, मिमीथास्, मिमीत, &c. *Impv.* मिमै, मिमीष्व, मिमीतां; मिमावहै, मिमाथां, मिमातां; मिमामहै, मिमीध्वं, मिमतां. *Perf.* ममे, ममिषे, ममे; ममिवहे, ममाथे, ममाते; ममिमहे, ममिध्वे, ममिरे. *1st Fut.* माताहे. *2d Fut.* मास्ये. *Aor.* (433. *a*) अमासि, अमास्थास्, अमास्त; अमास्वहि, अमासाथां, अमासातां; अमास्महि, अमाध्वं, अमासत. *Prec.* मासीय. *Cond.* अमास्ये. Pass., *Pres.* मीये; *Aor. 3d sing.* अमायि. Caus. मापयामि; *Aor.* अमीमपं. Des. मित्सामि, -त्से (503). Freq. मेमीये, मामामि or मामेमि. Part., *Pres.* मिमान; *Past pass.* मित; *Past indecl.* मित्वा, -माय, -मीय; *Fut. pass.* मातव्य, मानीय, मेय.

665. Root हा (337). *Inf.* हातुं 'to quit.' Par. *Pres.* जहामि, जहासि, जहाति; जहीवस् (or जहिवस्*), जहीथस् (or जहिथस्*), जहीतस् (or जहितस्*); जहीमस् (or जहिमस्*), जहीथ (or जहिथ*), जहति. *Impf.* अजहां, अजहास्, अजहात्; अजहीव (or अजहिव*), अजहीतं (or अजहितं*),

---

* According to Foster; but these alternatives are doubtful.

अजहीतां (or अजहितां*); अजहीत (or अजहित*), अजहीत (or अजहित*), अजहुः. *Pot.* जह्यां, जह्याम्, &c. *Impv.* जहानि, जहीहि or जहिहि or जहाहि, जहातु; जहाव, जहीतं (or जहितं*), जहीतां (or जहितां*); जहाम, जहीत (or जहित*), जहतु. *Perf.* जहौ, जहिथ or जहाथ, जहौ; जहिव, जहथुः, जहतुः; जहिम, जह, जहुः. *1st Fut.* हातास्मि. *2d Fut.* हास्यामि. *Aor.* (433) अहासिषं, अहासीः, अहासीत्; अहासिष्व, अहासिष्टं, अहासिष्टां; अहासिष्म, अहासिष्ट, अहासिषुः. *Prec.* हेयासं. *Cond.* अहास्यं. Pass., *Pres.* हीये; *Aor.* 3d *sing.* अहायि. Caus., *Pres.* हापयामि; *Aor.* अजीहपं. Des. जिहासामि. Freq. जेहीये, जाहामि or जाहेमि. Part., *Pres.* जहत् (141. *a*); *Past pass.* हीन; *Past indecl.* हित्वा, -हाय; *Fut. pass.* हातव्य, हानीय, हेय.

666. Root भी (333). *Inf.* भेतुं 'to fear.' Par. *Pres.* बिभेमि, बिभेषि, बिभेति; बिभीवः or बिभिवः, बिभीथः or बिभिथः, बिभीतः or बिभितः; बिभीमः or बिभिमः, बिभीथ or बिभिथ, बिभ्यति (34). *Impf.* अबिभेम्, अबिभेः, अबिभेत्; अबिभीव or अबिभिव, अबिभीतं or अबिभितं, अबिभीतां or अबिभितां; अबिभीम or अबिभिम, अबिभीत or अबिभित, अबिभयुः (330). *Pot.* बिभीयां or बिभियां, &c. *Impv.* बिभयानि, बिभीहि or बिभिहि, बिभेतु; बिभयाव, बिभीतं or बिभितं, बिभीतां or बिभितां; बिभयाम, बिभीत or बिभित, बिभ्यतु (34). *Perf.* (374) बिभाय, बिभयिथ or बिभेथ, बिभाय; बिभियिव, बिभ्यथुः, बिभ्यतुः; बिभियिम, बिभ्य, बिभ्युः. Or बिभयाञ्चकार (385. *c*). *1st Fut.* भेतास्मि. *2d Fut.* भेष्यामि. *Aor.* अभैषं, अभैषीः, अभैषीत्; अभैष्व, अभैष्टं, अभैष्टां; अभैष्म, अभैष्ट, अभैषुः. *Prec.* भीयासं. *Cond.* अभेष्यं. Pass., *Pres.* भीये; *Aor.* 3d *sing.* अभायि. Caus., *Pres.* भाययामि or -ये, or भापये or भीषये; *Aor.* अबीभयं or अबीभपं or अबीभिषं. Des. बिभीषामि. Freq. बेभीये or बेभेमि or बेभयीमि. Part., *Pres.* बिभ्यत् (141. *a*); *Past pass.* भीत; *Past indecl.* भीत्वा, -भीय; *Fut. pass.* भेतव्य, भयनीय, भेय.

a. Root ह्री. *Inf.* ह्रेतुं 'to be ashamed.' Par. *Pres.* जिह्रेमि, जिह्रेषि, जिह्रेति; जिह्रीवः, जिह्रीथः, जिह्रीतः; जिह्रीमः, जिह्रीथ, जिह्रियति (123. *a*). *Impf.* अजिह्रेम्, अजिह्रेः, अजिह्रेत्; अजिह्रीव, अजिह्रीतं, अजिह्रीतां; अजिह्रीम, अजिह्रीत, अजिह्रयुः (332). *Pot.* जिह्रीयां. *Impv.* जिह्रयाणि, जिह्रीहि, जिह्रेतु; जिह्रयाव, जिह्रीतं, जिह्रीतां; जिह्रयाम, जिह्रीत, जिह्रियतु. *Perf.* जिह्राय, जिह्रयिथ or जिह्रेथ, जिह्राय; जिह्रियिव (374. *c*), जिह्रियथुः, जिह्रियतुः; जिह्रियिम, जिह्रिय, जिह्रियुः. *1st Fut.* ह्रेतास्मि. *2d Fut.* ह्रेष्यामि. *Aor.* अह्रैषं, अह्रैषीः, अह्रैषीत्; अह्रैष्व, -ष्टं, -ष्टां; अह्रैष्म, -ष्ट, -षुः. *Prec.* ह्रीयासं. *Cond.* अह्रेष्यं. Pass., *Pres.* ह्रीये; *Aor.* 3d *sing.* अह्रायि. Caus., *Pres.* ह्रेपयामि; *Aor.* अजिह्रिपं†. Des. जिह्रीषामि. Freq. जेह्रीये, जेह्रेमि or

* According to Foster; but these alternatives are doubtful.

† So Foster. Westergaard gives अजिह्रपं.

जेह्रयीमि. Part., *Pres.* जिह्रियत् (141. *a*); *Past pass.* ह्रीण or ह्रीत; *Past indecl.* ह्रीत्वा; *Fut. pass.* ह्रेतव्य, ह्रयणीय, ह्रेय.

b. Root जन्. *Inf.* जनितुं 'to produce.' Par. *Pres.* जजन्मि, जजंसि, जजन्ति; जजन्वस्, जजन्थस्, जजन्तस्; जजन्मस्, जजन्थ, जज्ञति. *Impf.* अजजनं, अजजन् (292. *a*), अजजन्; अजजन्व, अजजन्तं, अजजन्तां; अजजन्म, अजजन्त, अजज्ञुस्. *Pot.* जजन्यां or जजायां. *Impv.* जजनानि, जजन्हि, जजन्तु; जजनाव, जजन्तं, जजन्तां; जजनाम, जजन्त, जज्ञतु. *Perf.* जजान or जजन, जजन्थ, जजान; जज्ञिव, जज्ञथुस्, जज्ञतुस्; जज्ञिम, जज्ञ, जज्ञुस्. *1st Fut.* जनितास्मि. *2d Fut.* जनिष्यामि. *Aor.* अजानिषं, अजानीस्, अजानीत्; अजानिष्व, &c. Or अजनिषं, &c.; see 427. *Prec.* जन्यासं or जायासं. *Cond.* अजनिष्यं. Pass., *Pres.* जाये (compare 617. *a*) or जन्ये; *Aor. 3d sing.* अजनि. Caus., *Pres.* जनयामि; *Aor.* अजीजनं. Des. जिजनिषे. Freq. जाजाये or जंजन्ये, जंजन्मि. Part., *Pres.* जज्ञत् (141. *a*); *Past pass.* जात, जनित; *Past indecl.* जनित्वा, -जन्य, -जाय; *Fut. pass.* जनितव्य, जननीय, जन्य.

EXAMPLES OF PRIMITIVE VERBS OF THE SEVENTH CONJUGATIONAL CLASS, EXPLAINED AT 342.

667. Root छिद् *ćhid.* Infin. छेत्तुम् *ćhettum*, 'to cut.'

PARASMAI-PADA. *Present tense*, 'I cut.'

छिनद्मि *ćhinadmi*	छिन्द्वस् *ćhindvas*	छिन्द्मस् *ćhindmas*
छिनत्सि *ćhinatsi*	छिन्थस् *ćhinthas* (345)	छिन्थ *ćhintha* (345)
छिनत्ति *ćhinatti*	छिन्तस् *ćhintas* (345)	छिन्दन्ति *ćhindanti*

Imperfect or *first preterite*, 'I was cutting,' or 'I cut.'

अच्छिनदम् *aćhinadam*	अच्छिन्द्व *aćhindva*	अच्छिन्द्म *aćhindma*
अच्छिनत् *aćhinat* (292)	अच्छिन्तम् *aćhintam*	अच्छिन्त *aćhinta*
अच्छिनत् *aćhinat* (292)	अच्छिन्ताम् *aćhintām*	अच्छिन्दन् *aćhindan*

Potential, 'I may cut.'

छिन्द्याम् *ćhindyām*	छिन्द्याव *ćhindyāva*	छिन्द्याम *ćhindyāma*
छिन्द्यास् *ćhindyās*	छिन्द्यातम् *ćhindyātam*	छिन्द्यात *ćhindyāta*
छिन्द्यात् *ćhindyāt*	छिन्द्याताम् *ćhindyātām*	छिन्द्युस् *ćhindyus*

Imperative, 'Let me cut.'

छिनदानि *ćhinadāni*	छिनदाव *ćhinadāva*	छिनदाम *ćhinadāma*
छिन्द्धि *ćhinddhi* *	छिन्तम् *ćhintam* (345)	छिन्त *ćhinta* (345)
छिनत्तु *ćhinattu*	छिन्ताम् *ćhintām* (345)	छिन्दन्तु *ćhindantu*

* Or छिन्धि *ćhindhi*, see 345.

Perf. चिच्छेद, चिच्छेदिथ, चिच्छेद; चिच्छिदिव, चिच्छिदथुस्, चिच्छिदतुस्; चिच्छिदिम, चिच्छिद, चिच्छिदुस्. *1st Fut.* छेत्तास्मि. *2d Fut.* छेत्स्यामि. *Aor.* अच्छिदं, अच्छिदस्, अच्छिदत्; अच्छिदाव, अच्छिदतं, अच्छिदतां; अच्छिदाम, अच्छिदत, अच्छिदन्. Or अच्छैत्सं, अच्छैत्सीस्, अच्छैत्सीत्; अच्छैत्स्व, अच्छैत्तं, अच्छैत्तां; अच्छैत्स्म, अच्छैत्त, अच्छैत्सुस्. *Prec.* छिद्यासं. *Cond.* अच्छेत्स्यं.

ÁTMANE-PADA. *Present tense* 'I cut.'

छिन्दे *ćhinde*	छिन्द्वहे *ćhindvahe*	छिन्द्महे *ćhindmahe*
छिन्त्से *ćhintse*	छिन्दाथे *ćhindáthe*	छिन्द्ध्वे *ćhinddhwe*
छिन्ते *ćhinte* (345)	छिन्दाते *ćhindáte*	छिन्दते *ćhindate*

Imperfect or *first preterite*, 'I was cutting,' or 'I cut.'

अच्छिन्दि *aćhindi*	अच्छिन्द्वहि *aćhindvahi*	अच्छिन्द्महि *aćhindmahi*
अच्छिन्त्थास् *aćhinthás*	अच्छिन्दाथाम् *aćhindáthám*	अच्छिन्द्ध्वम् *aćhinddhwam*
अच्छिन्त *aćhinta*	अच्छिन्दाताम् *aćhindátám*	अच्छिन्दत *aćhindata*

Potential, 'I may cut.'

छिन्दीय *ćhindíya*	छिन्दीवहि *ćhindívahi*	छिन्दीमहि *ćhindímahi*
छिन्दीथास् *ćhindíthás*	छिन्दीयाथाम् *ćhindíyáthám*	छिन्दीध्वम् *ćhindídhwam*
छिन्दीत *ćhindíta*	छिन्दीयाताम् *ćhindíyátám*	छिन्दीरन् *ćhindíran*

Imperative, 'Let me cut.'

छिनदै *ćhinadai*	छिनदावहै *ćhinadávahai*	छिनदामहै *ćhinadámahai*
छिन्त्स्व *ćhintswa*	छिन्दाथाम् *ćhindáthám*	छिन्द्ध्वम् *ćhinddhwam*
छिन्ताम् *ćhintám*	छिन्दाताम् *ćhindátám*	छिन्दताम् *ćhindatám*

Perf. चिच्छिदे, चिच्छिदिषे, चिच्छिदे; चिच्छिदिवहे, चिच्छिदाथे, चिच्छिदाते; चिच्छिदिमहे, चिच्छिदिध्वे, चिच्छिदिरे. *1st Fut.* छेत्ताहे. *2d Fut.* छेत्स्ये. *Aor.* अच्छित्सि, अच्छित्थास्, अच्छित्त; अच्छित्स्वहि, अच्छित्साथां, अच्छित्सातां; अच्छित्स्महि, अच्छिद्ध्वं, अच्छित्सत. *Prec.* छित्सीय. *Cond.* अच्छेत्स्ये. Pass., *Pres.* छिद्ये; *Aor. 3d sing.* अच्छेदि. Caus., *Pres.* छेदयामि; *Aor.* अचिच्छिदं. Des. चिच्छित्सामि, -त्से. Freq. चेच्छिद्ये, चेच्छेद्मि. Part., *Pres.* छिन्दत्; Átm. छिन्दान; *Past pass.* छिन्न; *Past indecl.* छित्त्वा, -छिद्य; *Fut. pass.* छेत्तव्य, छेदनीय, छेद्य.

EXAMPLES OF OTHER VERBS OF THE SEVENTH CONJUGATIONAL CLASS IN THE ORDER OF THEIR FINAL LETTERS.

668. Root अंज्. *Inf.* अंक्तुं 'to anoint,' 'to make clear.' Par. *Pres.* अनज्मि, अनक्षि (296), अनक्ति; अंज्वस्, अंक्थस्, अंक्तस्; अंज्मस्, अंक्थ, अंजन्ति. *Impf.* आनजं, आनक् (292), आनक्; आंज्व, आंक्तं, आंक्तां; आंज्म, आंक्त, आंजन्. *Pot.* अंज्यां. *Impv.* अनजानि, अंग्धि, अनक्तु; अनजाव, अंक्तं, अंक्तां;

अनजाम, अंक्त, अञ्जन्तु. *Perf.* आनञ्ज, आनञ्जिथ or आनंक्थ, आनञ्ज; आनञ्जिव, आनञ्जथुस्, आनञ्जतुस्; आनञ्जिम, आनञ्ज, आनञ्जुस्. *1st Fut.* अंक्तास्मि or अञ्जितास्मि. *2d Fut.* अंक्ष्यामि or अञ्जिष्यामि. *Aor.* आञ्जिषं, आञ्जीस्, आञ्जीत्; आञ्जिष्व, &c., see 427. *Prec.* अज्यासं (453). *Cond.* आंक्ष्यं or आञ्जिष्यं. Pass., *Pres.* अज्यते (469); *Aor. 3d sing.* आञ्जि. Caus., *Pres.* अञ्जयामि; *Aor.* आञ्जिजं. Des. अञ्जिजिषामि. Part., *Pres.* अञ्जत्; *Past pass.* अक्त; *Past indecl.* अञ्जित्वा or अंक्त्वा or अक्त्वा, -अज्य; *Fut. pass.* अंक्तव्य or अञ्जितव्य, अञ्जनीय, अंग्य or अंज्य.

668. Root भुज् (346). *Inf.* भोक्तुं 'to eat,' 'to enjoy.' Par. and Ātm. *Pres.* भुनज्मि, भुनक्षि, भुनक्ति; भुंज्वस्, भुंक्थस्, भुंक्तस्; भुंज्मस्, भुंक्थ, भुञ्जन्ति. Ātm. भुंजे, भुंक्षे, भुंक्ते; भुंज्वहे, भुञ्जाथे, भुञ्जाते; भुंज्महे, भुंग्ध्वे, भुञ्जते. *Impf.* अभुनजं, अभुनक् (292), अभुनक्; अभुंज्व, अभुंक्तं, अभुंक्तां; अभुंज्म, अभुंक्त, अभुञ्जन्. Ātm. अभुंजि, अभुंक्थास्, अभुंक्त; अभुंज्वहि, अभुञ्जाथां, अभुञ्जातां; अभुंज्महि, अभुंग्ध्वं, अभुञ्जत. *Pot.* भुंज्यां. Ātm. भुञ्जीय. *Impv.* भुनजानि, भुंग्धि, भुनक्तु; भुनजाव, भुंक्तं, भुंक्तां; भुनजाम, भुंक्त, भुञ्जन्तु. Ātm. भुनजै, भुंक्ष्व, भुंक्तां; भुनजावहै, भुञ्जाथां, भुञ्जातां; भुनजामहै, भुंग्ध्वं, भुञ्जतां. *Perf.* बुभोज, बुभोजिथ, बुभोज; बुभुजिव, बुभुजथुस्, बुभुजतुस्; बुभुजिम, बुभुज, बुभुजुस्. Ātm. बुभुजे, बुभुजिषे, बुभुजे; -जिवहे, -जाथे, -जाते; -जिमहे, -जिध्वे, -जिरे. *1st Fut.* भोक्तास्मि. Ātm. भोक्ताहे. *2d Fut.* भोक्ष्यामि. Ātm. भोक्ष्ये. *Aor.* अभौक्षं, -क्षीस्, -क्षीत्; अभौक्ष्व, अभौक्तं, -क्तां; अभौक्ष्म, अभौक्त, अभौक्षुस्. Ātm. अभुक्षि, अभुक्थास्, अभुक्त; अभुक्ष्वहि, अभुक्षाथां, अभुक्षातां; अभुक्ष्महि, अभुग्ध्वं, अभुक्षत. *Prec.* भुज्यासं. Ātm. भुक्षीय. *Cond.* अभोक्ष्यं. Ātm. अभोक्ष्ये. Pass., *Pres.* भुज्ये; *Aor. 3d sing.* अभोजि. Caus., *Pres.* भोजयामि, -ये; *Aor.* अबूभुजं. Des. बुभुक्षामि, -क्षे. Freq. बोभुज्ये, बोभोज्मि. Part., *Pres.* भुञ्जत्; Ātm. भुञ्जान; *Past pass.* भुक्त; *Past indecl.* भुक्त्वा, -भुज्य; *Fut. pass.* भोक्तव्य, भोजनीय, भोज्य or भोग्य.

669. Root भञ्ज् (347). *Inf.* भंक्तुं 'to break.' Par. *Pres.* भनज्मि, भनक्षि, भनक्ति; भंज्वस्, भंक्थस्, भंक्तस्; भंज्मस्, भंक्थ, भञ्जन्ति. *Impf.* अभनजं, अभनक् (292), अभनक्; अभंज्व, अभंक्तं, अभंक्तां; अभंज्म, अभंक्त, अभञ्जन्. *Pot.* भंज्यां. *Impv.* भनजानि, भंग्धि, भनक्तु; भनजाव, भंक्तं, भंक्तां; भनजाम, भंक्त, भञ्जन्तु. *Perf.* बभञ्ज, बभञ्जिथ or बभंक्थ, बभञ्ज; बभञ्जिव, बभञ्जथुस्, बभञ्जतुस्; बभञ्जिम, बभञ्ज, बभञ्जुस्. *1st Fut.* भंक्तास्मि. *2d Fut.* भंक्ष्यामि. *Aor.* अभांक्षं, -क्षीस्, -क्षीत्; अभांक्ष्व, अभांक्तं, -क्तां; अभांक्ष्म, अभांक्त, अभांक्षुस्. *Prec.* भज्यासं (453). *Cond.* अभंक्ष्यं. Pass., *Pres.* भज्ये (469); *Aor. 3d sing.* अभाजि. Caus., *Pres.* भञ्जयामि; *Aor.* अबभञ्जं. Des. बिभंक्षामि. Freq. बंभज्ये, बंभज्मि. Part., *Pres.* भञ्जत्; *Past pass.* भग्न; *Past indecl.* भंक्त्वा or भक्त्वा, -भज्य; *Fut. pass.* भंक्तव्य, भञ्जनीय, भंग्य.

670. Root युज्. *Inf.* योक्तुं 'to join,' 'to unite.' Par. and Ātm.

Pres. युनज्मि, युनक्षि, &c.; like भुज् 668. *a.* *Ātm.* युञ्जे, युङ्क्षे, &c. *Impf.* अयुनजं, अयुनक् (292), अयुनक्; अयुञ्ज्व, &c. *Ātm.* अयुञ्जि, अयुङ्क्थास्, &c. *Pot.* युञ्ज्यां. *Ātm.* युञ्जीय. *Impv.* युनजानि, युङ्ग्धि, युनक्तु; युनजाव, &c. *Ātm.* युनजै, युङ्क्ष्व, युङ्क्तां, &c. *Perf.* युयोज, युयोजिथ, युयोज; युयुजिव, &c.; like भुज् 668. *a.* *Ātm.* युयुजे. *1st Fut.* योक्तास्मि. *Ātm.* योक्ताहे. *2d Fut.* योक्ष्यामि. *Ātm.* योक्ष्ये. *Aor.* अयुजं, -जस्, -जत्; -जाव, -जतं, -जतां; -जाम, -जत, -जन्. Or अयौक्षं, -क्षीस्, -क्षीत्; अयौक्ष्व, &c. *Ātm.* अयुक्षि, अयुक्थास्, अयुक्त; अयुक्ष्वहि, &c. *Prec.* युज्यासं. *Ātm.* युक्षीय. *Cond.* अयोक्ष्यं. *Ātm.* अयोक्ष्ये. Pass., *Pres.* युज्ये; *Aor. 3d sing.* अयोजि, see 702. Caus., *Pres.* योजयामि; *Aor.* अयूयुजं. Des. युयुक्षामि, -क्षे. Freq. योयुज्ये, योयोज्मि. Part., *Pres.* युञ्जत्; *Ātm.* युञ्जान; *Past pass.* युक्त; *Past indecl.* युक्त्वा, -युज्य; *Fut. pass.* योक्तव्य, योजनीय, योग्य or योज्य.

671. Root रुध्. *Inf.* रोद्धुं 'to hinder.' Par. and *Ātm.* *Pres.* रुणध्मि, रुणत्सि, रुणद्धि; रुन्ध्वस्, रुन्द्धस्*, रुन्द्धस्*; रुन्ध्मस्, रुन्द्ध*, रुन्धन्ति. *Ātm.* रुन्धे, रुन्त्से, रुन्द्धे*; रुन्ध्वहे, रुन्धाथे, रुन्धाते; रुन्ध्महे, रुन्द्ध्वे, रुन्धते. *Impf.* अरुणधं, अरुणत् or अरुणद् or अरुणस् (292), अरुणत् or अरुणद्; अरुन्ध्व, अरुन्द्धं, अरुन्द्धां; अरुन्ध्म, अरुन्द्ध, अरुन्धन्. *Ātm.* अरुन्धि, अरुन्द्धास्, अरुन्द्ध; अरुन्ध्वहि, अरुन्धाथां, अरुन्धातां; अरुन्ध्महि, अरुन्द्ध्वं, अरुन्धत. *Pot.* रुन्ध्यां. *Ātm.* रुन्धीय. *Impv.* रुणधानि, रुन्द्धि, रुणद्धु; रुणधाव, रुन्द्धं*, रुन्द्धां*; रुणधाम, रुन्द्ध*, रुन्धन्तु. *Ātm.* रुणधै, रुन्त्स्व, रुन्द्धां; रुणधावहै, रुन्धाथां, रुन्धातां; रुणधामहै, रुन्द्ध्वं, रुन्धतां. *Perf.* रुरोध, रुरोधिथ, रुरोध; रुरुधिव, रुरुधथुस्, रुरुधतुस्; रुरुधिम, रुरुध, रुरुधुस्. *Ātm.* रुरुधे, रुरुधिषे, रुरुधे; रुरुधिवहे, रुरुधाथे, रुरुधाते; रुरुधिमहे, रुरुधिध्वे, रुरुधिरे. *1st Fut.* रोद्धास्मि. *Ātm.* रोद्धाहे. *2d Fut.* रोत्स्यामि. *Ātm.* रोत्स्ये. *Aor.* अरुधं, -धस्, -धत्; -धाव, -धतं, -धतां; -धाम, -धत, -धन्. Or अरौत्सं, अरौत्सीस्, अरौत्सीत्; अरौत्स्व, अरौद्धं, अरौद्धां; अरौत्स्म, अरौद्ध, अरौत्सुस्. *Ātm.* अरुत्सि, अरुद्धास्, अरुद्ध; अरुत्स्वहि, अरुत्साथां, अरुत्सातां; अरुत्स्महि, अरुद्ध्वं, अरुत्सत. *Prec.* रुध्यासं. *Ātm.* रुत्सीय. *Cond.* अरोत्स्यं. *Ātm.* अरोत्स्ये. Pass., *Pres.* रुध्ये; *Aor. 3d sing.* अरोधि. Caus., *Pres.* रोधयामि; *Aor.* अरूरुधं. Des. रुरुत्सामि, -त्से. Freq. रोरुध्ये, रोरोध्मि. Part., *Pres.* रुन्धत्; *Ātm.* रुन्धान; *Past pass.* रुद्ध; *Past indecl.* रुद्ध्वा, -रुध्य; *Fut. pass.* रोद्धव्य, रोधनीय, रोध्य.

672. Root शिष्. *Inf.* शेष्टुं 'to distinguish,' 'to separate,' 'to leave remaining.' Par. *Pres.* शिनष्मि, शिनक्षि, शिनष्टि; शिंष्वस्, शिंष्ठस्, शिंष्टस्; शिंष्मस्, शिंष्ठ, शिंषन्ति. *Impf.* अशिनषं, अशिनट् (292), अशिनट्; अशिंष्व, अशिंष्टं, अशिंष्टां; अशिंष्म, अशिंष्ट, अशिंषन्. *Pot.* शिंष्यां. *Impv.* शिनषाणि,

* रुन्धस् may be written for रुन्द्धस्. Similarly, रुन्ध for रुन्द्ध, रुन्धे for रुन्द्धे, &c. See 298. *a.*

छिंद्धि or छिन्द्धि (303, compare 345), छिनत्तु; छिनदाव, छिंत्तं, छिंत्तां; छिनदाम, छिंत्त, छिंदंतु. *Perf.* चिच्छेद, चिच्छेदिथ, चिच्छेद; चिच्छिदिव, चिच्छिदथुस्, चिच्छिदतुस्; चिच्छिदिम, चिच्छिद, चिच्छिदुस्. *1st Fut.* छेत्तास्मि. *2d Fut.* छेत्स्यामि. *Aor.* अच्छिदं, -दस्, -दत्; -दाव, -दतं, -दतां; -दाम, -दत, -दन्. *Prec.* छिद्यासं. *Cond.* अच्छेत्स्यं. Pass., *Pres.* छिद्ये; *Aor. 3d sing.* अच्छेदि. Caus., *Pres.* छेदयामि; *Aor.* अचिच्छिदं. Des. चिच्छित्सामि. Freq. चेच्छिद्ये, चेच्छेद्मि. Part., *Pres.* छिंदत्; *Past pass.* छिन्न; *Past indecl.* छित्त्वा, -छिद्य; *Fut. pass.* छेत्तव्य, छेदनीय, छेद्य.

673. Root हिंस्. *Inf.* हिंसितुं 'to injure.' Par. *Pres.* हिनस्मि, हिनस्सि*, हिनस्ति; हिंस्वस्, हिंस्थस्, हिंस्तस्; हिंस्मस्, हिंस्थ, हिंसंति. *Impf.* अहिनसं, अहिनत् or अहिनस् (292. *a*, 304. *a*), अहिनत्; अहिंस्व, अहिंस्तं, अहिंस्तां; अहिंस्म, अहिंस्त, अहिंसन्. *Pot.* हिंस्यां. *Impv.* हिनसानि, हिंधि or हिन्धि (304), हिनस्तु; हिनसाव, हिंस्तं, हिंस्तां; हिनसाम, हिंस्त, हिंसंतु. *Perf.* जिहिंस, जिहिंसिथ, जिहिंस; जिहिंसिव, जिहिंसथुस्, जिहिंसतुस्; जिहिंसिम, जिहिंस, जिहिंसुस्. *1st Fut.* हिंसितास्मि. *2d Fut.* हिंसिष्यामि. *Aor.* अहिंसिषं, अहिंसीस्, अहिंसीत्; अहिंसिष्व, अहिंसिष्टं, अहिंसिष्टां; अहिंसिष्म, अहिंसिष्ट, अहिंसिषुस्. *Prec.* हिंस्यासं. *Cond.* अहिंसिष्यं. Pass., *Pres.* हिंस्ये; *Aor. 3d sing.* अहिंसि. Caus., *Pres.* हिंसयामि; *Aor.* अजिहिंसं. Des. जिहिंसिषामि. Freq. जेहिंस्ये, जेहिंस्मि. Part., *Pres.* हिंसत्; *Past pass.* हिंसित; *Past indecl.* हिंसित्वा, -हिंस्य; *Fut. pass.* हिंसितव्य, हिंसनीय, हिंस्य.

674. Root तृह्. *Inf.* तर्हितुं or तर्ढुं 'to injure,' 'to kill.' Par. *Pres.* तृणेह्मि, तृणेक्षि (306), तृणेढि (305. *a*); तृंह्वस्, तृंढस् (345), तृंढस्; तृंह्मस्, तृंढ, तृंहंति. *Impf.* अतृणहं, अतृणेट् or अतृणेड् (292), अतृणेट् or अतृणेड्; अतृंह्व, अतृंढं, अतृंढां; अतृंह्म, अतृंढ, अतृंहन्. *Pot.* तृंह्यां. *Impv.* तृणहानि, तृंढि (see 306. *c*), तृणेढु; तृणहाव, तृंढं, तृंढां; तृणहाम, तृंढ, तृंहंतु. *Perf.* ततर्ह, ततर्हिथ or ततर्ढ, ततर्ह; ततृहिव, ततृहथुस्, ततृहतुस्; ततृहिम, ततृह, ततृहुस्. *1st Fut.* तर्हितास्मि or तर्ढास्मि. *2d Fut.* तर्हिष्यामि or तर्क्ष्यामि. *Aor.* अतर्हिषं, -हीस्, -हीत्; -हिष्व, -हिष्टं, -हिष्टां; -हिष्म, -हिष्ट, -हिषुस्. Or अतृक्षं, -क्षस्, -क्षत्; -क्षाव, -क्षतं, -क्षतां; -क्षाम, -क्षत, -क्षन्. *Prec.* तृह्यासं. *Cond.* अतर्हिष्यं or अतर्क्ष्यं. Pass., *Pres.* तृह्ये; *Aor. 3d sing.* अतर्हि. Caus., *Pres.* तर्हयामि; *Aor.* अततर्हं or अतीतृहं. Des. तितर्हिषामि or तितृक्षामि. Freq. तरीतृह्ये, तरीतर्ह्मि (*3d sing.* तरीतर्ढि). Part., *Pres.* तृंहत्; *Past pass.* (305. *a*) तृढ; *Past indecl.* तर्हित्वा or तृढ्वा, -तृह्य; *Fut. pass.* तर्हितव्य or तर्ढव्य, तर्हणीय, तृह्य.

---

* Final स् *s* preceded by *a* or *á* remains unchanged before the terminations *si* and *sva*; see 62. *b*.

EXAMPLES OF PRIMITIVE VERBS OF THE FIFTH CONJUGATIONAL CLASS, EXPLAINED AT 349.

675. Root वृ *vṛi*. Infin. वरितुम् *varitum* or वरीतुम् *varītum*, 'to cover,' 'to enclose,' 'to surround,' 'to choose *.'

Note, that the conjugational नु *nu* becomes णु *ṇu* after वृ *vṛi* by 58.

PARASMAI-PADA. *Present tense*, 'I cover.'

वृणोमि *vṛiṇomi*	वृणुवः *vṛiṇuvas* †	वृणुमः *vṛiṇumas* ‡
वृणोषि *vṛiṇoshi*	वृणुथः *vṛiṇuthas*	वृणुथ *vṛiṇutha*
वृणोति *vṛiṇoti*	वृणुतः *vṛiṇutas*	वृण्वन्ति *vṛiṇvanti*

Imperfect or first preterite, 'I was covering,' or 'I covered.'

अवृणवम् *avṛiṇavam*	अवृणुव *avṛiṇuva* §	अवृणुम *avṛiṇuma* ‖
अवृणोः *avṛiṇos*	अवृणुतम् *avṛiṇutam*	अवृणुत *avṛiṇuta*
अवृणोत् *avṛiṇot*	अवृणुताम् *avṛiṇutām*	अवृण्वन् *avṛiṇvan*

Potential, 'I may cover.'

वृणुयाम् *vṛiṇuyām*	वृणुयाव *vṛiṇuyāva*	वृणुयाम *vṛiṇuyāma*
वृणुयाः *vṛiṇuyās*	वृणुयातम् *vṛiṇuyātam*	वृणुयात *vṛiṇuyāta*
वृणुयात् *vṛiṇuyāt*	वृणुयाताम् *vṛiṇuyātām*	वृणुयुः *vṛiṇuyus*

Imperative, 'Let me cover.'

वृणवानि *vṛiṇavāni*	वृणवाव *vṛiṇavāva*	वृणवाम *vṛiṇavāma*
वृणु *vṛiṇu*	वृणुतम् *vṛiṇutam*	वृणुत *vṛiṇuta*
वृणोतु *vṛiṇotu*	वृणुताम् *vṛiṇutām*	वृण्वन्तु *vṛiṇvantu*

Perf. (369) ववार, ववर्थ or ववरिथ (see 370), ववार; ववृव, ववृथुः, ववृतुः; ववृम, ववृ, वव्रुः or ववरुः ¶. *1st Fut.* (393) वरितास्मि or वरीतास्मि. *2d Fut.* (393) वरिष्यामि or वरीष्यामि. *Aor.* अवारिषम्, अवारीः, अवारीत्; अवारिष्व, अवारिष्टम्, अवारिष्टाम्; अवारिष्म, अवारिष्ट, अवारिषुः. *Prec.* व्रियासम् or वूर्यासम् (448. *b*). *Cond.* अवरिष्यम् or अवरीष्यम्.

ĀTMANE-PADA. *Present tense*, 'I cover.'

वृण्वे *vṛiṇve*	वृणुवहे *vṛiṇuvahe* **	वृणुमहे *vṛiṇumahe* ††
वृणुषे *vṛiṇushe*	वृण्वाथे *vṛiṇvāthe*	वृणुध्वे *vṛiṇudhve*
वृणुते *vṛiṇute*	वृण्वाते *vṛiṇvāte*	वृण्वते *vṛiṇvate*

---

* In the sense of 'to choose,' this root generally follows the 9th conjugation; thus, Pres. वृणामि, वृणासि, वृणाति; वृणीवः, &c. See 686.

† Or वृण्वः *vṛiṇvas*. ‡ Or वृण्मः *vṛiṇmas*. § Or अवृण्व *avṛiṇva*. ‖ Or अवृण्म *avṛiṇma*.

¶ वृ is sometimes written with long *ṝī*, in which case 374. *k*. may be applied.

** Or वृण्वहे *vṛiṇvahe*. †† Or वृण्महे *vṛiṇmahe*.

Imperfect or first preterite, 'I was covering,' or 'I covered.'

अवृणि *avṛṇi*	अवृणुवहि *avṛṇuvahi**	अवृणुमहि *avṛṇumahi*†
अवृणुथास् *avṛṇuthās*	अवृण्वाथाम् *avṛṇvāthām*	अवृणुध्वम् *avṛṇudhvam*
अवृणुत *avṛṇuta*	अवृण्वाताम् *avṛṇvātām*	अवृण्वत *avṛṇvata*

Potential, 'I may cover.'

वृण्वीय *vṛṇvīya*	वृण्वीवहि *vṛṇvīvahi*	वृण्वीमहि *vṛṇvīmahi*
वृण्वीथास् *vṛṇvīthās*	वृण्वीयाथाम् *vṛṇvīyāthām*	वृण्वीध्वम् *vṛṇvīdhvam*
वृण्वीत *vṛṇvīta*	वृण्वीयाताम् *vṛṇvīyātām*	वृण्वीरन् *vṛṇvīran*

Imperative, 'Let me cover.'

वृणवै *vṛṇavai*	वृणवावहै *vṛṇavāvahai*	वृणवामहै *vṛṇavāmahai*
वृणुष्व *vṛṇushva*	वृण्वाथाम् *vṛṇvāthām*	वृणुध्वम् *vṛṇudhvam*
वृणुताम् *vṛṇutām*	वृण्वाताम् *vṛṇvātām*	वृण्वताम् *vṛṇvatām*

Perf. वव्रे (369) or ववरे ‡, वव्रिषे, वव्रे or ववरे; ववृवहे, वव्राथे, वव्राते; ववृमहे, ववृढ्वे, वव्रिरे. *1st Fut.* वरिताहे or वरीताहे. *2d Fut.* वरिष्ये or वरीष्ये. *Aor.* अवरिषि, अवरिष्ठास्, अवरिष्ट; अवरिष्वहि, अवरिषाथां, अवरिषातां; अवरिष्महि, अवरिढ्वं or -ध्वं, अवरिषत. Or अवरीषि, अवरीष्ठास्, &c. Or अवृषि, अवृथास्, अवृत; अवृष्वहि, अवृषाथां, अवृषातां; अवृष्महि, अवृढ्वं, अवृषत. Or अवूर्षि, अवूर्ष्ठास्, अवूर्ष्ट; अवूर्ष्वहि, अवूर्षाथां, अवूर्षातां; अवूर्ष्महि, अवूर्ढ्वं, अवूर्षत. *Prec.* वरिषीय or वृषीय or वूर्षीय (448. *b*). *Cond.* अवरिष्ये or अवरीष्ये. Pass. व्रियते; *Aor. 3d sing.* अवारि. Caus., *Pres.* वरयामि or -ये, or वारयामि or -ये; *Aor.* अवीवरं. Des. विवरिषामि or -षे, विवरीषामि or -षे, वुवूर्षामि or -र्षे (502). Freq. वेव्रीये (511) or वोवूर्मि, वर्वर्मि. Part., *Pres.* वृण्वत्; Ātm. वृण्वान; *Past pass.* वृत; *Past indecl.* वृत्वा, -वृत्य; *Fut. pass.* वरितव्य or वरीतव्य, वरणीय, वार्य.

EXAMPLES OF OTHER VERBS OF THE FIFTH CONJUGATIONAL CLASS IN THE ORDER OF THEIR FINAL LETTERS.

676. Root श्रु§. *Inf.* श्रोतुं 'to hear.' Par. *Pres.* शृणोमि, शृणोषि, शृणोति; शृणुवस् or शृण्वस्, शृणुथस्, शृणुतस्; शृणुमस् or शृण्मस्, शृणुथ, शृण्वन्ति. *Impf.* अशृणवं, अशृणोस्, अशृणोत्; अशृणुव or अशृण्व, अशृणुतं, अशृणुतां; अशृणुम or अशृण्म, अशृणुत, अशृण्वन्. *Pot.* शृणुयां. *Impv.* शृणवानि, शृणु, शृणोतु; शृणवाव, शृणुतं, शृणुतां; शृणवाम, शृणुत, शृण्वन्तु. *Perf.* (369) शुश्राव, शुश्रोथ, शुश्राव; शुश्रुव, शुश्रुवथुस्, शुश्रुवतुस्; शुश्रुम, शुश्रुव, शुश्रुवुस्. *1st Fut.* श्रोतास्मि. *2d Fut.* श्रोष्यामि. *Aor.* अश्रौषं, अश्रौषीस्,

* Or अवृण्वहि *avṛṇvahi*. † Or अवृण्महि *avṛṇmahi*.

‡ वृ is sometimes written with long *ṝ*, in which case 374. *k.* may be applied.

§ This root is placed by Indian grammarians under the 1st class.

अजहीतां (or अजहितां*); अजहीम (or अजहिम*), अजहीत (or अजहित*), अजहुः. *Pot.* जह्यां, जह्याः, &c. *Impv.* जहानि, जहीहि or जहिहि or जहाहि, जहातु; जहाव, जहीतं (or जहितं*), जहीतां (or जहितां*); जहाम, जहीत (or जहित*), जहतु. *Perf.* जहौ, जहिथ or जहाथ, जहौ; जहिव, जहथुः, जहतुः; जहिम, जह, जहुः. *1st Fut.* हातास्मि. *2d Fut.* हास्यामि. *Aor.* (433) अहासिषं, अहासीः, अहासीत्; अहासिष्व, अहासिष्टं, अहासिष्टां; अहासिष्म, अहासिष्ट, अहासिषुः. *Prec.* हेयासं. *Cond.* अहास्यं. Pass., *Pres.* हीये; *Aor. 3d sing.* अहायि. Caus., *Pres.* हापयामि; *Aor.* अजीहपं. Des. जिहासामि. Freq. जेहीये, जाहामि or जाहेमि. Part., *Pres.* जहत् (141. *a*); *Past pass.* हीन; *Past indecl.* हित्वा, -हाय; *Fut. pass.* हातव्य, हानीय, हेय.

666. Root भी (333). *Inf.* भेतुं 'to fear.' Par. *Pres.* बिभेमि, बिभेषि, बिभेति; बिभीवः or बिभिवः, बिभीथः or बिभिथः, बिभीतः or बिभितः; बिभीमः or बिभिमः, बिभीथ or बिभिथ, बिभ्यति (34). *Impf.* अबिभयं, अबिभेः, अबिभेत्; अबिभीव or अबिभिव, अबिभीतं or अबिभितं, अबिभीतां or अबिभितां; अबिभीम or अबिभिम, अबिभीत or अबिभित, अबिभयुः (330). *Pot.* बिभीयां or बिभियां, &c. *Impv.* बिभयानि, बिभीहि or बिभिहि, बिभेतु; बिभयाव, बिभीतं or बिभितं, बिभीतां or बिभितां; बिभयाम, बिभीत or बिभित, बिभ्यतु (34). *Perf.* (374) बिभाय, बिभयिथ or बिभेथ, बिभाय; बिभ्यिव, बिभ्यथुः, बिभ्यतुः; बिभ्यिम, बिभ्य, बिभ्युः. Or बिभयांचकार (385. *c*). *1st Fut.* भेतास्मि. *2d Fut.* भेष्यामि. *Aor.* अभैषं, अभैषीः, अभैषीत्; अभैष्व, अभैष्टं, अभैष्टां; अभैष्म, अभैष्ट, अभैषुः. *Prec.* भीयासं. *Cond.* अभेष्यं. Pass., *Pres.* भीये; *Aor. 3d sing.* अभायि. Caus., *Pres.* भाययामि or -ये, or भापये or भीषये; *Aor.* अबीभयं or अबीभपं or अबीभिषं. Des. बिभीषामि. Freq. बेभीये or बेभेमि or बेभयीमि. Part., *Pres.* बिभ्यत् (141. *a*); *Past pass.* भीत; *Past indecl.* भीत्वा, -भीय; *Fut. pass.* भेतव्य, भयनीय, भेय.

a. Root ह्री. *Inf.* ह्रेतुं 'to be ashamed.' Par. *Pres.* जिह्रेमि, जिह्रेषि, जिह्रेति; जिह्रीवः, जिह्रीथः, जिह्रीतः; जिह्रीमः, जिह्रीथ, जिह्रियति (123. *a*). *Impf.* अजिह्रयं, अजिह्रेः, अजिह्रेत्; अजिह्रीव, अजिह्रीतं, अजिह्रीतां; अजिह्रीम, अजिह्रीत, अजिह्रयुः (332). *Pot.* जिह्रीयां. *Impv.* जिह्रयाणि, जिह्रीहि, जिह्रेतु; जिह्रयाव, जिह्रीतं, जिह्रीतां; जिह्रयाम, जिह्रीत, जिह्रियतु. *Perf.* जिह्राय, जिह्रयिथ or जिह्रेथ, जिह्राय; जिह्रियिव (374. *e*), जिह्रियथुः, जिह्रियतुः; जिह्रियिम, जिह्रिय, जिह्रियुः. *1st Fut.* ह्रेतास्मि. *2d Fut.* ह्रेष्यामि. *Aor.* अह्रैषं, अह्रैषीः, अह्रैषीत्; अह्रैष्व, -ष्टं, -ष्टां; अह्रैष्म, -ष्ट, -षुः. *Prec.* ह्रीयासं. *Cond.* अह्रेष्यं. Pass., *Pres.* ह्रीये; *Aor. 3d sing.* अह्रायि. Caus., *Pres.* ह्रेपयामि; *Aor.* अजिह्रिपं†. Des. जिह्रीषामि. Freq. जेह्रीये, जेह्रेमि or

---

* According to Foster; but these alternatives are doubtful.

† So Foster. Westergaard gives अजिह्रेपं.

जेह्रेमि. Part., Pres. जिह्रियत् (141. a); Past pass. ह्रीण or ह्रीत; Past indecl. ह्रीत्वा; Fut. pass. ह्रेतव्य, ह्रयणीय, ह्रेय.

b. Root जन्. Inf. जनितुं 'to produce.' Par. Pres. जजन्मि, जजंसि, जजन्ति; जजन्वस्, जजाथस्, जजातस्; जजन्मस्, जजाथ, जज्ञति. Impf. अजजनं, अजजन् (292. a), अजजन्; अजजन्व, अजजातं, अजजातां; अजजन्म, अजजात, अजज्ञुस्. Pot. जजन्यां or जजायां. Impv. जजनानि, जजाहि, जजन्तु; जजनाव, जजातं, जजातां; जजनाम, जजात, जज्ञतु. Perf. जजान or जजन, जजनिथ, जजान; जज्ञिव, जज्ञथुस्, जज्ञतुस्; जज्ञिम, जज्ञ, जज्ञुस्. 1st Fut. जनितास्मि. 2d Fut. जनिष्यामि. Aor. अजानिषं, अजानीस्, अजानीत्; अजानिष्व, &c. Or अजनिषं, &c.; see 427. Prec. जन्यासं or जायासं. Cond. अजनिष्यं. Pass., Pres. जाये (compare 617. a) or जन्ये; Aor. 3d sing. अजनि. Caus., Pres. जनयामि; Aor. अजीजनं. Des. जिजनिषामि. Freq. जाजाये or जञ्जन्ये, जञ्जन्मि. Part., Pres. जजत् (141. a); Past pass. जात, जनित; Past indecl. जनित्वा, -जत्य, -जाय; Fut. pass. जनितव्य, जननीय, जन्य.

EXAMPLES OF PRIMITIVE VERBS OF THE SEVENTH CONJUGATIONAL CLASS, EXPLAINED AT 342.

667. Root छिद् ćhid. Infin. छेत्तुम् ćhettum, 'to cut.'

PARASMAI-PADA. *Present tense*, 'I cut.'

छिनद्मि *ćhinadmi*	छिन्द्वस् *ćhindvas*	छिन्द्मस् *ćhindmas*
छिनत्सि *ćhinatsi*	छिन्थस् *ćhinthas* (345)	छिन्थ *ćhintha* (345)
छिनत्ति *ćhinatti*	छिन्तस् *ćhintas* (345)	छिन्दन्ति *ćhindanti*

Imperfect or first preterite, 'I was cutting,' or 'I cut.'

अच्छिनदम् *aćhinadam*	अच्छिन्द्व *aćhindva*	अच्छिन्द्म *aćhindma*
अच्छिनत् *aćhinat* (291)	अच्छिन्तम् *aćhintam*	अच्छिन्त *aćhinta*
अच्छिनत् *aćhinat* (292)	अच्छिन्ताम् *aćhintám*	अच्छिन्दन् *aćhindan*

Potential, 'I may cut.'

छिन्द्याम् *ćhindyám*	छिन्द्याव *ćhindyáva*	छिन्द्याम *ćhindyáma*
छिन्द्यास् *ćhindyás*	छिन्द्यातम् *ćhindyátam*	छिन्द्यात *ćhindyáta*
छिन्द्यात् *ćhindyát*	छिन्द्याताम् *ćhindyátám*	छिन्द्युस् *ćhindyus*

Imperative, 'Let me cut.'

छिनदानि *ćhinadáni*	छिनदाव *ćhinadáva*	छिनदाम *ćhinadáma*
छिन्द्धि *ćhinddhi* *	छिन्तम् *ćhintam* (345)	छिन्त *ćhinta* (345)
छिनत्तु *ćhinattu*	छिन्ताम् *ćhintám* (345)	छिन्दन्तु *ćhindantu*

* Or छिन्धि *ćhindhi*, see 345.

अजहीतां (or अजहितां*); अजहीम (or अजहिम*), अजहीत (or अजहित*). अजहुः. *Pot.* जह्यां, जह्याः, &c. *Impv.* जहानि, जहीहि or जहिहि or जहाहि, जहातु; जहाव, जहीतं (or जहितं*), जहीतां (or जहितां*); जहाम, जहीत (or जहित*), जहतु. *Perf.* जहौ, जहिथ or जहाथ, जहौ; जहिव, जहथुः, जहतुः; जहिम, जह, जहुः. *1st Fut.* हातास्मि. *2d Fut.* हास्यामि. *Aor.* (433) अहासिषं, अहासीः, अहासीत्; अहासिष्व, अहासिष्टं, अहासिष्टां; अहासिष्म, अहासिष्ट, अहासिषुः. *Prec.* हेयासं. *Cond.* अहास्यं. Pass., *Pres.* हीये; *Aor. 3d sing.* अहायि. Caus., *Pres.* हापयामि; *Aor.* अजीहपं. Des. जिहासामि. Freq. जेहीये, जाहामि or जाहेमि. Part., *Pres.* जहत् (141. *a*); *Past pass.* हीन; *Past indecl.* हित्वा, -हाय; *Fut. pass.* हातव्य, हानीय, हेय.

666. Root भी (333). *Inf.* भेतुं 'to fear.' Par. *Pres.* बिभेमि, बिभेषि, बिभेति; बिभीवः or बिभिवः, बिभीथः or बिभिथः, बिभीतः or बिभितः; बिभीमः or बिभिमः, बिभीथ or बिभिथ, बिभ्यति (34). *Impf.* अबिभयं, अबिभेः, अबिभेत्; अबिभीव or अबिभिव, अबिभीतं or अबिभितं, अबिभीतां or अबिभितां; अबिभीम or अबिभिम, अबिभीत or अबिभित, अबिभयुः (330). *Pot.* बिभीयां or बिभियां, &c. *Impv.* बिभयानि, बिभीहि or बिभिहि, बिभेतु; बिभयाव, बिभीतं or बिभितं, बिभीतां or बिभितां; बिभयाम, बिभीत or बिभित, बिभ्यतु (34). *Perf.* (374) बिभाय, बिभयिथ or बिभेथ, बिभाय; बिभ्यिव, बिभ्यथुः, बिभ्यतुः; बिभ्यिम, बिभ्य, बिभ्युः. Or बिभयांचकार (385. *c*). *1st Fut.* भेतास्मि. *2d Fut.* भेष्यामि. *Aor.* अभैषं, अभैषीत्, अभैषीत्; अभैष्व, अभैष्टं, अभैष्टां; अभैष्म, अभैष्ट, अभैषुः. *Prec.* भीयासं. *Cond.* अभेष्यं. Pass., *Pres.* भीये; *Aor. 3d sing.* अभायि. Caus., *Pres.* भाययामि or -ये, or भापये or भीषये; *Aor.* अबीभयं or अबीभपं or अबीभिषं. Des. बिभीषामि. Freq. बेभीये or बेभेमि or बेभयीमि. Part., *Pres.* बिभ्यत् (141. *a*); *Past pass.* भीत; *Past indecl.* भीत्वा, -भीय; *Fut. pass.* भेतव्य, भयनीय, भेय.

a. Root ह्री. *Inf.* ह्रेतुं 'to be ashamed.' Par. *Pres.* जिह्रेमि, जिह्रेषि, जिह्रेति; जिह्रीवः, जिह्रीथः, जिह्रीतः; जिह्रीमः, जिह्रीथ, जिह्रियति (123. *a*). *Impf.* अजिह्रयं, अजिह्रेः, अजिह्रेत्; अजिह्रीव, अजिह्रीतं, अजिह्रीतां; अजिह्रीम, अजिह्रीत, अजिह्रयुः (332). *Pot.* जिह्रीयां. *Impv.* जिह्रयाणि, जिह्रीहि, जिह्रेतु; जिह्रयाव, जिह्रीतं, जिह्रीतां; जिह्रयाम, जिह्रीत, जिह्रियतु. *Perf.* जिह्राय, जिह्रयिथ or जिह्रेथ, जिह्राय; जिह्रियिव (374. *e*), जिह्रियथुः, जिह्रियतुः; जिह्रियिम, जिह्रिय, जिह्रियुः. *1st Fut.* ह्रेतास्मि. *2d Fut.* ह्रेष्यामि. *Aor.* अह्रैषं, अह्रैषीत्, अह्रैषीत्; अह्रैष्व, -ष्टं, -ष्टां; अह्रैष्म, -ष्ट, -षुः. *Prec.* ह्रीयासं. *Cond.* अह्रेष्यं. Pass., *Pres.* ह्रीये; *Aor. 3d sing.* अह्रायि. Caus., *Pres.* ह्रेपयामि; *Aor.* अजिह्रिपं†. Des. जिह्रीषामि. Freq. जेह्रीये, जेह्रेमि or

---

* According to Foster; but these alternatives are doubtful.

† So Foster. Westergaard gives अजिह्रीपं.

जोहवीमि. Part., *Pres.* जिह्वत् (141. *a*); *Past pass.* हूत or हुत; *Past indecl.* हुत्वा; *Fut. pass.* होतव्य, हवनीय, हेय.

b. Root जन्. *Inf.* जनितुं 'to produce.' Par. *Pres.* जजन्मि, जजंसि, जजन्ति; जजन्वस्, जजाथस्, जजातस्; जजन्मस्, जजाथ, जज्ञति. *Impf.* अजजनं, अजजन् (292. *a*), अजजन्; अजजन्व, अजजातं, अजजातां; अजजन्म, अजजात, अजज्ञुस्. *Pot.* जजन्यां or जजायां. *Impv.* जजनानि, जजाहि, जजन्तु; जजनाव, जजातं, जजातां; जजनाम, जजात, जज्ञतु. *Perf.* जजान or जजन, जजनिथ, जजान; जज्ञिव, जज्ञथुस्, जज्ञतुस्; जज्ञिम, जज्ञ, जज्ञुस्. *1st Fut.* जनितास्मि. *2d Fut.* जनिष्यामि. *Aor.* अजानिषं, अजानीस्, अजानीत्; अजानिष्व, &c. Or अजनिषं, &c.; see 427. *Prec.* जन्यासं or जायासं. *Cond.* अजनिष्यं. Pass., *Pres.* जाये (compare 617. *a*) or जन्ये; *Aor. 3d sing.* अजनि. Caus., *Pres.* जनयामि; *Aor.* अजीजनं. Des. जिजनिषे. Freq. जाजाये or जञ्जन्ये, जञ्जन्मि. Part., *Pres.* जजत् (141. *a*); *Past pass.* जात, जनित; *Past indecl.* जनित्वा, -जन्य, -जाय; *Fut. pass.* जनितव्य, जननीय, जन्य.

EXAMPLES OF PRIMITIVE VERBS OF THE SEVENTH CONJUGATIONAL CLASS, EXPLAINED AT 342.

667. Root छिद् *ćhid.* Infin. छेत्तुम् *ćhettum*, 'to cut.'

PARASMAI-PADA. *Present tense*, 'I cut.'

छिनद्मि *ćhinadmi*	छिन्द्वस् *ćhindvas*	छिन्द्मस् *ćhindmas*
छिनत्सि *ćhinatsi*	छिन्थस् *ćhinthas* (345)	छिन्थ *ćhintha* (345)
छिनत्ति *ćhinatti*	छिन्तस् *ćhintas* (345)	छिन्दन्ति *ćhindanti*

Imperfect or *first preterite*, 'I was cutting,' or 'I cut.'

अच्छिनदम् *aćhinadam*	अच्छिन्द्व *aćhindva*	अच्छिन्द्म *aćhindma*
अच्छिनत् *aćhinat* (292)	अच्छिन्तम् *aćhintam*	अच्छिन्त *aćhinta*
अच्छिनत् *aćhinat* (292)	अच्छिन्ताम् *aćhintām*	अच्छिन्दन् *aćhindan*

Potential, 'I may cut.'

छिन्द्याम् *ćhindyām*	छिन्द्याव *ćhindyāva*	छिन्द्याम *ćhindyāma*
छिन्द्यास् *ćhindyās*	छिन्द्यातम् *ćhindyātam*	छिन्द्यात *ćhindyāta*
छिन्द्यात् *ćhindyāt*	छिन्द्याताम् *ćhindyātām*	छिन्द्युस् *ćhindyus*

Imperative, 'Let me cut.'

छिनदानि *ćhinadāni*	छिनदाव *ćhinadāva*	छिनदाम *ćhinadāma*
छिन्द्धि *ćhinddhi* *	छिन्तम् *ćhintam* (345)	छिन्त *ćhinta* (345)
छिनत्तु *ćhinattu*	छिन्ताम् *ćhintām* (345)	छिन्दन्तु *ćhindantu*

* Or छिन्धि *ćhindhi*, see 345.

अजहीतां (or अजहितां*); अजहीम (or अजहिम*), अजहीत (or अजहित*), अजहुः. *Pot.* जह्यां, जह्याः, &c. *Impv.* जहानि, जहीहि or जहिहि or जहाहि, जहातु; जहाव, जहीतं (or जहितं*), जहीतां (or जहितां*); जहाम, जहीत (or जहित*), जहतु. *Perf.* जहौ, जहिथ or जहाथ, जहौ; जहिव, जहथुः, जहतुः; जहिम, जह, जहुः. *1st Fut.* हातास्मि. *2d Fut.* हास्यामि. *Aor.* (433) अहासिषं, अहासीः, अहासीत्; अहासिष्व, अहासिष्टं, अहासिष्टां; अहासिष्म, अहासिष्ट, अहासिषुः. *Prec.* हेयासं. *Cond.* अहास्यं. Pass., *Pres.* हीये; *Aor. 3d sing.* अहायि. Caus., *Pres.* हापयामि; *Aor.* अजीहपं. Des. जिहासामि. Freq. जेहीये, जाहामि or जाहेमि. Part., *Pres.* जहत् (141. a); *Past pass.* हीन; *Past indecl.* हित्वा, -हाय; *Fut. pass.* हातव्य, हानीय, हेय.

666. Root भी (333). *Inf.* भेतुं 'to fear.' Par. *Pres.* बिभेमि, बिभेषि, बिभेति; बिभीवः or बिभिवः, बिभीथः or बिभिथः, बिभीतः or बिभितः; बिभीमः or बिभिमः, बिभीथ or बिभिथ, बिभ्यति (34). *Impf.* अबिभयं, अबिभेः, अबिभेत्; अबिभीव or अबिभिव, अबिभीतं or अबिभितं, अबिभीतां or अबिभितां; अबिभीम or अबिभिम, अबिभीत or अबिभित, अबिभयुः (330). *Pot.* बिभीयां or बिभियां, &c. *Impv.* बिभयानि, बिभीहि or बिभिहि, बिभेतु; बिभयाव, बिभीतं or बिभितं, बिभीतां or बिभितां; बिभयाम, बिभीत or बिभित, बिभ्यतु (34). *Perf.* (374) बिभाय, बिभयिथ or बिभेथ, बिभाय; बिभियिव, बिभ्यथुः, बिभ्यतुः; बिभियिम, बिभ्य, बिभ्युः. Or बिभयांचकार (385. c). *1st Fut.* भेतास्मि. *2d Fut.* भेष्यामि. *Aor.* अभैषं, अभैषीः, अभैषीत्; अभैष्व, अभैष्टं, अभैष्टां; अभैष्म, अभैष्ट, अभैषुः. *Prec.* भीयासं. *Cond.* अभेष्यं. Pass., *Pres.* भीये; *Aor. 3d sing.* अभायि. Caus., *Pres.* भाययामि or -ये, or भापये or भीषये; *Aor.* अबीभयं or अबीभपं or अबीभिषं. Des. बिभीषामि. Freq. बेभीये or बेभेमि or बेभयीमि. Part., *Pres.* बिभ्यत् (141. a); *Past pass.* भीत; *Past indecl.* भीत्वा, -भीय; *Fut. pass.* भेतव्य, भयनीय, भेय.

a. Root ह्री. *Inf.* ह्रेतुं 'to be ashamed.' Par. *Pres.* जिह्रेमि, जिह्रेषि, जिह्रेति; जिह्रीवः, जिह्रीथः, जिह्रीतः; जिह्रीमः, जिह्रीथ, जिह्रियति (123. a). *Impf.* अजिह्रयं, अजिह्रेः, अजिह्रेत्; अजिह्रीव, अजिह्रीतं, अजिह्रीतां; अजिह्रीम, अजिह्रीत, अजिह्रयुः (332). *Pot.* जिह्रीयां. *Impv.* जिह्रयाणि, जिह्रीहि, जिह्रेतु; जिह्रयाव, जिह्रीतं, जिह्रीतां; जिह्रयाम, जिह्रीत, जिह्रियतु. *Perf.* जिह्राय, जिह्रयिथ or जिह्रेथ, जिह्राय; जिह्रियिव (374. e), जिह्रियथुः, जिह्रियतुः; जिह्रियिम, जिह्रिय, जिह्रियुः. *1st Fut.* ह्रेतास्मि. *2d Fut.* ह्रेष्यामि. *Aor.* अह्रैषं, अह्रैषीत्, अह्रैषीत्; अह्रैष्व, -ष्टं, -ष्टां; अह्रैष्म, -ष्ट, -षुः. *Prec.* ह्रीयासं. *Cond.* अह्रेष्यं. Pass., *Pres.* ह्रीये; *Aor. 3d sing.* अह्रायि. Caus., *Pres.* ह्रेपयामि; *Aor.* अजिह्रिपं†. Des. जिह्रीषामि. Freq. जेह्रीये, जेह्रेमि or

---

* According to Foster; but these alternatives are doubtful.

† So Foster. Westergaard gives अजिह्रेपं.

दोदोग्धि. Part., *Pres.* दुहत् (141. a); *Past pass.* दुग्ध or दुहित; *Past indecl.* दुग्ध्वा; *Fut. pass.* दोग्धव्य, दोहनीय, दोह्य.

b. Root जन्. *Inf.* जनितुं 'to produce.' Par. *Pres.* जजन्मि, जजंसि, जजन्ति; जजन्वस्, जजाथस्, जजातस्; जजन्मस्, जजाथ, जज्ञति. *Impf.* अजजनं, अजजन् (292. a), अजजन्; अजजन्व, अजजातं, अजजातां; अजजन्म, अजजात, अजजनुस्. *Pot.* जजन्यां or जजायां. *Impv.* जजनानि, जजाहि, जजन्तु; जजनाव, जजातं, जजातां; जजनाम, जजात, जज्ञतु. *Perf.* जजान or जजन, जजनिथ, जजान; जज्ञिव, जज्ञथुस्, जज्ञतुस्; जज्ञिम, जज्ञ, जज्ञुस्. *1st Fut.* जनितास्मि. *2d Fut.* जनिष्यामि. *Aor.* अजानिषं, अजानीस्, अजानीत्; अजानिष्व, &c. Or अजनिषं, &c.; see 427. *Prec.* जन्यासं or जायासं. *Cond.* अजनिष्यं. Pass., *Pres.* जाये (compare 617. a) or जन्ये; *Aor. 3d sing.* अजनि. Caus., *Pres.* जनयामि; *Aor.* अजीजनं. Des. जिजनिषे. Freq. जाजाये or जञ्जन्ये, जञ्जन्मि. Part., *Pres.* जज्ञत् (141. a); *Past pass.* जात, जनित; *Past indecl.* जनित्वा, -जन्य, -जाय; *Fut. pass.* जनितव्य, जननीय, जन्य.

EXAMPLES OF PRIMITIVE VERBS OF THE SEVENTH CONJUGATIONAL CLASS, EXPLAINED AT 342.

667. Root छिद् *ćhid.* Infin. छेत्तुम् *ćhettum*, 'to cut.'

PARASMAI-PADA. *Present tense*, 'I cut.'

छिनद्मि *ćhinadmi*	छिन्द्वस् *ćhindvas*	छिन्द्मस् *ćhindmas*
छिनत्सि *ćhinatsi*	छिन्थस् *ćhinthas* (345)	छिन्थ *ćhintha* (345)
छिनत्ति *ćhinatti*	छिन्तस् *ćhintas* (345)	छिन्दन्ति *ćhindanti*

Imperfect or *first preterite*, 'I was cutting,' or 'I cut.'

अच्छिनदम् *aćhinadam*	अच्छिन्द्व *aćhindva*	अच्छिन्द्म *aćhindma*
अच्छिनत् *aćhinat* (292)	अच्छिन्तम् *aćhintam*	अच्छिन्त *aćhinta*
अच्छिनत् *aćhinat* (292)	अच्छिन्ताम् *aćhintām*	अच्छिन्दन् *aćhindan*

Potential, 'I may cut.'

छिन्द्याम् *ćhindyām*	छिन्द्याव *ćhindyāva*	छिन्द्याम *ćhindyāma*
छिन्द्यास् *ćhindyās*	छिन्द्यातम् *ćhindyātam*	छिन्द्यात *ćhindyāta*
छिन्द्यात् *ćhindyāt*	छिन्द्याताम् *ćhindyātām*	छिन्द्युस् *ćhindyus*

Imperative, 'Let me cut.'

छिनदानि *ćhinadāni*	छिनदाव *ćhinadāva*	छिनदाम *ćhinadāma*
छिन्द्धि *ćhinddhi* *	छिन्तम् *ćhintam* (345)	छिन्त *ćhinta* (345)
छिनत्तु *ćhinattu*	छिन्ताम् *ćhintām* (345)	छिन्दन्तु *ćhindantu*

* Or छिन्धि *ćhindhi*, see 345.

Perf. चिच्छेद, चिच्छेदिथ, चिच्छेद; चिच्छिदिव, चिच्छिदथुस्, चिच्छिदतुस्; चिच्छिदिम, चिच्छिद, चिच्छिदुस्. *1st Fut.* छेत्तास्मि. *2d Fut.* छेत्स्यामि. *Aor.* अच्छिदं, अच्छिदस्, अच्छिदत्; अच्छिदाव, अच्छिदतं, अच्छिदतां; अच्छिदाम, अच्छिदत, अच्छिदन्. Or अच्छैत्सं, अच्छैत्सीस्, अच्छैत्सीत्; अच्छैत्स्व, अच्छैत्तं, अच्छैत्तां; अच्छैत्स्म, अच्छैत्त, अच्छैत्सुस्. *Prec.* छिद्यासं. *Cond.* अच्छेत्स्यं.

ĀTMANE-PADA. *Present tense* 'I cut.'

छिन्दे *ćhinde*	छिन्द्वहे *ćhindvahe*	छिन्द्महे *ćhindmahe*
छिन्त्से *ćhintse*	छिन्दाथे *ćhindāthe*	छिन्द्ध्वे *ćhinddhve*
छिन्ते *ćhinte* (345)	छिन्दाते *ćhindāte*	छिन्दते *ćhindate*

Imperfect or *first preterite*, 'I was cutting,' or 'I cut.'

अच्छिन्दि *aćhindi*	अच्छिन्द्वहि *aćhindvahi*	अच्छिन्द्महि *aćhindmahi*
अच्छिन्त्थास् *aćhinthās*	अच्छिन्दाथाम् *aćhindāthām*	अच्छिन्द्ध्वम् *aćhinddhvam*
अच्छिन्त *aćhinta*	अच्छिन्दाताम् *aćhindātām*	अच्छिन्दत *aćhindata*

Potential, 'I may cut.'

छिन्दीय *ćhindīya*	छिन्दीवहि *ćhindīvahi*	छिन्दीमहि *ćhindīmahi*
छिन्दीथास् *ćhindīthās*	छिन्दीयाथाम् *ćhindīyāthām*	छिन्दीध्वम् *ćhindīdhvam*
छिन्दीत *ćhindīta*	छिन्दीयाताम् *ćhindīyātām*	छिन्दीरन् *ćhindīran*

Imperative, 'Let me cut.'

छिनदै *ćhinadai*	छिनदावहै *ćhinadāvahai*	छिनदामहै *ćhinadāmahai*
छिन्त्स्व *ćhintsva*	छिन्दाथाम् *ćhindāthām*	छिन्द्ध्वम् *ćhinddhvam*
छिन्ताम् *ćhintām*	छिन्दाताम् *ćhindātām*	छिन्दताम् *ćhindatām*

Perf. चिच्छिदे, चिच्छिदिषे, चिच्छिदे; चिच्छिदिवहे, चिच्छिदाथे, चिच्छिदाते; चिच्छिदिमहे, चिच्छिदिध्वे, चिच्छिदिरे. *1st Fut.* छेत्ताहे. *2d Fut.* छेत्स्ये. *Aor.* अच्छित्सि, अच्छित्थास्, अच्छित्त; अच्छित्स्वहि, अच्छित्साथां, अच्छित्सातां; अच्छित्स्महि, अच्छिद्ध्वं, अच्छित्सत. *Prec.* छित्सीय. *Cond.* अच्छेत्स्ये. Pass., *Pres.* छिद्ये; *Aor. 3d sing.* अच्छेदि. Caus., *Pres.* छेदयामि; *Aor.* अचिच्छिदं. Des. चिच्छित्सामि, -त्से. Freq. चेच्छिद्ये, चेच्छेद्मि. Part., *Pres.* छिन्दत्; Ātm. छिन्दान; *Past pass.* छिन्न; *Past indecl.* छित्त्वा, -च्छिद्य; *Fut. pass.* छेत्तव्य, छेदनीय, छेद्य.

EXAMPLES OF OTHER VERBS OF THE SEVENTH CONJUGATIONAL CLASS IN THE ORDER OF THEIR FINAL LETTERS.

668. Root अञ्ज्. *Inf.* अंक्तुं 'to anoint,' 'to make clear.' Par. *Pres.* अनज्मि, अनक्षि (296), अनक्ति; अंज्वस्, अंक्थस्, अंक्तस्; अंज्मस्, अंक्थ, अंजन्ति. *Impf.* आनजं, आनक् (292), आनक्; आंज्व, आंक्तं, आंक्तां; आंज्म, आंक्त, आंजन्. *Pot.* अंज्यां. *Impv.* अनजानि, अंग्धि, अनक्तु; अनजाव, अंक्तं, अंक्तां;

अनजाम, अंक्त, अञ्जन्तु. *Perf.* आनञ्ज, आनञ्जिथ or आनंक्थ, आनञ्ज; आनञ्जिव, आनञ्जथुः, आनञ्जतुः; आनञ्जिम, आनञ्ज, आनञ्जुः. *1st Fut.* अंक्तास्मि or अञ्जितास्मि. *2d Fut.* अंक्ष्यामि or अञ्जिष्यामि. *Aor.* आञ्जिषं, आञ्जीः, आञ्जीत्; आञ्जिष्व, &c., see 427. *Prec.* अज्यासं (453). *Cond.* आंक्ष्यं or आञ्जिष्यं. Pass., *Pres.* अज्यते (469); *Aor. 3d sing.* आञ्जि. Caus., *Pres.* अञ्जयामि; *Aor.* आञ्जिजं. Des. अञ्जिजिषामि. Part., *Pres.* अञ्जत्; *Past pass.* अक्त; *Past indecl.* अञ्जित्वा or अंक्त्वा or अक्त्वा, -अज्य; *Fut. pass.* अंक्तव्य or अञ्जितव्य, अञ्जनीय, अंग्य or अंज्य.

a. Root भुज् (346). *Inf.* भोक्तुं 'to eat,' 'to enjoy.' Par. and Ātm. *Pres.* भुनज्मि, भुनक्षि, भुनक्ति; भुञ्ज्वः, भुंक्थः, भुंक्तः; भुञ्ज्मः, भुंक्थ, भुञ्जन्ति. Ātm. भुञ्जे, भुंक्षे, भुंक्ते; भुञ्ज्वहे, भुञ्जाथे, भुञ्जाते; भुञ्ज्महे, भुंग्ध्वे, भुञ्जते. *Impf.* अभुनजं, अभुनक् (292), अभुनक्; अभुञ्ज्व, अभुंक्तं, अभुंक्तां; अभुञ्ज्म, अभुंक्त, अभुञ्जन्. Ātm. अभुञ्जि, अभुंक्थाः, अभुंक्त; अभुञ्ज्वहि, अभुञ्जाथां, अभुञ्जातां; अभुञ्ज्महि, अभुंग्ध्वं, अभुञ्जत. *Pot.* भुञ्ज्यां. Ātm. भुञ्जीय. *Impv.* भुनजानि, भुंग्धि, भुनक्तु; भुनजाव, भुंक्तं, भुंक्तां; भुनजाम, भुंक्त, भुञ्जन्तु. Ātm. भुनजै, भुंक्ष्व, भुंक्तां; भुनजावहै, भुञ्जाथां, भुञ्जातां; भुनजामहै, भुंग्ध्वं, भुञ्जतां. *Perf.* बुभोज, बुभोजिथ, बुभोज; बुभुजिव, बुभुजथुः, बुभुजतुः; बुभुजिम, बुभुज, बुभुजुः. Ātm. बुभुजे, बुभुजिषे, बुभुजे; -जिवहे, -जाथे, -जाते; -जिमहे, -जिध्वे, -जिरे. *1st Fut.* भोक्तास्मि. Ātm. भोक्ताहे. *2d Fut.* भोक्ष्यामि. Ātm. भोक्ष्ये. *Aor.* अभौक्षं, -क्षीः, -क्षीत्; अभौक्ष्व, अभौक्तं, -क्तां; अभौक्ष्म, अभौक्त, अभौक्षुः. Ātm. अभुक्षि, अभुक्थाः, अभुक्त; अभुक्ष्वहि, अभुक्षाथां, अभुक्षातां; अभुक्ष्महि, अभुग्ध्वं, अभुक्षत. *Prec.* भुज्यासं. Ātm. भुक्षीय. *Cond.* अभोक्ष्यं. Ātm. अभोक्ष्ये. Pass., *Pres.* भुज्ये; *Aor. 3d sing.* अभोजि. Caus., *Pres.* भोजयामि, -ये; *Aor.* अबूभुजं. Des. बुभुक्षामि, -क्षे. Freq. बोभुज्ये, बोभोज्मि. Part., *Pres.* भुञ्जत्; Ātm. भुञ्जान; *Past pass.* भुक्त; *Past indecl.* भुक्त्वा, -भुज्य; *Fut. pass.* भोक्तव्य, भोजनीय, भोज्य or भोग्य.

669. Root भञ्ज् (347). *Inf.* भंक्तुं 'to break.' Par. *Pres.* भनज्मि, भनक्षि, भनक्ति; भञ्ज्वः, भंक्थः, भंक्तः; भञ्ज्मः, भंक्थ, भञ्जन्ति. *Impf.* अभनजं, अभनक् (292), अभनक्; अभञ्ज्व, अभंक्तं, अभंक्तां; अभञ्ज्म, अभंक्त, अभञ्जन्. *Pot.* भञ्ज्यां. *Impv.* भनजानि, भंग्धि, भनक्तु; भनजाव, भंक्तं, भंक्तां; भनजाम, भंक्त, भञ्जन्तु. *Perf.* बभञ्ज, बभञ्जिथ or बभंक्थ, बभञ्ज; बभञ्जिव, बभञ्जथुः, बभञ्जतुः; बभञ्जिम, बभञ्ज, बभञ्जुः. *1st Fut.* भंक्तास्मि. *2d Fut.* भंक्ष्यामि. *Aor.* अभांक्षं, -क्षीः, -क्षीत्; अभांक्ष्व, अभांक्तं, -क्तां; अभांक्ष्म, अभांक्त, अभांक्षुः. *Prec.* भज्यासं (453). *Cond.* अभंक्ष्यं. Pass., *Pres.* भज्ये (469); *Aor. 3d sing.* अभाजि. Caus., *Pres.* भञ्जयामि; *Aor.* अबभञ्जं. Des. बिभंक्षामि. Freq. बंभज्ये, बंभज्मि. Part., *Pres.* भञ्जत्; *Past pass.* भग्न; *Past indecl.* भंक्त्वा or भक्त्वा, -भज्य; *Fut. pass.* भंक्तव्य, भञ्जनीय, भंग्य.

670. Root युज्. *Inf.* योक्तुं 'to join,' 'to unite.' Par. and Ātm.

Pres. युनज्मि, युनक्षि, &c.; like भुज् 668. *a.* Âtm. युञ्जे, युङ्क्षे, &c. *Impf.* अयुनजं, अयुनक् (292), अयुनक्; अयुञ्ज्व, &c. Âtm. अयुञ्जि, अयुङ्क्थास्, &c. *Pot.* युञ्ज्यां. Âtm. युञ्जीय. *Impv.* युनजानि, युङ्ग्धि, युनक्तु; युनजाव, &c. Âtm. युनजै, युङ्क्ष्व, युङ्क्तां, &c. *Perf.* युयोज, युयोजिथ, युयोज; युयुजिव, &c.; like भुज् 668. *a.* Âtm. युयुजे. *1st Fut.* योक्तास्मि. Âtm. योक्ताहे. *2d Fut.* योक्ष्यामि. Âtm. योक्ष्ये. *Aor.* अयुजं, -जस्, -जत्; -जाव, -जतं, -जतां; -जाम, -जत, -जन्. Or अयौक्षं, -क्षीस्, -क्षीत्; अयौक्ष्व, &c. Âtm. अयुक्षि, अयुक्थास्, अयुक्त; अयुक्ष्वहि, &c. *Prec.* युज्यासं. Âtm. युक्षीय. *Cond.* अयोक्ष्यं. Âtm. अयोक्ष्ये. Pass., *Pres.* युज्ये; *Aor. 3d sing.* अयोजि, see 702. Caus., *Pres.* योजयामि; *Aor.* अयूयुजं. Des. युयुक्षामि, -क्षे. Freq. योयुज्ये, योयोज्मि. Part., *Pres.* युञ्जत्; Âtm. युञ्जान; *Past pass.* युक्त; *Past indecl.* युक्त्वा, -युज्य; *Fut. pass.* योक्तव्य, योजनीय, योग्य or योज्य.

671. Root रुध्. *Inf.* रोद्धुं 'to hinder.' Par. and Âtm. *Pres.* रुणध्मि, रुणत्सि, रुणद्धि; रुन्ध्वस्, रुन्द्धस्*, रुन्द्धस्*; रुन्ध्मस्, रुन्द्ध*, रुन्धन्ति. Âtm. रुन्धे, रुन्त्से, रुन्द्धे*; रुन्ध्वहे, रुन्धाथे, रुन्धाते; रुन्ध्महे, रुन्द्ध्वे, रुन्धते. *Impf.* अरुणधं, अरुणत् or अरुणद् or अरुणस् (292), अरुणत् or अरुणद्; अरुन्ध्व, अरुन्द्धं, अरुन्द्धां; अरुन्ध्म, अरुन्द्ध, अरुन्धन्. Âtm. अरुन्धि, अरुन्द्धास्, अरुन्द्ध; अरुन्ध्वहि, अरुन्धाथां, अरुन्धातां; अरुन्ध्महि, अरुन्द्ध्वं, अरुन्धत. *Pot.* रुन्ध्यां. Âtm. रुन्धीय. *Impv.* रुणधानि, रुन्द्धि, रुणद्धु; रुणधाव, रुन्द्धं*, रुन्द्धां*; रुणधाम, रुन्द्ध*, रुन्धन्तु. Âtm. रुणधै, रुन्त्स्व, रुन्द्धां; रुणधावहै, रुन्धाथां, रुन्धातां; रुणधामहै, रुन्द्ध्वं, रुन्धतां. *Perf.* रुरोध, रुरोधिथ, रुरोध; रुरुधिव, रुरुधथुस्, रुरुधतुस्; रुरुधिम, रुरुध, रुरुधुस्. Âtm. रुरुधे, रुरुधिषे, रुरुधे; रुरुधिवहे, रुरुधाथे, रुरुधाते; रुरुधिमहे, रुरुधिध्वे, रुरुधिरे. *1st Fut.* रोद्धास्मि. Âtm. रोद्धाहे. *2d Fut.* रोत्स्यामि. Âtm. रोत्स्ये. *Aor.* अरुधं, -धस्, -धत्; -धाव, -धतं, -धतां; -धाम, -धत, -धन्. Or अरौत्सं, अरौत्सीस्, अरौत्सीत्; अरौत्स्व, अरौद्धं, अरौद्धां; अरौत्स्म, अरौद्ध, अरौत्सुस्. Âtm. अरुत्सि, अरुद्धास्, अरुद्ध; अरुत्स्वहि, अरुत्साथां, अरुत्सातां; अरुत्स्महि, अरुद्ध्वं, अरुत्सत. *Prec.* रुध्यासं. Âtm. रुत्सीय. *Cond.* अरोत्स्यं. Âtm. अरोत्स्ये. Pass., *Pres.* रुध्ये; *Aor. 3d sing.* अरोधि. Caus., *Pres.* रोधयामि; *Aor.* अरूरुधं. Des. रुरुत्सामि, -त्से. Freq. रोरुध्ये, रोरोध्मि. Part., *Pres.* रुन्धत्; Âtm. रुन्धान; *Past pass.* रुद्ध; *Past indecl.* रुद्ध्वा, -रुध्य; *Fut. pass.* रोद्धव्य, रोधनीय, रोध्य.

672. Root शिष्. *Inf.* शेष्टुं 'to distinguish,' 'to separate,' 'to leave remaining.' Par. *Pres.* शिनष्मि, शिनक्षि, शिनष्टि; शिंष्वस्, शिंष्ठस्, शिंष्टस्; शिंष्मस्, शिंष्ठ, शिंषन्ति. *Impf.* अशिनषं, अशिनट् (292), अशिनट्; अशिंष्व, अशिंष्टं, अशिंष्टां; अशिंष्म, अशिंष्ट, अशिंषन्. *Pot.* शिंष्यां. *Impv.* शिनषाणि,

* रुन्धस् may be written for रुन्द्धस्. Similarly, रुन्ध for रुन्द्ध, रुन्धे for रुन्द्धे, &c. See 298. *a.*

शिंड्ढि or शिण्ड्ढि (303, compare 345), शिनष्टु; शिनषाव, शिंष्टं, शिंष्टां; शिनषाम, शिंष्ट, शिंषन्तु. *Perf.* शिशेष, शिशेषिथ, शिशेष; शिशिषिव, शिशिषथुस्, शिशिषतुस्; शिशिषिम, शिशिष, शिशिषुस्. *1st Fut.* शेष्टास्मि. *2d Fut.* शेक्ष्यामि. *Aor.* अशिषं, -षस्, -षत्; -षाव, -षतं, -षतां; -षाम, -षत, -षन्. *Prec.* शिष्यासं. *Cond.* अशेक्ष्यं. Pass., *Pres.* शिष्ये; *Aor. 3d sing.* अशेषि. Caus., *Pres.* शेषयामि; *Aor.* अशीशिषं. Des. शिशिक्षामि. Freq. शेशिष्ये, शेशेष्मि. Part., *Pres.* शिंषत्; *Past pass.* शिष्ट; *Past indecl.* शिष्ट्वा, -शिष्य; *Fut. pass.* शेष्टव्य, शेषणीय, शेष्य.

673. Root हिंस्. *Inf.* हिंसितुं 'to injure.' Par. *Pres.* हिनस्मि, हिनस्सि*, हिनस्ति; हिंस्वस्, हिंस्थस्, हिंस्तस्; हिंस्मस्, हिंस्थ, हिंसन्ति. *Impf.* अहिनसं, अहिनत् or अहिनस् (292. a, 304. a), अहिनत्; अहिंस्व, अहिंस्तं, अहिंस्तां; अहिंस्म, अहिंस्त, अहिंसन्. *Pot.* हिंस्यां. *Impv.* हिनसानि, हिन्धि or हिंधि (304), हिनस्तु; हिनसाव, हिंस्तं, हिंस्तां; हिनसाम, हिंस्त, हिंसन्तु. *Perf.* जिहिंस, जिहिंसिथ, जिहिंस; जिहिंसिव, जिहिंसथुस्, जिहिंसतुस्; जिहिंसिम, जिहिंस, जिहिंसुस्. *1st Fut.* हिंसितास्मि. *2d Fut.* हिंसिष्यामि. *Aor.* अहिंसिषं, अहिंसीस्, अहिंसीत्; अहिंसिष्व, अहिंसिष्टं, अहिंसिष्टां; अहिंसिष्म, अहिंसिष्ट, अहिंसिषुस्. *Prec.* हिंस्यासं. *Cond.* अहिंसिष्यं. Pass., *Pres.* हिंस्ये; *Aor. 3d sing.* अहिंसि. Caus., *Pres.* हिंसयामि; *Aor.* अजिहिंसं. Des. जिहिंसिषामि. Freq. जेहिंस्ये, जेहिंस्मि. Part., *Pres.* हिंसत्; *Past pass.* हिंसित; *Past indecl.* हिंसित्वा, -हिंस्य; *Fut. pass.* हिंसितव्य, हिंसनीय, हिंस्य.

674. Root तृह्. *Inf.* तर्हितुं or तर्ढुं 'to injure,' 'to kill.' Par. *Pres.* तृणेह्मि, तृणेक्षि (306), तृणेढि (305. a); तृंह्वस्, तृण्ढस् (345), तृण्ढस्; तृंह्मस्, तृण्ढ, तृंहन्ति. *Impf.* अतृणहं, अतृणेट् or अतृणेड् (292), अतृणेट् or अतृणेड्; अतृंह्व, अतृण्ढं, अतृण्ढां; अतृंह्म, अतृण्ढ, अतृंहन्. *Pot.* तृंह्यां. *Impv.* तृणहानि, तृण्ढि (see 306. c), तृणेढु; तृणहाव, तृण्ढं, तृण्ढां; तृणहाम, तृण्ढ, तृंहन्तु. *Perf.* ततर्ह, ततर्हिथ or ततर्ढ, ततर्ह; ततृहिव, ततृहथुस्, ततृहतुस्; ततृहिम, ततृह, ततृहुस्. *1st Fut.* तर्हितास्मि or तर्ढास्मि. *2d Fut.* तर्हिष्यामि or तर्क्ष्यामि. *Aor.* अतर्हिषं, -हीस्, -हीत्; -हिष्व, -हिष्टं, -हिष्टां; -हिष्म, -हिष्ट, -हिषुस्. Or अतृक्षं, -क्षस्, -क्षत्; -क्षाव, -क्षतं, -क्षतां; -क्षाम, -क्षत, -क्षन्. *Prec.* तृह्यासं. *Cond.* अतर्हिष्यं or अतर्क्ष्यं. Pass., *Pres.* तृह्ये; *Aor. 3d sing.* अतर्हि. Caus., *Pres.* तर्हयामि; *Aor.* अततर्हं or अतीतृहं. Des. तितर्हिषामि or तितृक्षामि. Freq. तरीतृह्ये, तरीतर्ह्मि (*3d sing.* तरीतर्ढि). Part., *Pres.* तृंहत्; *Past pass.* (305. a) तृढ; *Past indecl.* तर्हित्वा or तृढ्वा, -तृह्य; *Fut. pass.* तर्हितव्य or तर्ढव्य, तर्हणीय, तृह्य.

* Final स् *s* preceded by *a* or *á* remains unchanged before the terminations *si* and *se*; see 62. b.

EXAMPLES OF PRIMITIVE VERBS OF THE FIFTH CONJUGATIONAL CLASS, EXPLAINED AT 349.

675. Root वृ *vṛi*. Infin. वरितुम् *varitum* or वरीतुम् *varītum*, 'to cover,' 'to enclose,' 'to surround,' 'to choose *.'

Note, that the conjugational नु *nu* becomes णु *ṇu* after वृ *vṛi* by 58.

PARASMAI-PADA. *Present tense*, 'I cover.'

वृणोमि *vṛiṇomi*	वृणुवस् *vṛiṇuvas* †	वृणुमस् *vṛiṇumas* ‡
वृणोषि *vṛiṇoshi*	वृणुथस् *vṛiṇuthas*	वृणुथ *vṛiṇutha*
वृणोति *vṛiṇoti*	वृणुतस् *vṛiṇutas*	वृण्वन्ति *vṛiṇvanti*

Imperfect or *first preterite*, 'I was covering,' or 'I covered.'

अवृणवम् *avṛiṇavam*	अवृणुव *avṛiṇuva* §	अवृणुम *avṛiṇuma* ‖
अवृणोस् *avṛiṇos*	अवृणुतम् *avṛiṇutam*	अवृणुत *avṛiṇuta*
अवृणोत् *avṛiṇot*	अवृणुताम् *avṛiṇutām*	अवृण्वन् *avṛiṇvan*

Potential, 'I may cover.'

वृणुयाम् *vṛiṇuyām*	वृणुयाव *vṛiṇuyāva*	वृणुयाम *vṛiṇuyāma*
वृणुयास् *vṛiṇuyās*	वृणुयातम् *vṛiṇuyātam*	वृणुयात *vṛiṇuyāta*
वृणुयात् *vṛiṇuyāt*	वृणुयाताम् *vṛiṇuyātām*	वृणुयुस् *vṛiṇuyus*

Imperative, 'Let me cover.'

वृणवानि *vṛiṇavāni*	वृणवाव *vṛiṇavāva*	वृणवाम *vṛiṇavāma*
वृणु *vṛiṇu*	वृणुतम् *vṛiṇutam*	वृणुत *vṛiṇuta*
वृणोतु *vṛiṇotu*	वृणुताम् *vṛiṇutām*	वृण्वन्तु *vṛiṇvantu*

Perf. (369) ववार, ववर्थ or ववरिथ (see 370), ववार; ववृव, वव्रथुस्, वव्रतुस्; ववृम, वव्र, वव्रुस् or ववरुस् ¶. *1st Fut.* (393) वरितास्मि or वरीतास्मि. *2d Fut.* (393) वरिष्यामि or वरीष्यामि. *Aor.* अवारिषं, अवारीस्, अवारीत्; अवारिष्व, अवारिष्टं, अवारिष्टां; अवारिष्म, अवारिष्ट, अवारिषुस्. *Prec.* व्रियासं or वूर्यासं (448. *b*). *Cond.* अवरिष्यं or अवरीष्यं.

ĀTMANE-PADA. *Present tense*, 'I cover.'

वृण्वे *vṛiṇve*	वृणुवहे *vṛiṇuvahe* **	वृणुमहे *vṛiṇumahe* ††
वृणुषे *vṛiṇushe*	वृण्वाथे *vṛiṇvāthe*	वृणुध्वे *vṛiṇudhve*
वृणुते *vṛiṇute*	वृण्वाते *vṛiṇvāte*	वृण्वते *vṛiṇvate*

---

* In the sense of 'to choose,' this root generally follows the 9th conjugation; thus, Pres. वृणामि, वृणासि, वृणाति; वृणीवस्, &c. See 686.

† Or वृण्वस् *vṛiṇvas*. ‡ Or वृण्मस् *vṛiṇmas*. § Or अवृण्व *avṛiṇva*. ‖ Or अवृण्म *avṛiṇma*.

¶ वृ is sometimes written with long *ṝi*, in which case 374. *b*. may be applied.

** Or वृण्वहे *vṛiṇvahe*. †† Or वृण्महे *vṛiṇmahe*.

Imperfect or first preterite, 'I was covering,' or 'I covered.'

अवृणि *avṛiṇi*	अवृणुवहि *avṛiṇuvahi* *	अवृणुमहि *avṛiṇumahi* †
अवृणुथास् *avṛiṇuthās*	अवृण्वाथाम् *avṛiṇvāthām*	अवृणुध्वम् *avṛiṇudhvam*
अवृणुत *avṛiṇuta*	अवृण्वाताम् *avṛiṇvātām*	अवृण्वत *avṛiṇvata*

Potential, 'I may cover.'

वृण्वीय *vṛiṇvīya*	वृण्वीवहि *vṛiṇvīvahi*	वृण्वीमहि *vṛiṇvīmahi*
वृण्वीथास् *vṛiṇvīthās*	वृण्वीयाथाम् *vṛiṇvīyāthām*	वृण्वीध्वम् *vṛiṇvīdhvam*
वृण्वीत *vṛiṇvīta*	वृण्वीयाताम् *vṛiṇvīyātām*	वृण्वीरन् *vṛiṇvīran*

Imperative, 'Let me cover.'

वृणवै *vṛiṇavai*	वृणवावहै *vṛiṇavāvahai*	वृणवामहै *vṛiṇavāmahai*
वृणुष्व *vṛiṇushva*	वृण्वाथाम् *vṛiṇvāthām*	वृणुध्वम् *vṛiṇudhvam*
वृणुताम् *vṛiṇutām*	वृण्वाताम् *vṛiṇvātām*	वृण्वताम् *vṛiṇvatām*

Perf. वव्रे (369) or ववरे ‡, ववृषे, वव्रे or ववरे; ववृवहे, वव्राथे, वव्राते; ववृमहे, ववृढ्वे, वव्रिरे. *1st Fut.* वरिताहे or वरीताहे. *2d Fut.* वरिष्ये or वरीष्ये. *Aor.* अवरिषि, अवरिष्ठास्, अवरिष्ट; अवरिष्वहि, अवरिषाथां, अवरिषातां; अवरिष्महि, अवरिढ्वं or -ध्वं, अवरिषत. Or अवरीषि, अवरीष्ठास्, &c. Or अवृषि, अवृथास्, अवृत; अवृष्वहि, अवृषाथां, अवृषातां; अवृष्महि, अवृढ्वं, अवृषत. Or अवूर्षि, अवूर्ष्ठास्, अवूर्ष्ट; अवूर्ष्वहि, अवूर्षाथां, अवूर्षातां; अवूर्ष्महि, अवूर्ढ्वं, अवूर्षत. *Prec.* वरिषीय or वृषीय or वूर्षीय (448. *b*). *Cond.* अवरिष्ये or अवरीष्ये. Pass. व्रिये; *Aor. 3d sing.* अवारि. Caus., *Pres.* वरयामि or -ये, or वारयामि or -ये; *Aor.* अवीवरं. Des. विवरिषामि or -षे, विवरीषामि or -षे, वुवूर्षामि or -षे (502). Freq. वेव्रीये (511) or वोवूर्ये, वर्वर्मि. Part., *Pres.* वृण्वत्; Ātm. वृण्वान; *Past pass.* वृत; *Past indecl.* वृत्वा, -वृत्य; *Fut. pass.* वरितव्य or वरीतव्य, वरणीय, वार्य.

EXAMPLES OF OTHER VERBS OF THE FIFTH CONJUGATIONAL CLASS IN THE ORDER OF THEIR FINAL LETTERS.

676. Root श्रु §. *Inf.* श्रोतुं 'to hear.' Par. *Pres.* शृणोमि, शृणोषि, शृणोति; शृणुवस् or शृण्वस्, शृणुथस्, शृणुतस्; शृणुमस् or शृण्मस्, शृणुथ, शृण्वन्ति. *Impf.* अशृणवं, अशृणोस्, अशृणोत्; अशृणुव or अशृण्व, अशृणुतं, अशृणुतां; अशृणुम or अशृण्म, अशृणुत, अशृण्वन्. *Pot.* शृणुयां. *Impv.* शृणवानि, शृणु, शृणोतु; शृणवाव, शृणुतं, शृणुतां; शृणवाम, शृणुत, शृण्वन्तु. *Perf.* (369) शुश्राव, शुश्रोथ, शुश्राव; शुश्रुव, शुश्रुवथुस्, शुश्रुवतुस्; शुश्रुम, शुश्रुव, शुश्रुवुस्. *1st Fut.* श्रोतास्मि. *2d Fut.* श्रोष्यामि. *Aor.* अश्रौषं, अश्रौषीस्,

* Or अवृण्वहि *avṛiṇvahi*. † Or अवृण्महि *avṛiṇmahi*.

‡ वृ is sometimes written with long *ṛī*, in which case 374. *k.* may be applied.

§ This root is placed by Indian grammarians under the 1st class.

अश्रौषीत्; अश्रौष्व, अश्रौष्टं, -ष्टां; अश्रौष्म, अश्रौष्ट, अश्रौषुः. *Prec.* श्रूयासं. *Cond.* अश्रोष्यं. Pass., *Pres.* श्रूये; *Aor. 3d sing.* अश्रावि. Caus., *Pres.* श्रावयामि; *Aor.* अशिश्रवं or अशुश्रवं. Des. शुश्रूषे. Freq. शोश्रूये, शोश्रोमि or शोश्रवीमि. Part., *Pres.* शृण्वत्; *Past pass.* श्रुत; *Past indecl.* श्रुत्वा, -श्रुत्य; *Fut. pass.* श्रोतव्य, श्रवणीय, श्राव्य.

677. Root धू*. *Inf.* धवितुं or धोतुं 'to shake,' 'to agitate.' Par. and Ātm. *Pres.* धूनोमि, धूनोषि, धूनोति; धूनुवः or धून्वः, धूनुथः, धूनुतः; धूनुमः or धून्मः, धूनुथ, धून्वन्ति. Ātm. धून्वे, धूनुषे, धूनुते; धूनुवहे or धून्वहे, धून्वाथे, धून्वाते; धूनुमहे or धून्महे, धूनुध्वे, धून्वते. *Impf.* अधूनवं, अधूनोः, अधूनोत्; अधूनुव or अधून्व, अधूनुतं, अधूनुतां; अधूनुम or अधून्म, अधूनुत, अधून्वन्. Ātm. अधून्वि, अधूनुथाः, अधूनुत; अधूनुवहि or अधून्वहि, अधून्वाथां, अधून्वातां; अधूनुमहि, अधूनुध्वं, अधून्वत. *Pot.* धूनुयां. Ātm. धून्वीय. *Impv.* धूनवानि, धूनु, धूनोतु; धूनवाव, धूनुतं, धूनुतां; धूनवाम, धूनुत, धून्वन्तु. Ātm. धूनवै, धूनुष्व, धूनुतां; धूनवावहै, धून्वाथां, धून्वातां; धूनवामहै, धूनुध्वं, धून्वतां. *Perf.* (374. *g*) दुधाव, दुधविथ or दुधोथ, दुधाव; दुधुविव, दुधुवथुः, दुधुवतुः; दुधुविम, दुधुव, दुधुवुः. Ātm. दुधुवे, दुधुविषे, दुधुवे; दुधुविवहे, दुधुवाथे, दुधुवाते; दुधुविमहे, दुधुविध्वे or -ढ्वे, दुधुविरे. *1st Fut.* धवितास्मि or धोतास्मि. Ātm. धविताहे or धोताहे. *2d Fut.* धविष्यामि or धोष्यामि. Ātm. धविष्ये or धोष्ये. *Aor.** अधाविषं, अधावीः, अधावीत्; अधाविष्व, अधाविष्टं, अधाविष्टां; अधाविष्म, अधाविष्ट, अधाविषुः. Or अधौषं, -षीः, -षीत्; अधौष्व, अधौष्टं, -ष्टां; अधौष्म, अधौष्ट, अधौषुः. Ātm. अधविषि, अधविष्ठाः, अधविष्ट; अधविष्वहि, अधविषाथां, -षातां; अधविष्महि, अधविढ्वं (-ध्वं), अधविषत. Or अधोषि, अधोष्ठाः, अधोष्ट; अधोष्वहि, अधोषाथां, -षातां; अधोष्महि, अधोढ्वं, अधोषत. *Prec.* धूयासं. Ātm. धविषीय or धोषीय. *Cond.* अधविष्यं or अधोष्यं. Ātm. अधविष्ये or अधोष्ये. Pass., *Pres.* धूये; *Aor. 3d sing.* अधावि. Caus., *Pres.* धूनयामि or धावयामि; *Aor.* अदूधुनं or अदूधवं. Des. दुधूषामि, -षे. Freq. दोधूये, दोधोमि or दोधवीमि. Part., *Pres.* धून्वत्; Ātm. धून्वान; *Past pass.* धूत or धून; *Past indecl.* धूत्वा, -धूय; *Fut. pass.* धवितव्य or धोतव्य, धवनीय, धाव्य or धव्य.

a. Like धू may be conjugated सु 'to press out Soma juice,' which in native grammars is the model of the 5th class; thus, *Pres.* सुनोमि, &c. The two futures reject *i*; *1st Fut.* सोतास्मि, &c.

678. Root स्तृ or स्तॄ†. *Inf.* स्तरितुं or स्तरीतुं or स्तर्तुं 'to spread,' 'to

---

* This root may also be धुनोमि &c., and also in the 9th class; Pres. धुनामि, धुनासि, धुनाति; धुनीवः, &c.; see 686: and in the 6th (धुवामि 280). In the latter case the Aor. is अधुविषं, &c.; see 430.

† This root may also be conjugated as a verb of the 9th class; thus, Pres. स्तृणामि, स्तृणासि, स्तृणाति; स्तृणीवः, &c. See 686.

cover.' Par. and Ātm. *Pres.* वृणोमि, &c.; like सु at 675. Ātm. वृण्वे, वृणुषे, &c. *Impf.* अवृणवं. Ātm. अवृण्वि. *Pot.* वृणुयां. Ātm. वृण्वीय. *Impv.* वृणवानि. Ātm. वृणवै. *Perf.* (331. *c*, 374. *k*) ववार, ववर्थ, ववार; ववृव, ववृथुस्, ववृतुस्; ववृम, ववृ, ववृस्. Ātm. वव्रे, ववृषे, वव्रे; ववृवहे, वव्राथे, वव्राते; ववृमहे, ववृढ्वे or -ध्वे, वव्रिरे. *1st Fut.* वरितास्मि or वरीतास्मि or वर्तास्मि. Ātm. वरिताहे or वरीताहे or वर्ताहे. *2d Fut.* वरिष्यामि or वरीष्यामि. Ātm. वरिष्ये or वरीष्ये. *Aor.* अवारिषं, -रीस्, -रीत्; अवारिष्व, &c.; see 675. Or अवार्षं, -र्षीस्, -र्षीत्; अवार्ष्व, -र्ष्टं, -र्ष्टां; अवार्ष्म, -र्ष्ट, -र्षुस्. Ātm. अवरिषि or अवरीषि or अवृषि or अवार्षि. *Prec.* व्रियासं or वूर्यासं. Ātm. वृषीय or वरिषीय or वूर्षीय. *Cond.* अवरिष्यं or अवरीष्यं. Ātm. अवरिष्ये or अवरीष्ये. Pass., *Pres.* (467) व्रिये; *Aor.* 3d *sing.* अवारि. Caus., *Pres.* वारयामि; *Aor.* अवीवरं or अववरं. Des. विवरिषामि, -षे; or विवरीषामि, -षे; or वुवूर्षामि, -र्षे. Freq. वाव्रिये or वेव्रीये, वर्वर्मि or वरीवर्मि. Part., *Pres.* वृण्वत्; Ātm. वृण्वान; *Past pass.* वृत or वूर्ण (534); *Past indecl.* वृत्वा, -वार्य, -वृत्य; *Fut. pass.* वरितव्य or वरीतव्य or वर्तव्य, वरणीय, वार्य.

679. Root शक्*. *Inf.* शक्तुं 'to be able.' Par. *Pres.* शक्नोमि, शक्नोषि, शक्नोति; शक्नुवस्, शक्नुथस्, शक्नुतस्; शक्नुमस्, शक्नुथ, शक्नुवन्ति. *Impf.* अशक्नवं, अशक्नोस्, अशक्नोत्; अशक्नुव, अशक्नुतं, अशक्नुतां; अशक्नुम, अशक्नुत, अशक्नुवन्. *Pot.* शक्नुयां. *Impv.* शक्नवानि, शक्नुहि (291), शक्नोतु; शक्नवाव, शक्नुतं, शक्नुतां; शक्नवाम, शक्नुत, शक्नुवन्तु. *Perf.* शशाक, शेकिथ or शशक्थ, शशाक; शेकिव, शेकथुस्, शेकतुस्; शेकिम, शेक, शेकुस्. *1st Fut.* शक्तास्मि. *2d Fut.* शक्ष्यामि. *Aor.* अशकं, -कस्, -कत्; -काव, -कतं, -कतां; -काम, -कत, -कन्. Or अशकिषं, -कीस्, -कीत्; अशकिष्व, -किष्टं, -ष्टां; अशकिष्म, -किष्ट, -किषुस्. *Prec.* शक्यासं. *Cond.* अशक्ष्यं. Pass., *Pres.* शक्ये; *Aor.* 3d *sing.* अशाकि. Caus., *Pres.* शाकयामि; *Aor.* अशीशकं. Des. शिशक्षिषामि or शिक्षामि, -क्षे † (503). Freq. शाशक्ये, शाशक्मि or शाशकीमि. Part., *Pres.* शक्नुवत्; Ātm. शक्नुवान; *Past pass.* शक्त; *Past indecl.* शक्त्वा, -शक्य; *Fut. pass.* शक्तव्य, शकनीय, शक्य.

680. Root ऋध्. *Inf.* अर्धितुं 'to prosper,' 'to flourish,' 'to increase.' Par. *Pres.* ऋध्नोमि, ऋध्नोषि, ऋध्नोति; ऋध्नुवस्, ऋध्नुथस्, ऋध्नुतस्; ऋध्नुमस्, ऋध्नुथ, ऋध्नुवन्ति. *Impf.* (260. *a*) आर्ध्नवं, आर्ध्नोस्, आर्ध्नोत्; आर्ध्नुव, आर्ध्नुतं,

---

* शक् is also conjugated in the 4th class, Parasmai and Ātmane (Pres. शक्यामि &c., शक्ये); but it may then be regarded as a passive verb. See 253. *b*.

† This form of the Des. generally means 'to learn,' and is said by some to come from a root शिक्ष्.

आर्ध्नोत्; आर्ध्नुव, आर्ध्नुत, आर्ध्नुवन्. *Pot.* ऋध्नुयां. *Impv.* ऋध्नवानि, ऋध्नुहि, ऋध्नोतु; ऋध्नवाव, ऋध्नुतं, -तां; ऋध्नवाम, ऋध्नुत, ऋध्नुवन्तु. *Perf.* आनर्ध, आनर्धिथ, आनर्ध; आनृधिव, आनृधथुः, आनृधतुः; आनृधिम, आनृध, आनृधुः. *1st Fut.* अर्धितास्मि. *2d Fut.* अर्धिष्यामि. *Aor.* आर्धिषं, आर्धीः, आर्धीत्; आर्धिष्व, आर्धिष्टं, -ष्टां; आर्धिष्म, आर्धिष्ट, आर्धिषुः. Or आर्धं, -धः, -धत्; -धाव, &c. *Prec.* ऋध्यासं. *Cond.* आर्धिष्यं. Pass., *Pres.* ऋध्ये; *Aor. 3d sing.* आर्धि. Caus. अर्धयामि; *Aor.* आर्दिधं. Des. अर्दिधिषामि or ईर्त्सामि (503). Part., *Pres.* ऋध्नुवत्; *Past pass.* ऋद्ध; *Past indecl.* अर्धित्वा or ऋद्ध्वा, -ऋध्य; *Fut. pass.* अर्धितव्य, अर्धनीय, ऋध्य.

681. Root आप्. *Inf.* आप्तुं 'to obtain.' Par. *Pres.* आप्नोमि, आप्नोषि, आप्नोति; आप्नुवः, आप्नुथः, आप्नुतः; आप्नुमः, आप्नुथ, आप्नुवन्ति. *Impf.* आप्नवं, आप्नोः, आप्नोत्; आप्नुव, आप्नुतं, -तां; आप्नुम, आप्नुत, आप्नुवन्. *Pot.* आप्नुयां. *Impv.* आप्नवानि, आप्नुहि, आप्नोतु; आप्नवाव, आप्नुतं, -तां; आप्नवाम, आप्नुत, आप्नुवन्तु. *Perf.* आप, आपिथ, आप; आपिव, आपथुः, आपतुः; आपिम, आप, आपुः. *1st Fut.* आप्तास्मि. *2d Fut.* आप्स्यामि. *Aor.* आपं, आपः, आपत्; आपाव, आपतं, -तां; आपाम, आपत, आपन्. *Prec.* आप्यासं. *Cond.* आप्स्यं. Pass., *Pres.* आप्ये; *Aor. 3d sing.* आपि. Caus., *Pres.* आपयामि; *Aor.* आपिपं. Des. (503) ईप्सामि. Part., *Pres.* आप्नुवत्; *Past pass.* आप्त; *Past indecl.* आप्त्वा, -आप्य; *Fut. pass.* आप्तव्य, आपनीय, आप्य.

a. Root अश्. *Inf.* अशितुं or अष्टुं 'to obtain,' 'to enjoy,' 'to pervade.' Ātm. *Pres.* अश्नुवे, अश्नुषे, अश्नुते; अश्नुवहे, अश्नुवाथे, अश्नुवाते; अश्नुमहे, अश्नुध्वे, अश्नुवते. *Impf.* आश्नुवि, आश्नुथाः, आश्नुत; आश्नुवहि, आश्नुवाथां, आश्नुवातां; आश्नुमहि, आश्नुध्वं, आश्नुवत. *Pot.* अश्नुवीय. *Impv.* अश्नवै, अश्नुष्व, अश्नुतां; अश्नवावहै, अश्नुवाथां, अश्नुवातां; अश्नवामहै, अश्नुध्वं, अश्नुवतां. *Perf.* (367. c) आनशे, आनशिषे or आनक्षे, आनशे; आनशिवहे or आनश्वहे (371), आनशाथे, आनशाते; आनशिमहे or आनश्महे, आनशिध्वे or आनड्ढ्वे, आनशिरे. *1st Fut.* अशिताहे or अष्टाहे. *2d Fut.* अशिष्ये or अक्ष्ये. *Aor.* आक्षि, आष्ठाः, आष्ट; आश्वहि, आक्षाथां, आक्षातां; आश्महि, आड्ढ्वं, आक्षत. Or आशिषि, आशिष्ठाः, आशिष्ट; आशिष्वहि, आशिषाथां, आशिषातां; आशिष्महि, आशिढ्वं, आशिषत. *Prec.* अशिषीय or अक्षीय. *Cond.* आशिष्ये or आक्ष्ये. Pass., *Pres.* अश्ये; *Aor. 3d sing.* आशि. Caus., *Pres.* आशयामि; *Aor.* आशिशं. Des. अशिशिषे. Freq. अशाश्ये (511. a). Part., *Pres.* अश्नुवान; *Past pass.* अशित or अष्ट; *Past indecl.* अशित्वा or अष्ट्वा, -अश्य; *Fut. pass.* अशितव्य or अष्टव्य, अशनीय, आश्य.

EXAMPLES OF PRIMITIVE VERBS OF THE EIGHTH CONJUGATIONAL CLASS, EXPLAINED AT 353.

682. Root कृ *kṛi*. Infin. कर्तुम् *kartum*, 'to do' (355).

PARASMAI-PADA. *Present tense*, 'I do.'

करोमि *karomi*	कुर्वस्* *kurvas*	कुर्मस्* *kurmas*
करोषि *karoshi*	कुरुथस् *kuruthas*	कुरुथ *kurutha*
करोति *karoti*	कुरुतस् *kurutas*	कुर्वन्ति* *kurvanti*

Imperfect or *first preterite*, 'I was doing,' or 'I did.'

अकरवम् *akaravam*	अकुर्व *akurva* (73)	अकुर्म *akurma* (73)
अकरोस् *akaros*	अकुरुतम् *akurutam*	अकुरुत *akuruta*
अकरोत् *akarot*	अकुरुताम् *akurutām*	अकुर्वन् *akurvan*

Potential, 'I may do,' &c.

कुर्याम्* *kuryām*	कुर्याव *kuryāva*	कुर्याम *kuryāma*
कुर्यास् *kuryās*	कुर्यातम् *kuryātam*	कुर्यात *kuryāta*
कुर्यात् *kuryāt*	कुर्याताम् *kuryātām*	कुर्युस् *kuryus*

Imperative, 'Let me do,' &c.

करवाणि *karavāṇi*	करवाव *karavāva*	करवाम *karavāma*
कुरु *kuru*	कुरुतम् *kurutam*	कुरुत *kuruta*
करोतु *karotu*	कुरुताम् *kurutām*	कुर्वन्तु* *kurvantu*

Perfect or *second preterite*, 'I did,' or 'I have done.'

चकार *ćakāra* (368)	चकृव *ćakṛiva*	चकृम *ćakṛima*
चकर्थ *ćakartha*	चक्रथुस् *ćakrathus*	चक्र *ćakra*
चकार *ćakāra*	चक्रतुस् *ćakratus*	चक्रुस् *ćakrus*

First future, 'I will do.'

कर्तास्मि *kartāsmi*	कर्तास्वस् *kartāsvas*	कर्तास्मस् *kartāsmas*
कर्तासि *kartāsi*	कर्तास्थस् *kartāsthas*	कर्तास्थ *kartāstha*
कर्ता *kartā*	कर्तारौ *kartārau*	कर्तारस् *kartāras*

Second future, 'I shall do.'

करिष्यामि *karishyāmi*	करिष्यावस् *karishyāvas*	करिष्यामस् *karishyāmas*
करिष्यसि *karishyasi*	करिष्यथस् *karishyathas*	करिष्यथ *karishyatha*
करिष्यति *karishyati*	करिष्यतस् *karishyatas*	करिष्यन्ति *karishyanti*

* कुर्व्वस्, कुर्म्मस्, कुर्व्वी, &c., would be equally correct; see 73. An obsolete form कुर्मि for करोमि is found in Epic poetry.

Aorist or third preterite, 'I did.'

अकार्षम् *akársham*	अकार्ष्व *akárshva*	अकार्ष्म *akárshma*
अकार्षीस् *akárshís*	अकार्ष्टम् *akárshṭam*	अकार्ष्ट *akárshṭa*
अकार्षीत् *akárshít*	अकार्ष्टाम् *akárshṭám*	अकार्षुस् *akárshus*

Precative or benedictive, 'May I do.'

क्रियासम् *kriyásam*	क्रियास्व *kriyásva*	क्रियास्म *kriyásma*
क्रियास् *kriyás*	क्रियास्तम् *kriyástam*	क्रियास्त *kriyásta*
क्रियात् *kriyát*	क्रियास्ताम् *kriyástám*	क्रियासुस् *kriyásus*

Conditional, 'I should do.'

अकरिष्यम् *akarishyam*	अकरिष्याव *akarishyáva*	अकरिष्याम *akarishyáma*
अकरिष्यस् *akarishyas*	अकरिष्यतम् *akarishyatam*	अकरिष्यत *akarishyata*
अकरिष्यत् *akarishyat*	अकरिष्यताम् *akarishyatám*	अकरिष्यन् *akarishyan*

683. Átmane-pada. *Present tense*, 'I do.'

कुर्वे *kurve* (73)	कुर्वहे *kurvahe*	कुर्महे *kurmahe*
कुरुषे *kurushe*	कुर्वाथे *kurváthe*	कुरुध्वे *kurudhve*
कुरुते *kurute*	कुर्वाते *kurváte*	कुर्वते *kurvate*

Imperfect or first preterite, 'I was doing,' or 'I did.'

अकुर्वि *akurvi* (73)	अकुर्वहि *akurvahi*	अकुर्महि *akurmahi*
अकुरुथास् *akuruthás*	अकुर्वाथाम् *akurváthám*	अकुरुध्वम् *akurudhvam*
अकुरुत *akuruta*	अकुर्वाताम् *akurvátám*	अकुर्वत *akurvata*

Potential, 'I may do.'

कुर्वीय *kurvíya*	कुर्वीवहि *kurvívahi*	कुर्वीमहि *kurvímahi*
कुर्वीथास् *kurvíthás*	कुर्वीयाथाम् *kurvíyáthám*	कुर्वीध्वम् *kurvídhvam*
कुर्वीत *kurvíta*	कुर्वीयाताम् *kurvíyátám*	कुर्वीरन् *kurvíran*

Imperative, 'Let me do.'

करवै *karavai*	करवावहै *karavávahai*	करवामहै *karavámahai*
कुरुष्व *kurushva*	कुर्वाथाम् *kurváthám*	कुरुध्वम् *kurudhvam*
कुरुताम् *kurutám*	कुर्वाताम् *kurvátám*	कुर्वताम् *kurvatám*

Perfect or second preterite, 'I did,' or 'I have done.'

चक्रे *ćakre*	चकृवहे *ćakṛivahe*	चकृमहे *ćakṛimahe*
चकृषे *ćakṛishe*	चक्राथे *ćakráthe*	चकृढ्वे *ćakṛiḍhve*
चक्रे *ćakre*	चक्राते *ćakráte*	चक्रिरे *ćakrire*

First future, 'I will do.'

कर्ताहे *kartáhe*	कर्तास्वहे *kartásvahe*	कर्तास्महे *kartásmahe*
कर्तासे *kartáse*	कर्तासाथे *kartásáthe*	कर्ताध्वे *kartádhve*
कर्ता *kartá*	कर्तारौ *kartárau*	कर्तारस् *kartáras*

Second future, 'I shall do.'

करिष्ये *karishye*	करिष्यावहे *karishyávahe*	करिष्यामहे *karishyámahe*
करिष्यसे *karishyase*	करिष्येथे *karishyethe*	करिष्यध्वे *karishyadhve*
करिष्यते *karishyate*	करिष्येते *karishyete*	करिष्यन्ते *karishyante*

Aorist or third preterite, 'I did.'

अकृषि *akṛishi*	अकृष्वहि *akṛishvahi*	अकृष्महि *akṛishmahi*
अकृथास् *akṛithás*	अकृषाथाम् *akṛisháthám*	अकृढ्वम् *akṛiḍhvam*
अकृत *akṛita*	अकृषाताम् *akṛishátám*	अकृषत *akṛishata*

Precative or benedictive, 'May I do.'

कृषीय *kṛishíya*	कृषीवहि *kṛishívahi*	कृषीमहि *kṛishímahi*
कृषीष्ठास् *kṛishíshṭhás*	कृषीयास्थाम् *kṛishíyásthám*	कृषीढ्वम् *kṛishíḍhvam*
कृषीष्ट *kṛishíshṭa*	कृषीयास्ताम् *kṛishíyástám*	कृषीरन् *kṛishíran*

Conditional, 'I should do.'

अकरिष्ये *akarishye*	अकरिष्यावहि *akarishyávahi*	अकरिष्यामहि *akarishyámahi*
अकरिष्यथास् *akarishyathás*	अकरिष्येथाम् *akarishyethám*	अकरिष्यध्वम् *akarishyadhvam*
अकरिष्यत *akarishyata*	अकरिष्येताम् *akarishyetám*	अकरिष्यन्त *akarishyanta*

Pass., *Pres.* क्रियते; *Aor. 3d sing.* अकारि (701). Caus., *Pres.* कारयामि; *Aor.* अचीकरं. Des. चिकीर्षामि, -षे (502). Freq. चेक्रीये, चर्कर्मि or चरिकर्मि or चरीकर्मि or चर्करीमि or चरिकरीमि or चरीकरीमि. Part., *Pres.* कुर्वत्; Átm. कुर्वाण; *Past pass.* कृत; *Past indecl.* कृत्वा, -कृत्य; *Fut. pass.* कर्तव्य, करणीय, कार्य.

684. Only nine other roots are generally given in this class. Of these the commonest is तन् 'to stretch,' conjugated at 583. The others are, ऋण् 'to go,' क्षण् and क्षिण् 'to kill' or 'to hurt,' घृण् 'to shine,' तृण् 'to eat grass,' मन् 'to imagine,' Átm.; वन् 'to ask,' सन् 'to give.' As these end in nasals, their conjugation resembles that of verbs of the 5th class at 675; thus—

685. Root क्षण्. *Inf.* क्षणितुं 'to kill,' 'to hurt.' Par. and Átm. *Pres.* क्षणोमि, क्षणोषि, क्षणोति; क्षणुवस्, &c. Átm. क्षण्वे, क्षणुषे, &c. *Impf.* अक्षणवं, अक्षणोस्, &c. Átm. अक्षण्वि. *Pot.* क्षणुयां. Átm. क्षण्वीय. *Impv.* क्षणवानि. Átm. क्षणवै. *Perf.* चक्षाण, चक्षणिथ, चक्षाण; चक्षणिव, चक्षणथुस्, चक्षणतुस्; चक्षणिम, चक्षण, चक्षणुस्. Átm. चक्षणे,

जगृहिषे, जगृहे; जगृहिवहे, जगृहाथे, जगृहाते; जगृहिमहे, जगृहिढ्वे, जगृहिरे. *1st Fut.* ग्रहीतास्मि. *Ātm.* ग्रहीताहे. *2d Fut.* ग्रहीष्यामि. *Ātm.* ग्रहीष्ये. *Aor.* अग्रहीषं, -हीस्, -हीत्; अग्रहीष्व, -हीष्टं, -हीष्टां; अग्रहीष्म, -हीष्ट, -हीषुस्. *Ātm.* अग्रहीषि, अग्रहीष्ठास् or अग्रहीथास् (424. c), अग्रहीष्ट or अग्रहीत; अग्रहीष्वहि, -हीषाथां, -हीषातां; अग्रहीष्महि, -हीढ्वं, -हीषत. *Prec.* गृह्यासं. *Ātm.* ग्रहीषीय. *Cond.* अग्रहीष्यं. *Ātm.* अग्रहीष्ये. Pass., *Pres.* गृह्ये; *Aor. 3d sing.* अग्राहि. Caus., *Pres.* ग्राहयामि; *Aor.* अजिग्रहं. Des. जिघृक्षामि, -क्षे. Freq. जरीगृह्ये, जाग्रह्मि. Part., *Pres.* गृह्णत्; *Ātm.* गृह्णान; *Past pass.* गृहीत; *Past indecl.* गृहीत्वा or ग्रहीत्वा, -गृह्य; *Fut. pass.* ग्रहीतव्य, ग्रहणीय, ग्राह्य.

EXAMPLES OF PRIMITIVE VERBS OF THE NINTH CONJUGATIONAL CLASS, EXPLAINED AT 356.

686. Root यु *yu.* Infin. यवितुम् *yavitum,* 'to join,' 'to mix.'

PARASMAI-PADA. *Present tense,* 'I join.'

युनामि *yunámi*	युनीवस् *yunívas*	युनीमस् *yunímas*
युनासि *yunási*	युनीथस् *yunīthas*	युनीथ *yunītha*
युनाति *yunáti*	युनीतस् *yunītas*	युनन्ति *yunanti*

Imperfect or first preterite, 'I was joining,' or 'I joined.'

अयुनाम् *ayunám*	अयुनीव *ayunīva*	अयुनीम *ayunīma*
अयुनास् *ayunás*	अयुनीतम् *ayunītam*	अयुनीत *ayunīta*
अयुनात् *ayunát*	अयुनीताम् *ayunītám*	अयुनन् *ayunan*

Potential, 'I may join.'

युनीयाम् *yunīyám*	युनीयाव *yunīyáva*	युनीयाम *yunīyáma*
युनीयास् *yunīyás*	युनीयातम् *yunīyátam*	युनीयात *yunīyáta*
युनीयात् *yunīyát*	युनीयाताम् *yunīyátám*	युनीयुस् *yunīyus*

Imperative, 'Let me join.'

युनानि *yunáni*	युनाव *yunáva*	युनाम *yunáma*
युनीहि *yunīhi*	युनीतम् *yunītam*	युनीत *yunīta*
युनातु *yunátu*	युनीताम् *yunītám*	युनन्तु *yunantu*

Perf. युयाव, युयविथ or युयोथ, युयाव; युयुविव, युयुवथुस्, -वतुस्; युयुविम, युयुव, युयुवुस्. *1st Fut.* यवितास्मि or योतास्मि*. *2d Fut.* यविष्यामि. *Aor.*

* Some authorities give योतास्मि &c. as the only form. See Laghu Kaum. 724.

अयाविषं, -षीः, -षीत्; अयाविष्व, -ष्टं, -ष्टां; अयाविष्म, -ष्ट, -षुः. *Prec.* यूयात्. *Cond.* अयविष्यत्.

687. Ātmane-pada. *Present tense*, 'I join.'

युने *yune*	युनीवहे *yunīvahe*	युनीमहे *yunīmahe*
युनीषे *yunīshe*	युनाथे *yunāthe*	युनीध्वे *yunīdhve*
युनीते *yunīte*	युनाते *yunāte*	युनते *yunate*

Imperfect or *first preterite*, 'I was joining,' or 'I joined.'

अयुनि *ayuni*	अयुनीवहि *ayunīvahi*	अयुनीमहि *ayunīmahi*
अयुनीथास् *ayunīthās*	अयुनाथाम् *ayunāthām*	अयुनीध्वम् *ayunīdhvam*
अयुनीत *ayunīta*	अयुनाताम् *ayunātām*	अयुनत *ayunata*

Potential, 'I may join.'

युनीय *yunīya*	युनीवहि *yunīvahi*	युनीमहि *yunīmahi*
युनीथास् *yunīthās*	युनीयाथाम् *yunīyāthām*	युनीध्वम् *yunīdhvam*
युनीत *yunīta*	युनीयाताम् *yunīyātām*	युनीरन् *yunīran*

Imperative, 'Let me join.'

युनै *yunai*	युनावहै *yunāvahai*	युनामहै *yunāmahai*
युनीष्व *yunīshva*	युनाथाम् *yunāthām*	युनीध्वम् *yunīdhvam*
युनीताम् *yunītām*	युनाताम् *yunātām*	युनताम् *yunatām*

Perf. युयुवे, युयुविषे, युयुवे; युयुविवहे, युयुवाथे, युयुवाते; युयुविमहे, युयुविढ्वे or -ध्वे, युयुविरे. *1st Fut.* यविताहे. *2d Fut.* यविष्ये. *Aor.* अयविषि, -विष्ठाः, -विष्ट; अयविष्वहि, अयविषाथां, -षातां; अयविष्महि, -विढ्वं or -विध्वं, -विषत. *Prec.* यविषीय. *Cond.* अयविष्ये. Pass., *Pres.* यूये; *1st Fut.* याविताहे; *Aor. 3d sing.* अयावि. Caus., *Pres.* यावयामि; *Aor.* अयीयवं. Des. युयूषामि or यियविषामि. Freq. योयूये, योयोमि or योयवीमि. Part., *Pres.* युनत्; Ātm. युनान; *Past pass.* युत; *Past indecl.* युत्वा, -युत्य; *Fut. pass.* यवितव्य, यवनीय, याव्य or यव्य.

688. Root ज्ञा (361). *Inf.* ज्ञातुं 'to know.' Par. and Ātm. *Pres.* जानामि, जानासि, जानाति; जानीवस्, जानीथस्, जानीतस्; जानीमस्, जानीथ, जानन्ति. Ātm. जाने, जानीषे, जानीते; जानीवहे, जानाथे, जानाते; जानीमहे, जानीध्वे, जानते. *Impf.* अजानां, अजानास्, अजानात्; अजानीव, अजानीतं, अजानीतां; अजानीम, अजानीत, अजानन्. Ātm. अजानि, अजानीथास्, अजानीत; अजानीवहि, अजानाथां, अजानातां; अजानीमहि, अजानीध्वं, अजानत. *Pot.* जानीयां. Ātm. जानीय. *Impv.* जानानि, जानीहि, जानातु; जानाव, जानीतं, जानीतां; जानाम, जानीत, जानन्तु. Ātm. जानै, जानीष्व, जानीतां; जानावहै, जानाथां, जानातां; जानामहै, जानीध्वं, जानतां. *Perf.* (373) जज्ञौ, जज्ञिथ,

जज्ञौ; जज्ञिव, जज्ञथुस्, जज्ञतुस्; जज्ञिम, जज्ञ, जज्ञुस्. *Ātm.* जज्ञे, जज्ञिषे, जज्ञे; जज्ञिवहे, जज्ञाथे, जज्ञाते; जज्ञिमहे, जज्ञिध्वे, जज्ञिरे. *1st Fut.* ज्ञातास्मि. *2d Fut.* ज्ञास्यामि. *Aor.* (433) अज्ञासिषं, अज्ञासीस्, अज्ञासीत्; अज्ञासिष्व, अज्ञासिष्टं, -ष्टां; अज्ञासिष्म, -ष्ट, -षुस्. *Ātm.* अज्ञासि, अज्ञास्थास्, अज्ञास्त; अज्ञास्वहि, अज्ञासाथां, -साताम्; अज्ञास्महि, अज्ञाध्वं, अज्ञासत. *Prec.* ज्ञेयासं or ज्ञायासं. *Ātm.* ज्ञासीय. *Cond.* अज्ञास्यं. *Ātm.* अज्ञास्ये. Pass., *Pres.* (465. *a*) ज्ञाये; *Perf.* जज्ञे (473); *1st Fut.* ज्ञाताहे or ज्ञायिताहे (474); *2d Fut.* ज्ञास्ये or ज्ञायिष्ये; *Aor. 3d sing.* अज्ञायि. Caus., *Pres.* ज्ञापयामि or ज्ञपयामि; *Aor.* अजिज्ञपं. Des. जिज्ञासे (-सामि Ep.). Freq. जाज्ञाये, जाज्ञामि or जाज्ञेमि. Part., *Pres.* जानत्; *Ātm.* जानान; *Past pass.* ज्ञात; *Past indecl.* ज्ञात्वा, -ज्ञाय; *Fut. pass.* ज्ञातव्य, ज्ञानीय, ज्ञेय.

689. Root क्री. *Inf.* क्रेतुं 'to buy.' Par. and Ātm. *Pres.* क्रीणामि, क्रीणासि, क्रीणाति; क्रीणीवस्, क्रीणीथस्, क्रीणीतस्; क्रीणीमस्, क्रीणीथ, क्रीणन्ति. *Ātm.* क्रीणे, क्रीणीषे, क्रीणीते; क्रीणीवहे, क्रीणाथे, क्रीणाते; क्रीणीमहे, क्रीणीध्वे, क्रीणते. *Impf.* अक्रीणां, अक्रीणास्, अक्रीणात्; अक्रीणीव, अक्रीणीतं, अक्रीणीतां; अक्रीणीम, अक्रीणीत, अक्रीणन्. *Ātm.* अक्रीणि, अक्रीणीथास्, अक्रीणीत; अक्रीणीवहि, अक्रीणाथां, अक्रीणातां; अक्रीणीमहि, अक्रीणीध्वं, अक्रीणत. *Pot.* क्रीणीयां. *Ātm.* क्रीणीय. *Impv.* क्रीणानि, क्रीणीहि, क्रीणातु; क्रीणाव, क्रीणीतं, क्रीणीतां; क्रीणाम, क्रीणीत, क्रीणन्तु. *Ātm.* क्रीणै, क्रीणीष्व, क्रीणीतां; क्रीणावहै, क्रीणाथां, क्रीणातां; क्रीणामहै, क्रीणीध्वं, क्रीणतां. *Perf.* (374. *e*) चिक्राय, चिक्रयिथ or चिक्रेथ, चिक्राय; चिक्रियिव, चिक्रियथुस्, चिक्रियतुस्; चिक्रियिम, चिक्रिय, चिक्रियुस्. *Ātm.* चिक्रिये, चिक्रियिषे, चिक्रिये; चिक्रियिवहे, चिक्रियाथे, -याते; चिक्रियिमहे, चिक्रियिध्वे or -ढ्वे, चिक्रियिरे. *1st Fut.* क्रेतास्मि. *Ātm.* क्रेताहे. *2d Fut.* क्रेष्यामि. *Ātm.* क्रेष्ये. *Aor.* अक्रैषं, -षीस्, -षीत्; अक्रैष्व, -ष्टं, -ष्टां; अक्रैष्म, -ष्ट, -षुस्. *Ātm.* अक्रेषि, -ष्ठास्, -ष्ट; अक्रेष्वहि, -षाथां, -षातां; अक्रेष्महि, अक्रेढ्वं, अक्रेषत. *Prec.* क्रीयासं. *Ātm.* क्रेषीय. *Cond.* अक्रेष्यं. *Ātm.* अक्रेष्ये. Pass., *Pres.* क्रीये; *Aor. 3d sing.* अक्रायि. Caus., *Pres.* क्रापयामि; *Aor.* अचिक्रपं. Des. चिक्रीषामि, -षे. Freq. चेक्रीये, चेक्रेमि or चेक्रयीमि. Part., *Pres.* क्रीणत्; *Ātm.* क्रीणान; *Past pass.* क्रीत; *Past indecl.* क्रीत्वा, -क्रीय; *Fut. pass.* क्रेतव्य, क्रयणीय, क्रेय.

690. Like क्री is प्री 'to please.' *Pres.* प्रीणामि; *Ātm.* प्रीणे. Caus. प्रीणयामि or प्राययामि; *Aor.* अपिप्रणं or अपिप्रीणं*. Des. पिप्रीषामि. Freq. पेप्रीये.

691. लू, 'to cut,' follows पू, 'to purify,' at 583; thus, *Pres.* लुनामि; *Ātm.* लुने. *Pot.* लुनीयां; *Ātm.* लुनीय. *Perf.* लुलाव; *Ātm.* लुलुवे. *1st Fut.* लवितास्मि. *2d Fut.* लविष्यामि. *Aor.* अलाविषं.

* Foster gives अपिप्रणं; Westergaard, अपिप्रीणं.

692. Root बन्ध्. *Inf.* बन्द्धुं 'to bind.' Par. *Pres.* बध्नामि, बध्नासि, बध्नाति; बध्नीवस्, बध्नीथस्, बध्नीतस्; बध्नीमस्, बध्नीथ, बध्नन्ति. *Impf.* अबध्नां, अबध्नास्, अबध्नात्; अबध्नीव, अबध्नीतं, -तां; अबध्नीम, अबध्नीत, अबध्नन्. *Pot.* बध्नीयां. *Impv.* बध्नानि, बधान (357. a), बध्नातु; बध्नाव, बध्नीतं, -तां; बध्नाम, बध्नीत, बध्नन्तु. *Perf.* बबन्ध, बबन्धिथ or बबन्द्ध or बबन्ध (298. a), बबन्ध; बबन्धिव, बबन्धथुस्, बबन्धतुस्; बबन्धिम, बबन्ध, बबन्धुस्. *1st Fut.* बन्द्धास्मि. *2d Fut.* भन्त्स्यामि (299. a). *Aor.* अभान्त्सं (299. a), अभान्त्सीस्, अभान्त्सीत्; अभान्त्स्व, अबान्द्धं, अबान्द्धां; अभान्त्स्म, अबान्द्ध, अभान्त्सुस्. *Prec.* बध्यासं. *Cond.* अभन्त्स्यं. Pass., *Pres.* (469) बध्ये. Caus., *Pres.* बन्धयामि; *Aor.* अबबन्धं. Des. बिभन्त्सामि (299. a). Freq. बाबध्ये, बाबन्धिम, बाबन्धीमि. Part., *Pres.* बध्नत्; *Past pass.* बद्ध; *Past indecl.* बद्ध्वा, -बध्य; *Fut. pass.* बन्द्धव्य, बन्धनीय, बन्ध्य.

693. Root ग्रन्थ्. *Inf.* ग्रन्थितुं 'to string,' 'to tie.' Par. *Pres.* ग्रथ्नामि, ग्रथ्नासि, ग्रथ्नाति; ग्रथ्नीवस्, ग्रथ्नीथस्, ग्रथ्नीतस्; ग्रथ्नीमस्, ग्रथ्नीथ, ग्रथ्नन्ति. *Impf.* अग्रथ्नां, अग्रथ्नास्, अग्रथ्नात्; अग्रथ्नीव, अग्रथ्नीतं, -तां; अग्रथ्नीम, अग्रथ्नीत, अग्रथ्नन्. *Pot.* ग्रथ्नीयां. *Impv.* ग्रथ्नानि, ग्रथान*, ग्रथ्नातु; ग्रथ्नाव, ग्रथ्नीतं, -तां; ग्रथ्नाम, ग्रथ्नीत, ग्रथ्नन्तु. *Perf.* (375. b) जग्रन्थ*, जग्रन्थिथ or ग्रेथिथ, जग्रन्थ*; जग्रन्थिव or ग्रेथिव, जग्रन्थथुस् or ग्रेथथुस्, जग्रन्थतुस् or ग्रेथतुस्; जग्रन्थिम or ग्रेथिम, जग्रन्थ or ग्रेथ, जग्रन्थुस् or ग्रेथुस्. *1st Fut.* ग्रन्थितास्मि. *2d Fut.* ग्रन्थिष्यामि. *Aor.* अग्रन्थिषं, -न्थीस्, -न्थीत्, &c. *Prec.* ग्रथ्यासं. *Cond.* अग्रन्थिष्यं. Pass., *Pres.* (469) ग्रथ्ये. Caus., *Pres.* ग्रन्थयामि; *Aor.* अजग्रन्थं. Des. जिग्रन्थिषामि. Freq. जाग्रथ्ये, जंग्रन्थ्मि, जंग्रन्थीमि. Part., *Pres.* ग्रथ्नत्; *Past pass.* ग्रथित; *Past indecl.* ग्रथित्वा or ग्रन्थित्वा, -ग्रथ्य; *Fut. pass.* ग्रन्थितव्य, ग्रन्थनीय, ग्रन्थ्य.

a. Like ग्रन्थ् is conjugated श्रन्थ् 'to loosen,' मन्थ् 'to churn.'

694. Root क्षुभ्†. *Inf.* क्षोभितुं 'to agitate.' Par. *Pres.* क्षुभ्णामि, क्षुभ्णासि, क्षुभ्णाति; क्षुभ्णीवस्, क्षुभ्णीथस्, क्षुभ्णीतस्; क्षुभ्णीमस्, क्षुभ्णीथ, क्षुभ्णन्ति. *Impf.* अक्षुभ्णां, अक्षुभ्णास्, अक्षुभ्णात्; अक्षुभ्णीव, अक्षुभ्णीतं, -तां; अक्षुभ्णीम, अक्षुभ्णीत, अक्षुभ्णन्. *Pot.* क्षुभ्णीयां. *Impv.* क्षुभ्णानि, क्षुभाण (357. a, 58), क्षुभ्णातु; क्षुभ्णाव, क्षुभ्णीतं, -तां; क्षुभ्णाम, क्षुभ्णीत, क्षुभ्णन्तु. *Perf.* चुक्षोभ, चुक्षोभिथ, चुक्षोभ; चुक्षुभिव, चुक्षुभथुस्, -भतुस्; चुक्षुभिम, चुक्षुभ, चुक्षुभुस्. *1st Fut.* क्षोभितास्मि. *2d Fut.* क्षोभिष्यामि. *Aor.* अक्षोभिषं, -भीस्, -भीत्, &c. Or अक्षुभं, -भस्, -भत्; -भाव, -भतं, -भतां; -भाम, -भत, -भन्. *Prec.* क्षुभ्यासं. *Cond.* अक्षोभिष्यं. Pass., *Pres.* क्षुभ्ये; *Aor. 3d sing.* अक्षोभि. Caus., *Pres.* क्षोभयामि; *Aor.*

* Some authorities give ग्रन्थान in 2d sing. Impv.; and the option of जग्राथ in the 1st and 3d of the Perf. Compare 339.

† Also neuter, 4th c. 'to be agitated;' Pres. क्षुभ्यामि 612.

अचुक्षुभं. Des. चुक्षोभिषामि or चुक्षुभिषामि. Freq. चोक्षुभ्यते, चोक्षोभ्मि (3d sing. चोक्षोब्धि). Part., Pres. क्षुभ्नत्; Past pass. क्षुब्ध or क्षुभित; Past indecl. क्षुब्ध्वा or क्षुभित्वा, -क्षुभ्य; Fut. pass. क्षोभितव्य, क्षोभणीय (58), क्षोभ्य.

695. Root स्तम्भ्*. Inf. स्तम्भितुं 'to stop,' 'to support.' Par. Pres. स्तभ्नामि; like क्षुभ् 694. Impf. अस्तभ्नां. Pot. स्तभ्नीयां. Impv. स्तभ्नानि, स्तभान (357. a), स्तभ्नातु; स्तभ्नाव, स्तभ्नीतं, -तां; स्तभ्नाम, स्तभ्नीत, स्तभ्नन्तु. Perf. तस्तम्भ, तस्तम्भिथ, तस्तम्भ; तस्तम्भिव, तस्तम्भथुस्, -अतुस्; तस्तम्भिम, तस्तम्भ, तस्तम्भुस्. 1st Fut. स्तम्भितास्मि. 2d Fut. स्तम्भिष्यामि. Aor. अस्तम्भिषं, -भीस्, -भीत्, &c. Or अस्तभं, -अस्, -अत्; -आव, -अतं, -अतां; -आम, -अत, -अन्. Prec. स्तभ्यासं. Cond. अस्तम्भिष्यं. Pass., Pres. स्तभ्यते. Caus., Pres. स्तम्भयामि; Aor. अतस्तम्भं. Des. तिस्तम्भिषामि. Freq. तास्तभ्यते, तास्तम्भ्मि or तास्तम्भीमि. Part., Pres. स्तभ्नत्; Past pass. स्तब्ध; Past indecl. स्तब्ध्वा or स्तम्भित्वा; Fut. pass. स्तम्भितव्य, स्तम्भनीय, स्तम्भ्य.

696. Root अश्†. Inf. अशितुं 'to eat.' Par. Pres. अश्नामि, अश्नासि, अश्नाति; अश्नीवस्, अश्नीथस्, अश्नीतस्; अश्नीमस्, अश्नीथ, अश्नन्ति. Impf. आश्नां, आश्नास्, आश्नात्; आश्नीव, आश्नीतं, -तां; आश्नीम, आश्नीत, आश्नन्. Pot. अश्नीयां. Impv. अश्नानि, अशान (357. a), अश्नातु; अश्नाव, अश्नीतं, -तां; अश्नाम, अश्नीत, अश्नन्तु. Perf. आश, आशिथ, आश; आशिव, आशथुस्, आशतुस्; आशिम, आश, आशुस्. 1st Fut. अशितास्मि. 2d Fut. अशिष्यामि. Aor. आशिषं, आशीस्, आशीत्; आशिष्व, आशिष्टं, आशिष्टां; आशिष्म, आशिष्ट, आशिषुस्. Prec. अश्यासं. Cond. आशिष्यं. Pass., Pres. अश्यते. Caus., Pres. आशयामि; Aor. आशिशं. Des. अशिशिषामि. Freq. अशाश्यते (508. a). Part., Pres. अश्नत्; Past pass. अशित; Past indecl. अशित्वा, -अश्य; Fut. pass. अशितव्य, अशनीय, आश्य.

697. Root क्लिश्. Inf. क्लेशितुं or क्लेष्टुं 'to harass.' Par. Pres. क्लिश्नामि; like अश् 696. Impf. अक्लिश्नां, अक्लिश्नास्, अक्लिश्नात्; अक्लिश्नीव, अक्लिश्नीतं, -तां; अक्लिश्नीम, अक्लिश्नीत, अक्लिश्नन्. Pot. क्लिश्नीयां. Impv. क्लिश्नानि, क्लिशान, &c. Perf. चिक्लेश, चिक्लेशिथ or चिक्लेष्ठ, चिक्लेश; चिक्लिशिव or चिक्लिश्व (371), चिक्लिशथुस्, -शतुस्; चिक्लिशिम or चिक्लिश्म, चिक्लिश, चिक्लिशुस्. 1st Fut. क्लेशितास्मि or क्लेष्टास्मि. 2d Fut. क्लेशिष्यामि or क्लेक्ष्यामि. Aor. अक्लेशिषं, -शीस्, -शीत्; अक्लेशिष्व, -शिष्टं, -शिष्टां; अक्लेशिष्म, -शिष्ट, -शिषुस्. Or अक्लिक्षं, -क्षस्, -क्षत्; -क्षाव, -क्षतं, -क्षतां; -क्षाम, -क्षत, -क्षन् (439). Prec. क्लिश्यासं. Cond. अक्लेशिष्यं or अक्लेक्ष्यं. Pass., Pres. क्लिश्यते; Aor. 3d sing. अक्लेशि. Caus., Pres. क्लेशयामि; Aor. अचिक्लिशं. Des. चिक्लिशिषामि or चिक्लेशिषामि or चिक्लिक्षामि. Freq. चेक्लिश्यते, चेक्लेष्मि. Part., Pres. क्लिश्नत्;

---

* This root also follows the 5th conjugation; thus, Pres. स्तभ्नोमि. See 675.

† This is a different root from अश् 5th conjugation. See 681.

Past pass. क्लिष्ट or क्लिशित; *Past indecl.* क्लिष्ट्वा or क्लिशित्वा, -क्लिश्य; *Fut. pass.* क्लेशितव्य or क्लेष्टव्य, क्लेशनीय, क्लेश्य.

698. Root पुष्. *Inf.* पोषितुं 'to nourish.' Par. *Pres.* पुष्णामि, पुष्णासि, पुष्णाति; पुष्णीवस्, पुष्णीथस्, पुष्णीतस्; पुष्णीमस्, पुष्णीथ, पुष्णन्ति. *Impf.* अपुष्णां, अपुष्णास्, अपुष्णात्; अपुष्णीव, अपुष्णीतं, -तां; अपुष्णीम, अपुष्णीत, अपुष्णन्. *Pot.* पुष्णीयां. *Impv.* पुष्णानि, पुषाण (357.*a*), पुष्णातु; पुष्णाव, पुष्णीतं, -तां; पुष्णाम, पुष्णीत, पुष्णन्तु. For the rest, see पुष् 4th c., 621.

699. Root ग्रह् (359, 399.*a*). *Inf.* ग्रहीतुं 'to take.' Par. and Ātm. *Pres.* गृह्णामि, गृह्णासि, गृह्णाति; गृह्णीवस्, गृह्णीथस्, गृह्णीतस्; गृह्णीमस्, गृह्णीथ, गृह्णन्ति. Ātm. गृह्णे, गृह्णीषे, गृह्णीते; गृह्णीवहे, गृह्णाथे, गृह्णाते; गृह्णीमहे, गृह्णीध्वे, गृह्णते. *Impf.* अगृह्णां, अगृह्णास्, अगृह्णात्; अगृह्णीव, अगृह्णीतं, अगृह्णीतां; अगृह्णीम, अगृह्णीत, अगृह्णन्. Ātm. अगृह्णि, अगृह्णीथास्, अगृह्णीत; अगृह्णीवहि, अगृह्णाथां, अगृह्णातां; अगृह्णीमहि, अगृह्णीध्वं, अगृह्णत. *Pot.* गृह्णीयां. Ātm. गृह्णीय. *Impv.* गृह्णानि, गृहाण, गृह्णातु; गृह्णाव, गृह्णीतं, गृह्णीतां; गृह्णाम, गृह्णीत, गृह्णन्तु. Ātm. गृह्णै, गृह्णीष्व, गृह्णीतां; गृह्णावहै, गृह्णाथां, गृह्णातां; गृह्णामहै, गृह्णीध्वं, गृह्णतां. *Perf.* (384) जग्राह, जग्रहिथ, जग्राह; जगृहिव, जगृहथुस्, जगृहतुस्; जगृहिम, जगृह, जगृहुस्. Ātm. जगृहे, जगृहिषे, जगृहे; जगृहिवहे, जगृहाथे, जगृहाते; जगृहिमहे, जगृहिध्वे or -ढ्वे, जगृहिरे. *1st Fut.* ग्रहीतास्मि (399.*a*). Ātm. ग्रहीताहे. *2d Fut.* ग्रहीष्यामि. Ātm. ग्रहीष्ये. *Aor.* अग्रहीषं, अग्रहीस्, अग्रहीत्; अग्रहीष्व, अग्रहीष्टं, अग्रहीष्टां; अग्रहीष्म, अग्रहीष्ट, अग्रहीषुस्. Ātm. अग्रहीषि, अग्रहीष्ठास्, अग्रहीष्ट; अग्रहीष्वहि, अग्रहीषाथां, अग्रहीषातां; अग्रहीष्महि, अग्रहीढ्वं, अग्रहीषत. *Prec.* गृह्यासं. Ātm. ग्रहीषीय. *Cond.* अग्रहीष्यं. Ātm. अग्रहीष्ये. Pass., *Pres.* गृह्ये; *Perf.* जगृहे; *1st Fut.* ग्रहीताहे or ग्राहिताहे; *2d Fut.* ग्रहीष्ये or ग्राहिष्ये; *Aor. 3d sing.* अग्राहि, *3d pl.* अग्रहीषत or अग्राहिषत. Caus., *Pres.* ग्राहयामि; *Aor.* अजिग्रहं. Des. जिघृक्षामि, -क्षे (503). Freq. जरीगृह्ये, जाग्रह्मि (*3d sing.* जाग्राढि) or जाग्रहीमि (711). Part., *Pres.* गृह्णत्; Ātm. गृह्णान; *Past pass.* गृहीत; *Past indecl.* गृहीत्वा, -गृह्य; *Fut. pass.* ग्रहीतव्य, ग्रहणीय, ग्राह्य.

EXAMPLES OF PASSIVE VERBS, EXPLAINED AT 461.

700. Root दा *dá* (465). Infin. दातुम् *dátum*, 'to be given.'

Present, 'I am given.'

दीये *díye*	दीयावहे *díyávahe*	दीयामहे *díyámahe*
दीयसे *díyase*	दीयेथे *díyethe*	दीयध्वे *díyadhve*
दीयते *díyate*	दीयेते *díyete*	दीयन्ते *díyante*

Imperfect or first preterite, 'I was given.'

अदीये *adíye*	अदीयावहि *adíyávahi*	अदीयामहि *adíyámahi*
अदीयथास् *adíyathás*	अदीयेथाम् *adíyethám*	अदीयध्वम् *adíyadhvam*
अदीयत *adíyata*	अदीयेताम् *adíyetám*	अदीयन्त *adíyanta*

Potential, 'I may be given.'

दीयेय *díyeya*	दीयेवहि *díyevahi*	दीयेमहि *díyemahi*
दीयेथास् *díyethás*	दीयेयाथाम् *díyeyáthám*	दीयेध्वम् *díyedhvam*
दीयेत *díyeta*	दीयेयाताम् *díyeyátám*	दीयेरन् *díyeran*

Imperative, 'Let me be given.'

दीयै *díyai*	दीयावहै *díyávahai*	दीयामहै *díyámahai*
दीयस्व *díyasva*	दीयेथाम् *díyethám*	दीयध्वम् *díyadhvam*
दीयताम् *díyatám*	दीयेताम् *díyetám*	दीयन्ताम् *díyantám*

Perfect or second preterite, 'I have been given.'

ददे *dade*	ददिवहे *dadivahe*	ददिमहे *dadimahe*
ददिषे *dadishe*	ददाथे *dadáthe*	ददिध्वे *dadidhve*
ददे *dade*	ददाते *dadáte*	ददिरे *dadire*

First future, 'I shall be given.'

दाताहे *dátáhe* or	दातास्वहे *dátásvahe*	दातास्महे *dátásmahe*, &c.
दायिताहे *dáyitáhe*	दायितास्वहे *dáyitásvahe*	दायितास्महे *dáyitásmahe*, &c.

Second future, 'I shall be given.'

दास्ये *dásye* or	दास्यावहे *dásyávahe*	दास्यामहे *dásyámahe*, &c.
दायिष्ये *dáyishye*	दायिष्यावहे *dáyishyávahe*	दायिष्यामहे *dáyishyámahe*, &c.

Aorist or third preterite, 'I was given.'

अदिषि *adishi* or	अदिष्वहि *adishvahi*	अदिष्महि *adishmahi*
अदायिषि *adáyishi*	अदायिष्वहि *adáyishvahi*	अदायिष्महि *adáyishmahi*
अदिथास् *adithás* or	अदिषाथाम् *adisháthám*	अदिढ्वम् *adiḍhvam*
अदायिष्ठास् *adáyishṭhás*	अदायिषाथाम् *adáyisháthám*	अदायिढ्वम् *adáyiḍhvam*
अदायि *adáyi*, 'it was given,'	अदिषाताम् *adishátám*	अदिषत *adishata*
	अदायिषाताम् *adáyishátám*	अदायिषत *adáyishata*

Prec. दासीय or दायिषीय, &c. *Cond.* अदास्ये or अदायिष्ये.

701. Root कृ *kṛi* (467). Infin. कर्तुम् *kartum*, 'to be made' or 'done.'

Present, 'I am made.'			*Imperfect or first preterite*, 'I was made.'		
क्रिये	क्रियावहे	क्रियामहे	अक्रिये	अक्रियावहि	अक्रियामहि
क्रियसे	क्रियेथे	क्रियध्वे	अक्रियथास्	अक्रियेथाम्	अक्रियध्वम्
क्रियते	क्रियेते	क्रियन्ते	अक्रियत	अक्रियेताम्	अक्रियन्त

Potential, 'I may be made.'			*Second preterite.*		
क्रियेय	क्रियेवहि	क्रियेमहि	चक्रे	चकृवहे	चकृमहे
क्रियेथास्	क्रियेयाथां	क्रियेध्वं	चकृषे	चक्राथे	चकृढ्वे
क्रियेत	क्रियेयातां	क्रियेरन्	चक्रे	चक्राते	चक्रिरे

Imperative, 'Let me be made.'			*First future*		
क्रियै	क्रियावहै	क्रियामहै	कर्ताहे	कर्तास्वहे	कर्तास्महे, &c.
क्रियस्व	क्रियेथां	क्रियध्वं	or कारिताहे	कारितास्वहे	कारितास्महे, &c.
क्रियतां	क्रियेतां	क्रियन्तां	*Second fut.* करिष्ये or कारिष्ये, &c.		

Aorist or third preterite.

SING.	DUAL.	PLURAL.
अकृषि or अकारिषि	अकृष्वहि or अकारिष्वहि	अकृष्महि or अकारिष्महि
अकृथास् or अकारिष्ठास्	अकृषाथां or अकारिषाथां	अकृढ्वं or अकारिढ्वं, -ढ्वं
अकारि 'it was done'	अकृषातां or अकारिषातां	अकृषत or अकारिषत

Prec. कृषीय or कारिषीय. *Cond.* अकरिष्ये or अकारिष्ये.

702. Example of a passive from a root ending in a consonant:

Root युज् *yuj*. Infin. योक्तुम् *yoktum*, 'to be fitting.'

Pres. युज्ये, युज्यसे, युज्यते, &c. *Impf.* अयुज्ये, अयुज्यथास्, अयुज्यत, &c. *Pot.* युज्येय. *Impv.* युज्यै, युज्यस्व, युज्यतां, &c. *Perf.* युयुजे, युयुजिषे, युयुजे, &c. *1st Fut.* योक्ताहे, योक्तासे, योक्ता, &c. *2d Fut.* योक्ष्ये, योक्ष्यसे, &c. *Aor.* अयुक्षि, अयुक्थास्, अयोजि; अयुक्ष्वहि, &c. *Prec.* युक्षीय. *Cond.* अयोक्ष्ये.

EXAMPLE OF CAUSAL VERBS, EXPLAINED AT 479.

703. Root भू *bhú*. Infin. भावयितुम् *bhávayitum*, 'to cause to be.'

PARASMAI-PADA.			ĀTMANE-PADA.		
Present, 'I cause to be.'					
भावयामि	भावयावस्	भावयामस्	भावये	भावयावहे	भावयामहे
भावयसि	भावयथस्	भावयथ	भावयसे	भावयेथे	भावयध्वे
भावयति	भावयतस्	भावयन्ति	भावयते	भावयेते	भावयन्ते
Imperfect or first preterite, 'I was causing to be,' or 'I caused,' &c.					
अभावयम्	अभावयाव	अभावयाम	अभावये	अभावयावहि	अभावयामहि
अभावयस्	अभावयतं	अभावयत	अभावयथास्	अभावयेथां	अभावयध्वं
अभावयत्	अभावयतां	अभावयन्	अभावयत	अभावयेतां	अभावयन्त
Potential, 'I may cause to be.'					
भावयेयं	भावयेव	भावयेम	भावयेय	भावयेवहि	भावयेमहि
भावयेस्	भावयेतं	भावयेत	भावयेथास्	भावयेयाथां	भावयेध्वं
भावयेत्	भावयेतां	भावयेयुस्	भावयेत	भावयेयातां	भावयेरन्

Imperative, 'Let me cause to be.'

भावयानि	भावयाव	भावयाम	भावयै	भावयावहै	भावयामहै
भावय	भावयतं	भावयत	भावयस्व	भावयेथां	भावयध्वं
भावयतु	भावयतां	भावयन्तु	भावयतां	भावयेतां	भावयन्तां

Perfect or second preterite, 'I caused to be.'

भावयाञ्चकार	भावयाञ्चकृव	भावयाञ्चकृम	भावयाञ्चक्रे	भावयाञ्चकृवहे	भावयाञ्चकृमहे
भावयाञ्चकर्थ	भावयाञ्चक्रथुस्	भावयाञ्चक्र	भावयाञ्चकृषे	भावयाञ्चक्राथे	भावयाञ्चकृढ्वे
भावयाञ्चकार	भावयाञ्चक्रतुस्	भावयाञ्चक्रुस्	भावयाञ्चक्रे	भावयाञ्चक्राते	भावयाञ्चक्रिरे

First future, 'I will cause to be.'

भावयितास्मि	भावयितास्वस्	भावयितास्मस्	भावयिताहे	भावयितास्वहे	भावयितास्महे
भावयितासि	भावयितास्थस्	भावयितास्थ	भावयितासे	भावयितासाथे	भावयिताध्वे
भावयिता	भावयितारौ	भावयितारस्	भावयिता	भावयितारौ	भावयितारस्

Second future, 'I shall or will cause to be.'

भावयिष्यामि	भावयिष्यावस्	भावयिष्यामस्	भावयिष्ये	भावयिष्यावहे	भावयिष्यामहे
भावयिष्यसि	भावयिष्यथस्	भावयिष्यथ	भावयिष्यसे	भावयिष्येथे	भावयिष्यध्वे
भावयिष्यति	भावयिष्यतस्	भावयिष्यन्ति	भावयिष्यते	भावयिष्येते	भावयिष्यन्ते

Aorist or third preterite, 'I caused to be.'

अबीभवम्	अबीभवाव	अबीभवाम	अबीभवे	अबीभवावहि	अबीभवामहि
अबीभवस्	अबीभवतं	अबीभवत	अबीभवथास्	अबीभवेथां	अबीभवध्वं
अबीभवत्	अबीभवतां	अबीभवन्	अबीभवत	अबीभवेतां	अबीभवन्त

Precative or benedictive, 'May I cause to be.'

भाव्यासम्	भाव्यास्व	भाव्यास्म	भावयिषीय	भावयिषीवहि	भावयिषीमहि
भाव्यास्	भाव्यास्तं	भाव्यास्त	भावयिषीष्ठास्	भावयिषीयास्थां	भावयिषीढ्वं
भाव्यात्	भाव्यास्तां	भाव्यासुस्	भावयिषीष्ट	भावयिषीयास्तां	भावयिषीरन्

Conditional, 'I should cause to be.'

अभावयिष्यम्	अभावयिष्याव	अभावयिष्याम	अभावयिष्ये	अभावयिष्यावहि	अभावयिष्यामहि
अभावयिष्यस्	अभावयिष्यतं	अभावयिष्यत	अभावयिष्यथास्	अभावयिष्येथां	अभावयिष्यध्वं
अभावयिष्यत्	अभावयिष्यतां	अभावयिष्यन्	अभावयिष्यत	अभावयिष्येतां	अभावयिष्यन्त

704. After this model, and after the model of primitive verbs of the 10th class at 638, may be conjugated all causal verbs.

EXAMPLES OF DESIDERATIVE VERBS, EXPLAINED AT 498.

705. Root भू *bhú*. Infin. बुभूषितुम् *bubhúshitum*, 'to wish to be.'

PARASMAI-PADA. ÁTMANE-PADA.

Present, 'I wish to be.'

बुभूषामि	बुभूषावस्	बुभूषामस्	बुभूषे	बुभूषावहे	बुभूषामहे
बुभूषसि	बुभूषथस्	बुभूषथ	बुभूषसे	बुभूषेथे	बुभूषध्वे
बुभूषति	बुभूषतस्	बुभूषन्ति	बुभूषते	बुभूषेते	बुभूषन्ते

Imperfect or first preterite, 'I was wishing to be,' or 'I wished,' &c.

अबुभूषम्	अबुभूषाव	अबुभूषाम	अबुभूषे	अबुभूषावहि	अबुभूषामहि
अबुभूषस्	अबुभूषतं	अबुभूषत	अबुभूषथास्	अबुभूषेथां	अबुभूषध्वं
अबुभूषत्	अबुभूषतां	अबुभूषन्	अबुभूषत	अबुभूषेतां	अबुभूषन्त

Potential, 'I may wish to be.'

बुभूषेयं	बुभूषेव	बुभूषेम	बुभूषेय	बुभूषेवहि	बुभूषेमहि
बुभूषेस्	बुभूषेतं	बुभूषेत	बुभूषेथास्	बुभूषेयाथां	बुभूषेध्वं
बुभूषेत्	बुभूषेतां	बुभूषेयुस्	बुभूषेत	बुभूषेयातां	बुभूषेरन्

Imperative, 'Let me wish to be.'

बुभूषाणि	बुभूषाव	बुभूषाम	बुभूषै	बुभूषावहै	बुभूषामहै
बुभूष	बुभूषतं	बुभूषत	बुभूषस्व	बुभूषेथां	बुभूषध्वं
बुभूषतु	बुभूषतां	बुभूषन्तु	बुभूषतां	बुभूषेतां	बुभूषन्तां

Perfect or second preterite, 'I wished to be.'

बुभूषाञ्चकार*	बुभूषाञ्चकृव	बुभूषाञ्चकृम	बुभूषाञ्चक्रे	बुभूषाञ्चकृवहे	बुभूषाञ्चकृमहे
बुभूषाञ्चकर्थ	बुभूषाञ्चक्रथुस्	बुभूषाञ्चक्र	बुभूषाञ्चकृषे	बुभूषाञ्चक्राथे	बुभूषाञ्चकृढ्वे
बुभूषाञ्चकार	बुभूषाञ्चक्रतुस्	बुभूषाञ्चक्रुस्	बुभूषाञ्चक्रे	बुभूषाञ्चक्राते	बुभूषाञ्चक्रिरे

First future, 'I will wish to be.'

बुभूषितास्मि	बुभूषितास्वस्	बुभूषितास्मस्	बुभूषिताहे	बुभूषितास्वहे	बुभूषितास्महे
बुभूषितासि	बुभूषितास्थस्	बुभूषितास्थ	बुभूषितासे	बुभूषितासाथे	बुभूषिताध्वे
बुभूषिता	बुभूषितारौ	बुभूषितारस्	बुभूषिता	बुभूषितारौ	बुभूषितारस्

Second future, 'I will or shall wish to be.'

बुभूषिष्यामि	बुभूषिष्यावस्	बुभूषिष्यामस्	बुभूषिष्ये	बुभूषिष्यावहे	बुभूषिष्यामहे
बुभूषिष्यसि	बुभूषिष्यथस्	बुभूषिष्यथ	बुभूषिष्यसे	बुभूषिष्येथे	बुभूषिष्यध्वे
बुभूषिष्यति	बुभूषिष्यतस्	बुभूषिष्यन्ति	बुभूषिष्यते	बुभूषिष्येते	बुभूषिष्यन्ते

Aorist or third preterite, 'I wished to be.'

अबुभूषिषम्	अबुभूषिष्व	अबुभूषिष्म	अबुभूषिषि	अबुभूषिष्वहि	अबुभूषिष्महि
अबुभूषीस्	अबुभूषिष्टं	अबुभूषिष्ट	अबुभूषिष्ठास्	अबुभूषिषाथां	अबुभूषिढ्वं
अबुभूषीत्	अबुभूषिष्टां	अबुभूषिषुस्	अबुभूषिष्ट	अबुभूषिषातां	अबुभूषिषत

Precative or benedictive, 'May I wish to be.'

बुभूष्यासम्	बुभूष्यास्व	बुभूष्यास्म	बुभूषिषीय	बुभूषिषीवहि	बुभूषिषीमहि
बुभूष्यास्	बुभूष्यास्तं	बुभूष्यास्त	बुभूषिषीष्ठास्	बुभूषिषीयास्थां	बुभूषिषीढ्वं
बुभूष्यात्	बुभूष्यास्तां	बुभूष्यासुस्	बुभूषिषीष्ट	बुभूषिषीयास्तां	बुभूषिषीरन्

Conditional, 'I should wish to be.'

अबुभूषिष्यम्	अबुभूषिष्याव	अबुभूषिष्याम	अबुभूषिष्ये	अबुभूषिष्यावहि	अबुभूषिष्यामहि
अबुभूषिष्यस्	अबुभूषिष्यतं	अबुभूषिष्यत	अबुभूषिष्यथास्	अबुभूषिष्येथां	अबुभूषिष्यध्वं
अबुभूषिष्यत्	अबुभूषिष्यतां	अबुभूषिष्यन्	अबुभूषिष्यत	अबुभूषिष्येतां	अबुभूषिष्यन्त

* Or बुभूषाञ्चकर.

EXAMPLES OF FREQUENTATIVE OR INTENSIVE VERBS, EXPLAINED AT 507.

706. Root भू *bhú.* Infin. बोभूयितुम् *bobhúyitum,* 'to be repeatedly.'

ÁTMANE-PADA FORM (509).

Present, 'I am repeatedly.'

बोभूये	बोभूयावहे	बोभूयामहे
बोभूयसे	बोभूयेथे	बोभूयध्वे
बोभूयते	बोभूयेते	बोभूयन्ते

Imperfect or *first preterite,* 'I was frequently.'

अबोभूये	अबोभूयावहि	अबोभूयामहि
अबोभूयथास्	अबोभूयेथां	अबोभूयध्वं
अबोभूयत	अबोभूयेतां	अबोभूयन्त

Potential, 'I may be frequently.'

बोभूयेय	बोभूयेवहि	बोभूयेमहि
बोभूयेथास्	बोभूयेयाथां	बोभूयेध्वं
बोभूयेत	बोभूयेयातां	बोभूयेरन्

Imperative, 'Let me be frequently.'

बोभूयै	बोभूयावहै	बोभूयामहै
बोभूयस्व	बोभूयेथां	बोभूयध्वं
बोभूयतां	बोभूयेतां	बोभूयन्तां

Perfect or *second preterite,* 'I was frequently.'

बोभूयाञ्चक्रे	बोभूयाञ्चकृवहे	बोभूयाञ्चकृमहे
बोभूयाञ्चकृषे	बोभूयाञ्चक्राथे	बोभूयाञ्चकृढ्वे
बोभूयाञ्चक्रे	बोभूयाञ्चक्राते	बोभूयाञ्चक्रिरे

First future, 'I will be frequently.'

बोभूयिताहे	बोभूयितास्वहे	बोभूयितास्महे
बोभूयितासे	बोभूयितासाथे	बोभूयिताध्वे
बोभूयिता	बोभूयितारौ	बोभूयितारस्

Second future, 'I will or shall be frequently.'

बोभूयिष्ये	बोभूयिष्यावहे	बोभूयिष्यामहे
बोभूयिष्यसे	बोभूयिष्येथे	बोभूयिष्यध्वे
बोभूयिष्यते	बोभूयिष्येते	बोभूयिष्यन्ते

Aorist or *third preterite,* 'I was frequently.'

अबोभूयिषि	अबोभूयिष्वहि	अबोभूयिष्महि
अबोभूयिष्ठास्	अबोभूयिषाथां	अबोभूयिढ्वं or -ध्वं
अबोभूयिष्ट	अबोभूयिषातां	अबोभूयिषत

Precative or benedictive, 'May I be frequently.'

बोभूयिषीय	बोभूयिषीवहि	बोभूयिषीमहि
बोभूयिषीष्ठास्	बोभूयिषीयास्थां	बोभूयिषीध्वं or -ढ्वं
बोभूयिषीष्ट	बोभूयिषीयास्तां	बोभूयिषीरन्

Conditional, 'I should be frequently.'

अबोभूयिष्ये	अबोभूयिष्यावहि	अबोभूयिष्यामहि
अबोभूयिष्यथास्	अबोभूयिष्येथां	अबोभूयिष्यध्वं
अबोभूयिष्यत	अबोभूयिष्येतां	अबोभूयिष्यन्त

707. PARASMAI-PADA FORM (514).

Present, 'I am frequently.'

बोभवीमि or बोभोमि	बोभूवस्	बोभूमस्
बोभवीषि or बोभोषि	बोभूथस्	बोभूथ
बोभवीति or बोभोति	बोभूतस्	बोभुवति

Imperfect or first preterite, 'I was frequently.'

अबोभवम्	अबोभूव	अबोभूम
अबोभवीस् or अबोभोस्	अबोभूतं	अबोभूत
अबोभवीत् or अबोभोत्	अबोभूतां	अबोभवुस्

Potential, 'I may be frequently.'

बोभूयां	बोभूयाव	बोभूयाम
बोभूयास्	बोभूयातं	बोभूयात
बोभूयात्	बोभूयातां	बोभूयुस्

Imperative, 'May I be frequently.'

बोभवानि	बोभवाव	बोभवाम
बोभूहि	बोभूतं	बोभूत
बोभवीतु or बोभोतु	बोभूतां	बोभुवतु

Perfect or second preterite, 'I was frequently.'

बोभुवाम्बभूव, &c.	बोभुवाम्बभूविव, &c.	बोभुवाम्बभूविम, &c.
or	or	or
बोभाव or बोभूव	बोभुविव or बोभूविव	बोभुविम or बोभूविम
बोभूविथ	बोभुवथुस् or बोभूवथुस्	बोभुव or बोभूव
बोभाव or बोभूव	बोभुवतुस् or बोभूवतुस्	बोभुवुस् or बोभूवुस्

First future, 'I will be frequently.'

बोभवितास्मि	बोभवितास्वस्	बोभवितास्मस्
बोभवितासि	बोभवितास्थस्	बोभवितास्थ
बोभविता	बोभवितारौ	बोभवितारस्

Second future, 'I will or shall be frequently.'

बोभविष्यामि	बोभविष्यावः	बोभविष्यामः
बोभविष्यसि	बोभविष्यथः	बोभविष्यथ
बोभविष्यति	बोभविष्यतः	बोभविष्यन्ति

Aorist or third preterite, 'I was frequently.'

अबोभूवम्	अबोभूव	अबोभूम
अबोभूः	अबोभूतम्	अबोभूत
अबोभूत्	अबोभूताम्	अबोभूवुः
or	or	or
अबोभाविषम्	अबोभाविष्व	अबोभाविष्म
अबोभावीः	अबोभाविष्टं	अबोभाविष्ट
अबोभावीत्	अबोभाविष्टां	अबोभाविषुः

Precative or *benedictive*, 'May I be frequently.'

बोभूयासं	बोभूयास्व	बोभूयास्म
बोभूयाः	बोभूयास्तं	बोभूयास्त
बोभूयात्	बोभूयास्तां	बोभूयासुः

Conditional, 'I should be frequently.'

अबोभविष्यम्	अबोभविष्याव	अबोभविष्याम
अबोभविष्यः	अबोभविष्यतं	अबोभविष्यत
अबोभविष्यत्	अबोभविष्यतां	अबोभविष्यन्

708. Root हन् 'to kill' (323, 654). Parasmai form of Frequentative, 'to kill repeatedly.' *Pres.* जङ्घन्मि or जङ्घनीमि, जङ्घंसि or जङ्घनीषि, जङ्घन्ति or जङ्घनीति; जङ्घन्वः, जङ्घथः, जङ्घतः; जङ्घन्मः, जङ्घथ, जङ्घ्नति or जंघ्नति. *Impf.* अजङ्घनं, अजङ्घन् or अजङ्घनीः, अजङ्घन् or अजङ्घनीत्; अजङ्घन्व, अजङ्घतं, -तां; अजङ्घन्म, अजङ्घत, अजङ्घ्नुः or अजंघ्नुः. *Pot.* जङ्घन्यां. *Impv.* जङ्घनानि, जङ्घहि, जङ्घन्तु or जङ्घनीतु; जङ्घनाव, जङ्घतं, -तां; जङ्घनाम, जङ्घत, जङ्घ्नतु or जंघ्नतु. *Perf.* जङ्घनाम्बभूव or जङ्घनाञ्चकार, &c. &c.

709. Root गम् 'to go' (602, 270). Parasmai form of Frequentative, 'to go frequently.' *Pres.* जङ्गन्मि or जङ्गमीमि, जङ्गंसि or जङ्गमीषि, जङ्गन्ति or जङ्गमीति; जङ्गन्वः, जङ्गथः, जङ्गतः; जङ्गन्मः, जङ्गथ, जङ्ग्मति or जंग्मति. *Impf.* अजङ्गमं, अजङ्गन् or अजङ्गमीः, अजङ्गन् or अजङ्गमीत्; अजङ्गन्व, अजङ्गतं, -तां; अजङ्गन्म, अजङ्गत, अजङ्ग्मुः or अजंग्मुः. *Pot.* जङ्गम्यां. *Impv.* जङ्गमानि, जङ्गहि, जङ्गन्तु or जङ्गमीतु; जङ्गमाव, जङ्गतं, जङ्गतां; जङ्गमाम, जङ्गत, जङ्ग्मतु or जंग्मतु. *Perf.* जङ्गमाम्बभूव or जङ्गमाञ्चकार, &c. &c.

710. Root क्षिप् 'to throw' (635). Parasmai form of Frequentative. *Pres.* चेक्षेप्मि or चेक्षिपीमि, चेक्षेप्सि or चेक्षिपीषि, चेक्षेप्ति or चेक्षिपीति;

बेभिद्वस्, बेभित्थस्, बेभित्तस्; बेभिद्मस्, बेभित्थ, बेभिदति. *Impf.* अबेभेदं, अबेभेत् or अबेभिदीस्, अबेभेत् or अबेभिदीत्; अबेभिद्व, अबेभित्तं, -त्तां; अबेभिद्म, अबेभित्त, अबेभिदुस्. *Pot.* बेभिद्यां, &c. *Impv.* बेभेदानि, बेभिद्धि, बेभेत्तु or बेभिदीतु; बेभेदाव, बेभित्तं, -त्तां; बेभेदाम, बेभित्त, बेभिदतु. *Perf.* बेभिदाम्बभूव or बेभिदाञ्चकार, &c. &c.

711. Root ग्रह् 'to take' (699, 359). Parasmai form of Frequentative. *Pres.* जाग्रह्मि or जाग्रहीमि, जाघर्क्षि (306. *a*) or जाग्रहीषि, जाग्राढि (305. *a*) or जाग्रहीति; जागृह्वस्, जागृढस्, जागृढस्; जागृह्मस्, जागृढ, जागृहति. *Impf.* अजाग्रहं, अजाघर्ट् (292. *b*, 43. *c*) or अजाग्रहीस्, अजाघर्ट् or अजाग्रहीत्; अजागृह्व, अजागृढं, -ढां; अजागृह्म, अजागृढ, अजागृहुस् (332). *Pol.* जागृह्यां. *Impv.* जाग्रहाणि, जागृढि, जाग्राढु or जाग्रहीतु; जाग्रहाव, जागृढं, -ढां; जाग्रहाम, जागृढ, जागृहतु, &c. &c.

CHAPTER VII.

INDECLINABLE WORDS.

ADVERBS.

712. ADVERBS (*nipáta*), like nouns and verbs, may be divided into simple and compound. The latter are treated of in the next Chapter on Compound Words.

There are in Sanskrit a number of aptote or monoptote nouns called *indeclinables*. Some of these indeclinable nouns are as follows: अस्तम् 'setting,' 'decline;' अस्ति 'what exists,' 'existence;' ओम् 'mystical ejaculation, typical of the Hindú Triad;' कम् 'water,' 'ease,' 'head;' क्षमा 'on the ground;' अलम् 'satisfaction,' 'food;' नमस् 'reverence;' नास्ति 'non-existence;' वदि 'the fortnight of the moon's wane;' भुवस् 'sky;' भूर् 'earth;' संवत् 'a year;' सुदि or शुदि 'the fortnight of the moon's increase;' स्वर् 'heaven;' स्वस्ति 'salutation;' स्वधा 'interjection at oblation to the manes;' शम् 'ease.' Others will be mentioned at 713—717, as it will be convenient to classify simple adverbs under four heads; 1st, those formed from the cases of nouns and obsolete words; 2dly, other adverbs of less obvious derivation; 3dly, adverbial affixes; 4thly, adverbial prefixes.

Formed from the Cases of Nouns and Obsolete Words.

713. The nominative or accusative neuter of any adjective;

As, सत्यं 'truly;' बहु 'much;' शीघ्रं, क्षिप्रं, 'quickly;' युक्तं 'fitly;' समीपं 'near;'

Second future, 'I will or shall be frequently.'

बोभविष्यामि	बोभविष्यावः	बोभविष्यामः
बोभविष्यसि	बोभविष्यथः	बोभविष्यथ
बोभविष्यति	बोभविष्यतः	बोभविष्यन्ति

Aorist or *third preterite*, 'I was frequently.'

अबोभूवम्	अबोभूव	अबोभूम
अबोभूः	अबोभूतं	अबोभूत
अबोभूत्	अबोभूतां	अबोभूवुः
or	or	or
अबोभाविषम्	अबोभाविष्व	अबोभाविष्म
अबोभावीः	अबोभाविष्टं	अबोभाविष्ट
अबोभावीत्	अबोभाविष्टां	अबोभाविषुः

Precative or *benedictive*, 'May I be frequently.'

बोभूयासं	बोभूयास्व	बोभूयास्म
बोभूयाः	बोभूयास्तं	बोभूयास्त
बोभूयात्	बोभूयास्तां	बोभूयासुः

Conditional, 'I should be frequently.'

अबोभविष्यम्	अबोभविष्याव	अबोभविष्याम
अबोभविष्यः	अबोभविष्यतं	अबोभविष्यत
अबोभविष्यत्	अबोभविष्यतां	अबोभविष्यन्

708. Root हन् 'to kill' (323, 654). Parasmai form of Frequentative, 'to kill repeatedly.' *Pres.* जङ्घन्मि or जङ्घनीमि, जङ्घंसि or जङ्घनीषि, जङ्घन्ति or जङ्घनीति; जङ्घन्वः, जङ्घथः, जङ्घतः; जङ्घन्मः, जङ्घथ, जङ्घनति or जङ्घ्नति. *Impf.* अजङ्घनं, अजङ्घन् or अजङ्घनीः, अजङ्घन् or अजङ्घनीत्; अजङ्घन्व, अजङ्घतं, -तां; अजङ्घन्म, अजङ्घत, अजङ्घनुः or अजङ्घ्नुः. *Pot.* जङ्घन्यां. *Impv.* जङ्घनानि, जङ्घहि, जङ्घन्तु or जङ्घनीतु; जङ्घनाव, जङ्घतं, -तां; जङ्घनाम, जङ्घत, जङ्घनतु or जङ्घ्नतु. *Perf.* जङ्घनाम्बभूव or जङ्घनाञ्चकार, &c. &c.

709. Root गम् 'to go' (602, 270). Parasmai form of Frequentative, 'to go frequently.' *Pres.* जङ्गन्मि or जङ्गमीमि, जङ्गंसि or जङ्गमीषि, जङ्गन्ति or जङ्गमीति; जङ्गन्वः, जङ्गथः, जङ्गतः; जङ्गन्मः, जङ्गथ, जङ्गमति or जङ्ग्मति. *Impf.* अजङ्गमं, अजङ्गन् or अजङ्गमीः, अजङ्गन् or अजङ्गमीत्; अजङ्गन्व, अजङ्गतं, -तां; अजङ्गन्म, अजङ्गत, अजङ्गमुः or अजङ्ग्मुः. *Pot.* जङ्गम्यां. *Impv.* जङ्गमानि, जङ्गहि, जङ्गन्तु or जङ्गमीतु; जङ्गमाव, जङ्गतं, जङ्गतां; जङ्गमाम, जङ्गत, जङ्गमतु or जङ्ग्मतु. *Perf.* जङ्गमाम्बभूव or जङ्गमाञ्चकार, &c. &c.

710. Root क्षिप् 'to throw' (635). Parasmai form of Frequentative. *Pres.* चेक्षेप्मि or चेक्षिपीमि, चेक्षेप्सि or चेक्षिपीषि, चेक्षेप्ति or चेक्षिपीति;

वेविद्वस्, वेवित्थस्, वेवित्तस्; वेविद्मस्, वेवित्थ, वेविदति. *Impf.* अवेवेदं, अवेवेत् or अवेविदीस्, अवेवेत् or अवेविदीत्; अवेविद्व, अवेवित्तं, -त्तां; अवेविद्म, अवेवित्त, अवेविदुस्. *Pot.* वेविद्यां, &c. *Impv.* वेवेदानि, वेविद्धि, वेवेत्तु or वेविदीतु; वेवेदाव, वेवित्तं, -त्तां; वेवेदाम, वेवित्त, वेविदतु. *Perf.* वेविदाम्बभूव or वेविदाञ्चकार, &c. &c.

711. Root ग्रह् 'to take' (699, 359). Parasmai form of Frequentative. *Pres.* जाग्रह्मि or जाग्रहीमि, जाघक्षि (306. *a*) or जाग्रहीषि, जाग्राढि (305. *a*) or जाग्रहीति; जागृह्वस्, जागृढस्, जागृढस्; जागृह्मस्, जागृढ, जागृहति. *Impf.* अजाग्रहं, अजाघक् (292. *b*, 43. *c*) or अजाग्रहीस्, अजाघक् or अजाग्रहीत्; अजागृह्व, अजागृढं, -ढां; अजागृह्म, अजागृढ, अजागृहुस् (332). *Pot.* जागृह्यां. *Impv.* जाग्रहाणि, जागृढि, जाग्राढु or जाग्रहीतु; जाग्रहाव, जागृढं, -ढां; जाग्रहाम, जागृढ, जागृहतु, &c. &c.

CHAPTER VII.

INDECLINABLE WORDS.

ADVERBS.

712. ADVERBS (*nipáta*), like nouns and verbs, may be divided into simple and compound. The latter are treated of in the next Chapter on Compound Words.

There are in Sanskrit a number of aptote or monoptote nouns called *indeclinables*. Some of these indeclinable nouns are as follows: अस्तम् 'setting,' 'decline;' अस्ति 'what exists,' 'existence;' ओम् 'mystical ejaculation, typical of the Hindú Triad;' कम् 'water,' 'ease,' 'head;' क्ष्मा 'on the ground;' चनस् 'satisfaction,' 'food;' नमस् 'reverence;' नास्ति 'non-existence;' वदि 'the fortnight of the moon's wane;' भुवस् 'sky;' भूर् 'earth;' संवत् 'a year;' शुदि or सुदि 'the fortnight of the moon's increase;' स्वर् 'heaven;' स्वस्ति 'salutation;' स्वधा 'interjection at oblation to the manes;' शम् 'ease.' Others will be mentioned at 713—717, as it will be convenient to classify simple adverbs under four heads; 1st, those formed from the cases of nouns and obsolete words; 2dly, other adverbs of less obvious derivation; 3dly, adverbial affixes; 4thly, adverbial prefixes.

Formed from the Cases of Nouns and Obsolete Words.

713. The nominative or accusative neuter of any adjective;

As, सत्यं 'truly;' बहु 'much;' शीघ्रं, क्षिप्रं, 'quickly;' युक्तं 'fitly;' समीपं 'near;'

Second future, 'I will or shall be frequently.'

बोभविष्यामि	बोभविष्यावस्	बोभविष्यामस्
बोभविष्यसि	बोभविष्यथस्	बोभविष्यथ
बोभविष्यति	बोभविष्यतस्	बोभविष्यन्ति

Aorist or *third preterite*, 'I was frequently.'

अबोभूवम्	अबोभूव	अबोभूम
अबोभूस्	अबोभूतं	अबोभूत
अबोभूत्	अबोभूतां	अबोभूवन्
or	or	or
अबोभाविषम्	अबोभाविष्व	अबोभाविष्म
अबोभावीस्	अबोभाविष्टं	अबोभाविष्ट
अबोभावीत्	अबोभाविष्टां	अबोभाविषुस्

Precative or *benedictive*, 'May I be frequently.'

बोभूयासं	बोभूयास्व	बोभूयास्म
बोभूयास्	बोभूयास्तं	बोभूयास्त
बोभूयात्	बोभूयास्तां	बोभूयासुस्

Conditional, 'I should be frequently.'

अबोभविष्यम्	अबोभविष्याव	अबोभविष्याम
अबोभविष्यस्	अबोभविष्यतं	अबोभविष्यत
अबोभविष्यत्	अबोभविष्यतां	अबोभविष्यन्

708. Root हन् 'to kill' (323, 654). Parasmai form of Frequentative, 'to kill repeatedly.' *Pres.* जङ्घन्मि or जङ्घनीमि, जङ्घंसि or जङ्घनीषि, जङ्घन्ति or जङ्घनीति; जङ्घन्वस्, जङ्घथस्, जङ्घतस्; जङ्घन्मस्, जङ्घथ, जङ्घ्नति or जंघ्नति. *Impf.* अजङ्घनं, अजङ्घन् or अजङ्घनीस्, अजङ्घन् or अजङ्घनीत्; अजङ्घन्व, अजङ्घतं, -तां; अजङ्घन्म, अजङ्घत, अजङ्घ्नुस् or अजंघ्नुस्. *Pot.* जङ्घन्यां. *Impv.* जङ्घनानि, जंघहि, जङ्घन्तु or जङ्घनीतु; जङ्घनाव, जङ्घतं, -तां; जङ्घनाम, जङ्घत, जङ्घ्नतु or जंघ्नतु. *Perf.* जङ्घनाम्बभूव or जङ्घनाञ्चकार, &c. &c.

709. Root गम् 'to go' (602, 270). Parasmai form of Frequentative, 'to go frequently.' *Pres.* जङ्गन्मि or जङ्गमीमि, जङ्गंसि or जङ्गमीषि, जङ्गन्ति or जङ्गमीति; जङ्गन्वस्, जङ्गथस्, जङ्गतस्; जङ्गन्मस्, जङ्गथ, जङ्ग्मति or जंग्मति. *Impf.* अजङ्गमं, अजङ्गन् or अजङ्गमीस्, अजङ्गन् or अजङ्गमीत्; अजङ्गन्व, अजङ्गतं, -तां; अजङ्गन्म, अजङ्गत, अजङ्ग्मुस् or अजंग्मुस्. *Pot.* जङ्गम्यां. *Impv.* जङ्गमानि, जङ्गहि, जङ्गन्तु or जङ्गमीतु; जङ्गमाव, जङ्गतं, जङ्गतां; जङ्गमाम, जङ्गत, जङ्ग्मतु or जंग्मतु. *Perf.* जङ्गमाम्बभूव or जङ्गमाञ्चकार, &c. &c.

710. Root क्षिप् 'to throw' (635). Parasmai form of Frequentative. *Pres.* चेक्षेप्मि or चेक्षिपीमि, चेक्षेप्सि or चेक्षिपीषि, चेक्षेप्ति or चेक्षिपीति;

वेविष्वः, वेविष्ठः, वेविष्टः; वेविष्मः, वेविष्ठ, वेविषति. *Impf.* अवेवेषम्, अवेवेट् or अवेविषीत्, अवेवेट् or अवेविषीत्; अवेविष्व, अवेविष्टम्, -ष्टां; अवेविष्म, अवेविष्ट, अवेविषुः. *Pot.* वेविष्यां, &c. *Impv.* वेवेषाणि, वेविड्ढि, वेवेष्टु or वेविषीतु; वेवेषाव, वेविष्टं, -ष्टां; वेवेषाम, वेविष्ट, वेविषतु. *Perf.* वेविषाम्बभूव or वेविषाञ्चकार, &c. &c.

711. Root ग्रह् 'to take' (699, 359). Parasmai form of Frequentative. *Pres.* जाग्रह्मि or जाग्रहीमि, जाघ्रक्षि (306. *a*) or जाग्रहीषि, जाग्राढि (305. *a*) or जाग्रहीति; जागृह्वः, जागृढः, जागृढः; जागृह्मः, जागृढ, जागृहति. *Impf.* अजाग्रहं, अजाघ्रट् (292. *b*, 43. *c*) or अजाग्रहीः, अजाघ्रट् or अजाग्रहीत्; अजागृह्व, अजागृढं, -ढां; अजागृह्म, अजागृढ, अजाग्रहुः (332). *Pot.* जागृह्यां. *Impv.* जाग्रहाणि, जागृढि, जाग्राढु or जाग्रहीतु; जाग्रहाव, जागृढं, -ढां; जाग्रहाम, जागृढ, जागृहतु, &c. &c.

CHAPTER VII.

INDECLINABLE WORDS.

ADVERBS.

712. Adverbs (*nipáta*), like nouns and verbs, may be divided into simple and compound. The latter are treated of in the next Chapter on Compound Words.

There are in Sanskṛit a number of aptote or monoptote nouns called *indeclinables*. Some of these indeclinable nouns are as follows: अस्तम् 'setting,' 'decline;' अस्ति 'what exists,' 'existence;' ओम् 'mystical ejaculation, typical of the Hindú Triad;' कम् 'water,' 'ease,' 'head;' क्ष्मा 'on the ground;' चनस् 'satisfaction,' 'food;' नमस् 'reverence;' नास्ति 'non-existence;' बदि 'the fortnight of the moon's wane;' भुवस् 'sky;' भूर् 'earth;' संवत् 'a year;' सुदि or शुदि 'the fortnight of the moon's increase;' स्वर् 'heaven;' स्वस्ति 'salutation;' स्वधा 'interjection at oblation to the manes;' शम् 'ease.' Others will be mentioned at 713—717, as it will be convenient to classify simple adverbs under four heads; 1st, those formed from the cases of nouns and obsolete words; 2dly, other adverbs of less obvious derivation; 3dly, adverbial affixes; 4thly, adverbial prefixes.

Formed from the Cases of Nouns and Obsolete Words.

713. The nominative or accusative neuter of any adjective;

As, सत्यं 'truly;' बहु 'much;' क्षिप्रं, शीघ्रं, 'quickly;' युक्तं 'fitly;' समीपं 'near;'

Second future, 'I will or shall be frequently.'

बोभविष्यामि	बोभविष्यावः	बोभविष्यामः
बोभविष्यसि	बोभविष्यथः	बोभविष्यथ
बोभविष्यति	बोभविष्यतः	बोभविष्यन्ति

Aorist or *third preterite*, 'I was frequently.'

अबोभूवम्	अबोभूव	अबोभूम
अबोभूः	अबोभूतं	अबोभूत
अबोभूत्	अबोभूतां	अबोभूवन्
or	or	or
अबोभाविषम्	अबोभाविष्व	अबोभाविष्म
अबोभावीः	अबोभाविष्टं	अबोभाविष्ट
अबोभावीत्	अबोभाविष्टां	अबोभाविषुः

Precative or *benedictive*, 'May I be frequently.'

बोभूयासं	बोभूयास्व	बोभूयास्म
बोभूयाः	बोभूयास्तं	बोभूयास्त
बोभूयात्	बोभूयास्तां	बोभूयासुः

Conditional, 'I should be frequently.'

अबोभविष्यम्	अबोभविष्याव	अबोभविष्याम
अबोभविष्यः	अबोभविष्यतं	अबोभविष्यत
अबोभविष्यत्	अबोभविष्यतां	अबोभविष्यन्

708. Root हन् 'to kill' (323, 654). Parasmai form of Frequentative, 'to kill repeatedly.' *Pres.* जङ्घन्मि or जङ्घनीमि, जङ्घंसि or जङ्घनीषि, जङ्घन्ति or जङ्घनीति; जङ्घन्वः, जङ्घथः, जङ्घतः; जङ्घन्मः, जङ्घथ, जङ्घ्नति or जंघ्नति. *Impf.* अजङ्घनं, अजङ्घन् or अजङ्घनीः, अजङ्घन् or अजङ्घनीत्; अजङ्घन्व, अजङ्घतं, -तां; अजङ्घन्म, अजङ्घत, अजङ्घनुः or अजंघ्नुः. *Pot.* जङ्घन्यां. *Impv.* जङ्घनानि, जंघहि, जङ्घन्तु or जङ्घनीतु; जङ्घनाव, जङ्घतं, -तां; जङ्घनाम, जङ्घत, जङ्घ्नन्तु or जंघ्नन्तु. *Perf.* जङ्घनाम्बभूव or जङ्घनाञ्चकार, &c. &c.

709. Root गम् 'to go' (602, 270). Parasmai form of Frequentative, 'to go frequently.' *Pres.* जङ्गन्मि or जङ्गमीमि, जङ्गंसि or जङ्गमीषि, जङ्गन्ति or जङ्गमीति; जङ्गन्वः, जङ्गथः, जङ्गतः; जङ्गन्मः, जङ्गथ, जङ्गमति or जंग्मति. *Impf.* अजङ्गमं, अजङ्गन् or अजङ्गमीः, अजङ्गन् or अजङ्गमीत्; अजङ्गन्व, अजङ्गतं, -तां; अजङ्गन्म, अजङ्गत, अजङ्गमुः or अजंग्मुः. *Pot.* जङ्गम्यां. *Impv.* जङ्गमानि, जङ्गहि, जङ्गन्तु or जङ्गमीतु; जङ्गमाव, जङ्गतं, जङ्गतां; जङ्गमाम, जङ्गत, जङ्गमतु or जंग्मतु. *Perf.* जङ्गमाम्बभूव or जङ्गमाञ्चकार, &c. &c.

710. Root क्षिप् 'to throw' (635). Parasmai form of Frequentative. *Pres.* चेक्षेप्मि or चेक्षिपीमि, चेक्षेप्सि or चेक्षिपीषि, चेक्षेप्ति or चेक्षिपीति;

चेच्छिद्वस्, चेच्छित्थस्, चेच्छित्तस्; चेच्छिद्मस्, चेच्छित्थ, चेच्छिदति. *Impf.* अचेच्छेदं, अचेच्छेत् or अचेच्छिदीत्, अचेच्छेत् or अचेच्छिदीत्; अचेच्छिद्व, अचेच्छित्तं, -त्तां; अचेच्छिद्म, अचेच्छित्त, अचेच्छिदुस्. *Pot.* चेच्छिद्यां, &c. *Impv.* चेच्छेदानि, चेच्छिन्द्धि, चेच्छेत्तु or चेच्छिदीतु; चेच्छेदाव, चेच्छित्तं, -त्तां; चेच्छेदाम, चेच्छित्त, चेच्छिदतु. *Perf.* चेच्छिदाम्बभूव or चेच्छिदाञ्चकार, &c. &c.

711. Root ग्रह् 'to take' (699, 359). Parasmai form of Frequentative. *Pres.* जाग्रह्मि or जाग्रहीमि, जाघर्क्षि (306. a) or जाग्रहीषि, जाग्राढि (305. a) or जाग्रहीति; जागृह्वस्, जागृढस्, जागृढस्; जागृह्मस्, जागृढ, जागृहति. *Impf.* अजाग्रहं, अजाघर्ट् (292. b, 43. c) or अजाग्रहीस्, अजाघर्ट् or अजाग्रहीत्; अजागृह्व, अजागृढं, -ढां; अजागृह्म, अजागृढ, अजागृहुस् (332). *Pot.* जागृह्यां. *Impv.* जाग्रहाणि, जागृढि, जाग्राढु or जाग्रहीतु; जाग्रहाव, जागृढं, -ढां; जाग्रहाम, जागृढ, जागृहतु, &c. &c.

CHAPTER VII.

INDECLINABLE WORDS.

ADVERBS.

712. ADVERBS (*nipáta*), like nouns and verbs, may be divided into simple and compound. The latter are treated of in the next Chapter on Compound Words.

There are in Sanskrit a number of aptote or monoptote nouns called *indeclinables*. Some of these indeclinable nouns are as follows: अस्तम् 'setting,' 'decline;' अस्ति 'what exists,' 'existence;' ओम् 'mystical ejaculation, typical of the Hindú Triad;' कम् 'water,' 'ease,' 'head;' क्षमा 'on the ground;' [illegible] 'satisfaction,' 'food;' नमस् 'reverence;' नास्ति 'non-existence;' बदि 'the fortnight of the moon's wane;' भुवस् 'sky;' भूर् 'earth;' संवत् 'a year;' सुदि or शुदि 'the fortnight of the moon's increase;' स्वर् 'heaven;' स्वस्ति 'salutation;' स्वधा 'interjection at oblation to the manes;' शम् 'ease.' Others will be mentioned at 713—717, as it will be convenient to classify simple adverbs under four heads; 1st, those formed from the cases of nouns and obsolete words; 2dly, other adverbs of less obvious derivation; 3dly, adverbial affixes; 4thly, adverbial prefixes.

Formed from the Cases of Nouns and Obsolete Words.

713. The nominative or accusative neuter of any adjective;

As, सत्यं 'truly;' बहु 'much;' शीघ्रं, क्षिप्रं, 'quickly;' नित्यं 'daily;' समीपं 'near;'

ध्रुवं 'certainly;' लघु 'lightly;' निर्भरं, अत्यन्तं, गाढं, भृशं, 'exceedingly;' अवश्यं 'certainly;' नित्यं 'constantly;' चिरं 'for a long while;' बलवत् 'strongly;' भूयस् 'again,' 'repeatedly' (194); केवलं 'only,' 'merely;' साधु 'very well.'

a. The nom. or acc. neuter of certain pronouns; as, तत् 'therefore,' 'then;' यत् 'wherefore,' 'when,' 'since;' तावत् 'so long,' 'so soon;' यावत् 'as long as,' 'as soon as;' किम् 'why?'

b. The nom. or acc. neuter of certain substantives and obsolete words; as, रहस् 'secretly;' कामं 'willingly;' स्वयं 'of one's own accord,' 'of one's self,' 'spontaneously;' नाम 'by name,' 'that is to say;' वारं वारं 'repeatedly;' चिरं 'long ago;' सुखं 'pleasantly;' साम्प्रतं 'now;' नक्तं 'by night' (*noctu*); सायम् 'in the evening' (this last may be an ind. part. of *so*, 'to finish').

714. The instrumental case of nouns, pronouns, and obsolete words;

As, धर्मेण 'virtuously;' दक्षिणेन 'southwards' or 'to the right;' उत्तरेण 'northwards;' अतिरेकेण 'without;' उच्चैस् 'above,' 'aloud;' नीचैस् 'below;' शनैस् or शनकैस् 'slowly;' तेन 'therefore;' येन 'wherefore;' अन्तरा or अन्तरेण 'without,' 'except;' क्षणेन 'instantly;' चिरेण 'for a long time;' अचिरेण 'in a short time;' साकल्येन 'entirely;' दिवा 'by day;' दिष्ट्या 'fortunately;' सहसा, अञ्जसा, 'quickly;' अधुना 'now;' विहायसा 'in the air;' पुरा 'formerly.'

a. The dative case more rarely;

As, चिराय 'for a long time;' चिररात्राय 'for a period of many nights;' अर्थाय 'for the sake of.'

715. The ablative case of nouns, pronouns, and obsolete words;

As, बलात् 'forcibly;' हर्षात् 'joyfully;' दूरात् 'at a distance;' तस्मात् 'therefore;' कस्मात् 'wherefore?' अकस्मात् 'without cause,' 'unexpectedly;' उत्तरात् 'from the north;' चिरात् 'for a long time;' पश्चात् 'afterwards;' तत्क्षणात् 'at that instant;' समन्तात् 'from all quarters.'

716. The locative case of nouns and obsolete words;

As, रात्रौ 'at night;' दूरे 'far off;' प्रभाते 'in the morning;' पूर्वाह्णे 'in the forenoon;' स्थाने 'suitably;' अग्रे 'in front;' एकपदे 'at once;' सपदि 'instantly;' ऋते 'except;' अन्तरे 'within;' दक्षिणे 'towards the south;' समीपे or अभ्याशे 'near;' एकान्ते 'in private;' सायाह्ने 'in the evening;' हेतौ 'by reason of.'

Other Adverbs and Particles of less obvious Derivation.

717. Of *affirmation.*—नूनं, अङ्ग, किल, एव, अद्धा, 'indeed;' अथ किम् 'yes, sure enough.'

a. Of *negation.*—न, नो, नहि, 'not.' मा, मास्म, are prohibitive; as, मा कुरु, मा कार्षीः, 'do not.' See 889.

b. Of *interrogation.*—किम्, किमु, कच्चित्, नु, ननु, किंनु, किंस्वित्, 'whether?'

c. Of *comparison.*—इव 'like;' तथा, एवं, 'so;' किंपुनर् 'how much rather;' तथैव (तथा+एव) 'in like manner.'

d. Of *quantity.*—अतीव 'exceedingly;' ईषत् 'a little;' सकृत् 'once;' असकृत्, पुनः पुनर्, मुहुर्, 'repeatedly.'

e. Of *manner.*—इति, एवं, 'so,' 'thus;' पुनर् 'again;' प्रायस् 'for the most part;' नाना 'variously;' पृथक् 'separately;' मृषा, मिथ्या, 'falsely;' वृथा, मुधा, 'in vain;' अलं 'enough;' झटिति, आशु (cf. ὠκύς), 'quickly;' तूष्णीं 'silently;' मिथस् 'reciprocally,' 'together.'

f. Of *time.*—अद्य 'to-day,' 'now;' श्वस् 'to-morrow;' ह्यस् 'yesterday;' परश्वस् 'the day after to-morrow;' सम्प्रति 'now;' पुरा 'formerly;' पुरस्, पुरस्तात्, प्राक्, 'before;' युगपत् 'at once;' सद्यस् 'instantly;' प्रेत्य 'after death;' परं 'afterwards;' जातु 'ever;' न जातु 'never;' अन्येद्युस्, परेद्युस्, 'another day,' 'next day.'

g. Of *place.*—इह 'here;' क्व 'where?' बहिस् 'without.'

h. Of *doubt.*—स्वित्, किंस्वित्, अपिनाम, उत, उताहो, उताहो स्वित्, आहो स्वित्, 'perhaps,' &c.

i. अपि 'even,' एव 'indeed,' ह 'just,' are placed after words to modify their sense, or for emphatic affirmation. इत्, ईम्, घ, are particles of this kind used in the Veda.

Observe—Some of the above are properly conjunctions; see 727.

Adverbial Affixes.

718. चित् *ćit*, अपि *api*, and चन *ćana*, may form *indefinite* adverbs of *time* and *place*, when affixed to interrogative adverbs;

As, from कदा 'when?' कदाचित्, कदापि, and कदाचन, 'sometimes;' from कुत्र and क्व 'where?' कुत्रचित्, कुत्रापि, क्वचित्, क्वापि, 'somewhere;' from कुतस् 'whence?' कुतश्चित् and कुतश्चन 'from somewhere;' from कति 'how many?' कतिचित् 'a few;' from कर्हि 'when?' कर्हिचित् 'at some time;' from कथं 'how?' कथमपि, कथंचन, 'somehow or other,' 'with some difficulty.' Compare 228, 230.

a. अपि following a word, generally signifies 'even,' but after numerals, 'all,' as त्रयोऽपि 'all three;' सर्वेऽपि 'all together.'

719. तस् *tas* (changeable to तः or तो by 63, 64) may be added to any noun, and to some pronouns, to form adverbs;

As, from यत्न, यत्नतस् 'with effort;' from आदि, आदितस् 'from the beginning;' from त (the proper base of the pronoun तद्), ततस् 'thence,' 'then,' 'thereupon,' 'therefore:' similarly, यतस् 'whence,' 'since,' 'because;' अतस्, इतस्, अमुतस्, 'hence,' 'hereupon.'

Observe—In affixing *tas* to pronouns, the base त is used for तद्, य for यद्, इ for इदं, अमु for अदस्, अ for एतद्, कु for किम्.

a. This affix usually gives the sense of the prepositions *with* and *from*, and is often equivalent to the ablative case; as in मत्तस् 'from me;' त्वत्तस् 'from thee*;' पितृतस् 'from the father;' शत्रुतस् 'from an enemy.'

b. But it is sometimes vaguely employed to express other relations; as, पृष्ठतस् 'behind the back;' अन्यतस् 'to another place,' 'elsewhere;' प्रथमतस् 'in the first place;' इतस्ततस् 'here and there,' 'hither and thither;' समन्ततस् 'on all sides;' समीपतस् 'in the neighbourhood;' पुरतस्, अग्रतस्, 'in front;' अन्तिकतस् 'near to;' विभवतस् 'in pomp or state.'

c. तात् is an affix which generally denotes 'place' or 'direction;' as, from अधस्, अधस्तात् 'downwards;' from उपरि (which becomes उपरिष्), उपरिष्टात् 'above.'

720. त्र *tra*, forming adverbs of *place*;

As, अत्र 'here;' तत्र 'there;' कुत्र 'where?' यत्र 'where;' सर्वत्र 'every where;' अन्यत्र 'in another place;' एकत्र 'in one place;' बहुत्र 'in many places;' अमुत्र 'there,' 'in the next world.'

721. था *thá* and थम् *tham*, forming adverbs of *manner*;

As, तथा 'so,' 'in like manner;' यथा 'as;' सर्वथा 'in every way,' 'by all means;' अन्यथा 'otherwise;' कथं 'how?' इत्थं 'thus.'

722. दा *dá*, र्हि *rhi*, नीम् *ním*, forming adverbs of *time* from pronouns, &c.;

As, तदा 'then;' यदा 'when;' कदा 'when?' एकदा 'once;' नित्यदा 'constantly;' सर्वदा, सदा, 'always;' तर्हि, तदानीम्, 'then;' इदानीम् 'now.'

723. धा *dhá*, forming adverbs of *distribution* from numerals;

As, एकधा 'in one way;' द्विधा 'in two ways;' षोढा 'in six ways;' शतधा 'in a hundred ways;' सहस्रधा 'in a thousand ways;' बहुधा or अनेकधा 'in many ways.'

a. कृत्वस्, signifying 'times,' is added to पञ्च, 'five,' and other numerals, as explained at 215. सकृत्, 'once,' may be a corruption of सकृत्वस् ('this time'); and only स् is added to द्वि, त्रि, and dropped after चतुर् 'four times.'

724. वत् *vat* may be added to any noun to form adverbs of *comparison* or *similitude*;

As, from सूर्य, सूर्यवत् 'like the sun;' from पूर्व, पूर्ववत् 'as before.' It may be used in connexion with a word in the accusative case. See 918.

a. This affix *often* expresses 'according to;' as, विधिवत् 'according to rule;' प्रयोजनवत् 'according to need.' It may also be added to adverbs; as, यथावत् 'truly' (exactly as it took place).

---

* These are the forms generally used for the ablative case of the personal pronouns, the proper ablative cases मत्, त्वत् being rarely used, except as substitutes for the crude base in compound words.

725. शस् *śas*, forming adverbs of *quantity*, &c.;

As, बहुशस् 'abundantly;' अल्पशस् 'in small quantities;' सर्वशस् 'wholly;' एकशस् 'singly;' शतसहस्रशस् 'by hundreds and thousands;' क्रमशस् 'by degrees;' मुख्यशस् 'principally;' पादशस् 'foot by foot.'

a. सात् is added to nouns in connexion with the roots कृ, अस्, and भू, to denote a complete change *to* the condition of the thing signified by the noun; as, अग्निसात् 'to the state of fire.' See 789, and compare 70. *g.*

Adverbial Prefixes.

726. अ *a*, prefixed to nouns and even to participles with a privative or negative force, corresponding to the Greek *α*, the Latin *in*, and the English 'in,' 'im,' 'un;' as, from शक्य 'possible,' अशक्य 'impossible;' from स्पृशत् 'touching' (pres. part.), अस्पृशत् 'not touching;' from कृत्वा 'having done' (indecl. part.), अकृत्वा 'not having done.' When a word begins with a vowel, अन् is euphonically substituted; as, अन्त 'end;' अनन्त 'endless.'

a. अति *ati*, 'excessively,' 'very;' as, अतिमहत् 'very great.'

b. आ *á*, prefixed to imply 'diminution;' as, आपाण्डु 'somewhat pale.' ईषत् is prefixed with the same sense.

c. का *ká* or कु *ku*, prefixed to words to imply 'disparagement;' as, कापुरुष 'a coward;' कुरूप 'deformed.'

d. दुस् *dus* or दुर् *dur*, prefixed to imply 'badly' or 'with difficulty;' as, दुष्कृत 'badly done' (see 72); दुर्भेद 'not easily broken.' It is opposed to सु, and corresponds to the Greek δυσ.

e. निस् *nis* or निर् *nir* and वि *vi* are prefixed to nouns like अ *a* with a privative or negative sense; as, निर्बल 'powerless;' निष्फल 'without fruit' (see 72); विशस्त्र 'unarmed:' but not to participles.

f. सु *su*, prefixed to imply 'well,' 'easily;' as, सुकृत 'well done;' सुभेद 'easily broken.' In this sense it is opposed to दुर्, and corresponds to the Greek εὐ. It is also used for अति, to imply 'very,' 'excessively;' as, सुमहत् 'very great.'

CONJUNCTIONS.

Copulative.

727. च *ća*, 'and,' 'also,' corresponding to the Latin *que* and not to *et*. It can never, therefore, stand as the *first word* in a sentence, but follows the word of which it is the copulative. चैव (च एव), 'also,' is a common combination.

a. उत 'and,' 'also,' is sometimes copulative. Sometimes it implies *doubt or interrogation*.

b. तथा 'so,' 'thus,' 'in like manner' (see 721), is not unfrequently used for च, in the sense of 'also;' and like च is then generally placed after the word which it connects with another.

c. अथ 'now,' 'and,' अथो 'then,' are inceptive, being frequently used at the commencement of sentences or narratives. अथ is often opposed to इति, which marks the close of a story or chapter.

d. हि, 'for,' is a causal conjunction; like च it is always placed after its word, and never admitted to the first place in a sentence.

e. यदि, चेद्, both meaning 'if,' are conditional conjunctions.

f. ततस् 'upon that,' 'then' (see 719), तद् 'then,' अपरम्, किञ्च, अपरञ्च, परञ्च, अपिच, 'again,' 'moreover,' are all copulatives, used very commonly in narration.

Disjunctive.

728. वा *vá*, 'or,' corresponds to the Latin *ve*, and is always placed after its word, being never admitted to the first place in a sentence.

a. तु, किन्तु, 'but;' the former is placed after its word.

b. यद्यपि 'although;' तथापि 'nevertheless,' 'yet,' sometimes used as a correlative to the last; अथवा, किम्वा, 'or else;' नवा 'or not;' यदिवा 'whether,' 'whether or no.'

c. अथवा may also be used to correct or qualify a previous thought, when it is equivalent to 'but no,' 'yet,' 'however.'

d. स्म, ह, तु, वै, are expletives, often used in poetry to fill up the verse.

PREPOSITIONS.

729. There are about twenty prepositions (see 783), but in later Sanskrit they are generally prefixes, qualifying the sense of verbs (and then called *upasarga*) or of verbal derivatives (and then called *gati*). About ten may be used separately or detached in government with the cases of nouns (and then called *karma-pravaćaníya*); e.g. आ, प्रति, अनु, अति, अधि, अभि, परि, अप, अपि and सु; but of these the first three only are commonly found as separable particles in classical Sanskrit.

730. आ *á*, generally signifying 'as far as,' 'up to,' 'until,' with an ablative case; as, आसमुद्रात् 'as far as the ocean;' आमनोः 'up to Manu:' and rarely with an accusative; as, शतम् आजातीन् 'for a hundred births.'

a. आ *á* may sometimes express 'from;' as, आमूलात् 'from the beginning;' आप्रथमदर्शनात् 'from the first sight.'

b. It may also be compounded with a word in the accusative neuter forming with it an Avyayí-bháva (see 760); thus, आमेखलं 'as far as the girdle' (where मेखलं is for मेखलां).

c. प्रति *prati*, generally a postposition, signifying 'at,' 'with regard to,' '*to*,' 'towards,' 'against,' with accusative; as, गङ्गां प्रति 'at the Ganges;' धर्मं प्रति 'with regard to justice;' शत्रुं प्रति 'against an enemy.' It may have the force of *apud*; as, मां प्रति 'as far as regards me.' When denoting 'in the place of,' it governs the ablative.

d. अनु 'after,' with accusative, and rarely with ablative or genitive; as, गङ्गाया अनु 'along the Ganges;' तदनु or ततोऽनु 'after that.'

e. प्रति, and more rarely अनु and अभि, may be used distributively to signify 'each,' 'every;' thus, वृक्षमनु 'tree by tree.' They may also be prefixed to form Avyayí-bhávas; प्रतिवत्सरं or अनुवत्सरं 'every year,' 'year by year.' See 760.

f. अति, अभि, परि, are said to require the accusative; अधि the locative or accusative; अप and परि, in the sense 'except,' the ablative; उप the locative and accusative; but examples of such syntax are not common in classical Sanskrit.

g. Instances, of course, are common of prepositions united with the neuter form or accusative case of nouns, so as to form compounds, see 760. *b.*; as, प्रतिस्कन्धं 'upon the shoulders;' प्रतिमुखं 'face to face;' अधिवृक्षं 'upon the tree;' अनुगङ्गं 'along the Ganges.'

ADVERBS USED FOR PREPOSITIONS IN GOVERNMENT WITH NOUNS.

731. There are many adverbs used like the preceding prepositions in government with nouns, and often placed after the nouns which they govern.

a. These are, ऋते 'besides,' 'without,' 'except,' with the accusative and sometimes ablative case. यावत् 'up to,' 'as far as,' sometimes found with the accusative. सह, साकं, समं, सार्धं, 'with,' 'along with,' with the instrumental. विना 'without,' with the instrumental or accusative, or sometimes the ablative. बहिस् 'out;' प्रभृति, '*inde a*,' 'from a particular time,' 'beginning with,' with the ablative, or placed after the crude base. अर्थे, अर्थं, अर्थाय, हेतोस्, हेतौ, कृते, निमित्ते, कारणात्, 'on account of,' 'for the sake of,' 'for,' with the genitive, or usually placed after the crude base *; अधस्तात् 'under;' उपरि, ऊर्ध्वं, 'above,' 'over,' 'upon'

* अर्थे is generally found in composition with a crude base, and may be compounded adjectively to agree with another noun; as, द्विजार्थः सूपस् 'broth for the Bráhman;' द्विजार्थं पयस् 'milk for the Bráhman.' See 760.

(cf. ὑπέρ, super), with the genitive and accusative: so अधस् or अधस्तात् 'below;' अनन्तरं 'after,' 'afterwards;' समीपे, सन्निधम्, निकटे, अभ्याशे, सकाशे, 'near;' सकाशात् 'from;' अग्रे, पुरस्तात्, समक्षं, साक्षात्, 'before the eyes,' 'in the presence of;' परतस् 'behind;' पश्चात् 'after;' उत्तरात् 'to the north;' दक्षिणात् 'to the south:' all with the genitive. प्राक्, पूर्वं, 'before,' with ablative, rarely genitive and accusative; परं, परेण, ऊर्ध्वं, परतस्, 'after,' 'beyond,' with the ablative; अन्तरेण 'without,' 'except,' 'with regard to,' मध्ये 'in the middle,' पारे 'on the further side,' with the genitive or accusative; अन्तर् 'within,' with the genitive. All the above may be placed after the crude base. उपरि and अधस् are sometimes doubled; thus, उपर्युपरि, अधोऽधस्. The adverb अलं, 'enough,' is used with the instrumental case.

b. Some of the adverbs enumerated at 714, 715, may be used in government with the cases of nouns; thus, दक्षिणेन 'to the south' or 'to the right,' उत्तरेण 'to the north,' may govern a genitive or accusative case; व्यतिरेकेण, 'without,' is generally placed after the crude base.

INTERJECTIONS.

732. भोस्, भो, हे, are vocative; रे, अरे, less respectfully vocative, or sometimes expressive of 'contempt.' धिक् expresses 'contempt,' 'abhorrence,' 'fie!' 'shame!' (with accusative case); आस्, अहो, अहह, 'surprise,' 'alarm;' हा, हाहा, अहो, अहोबत, बत, 'grief;' साधु, सुष्ठु, 'approbation;' स्वस्ति, 'salutation.'

CHAPTER VIII.

COMPOUND WORDS.

733. Compounds abound in Sanskṛit to a degree wholly unequalled in any other language, and it becomes necessary to study the principles on which they are constructed, before the learner can hope to understand the simplest sentence in the most elementary book. In the foregoing chapters we have treated of simple nouns, simple verbs, and simple adverbs. We have now to treat of compound nouns, compound verbs, and compound adverbs.

a. Observe, that in this chapter the nom. case, and not the crude base, of a substantive terminating a compound will be given; and in the instance of an adjective forming the last member of a compound, the nom. case masc., fem., and neut. The examples are chiefly taken from the Hitopadeśa, and sometimes the oblique cases in which they are there found have been retained. A dot placed underneath marks the division of the words in a compound.

SECTION I.

COMPOUND NOUNS.

734. The student has now arrived at that portion of the grammar in which the use of the crude base of the noun becomes most strikingly apparent. This use has been already noticed at 77, p. 52; and its formation explained at pp. 54—64.

a. In almost all compound nouns the last word alone admits of declension, and the preceding word or words require to be placed in the crude form or base, to which a plural as well as singular signification may be attributed. Instances, however, will be given in which the characteristic signs of case and number are retained in the first member of the compound, but these are exceptional.

b. It may here be noted, that while Sanskṛit generally exhibits the first member or members of a compound in the crude base with the final letter unchanged, except by the usual euphonic laws, Latin frequently and Greek less frequently change the final vowel of the base into the light vowel *i*; and both Greek and Latin often make use of a vowel of conjunction, which in Greek is generally *o*, but occasionally *i*: thus, *coeli-cola* for *coelu-cola* or *coelo-cola*; *lani-ger* for *lana-ger*; χαλκί-ναος, ἰχθυ-ο-φάγος, *foeder-i-fragus*. Both Greek and Latin, however, possess many compounds which are completely analogous to Sanskṛit formations. In English we have occasional examples of the use of a conjunctive vowel, as in 'handicraft' for 'hand-craft.'

735. Native grammarians class compound nouns under six heads; the 1st they call DVANDVA, or those formed by the aggregation into one compound of two or more nouns (the last word being, according to circumstances, either in the dual, plural, or neuter singular, and the preceding word or words being in the crude base), when, if uncompounded, they would all be in the same case, connected by a copulative conjunction; as, गुरुशिष्यौ 'master and pupil' (for गुरुः शिष्यश्च); मरणव्याधिशोकाः 'death, sickness, and sorrow' (for मरणं व्याधिः शोकश्च); पाणिपादं 'hand and foot' (for पाणी पादौ च). The 2d, TAT-PURUSHA, or those composed of two nouns, the first of which (being in the crude base) would be, if uncompounded, in a case different from, or dependent on, the last; as, चन्द्रप्रभा 'moon-light' (for चन्द्रस्य प्रभा 'the light of the moon'); शस्त्रकुशलः, -ला, -लं, 'skilled in arms' (for शस्त्रेषु कुशलः); मणिभूषितः, -ता, -तं, 'adorned with gems' (for मणिभिर् भूषितः). The 3d, KARMA-DHĀRAYA, or those composed of an adjective or participle and substantive, the adjective or participle

being placed first in its crude base, when, if uncompounded, it would be in grammatical concord with the substantive; as, साधुशीलम् 'a good disposition' (for साधु शीलम्); सर्वद्रव्याणि 'all things' (for सर्वाणि द्रव्याणि). The 4th, DVIGU, or those in which a numeral in its crude base is compounded with a noun, either so as to form a singular collective noun, or an adjective; as, त्रिगुणं 'three qualities' (for त्रयो गुणाः); त्रिगुणस्, -णा, -णं, 'possessing the three qualities.' The 5th, BAHU-VRÍHI, or attributive compounds, generally epithets of other nouns. These, according to Páṇini (II. 2, 24), are formed by compounding two or more words to qualify the sense of another word; thus, प्राप्तोदको ग्रामः for प्राप्तम् उदकं यं ग्रामं, 'a village to which the water has come.' The 6th, AVYAYÍ-BHÁVA, or those resulting from the combination of a preposition or adverbial prefix with a noun. The latter, whatever may be its gender, always takes the form of an accusative neuter and becomes indeclinable.

a. Observe—These names either furnish examples of the several kinds of compounds, or give some sort of definition of them: thus, द्वन्द्वः is a definition of the 1st kind, meaning 'conjunction;' तत्पुरुषः, 'his servant,' is an example of the 2d kind (for तस्य पुरुषः); कर्मधारयः is a somewhat obscure definition of the 3d kind, i. e. 'that which contains or comprehends (धारयति) the object' (कर्म); द्विगुः is an example of the 4th kind, meaning 'any thing to the value of two cows;' बहुव्रीहिः is an example of the 5th kind, meaning 'possessed of much rice.' The 6th class, अव्ययीभावः *avyayí-bhávaḥ*, means 'the indeclinable state' ('that which does not change,' as *vyeti*).

736. It should be stated, however, that the above six kinds of compounds really form, according to the native theory, only four classes, as the 3d and 4th (i. e. the Karma-dháraya and Dvigu) are regarded as subdivisions of the Tat-purusha class.

As such a classification appears to lead to some confusion from the absence of sufficient distinctness and opposition between the several parts or members of the division, the subject is discussed in the following pages according to a different method, although it has been thought desirable to preserve the Indian names and to keep the native arrangement in view.

737. Compound nouns may be regarded either as *simply* or *complexly* compounded. The latter have reference to a class of compounds within compounds, very prevalent in poetry, involving two or three species of simple compounds under one head.

SIMPLY COMPOUNDED NOUNS.

738. These we will divide into, 1st, Dependent compounds or compounds dependent in case (corresponding to *Tat-purusha*); 2d, Copulative (or Aggregative, *Dvandva*); 3d, Descriptive * (or Determinative, *Karma-dhāraya*); 4th, Numeral (or Collective, *Dvigu*); 5th, Adverbial (or Indeclinable, *Avyayī-bhāva*); 6th, Relative (*Bahu-vrīhi*). This last consists of, *a.* Relative form of absolute Dependent compounds, terminated by substantives; *b.* Relative form of Copulative or Aggregative compounds; *c.* Relative form of Descriptive or Determinative compounds; *d.* Relative form of Numeral or Collective compounds; *e.* Relative form of Adverbial compounds.

a. Observe—A list of the substitutions which take place in the final syllables of certain words in compounds is given at 778.

DEPENDENT COMPOUNDS (TAT-PURUSHA).

Accusatively Dependent.

739. These comprehend all those compounds in which the relation of the first word (being in the crude base) to the last is equivalent to that of an accusative case. They are generally composed of a noun in the first member, and a participle, root, or noun of agency in the last; as, स्वर्गप्राप्तस्, -प्ता, -प्तं, 'one who has obtained heaven' (equivalent to स्वर्गं प्राप्तस्); प्रियवादी 'one who speaks kind words;' बहुदस् 'one who gives much;' शस्त्रभृत् 'one who bears arms;' पत्रगतस्, -ता, -तं, 'committed to a leaf,' 'committed to paper' (as 'writing'); चित्रगतस्, -ता, -तं, 'committed to painting;' दर्शनीयमानी, -मानिनी, -मानि, 'thinking one's self handsome.'

a. गत 'gone' (past pass. part. of गम् 'to go') is used loosely at the end of compounds of this description to express relationship and connexion, without any necessary implication of motion. In the above compound, and in many others (such as शिलाभेदगतो मणिस् 'a jewel lying in the cleft of a rock;' हस्ततलगतस्, -ता, -तं 'lying in the palm of the hand'), it has the sense of स्थ 'staying;' but it may often have other senses; as, गोष्ठीगतस्, -ता, -तं, 'engaged in conversation;' सखीगतं किंचित् 'something relating to a friend.'

b. In theatrical language आत्मगतं and स्वगतं (lit. 'gone to one's self') mean 'spoken to one's self,' 'aside.'

---

* As being composed of an adjective or participle preceding a substantive, and always descriptive of the substantive. Prof. Bopp calls them 'Determinativa,' a word of similar import.

c. Before nouns of agency and similar forms the accusative case is often retained, especially in poetry; as, अरिन्दमस्, -मा, -मं, 'enemy-subduing;' हृदयङ्गमस्, -मा, -मं, 'heart-touching;' भयङ्करस्, -रा, -रं, 'fear-inspiring' (see 580); सागरङ्गमस्, -मा, -मं, 'going to the ocean;' पण्डितम्मन्यस्, -न्या, -न्यं, 'one who thinks himself learned;' रात्रिम्मन्यस् 'one who thinks it night.'

Instrumentally Dependent,

740. Or those in which the relation of the first word (being in the crude base) to the last is equivalent to that of an instrumental case. These are very common, and are, for the most part, composed of a substantive in the first member, and a passive participle in the last; as, लोभमोहितस्, -ता, -तं, 'beguiled by avarice' (for लोभेन मोहितस्); वस्त्रवेष्टितस्, -ता, -तं, 'covered with clothes;' राजपूजितस्, -ता, -तं, 'honoured by kings;' विद्याहीनस्, -ना, -नं, 'deserted by (i. e. destitute of) learning;' बुद्धिरहितस्, -ता, -तं, 'destitute of intelligence;' दुःखार्तस्, -र्ता, -र्तं, 'pained with grief;' आत्मकृतस्, -ता, -तं, 'done by one's self;' आदित्यसदृशस्, -शी, -शं, 'like the sun' (for आदित्येन सदृशस्, see 826); अस्मदुपार्जितस्, -ता, -तं, 'acquired by us.'

a. Sometimes this kind of compound contains a substantive or noun of agency in the last member; as, विद्याधनं 'money acquired by science;' शस्त्रोपजीवी 'one who lives by arms.'

Datively Dependent,

741. Or those in which the relation of the first word to the last is equivalent to that of a dative; as, वल्कलवस्त्रं 'bark for clothing;' पादोदकं 'water for the feet;' यूपदारु 'wood for a stake;' शरणागतस्, -ता, -तं, 'come for protection' (for शरणाय आगतस्). This kind of compound is not very common, and is generally supplied by the use of अर्थं (731. a); as, शरणार्थम् आगतस्.

a. The grammatical terms *Parasmai-padam* and *Ātmane-padam* (see 243) are instances of compounds in which the sign of the dative case is retained.

Ablatively Dependent,

742. Or those in which the relation of the first word to the last is equivalent to that of an ablative; as, पितृप्राप्तस्, -ता, -तं, 'received from a father;' राज्यभ्रष्टस्, -ष्टा, -ष्टं, 'fallen from the kingdom' (for राज्याद् भ्रष्टस्); तरङ्गचञ्चलतरस्, -रा, -रं, 'more changeable than a wave;' भवदन्यस् 'other than you' (for भवतोऽन्यस्); भवद्भयं 'fear of you' (814. d); कुक्कुरभयं 'fear of a dog;' ग्रन्थपराङ्मुखस्, -खी, -खं, 'turning the face from books,' 'averse to study.'

Genitively Dependent.

743. Or those in which the relation of the first word to the last is equivalent to that of a genitive. These are the most common of all dependent compounds, and may generally be expressed by a similar compound in English. They are for the most part composed of two substantives; as, समुद्रतीरं 'sea-shore' (for समुद्रस्य तीरं 'shore of the sea').

a. Other examples are, अश्वपृष्ठं 'horse-back;' धनुर्गुणम् 'bow-string;' इष्टकागृहं 'brick-house;' गिरिनदी 'mountain-torrent;' जलतीरं 'water's edge;' अर्थोपार्जनम् or अर्थोपार्जना 'acquisition of wealth;' विपद्दशा 'state of misfortune;' सुहृद्भेदम् 'separation of friends;' यद्भ्रुवि 'on whose brow' (loc. c.); तद्वचस् 'his words;' जन्मस्थानं or जन्मभूमिस् 'birth-place;' मूर्खशतैस् 'with hundreds of fools' (instrum. c. plur.); श्लोकद्वयं 'a couple of Ślokas;' भूतलं 'the surface of the earth;' पृथिवीपतिस् 'lord of the earth;' तद्भरणाय 'for his support' (dat. c.); ब्राह्मणपुत्रास् 'the sons of a Bráhman;' अस्मत्पुत्रास् 'our sons;' त्वत्कृतं 'thy deed;' पितृवचनं 'a father's speech;' मृत्युद्वारं 'the gate of death;' इच्छासम्पद् 'fulfilment of wishes;' मात्रानन्दम् 'a mother's joy;' जलाशयम् 'a receptacle of water,' 'a lake;' विद्यार्थी 'seeker of knowledge,' 'a scholar;' कुक्कुटाण्डं (for कुक्कुट्या अण्डं) 'a hen's egg.'

b. Sometimes an adjective in the superlative degree, used substantively, occupies the last place in the compound; as, नरश्रेष्ठस् or पुरुषोत्तमस् 'the best of men.'

c. In occasional instances the genitive case is retained; as, विशाम्पतिस् 'lord of men;' दिवस्पतिस् 'lord of the sky.'

d. Especially in terms of reproach; as, दास्याःपुत्रस् (or दासीपुत्रस्) 'son of a slave girl.'

Locatively Dependent.

744. Or those in which the relation of the first word to the last is equivalent to that of a locative case; as, पङ्कमग्नस्, -ग्ना, -ग्नं, 'sunk in the mud' (for पङ्के मग्न); गगनविहारी 'sporting in the sky;' जलक्रीडा 'sport in the water;' ग्रामवासी 'a dweller in a village;' जलचरस् 'going in the water;' जलजस् 'born in the water;' शिरोरत्नं 'gem on the head.'

a. The sign of the locative case is retained in some cases, especially before nouns of agency; as, ग्रामेवासी 'a villager;' जलेचरस् 'going in the water;' उरसिभूषितस्, -ता, -तं, 'ornamented on the breast;' अग्रेगस् or अग्रेसरस् 'going in front;' दिविषद् 'abiding in the sky;' दिविस्पृश् (rt. स्पृश्) 'touching the sky;' युधिष्ठिरस् 'firm in war.'

Dependent in more than one Case.

745. Dependent compounds do not always consist of two words. They may be composed of almost any number of nouns, all depending upon each other, in the

manner that one case depends upon another in a sentence; thus, चक्षुर्विषयातिक्रान्तः, -न्ता, -न्तं, 'passed beyond the range of the eye' (for चक्षुषो विषयम् अतिक्रान्तः); रथमध्यस्थः 'standing in the middle of the chariot;' भीतपरित्राणवस्तूपालम्भपण्डितः 'skilful in censuring the means of rescuing those in danger.'

a. There is an anomalous form of Tat-purusha compound, which is really the result of the elision of the second or middle member (*uttara-pada-lopa*, *madhyama-pada-lopa*) of a complex compound; thus, अभिज्ञानशकुन्तला 'token-Śakuntalā' for अभिज्ञानस्मृतशकुन्तला 'Śakuntalā (recognised) by the token.'

b. Dependent compounds abound in all the cognate languages. The following are examples from Greek and Latin; *οἰνο-θήκη*, *οἰκο-φύλαξ*, *λιθό-στρωτος*, *γυναικο-κήρυκτος*, *ἀνθρωπο-δίδακτος*, *θεό-δοτος*, *θεό-τρεπτος*, *χειρο-ποίητος*, *auri-fodina*, *manu-pretium*, *parri-cida* for *patri-cida*, *parri-cidium*, *matri-cidium*, *marti-cultor*, *mus-cerda*. English furnishes innumerable examples of dependent compounds, e.g. 'ink-stand,' 'snow-drift,' 'moth-eaten,' 'priest-ridden,' 'door-mat,' 'writing-master,' &c.

COPULATIVE (OR AGGREGATIVE) COMPOUNDS (DVANDVA).

746. This class of compounds has no exact parallel in other languages.

When two or more persons or things are enumerated together, it is usual in Sanskrit, instead of connecting them by a copulative, to aggregate them into one compound word. No syntactical dependence of one case upon another subsists between the members of Dvandva compounds, since they must always consist of words which, if uncompounded, would be in the *same case*. The only grammatical connexion between the members is that which would be expressed by the copulative conjunction *and* in English, or च in Sanskrit. In fact, the difference between this class and the last turns upon this dependence *in case* of the words compounded on each other; insomuch that the existence or absence of such dependence, as deducible from the context, is, in some cases, the only guide by which the student is enabled to refer the compound to the one head or to the other: thus, गुरुशिष्यसेवकाः may either be a Dependent compound, and mean 'the servants of the pupils of the Guru,' or a Copulative, 'the Guru, and the pupil, and the servant.' And मांसशोणितम् may either be Dependent, 'the blood of the flesh,' or Copulative, 'flesh and blood.' This ambiguity, however, can never occur in Dvandvas inflected in the dual, and rarely occasions any practical difficulty.

747. There are three kinds of Copulative compounds: 1st, in-

flected in the plural; 2d, inflected in the dual; 3d, inflected in the singular. In the first two cases the final letter of the base of the word terminating the compound determines the declension, and its gender the particular form of declension; in the third case it seems to be a law that this kind of compound cannot be formed unless the last word ends in अ *a*, or in a vowel changeable to अ *a*, or in a consonant to which अ *a* may be subjoined; and the gender is invariably neuter, whatever may be the gender of the final word.

Inflected in the Plural.

748. When *more than two* animate objects are enumerated, the last is inflected in the plural, the declension following the gender of the last member of the compound; as, इन्द्रानिलयमार्काः 'Indra, Anila, Yama, and Arka' (for इन्द्रः, अनिलः, यमः, अर्कः); रामलक्ष्मणभरताः 'Ráma, Lakshmaṇa, and Bharata;' मृगव्याधसर्पशूकराः 'the deer, the hunter, the serpent, and the hog.' The learner will observe, that although the last member of the compound is inflected in the plural, each of the members has here a singular acceptation. But a plural signification may often be inherent in some or all of the words constituting the compound; thus, ब्राह्मणक्षत्रियवैश्यशूद्राः 'Bráhmaṇas, Kshatriyas, Vaiśyas, and Śúdras;' मित्रोदासीनशत्रवः 'friends, neutrals, and foes' (for मित्राणि, उदासीनाः, शत्रवः); ऋषिदेवपितृतिथिभूतानि 'sages, gods, ancestors, guests, and spirits' (for ऋषयः, देवाः, पितरः, अतिथयः, भूतानि च); सिंहव्याघ्रमहोरगाः 'lions, tigers, and serpents;' श्वगृध्रकङ्ककाकोलभासगोमायुवायसाः 'dogs, vultures, herons, ravens, kites, jackals, and crows.'

749. So also when *more than two* inanimate objects are enumerated, the last may be inflected in the plural; as, धर्मार्थकाममोक्षाः 'virtue, wealth, enjoyment, and beatitude' (for धर्मः, अर्थः, कामः, मोक्षः); इज्याध्ययनदानानि 'sacrifice, study, and liberality' (for इज्या, अध्ययनं, दानं च). In some of the following a plural signification is inherent; as, पुष्पमूलफलानि 'flowers, roots, and fruits;' अजातमृतमूर्खाणां 'of the unborn, the dead, and the foolish' (for अजातानां, मृतानां, मूर्खाणां च); नेत्रमनःस्वभावाः 'eyes, mind, and disposition;' रोगशोकपरीतापबन्धनव्यसनानि 'sickness, sorrow, anguish, bonds, and afflictions;' काष्ठजलफलमूलमधूनि 'wood, water, fruit, roots, and honey.'

750. So also when *only two* animate or inanimate objects are enumerated, in which a *plural* signification is inherent, the last is

inflected in the plural; as, देवमनुष्यास् 'gods and men;' पुत्रपौत्रास्, 'sons and grandsons;' पातोत्पातास् 'falls and rises;' प्राकारपरिखास् 'ramparts and trenches;' सुखदुःखेषु 'in pleasures and pains' (for सुखेषु, दुःखेषु च); पापपुण्यानि 'sins and virtues.'

Inflected in the Dual.

751. When *only two* animate objects are enumerated, in each of which a *singular* signification is inherent, the last is inflected in the dual, the declension following the gender of the last member; as, रामलक्ष्मणौ 'Ráma and Lakshmaṇa' (for रामस्, लक्ष्मणश् च); चन्द्रसूर्यौ 'the moon and sun;' मृगकाकौ 'a deer and a crow;' भार्यापती 'wife and husband;' मयूरीकुक्कुटौ 'pea-hen and cock;' कुक्कुटमयूर्यौ 'cock and pea-hen.'

752. So also when *only two* inanimate objects are enumerated, in each of which a *singular* signification is inherent, the last is inflected in the dual; as, आरम्भावसाने 'beginning and end' (for आरम्भम्, अवसानं च); अनुरागापरागौ 'affection and enmity' (for अनुरागस्, अपरागश् च); हर्षविषादौ 'joy and sorrow;' क्षुत्पिपासे 'hunger and thirst' (for क्षुत्, पिपासा च); क्षुद्व्याधी 'hunger and sickness;' स्थानासनाभ्यां 'by standing and sitting' (for स्थानेन, आसनेन च); मधुसर्पिषी 'honey and ghee;' सुखदुःखे 'pleasure and pain;' उलूखलमुसले 'mortar and pestle;' अभ्युत्थानाभिवादनाभ्यां 'by rising and saluting;' मृदद्भ्यां 'by earth and water.'

Inflected in the Singular Neuter.

753. When two or more *inanimate* objects are enumerated, whether singular or plural in their signification, the last may either be inflected as above (748, 749, 750, 751), or in the singular number, neut. gender; as, पुष्पमूलफलं 'flowers, roots, and fruits' (for पुष्पाणि, मूलानि, फलानि च); तृणान्नोदकेन्धनं 'grass, food, water, and fuel' (for तृणम्, अन्नं, उदकं, इन्धनं च); अहोरात्रं 'a day and night' (for अहस्, रात्रिश् च. A form अहोरात्रस् in the masc. sing. also occurs); दिग्देशं 'quarters and countries' (for दिशस्, देशाश् च); द्युनिशं or दिवानिशं 'day and night;' शिरोग्रीवं 'head and neck;' चर्ममांसरुधिरं 'skin, flesh, and blood.'

a. Sometimes two or more animate objects are thus compounded; as, पुत्रपौत्रं 'sons and grandsons;' हस्त्यश्वं 'elephants and horses;' especially inferior objects: as, श्वचाण्डालं 'a dog and an outcast.'

754. In enumerating two qualities the opposite of each other, it is common to

form a Dvandva compound of this kind, by doubling an adjective or participle, and interposing the negative अ *a*; as, चराचरं 'moveable and immoveable' (for चरम् अचरं च); शुभाशुभे 'good and evil;' प्रियाप्रिये 'in agreeable and disagreeable' (for प्रिये अप्रिये च); दृष्टादृष्टे 'seen and not seen;' कृताकृते 'done and not done;' मृदुक्रूरे 'gentle and cruel.'

a. In the Dvandvas which occur in the Vedas the first member of the compound, as well as the last, may sometimes take a dual termination; thus, मित्रा-वरुणौ (see 97. *a*), इन्द्रा-विष्णू, पितरा-मातरौ; and some of the anomalous Dvandvas used in more modern Sanskṛit are probably Vaidik in their character; thus, द्यावा-पृथिवी 'heaven and earth;' माता-पितरौ 'mother and father,' &c.

b. It is a general rule, however, that if a compound consists of two crude bases in *ṛi*, the final of the first becomes आ, as in मातापितरौ above. This also happens if the last member of the compound be पुत्र, as पिता-पुत्रौ 'father and son.'

c. Greek and Latin furnish examples of complex compounds involving Dvandvas; thus, *Βατραχο-μυο-μαχία*, 'frog-mouse war;' *su-ovi-taurilia*, 'pig-sheep-bull sacrifice;' *ζωό-φυτον*, 'animal-plant.' *Zoophyte* is thus a kind of Dvandva. In English, compounds like 'plano-convex,' 'convexo-concave,' are examples of the relative form of Dvandva explained at 765.

DESCRIPTIVE (OR DETERMINATIVE) COMPOUNDS (KARMA-DHÁRAYA).

755. In describing, qualifying, or defining a substantive by means of an adjective or participle, it is common in Sanskṛit to compound the two words together, placing the adjective or participle in the first member of the compound in its crude base; as, साधु-जनः 'a good man' (for साधुर् जनः); चिर-मित्रम् 'an old friend' (for चिरं मित्रम्); क्षुभितार्णवः 'a troubled ocean;' पुण्य-कर्म 'a holy act;' अनन्तात्मा 'the infinite soul;' संस्कृतोक्तिः 'polished speech;' पुण्य-कर्माणि 'holy acts' (for पुण्यानि कर्माणि); उत्तम-नराणाम् 'of the best men' (for उत्तमानां नराणाम्); महा-पातकं 'a great crime' (see 778); महा-राजः 'a great king' (see 778); प्रिय-सखः 'a dear friend' (see 778); दीर्घ-रात्रः 'a long night' (see 778).

a. The feminine bases of adjectives do not generally appear in compounds; thus, प्रियभार्या 'a dear wife' (for प्रिया भार्या); महाभार्या 'a great wife' (for महती भार्या, see 778); रूपवद्भार्या 'a beautiful wife' (for रूपवती भार्या); पाचक-स्त्री 'a she-cook' (for पाचिका स्त्री).

b. There are, however, a few examples of feminine adjective bases in compounds, e.g. वामोरुभार्या 'a wife with beautiful thighs;' कामिनी-जनः 'an impassioned woman,' where कामिनी is perhaps used substantively. See also 766. *c*, note.

756. An indeclinable word or prefix may sometimes take the place of an adjective

in this kind of compound; thus, सुपथः 'a good road;' सुदिनं 'a fine day;' सुभाषितं 'good speech;' दुश्चरितं 'bad conduct;' अभयं 'not fear,' &c.; बहिःशौचं 'external cleanliness' (from *bahis*, 'externally,' and *śauca*, 'purity'); अन्तःशौचं 'internal purity;' ईषद्दर्शनं 'a slight inspection;' कुपुरुषः 'a bad man.'

757. Adjectives sometimes occupy the last place in Descriptive compounds; as, परमधार्मिकः 'a very just man;' परमाद्भुतं 'a very wonderful thing.'

a. In the same manner, substantives, used adjectively, may occupy the first place; as, मलद्रव्याणि 'impure substances;' राजर्षिः 'a royal sage.'

758. Descriptive compounds expressing 'excellence' or 'eminence' fall under this class, and are composed of two substantives, one of which is used as an adjective to describe or define the other, and is placed last, being generally the name of an animal denoting 'superiority;' as, पुरुषव्याघ्रः 'man-tiger,' पुरुषपुङ्गवः 'man-bull,' पुरुषसिंहः 'man-lion,' पुरुषर्षभः 'man-bull,' equivalent to 'an illustrious man.' Similarly, स्त्रीरत्नं 'an excellent woman' (gem of a woman).

a. No other compounds expressive of 'comparison' or 'resemblance' are usually included in native grammars under the Descriptive or Karma-dhāraya class. In these the adjective is placed last; as, छायाचञ्चलम्, -ला, -लं, 'fickle as a shadow;' अम्बुदश्यामम्, -मा, -मं, 'dark as a cloud;' भूधरविस्तीर्णम्, -र्णा, -र्णं, 'spread out like a mountain.'

b. The following are examples of Greek and Latin compounds falling under this class; *μεγαλο-μήτηρ, ἰσό-θεος, μεγαλό-νοια, ἡμι-κύων, sacri-portus, meri-dies* (for *medi-dies*), *decem-viri, semi-deus*. Parallel compounds in English are, 'good-will,' 'good-sense,' 'ill-nature,' &c.

NUMERAL (OR COLLECTIVE) COMPOUNDS (DVIGU).

759. A numeral is often compounded with a substantive to form a collective noun, but the last member of the compound is generally in the neuter singular; thus, चतुर्युगं 'the four ages' (for चत्वारि युगानि); चतुर्दिशं 'the four quarters;' त्रिदिनं 'three days' (*triduum*); त्रिरात्रं 'three nights' (रात्र being substituted for रात्रि, see 778); त्र्यब्दं 'three years' (*triennium*); पञ्चाग्नि 'the five fires.'

a. Rarely numerals in their crude state are compounded with plural substantives; as, चतुर्वर्णम् 'the four castes;' पञ्चबाणम् 'five arrows;' सप्तर्षिवम् 'the seven stars of Ursa Major.'

b. Compare Greek and Latin compounds like *τετραόδιον, τριώνυμον, τέθριππον, triduum, triennium, trinoctium, quadrivium, quinquertium*.

c. Sometimes the last member of the compound is in the feminine singular, with the termination ई; as, त्रिलोकी 'the three worlds.'

ADVERBIAL OR INDECLINABLE COMPOUNDS (AVYAYĪ-BHĀVA).

760. In this class of indeclinable (*avyaya*, i. e. *na vyeti*, 'what does not change') compounds the first member must be either a preposition

(such as अति, अधि, अनु, प्रति, &c., at 783) or an adverbial prefix (such as यथा 'as,' यावत् 'as far as,' अ or अन् 'not,' सह 'with,' &c.). The last member is a substantive which takes the form of an accusative case neuter, whatever may be the termination of its crude base; thus, यथाश्रद्धं 'according to faith' (from यथा and श्रद्धा); प्रतिनिशं 'every night' (from प्रति and निशा); प्रतिदिशं 'in every quarter' (from प्रति and दिश्); अतिनु 'beyond the ship' (from अति and नौ).

a. Many of these compounds are formed with the adverbial preposition सह, generally contracted into स; thus, सक्रोधं 'with anger' (from स and क्रोध); सादरं 'with respect' (स आदरं); साष्टाङ्गपातं 'with prostration of eight parts of the body.' Páṇini (II. 1, 9, &c.) gives some unusual forms with postpositions; as, सूपप्रति 'a little sauce.'

b. The following are examples of indeclinable compounds with other prefixes; अनुज्येष्ठं 'according to seniority;' प्रत्यङ्गं 'over every limb;' प्रतिमासं 'every month' (730. *d*); यथाविधि 'according to rule;' यथाशक्ति or यावच्छक्यं (49) 'according to one's ability;' यथासुखं 'happily;' यथार्हं 'suitably,' 'worthily;' यथोक्तं 'as described;' अनुक्षणं 'every moment;' समक्षं 'before the eyes' (778); अधिस्कन्धं 'upon the shoulders;' अधिवृक्षं 'upon the tree;' असंशयं 'without doubt;' निर्विशेषं 'without distinction;' मध्येगङ्गं 'in the middle of the Ganges.'

c. Analogous indeclinable compounds are found in Latin and Greek, such as *admodum*, *obviam*, *affatim*, ἀντιβίην, ἀντίβιον, ὑπέρμορον, παραχρῆμα. In these, however, the original gender is retained, whereas, according to the Sanskrit rule, *obvium* would be written for *obviam*, and *affate* for *affatim*. In Greek compounds like σήμερον, the feminine ἡμέρα appends a neuter form, as in Sanskrit.

d. The neuter word अर्थं 'for the sake of,' 'on account of' (see 731. *a*), is often used at the end of compounds; thus, स्वापार्थं 'for the sake of sleep;' कार्यानुष्ठानार्थं 'for the sake of the performance of business.' See, however, 731, note.

e. There is a peculiar adverbial compound formed by doubling a crude base, the final of the first member of the compound being lengthened, and the final of the last changed to इ *i*. It generally denotes mutual contact, reciprocity, or opposition; thus, मुष्टीमुष्टि 'fist to fist;' दण्डादण्डि 'stick to stick' (fighting); भागाभागि 'share by share;' केशाकेशि 'pulling each other's hair;' अङ्गाङ्गि 'body to body;' बाहूबाहवि 'arm to arm.'

f. Something in the same manner, अन्य and पर, 'another,' are doubled; thus, अन्योन्यं, परस्परं, 'one another,' 'mutually,' 'together.'

RELATIVE COMPOUNDS (MOSTLY EQUIVALENT TO BAHU-VRÍHI).

761. The greater number of compounds in the preceding four divisions are terminated by substantives, the sense of each being in that case absolute and complete in itself. All such compounds may be used *relatively*, that is, as epithets of other words, the final

substantive becoming susceptible of three genders, like an adjective (see 108, 119, 130, 134. *a*). We have given the name *relative* to compounds when thus used, not only for the obvious reason of their being relatively and not absolutely employed, but also because they usually involve a relative pronoun, and are sometimes translated into English by the aid of this pronoun, and are, moreover, resolved by native commentators into their equivalent uncompounded words by the aid of the genitive case of the relative (यस्य). Thus, महद्धनं is a Descriptive compound, meaning 'great wealth,' and may be used adjectively in relation to पुरुषम्, thus महाधनः पुरुषः 'a man *who* has great wealth;' or to स्त्री, thus महाधना स्त्री 'a woman *who* has great wealth;' and would be resolved by commentators into यस्य or यस्या महद् धनं. In English we have similar compounds, as 'high-minded,' 'left-handed,' and the like, where the substantive terminating the compound is converted into an adjective.

Relative form of Tat-purusha or Dependent Compounds.

762. Many Dependent compounds (especially those that are instrumentally dependent at 740) are already *in their own nature* relative, and cannot be used except in connexion with some other word in the sentence. But, on the other hand, many others, and especially those which are genitively dependent, constituting by far the largest number of this class of compounds, are in their nature absolute, and yield a sense complete in itself. These may be made relative by declining the final substantive after the manner of an adjective; thus, चन्द्राकृतिस्, -तिस्, -ति, 'moon-shaped' (see 119), from the absolute compound चन्द्राकृतिस् 'the shape of the moon.'

a. Other examples are, देवरूपस्, -पी, -पं, 'whose form is godlike' (see 108); सूर्यप्रभावस्, -वा, -वं, 'splendid as the sun' (108); हस्तिपादस्, -दा, -दं*, 'elephant-footed' (see 57); सागरान्तस्, -न्ता, -न्तं, 'ending at the sea;' मरणान्तस्, -न्ता, -न्तं, 'terminated by death;' कर्णपुरोगमस्, -मा, -मं, or कर्णमुखस्, -खा, -खं, 'headed by Karṇa;' विष्णुशर्मनामा, -मा, -म, 'named Vishṇuśarma' (see 154); पुण्डरीकाक्षस्, -क्षी, -क्षं, 'lotus-eyed' (see 778); नारायणाख्यस्, -ख्या, -ख्यं, 'called Náráyaṇa;' धनमूलस्, -ला, -लं, 'founded on wealth;' लक्षसंख्यानि (agreeing with धनानि), 'money to the amount of a lac;' गदाहस्तस्, -स्ता, -स्तं, 'having a club in the hand,' or 'club in hand;' शस्त्रपाणिस्, -णिस्, -णि, 'arms in hand;' जालहस्तस्, -स्ता, -स्तं, 'net in hand;' दुष्यन्तविषयस्, -या, -यं, 'on the subject of

* पाद् may be substituted for पाद in compounds of this kind, but not after हस्तिन्. See 778.

flowers,' 'relating to flowers;' ध्यानपरम्, -रा, -रं, 'having meditation for one's chief or highest occupation;' तद्विद्यम्, -द्या, -द्यं, 'having his knowledge.' These examples are not distinguishable from absolute dependent compounds, except by declension in three genders.

b. Note—Parallel compounds are found in Greek, e. g. ἱππό-γλωσσος, 'having a tongue like a horse.'

763. Many of them, however, are not found, except as relatives; and if used absolutely would yield a different sense; thus, कर्णमुखं means 'the face of Karṇa,' but when used relatively to राजानस्, 'the kings headed by Karṇa.' So also चारचक्षुस् signifies 'the eye of the spy,' but when used relatively to राजा, 'a king who sees by means of his spies.' See 166. *c.*

764. The substantive आदि, 'a beginning,' when it occurs in the last member of a compound of this nature, is used relatively to some word expressed or understood, and yields a sense equivalent to *et cetera*. It is generally found either in the plural or neuter singular; as, इन्द्रादयस् 'Indra and the others' (agreeing with the nom. case सुरास् expressed or understood, 'the gods commencing with Indra'); अग्न्यादीनां 'of Agni and the others' (agreeing with पूर्वोक्तानां understood, 'of those above-named things of which Agni was the first'); चक्षुरादीनि 'the eyes, &c.' (agreeing with इन्द्रियाणि 'the senses commencing with the eyes'). When used in the neut. sing. it either agrees with पूर्वोक्तं, 'the aforesaid,' understood, or with a number of things taken collectively, and the adverb *iti* * may be prefixed; as, देवानित्यादि 'the word *devān*, &c.' (agreeing with पूर्वोक्तं understood, 'the aforesaid sentence of which *devān* is the first word'); दानादिना 'by liberality, &c.' (agreeing with some class of things understood, 'by that class of things of which liberality is the first'). See also 772.

a. It may occasionally be used in the masc. sing.; as, मार्जन्यादिम् 'brooms, &c.' (agreeing with उपस्करम् 'furniture').

b. Sometimes आदिक is used for आदि; as, दानादिकं 'gifts, &c.:' and sometimes आद्य; as, इन्द्राद्यास् सुरास् 'the gods of whom Indra is the first.'

c. The feminine substantive प्रभृति 'manner,' 'kind,' may be used in the same way; thus, इन्द्रप्रभृतयस् सुरास् 'the gods, Indra and the others;' तेषां ग्रामनिवासिप्रभृतीनां 'of those villagers, &c.'

d. Observe—The neuter of आदि may optionally take the terminations of the masculine in all but the nom. and accus. cases; thus, हस्त्यश्वादेस् 'of elephants, horses, &c.' (agreeing with बलस्य gen. neut. of बलं 'an army').

Relative form of Dvandva or Copulative Compounds.

765. Copulative (or Aggregative) compounds are sometimes used

* Sometimes *evam* is prefixed; as, एवमादीनि प्रलापानि 'lamentations beginning thus.'

relatively; especially in the case of adjectives or participles; as, कृष्णशुक्लस्, -क्ला, -क्लं, 'black and white;' स्नातानुलिप्तस्, -प्ता, -प्तं, 'bathed and anointed;' पौरजानपदस्, -दा, -दं, 'city and country;' कृतापकृतस्, -ता, -तं, 'done and done badly;' शुभाशुभस्, -भा, -भं, 'good and evil' (754); सान्द्रस्निग्धस्, -ग्धा, -ग्धं, 'thick and unctuous;' निःशब्दस्तिमितस्, -ता, -तं, 'noiseless and motionless' (night); गृहीतप्रतिमुक्तस्य 'of him taken and let loose.' Compare λευκο-μέλας, 'white and black.' See other examples under Complex Compounds.

a. Be it remembered, that many compounds of this kind are classed by native grammarians under the head of Tat-purusha (Pāṇ. II. 1, 69), though the accent in many conforms to the rule for Bahu-vríhi (VI. 2, 3).

Relative form of Karma-dháraya or Descriptive Compounds.

766. A greater number of compound words may be referred to this head than to any other. Every style of writing abounds with them; thus, अल्पशक्तिस्, -क्तिस्, -क्ति, 'whose strength is small' (119).

a. Other examples are, महाबलस्, -ला, -लं, 'whose strength is great' (108, see also 778); महातेजास्, -जास्, -जस्, 'whose glory is great' (164. *a*); अल्पधनस्, -ना, -नं, 'whose wealth is small;' महात्मा, -त्मा, -त्म, 'high-minded' (151); उदारचरितस्, -ता, -तं, 'of noble demeanour;' बहुमत्स्यस्, -त्स्या, -त्स्यं, 'having many fish;' स्वल्पसलिलस्, -ला, -लं, 'having very little water;' पण्डितबुद्धिस्, -द्धिस्, -द्धि, 'of wise intellect' (119); प्रियभार्यस्, -र्या, -र्यं, 'having a dear wife;' अशक्यसन्धानस्, -ना, -नं, 'not to be reconciled;' संवृतसंवार्यस्, agreeing with राजा, 'a king who conceals what ought to be concealed.'

767. Although a passive participle is not often prefixed to a noun in an absolute sense, this kind of combination prevails most extensively in the formation of relative compounds; as, प्राप्तकालस्, -ला, -लं, 'whose time has arrived.'

a. Other examples are, जितेन्द्रियस्, -या, -यं, 'whose passions are subdued;' शान्तचेतास्, -तास्, -तस्, 'whose mind is composed;' संहृष्टमनास्, -नास्, -नस्, 'whose mind is rejoiced' (see 164); भग्नाशस्, -शा, -शं 'whose hopes are broken;' हृतराज्यस्, -ज्या, -ज्यं, 'whose kingdom is taken away;' अमिततेजास्, -जास्, -जस्, 'whose glory is boundless;' आसन्नमृत्युस्, -त्युस्, -त्यु, 'whose death is near;' कृतकामस्, -मा, -मं, 'whose desire is accomplished,' i. e. 'successful;' कृतभोजनस्, -ना, -नं, 'one who has finished eating;' अनधिगतशास्त्रस्, -स्त्रा, -स्त्रं, 'one by whom the Śástras have not been read;' भिन्नहृदयस्, -या, -यं, or दलितहृदयस्, 'whose heart is pierced;' जितशत्रुस्, -त्रुस्, -त्रु, 'who has conquered his enemies;' छिन्नकेशस्, -शा, -शं, 'having the hair cut;' मिताशनस्, -ना, -नं, 'eating sparingly;' पूतपापस्, -पा, -पं, 'purified from sin.'

b. Occasionally the feminine of the adjective appears in the compound; as, षष्ठीभार्यस् 'having a sixth wife.' Compare 755. *a.*

c. The affix क *ka* is often added; as, हतश्रीकस्, -का, -कं, 'reft of fortune;' हृतश्मश्रुकस्, -श्रुका, -श्रुकं, 'shorn of (his) beard.'

d. Examples of Greek and Latin compounds of this kind are, *μεγαλο-κέφαλος, μεγαλό-μητις, λευκό-πτερος, πολύ-χρυσος, χρυσεο-στέφανος, ἡδύ-γλωσσος, ἐρημό-πολις, magn-animus, longi-manus, multi-comus, albi-comus, multi-vius, atri-color.*

e. In English compounds of this kind abound; e. g. 'blue-eyed,' 'narrow-minded,' 'good-tempered,' 'pale-faced,' &c.

Relative form of Dvigu or Numeral Compounds.

768. Numeral or Dvigu compounds may be used relatively; as, द्विपर्णस्, -र्णी, -र्णं, 'two-leaved;' त्रिलोचनस्, -ना, -नं, 'tri-ocular.'

a. Other examples are, त्रिमूर्द्धस्, -र्द्धा, -र्द्धं, 'three-headed' (मूर्द्ध being substituted for मूर्द्धन्, see 778); चतुर्मुखस्, -खी, -खं, 'four-faced;' चतुष्कोणस्, -णा, -णं, 'quadrangular;' शतद्वारस्, -रा, -रं, 'hundred-gated;' चतुर्विद्यस्, -द्या, -द्यं, 'possessed of the four sciences;' सहस्राक्षस्, -क्षी, -क्षं, 'thousand-eyed' (see 778); पञ्चगवधनस्, -ना, -नं, 'having the wealth of five bullocks.'

Relative form of Compounds with Adverbial Prefixes.

769. The adverbial compounds most frequently employed relatively as adjectives are those formed with the adverbial preposition सह 'with,' contracted into स; thus, सक्रोधस्, -धा, -धं, 'angry' (lit. 'with-anger,' 'having anger'); सफलस्, -ला, -लं, 'fruitful' (108); सबन्धुस्, -न्धुस्, -न्धु, 'possessed of kindred' (119); सपक्षस्, -क्षा, -क्षं, 'energetic;' सजीवस्, -वा, -वं, 'possessed of life,' 'living;' सानन्दस्, -न्दा, -न्दं, 'joyful;' ससचिवस्, -वा, -वं, 'accompanied by ministers;' सभार्यस् 'accompanied by a wife,' 'having a wife;' सज्यस्, -ज्या, -ज्यं, 'strung' (as a bow, lit. 'with-bowstring').

a. The affix क *ka* is often added to this kind of compound; as, सश्रीकस्, -का, -कं, 'possessed of fortune;' सस्त्रीकस्, -का, -कं, 'accompanied by women.' Compare 80. XVII.

b. In some compounds सह remains; as, सहवाहनम् 'with his army;' सहपुत्रम् 'along with his son.'

c. स is also used for समान 'same;' as, सगोत्रस्, -त्रा, -त्रं, 'of the same family.'

d. There are of course many examples of nouns combined with adverbial prefixes, so as to form relative compounds, which cannot be regarded as relative forms of Avyayí-bháva; thus, उद्यतायुधस्, -धा, -धं, 'with uplifted weapon;' नानाप्रकारस्, -रा, -रं, 'of various shapes;' किंनिवासस्, -सा, -सं, 'where dwelling?' कुत्रजन्मा, -न्मा, -न्म, 'where born?' निरपराधस्, -धा, -धं, 'without fault;' निराहारस्,

-न्ना, -न्नं, 'having no food;' अपभीस्, -भीस्, -भि, 'fearless' (123. b); तथाविधस्, -धा, -धं, 'of that kind,' 'in such a state;' दुर्बुद्धिस्, -द्धिस्, -द्धि, 'weak-minded;' दुष्प्रकृतिस्, -तिस्, -ति, 'ill-natured' (see 72); सुमुखस्, -खी, -खं, 'handsome-faced;' सुबुद्धिस्, -द्धिस्, -द्धि, 'of good understanding.' Some of the above may be regarded as relative forms of Descriptive compounds, formed with indeclinable prefixes; see 756. Similar compounds in Greek and Latin are, *ἀν-ήμερος*, *εὔ-δηλος*, *in-imicus*, *in-felix*, *dis-similis*, *semi-plenus*.

e. Observe—The adverbial prefixes दुस् and सु (726. *d. f*) impart a passive sense to participial nouns of agency, just as δυσ and εὖ in Greek; thus, दुष्कर 'difficult to be done,' सुकर 'easy to be done;' दुर्लभ 'difficult to be obtained,' सुलभ 'easy to be attained;' दुस्तर 'difficult to be crossed.' Compare the Greek εὔφορος, 'easy to be borne;' δύσπορος, 'difficult to be passed,' &c.

f. स्वामिकस्, -का, -कं, 'possessed of a master,' is sometimes used at the end of compounds to denote simply 'possessed of,' 'furnished with;' thus, वितानस्वामिकं शिलासनं 'a stone-seat furnished with a canopy;' शिलापट्टस्वामिको लतागृहः 'an arbour having a marble-slab as its master,' i. e. 'furnished with,' 'provided with,' &c. Similarly, बहुबकस्वामिको वटपादपः 'a fig-tree occupied by a number of cranes.'

g. Observe—The relative form of a compound would be marked in Vedic Sanskrit by the accent. In the Karma-dháraya compound *mahá-báhu*, 'great arm,' the accent would be on the last syllable, thus महाबाहु; but in the Relative *mahá-bāhu*, 'great armed,' on the ante-penultimate, thus महाबाहु. So, native commentators often quote as an example of the importance of right accentuation, the word *Indra-śatru*, which, accented on the first syllable, would be Bahu-vrīhi (see Pāṇ. VI. 2, 1, by which the first member retains its original accent); but accented on the penultimate would be Tat-purusha. The sense in the first case is 'having Indra for an enemy;' in the second, 'the enemy of Indra.'

h. Note, that आत्मक and रूप are used at the end of relative compounds to denote 'composed of,' 'consisting of;' but are more frequently found at the end of complex relatives; see 774.

COMPLEX COMPOUND NOUNS.

770. We have now to speak of complex compound words, or compounds within compounds, which form a most remarkable feature in Sanskrit composition. Instances might be given of twenty or thirty words thus compounded together; but these are the productions of the vitiated taste of more modern times, and are only curious as showing that the power of compounding words may often be extravagantly abused. But even in the best specimens of Sanskrit composition, and in the simplest prose writings, four, five, or even six words are commonly compounded together, involving two or three forms under one head. It will be easy, however, to

determine the character of the forms involved, by the rules propounded in the preceding pages; in proof of which the student has only to study attentively the following examples.

Instances of absolute complex compounds, whose sense is complete and unconnected, are not rare.

a. The following are examples: कालान्तरावृत्तिशुभाशुभानि 'good and evil (occurring) in the revolutions of the interval of time,' the whole being a dependent, involving a dependent and a copulative; सेनापतिबलाध्यक्षौ 'the general of the army and the overseer of the forces,' the whole being a copulative, involving two dependents; शोकारातिभयत्राणं 'the protection from sorrow, enemies, and perils,' the whole being a dependent, involving an aggregative; अवधीरितसुहृद्वाक्यं 'the disregarded words of a friend,' the whole being a descriptive, involving a dependent; शुक्लाम्बरमाल्यदाम 'a white robe and a string of garlands,' the whole being a copulative, involving a descriptive and dependent; सर्वशास्त्रपारगः 'one who has gone to the opposite bank (*pára*) of all the Sástras,' i. e. 'one who has read them through;' मृतसिंहास्थीनि 'the bones of a dead lion.'

771. The greater number of complex compounds are used as adjectives, or relatively, as epithets of some other word in the sentence; thus, गलितनखनयनः, -ना, -नं, 'whose nails and eyes were decayed,' the whole being the relative form of descriptive, involving a copulative; क्षुत्क्षामकण्ठः 'having a throat emaciated with hunger,' the whole being the relative form of descriptive, involving a dependent.

a. Other examples are, शुक्लमाल्यानुलेपनः, -ना, -नं, 'having a white garland and unguents,' the whole being the relative form of copulative, involving a descriptive; पीनस्कन्धोरुबाहु 'broad-shouldered and strong-armed,' the whole being a copulative, involving two descriptives; पूर्वजन्मकृतः, -ता, -तं, 'done in a former birth,' the whole being a dependent, involving a descriptive; विद्यावयोवृद्धः, -द्धा, -द्धं, 'advanced in learning and age,' the whole being a dependent, involving a copulative; अम्लानस्रग्रजोहीनः, -ना, -नं, 'having fresh garlands, and being free from dust,' the whole being the relative form of copulative, involving a descriptive and dependent; अभिषेकार्द्रशिराः, -राः, -रः, 'whose head was moist with unction;' यथेप्सितमुखः, -खा, -खं, 'having the face turned in any direction one likes;' शूलमुद्गरहस्तः, -स्ता, -स्तं, 'spear and club in hand;' एकरात्रनिर्वाहोचितः, -ता, -तं, 'sufficient for support during one night' (see 778); ऋग्यजुःसामाख्यवेदत्रयार्थवित् 'acquainted with the meaning of the three Vedas, called Rig, Yajur, and Sáma;' सन्दष्टदशनच्छदरक्तनेत्राः 'biting their lips and having red eyes' (agreeing with राजानः); परद्रोहकर्मधीः 'injuring another by action or by intention.'

772. The substantive आदि, 'a beginning,' often occurs in complex relative

compounds, with the force of *et cetera*, as in simple relatives at 764: thus, शुक-सारिकाद्यम् 'parrots, starlings, &c.' (agreeing with पक्षिगणम् 'birds beginning with parrots and starlings'), the whole being the relative form of dependent, involving an aggregative; सन्धि-विग्रहादि 'peace, war, &c.' (agreeing with पूर्वोक्तं understood); गृह-देवागारादि-युक्त, -क्ता, -क्तं, 'possessed of houses, temples, &c.;' करि-तुरग-कोषादि-परिच्छद-युक्त, -क्ता, -क्तं, 'possessed of elephants, horses, treasuries, and other property.'

a. Similarly, आद्य in the example उत्तम-गन्धाद्याः (agreeing with स्रजः 'garlands possessing the best odour and other qualities').

773. Long complex compounds may be generally translated by beginning at the last word and proceeding regularly backwards, as in the following; मत्त-मधुकर-निकर-गुञ्ज-झङ्कार-मिलित-कोकिल-कलाप-सङ्गीत-सुखावहः, -हा, -हं, 'causing pleasure by the music of the voice of the cuckoo, blended with the hum emitted by the swarms of joyous bees.'

774. आत्मक or रूप, as occupying the last place in a complex relative, denotes 'composed of;' thus, हस्त्यश्व-रथ-पदाति-कर्मकरात्मकं बलं 'a force consisting of elephants, horses, chariots, infantry, and servants;' प्राग्जन्म-कृत-सुकृत-दुष्कृत-रूपे कर्मणी 'the two actions consisting of the good and evil done in a former birth.'

775. Complex compounds may sometimes have their second or middle member elided or omitted; thus, अभिज्ञान-शकुन्तला is really a complex compound, the whole being a descriptive, involving a dependent; but the middle member स्मृत is elided: see 745. *a.* Similarly, शाक-पार्थिवः 'the era-king' is for शाक-प्रिय-पार्थिवः 'the king (beloved) by the era;' विक्रमोर्वशी for विक्रम-प्राप्तोर्वशी 'Urvaśī gained by valour.'

a. Complex compounds expressive of comparison are not uncommon; as, जल-बिन्दु-लोल-चपलम्, -ला, -लं, 'unsteady as a trembling drop of water;' नलिनी-दल-तोय-तरलम्, -ला, -लं, 'tremulous as water on the leaf of a lotus;' the last two examples are complex. Compare 758. *a.*

b. A peculiar compound of this kind is formed from Dvandvas by adding the affix *iya*; thus, काक-तालीयम्, -या, -यं, 'like the story of the crow and the palm tree;' श्येन-कपोतीयम्, -या, -यं, 'like the story of the hawk and the pigeon.'

c. The substantive verb must often be supplied in connexion with a relative compound; as, आरम्भ-सदृशोदयम् 'his success was proportionate to his undertakings;' पीताम्भसि 'on his drinking water,' for तेन अम्भसि पीते सति.

776. Complex compound adverbs, or indeclinable compounds, involving other compounds, are sometimes found; as, स्व-गृह-निर्विशेषम् 'not differently from one's own house;' शब्दोच्चारणानन्तरं 'after uttering a sound;' स्तन-भार-विनमन्-मध्य-भङ्गानपेक्षं 'regardlessly of the curving of her waist bending under the weight of her bosom;' यथा-दृष्ट-श्रुतं 'as seen and heard.'

ANOMALOUS COMPOUNDS.

777. There are certain compounds which are too anomalous in their *formation* to admit of ready classification under any one of the preceding heads.

a. कल्प, देशीय, देश्य, रूपक, मात्र, affixed to crude bases, form anomalous compounds; see 80. XX. XXI.

b. There is a common compound formed by placing अन्तर after a crude base, to express 'another,' 'other;' as, स्थानान्तरं or देशान्तरं 'another place;' राजान्तरेण सह 'along with another king;' जन्मान्तराणि 'other births.'

c. Similarly, मात्र is added to express 'mere;' see 919.

d. पूर्व or पूर्वक or पुरःसर (meaning literally 'preceded by') may be added to crude bases to denote the manner in which any thing is done; as, क्रोधपूर्वं 'with anger;' पूजापूर्वकम् अन्नं ददौ 'he gave food with reverence.' See 792.

e. A peculiar compound is formed by the use of an ordinal number as the last member; thus, सारसद्वितीयम् 'accompanied by the Sáras;' सीतातृतीयम् (agreeing with रामम्) 'having Sítá *for* his third (companion),' i. e. including Lakshmaṇa; छायाद्वितीयम् (नलम्) 'Nala made double by his shadow;' मातृषष्ठाः (पाण्डवाः) 'the Páṇḍavas with their mother as the sixth;' वेदा आख्यानपञ्चमाः 'the Vedas with the Ákhyánas as a fifth.'

f. The following are peculiar; त्यक्तजीवितयोधी 'a fighter who abandons life;' अकुतोभयम्, -या, -यं, 'having no fear from any quarter;' अदृष्टपूर्वम्, -र्वा, -र्वं, 'never before seen;' सप्तरात्रोषितः 'one who has lodged seven nights.'

g. With regard to compounds like गन्तुकाम 'desirous of going,' see 871.

h. The Veda has some peculiar compounds; e.g. *vidad-vasu*, 'granting wealth;' *yávayad-dveshas*, 'defending from enemies;' *kshayad-víra*, 'ruling over men.' These are a kind of inverted Tat-purusha.

CHANGES OF CERTAIN WORDS IN CERTAIN COMPOUNDS.

778. The following is an alphabetical list of the substitutions and changes which take place in the final syllables of certain words when used in certain compounds.

अक्ष m. at end of various compounds for अक्षि n. 'the eye;' e.g. गवाक्ष 'a bull's eye (window);' लोहिताक्षम्, -क्षी, -क्षं, 'red-eyed.'—अङ्गुल for अङ्गुलि f. 'the finger;' e.g. द्व्यङ्गुलम्, -ला, -लं, 'measuring two fingers.'—अञ्जल m. for अञ्जलि m. 'joining the hands in reverence.'—अध्व for अध्वन् m. 'a road;' e.g. दूराध्वम्, -ध्वा, -ध्वं, 'distant (as a road).'—अनडुह in Dvandvas for अनडुह् m. 'a bull;' e.g. धेन्वनडुहे or -हौ 'cow and bull.'—अनस in Karma-dhárayas for अनस् n. 'a cart,' 'a carriage;' e.g. महानसम् 'a large cart.'—अयस in Karma-dhárayas for अयस् n. 'iron.'—अश्म in Karma-dhárayas for अश्मन् m. 'a stone.'—अष्टा in Dvigus and relative compounds for अष्टन्; e.g. अष्टागवं 'a car drawn by eight oxen;' अष्टाकपालम्, -ला, -लं, 'having eight receptacles.'—अष्ठीव in Dvandvas for अष्ठीवत् m. n. 'the knee;' e.g. ऊर्वष्ठीवं 'thigh and knee.'—अस्र for अस्रि f. 'an angle;' e.g. चतुरस्रम्, -स्रा, -स्रं, 'quadrangular.'—अह or अहृ for अहन् n. 'a day;' e.g. एकाहम् 'the period of one day;' पुण्याहं 'a holy-day;' अहर्पतिम् 'the lord of day.'—अह्न for अहन् n. 'a day;' e.g. पूर्वाह्णम् 'the forenoon.'—ईप for अप् f. 'water;' e.g. द्वीपम् 'an island;' अन्तरीपम् 'an island.'—ईर्म for ईर्मि 'a wound.'—उक्ष in Karma-dhárayas for उक्षन् m. 'an ox;' e.g. महोक्षम् 'a large ox.'—उद for उदक n. 'water;' e.g. उद-कुम्भस् 'a water-jar;' क्षीरोदस् 'the sea of milk.'—उरस in Karma-dhárayas for उरस् n. 'the breast;' e.g. अश्वोरसस्, -सी, -सं, 'broad-chested as a horse.'—उषासा an old dual form in Dvandvas for उषस् m. f. 'the dawn;' e.g. उषासा-सूर्यं 'dawn and sun.'—ऊधन् (f. ऊध्नी) for ऊधस् n. 'an udder;' e.g. पीनोध्नी 'having a full udder.'—ऊप for अप् f. 'water;' e.g. अनूपस्, -पा, -पं, 'waters.'—ऋच for ऋच्; see 779.—ककुद् for ककुद m. 'the top,' 'head;' e.g. त्रि-ककुद् 'three-peaked (mountain).'—कद् or का or कव for कु expressing *inferiority or diminution*; e.g. कदुष्ण or कोष्ण or कवोष्ण 'slightly warm;' कदक्षरं 'a bad letter;' कापुरुषस् 'a coward.'—काकुद् at end of Bahu-vrihis for काकुद m. 'the palate;' e.g. विकाकुद् 'having no palate.'—कुक्ष for कुक्षि m. 'the belly.'—खार for खारी; e.g. अर्धखारं 'half a khárí' (a measure).—गन्धि for गन्ध m. 'smell;' e.g. पूतिगन्धिस्, -न्धिस्, -न्धि, 'fetid.'—गव in Dvigus for गो m. f. 'an ox;' e.g. पञ्चगवं 'a collection of five cows.'—चतुर for चतुर् 'four;' see 779.—जम् for जाया 'a wife;' e.g. जम्पती du. 'husband and wife.'—जम्भन् for जम्भ 'a tooth;' e.g. तृण-जम्भा, -म्भा, -म्भ, 'grass-toothed,' 'graminivorous.'—जानि for जाया f. 'a wife;' e.g. युव-जानिस् 'having a young wife.'—ज्ञ and ज्ञु in Bahu-vrihis for जानु n. 'the knee;' e.g. प्रज्ञुस्, -ज्ञुस्, -ज्ञु, or प्रज्ञस्, -ज्ञा, -ज्ञं, 'bandy-kneed.'—तक्ष for तक्षन् m. 'a carpenter;' e.g. कौटतक्षस् 'an independent carpenter;' ग्रामतक्षस् 'the village carpenter.'—तमस in Karma-dhárayas (preceded by सम्, अव, or अन्ध) for तमस् n. 'darkness;' e.g. अवतमसं 'slight darkness.'—त्वच for त्वच्; see 779.—दत् (f. दती) for दन्त m. 'a tooth;' e.g. सुदन्, -दती, -दत्, 'having beautiful teeth.'—दम for जाया 'a wife;' e.g. दम्पती 'husband and wife' (according to some, 'the two lords of *dama* the house').—दिव at end and दिवा at beginning for दिवस m. 'the day;' e.g. नक्तं-दिवं 'night and day;' दिवा-निशं 'day and night.'—दुघ at end for दुह् 'yielding milk;' e.g. काम-दुघा 'the cow of plenty.'—द्यावा an old dual form for दिव् f. 'heaven;' द्यावापृथिव्यौ du. 'heaven and earth.'—धन्वन् at end of Bahu-vrihis for धनुस् n. 'a bow;' e.g. दृढ-धन्वा, -न्वा, -न्व, 'a strong archer.'—धर्मन् at end for धर्म m. 'virtue,' 'duty;' e.g. कल्याण-धर्मा, -र्मा, -र्म, 'virtuous.'—धुर for धुर् f. 'a load;' e.g. राज-धुरम् 'a royal load.'—न at the beginning of a few compounds for अ 'not;' e.g. नपुंसकम् 'a eunuch.'—नद for नदी 'a river;' e.g. पञ्चनदं 'the Panjáb.'—नस or नस् for नासिका 'nose;' e.g. खर-णास्, -णास्, -णस्, or खरणसस्, -सा, -सं, 'sharp-nosed.'—नाभ for नाभि f. 'the navel;' e.g. पद्म-नाभस् 'lotus-naveled,' a name of Vishṇu.—नाव for नौ f. 'a ship;' e.g. अर्धनावं 'half of a boat.'—पथ for पथिन् m. 'a road;' e.g. सुपथस् 'a good road.'—पद् and पाद् (fem. पदी) for पाद m. 'the foot;' e.g. पद्धिमं 'coldness of the feet;' द्विपाद्, -पदी, -पद्, 'a biped;' चतुष्पाद् 'a quadruped.'—पद् for पाद m. 'the foot;' e.g. पद्गस्, -गा, -गं, 'going on foot.'—पृत् for पृतना f. 'an army.'—पुंस in Dvandvas for पुंस् m. 'a male;' e.g. स्त्रीपुंसौ nom. du. 'man and woman.'—प्रजस् at end of Bahu-vrihis (preceded by अ, सु, or दुर्) for प्रजा f. 'people,' 'progeny;' e.g. बहुप्रजास्, -जास्, -जस्, 'having a numerous progeny.'—ब्रह्म for ब्रह्मन् m. 'a Brahman;' e.g. कुब्रह्म 'a contemptible Brahman.'—भूम for भूमि f. 'the earth;' e.g. उदग्भूमम् 'land towards the north.'—भ्रुव in Dvandvas for भ्रू f. 'the eye-brow;' e.g. अक्षिभ्रुवं 'eye and brow.'—मनस in Dvandvas for मनस् n. 'the mind;' e.g. वाङ्मनसे nom. du. n. 'speech and heart.'—मह and मही (preceded by पिता, माता, &c., 754. a) for महत् 'great;' e.g. पितामहस् 'grandfather.'—महा at beginning of Karma-dhárayas and Bahu-vrihis for महत् m. f. n. 'great;' but in Tat-purusha or dependent compounds महत् is retained, as in महदाश्रयः 'recourse to the great;' also before भूत 'become,' and words of a similar import, as महद्भूतस् 'one who has become great;' but महाभूतं 'an element.'—मूर्ध or मूर्ध at end of Bahu-vrihis (preceded by द्वि, त्रि, &c.) for मूर्धन् m. 'the head;' e.g. त्रिमूर्धस्, -र्धा, -र्धं.—मेधस् at end of Bahu-vrihis (preceded by अ, सु, दुर्, अल्प, मन्द) for मेधा f. 'intellect;' e.g. अल्पमेधास्, -धास्, -धस्.—रहस for रहस्, after अनु, अव, and तप्त; e.g. अनुरहसम् 'solitary.'—राज at end of Karma-dhárayas and Tat-purushas for राजन् m. 'a king' (see 151. a); e.g. परमराजस् 'a supreme monarch;' देवराजस् 'the king of the gods.' But occasional instances occur of राजन् at the end of Tat-purushas; e.g. विदर्भराजस्य gen. c. 'of the king of Vidarbha' (Nal. XI. 21).—रात्र at end of Dvigus, Karma-dhárayas, and Dvandvas, for रात्रि f. 'night;' e.g. अहोरात्रं 'day and night;' द्विरात्रं 'a period of two nights;' मध्यरात्रस् 'midnight.'—लोम (after अनु, अव, and प्रति) for लोमन् n. 'hair;' e.g. अनुलोमस्, -मा, -मं, 'with the hair.'—वर्चस in Karma-dhárayas for वर्चस् n. 'splendour;' e.g. ब्रह्मवर्चसं 'the power of a Brahman.'—श्रेयस in Karma-dhárayas and Bahu-vrihis for श्रेयस् n. 'virtue,' 'felicity;' e.g. निःश्रेयसस्, -सी, -सं, 'destitute of excellence or happiness.'—श्व or श्वा for श्वन् m. 'a dog;' e.g. अतिश्वस्, -श्वी, -श्वं, 'worse than a dog;' श्वापद m. 'a beast of prey;' श्वादन्त m. 'a dog's tooth.'—स at beginning of Avyayí-bhávas and Bahu-vrihis for सह 'with;' e.g. सकोपं 'with anger;' सपुत्रस् 'accompanied by a son' (सहपुत्र would be equally correct).—स for समान 'same;' e.g. सपिण्डस् 'one who eats the same cake.'—सक्थ in Karma-dhárayas and Bahu-vrihis for सक्थि n. 'the thigh;' e.g. असक्थस्, -क्था, -क्थं, 'having no thighs.'—सख in Karma-dhárayas and Dvigus for सखि m. 'a friend;' e.g. मरुत्सखस् 'the friend of the winds' (Indra).—सरस in Karma-dhárayas for सरस् n. 'a lake;' e.g. महासरसम् 'a great lake.'—साम (after अनु, अव, प्रति) for सामन् n. 'conciliation;' e.g. अनुसामम् 'friendly.'—हल for हलि m. 'a furrow;' e.g. अहलस्, -ला, -लं, 'unploughed.'—हृद् for हृदय n. 'the heart;' e.g. हृच्छयः 'sleeping in the heart;' सुहृद् m. 'a friend.'

779. It is evident from the above list that the most common substitution is that of अ *a* for the final vowel or final consonant and vowel of a word. Other bases ending in च्, ज्, श्, ष्, द्, म्, न्, र्, may add *a*; as, त्वच for त्वच् in वाक्त्वचं 'voice and skin;' यजुष for यजुस् in ऋग्यजुषं 'the Ṛig and Yajur-veda.' Also दृषद for दृषद्, आयुष for आयुस्, &c. Also ऋच for ऋच् in अर्धर्च, -र्चं, 'half a verse of the Veda;' and बह्वृच 'one conversant with the Ṛig-veda.'

a. Some words as the first member of a compound lengthen their finals; e.g. कोटर before वन (कोटरावणं 'a wood full of hollow trees'); अञ्जन before गिरि (अञ्जनागिरि 'name of a mountain'); विश्व before राज् and मित्र (विश्वाराट् 'a universal sovereign;' विश्वामित्र 'Viśvámitra'). This is more common in the Veda.

b. Some few shorten their finals, when they stand as the first member, especially nouns terminating in ऊ *ú* or ई *í*; e.g. भ्रु for भ्रू in भ्रुकुटि *f.* 'a frown;' ग्रामणि for ग्रामणी in ग्रामणिपुत्र 'the son of a harlot:' so लक्ष्मि-सम्पन्न for लक्ष्मीसम्पन्न 'endowed with good fortune,' Rámay. I. 19. 21.

c. A few feminine words in आ *á* (such as छाया, सभा, निशा, शाला, सेना) may be made neuter at the end of certain compounds; e.g. इक्षुच्छायं 'the shade of sugar-canes;' ईश्वरसभं 'an assembly of princes;' स्त्रीसभं 'an assembly of women;' श्वनिशं (or -शा) 'a night when dogs howl.'

d. A sibilant is sometimes inserted between two members of a compound; as, प्रायश्चित्तं, 'expiation of sin,' for प्राय-चित्तं; गोष्पदं 'a spot trodden by kine.'

780. Numerals, when preceded by particles, prepositions, or other numerals, may change their finals to अ *a*; or if their final letter be a consonant, may either drop that consonant or add अ *a* to it; thus, द्वित्र (nom. -त्रास्, -त्राः, -त्राणि) 'two or three;' पञ्चष (nom. -षास्, -षाः, -षाणि) 'five or six;' उपचतुर (nom. -रास्) 'nearly four.'

e. अहं is found in the beginning of certain anomalous compounds (such as अहङ्कार, अहम्पूर्विका, &c.) for मद् or अस्मद् 'I.'

Compound Nouns formed from roots combined with Prepositions.

781. In the next section it will be shown that the combination of roots with prepositions prevails most extensively in Sanskṛit. From roots thus combined nouns of the most various significations may be formed; thus, from हृ 'to seize,' with वि and अव, is formed व्यवहार 'practice;' from कृ 'to do,' with अनु, अनुकार 'imitation.' Almost every line in every Sanskṛit book affords an example of this kind of compound.

SECTION II.

COMPOUND VERBS.

782. The learner might look over the list of 2000 simple roots, and well imagine that in some of these would be contained every

possible variety of idea, and that the aid of prepositions and adverbial prefixes to expand and modify the sense of each root would be unnecessary. But in real fact there are comparatively few Sanskrit roots in common use; and whilst those that are so appear in a multitude of different forms by the prefixing of one or two or even three prepositions, the remainder are almost useless for any practical purposes, except the formation of nouns. Hence it is that compound verbs are of more frequent occurrence than simple ones.

They are formed in two ways: 1st, by combining roots with prepositions; 2dly, by combining the auxiliaries कृ 'to do' and भू 'to be' with adverbs, or nouns converted into adverbs.

Compound Verbs formed by combining Prepositions with roots.

783. The following list exhibits the prepositions chiefly used in combination with roots:

a. अति *ati*, 'across,' 'beyond,' 'over;' as, अतिया, अती (pres. अत्येति, &c.), अतिक्रम्, 'to pass by,' 'to pass along,' 'to transgress.'

b. अधि *adhi*, 'above,' 'upon,' 'over;' as, अधिष्ठा 'to stand over,' 'to preside' (pres. अधितिष्ठति); अधिरुह् 'to climb upon;' अधिशी 'to lie upon;' अधिगम् 'to go over towards;' अधी 'to go over,' in the sense of 'reading.' The initial अ *a* is rarely rejected in Epic poetry; as, धिष्ठित for अधिष्ठित.

c. अनु *anu*, 'after;' as, अनुचर् 'to follow;' अनुष्ठा 'to follow,' in the sense of 'performing;' अनुकृ 'to imitate;' अनुमन् 'to assent.' With भू it signifies 'to experience,' 'to enjoy.'

d. अन्तर् *antar*, 'between,' 'within' (Latin *inter*); as, अन्तर्धा 'to place within,' 'to conceal,' in pass. 'to vanish;' अन्तर्भू 'to be within;' अन्तश्चर् 'to walk in the midst.'

e. अप *apa*, 'off,' 'away,' 'from' (ἀπό); as, अपगम्, अपया, अपे (from अप and इ), 'to go away;' अपनी 'to lead away;' अपकृष् 'to abstract;' अपवह् 'to bear away.' It also implies 'detraction;' as, अपवद् 'to defame.'

f. अपि *api*, 'on,' 'over' (ἐπί), only used with धा and नह्; as, अपिधा 'to cover over;' अपिनह् 'to bind on.' The initial अ *a* is often rejected, leaving पिधा, पिनह्.

g. अभि *abhi*, 'to,' 'unto,' 'towards;' as, अभिया, अभी, 'to go towards;' अभिधाव् 'to run towards;' अभिवीक्ष् 'to behold;' अभिवद् or अभिधा (see धा at 664) 'to address,' 'to accost,' 'to speak to,' 'to salute.'

h. अव *ava*, 'down,' 'off;' as, अवरुह्, अवतॄ, 'to descend;' अवेक्ष् 'to look down;' अवक्षिप् 'to throw down,' 'to scatter;' अवकृत् 'to cut off.' It also implies 'disparagement;' as, अवज्ञा 'to despise;' अवधीर् 'to insult.' With धा (3d c. अवदधाति), 'to attend.' The initial अ *a* may be optionally rejected from अवगाह 'bathing.'

i. आ *ā*, 'to,' 'towards,' 'near to' (Latin *ad*); as, आविश् 'to enter;' आक्रम् 'to go towards;' आरुह् 'to mount up.' When prefixed to गम्, या, and इ, 'to go,' and दा 'to give,' it reverses the action; thus, आगम्, आया, आइ, 'to come;' आदा 'to take.' With चर्, 'to practise.'

j. उद् *ud* or उत् *ut*, 'up,' 'upwards,' 'out' (opposed to नि); as, उच्चर् (48), उदि, 'to go up,' 'to rise' (pres. उदयामि, 1st conj.); उड्डी 'to fly up;' उद्धन् 'to strike up' (उद् and हन्, 50); उद्धृ (उद् and हृ, see 50) 'to extract;' उन्मिष् and उन्मील् (47) 'to open the eyes;' उच्छिद्, उत्कृत्, 'to cut up;' उन्मूल् 'to root up;' उत्क्षिप् 'to lift up' (उद् and क्षिप्, 49).

When prefixed *immediately* to स्था and स्तम्भ् it causes the elision of *s*; as, उत्था 'to stand up;' उत्तम्भ् 'to prop up.' In some cases it reverses the action; as, from पत् 'to fall,' उत्पत् 'to leap up;' from नम् 'to bend down,' उन्नम् (47) 'to raise up;' from यम् 'to keep down,' उद्यम् 'to lift up.'

k. उप *upa*, 'to,' 'towards' (ὑπό), 'near,' 'down,' 'under,' joined like आ and अभि to roots of motion; as, उपया 'to approach;' उपचर् 'to wait upon;' उपस्था 'to stay near,' 'to be present,' 'to arrive.' With विश् (6th c. उपविशामि), 'to sit down;' with आस्, 'to sit near.' Observe—उप with ओषति (from उष्) = उपोषति 'he burns;' see 784. *a.*

l. नि *ni*, 'in,' 'on,' 'down,' 'downwards,' 'under' (opposed to उद्); as, निपत् 'to fall down;' नियम् 'to suppress;' निमिष् and निमील् 'to close the eyes;' निक्षिप्, निधा, न्यस्, 'to lay down,' 'to deposit;' निविश् 'to go within,' 'to encamp.' With वृत् 'to return,' 'to desist;' with शम्, 'to hear.' In some cases it does not alter, or simply intensifies the sense; as, निहन् 'to kill outright.'

m. निस् *nis* or निर् *nir*, 'out;' as, निष्क्रम् (see 72), निर्गम्, निःसृ (71. *a. c*), 'to go out,' 'to come out;' निष्कृत् 'to cut up;' निर्वृत् 'to come to an end,' 'to cease;' निश्चि (71. *b*) 'to determine.'

n. परा *parā*, 'back,' 'backwards' (παρά), combined with जि and भू in the sense of 'defeat;' as, पराजि 'to overcome' (cf. παρανικάω, Æsch. Choë.); पराभू 'to be defeated.' When joined with इ, 2d conj., it signifies 'to retire towards' (pres. परैमि); when with इ or अय्, 1st c. Ātm., 'to run away,' 'to retreat,' *r* being changed to *l* (pres. पलाये).

o. परि *pari*, 'around,' 'about' (περί, *per*); as, परिवेष्ट्, परिवृ, 'to surround;' परिचर्, परिगम्, 'to go round;' परीक्ष् 'to look round,' 'to examine;' परिवृत् 'to turn round;' परिधाव् 'to run round.' When prefixed to कृ it signifies 'to adorn,' and स् is inserted, परिष्कृ. With भू, 'to despise,' and with हृ, 'to avoid.' It sometimes merely gives intensity or completeness to the action; as, परित्यज् 'to abandon altogether;' परिज्ञा 'to ascertain completely.'

p. प्र *pra*, 'before,' 'forward' (πρό, *pro*, *pra*); as, प्रगम्, प्रसृ, 'to proceed;' प्रयम् 'to set before,' 'to present;' प्रारभ् 'to begin;' प्रवृत् 'to proceed,' 'to begin;' प्रधाव् 'to run forward;' प्रस्था 'to set out,' 'to advance;' प्रभू 'to be superior,' 'to prevail;' प्रदृश् 'to foresee.' With लभ्, 'to deceive.' Observe—प्र with ऋच्छति 'he goes,' makes प्रार्च्छति (or प्रार्छति) 'he goes on quickly;' प्र with एषय्, causal base of इष् 'to go,' makes प्रेषयामि 'I send.' Similarly, प्र + एजते = प्रेजते 'he trembles;' and प्र + ओषति (from उष्) = प्रोषति 'he burns.' See 784. *a.*

The *r* of *pra* influences a following nasal by 58; as, प्रणम् 'to bend before,' 'to salute.' Sometimes प्र does not alter the sense of a root, as in प्राप् 'to obtain' (5th c.; see 681).

q. प्रति *prati*, 'against,' 'to,' 'towards,' 'back again' (πρός); as, प्रतियुध् 'to fight against;' प्रती 'to go towards' (pres. प्रत्येमि); प्रतिगम् 'to go towards,' 'to return;' प्रतिकृ 'to counteract;' प्रतिहन् 'to beat back,' 'to repel;' प्रतिवच् 'to answer;' प्रतिलभ् 'to recover;' प्रतिनी 'to lead back;' प्रतिनन्द् 'to re-salute.' With श्रु, 'to promise;' with पद्, 'to arrive at,' 'to obtain;' with ईक्ष्, 'to wait for,' 'to expect.' Sometimes it alters the sense very slightly; as, प्रतिवस् 'to dwell near or at.'

r. वि *vi*, 'apart,' 'asunder,' implying 'separation,' 'distinction,' 'distribution,' 'dispersion' (Latin *dis*, *se*); as, विचर् 'to wander about;' विचल् 'to vacillate;' विहृ 'to roam for pleasure;' विकृ 'to dissipate;' विदृ 'to tear asunder;' विभज् 'to divide;' विविच् 'to distinguish.' Sometimes it gives a privative signification; as, वियुज् 'to disunite;' विस्मृ 'to forget;' विक्री 'to sell.' With कृ, 'to change for the worse.' Sometimes it has little apparent influence on the root; as, विनश् 'to perish,' or 'to perish entirely;' विचिन्त् 'to think.'

s. सम् *sam*, 'with,' 'together with' (σύν, con); as, सञ्चि, सङ्ग्रह्, 'to collect;' संयुज् 'to join together;' सङ्गम् 'to meet together;' सम्पद् 'to happen;' संक्षिप् 'to contract.' With कृ it signifies 'to perfect,' and स् is inserted, संस्कृ. It is often prefixed without altering the sense; as, सञ्जन् 'to be produced.'

t. दुस् *dus* or दुर् *dur*, 'badly,' and सु *su*, 'well,' are also prefixed to verbs; see 726. *d. f.*

u. Also other indeclinable prefixes; thus, अस्तम् 'decline' is compounded with इ 'to go,' in the sense of 'to go down,' 'to set;' तिरस् 'across,' with धा in the sense of 'to conceal,' with गम् 'to disappear,' with कृ 'to revile;' श्रत् with धा 'to believe.'

784. Two prepositions are often combined with a root; as, व्यादा (वि + आ) 'to open;' व्यापद् (10th c.) 'to kill;' उपागम् (उप + आ) 'to go under,' 'to undergo,' 'to arrive at;' समे (सम् + आ + root इ) 'to assemble;' प्रणिपत् (प्र + नि, 58) 'to prostrate one's self;' प्रोद्धृ (प्र + उद् + root हृ) 'to raise up:' and occasionally three; as, प्रव्याहृ (प्र + वि + आ) 'to predict;' प्रत्युदाहृ (प्रति + उद् + आ) 'to answer.' Other combinations of three prepositions, occasionally prefixed to roots, are सं + उप + आ; अभि + वि + आ; सं + अभि + प्र; उप + सं + प्र; अनु + सं + वि.

a. Observe—Final अ *a* and आ *á* of a preposition combine with the initial ऋ *ri* of a root into *ár*, and are rejected before initial ए *e* and ओ *o* (except in forms from the roots इ *i*, 'to go,' and एध् 'to increase'). See 38 *e. i*; and see प्र and उप above: but in other cases prepositions ending in vowels combine with roots beginning with vowels according to the rules of Sandhi; thus, आ with इ 'to go' becomes ए (32), and in pres. ऐमि (आ + इमि 33), &c.; in impf. आयम्, ऐत् (64.–33), &c.; in pot. एयां (आ + इयां), &c.; in impv. आयानि (आ + अयानि), &c. Similarly, अव with इमि becomes अवैमि by 33.

b. Observe also, a sibilant is generally inserted between the prepositions सम्, उप, परि, प्रति, अव, and the roots कृ 'to do' and कॄ 'to scatter;' see above under परि and सम्. Similarly, from अप and कॄ is formed अपस्कर 'excrement.'

c. The final *i* of अभि, प्रति, परि, नि, is optionally lengthened in forming certain nouns from compound verbs; as, अभीसार, प्रतीकार, परीहास, नीहार.

785. In conjugating compound verbs formed with prepositions, neither the augment nor the reduplication change their position, but remain attached to the root*; as, पर्यणयं, impf. of नी, with परि; उपाविशं, impf. of विश्, with उप; अन्वतिष्ठं, impf. of स्था, with अनु; अभिचक्राम, perf. of क्रम्, with अभि; उपसंजहार, perf. of हृ, with उप and सम्.

a. In the Veda, as in Homer, prepositions may be separated from the root by other words; as, आ त्वा विशन्तु 'let them enter thee.'

786. Grammarians restrict certain roots to either Parasmai-pada or Átmane-pada when in combination with particular prepositions or when peculiar meanings are involved†. Some instances have been already given at 243. *a.* Most of the examples specified by Páṇini in the 3d ch. of his 1st Adhyáya are here added. The 3d sing. present will be given, the termination either in *ti* or *te* marking the pada to which in each case the root is supposed to be limited.

अस् 'to throw' is generally Parasmai, and ऊह् 'to reason' is generally Átmane, but combined with any prep. may take either pada.—कृ 'to do;' *anu-karoti*, 'he imitates;' *pará-karoti*, 'he does well;' *adhi-kurute*, 'he overcomes;' *ut-kurute*, 'he informs against,' 'reviles;' *ud-á-kurute*, 'he reviles;' *upa-kurute*, 'he worships;' *upa-s-kurute* (784. *b*), 'he prepares;' *upa-s-karoti*, 'he polishes;' *pará-karoti*, 'he rejects;' *pra-kurute*, 'he offers violence,' 'he recites (stories).'—कॄ 'to scatter;' *apa-s-kirate* (784. *b*), 'he (the cock) throws up earth;' but *apa-kirati*, 'he scatters (as flowers).'—क्रम् 'to go;' *á-kramate*, 'he (the sun) ascends;' but *á-krámati* when not in the sense of 'the rising of a luminary, &c.;' *vi-kramate*, 'he (the horse) steps out;' but *vi-krámati*, 'it (the joint) splits in two;' *upa-kramate* or *pra-kramate*, 'he is valiant;' but *upa-krámati*, 'he approaches;' and *pra-krámati*, 'he departs.'—क्री 'to buy;' *ava-kríṇíte*, *pari-kríṇíte*, 'he buys;' *vi-kríṇíte*, 'he sells;' but *krí* alone takes either pada.—क्रीड् 'to play;' *á-kríḍate* or *anu-kríḍate*, 'he sports;' *pari-kríḍate*, 'he plays about;' *san-(sam)-kríḍate*, 'he

* There are a few exceptions to this rule in the Mahá-bhárata; as in अभ्यववदत् (Mahá-bhár. Selections, p. 33).

† In Epic poetry, however, there is much laxity; e. g. लभ् and भाष्, which are properly Átmane-pada, are found in Parasmai. Instances of passive verbs taking Parasmai terminations have been given at 253. *b*. On the other hand, मुद् 'to rejoice,' which is properly a Parasmai-pada verb, is found in the Átmane.

plays;' but sam-(sam)-kriḍati, 'it (the wheel) creaks.'—क्षिप् 'to throw;' ati-kshipati, 'he throws beyond;' abhi-kshipati, 'he throws on;' prati-kshipati, 'he throws back or towards.'—क्ष्णु 'to sharpen;' sam-(sam)-kshṇute, 'he sharpens.'—गम् 'to go;' á-gamayate, 'he delays or waits patiently;' vy-ati-gaććhanti, 'they go against each other;' sam-(sam)-gaććhati when motion towards any thing is implied, as 'he goes towards (the village);' but Átmane in the sense of 'he goes with' or 'agrees with.'—गॄ 'to swallow;' sam-(for sam)-girate, 'he promises,' 'he proclaims;' but sam-girati, 'he swallows;' ava-girate, 'he swallows.'—चर् 'to go;' uć(for ud)-ćarate, 'he goes astray;' uć-ćarati, 'it (the tear) overflows;' sam-(for sam)-ćarate or sam-ud-á-ćarate, 'he goes in a chariot.'—जि 'to conquer;' see 243. a.—ज्ञा 'to know;' apa-jánite, 'he denies (the debt);' prati-jánite or sam-jánite, 'he acknowledges.' Without a prep. this root is restricted to either pada if certain meanings are involved; as, sarpisho (for sarpishá) jánite, 'he engages (in sacrifice) by means of ghee;' gám jánite, 'he knows (his own) cow;' svám gám jánáti or jánite, 'he knows his own cow.'—नी 'to lead;' un(for ud)-nayate, 'he lifts up;' upa-nayate, 'he invests (with the sacred thread);' vi-nayate, 'he pays,' or 'he grants,' or 'he restrains;' vi-nayati, 'he takes away' (as 'the anger of his master'); vi-nayati, 'he turns away (his cheek).' Without a prep. this root is Átmane if it means 'to excel,' or 'to ascertain.'—नु 'to praise;' á-nute, 'he praises.'—तप् 'to burn;' ut-tapate or vi-tapate, 'he warms;' ut-tapate or vi-tapate, 'he warms (his own hand, &c.).' Without a prep. this root is Átmane, 4th c., if it means 'to perform penance.'—दा 'to give;' á-datte, 'he receives;' vy-á-dadáti, 'he opens (his mouth);' vy-á-datte, 'he opens (the mouth of another);' sam-yaććhate, 'he gives' (as dásyá, 'to the female slave,' the instr. being used for the dative).—दृश् 'to see;' sam-paśyate, 'he considers thoroughly.'—नाथ् 'to ask for;' always Átmane if used with gen. c., as madhuna náthate, 'he asks for honey.'—प्रछ् 'to ask;' á-priććhate, 'he bids adieu to;' sam-priććhate, 'he interrogates.'—भुज् 'to eat' is Átmane if it means 'to eat,' 'to possess,' or 'to suffer;' but Parasmai if it means 'to protect.'—मृष् 'to bear;' pari-mrishyati, 'he endures or forgives.'—यम् 'to restrain;' á-yaććhate, '(the tree) spreads;' á-yaććhate, 'he stretches out (his hand);' but á-yaććhati, 'he draws up' (as a rope from a well); upa-yaććhate, 'he takes (a woman) to wife;' but upa-yaććhati, 'he takes the wife (of another);' á-yaććhate, 'he puts on (clothes);' ud-yaććhate, 'he takes up (a load);' but ud-yaććhati, 'he studies vigorously (the Veda, &c.);' sam-yaććhate, 'he collects' (or stacks as rice, &c.)—युज् 'to join;' ud-yun-kte, 'he makes effort;' anu-yun-kte, 'he examines;' ni-yun-kte, 'he appoints;' pra-yun-kte, 'he applies;' but pra-yunakti, 'he sets in order (sacrificial vessels).'—रम् 'to sport;' upa-ramati, 'he causes to refrain*;' á-ramati, 'he rests;' see also vi-ramati 243. a.—लू 'to cut;' vy-ati-lunite, 'he performs cutting (of wood) which was the office of another.'—वद् 'to speak;' anu-vadate, 'he speaks after or like' (with gen.); but anu-vadati, 'he imitates' (as giram, 'a voice,' acc. c.); upa-vadate, 'he coaxes,' 'he advises;' vi-pra-vadante or vi-pra-vadanti, 'they dispute;'

* This is an instance of a simple verb involving the sense of a causal.

sam-pra-vadante, 'they speak together;' but *sam-pra-vadanti*, 'they (the birds) sing together;' *apa-vadate*, 'he reviles improperly;' but *apa-vadati*, 'he speaks against.' Without prep. *vad* is Átmane, 'to be learned in interpreting' (the Śástras), or 'to be earnest in the study of any thing' (as agriculture, &c.).—वह् 'to carry;' *pra-vahati*, 'it (the river) flows along.'—विद् 'to know;' *saṃ-vitte*, 'he is conscious;' *saṃ-vidate* or *saṃ-vidrate*, 'they are conscious' (308).—विश् 'to enter;' see 243. *a.*—शप् 'to swear;' *śapate*, 'he swears at' (with dat.).—श्रु 'to hear;' *saṃ-śṛiṇoti*, 'he hears (the speech);' but *saṃ-śṛiṇute*, 'he hears well' (intransitively).—स्था 'to stand;' *ava-tishṭhate*, 'he waits patiently;' *pra-tishṭhate*, 'he sets out;' *vi-tishṭhate*, 'he stands apart;' *san(for sam)-tishṭhate*, 'he stays with;' *upa-tishṭhate*, 'he worships,' 'he attends on.' Without prep. *sthá* takes the Átmane when it denotes 'adhering to,' 'depending on,' as *tishṭhate Kṛishṇáya*, 'he places his trust in Kṛishṇa;' but *upa-tishṭhati*, 'he waits on' (not in a religious sense, and governing an accus. c.); *ut-tishṭhate*, 'he aspires' (as 'to salvation'); but *ut-tishṭhati*, 'he rises' (as 'from a seat').—हन् 'to strike;' *á-hate* (see 654), 'he or it strikes' ('himself or itself,' the object being omitted); but *á-hanti vṛishabham*, 'he strikes the bull.'—स्वृ 'to sound;' *saṃ-svarate*, 'it sounds clearly.'—हृ 'to seize;' *anu-harate*, 'he takes after (the disposition of his father or mother),' otherwise *anu-harati*.—ह्वे 'to call;' *upa-hvayate* or *ni-hvayate* or *vi-hvayate* or *saṃ-hvayate*, 'he calls,' 'he invokes;' *á-hvayate*, 'he challenges' (as an enemy); but *á-hvayati*, 'he calls (his son).'

a. Some causals are also restricted to either Parasmai or Átmane, according to the preposition prefixed or the meaning involved; thus the causal of मुह् with परि, meaning 'to bewitch,' is limited to the Átmane. So also, गृध् 'to be greedy,' when its causal means 'to deceive,' is restricted to the Átmane: and the causal of वञ्च्, meaning 'to deceive,' takes the Átmane; meaning 'to avoid,' the Parasmai. Again, कृ in the causal, when joined with *mithyá*, and signifying 'to pronounce badly,' takes the Parasmai; but only in the sense of doing so *once*. In the sense of 'causing a false alarm' it requires the Átmane; but the above specimens will suffice to show the little profit likely to be derived from pursuing this part of the subject farther.

Compound Verbs formed by combining Adverbs with the roots कृ kṛi *and* भू bhú.

787. These are of two kinds; 1st, those formed by combining adverbs with कृ 'to make' and भू 'to become;' 2dly, those formed by combining nouns used adverbially with these roots.

a. Examples of the first kind are, अलंकृ 'to adorn;' आविष्कृ 'to make manifest' (see 72); बहिष्कृ 'to eject;' पुरस्कृ 'to place in front,' 'to follow;' तिरस्कृ 'to deprive;' सत्कृ 'to entertain as a guest;' नमस्कृ 'to revere;' आविर्भू, प्रादुर्भू, 'to become manifest,' &c.

788. In forming the second kind, the final of a crude word, being

a or *á*, is changed to *í*; as, from सज्ज, सज्जीकृ 'to make ready,' सज्जीभू 'to become ready;' from कृष्ण, कृष्णीकृ 'to blacken;' from परिखा 'a ditch,' परिखीकृ 'to convert into a ditch:' and sometimes *a* becomes *á*; as, प्रियाकृ 'to please,' from प्रिय. A final *i* or *u* is lengthened; as, from शुचि, शुचीभू 'to become pure;' from लघु, लघूकृ 'to lighten.' A final *ṛi* is changed to री *rí*; as, from मातृ, मात्रीभू 'to become a mother.' A final *as* and *an* become *í*; as, from सुमनस्, सुमनीभू 'to be of good mind;' from राजन्, राजीभू 'to be a king.'

a. But the greater number of compounds of this kind are formed from crude nouns in *a*. The following are other examples: तृणीकृ 'to esteem as a straw;' काष्ठीकृ 'to stiffen;' एकचित्तीभू 'to fix the mind on one object;' स्वीकृ 'to make one's own,' 'to claim as one's own;' मैत्रीभू 'to become friendly.' Substantives are sometimes formed from these; as, मैत्रीभाव 'the state of being friendly,' 'friendship.'

b. Observe—This change of a final to *í* before *kṛi* and *bhú* is technically said to be caused by the affix *cvi*, and the change to *á* by *ḍác*. These compounds often occur as passive participles; thus, अलंकृत 'adorned;' प्रादुर्भूत 'become manifest;' सज्जीकृत 'made ready;' लघूकृत 'lightened;' स्वीकरणीय 'to be agreed to.'

789. Sometimes सात्, placed after a crude noun, is used to form a compound verb of this kind; as, from जल 'water,' जलसात्कृ 'to reduce to liquid;' from भस्मन् 'ashes,' भस्मसात्कृ (57) 'to reduce to ashes.' Compare 725. *e*.

SECTION III.

COMPOUND ADVERBS.

790. Compound adverbs are formed, 1st, by combining adverbs, prepositions, and adverbial prefixes, with nouns in the nom. or accus. singular neuter; 2dly, by placing adverbs, or adjectives used as adverbs, after the crude base of nouns.

a. The first kind are identical with indeclinable compounds; see 760.

791. Most of the adverbs at 731 may be placed after the crude base of nouns; thus, बालकसमीपं 'near the child;' रक्षार्थं 'for the sake of protection;' प्रजार्थं 'for the sake of offspring;' किमर्थं 'on what account?' शब्दोच्चारणानन्तरं 'after uttering a sound.' See also 777. *d*.

792. The indeclinable participle आरभ्य, 'having begun,' is joined with अद्य, 'to-day' (अद्यारभ्य), in the sense of 'from this time forward;' and with the crude of words to express 'beginning from;' see 925. प्रभृति is used adverbially in the same sense; as, जन्मप्रभृति 'from birth upwards;' तदाप्रभृति 'from that time forward.'

CHAPTER IX.

SYNTAX.

793. Sanskrit syntax, unlike that of Greek and Latin, offers fewer difficulties to the student than the other portions of the Grammar. In fact, the writer who has fully explained the formation of compounds has already more than half completed his exposition of the laws which regulate the order, arrangement, and collocation of the words in a sentence (*vākya-vinyāsa, vākya-viveka, padānvaya*).

794. Observe—In the present chapter on Syntax, that the subject may be made as clear as possible, each word will be separated from the next, and vowels will not be allowed to coalesce, although such coalition be required by the laws of combination. When compounds are introduced into the examples, a dot will often be placed underneath, to mark the division of the words. Much vagueness and uncertainty, however, may be expected to attach to the rules propounded, when it is remembered that Sanskṛit literature consists almost entirely of poetry, and that the laws of syntax are ever prone to yield to the necessities of metrical composition.

THE ARTICLE.

795. There is no indefinite article in classical Sanskṛit; but कश्चित् (228) and in modern Sanskṛit एक (238) are sometimes used to supply the place of such an article; thus, एकस्मिन् प्रदेशे 'in a certain country;' कश्चित् शृगालः 'a certain jackal.' The definite article may not unfrequently be expressed by the pronoun स (220); thus, स पुरुषः may mean simply 'the man,' not necessarily 'that man.'

CONCORD OF THE VERB WITH THE NOMINATIVE CASE.

796. The verb must agree with the nominative case in number and person; as, अहं करवाणि 'I must perform.'

a. Other examples are, त्वम् अवधेहि 'do thou attend;' स ददाति 'he gives;' आवां ब्रूवः 'we two say;' कपोता ऊचुः 'the pigeons said;' राजा मन्त्री च जग्मतुः 'the king and minister went;' यावत् चन्द्रार्कौ तिष्ठतः 'as long as the moon and sun remain;' युवां विमृशतं 'do you two reflect;' यूयम् आयात 'do ye come;' सज्जनाः पूज्यन्ते 'good men are honoured;' वाति पवनः 'the wind blows;' उदयति शशाङ्कः 'the moon rises;' स्फुटति पुष्पं 'the flower blossoms.'

b. Observe—The verb is commonly, though not always, placed last in the sentence.

797. When a participle takes the place of the verb, it must agree with the nominative in number and *gender*; as, स गतः 'he went;'

सा गता 'she went;' नार्याव् ऊचतुः 'the two women spoke;' राजा हतः 'the king was killed;' बन्धनानि छिन्नानि 'the bonds were cut.'

a. Sometimes, when it is placed between two or more nominative cases, it agrees with one only; as, तद्वधूः प्रबोधिता पुत्रश्च 'his wife and son were awakened.'

b. Very often the copula, or verb which connects the subject with the predicate, is omitted; when, if an adjective stand in the place of the verb, it will follow the rules of concord in gender and number; as, धनं दुर्लभं 'wealth is difficult of attainment;' आवां कृताहारौ 'we two have finished eating.' But if a substantive stand in the place of the verb, no concord of gender or number need take place; as, सम्पदः पदम् आपदां 'successes are the road to misfortune.'

CONCORD OF THE ADJECTIVE WITH THE SUBSTANTIVE.

798. An adjective, participle, or adjective pronoun, qualifying a substantive, when not compounded with it, must agree with the substantive in gender, number, and case; as, साधुः पुरुषः 'a good man;' महद् दुःखं 'great pain;' एतेषु पूर्वोक्तेषु देशेषु 'in these before-mentioned countries;' त्रीणि मित्राणि 'three friends.'

CONCORD OF THE RELATIVE WITH THE ANTECEDENT.

799. The relative must agree with the antecedent noun in gender, number, and person; but in Sanskrit the relative pronoun generally precedes the noun to which it refers, this noun being put in the same case with the relative, and the pronoun स follows in the latter clause of the sentence; as, यस्य नरस्य बुद्धिः स बलवान् 'of whatever man there is intellect, he is strong.'

a. The noun referred to by the relative may also be joined with स, as यस्य बुद्धिः स नरो बलवान्; or may be omitted altogether, as यद् प्रतिज्ञातं तद् पालय 'what you have promised, that abide by;' येषाम् अपत्यानि खादितानि तैः (पक्षिभिः understood) जिज्ञासा समारब्धा 'by those (birds) whose young ones were devoured an inquiry was set on foot;' यः सर्वान् विषयान् प्राप्नुयाद् यश्च एतान् उपेक्षेत तयोर् विषयोपेक्षकः श्रेयान् 'he who would obtain all objects of sense, and he who despises them, of the two the despiser is the best.'

800. The relative sometimes stands alone, an antecedent noun or pronoun being understood, from which it takes its gender and number; as, श्रुतेन किं यो न धर्मम् आचरेत् 'Of what use is scriptural knowledge (to one) who does not practise virtue!' धनेन किं यो न ददाति 'What is the use of wealth (to him) who does not give!'

a. Sometimes, though rarely, the antecedent noun precedes the relative in the natural order; as, न सा भार्या यस्यां भर्ता न तुष्यति 'she is not a wife in whom the husband does not take pleasure.'

801. तावत् and यावत् stand to each other in the relation of demonstrative and

relative; as, यावन्ति तस्य द्वीपस्य वस्तूनि तावन्ति अस्माकम् उपनेतव्यानि 'as many products as belong to that island, so many are to be brought to us.' See also 876.

a. Similarly, यादृश and तादृश; as, यादृशं वृत्तं तादृशं तस्मै कथितवन्तः 'as the event occurred, so they related it to him.'

SYNTAX OF SUBSTANTIVES.

802. Under this head it is proposed to explain the construction of substantives, without special reference to the verbs which govern them; and for this purpose it will be desirable to exhibit examples beginning with the nominative case.

Nominative case.

803. A substantive simply and absolutely expressed must be placed in the nominative case; as, हितोपदेशः 'the Hitopadeśa;' भट्टिकाव्यं 'the poem of Bhaṭṭi.'

a. Two nominative cases in different numbers may be placed in apposition to each other; as, तृणानि शय्या 'grass as a bed.'

Accusative case.

804. Substantives are not found in the accusative, unconnected with verbs or participles, except as expressing '*duration of time*' or '*space*.' See 821.

Instrumental case.

805. This case yields a variety of senses. The most usual is that of '*the agent*' and '*the instrument*' or '*means*' by which any thing is done; as, मया (उक्तं) 'by me it was said;' व्याधेन (पाशो योजितः) 'by the fowler a snare was laid;' वेदाध्ययनेन 'by the study of the Vedas;' स्वचक्षुषा 'with one's own eye.'

806. It also has the force of '*with*' in expressing other collateral ideas; as, बलीयसा स्पर्द्धा 'vying with the strong;' मित्रेण संलापः 'conversation with a friend;' पशुभिः साम्यं 'equality with beasts;' पितृगोचरेण 'with the knowledge of (his) father:' especially when '*accompaniment*' is intended; as, शिष्येण गुरुः 'the master with his pupil;' आत्मना पञ्चमः 'the fifth with myself,' i. e. 'myself and four others.'

807. The other senses yielded by this case are, '*through*,' '*by reason of*,' '*on account of*;' as, कृपया 'through compassion;' तेन अपराधेन 'on account of that transgression:' especially in the case of abstract nouns formed with ता (80. XXIII); as, मूढतया 'through infatuation.'

a. '*According to,*' '*by:*' as, विधिना 'according to rule;' मम सम्मतेन 'according to my opinion;' जात्या 'by birth.'

b. '*The manner*' in which any thing is done, as denoted in English by the adverbial affix 'ly,' or by the prepositions 'in,' 'at;' as, बाहुल्येन 'in abundance;' धर्मेण 'virtuously;' यथेच्छया or स्वेच्छया 'at pleasure;' सुखेन 'at ease;' अनेन विधिना 'in this way;' महता स्नेहेन (निवसतः) 'they both dwell together in great intimacy;' (नृपः सर्वभूतानि अभिभवति) तेजसा 'a king surpasses all beings in glory;' मनसा (न कर्तव्यं) 'such a deed must not even be imagined in the mind;' मानुषरूपेण 'in human form;' प्रतिबन्धेन 'for a hindrance.'

808. Substantives expressive of '*want*,' '*need*,' may be joined with the instrumental of the thing wanted; as, चर्चया न प्रयोजनं 'there is no occasion for inquiry;' मम सेवकेन न प्रयोजनं 'there is no need of me as a servant;' तृणेन कार्यं 'there is use for a straw.'

809. '*The price*' for which any thing is done may be in the instrumental; as, पञ्चभिः पुराणैर् (याति दासतां) 'for five Purāṇas he becomes a slave;' महद्भिर् धनैर् (युध्यन्ते) 'they fight for great rewards.' Similarly, प्राणपरित्यागमूल्येन (श्रीर् न लभ्यते) 'fortune is not obtained at the price of the sacrifice of life.'

a. So also '*difference between*' two things; as, त्वया समुद्रेण च महद् अन्तरं 'there is great difference between you and the ocean.'

b. '*Separation from*,' either with or without सह; as, भर्त्रा वियोगः 'separation from a husband' (or भर्त्रा सह वियोगः). Similarly, वियोगो हरिणा सह 'separation from Hari.'

c. The English expression '*under the idea that*' is expressed by the instrumental case of the substantive बुद्धि; as, व्याघ्रबुद्ध्या 'under the idea that he was a tiger.'

Double Instrumental.

810. Sometimes when two substantives come together, expressing '*parts*' of a common idea, they are both placed in the instrumental, instead of one in the genitive; as, बकुलैः पुष्पैर् वास्यते '(an odour is emitted) by the bakul-plants by their flowers' (for बकुलानां पुष्पैः). Similarly, ताम् आश्वासयामास सखीभिश् चन्दनोदकैः '(he caused her to revive) by her attendants by sandal-water.'

Dative case.

811. This case is of very limited applicability, and its functions, irrespectively of the influence of verbs, are restricted to the expression of '*the object*,' '*motive*,' or '*cause*' for which any thing is done, or '*the result*' to which any act tends; as, आत्मविवृद्धये 'for self-aggrandizement;' आपत्प्रतीकाराय 'for the counteraction of calamity;' शस्त्रं च शास्त्रं च प्रतिपत्तये 'arms and books (lead) to renown.'

a. When, as in the last example, '*the result*' or '*end*' to which any thing leads is denoted by this case, the verb is seldom expressed, but appears to be involved in the case itself. The following are other examples: यत्र चास्ते विषसंसर्गोऽमृतं तदपि मृत्यवे 'where there is admixture of poison, then even nectar (leads) to death;' उपदेशो मूर्खाणां प्रकोपाय न शान्तये 'advice to fools (leads) to irritation, not to conciliation;' स वृद्धपतिस् तस्याः सन्तोषाय न अभवत् 'that old husband was not to her liking;' स राजा तस्या रुचये न बभूव 'that king was not to her liking.'

b. It will be seen hereafter that certain verbs of *giving* and *relating* govern the dative. Substantives derived from such verbs exercise a similar influence; as, अन्यस्मै दानं 'the *giving* to another;' अन्यस्मै कथनं 'the *telling* to another.'

c. Words expressive of '*salutation*' or '*reverence*' are joined with the dative; as, गणेशाय नमः 'reverence to Gaṇeśa;' कुशलं ते 'health to thee.'

Ablative case.

812. The proper force of the ablative case is expressed by '*from*;' as, लोभात् (क्रोधः प्रभवति) 'from avarice anger arises;' गिरेः पतनं 'falling from a mountain;' चाराणां मुखात् 'from the mouth of the spies.'

813. Hence this case passes to the expression of various correlative ideas; as, आहारात् किंचित् 'a portion of (from) their food:' and like the instrumental it very commonly signifies '*because*,' '*by reason of*,' '*in consequence of*;' as, गोमनुष्याणां वधात् 'on account of the slaughter of cows and men;' अनवसरप्रवेशात् (पुत्रं निन्दति) 'he blames his son for entering inopportunely;' दण्डभयात् 'through fear of punishment;' अस्मद्भाग्योदयात् 'by reason of my good fortune;' फलतो ऽविशेषात् 'because (there is) no difference as to the result.'

a. '*According to*;' as, मन्त्रिवचनात् 'according to the advice of the minister.' Abstract nouns in त्व are often found in this case to express some of these ideas; as, अनवस्थितचित्तत्वात् 'by reason of the unsteadiness of his mind;' especially in the writings of commentators; as, वक्ष्यमाणत्वात् 'according to what will be said hereafter;' स्पृष्टेषत्स्पृष्टेषद्विवृतविवृतसंवृतभेदात् 'according to the division of touched, slightly touched, slightly open, open and contracted.'

814. It also expresses '*through the means*' or '*instrumentality of*;' as, शृगालात् पाशबद्धः 'caught in the toils through the instrumentality of the jackal;' न औषधपरिज्ञानाद् (व्याधेः शान्तिर् भवेत्) 'the alleviation of disease is not effected by the mere knowledge of the medicine.'

a. '*The manner*' in which any thing is done is often expressed by the ablative; it is then used adverbially (compare 715); as, यत्नात् 'with diligence,' or 'diligently;' बलात् 'forcibly;' कुतूहलात् 'with wonder;' उपचारात् 'figuratively;' मूलाद् उद्धरणं 'tearing up by the roots:' or by the ablative affix तस्; as, स्वेच्छातस् 'at one's own pleasure' (see 719. *a. b*).

b. This case also denotes '*after*;' as, शरीरविगमात् 'after separation from the body;' मुख्यप्रतिबन्धनात् 'after the imprisonment of the Chief;' तस्य आगमनात् 'since his arrival.'

c. So also, in native grammars the ablative case is used to express '*after;*' thus, रहाभ्यां 'after the letters *ra* and *ha;*' ङात् 'after the letter *ṅa;*' ऋवर्णात् नस्य णत्वं वाच्यं 'it should be stated that after the letters *ṛi* and *ṛī* the cerebral ण् *ṇ* is substituted in place of the dental न् *n.*'

d. In reference to *time*, '*within;*' as, त्रिपक्षात् 'within three fortnights.'

e. Nouns expressive of '*fear*' are joined with the ablative of the thing feared; as, मृत्योर् भयं 'fear of death;' चौरेभ्यो भयं 'fear of robbers.'

Genitive case.

815. This and the locative case are of the most extensive application, and are often employed, in a vague and indeterminate manner, to express relations properly belonging to the other cases.

a. The true force of the genitive is equivalent to '*of,*' and this case appears most frequently when two substantives are to be connected, so as to present one idea; as, मित्रस्य वचनं 'the speech of a friend;' स्त्रीणां भर्ता परं भूषणं 'the best ornament of a woman is her husband;' न नरस्य नरो दासो दासस् तु अर्थस्य 'man is not the slave of man, but the slave of wealth.'

816. '*Possession*' is frequently expressed by the genitive case alone, without a verb; as, सर्वाः सम्पत्तयस् तस्य सन्तुष्टं यस्य मानसं 'all riches belong to him who has a contented mind;' धन्यो ऽहं यस्य ईदृशी भार्या 'happy am I in possessing such a wife.'

a. It often, however, has the force of '*to,*' and is very generally used to supply *the place of the dative;* as, आत्मा आत्मनो ऽभीष्टः 'one's own life is dear to one's self;' न योजनशतं दूरं वाह्यमानस्य तृष्णया 'a hundred yojanas is not far to one borne away by thirst (of gain);' किं ज्ञानवताम् अविदितं 'What is unknown to the wise?' किम् अन्धस्य (प्रकाशयति) प्रदीपः 'What does a lamp (show) to a blind man?' किं मया अपकृतं राज्ञः 'What offence have I committed towards the king;' किम् अयम् अस्माकं (कर्तुं समर्थः) 'What can this man (do to us)?'

b. And not unfrequently of '*in*' or '*on;*' as, स्त्रीणां विश्वासः 'confidence in women;' मम आयत्तत्वं 'dependence on me.'

c. It is even equivalent occasionally to '*from*' or '*by,*' as usually expressed by the ablative or instrumental; as, न कस्यापि (उपायनं गृह्णीयात्) 'one ought not to accept a present from any one;' अस्माकं (वनं त्याज्यं) 'the wood is to be abandoned by us;' स धन्यो यस्य अर्थिनो न यान्ति विमुखाः 'he is blessed from whom suppliants do not depart in disappointment;' नलस्य उपसंस्कृतं मांसं 'meat cooked by Nala.'

d. '*Difference between two things*' is expressed by this case; as, स्वामि-सेवकयोर् महद् अन्तरं 'there is great difference between the master and the servant.' Compare 807. *a.*

e. In native grammars it expresses '*in place of*;' as, उरण् रपरः 'ar in place of *ṛi* is followed by *ra*.'

Locative case.

817. The locative, like the genitive, expresses the most diversified relations, and frequently usurps the functions of the other cases. Properly it has the force of '*in*,' '*on*,' or '*at*,' as expressive of many collateral and analogous ideas; thus, रात्रौ 'in the night;' ग्रामे 'in the village;' पृष्ठे 'on the back;' त्वयि विश्वासः 'confidence in you;' मरुस्थल्यां वृष्टिः 'rain on desert ground;' प्रथमबुभुक्षायां 'at the first desire of eating;' पृथिव्यां रोपितो वृक्षः 'a tree planted in the earth.'

818. Hence it passes into the sense '*towards*;' as, दया शत्रौ च मित्रे च 'lenicency towards an enemy as well as a friend;' सर्वभूतेषु दया 'compassion towards all creatures;' सुहृत्सु आर्जवः 'upright towards friends;' सुकृतशतम् असत्सु नष्टं 'a hundred good offices are thrown away upon the wicked;' नले ऽनुरागः 'love for Nala;' तस्याम् अनुरागः 'affection for her.'

819. Words signifying '*cause*,' '*motive*,' or '*need*,' are joined with the locative; as, नम्रत्वे हेतुः 'the cause of his modesty;' युवराजयोर् विग्रहे भवद्वचनं निदानं 'your speech was the cause of the war between the two princes;' प्रार्थकाभावः सतीत्वे कारणं स्त्रियाः 'the absence of a suitor is the cause of a woman's chastity;' नौकायां किं प्रयोजनं 'What need of a boat!' Also words signifying '*employment*' or '*occupation*;' as, अर्थार्जने प्रवृत्तिः 'engaging in the acquisition of wealth.'

a. So words derived from the root *yuj* usually require the locative; as, मम राज्यरक्षणम् उपयोगः 'I am of service in preserving the kingdom.'

b. This case may yield other senses equivalent to '*by reason of*,' '*for*,' &c.; as, मे छिद्रेषु 'through my faults;' चारः परराष्ट्राणाम् अवलोकने 'a spy is *for the sake* of examining the territory of one's enemies;' युद्धे कालो ऽयं 'this is the time *for* battle;' उपदेशे ऽनादरः 'disregard for advice;' का चिन्ता मरणे रणे 'What anxiety *about* dying in battle!' कालं मन्ये पलायने 'I think the time has come for escaping;' पुत्रस्य अनुमते 'with the consent of a son.'

c. It is also used in giving the meaning of a root; as, ग्रह् उपादाने 'the root *grah* is in *taking*,' i. e. conveys the idea of 'taking.'

d. In native grammars it expresses '*followed by*;' thus ञिति means 'when any thing having an indicatory *ñ* follows.' So again, मान्तस्य पदस्य अनुस्वारो हलि 'in the room of *m* final in a word followed by any consonant (*hal*) there is Anusvára.'

e. The locative case is often used absolutely; see 840.

SYNTAX OF NOUNS OF TIME.

820. When reference is made to *any particular division* of time, the instrumental case is usually required; as, त्रिभिर् वर्षैः 'in three years;' द्वादशभिर् मासैः 'in twelve months;' क्षणेन 'in an instant;'

कियता कालेन 'In how long time?' वर्षशतैः 'in hundreds of years;' कालपर्यायेण (or simply कालेन) 'in process of time;' मासेन 'in a month;' मासमात्रेण 'in the space of a month;' एतावता कालेन 'in so much time.'

821. When to *duration of time*, the accusative case is generally used; as, क्षणं 'for a moment;' अनेककालं 'for a long time;' कियन्तं कालं 'for some time;' एकं मासं 'for one month;' विंशतिं मासान् 'for twenty months;' द्वौ मासौ 'for two months;' वर्षशतं 'for a hundred years;' शाश्वतीः समाः 'to all eternity;' शतं वर्षाणि 'for a hundred years;' बहूनि अहानि 'for many days.' The instrumental, however, is sometimes used in this sense, and to express other relations of time; as, द्वादशभिर् वर्षैर् वाणिज्यं कृत्वा 'having traded for twelve years;' कतिपयदिवसैः 'for a few days;' and even the genitive; as, चिरस्य कालस्य (or simply चिरस्य) 'for a long time;' कतिपयाहस्य 'after a few days.'

822. When any *particular day or epoch* is referred to, as the date on which any action has taken place or will take place, the locative may be employed; as, कस्मिंश्चिद् दिवसे 'on a certain day;' तृतीये दिवसे 'on the third day;' द्वादशे ऽह्नि 'on the twelfth day;' 'seventeen days from this time,' इतः सप्तदशे ऽहनि. Or sometimes the accusative; as, यां रात्रिं ते दूताः प्रविशन्ति स्म पुरीं तां रात्रिं भरतेन स्वप्नो दृष्टः 'on the night when the ambassadors entered the city, on that night a dream was seen by Bharata.'

a. The adverbs at 731 may often be found expressing *relations of time;* as, षण्मासाद् ऊर्ध्वं or परं 'after six months;' षण्मासेन or षण्मासाभ्यन्तरेण पूर्वं 'six months ago;' or (employing the locative absolute) पूर्णे वर्षसहस्रे 'after a thousand years.'

NOUNS OF PLACE AND DISTANCE.

823. Nouns expressive of '*distance between two places*' (according to Carey) may be in the nominative; as, कृष्णः शतं क्रोशाः सोमनाथात् 'Kṛishṇa is a hundred kos from Somanáth.' '*Space*' may also be expressed by the accusative; as, योजनं 'for a yojana;' क्रोशं गिरिः 'a hill for a kos;' or by the instrumental; as, क्रोशेन गत्वा 'having gone for a kos.' '*The place*' in which any thing is done is expressed by the locative; as, विदर्भेषु 'in Vidarbha.'

SYNTAX OF ADJECTIVES.

Accusative after the Adjective.

824. Adjectives formed from *desiderative* bases govern an accu-

sative; as, स्वगृहं जिगमिषुः 'desirous of going home;' पुत्रम् अभीप्सुः 'desirous of obtaining a son;' राजानं दिदृक्षुः 'desirous of seeing the king.'

Instrumental after the Adjective.

825. Adjectives, or participles used adjectively, expressive of '*want*' or '*possession*,' require this case; as, अर्थेन हीनः 'destitute of wealth;' अर्थैः समायुक्तः 'possessed of riches;' वारिणा पूर्णो घटः 'a jar full of water.'

826. So also of '*likeness*,' '*comparison*,' or '*equality*;' as, अनेन सदृशो लोके न भूतो न भविष्यति 'there has never been, nor will there ever be, any one like him in this world;' ब्राह्मणेन तुल्यम् अधीते 'he reads like a Bráhman;' आरम्भैः सदृश उदयः 'his success was equal to his undertakings;' प्राणैः समा पत्नी 'a wife as dear as life;' दाता ऽभ्यधिको नृपैः 'more liberal than (other) kings;' आदित्येन तुल्यः 'equal to the sun.' These are sometimes joined with a genitive; see 827. *b*.

Genitive after the Adjective.

827. Adjectives signifying '*dear to*,' or *the reverse*, are joined with the genitive; as, राज्ञां प्रियः 'dear to kings;' भर्तारः स्त्रीणां प्रियाः 'husbands are dear to women;' न कश्चित् स्त्रीणाम् अप्रियः 'women dislike nobody;' द्वेष्यो भवति मन्त्रिणां 'he is *detestable to* his ministers.'

a. Adjectives expressive of '*fear*' may govern the genitive or ablative; as, ऋषेर् भीतः 'afraid of the sage.'

b. Adjectives expressive of '*equality*,' '*resemblance*,' '*similitude*,' often require this case as well as the Instrumental; thus, सर्वस्य समः 'equal to all;' तस्य अनुरूपः 'like him;' चन्द्रस्य सदृशः 'like the moon;' न तस्य तुल्यः कश्चन 'nobody is equal to him.' Compare 826.

c. So also other adjectives; as, परोपदेशः सर्वेषां सुकरः नृणां 'giving advice to others is *easy* to all men;' सुखानाम् उचितः '*worthy* of happiness;' उचितः क्लेशानां '*capable* of toil;' प्रमाणानाम् परिहीनः '*destitute of* proof;' अज्ञातं धृतराष्ट्रस्य '*unknown to* Dhrita-ráshtra.'

Locative after the Adjective.

828. Adjectives, or participles used adjectively, expressive of '*power*' or '*ability*,' are joined with this case; as, अध्वनि क्षमा अश्वाः 'horses able for the journey;' महति शत्रौ क्षमो राजा 'a king who is a match for a great enemy;' अशक्तो गृहकरणे शक्तो गृहभञ्जने 'unable to build a house, but able to demolish one.'

a. So also other adjectives; as, शस्त्रेषु कुशलः '*skilled* in arms;' अल्पेषु प्राज्ञः '*wise* in trifles;' त्वयि अनुरक्तो विरक्तो वा स्वामी 'Is your master *attached* or *adverse* to you?' अनुजीविषु मन्दादरः '*neglectful* of his dependants.'

SYNTAX OF THE COMPARATIVE AND SUPERLATIVE DEGREE.

829. Adjectives in the comparative degree require the ablative case; as, भार्या प्राणेभ्यो ऽपि गरीयसी 'a wife *dearer even than* one's life;' पुत्रस्पर्शात् सुखतरः स्पर्शो लोके न विद्यते 'there is no pleasanter touch in this world than the touch of a son;' वर्धनात् प्रजारक्षणं श्रेयः 'the protection of one's subjects is *better than* aggrandizement;' न मत्तो (719. *a*) दुःखिततरः पुमान् अस्ति 'there is not a more wretched man than I;' मतिर् बलाद् बलीयसी 'mind is more powerful than strength.'

830. Sometimes they govern the instrumental; as, प्राणैः प्रियतरः 'dearer than life;' न अस्ति मया कश्चिद् अल्पभाग्यतरो भुवि 'there is nobody upon earth more unfortunate than I.'

a. When it is intended to express '*the better of two things*' the genitive may be used; as, अनयोर् देशयोः को देशो भद्रतरः 'Of these two countries which is the better?'

831. The comparative in Sanskrit is often resolved into the expression '*better and not*' or '*but not*;' as, वरं प्राणपरित्यागो न पुनर् ईदृशे कर्मणि प्रवृत्तिः 'better abandon life than (but not) engage in such an action;' वरं मौनं कार्यं न च वचनम् उक्तं यद् अनृतं 'it is better that silence should be kept than a speech uttered which is untrue;' विद्ययैव सह वेदाध्यापकेन वरं मर्तव्यं न तु अध्यापनयोग्यशिष्याभावे अपात्राय एनां प्रतिपादयेत् 'a teacher of the Veda should rather die with his learning than commit it to an unworthy object, in the absence of a pupil worthy to be instructed in it.'

832. The superlative degree is usually joined with the genitive; as, ब्राह्मणो द्विपदां श्रेष्ठो गौर् वरिष्ठा चतुष्पदां । गुरुर् गरीयसां श्रेष्ठः पुत्रः स्पर्शवतां वरः 'a Bráhmaṇ is the best of all bipeds, a cow of quadrupeds, a Guru of venerable things, a son of things possessed of touch;' but sometimes with the locative; as, नरेषु बलवत्तमः 'the most powerful of men;' and even with an ablative; as, धान्यानां संग्रह उत्तमः सर्वसंग्रहात् 'a store of grain is the best of all stores.'

a. A superlative degree may even take a comparative affix, and govern the genitive; as, तेषां ज्येष्ठतरः 'the eldest of them.' See 194.

b. A comparative word may have a superlative sense; as, दृढतरः 'very firm.'

833. '*Comparison*' is often expressed by an adjective in the *positive* degree,

joined with a noun in the ablative or instrumental case; as, नास्ति तस्मात् पुण्यवान् 'there is not a happier than he;' स मत्तो (719. a) महान् 'he is greater than me.' Similarly, सर्वैर् विशिष्टतः 'more excellently than all.'

a. In more modern Sanskrit 'comparison' is sometimes expressed by the use of अपेक्ष्य 'regarding,' 'with reference to' (indecl. part. of the root ईक्ष् with अप), which may take the place of 'than' in English; thus, दशोपाध्यायान् अपेक्ष्य आचार्य आचार्यशतम् अपेक्ष्य पिता गौरवेण अतिरिक्तो भवति 'an Áchárya ought to be higher in estimation than ten Upádhyáyas, a father than a hundred Áchâryas.'

834. Many words have a kind of comparative influence, and require an ablative case, especially वरं, अवरं, अन्य, अन्यत्र, अन्यतस्, इतर, पर, पूर्व, अधिक, ऊन, अवशिष्ट; as, प्रक्षालनाद् हि पङ्कस्य अस्पर्शनं वरं 'it is better not to touch mud than to wash it off;' दारिद्र्यम् अवरं मरणात् 'poverty is less desirable than death;' को मां मित्राद् अन्यस् त्रातुं समर्थः 'Who is able to rescue me, other than a friend?' किन्नु दुःखम् अतः परं 'What grief is greater than this?' न श्रुताद् अन्यद् विब्रूयात् 'one ought not to speak differently from what one has heard;' तत्कालाद् अन्यदा 'at another time than the present;' नरस्य न अन्यतो मरणाद् भयं 'there is no cause of fear to man from any other quarter than from death;' श्राद्धात् (731. a, 778) पूर्वेद्युः 'on the day before that of the Śráddha;' योजनशताद् अधिकं 'more than a hundred yojanas;' कामोदन्तः सङ्गमात् किञ्चिद् ऊनः 'intelligence of a lover is something less than a meeting;' अन्नाद् अवशिष्टं 'the remainder of the food.'

NUMERALS.

835. The syntax of numerals is explained at 206, 207. The following examples may be added: नवतेर् नराणां 'of ninety men;' षष्टेर् नराणां 'of sixty men;' सहस्रस्य नराणां 'of a thousand men;' सहस्रं पितरः 'a thousand ancestors;' त्रिभिर् गुणितं शतं 'one hundred multiplied by three;' फलसहस्रे द्वे 'two thousand fruits;' एषां त्रयाणां मध्याद् अन्यतमः 'one of these three;' अयुतं गा ददौ 'he gave ten thousand cows;' पञ्चशतं मृगान् जघान 'he killed five hundred deer.'

a. Sometimes the plural of the numerals from एकविंशति upwards may be used; as, पञ्चाशद्भिर् बाणैः 'with fifty arrows.'

b. The aggregative numerals may be employed at the end of compounds for the cardinals; thus सैन्यद्वयं 'two armies;' विवाहचतुष्टयं 'four marriages.' See 214.

c. Numerals may take the genitive after them of the things numbered; as, अश्वानां शतसहस्राणि 'a hundred thousand of horses;' पत्तीनां सप्तशतानि 'seven hundred foot-soldiers;' शतम् आचार्याणां 'a hundred preceptors;' गवां पञ्चशतानि षष्टिश् च 'five hundred and sixty cows;' अध्यायानां षट् शतानि विंशतिश् च 'six hundred and twenty chapters;' नराणां त्रिंशदधिकशते द्वे सहस्रे च 'two thousand one hundred and thirty men;' पञ्च रथसहस्राणि 'five thousand chariots.'

d. When numerals are used comparatively they may take an ablative; as, विवादाद् द्विगुणो दमः 'a fine the double of that in dispute.'

SYNTAX OF PRONOUNS.

836. The chief peculiarities in the syntax of pronouns have already been noticed in Chapter V, pp. 112—120.

With regard to the alternative of एनं, &c. (see 223), it is properly only allowed in case of the re-employment (*anvâdeśa*) of this pronoun in the subsequent part of a sentence in which इदं or एतद् have already been used; thus, अनेन व्याकरणम् अधीतम् एनं छन्दो ऽध्यापय 'the grammar has been studied by him, now set him to study the Veda.' It is an enclitic, and ought not to begin a sentence.

a. In the use of the relative and interrogative pronouns a very peculiar *attraction* is often to be observed; that is, when either a relative or interrogative pronoun has been used, and an indefinite pronoun would naturally be expected to follow, the relative or interrogative are repeated, as in the following examples: यो यस्य (for यस्यचित्) भावः स्यात् 'whatever may be the disposition of whom (i.e. any one);' यद् रोचते यस्मै 'whatever is pleasing to any one;' यो यस्य मांसम् अश्नाति 'whoever eats the flesh of any animal;' यस्य ये गुणाः सन्ति 'whatever excellencies belong to any one;' यद् येन युज्यते 'whatever corresponds with any thing;' केषां किं शास्त्रम् अध्ययनीयं 'What book is to be read by whom?'

837. The relative and interrogative are sometimes used together, in an indefinite distributive sense; as, यानि कानि मित्राणि 'any friends whatever:' or more usually with चिद् affixed to the interrogative; as, यस्मै कस्मैचिद् 'to any one whatever.'

a. The neuter of the interrogative (किं) is often joined with the instrumental to signify 'What is the use of?' 'there is no need of;' as, श्रुतेन किं यो न धर्मम् आचरेत् किम् आत्मना यो न जितेन्द्रियो भवेत् 'Of what use is scriptural knowledge (to one) who does not practice virtue? Of what use is a soul (to one) whose passions are not kept in subjection?' किं ते ऽनेन प्रश्नेन 'What business have you to make this inquiry?' किं बहुना 'What need of more?' 'in short.'

b. As already shown at 761, a relative pronoun is sometimes rendered unnecessary by the use of the relative compound; thus, नगरी चन्द्रिकाधौतहर्म्या is equivalent to नगरी यस्याश् चन्द्रिकाधौतानि हर्म्याणि 'a city whose palaces were silvered by the moon-beams.'

c. The relative, when followed by a pluperfect tense, may sometimes be expressed by the indeclinable participle; thus, सिंहो व्याधं हत्वा 'a lion having killed a hunter,' or 'a lion who had killed a hunter.'

838. The following examples will illustrate the use of pronouns of quantity and pronominals: यावतः (or यावत्संख्यकान्) ग्रासान् भुङ्क्ते तावतः (or तावत्संख्यकान्) ददाति 'as many mouthfuls as he eats, so many he gives away;' यदि एतावन् मह्यं दीयते तदा एतावद् अध्यापयामि 'if so much is given to me, then I will give so much instruction;' तेषां सर्वेषां मध्याद् एकतमः 'one out of all those.' See also 801.

SYNTAX OF VERBS.

839. Nothing is more common in Sanskṛit syntax than for the verb to be omitted altogether, or supplied from the context.

a. This is more especially the case with the copula, or substantive verb; thus, यावन् मेरुस्थिता देवा यावद् गङ्गा महीतले । चन्द्रार्कौ गगने यावत् तावद् विप्रकुले वयं 'as long as the gods have existed in Meru, as long as the Ganges upon earth, as long as the sun and moon in the sky, so long have we (existed) in the family of Brahmans;' विवेकः प्राज्ञे 'discrimination (in) wisdom.'

Locative, Genitive, and Nominative absolute.

840. The locative case is very commonly used absolutely with participles; as, तस्मिन् जीवति जीवामि मृते तस्मिन् म्रिये पुनः 'he living I live, he dying I die;' अवसन्नायां रात्रौ 'the night being ended;' ज्येष्ठे भ्रातरि अनूढे 'the elder brother being unmarried;' असति उपायान्तरे 'there being no other expedient;' तथा सति 'it being so.' Sometimes the verb is omitted; as, दूरे भये 'the danger (being) distant.' When the passive participle is thus used absolutely with a noun in the locative case, the present participle of अस्, 'to be,' is often redundantly added; as, तथा कृते सति or तथा अनुष्ठिते 'it being so done *.'

a. The genitive is less commonly used absolutely; as, आपदाम् आपतन्तीनां 'calamities impending;' पश्यतां नराणां 'the men looking on.'

b. The nominative is very rarely thus used; as, सुहृन् मे समायातः सुखवान् अस्मि 'my friend having arrived, I am happy.'

c. It is evident that the locative and genitive absolute may often take the place of the English particles 'when,' 'while,' 'since,' 'although;' and may supply the place of a *pluperfect tense;* thus, तस्मिन् अपक्रान्ते 'when he had departed.'

Nominative case after the Verb.

841. Verbs signifying 'to be,' 'to become,' 'to appear,' 'to be called,' or 'to be esteemed,' and other passive verbs used denominatively, may take a nominative after them; as, राजा प्रजापालकः स्यात् 'let a king be the protector of his subjects;' सा विरसवदना प्रतिभाति 'she appears sorrowful;' ग्रामो ऽरण्यं प्रतिभाति 'the village appears like a desert;' राजा धर्मो ऽभिधीयते 'a king is called Justice.'

---

* Possibly the object of adding the word *sati* may be to show that the passive participle is here used as a participle, and not as a past tense. So also in commentaries सति is placed after a word like गच्छति, to indicate the loc. c. sing. of the pres. part., as distinguished from the 3d sing. of the pres. tense.

Accusative case after the Verb.

842. Transitive verbs generally govern this case; as, विश्वं ससर्ज वेधाः 'Brahmá *created* the universe;' पुष्पाणि चिनोति नारी 'the woman *gathers* flowers;' प्राणान् जहौ मुमूर्षुः 'the dying man *gave up* the ghost;' मधु वर्जयेत् 'one should *avoid* wine;' सत्यं ब्रूहि '*speak* the truth.'

a. Verbs of *speaking to* or *addressing* take this case; as, तम् अब्रवीत् 'he said to him;' इति उवाच अर्जुनं 'he thus addressed Arjuna.'

843. So also verbs of *motion*; as, व्रजति तीर्थं मुनिः 'the holy man *goes* to the place of pilgrimage;' नद्यः समुद्रं द्रवन्ति 'rivers *run* into the ocean;' भ्रमति महीं 'he *wanders* over the earth.'

844. Verbs of motion are not unfrequently used with substantives, to supply the place of other verbs; as, ख्यातिं याति 'he goes to fame,' for 'he becomes famous;' समताम् एति 'he goes to equality,' for 'he becomes equal;' तयोर् मित्रताम् आजगाम 'he came to the friendship of those two,' for 'he became a friend of those two;' पञ्चत्वं गतः 'he went to death,' for 'he died;' नृपतिं तुष्टिं नयति 'he leads the king to satisfaction,' for 'he satisfies,' &c.

a. The following are other examples: परेषां पीडां परिहरति 'he *avoids* paining others;' अप्राप्यम् इच्छति 'he *desires* what is unattainable;' विद्यां चिन्तयेत् 'he should *think on* wisdom;' अश्वम् आरोहति 'he *mounts* his horse;' कर्माणि आरेभिरे 'they *began* the business;' गतान् मा शुचः '*grieve not for* the departed;' सर्वलोकाधिपत्यम् अर्हति 'he *deserves* the sovereignty of the universe;' पर्वतगह्वरम् अधिशेते 'he *lies down* in a cave of the mountain;' गां क्षीरं पिबन्तीं न निवारयेत् 'one ought not to *prevent* a cow from drinking milk.'

845. There are certain verbs which take a redundant accusative case after them of a substantive derived from the same root; as, शपथं शेपे 'he swore an oath;' वसति वासं 'he dwells;' वर्तते वृत्तिं 'he conducts himself;' वाक्यं वदति 'he speaks a speech;' जीविकां जीवति 'he lives a life;' नदति नादं 'he raises a cry' (cf. the Greek expressions λέγω λόγον, χαίρω χαράν, &c.).

Double Accusative after the Verb.

846. Verbs of *asking* govern a double accusative; as, देवं वरं याचते 'he seeks a boon of the god;' धनं राजानं प्रार्थयते 'he begs money from the king.' Of *speaking*; as, राजानं वचनम् अब्रवीत् 'he addressed a speech to the king.' Of *leading*; as, तं गृहं नयति 'he leads him home;' राजसुतां राजान्तरं निनाय 'he led the princess to another king.'

847. Causal verbs; as, अतिथिं भोजयति अन्नं 'he causes the guest to eat food;' त्वां बोधयामि यत् ते हितं 'I cause you to know what is *for your interest*;' शिष्यं वेदान् अध्यापयति गुरुः 'the Guru teaches his pupil the Vedas;' तां गृहं प्रवेशयति 'he causes her to enter the house;' फलपुष्पोदकं ग्राहयामास नृपात्मजं 'he presented the king's son with fruits, flowers, and water;' सुतम् अश्वम् आरोहयति 'she causes

her son to sit on her lap' (literally, 'her hip'); विद्या नरं नृपं सङ्गमयति 'learning causes a man to have access to a king.'

a. Other examples are, गां दोग्धि पयः 'he *milks milk* from the cow;' दुदुहुर् धरित्रीं रत्नानि 'they *milked* jewels out of the earth;' अभीप्सितं द्यौर् दुग्धा 'the sky has been *milked* of (your) wish,' i.e. 'your wish has been *milked* out *of* the sky;' जित्वा नलं राज्यं 'having won his kingdom from Nala,' i.e. 'having by play deprived Nala of his kingdom;' जितो राज्यं वसूनि च '*deprived* by *defeat* in play of his kingdom and property;' तं सेनापतिम् अभिषिषिचुः 'they *inaugurated* him general,' more usually joined with an acc. and loc.; देवं पतिं वरयति 'she *chooses* a god for her husband;' अवचिनोति कुसुमानि वृक्षात् 'she *gathers* blossoms from the trees;' तान् प्राहिणोद् यमसादनं 'he *sent* them to the abode of Yama;' स्वकर्माणि नरं गुरुत्वं विपरीततां वा नयन्ति 'his own acts *lead* a man to eminence or the reverse;' शिक्षयामास तान् अस्त्राणि 'he *taught* them the use of arms.'

Instrumental case after the Verb.

848. Any verb may be joined with the instrumental, to express '*the agent*,' '*instrument*,' or '*cause*,' or '*manner*' of the action; as, पुष्पं वातेन म्लायति 'the flower fades by reason of the wind;' अक्षैः क्रीडति 'he plays with dice;' मेघो वह्निं वर्षैर् निर्वापयति 'the cloud puts out the fire with its rain;' सुखेन जीवति 'he lives happily.' See 865.

a. In this sense many causals take an instrumental; as, तां मिष्टान्नैर् भोजयामास 'he caused her to eat sweetmeats;' पक्षिभिः पिण्डान् खादयति 'he causes the pieces to be eaten by the birds.'

849. After verbs of motion this case is used in reference either to *the vehicle by which*, or *the place on which*, the motion takes place; as, रथेन प्रयाति 'he goes *in a chariot*;' अश्वेन संचरति 'he goes *on horseback*;' मार्गेण गच्छति 'he goes *on the road*;' सस्यक्षेत्रेण गच्छति 'he goes *through a field of corn*;' पुप्लुवे सागरं नौकया 'he navigated the ocean *in a boat*.' Similarly, सुस्राव नयनैः सलिलं 'tears flowed *through the eyes*.'

a. After verbs of *carrying*, *placing*, &c., it is used in reference to 'the place' on which any thing is carried or placed; as, वहति काष्ठं मूर्ध्ना 'he bears fagots *on his head*;' कुक्कुरः स्कन्धेन उह्यते 'the dog is borne *on the shoulders*.' कृ is found with this case in the sense of *placing*; as, शिरसा पुत्रम् अकरोत् 'he *placed* his son on his head.' The following are other examples: शिष्येण गच्छति गुरुः 'the master *goes in company with* the pupil;' सममन्त्रयत मन्त्रिभिः 'he *consulted with* his ministers;' but in this sense सह is usually placed after it. पतिर् भार्यया सङ्गच्छति 'the husband *meets* the wife;' संयोजयति रथं हयैः 'he *harnesses* the horses to the chariot;' देहेन वियुज्यते 'he *is separated from* the body,' more usually with the ablative. युध्यते शत्रुभिः 'he *fights* his enemies,' or शत्रुभिः सह, &c.; वैरं न केनचित् सह कुर्वीत 'one ought not to be at *enmity* with any one;' मां दोषेण परिशङ्कते 'he *suspects* me of a crime.'

850. Verbs of *boasting*: as, विद्यया विकत्थसे 'you *boast* of your learning;' परेषां यशसा श्लाघसे 'you *glory* in the fame of others.' Of *swearing*: as, धनुषा शेपे 'he *swore* by his bow.' Of *thinking, reflecting*: as, मनसा विचिन्त्य '*thinking* in his mind.'

a. Verbs of *comparing*: as, जलौकसा उपमीयते प्रमदा 'a beautiful woman is *compared* to a leech.'

851. Verbs denoting *liberation, freedom from*, sometimes take an instrumental after them; as, सर्वैः पापैः प्रमुच्यते 'he is *released from* all sins.'

852. Verbs of *buying* and *selling* take the instrumental of the price; as, सहस्रैर् अपि मूर्खाणाम् एकं क्रीणीष्व पण्डितं '*buy* one wise man even for thousands of fools;' गवां सहस्रेण गृहं विक्रीणीते 'he *sells* his house for a thousand cows;' क्रीणीष्व तद् दशभिः सुवर्णैः '*buy* that for ten suvarṇas.'

Dative after the Verb.

853. All verbs in which a sense of *imparting* or *communicating* any thing to any object is inherent, may take an accusative of the thing imparted, and a dative of the object to which it is imparted. (Frequently, however, they take a genitive or even a locative of the object; see 857.) पुत्राय मोदकान् ददाति 'he *gives* sweetmeats to his son;' विप्राय गां प्रतिशृणोति 'he *promises* a cow to the Bráhman;' देवदत्ताय धनं धारयति 'he *owes* money to Devadatta;' कन्यां तस्मै प्रतिपादय '*consign* the maiden to him,' more usually with the locative; see 861.

a. Other examples of the dative are, तेषां विनाशाय प्रकुरुते मनः 'he *sets his mind* on their destruction;' गमनाय मतिं दधौ 'he *set his mind* on departure,' or with the locative. तन् मह्यं रोचते 'that *is pleasing to* me;' शिष्येभ्यः प्रवक्ष्यामि तद् 'I will *declare* this to my pupils;' सर्वं राज्ञे विज्ञापयति 'he *makes known* all to the king,' these are also joined with the genitive of the person. अमृतत्वाय कल्पते 'he *is rendered fit for* immortality;' प्रभवति मम वधाय 'he *has the power* to kill me;' तान् मातुर् वधाय अचोदयत् 'he *incited* them to the murder of their mother;' पुत्राय क्रुध्यति 'he is *angry* with his son;' इयं मांसपेशी जाता पुत्रशताय 'this lump of flesh *is produced for* a hundred sons;' नाशंसे विजयाय 'I had no *hopes of* success' (Mahá-bhár. I. 148).

Ablative after the Verb.

854. All verbs may take an ablative of 'the object' from which any thing proceeds, or arises, or is produced; as, पतति वृक्षात् पर्णं 'the leaf *falls* from the tree;' रुधिरं स्रवति गात्रात् 'blood *flows* from the body;' आसनाद् उत्तिष्ठति 'he *rises* from his seat;' मृत्पिण्डतः (719) कर्ता कुरुते यद् यद् इच्छति 'from the lump of clay the artist *makes* whatever he wishes;' विनयाद् याति पात्रतां 'from education a person *attains* capacity;' निर्जगाम नगरात् 'he *went* out from the city.'

855. Verbs of *fearing* are joined with the ablative, and sometimes with the genitive; as, साधुर् न तथा मृत्योर् बिभेति यथा अनृतात् 'a good man does not *fear* death so much as falsehood;' मा शब्दाद् बिभीत 'be not *afraid of* a noise;' दण्डाद् उद्विजते जगत् 'the whole world *stands in awe* of punishment;' दाम्भिकस्य ते कृतपश्चात्तापस्य बिभेमि 'I *fear* thee, a cunning penitent;' see 859.

856. Verbs which express *superiority* or *comparison* govern an ablative; as, प्रापणात् कामानां परित्यागो विशिष्यते 'the abandonment of pleasure is *superior* to (better than) the possession.'

a. Other examples of verbs followed by ablative cases are, प्रासादाद् अवरोहति 'he *descends from* the palace;' विष्णुः स्वर्गाद् अवततार 'Vishṇu *descended from* heaven;' कनककेयूरम् अङ्गाद् अवतारयति 'he *takes off* (causes to descend) the golden bracelet from his body;' निवर्तते पापात् 'he *ceases from* wickedness;' वचनाद् विरराम 'he *left off* speaking;' नरकात् पितरं त्रायते पुत्रो धार्मिकः 'a virtuous son *saves* his father from hell;' अश्वमेधसहस्रात् सत्यम् अतिरिच्यते 'truth *is superior to* a thousand sacrifices;' स्वहितात् प्रमाद्यति 'he *neglects* his own interest;' मित्रम् अकुशलाद् निवारयति 'a friend *guards* one from evil.'

Genitive after the Verb.

857. The genitive in Sanskṛit is constantly interchangeable with the dative, locative, or even instrumental and accusative*. It is more especially, however, used to supply the place of the first of these cases, so that almost all verbs may take a genitive as well as dative of 'the object' to which any thing is imparted. For example, दरिद्रस्य धनं ददाति 'he *gives* money to the poor.'

858. It may be used for the locative after verbs of *consigning*, as निक्षेपं मम अर्पयति 'he *deposits* a pledge with me;' or of *trusting*, as न कश्चित् स्त्रीणां श्रद्दधाति 'nobody puts *trust* in women;' and for the accusative in examples such as अविचिन्तितानि दुःखानि आयान्ति देहिनां 'unexpected ills *come upon* corporeal beings.'

859. It is sometimes used after verbs of *fearing*; as, तस्य किं न बिभेषि 'Why art thou not *afraid of* him?' see 855. Also after verbs of *longing for*, *desiring*, *envying*; as, अवमानस्य आकाङ्क्षेत् 'he should *desire* contempt;' स्पृहयामि पुरुषाणां चक्षुष्मतां 'I *envy* men who possess eyes.'

a. Other examples of verbs followed by genitive cases are, अजानताम् अस्माकं कथय कस्य असि भार्या '*tell* us, who are ignorant *of* it, whose wife you are;' कस्य (for कस्मात्) बिभ्यति धार्मिकाः 'Of whom are the righteous *afraid*?' यद् अन्यस्य प्रतिजानीते न तद् अन्यस्य दद्यात् 'one should not *give* to one what one *promises* to another;' मम न शृणोति 'he does not *hear* me' (cf. the Greek usage);

* This vague use of the genitive to express 'various relations' prevails also in early Greek.

मम स्मरेः '*remember me*,' or with the accusative. अस्माकं मृत्युः प्रभवति 'death *overcomes* us;' अग्निस् न तृप्यति काष्ठानां 'fire is not *satisfied with* fuel;' तेषां क्षमेथाः '*forgive* them;' किं मया तस्य अपकृतं 'What *offence have I given him?*'

Locative after the Verb.

860. This case is very widely applicable, but, as elsewhere remarked, is frequently interchangeable with the dative and genitive. The first sense of the locative requires that it should be united with verbs in reference only to 'the place' or 'time' in which any thing is done; as, पङ्के मज्जति 'he *sinks* in the mud;' पुरे वसति 'he *dwells* in the city;' रणमूर्ध्नि तिष्ठति 'he *stands* in the front of the fight;' सूर्योदये प्रबुध्यते 'at sunrise he *awakes*.'

861. The transition from 'the place' to 'the object' or 'recipient' of any action is natural; and hence it is that verbs are found with the locative of 'the object' to which any thing is imparted or communicated, as in the following examples: मा प्रयच्छ ईश्वरे धनं '*bestow* not money on the mighty;' तस्मिन् कार्याणि निक्षिपामि 'I *entrust* my affairs to him;' पुत्रे अङ्गुलीयकं समर्पयति 'he *consigns* a ring to his son;' योग्ये सचिवे न्यस्यति राज्यभारं 'he *entrusts* the burden of the kingdom to a capable minister;' राज्ञि or राजकुले निवेदयति 'he *informs* the king;' नले वद '*say to* Nala.'

a. प्रेतं भूमौ निदध्यात् 'one should *place* (bury) a dead man in the ground;' धर्मे मनो दधाति 'he *applies* his mind to virtue.' In this sense कृ may be used; as, पृष्ठे इन्धनम् अकरोत् 'he *placed* the wood on his back;' मतिं पापे करोति 'he *applies* his mind to sin.'

862. When दा, 'to give,' is used for 'to put,' it follows the same analogy; as, तस्य पुच्छाग्रे हस्तं देहि '*put* your hand on the end of its tail;' भस्मचये पदं ददौ 'he *placed* his foot on a heap of ashes.' Similarly, वस्त्राञ्चले धृतो ऽस्ति 'he was *held* by the skirt of his garment.' So also verbs of *seizing, striking*; as, केशेषु गृह्णाति or आकर्षति 'he *seizes* or *drags* him by the hair;' सुप्ते प्रहरति 'he *strikes* a sleeping man;' गृहीत्वा तं दक्षिणे पाणौ 'having *taken* hold of him by the right hand.'

863. The locative is often put for the dative in sentences where the latter case stands for the infinitive; thus, भर्तुर् अन्वेषणे त्वरस्व '*hasten* to seek thy spouse;' नलस्य आनयने यतस्व '*strive* to bring Nala hither;' न शेकुस् तस्य धनुषो ग्रहणे 'they could not *hold* that bow;' न शक्तो ऽभवत् निवारणे 'he *was not able to* prevent it.'

a. Other examples are, उग्रे तपसि वर्तते 'he is *engaged* in a very severe penance;' परकार्येषु मा व्यापृतो भूः 'do not *busy yourself* about other people's affairs;' विषयेषु सज्जते 'he is *addicted to* objects of sense;' सर्वलोकहिते रमते 'he *delights* in the good of all the world;' दुर्गाधिकारे नियुज्यते 'he is *appointed to* the command of the fort;' द्वौ वृषभौ धुरि नियोजयति 'he *yokes* two bulls to the pole;' सैनापत्ये ऽभिषिञ्च मां '*anoint* me to the generalship;' धर्मे व्याप्रियते 'he *strives to suppress evil-doers;'* कोपस् तेषाम् आसीन् नृपे 'they had *anger against* the king;' परीक्षां कुरु बाहुके '*make trial of* Vāhuka;' आधास्ये त्वयि दोषं '*I will lay the blame* on you;' वरयस्व तं पतित्वे '*choose him for* thy husband;' देवा अमृते यत्नवन्तो बभूवुः 'the gods exerted themselves for the nectar.'

b. न मादृशे युज्यते वाक्यम् ईदृशं 'such language is not *suited* to a person like me;' प्रभुत्वं त्वयि युज्यते 'sovereignty is *suited* to you;' आसने उपाविशत् 'he *reclined* on a seat;' कुथाम् आसस्व* '*sit* thou on a cushion;' शत्रुषु विश्वसिति 'he *confides* in his enemies;' चरणयोः पतति 'it *falls* at his feet;' लुठति पादेषु 'it *rolls* at the feet.'

Change of case after the same Verb.

864. This sometimes occurs; as, विदुरो धृतराष्ट्राय कुन्ती च गान्धार्याः सर्वं न्यवेदयेतां 'Vidhura and Kuntí *announced* every thing, the one to Dhṛita-ráshṭra, the other to Gándhárí' (Astrasiksha 34), where the same verb governs a dative and genitive. Similarly, in the Hitopadeśa, शृङ्गिणां विश्वासो न कर्तव्यः स्त्रीषु च 'confidence is not to be *placed* in horned animals or women.'

INSTRUMENTAL CASE AFTER PASSIVE VERBS.

865. The prevalence of a passive construction is the most remarkable feature in the syntax of this language. Passive verbs are joined with 'the agent, instrument, or cause,' in the instrumental case†, and agree with 'the object' in number and person; as, वातेन रज उद्धूयते 'the dust is raised by the wind;' तेन सर्वद्रव्याणि सज्जीक्रियन्तां 'let all things be prepared by him;' इषुभिर् आदित्यो ऽन्तरधीयत 'the sun was concealed by arrows.'

866. But the passive participle usually takes the place of the *past tenses* of the passive verb, and agrees with 'the object' in *gender* and *case* as well as number; as, नेत्राणि बाष्पाकुलानि आसन् '(their) eyes were suffused with tears;' तेन उक्तं (इदं being understood) 'it was said by him.' Compare 895.

a. This instrumental construction after passive verbs is a favourite idiom in Sanskṛit prose composition, and the love for it is remarkably displayed in such phrases as the following: दुःखेन गम्यते, 'he is gone to by misery,' for दुःखं गच्छति; and आगम्यतां देवेन, 'let it be come by your majesty,' for आगच्छतु देवः; and again, अस्माभिर् एकत्र स्थीयतां, 'let it be remained by us in one spot,' for 'let us remain in one spot;' येन मार्गेण इष्टं तेन गम्यतां 'by whatever road it is desired, by that let it be gone.'

b. Active or causal verbs, which take a double accusative, will retain one accusa-

---

* आसस्व Epic form for आस्स्व or आस्व.

† There are a *few* instances of the agent in the genitive case; as, मम कृतं पापं, 'a crime committed by me,' for मया.

tive when constructed passively; but the other accusative passes into a nominative case: thus, instead of स मां परुषाणि उवाच, 'he addressed me in harsh words,' may be written तेन अहं परुषाणि उक्तः, 'by him I was addressed in harsh words.'

SYNTAX OF THE INFINITIVE MOOD.

867. The infinitive in Sanskrit cannot be employed with the same latitude as in other languages. Its use is very limited, corresponding to that of the Latin *supines*, as its termination *tum* indicates.

a. Let the student, therefore, distinguish between the infinitive of Sanskrit and that of Latin and Greek. In these latter languages we have the infinitive made the subject of a proposition; or, in other words, standing in the place of a nominative, and an accusative case often admissible before it. We have it also assuming different forms, to express present, past, or future time, and completeness or incompleteness in the progress of the action. The Sanskrit infinitive, on the other hand, can never be made the subject or nominative case to a verb, admits of no accusative before it, and can only express indeterminate time and incomplete action. Wherever it occurs it must be considered as the object, and never the subject, of some verb expressed or understood. As the object of the verb, it may be regarded as equivalent to an indeclinable substantive, in which the force of two cases, an accusative and dative, is inherent, and which differs from other substantives in its power of governing a case. Its use as a substantive, with the force of the *accusative* case, corresponds to one use of the Latin infinitive; thus, तत् सर्वं श्रोतुम् इच्छामि 'I desire to hear all that,' '*id audire cupio*,' where श्रोतुं and *audire* are both equivalent to accusative cases, themselves also governing an accusative. Similarly, रोदितुं प्रवृत्ता 'she began to weep;' and महीं जेतुम् आरेभे 'he began to conquer the earth,' where महीजयम् आरेभे, 'he began the conquest of the earth,' would be equally correct.

b. Bopp considers the termination of the infinitive to be the accusative of the affix *tu* (459. *a*), and it is certain that in the Veda other cases of nouns formed with this affix in the sense of infinitives occur; e.g. a dative in *tave* or *tavai*, as from *han* comes *hantave*, 'to kill;' fr. *anu-i*, *anvetave*, 'to follow;' fr. *man*, *mantavai*, 'to think:' there is also a form in *tos*, generally in the sense of an ablative, e.g. fr. *i* comes *etos*, 'from going;' fr. *han*, *hantos*, as in *purá hantos*, 'before killing:' and a form in *tví* corresponding to the indeclinable participle in *tvá* of the classical language, e.g. fr. *han*, *hatví*, 'killing;' fr. *bhú*, *bhútví*, 'being.' Infinitives may also be formed in the Veda by simply adding the usual case-terminations to the root; e.g. in the sense of an accusative, fr. *á-ruh* may come *áruham*, 'to ascend;' fr. *á-sad*, *ásadam*, 'to sit down:' of a dative, fr. *á-dhṛish*, *ádhṛishe*, 'to get at,' 'subdue;' fr. *sam-ćaksh*, *samćakshe*, 'to survey:' of an ablative, fr. *ava-pad*, *avapadas*, 'from falling down.' Infinitives are also formed by changing the final *á* of roots ending in this letter to *ai*, e.g. fr. *pra-yá*, *prayai*, 'to approach:' or by adding *se* (liable to be changed to *she*) to a root, as fr. *ji* comes *jishe*, 'to conquer:' or by adding *ase*, e. g. fr. *jīv*, *jīvase*, 'to live:' or *adhyai*, e. g. fr. *bhṛi*, *bharadhyai*, 'to bear;' fr. *yaj*, *yajadhyai*, 'to sacrifice,' &c.

868. But the Sanskṛit infinitive most commonly involves a sense which belongs especially to the Sanskṛit dative, viz. that of 'the end' or 'purpose' for which any thing is done; thus, शावकान् भक्षितुम् आगच्छति 'he comes to devour the young ones;' शत्रून् योद्धुं सैन्यं प्राहिणोत् 'he sent an army to fight the enemy.'

a. In these cases it would be equally correct in Sanskṛit to substitute for the infinitive the dative case of the verbal noun, formed with the affix *ana*; thus, भक्षणाय, 'for the eating,' for भक्षितुं; योधनाय, 'for the fighting,' for योद्धुं; and in Latin the infinitive could not be used at all, but either the supine, *devoratum*, *pugnatum*, or, still more properly, the conjunction *ut* with the subjunctive mood, '*ut devoret*,' '*ut pugnaret*.' The following are other examples in which the infinitive has a dative force in expressing '*the purpose*' of the action: पानीयं पातुं नदीम् अगमत् 'he went to the river to drink water;' मम बन्धनं छेत्तुम् उपसर्पति 'he comes to cut asunder my bonds;' मां त्रातुं समर्थः (अस्ति being understood) 'he is able to rescue me;' पाशान् संवरितुं यत्नो बभूव 'he busied himself about collecting together the snares.'

b. The best Paṇḍits think that the infinitive ought not to be used when the verb which is connected with it refers to a different person, or is not समानाधिकरणे; thus तं गन्तुम् आज्ञापय, 'command him to go,' would be better expressed by तं गमनाय आज्ञापय.

c. The infinitive cannot be used after an accusative to express '*that*,' as in Latin; thus, 'having heard that Duryodhana was killed' would be expressed by हतं दुर्योधनं श्रुत्वा.

869. The Sanskṛit infinitive, therefore, has more of the character of a supine than an infinitive; and in its character of supine is susceptible of either an active or passive signification. In its passive character, however, like the Latin *supine* in *u*, it is joined with certain words only, the most usual being the passive verbs शक् 'to be able' and युज् 'to be fitting,' and their derivatives; thus, त्यक्तुं न शक्यते 'it cannot be abandoned;' पाशो न छेत्तुं शक्यते 'the snare cannot be cut;' न शक्याः समाधातुं ते दोषाः 'those evils cannot be remedied;' श्रोतुं न युज्यते 'it is not fitting to be heard;' छेत्तुम् अयोग्यः 'unfit to be cut;' अवज्ञा न युक्तम् अवमानम् तस्य कर्तुं 'contempt is not proper to be shown by thee for him;' कीर्तयितुं योग्यः 'worthy to be celebrated.'

a. The following are other instances: मण्डपः कारयितुम् आरब्धः 'the shed was begun to be built;' राज्ये अभिषेक्तुं भवान् निरूपितः 'your honour has been selected to be inaugurated to the kingdom;' अर्हति कर्तुं 'it deserves to be done;' कर्तुम् अनुचितं 'improper to be done' (cf. *factu indignum* and ποιεῖν αἰσχρόν);

सा मोचयितुं न्याय्या 'she ought to be released;' किम् इदं कर्तुं युक्तं 'what is sought to be done.' The infinitive of neuter verbs, which have a passive sense, will of course be passive; as, क्रोद्धुं न अर्हसि 'deign not to be angry.'

870. The root अर्ह् 'to deserve,' when used in combination with an infinitive, is usually equivalent to 'an entreaty' or 'respectful imperative;' as, धर्मान् नो वक्तुम् अर्हसि 'deign (or simply 'be pleased') to tell us our duties.' It sometimes has the force of the Latin *debet*; as, न मादृशी त्वाम् अभिभाषितुम् अर्हति 'such a person as I ought not to address you;' न एनं शोचितुम् अर्हसि 'you ought not to bewail him.'

871. The infinitive is sometimes joined with the noun काम, 'desire,' to form a kind of compound adjective, expressive of wishing to do any thing, but the final *m* is then rejected; thus, द्रष्टुकामः, -मा, -मं, 'desirous of seeing;' जेतुकामः, -मा, -मं, 'wishing to conquer.'

a. Sometimes the infinitive is joined in the same way with मनस्; thus, स द्रष्टुमनाः 'he has a mind to see.'

872. When *kim* follows the infinitive a peculiar transposition sometimes takes place, of which the 1st Act of Sakuntalá furnishes an example; thus, सख्यास् ते ज्ञातुम् इच्छामि किम् अनया वैखानसं व्रतं निषेवितव्यम्, 'I wish to know thy friend, whether this monastic vow is to be observed by her,' for ज्ञातुम् इच्छामि किं सख्या ते &c. 'I wish to know whether this vow is to be observed by thy friend.'

USE AND CONNEXION OF THE TENSES.

873. PRESENT TENSE.—This tense, besides its proper use, is often used for the future; as, क्व गच्छामि 'Whither shall I go?' कदा त्वां द्रक्ष्यामि 'When shall I see thee?' किं करोमि 'What shall I do?' and sometimes for the imperative; as, तत् कुर्मः 'let us do that.'

874. In *narration* it is commonly used for the past tense; as, स भूमिं स्पृष्ट्वा कर्णौ स्पृशति ब्रूते च 'he, having touched the ground, touches his ears, and says.'

875. It may denote '*habitual*' or '*repeated*' action; as, मृगः प्रत्यहं तत्र गत्वा शस्यं खादति 'the deer going there every day was in the habit of eating the corn;' यदा स मूषिकशब्दं शृणोति तदा बिडालं संवर्धयति 'whenever he heard the noise of the mouse, then he would feed the cat.'

876. It is usually found after यावत् and तावत्; as, यावन् मे दन्ता न त्रुट्यन्ति तावत् तव पाशं छिनद्मि 'as long as my teeth do not break, so long will I gnaw asunder your fetters.' (Compare the use of the Latin *dum*.)

877. The present tense of the root आस्, 'to sit,' 'to remain,' is used with the present participle of another verb, to denote '*continuous*' or '*simultaneous*' action; as, पशूनां वधं कुर्वन् आस्ते 'he keeps making a slaughter of the beasts;' मम पश्चाद् आगच्छन् आस्ते 'he is in the act of coming after me.'

878. The particle स्म, when used with the present, gives it the force of a perfect: as, प्रविशन्ति स्म पुरीं 'they entered the city;' निवसन्ति स्म 'they dwelt.'

879. POTENTIAL.—The name of this tense is no guide to its

numerous uses. Perhaps its most common force is that of '*fitness*' in phrases, where in Latin we should expect to find *oportet* with the infinitive; as, आगतं भयं वीक्ष्य नरः कुर्याद् यथोचितं 'having beheld danger actually present, a man should act in a becoming manner.'

880. It is also employed, as might be expected, in *indefinite general expressions*; as, यस्य यो भावः स्यात् 'whatever may be the disposition of any one;' यदा राजा स्वयं न कुर्यात् कार्य-दर्शनं 'when the king may not himself make investigation of the case;' अकाल-सह-वचनं ब्रुवन् प्राप्नुयाद् अपमानं 'by uttering unseasonable words one may meet with dishonour.'

a. Especially in *conditional sentences*; as, यदि राजा दण्डं न प्रणयेत् स्वाम्यं कस्मिंश्चिन् न स्यात् सर्व-सेतवश्च भिद्येरन् 'if the king were not to inflict punishment, ownership would remain with nobody, and all barriers would be broken down.' Sometimes the conjunction is omitted; as, न भवेत् 'should it not be so;' न स्यात् पराधीनः 'were he not subject to another.'

881. The potential often occurs as a *softened imperative*, the Sanskrit language, in common with others in the East, being averse to the more abrupt *form*; thus, गच्छेः, 'do thou go,' *for* गच्छ; and भक्षयेत् फलानि, 'let him eat fruits,' *for* भक्षयतु.

882. IMPERATIVE.—This tense yields the usual force of '*command*' or '*entreaty*;' as, आश्वसिहि 'take courage;' माम् अनुस्मर 'remember me.'

मा, *and not* न, *must be used in prohibition*; as, अनृतं मा ब्रूहि 'do not tell a falsehood;' मा लज्जस्व 'be not ashamed;' see 889. The first person is used to express '*necessity*,' see example at 796.

a. The 3d pers. singular is sometimes used interjectionally; thus, अस्तु 'Be it so!' 'Well!' यातु 'Let it go!' 'Come along!' 'Come!'

883. It is sometimes employed in conditional phrases to express '*contingency*;' as, अनुजानीहि मां गच्छामि 'permit me, (and) I will go,' i.e. 'if you will permit me, I will go;' आज्ञापय हन्मि दुर्-आत्मानं 'if you command me, I will kill the villain;' अभय-वाचं मे यच्छ गच्छामि 'if you give me a promise of security, I will go.'

884. IMPERFECT OR FIRST PRETERITE.—Although this tense, as explained at 242, properly has reference to '*past incomplete action*,' and has been so rendered in the paradigms of verbs, yet it is commonly used to denote '*indefinite past time*,' without any necessary connexion with another action; as, अर्थं ग्रहीतुं यत्नम् अकरवं 'I made an effort to collect wealth,' not necessarily 'I was making.' The augment may be cut off after मा, as in the aorist; thus, मा स्म भवत् 'May he not become?' See Pāṇini VI. 4. 74.

885. PERFECT OF SECOND PRETERITE.—As explained at 242, this tense is properly used to express '*an action done at some definite period of past time;*' as, कौशल्यादयो नृपतिं दशरथं चक्रन्दुः 'Kauśalyá and the others bewailed king Daśaratha.' It is frequently, however, employed indeterminately.

886. FIRST FUTURE.—This tense, as remarked at 242, expresses '*definite* but *not immediate* futurity;' as, तासु दिक्षु कामस्य फलं लब्धासि 'in those regions thou shalt (one day) obtain the fruit of thy desire.'

887. SECOND FUTURE.—This tense, although properly indefinite, is employed to express '*all degrees and kinds of futurity*,' immediate or remote, definite or indefinite; as, स्वादु पयः पास्यसि 'thou shalt drink sweet water;' तत्र अवश्यं भार्यां द्रक्ष्यति 'there certainly he will see his wife;' अद्य गमिष्यसि 'this very day thou shalt go.'

a. It is sometimes used for the imperative; as, यद् देयं तद् दास्यसि 'whatever is to be given, that you will give,' (do thou give.)

888. AORIST OF THIRD PRETERITE.—This tense properly expresses '*time indefinitely past;*' as, अभूत् नृपः 'there lived (in former times) a king;' see 242.

889. It is also employed to supply the place of the imperative, after the prohibitive particle मा or मास्म, the augment being omitted; as, मा कृथाः 'do not make;' मा त्याक्षीः समयं 'do not lose the opportunity;' मास्म अनृतं वादीः 'do not tell an untruth;' मा क्रुधः 'do not be angry;' मा शुचः 'do not grieve;' मा हिंसीः 'do not injure;' मा भीभिदः 'do not destroy;' एवं वोचः 'do not speak so;' मा भैषीः 'be not afraid' (contracted into मा भैः in Nala XIV).

890. PRECATIVE OF BENEDICTIVE.—Only one example of this tense occurs in the Hitopadeśa: नित्यं भूयात् सकल-सुख-वसतिः 'May he constantly be the abode of all happiness!' It is chiefly used in pronouncing benedictions. Also in imprecations.

a. In the latter case a noun formed with an affix *ani* is frequently used; thus, अजीवनिस् ते भूयात् 'May there be loss of life to thee!' 'Mayst thou perish!'

891. CONDITIONAL.—This tense is even less frequent than the last. Its use is explained at 242. The following are other examples: यदि राजा दण्डं न प्रणयेत् तदा शूले मत्स्यान् इव अपक्ष्यन् दुर्बलान् बलवत्तराः 'if the king were not to inflict punishment, then the stronger would roast the weak like fish on a spit;' or, according to the Scholiast, हिंसाम् अकरिष्यन् 'would cause injury;' सुवृष्टिश् चेद् अभविष्यत् तदा सुभिक्षम् अभविष्यत् 'if there should be abundant rain then there would be abundance of food.' According to Pánini (III. 3. 139) it is used क्रियातिपत्तौ 'when the action is supposed to pass by unaccomplished' (क्रियाया अनिष्पत्तौ Schol.).

a. LEṬ.—The Vedic mood, called *Leṭ* by native grammarians, corresponds to the subjunctive of the Greek language. In forming it from the indicative a short *a* is inserted between the conjugational base and the termination, or if the conjugational base ends in *a*, this letter is lengthened; at the same time the augment of the imperfect and aorist is dropped, e. g. from *han* comes pres. ind. *han-ti*; but subj. *han-a-ti*: from *pat*, pres. ind. *pata-ti*; subj. *patá-ti*: from *aś*, impf. ind. *áśno-t*; subj. *aśnava-t*, i. e. *aśno + a + t*. So also, from *pat*, impf. ind. *apata-t*; subj. *patá-t*: from *dṛś*, aor. ind. *adrāk* (for *adrāksh-t*, cf. du. *adrāksh-va*, &c.); subj. *drāksh-a-t*. It may also be mentioned that in the Ātmane the final *e* may optionally be changed to *ai*, e. g. *mādayādhvai*; and that the subjunctive of the aorist sometimes takes the terminations of the present tense without lengthening *a*, e. g. from *vad* comes aor. ind. *avadat*, subj. *vadāti*.

Observe—The characteristic of *Leṭ* is the insertion of *a*.

SYNTAX OF PARTICIPLES.

892. Participles in Sanskṛit often discharge the functions of the tenses of verbs. They are constantly found occupying the place of past and future tenses, and more especially of passive verbs.

893. Participles govern the cases of the verbs whence they are derived; as, व्याधं पश्यन् 'seeing the fowler;' वने चरन् 'walking in the forest;' तत् कृतवान् 'he did that;' शब्दम् आकर्ण्य 'having heard a noise;' पानीयम् अपीत्वा गतः 'he went away without drinking water.'

a. In the case of passive participles, as will presently appear, the agent is put in the instrumental case; and the participle agrees with the object, like an adjective.

Present Participles.

894. These are not so commonly used in Sanskṛit composition as past and future participles, but they are often idiomatically employed, especially where in English the word 'while' or 'whilst' is introduced; thus, अहं दक्षिणारण्ये चरन् अपश्यं 'whilst walking in the southern forest, I beheld,' &c.

Past Passive Participle.

895. This most useful participle is constantly used to supply the place of a *perfect tense passive*, sometimes in conjunction with the auxiliary verbs *as* and *bhū*, 'to be;' thus, आदिष्टो ऽस्मि 'I am commanded;' वयं विस्मिताः स्मः 'we are astonished;' उषितो ऽस्मि 'I have dwelt' (compare 866). Of course the participle is made to agree adjectively with the object in gender, number, and case, as in Latin;

and the agent, which in English would probably be in the nominative, and in Latin in the ablative, becomes in Sanskrit instrumental. Thus, in Sanskrit, the phrase 'I wrote a letter' would not be so idiomatically expressed by अहं पत्रं लिलेख, as by मया पत्रं लिखितं or मया पत्रं लिखितम् आसीत् 'by me a letter was written,' '*a me epistola scripta.*' So again, तेन बन्धनानि छिन्नानि 'by him the bonds were cut' is more idiomatic than स बन्धनानि चिच्छेद 'he cut the bonds;' and तेन उक्तं 'by him it was said' is more usual than स उवाच 'he said*.'

a. This participle may often be used impersonally, when, if the verb belong to the first group of classes, it may optionally be guṇated; as, द्युतितं or द्योतितं सूर्येण 'it is shone by the sun.' The same holds good if the beginning of an action is denoted; as, सूर्यः प्रद्युतितः or प्रद्योतितः 'the sun has begun to shine.'

b. When a verb governs a double accusative case (see 846), one accusative will be preserved after the passive participle; as, विश्वामित्रेण दशरथो रामं याचितः 'Daśaratha was asked for Ráma by Viśvámitra.'

896. But frequently the past passive participle is used for the active past participle; in which case it may sometimes govern the accusative case, like a perfect tense active; thus, स वृक्षम् आरूढः 'he ascended the tree;' स गृहं गतः or आगतः 'he went home;' मार्गं तीर्णः 'having crossed the road;' अहं पदवीम् अवतीर्णो ऽस्मि 'I have descended to the road;' अहं नगरीम् अनुप्राप्तः 'I reached the city;' आवाम् आश्रमं प्रविष्टौ स्वः 'we two have entered the hermitage.' But observe, that its use for the active participle is generally, though not invariably, restricted to intransitive verbs which involve the idea of '*motion*,' and to a few other neuter verbs. The following are other examples: पक्षिण उत्पतिताः 'the birds flew away;' स मृतः 'he died;' व्याधो निवृत्तः 'the fowler returned;' स भोक्तुं प्रवृत्तः 'he proceeded to eat;' स आश्रितः 'he had recourse to;' स प्रसुप्तः 'he fell asleep;' ते स्थिताः 'they stood;' उषितः 'he lodged.'

a. This participle has sometimes a *present signification*; thus, स्थित 'stood' may occasionally be translated 'standing,' भीत 'fearing,' स्मित 'smiling,' आश्लिष्ट 'embracing;' and all verbs characterised by the anubandha ञि may optionally use this participle in the sense of the present. See 75. c.

b. The neuter of the passive participle is sometimes used as a substantive; thus, दत्तं 'a gift;' खातं 'an excavation;' अन्नं 'food;' दुग्धं 'milk.'

---

* This instrumental or passive construction, which is so prevalent in Sanskrit, has been transferred from it to Hindí, Maráthí, Gujaráthí, and other dialects of India. The particle *ne* in Hindí and Hindústání corresponds to the Sanskrit न *na*, the final letter of the commonest termination for the instrumental case, and can never occasion any difficulty if so regarded.

Active Past Participle.

897. This participle is much used (especially in modern Sanskṛit and the writings of commentators) to supply the place of a *perfect tense active.* It may govern the case of the verb; as, सर्वं श्रुतवान् 'he heard every thing;' पत्नी पतिम् आलिङ्गितवती 'the wife embraced her husband;' राज्ञो हस्ते फलं दत्तवान् 'he gave the fruit into the hand of the king;' तत् कृतवती 'she did that.' This participle may also be used with the auxiliaries *as* and *bhū*, 'to be,' to form a compound perfect tense; thus, तत् कृतवान् अस्ति 'he has done that;' तत् कृतवान् भविष्यति 'he will have done that.'

Indeclinable Past Participles.

898. The sparing use made in Sanskṛit composition of relative pronouns, conjunctions, and connective particles, is mainly to be attributed to these participles, by means of which the sense of a clause may be suspended, and sentence after sentence strung together without the aid of a single copulative. They occur in narration more commonly than any other kind of participle; and some of the chief peculiarities of Sanskṛit syntax are to be traced to the frequency of their occurrence.

899. They are generally used for the *past tense*, as united with a copulative conjunction, and are usually translatable by the English 'having,' 'when,' 'after,' 'by,' see 555; thus, इदं आकर्ण्य निश्चितम् एष ध्रुवं कुक्कुर इति मत्वा छागं त्यक्त्वा स्नात्वा स्वगृहं ययौ 'having heard this, having thought to himself "this is certainly a dog," having abandoned the goat, having bathed, he went to his own house.' In all these cases we should use in English the past tense with a conjunction; thus, 'When he had heard this, he thought to himself that it must certainly be a dog. He then abandoned the goat, and, when he had bathed, went to his own house.'

a. It is evident from the above example that the indeclinable participles often stand in the place of a *pluperfect* tense, a tense which does not really exist in Sanskṛit.

b. But although they always refer to something past, it should be observed that they are frequently rendered in English by the present participle, as in the fifth sentence of the story at 930.

900. Another, though less frequent use of them is as *gerunds* in *do*; thus, नराः शास्त्राणि अधीत्य * भवन्ति पण्डिताः 'men become wise *by* reading the Śástras;'

---

* As the Latin gerund is connected with the future part. in *dus*, so the Sanskṛit indeclinable part. in *ya* is probably connected with the future passive part. in *ya*.

भार्या शतम् अपराद्धं कृत्वा भर्तव्या 'a wife is to be supported even *by* doing a hundred wrong things;' किं पौरुषं हत्वा सुप्तं 'What bravery is there in killing a sleeping man?'

Observe—This participle is occasionally capable of a passive sense.

901. Note—The termination त्वा *tvā* is probably the instrumental case of the same affix of which the infinitive termination (*tum*) is the accusative; see 458. It is certain at least that the indeclinable participle bears about it much of the character of an instrumental case, as it is constantly found in grammatical connexion with the agent in this case; thus, सर्वैः पशुभिर् मिलित्वा सिंहो विज्ञप्तः 'by all the beasts having met together the lion was informed;' सर्वैर् जालम् आदाय उड्डीयतां 'by all having taken up the net let it be flown away.'

a. Another and stronger proof of its instrumental character is, that the particle अलं, which always governs the instrumental case, is not unfrequently joined with the indeclinable participle; thus, अलं भोजनेन, 'enough of eating,' is with equal correctness of idiom expressed by अलं भुक्त्वा; see 918. *a.*

Future Passive Participles.

902. The usual sense yielded by this participle is that of '*fitness*,' '*obligation*,' '*necessity*' (see 568); and the usual construction required is, that the agent on whom the duty or necessity rests be in the instrumental case, and the participle agree with the object; as, त्वया प्रवृत्तिर् न विधेया 'by you the attempt is not to be made.'

a. Sometimes, however, the agent is in the genitive case; thus, द्विजातीनां भक्तम् भक्ष्यं 'boiled rice is to be eaten by Brāhmaṇs.' Compare 865, note.

903. Occasionally the future passive participle may yield a sense equivalent to '*worthy of*,' '*deserving of*:' thus, कश्य 'deserving a whipping;' ताडनीय 'worthy of being beaten;' मुसल्य 'deserving death by pounding;' वध्य 'worthy of death.'

904. If the verb govern two accusatives, one may be retained after the future passive participle; as, नयनसलिलं त्वया शान्तिं नेयं 'the tear of the eye is to be brought to assuagement by thee.'

905. Occasionally the neuter of this participle is used impersonally; in which case it does not agree with the object, but may govern it in the manner of the verb; thus, मया ग्रामं गन्तव्यं, 'it is to be gone by me to the village,' for मया ग्रामो गन्तव्यः. So also, त्वया सभां प्रवेष्टव्यं 'by you it is to be entered into the assembly.'

a. The neuter भवितव्यं (from भू) is thus used, and, in accordance with 841, requires the instrumental after it, as well as before; thus, केनापि कारणेन भवितव्यं 'by something it must become the cause,' i. e. 'there must be some cause;' स्वामिना सविवेकेन भवितव्यं 'a ruler ought to be possessed of discrimination;' मया तव अनुचरेण भवितव्यं 'I must become your companion;' भार्यया प्रवहणारूढया भवितव्यं 'the lady must be seated in the carriage.'

906. Similarly, the neuter of शक्य may be adverbially used, and impart at the same time a passive sense to the infinitive; thus, पवनः शक्यम् आलिङ्गितुम् अङ्गैः for पवनः शक्यः &c. 'the breeze is able to be embraced by the limbs' (Śak. Act III). Again, शक्यम् अञ्जलिभिः पातुं वाताः 'the breezes are able to be drunk by the hollowed palms;' विभूतयः शक्यम् अवाप्तुं 'great successes are able to be obtained.'

907. It is not uncommon to find this participle standing merely in the place of a future tense, no propriety or obligation being implied, just as the past passive participle stands in the place of a past tense; thus, नूनम् अनेन लुब्धकेन मृगमांसार्थिना गन्तव्यं 'in all probability this hunter will go in quest of the deer's flesh,' where गन्तव्यं is used impersonally; त्वां दृष्ट्वा लोकैः किञ्चिद् वक्तव्यं 'when the people see you, they will utter some exclamation;' यदि पक्षी पतति तदा मया खादितव्यः 'if the bird falls, then it shall be eaten by me.' See also the eleventh sentence of the story at 930.

908. The neuter of this participle is sometimes used infinitively or substantively, as expressive merely of 'the indeterminate action' of the verb, without implying 'necessity' or 'fitness.' In such cases इति may be added; thus, वञ्चयितव्यम् इति 'the being about to deceive,' 'deception' (Hitop. I. 416); मर्तव्यम् इति 'the being about to die,' 'dying:' but not always; as, जीवितव्यं 'life.'

Participial Nouns of Agency.

909. The first of these nouns of agency (580) is constantly used in poetry as a substitute for the present participle; implying, however, 'habitual action,' and therefore something more than present time. It is sometimes found governing the same case as the present participle, but united with the word which it governs in one compound; thus, पुरंजय 'city-conquering;' प्रियंवद 'speaking kind words;' जलेचर 'going in the water;' सरसिज 'lake-born.' But the word governed is often in the crude base; thus, तेजस्कर, 'light-making' (see 69), from *tejas* and *kri*; मनोहर, 'mind-captivating,' from *manas* and *hri* (64); बहुद, 'giving much,' from *bahu* and *dá*; आत्मज्ञ, 'self-knowing,' from *átman* and *jñá* (57. *b*).

910. The second (581) is sometimes, but rarely, found as a participle governing the case of the verb; thus, वाक्यं वक्ता 'speaking a speech;' गङ्गां धर्ता 'bearing the Ganges.'

911. The first and second species of the third (582. a. b), like the first, have often the sense of present participles, and are then always united with the crude base of the word which they govern in one compound; thus, मनोहारिन्, 'mind-captivating,' from *manas* and *hri*; कार्यसाधक, 'effective of the business,' from *kárya* and *sidh*. They may sometimes govern the case of the verb whence they are derived, and may then be compounded, or not, with the word which they govern; thus, ग्रामेवासिन्, 'dwelling in a village,' or ग्रामे वासिन्; कुड्मलानि चुम्बक 'kisser of the buds' (Ratnávali, p. 7).

SYNTAX OF CONJUNCTIONS, PREPOSITIONS, ADVERBS, &c.

Conjunctions.

912. च 'and' (727) is always placed after the word which it connects with another, like *que* in Latin, and can never stand first in a sentence, or in the same place as 'and' in English; thus, परिक्रम्य अवलोक्य च 'walking round and looking.' Unlike *que*, however, which must always follow the word of which it is the copulative, it may be admitted to any other part of the sentence, being only excluded from the first place; thus, तनयम् अचिरात् प्राची इव अर्कं प्रसूय च पावनं 'and having after a short time given birth to a pure son, as the eastern quarter (gives birth to) the sun.'

a. Sometimes two *ća's* are used, when one may be redundant or equivalent to the English 'both;' or the two *ća's* may be employed antithetically or disjunctively, or to express the contemporaneousness of two events; thus, अहश्च रात्रिश्च 'both day and night;' क्व हरिणकानां जीवितं च अतिलोलं क्व च शरास् ते 'Where on the one hand is the frail existence of fawns? Where on the other are thy arrows?' क्रन्दितुं च प्रवृत्ता स्त्रीसंस्थानं च ज्योतिर् उत्क्षिप्य एनां जगाम 'no sooner had she began to weep, than a shining apparition in female shape, having snatched her up, departed' (Śak. Act V).

b. Observe—When क्व, 'where?' is used as in the above example, it implies '*excessive incompatibility*,' or '*incongruity*.'

c. Sometimes च is used as an emphatic particle, and not as a copulative; thus, किं च मया परिणीतपूर्वा 'Was she indeed married by me formerly?'

913. तथा 'so,' 'likewise' (727. *b*), frequently supplies the place of च; thus, अनागतविधाता च प्रत्युत्पन्नमतिस् तथा 'both Anágata-vidhátá and Pratyutpanna-matis' (names of the two fish in Hitop. book IV).

914. हि 'for,' तु 'but,' वा 'or' (727. *d*, 728. *a*), like च, are excluded from the first place in a sentence; thus, पूर्वावधीरितं श्रेयो दुःखं हि परिवर्तते 'for happiness formerly scorned turns to misery;' विपर्यये तु 'but on the contrary;' एनां त्यज वा गृहाण वा 'either abandon her or take her.'

915. यदि 'if' and चेद् 'if' (727. *b*) may govern the potential or conditional (see 891), but are also used with the indicative; thus, यदि जीवति भद्राणि पश्यति 'if he live, he will behold prosperity;' यदि मया प्रयोजनम् अस्ति 'if there is need of me;' तृष्णा चेद् परित्यक्ता को दरिद्रः 'If avarice were abandoned, who would be poor?'

Prepositions and Adverbs.

916. Prepositions are often used in government with nouns. See 729, 730. *a. b. c. d. e. f. g.*

The following examples illustrate the construction of adverbs as described at 731.

917. आ मणिबन्धनात् 'as far as the wrist;' आमृत्योः 'till death;' आसमाप्तेः 'to the completion;' आ व्रतस्य समापनात् 'till the completion of his vow;'

आ शरीरविमोक्षणात् 'till his release from the body;' आजन्मनः 'from birth;' न दण्डाद् ऋते शक्यः कर्तुं पापविनिग्रहः 'the restraint of crime cannot be made *without* punishment;' शतं जन्मानि यावत् '*for* a hundred births;' सर्पविवरं यावत् '*up to* the serpent's hole;' पुत्रेण सह '*along with* his son;' हेतुं विना '*without* cause;' अपराधेन विना '*without* fault;' विवराद् बहिर् निःसृत्य 'creeping *out of* the hole;' अवलोकनक्षणात् प्रभृति 'from the moment of seeing (him);' जन्मप्रभृति '*from* birth;' ततः प्रभृति '*from that time forward*;' उपनयनात् प्रभृति '*from the time of* investiture;' धनस्य अर्थे, or more usually धनार्थं, '*for the sake of* wealth;' तस्याः कृते or तत्कृते 'for her *sake*;' पुत्रहेतोः '*for the sake of* a son;' तन्निमित्ते '*on that account*;' तव कारणात् 'on thy *account*.' उपरि, with the genitive, occurs rather frequently, and with some latitude of meaning; thus, नाभेर् उपरि '*above* the navel;' सिंहस् तस्य उपरि पपात 'the lion fell *upon* him;' मम उपरि विकारितः 'changed in his feelings *towards* me;' तव उपरि असद्व्यवहारी 'not behaving properly *towards* thee;' पुत्रस्य उपरि क्रुद्धः 'angry *with* his son;' नाभेर् ऊर्ध्वं '*above* the navel;' नाभेर् अधस्तात् '*below* the navel;' वृक्षस्य अधस्तात् '*beneath* the tree;' भोजनानन्तरं '*after* eating;' राज्ञः समीपं '*near* the king;' पितुः सकाशाद् धनम् आददाति 'he receives money *from* his father;' मांसं शुनो ऽग्रे निक्षिप्तं 'flesh thrown *before* the dog;' मम समक्षं 'in my *presence*.' साक्षात् may take an instrumental; as, अन्यैः साक्षात् '*before* others;' अस्माकं पश्चात् '*after* us;' प्राङ् निवेदनात् '*before* telling;' प्राग् उपनयनात् '*before* investiture;' भोजनात् प्राक् '*before* eating;' स्नानात् पूर्वं '*before* bathing;' विवाहात् पूर्वं '*before* marriage.' प्राक् may take an accusative; as, प्राग् द्वादशसमाः '*before* twelve years are over;' अभिवादनात् परं '*after* saluting;' तदवधेर् ऊर्ध्वं '*after* that period;' संवत्सराद् ऊर्ध्वं '*after* a year,' i. e. '*above a year* having expired;' विवाहाद् अर्वाक् '*after* marriage;' अर्वाक् सञ्चयनाद् अस्थ्नां '*after* collecting the bones;' फलम् अन्तरेण '*without* fruit;' भर्तुर् अनुमतिम् अन्तरेण '*without the* consent of her husband;' वाटिकाया दक्षिणेन '*to the right of* the garden;' प्राणिहिंसाव्यतिरेकेण 'without injury to living beings.'

918. अलं, 'enough,' is used with the instrumental, with the force of a prohibitive particle; as, अलं शङ्कया 'away with fear,' 'do not fear.'

a. It is also used with the indeclinable participle; as, अलं विचार्य 'enough of consideration;' see also 901. *a.*

b. It is sometimes followed by an infinitive; as, न अलम् अस्मि हृदयं निवर्तयितुं 'I am not able to turn back my heart.'

919. मात्रं 'even,' 'merely,' when compounded with another word is declinable; as, उत्तरमात्रं न ददाति 'he does not even give an answer;' न शब्दमात्राद् भेतव्यं 'one ought not to be afraid of mere noise;' शब्दमात्रेण 'by mere sound;' वचनमात्रेण 'by mere words;' उक्तमात्रे वचने 'immediately on the mere utterance of the speech.'

920. तथा and यथा, when used as correlatives, are equivalent to the English 'so that,' and the Latin *ita ut*; thus, यथा स्वामी जागर्ति तथा मया कर्तव्यं 'I must so act that my master awake,' i. e. 'I must do something to make my master awake.' So also, किं न जानासि यथा गृहरक्षां करोमि 'Do not you know that I keep watch in the house?'

a. ईदृशं, तादृशं, and यादृशं, may be used in the same way; thus, तादृशम् अनायुष्यं न किञ्चिद् विद्यते यादृशं परदारगमनं 'nothing is so opposed to length of life as intercourse with the wife of another.'

b. यत्, as well as यथा, is used for 'that;' thus, अयं नूतनो न्यायो यद् अरातिं हत्वा सन्तापः क्रियते 'this is a new doctrine, that having killed an enemy remorse should be felt.'

921. किं, 'why?' may often be regarded as a mark of interrogation which is not to be translated, but affects only the tone of voice in which a sentence is uttered; as, जातिमात्रेण किं कश्चित् पूज्यते 'Is any one honoured for mere birth?'

a. It sometimes has the force of 'whether;' as, ज्ञायतां किम् उपयुक्त एतावद् वर्तनं गृह्णाति अनुपयुक्तो वा 'let it be ascertained whether he is worthy to receive so large a salary, or whether he is unworthy;' मन्त्री वेत्ति किं गुणयुक्तो राजा न वा 'the minister knows whether the king is meritorious or not.'

922. वत् (technically *vati*) as an affix of comparison or similitude (724) may be compounded with a word in the crude base, which if uncompounded would be in the accusative case; thus, आत्मानं मृतवत् सन्दर्श्य 'showing himself as if dead;' आश्चर्यवद् इदं पश्यति 'he regards it as a wonder.' Also in the locative or genitive case; thus, मथुरावत् स्रुघ्ने प्राकारः 'a wall in Srughna like that in Mathurá.' According to Páṇini V. 1, 115, it is used in place of the instr. c. after adjectives of comparison, when some action is expressed; thus, ब्राह्मणेन तुल्यम् अधीते (see 826) may be rendered ब्राह्मणवद् अधीते, but it would not be correct to say पुत्रवत् स्थूलः for पुत्रेण तुल्यः स्थूलः.

923. The negative न is sometimes repeated to give intensity to an affirmation; thus, न न वक्ष्यति 'he will not not say' = वक्ष्यति एव 'he will certainly say.'

924. The indeclinable participle of *diś* with *ut* is sometimes used adverbially to express 'on account of,' 'with reference to,' 'towards,' and governs an accusative; thus, किम् उद्दिश्य 'On account of what?' तम् उद्दिश्य 'with reference to him.'

925. The indeclinable participle of रभ् with आ ('to begin') is used adverbially to express 'from,' 'beginning with,' and may either govern an ablative or be placed after the crude base; thus, निमन्त्रणाद् आरभ्य श्राद्धं यावत् 'from the time of invitation to the time of the Śráddha.' निमन्त्रणारभ्य would be equally correct.

926. The interjections धिक् and हा require the accusative; as, धिक् पापिष्ठं 'Woe to the wretch!' and the vocative interjections the vocative case; as, भोः पान्थ 'O traveller!'

a. Adverbs are sometimes used for adjectives in connexion with substantives; as, तत्र शालायां for तस्यां शालायां 'in that hall;' अमात्येषु मुख्यतः for अमात्येषु मुख्येषु 'among the principal ministers.'

ON THE USE OF THE PARTICLE इति.

927. All the languages of the East are averse to the use of the *obliqua oratio*. In Sanskṛit it is rarely admitted; and when any one relates the words or describes the sentiments or thoughts of another, the relator generally represents him as speaking the actual words, or thinking the thoughts, in his own person.

a. In such cases the particle इति (properly meaning 'so,' 'thus') is often placed after the words quoted, and may be regarded as serving the purpose of inverted commas; thus, शिष्या ऊचुः कृतकृत्या वयम् इति 'the pupils said, "We have accomplished our object;"' not, according to the English or Latin idiom, 'the pupils said *that they had* accomplished their object.' So also, कलहकारी इति त्वां भर्त्ता 'your husband calls you "quarrelsome,"' where कलहकारी is in the nominative case, as being the actual word supposed to be spoken by the husband himself in his own person. So again, त्वाम् विश्वासभूमय इति सर्वे पक्षिणो मम अग्रे प्रस्तुवन्ति 'all the birds praise you in my presence, saying, "He is an object of confidence,"' where the particle इति is equivalent to 'saying,' and the word विश्वासभूमयः is not in the accusative, to agree with त्वाम्, as might be expected, but in the nominative, as being the actual word supposed to be uttered by the birds in their own persons. In some cases, however, the accusative is retained before इति, as in the following example from Manu: अज्ञं बालम् इत्य् आहुः 'they call an ignorant man "child."' But in the latter part of the same line it passes into a nominative; as, पितेत्य् एव तु मन्त्रदं 'but (they call) a teacher of scripture "father."' II. 153.

928. In narratives and dialogues इति is often placed redundantly at the end of a speech. Again, it may have reference merely to what is passing in the mind either of another person or of one's self. When so employed, it is usually joined with the indeclinable participle, or of some other part of a verb signifying 'to think,' 'to suppose,' &c., and may be translated by the English conjunction 'that,' to which, in fact, it may be regarded as equivalent; thus, मर्कटो घण्टां वादयति इति परिज्ञाय 'having ascertained *that* it is a monkey who rings the bell;' पुनर् अर्थवृद्धिः कर्तव्या इति मतिर् बभूव 'his idea was *that* an increase of wealth ought again to be made;' धन्यो ऽहं यस्य एतादृशी भार्या इति मनसि विचार्य 'reflecting in his mind *that* I am happy in possessing such a wife.' The accusative is also retained before इति in this sense; as, मृतम् इति मत्वा 'thinking that he was dead.' In all these examples the use of इति indicates that a quotation is made of the thoughts of the person at the time when the event took place.

929. Not unfrequently the participle 'saying,' 'thinking,' 'supposing,' &c., is omitted altogether, and इति itself involves the sense of such a participle; as, बालो ऽपि न अवमन्तव्यो मनुष्य इति भूमिपः 'a king, even though a child, is not to be despised, *saying to one's self*, "He is a mortal;"' सौहार्दाद् वा विधुर इति वा

मय्य् अनुक्रोशात् 'either through affection or through compassion towards me, *saying to yourself*, "What a wretched man he is;"' अयं वराहः । अयं शार्दूल इति वन.वर्त्मसु आहिण्ड्यते 'There's a boar! Yonder's a tiger! *so crying out*, it is wandered about (by us) in the paths of the woods.'

CHAPTER X.

EXERCISES IN TRANSLATION AND PARSING.

930. STORY OF THE SAGE AND THE MOUSE, FROM 'THE HITOPADEŚA,' TRANSLATED AND PARSED.

1st sentence. अस्ति गौतमस्य मुनेस् तपो.वने महा.तपा नाम मुनिः । 'There is in the sacred grove of the sage Gautama a sage named Mahátapás (Great-devotion).'

2d. तेनाश्रम.सन्निधाने मूषिक.शावकः काक.मुखाद् भ्रष्टो दृष्टः । 'By him, in the neighbourhood of his hermitage, a young mouse, fallen from the beak of a crow, was seen.'

3d. ततो दया.युक्तेन तेन मुनिना नीवार.कणैः संवर्धितः । 'Then by that sage, touched with compassion, with grains of wild rice it was reared.'

4th. तदनन्तरं मूषिकं खादितुम् अनुधावन् विडालो मुनिना दृष्टः । 'Soon after this, a cat was observed by the sage running after the mouse to devour it.'

5th. तं मूषिकं भीतम् आलोक्य तपःप्रभावात् तेन मुनिना मूषिको बलिष्ठो विडालः कृतः । 'Perceiving the mouse terrified, by that sage, through the efficacy of his devotion, the mouse was changed into a very strong cat.'

6th. स विडालः कुक्कुराद् बिभेति । ततः कुक्कुरः कृतः । कुक्कुरस्य व्याघ्रान् महद् भयं । तदनन्तरं स व्याघ्रः कृतः । 'The cat fears the dog: upon that it was changed into a dog. Great is the dread of the dog for a tiger: then it was transformed into a tiger.'

7th. अथ व्याघ्रम् अपि मूषिकनिर्विशेषं पश्यति मुनिः । 'Now the sage regards even the tiger as not differing at all from the mouse.'

8th. अतः सर्वे तत्रस्था जनास् तं व्याघ्रं दृष्ट्वा वदन्ति । 'Then all the persons residing in the neighbourhood, seeing the tiger, say.'

9th. अनेन मुनिना मूषिकोऽयं व्याघ्रतां नीतः । 'By this sage this mouse has been brought to the condition of a tiger.'

10th. एतच् छ्रुत्वा स व्याघ्रः सव्यथोऽचिन्तयत् । 'The tiger overhearing this, being uneasy, reflected.'

11th. यावद् अनेन मुनिना जीवितव्यं तावद् इदं मम स्वरूपाख्यानम् अकीर्तिकरं न पलायिष्यते । 'As long as it shall be lived by this sage, so long this disgraceful story of my original condition will not die away.'

12th. इति समालोच्य मुनिं हन्तुं समुद्यतः । 'Thus reflecting, he prepared (was about) to kill the sage.'

13th. मुनिस् तस्य चिकीर्षितं ज्ञात्वा पुनर् मूषिको भव इत्य् उक्त्वा मूषिक एव कृतः । 'The sage discovering his intention, saying, "Again become a mouse," he was reduced to (his former state of) a mouse.'

931. Observe in this story: 1st, the simplicity of the style; 2dly, the prevalence of compound words; 3dly, the scarcity of verbs; 4thly, the prevalence of the past passive participle with the agent in the instrumental case for expressing indefinite past time, in lieu of the past tense active with the nominative: see 895, with note.

932. First sentence.—*Asti*, 'there is,' 3d sing. pres. of the root *as*, 2d c. (see 584). *Gautamasya*, 'of Gautama,' gen. case m. (103). *Munes*, 'of the sage,' gen. case m. (110): final *s* remains by 62. *Tapo-vane*, 'in the sacred grove,' or 'grove of penance,' genitively dependent compound (743); the first member formed by the crude noun *tapas*, 'penance,' *as* being changed to *o* by 64; the last member, by the loc. case of *vana*, 'grove,' neut. (104). *Mahā-tapāḥ*, 'great-devotion,' relative form of descriptive compound (766); the first member formed by the crude adjective *mahā* (substituted for *mahat* 778), 'great;' the last member, by the nom. case of *tapas*.

'devotion,' neut. (164): final *s* dropped by 66. *a*. *Náma*, 'by name,' an adverb (713). *Muniḥ*, 'a sage,' masc., nom. case (110): final *s* passes into Visarga by 63. *a*.

Second sentence.—*Tena*, 'by him,' instr. case of the pronoun *tat* at 220. *Áśrama-sannidháne*, 'in the neighbourhood of his hermitage,' genitively dependent compound (743): the first member formed by the crude noun *áśrama*, 'hermitage;' the last member, by the loc. case of *sannidhána*, 'neighbourhood,' neut. (104). The final *a* of *tena* blends with the initial *á* of *áśrama* by 31. *Múshika-śávakaḥ*, 'a young mouse,' or 'the young of a mouse,' genitively dependent compound (743); the first member formed by the crude noun *múshika*, 'a mouse;' the last, by the nom. case of *śávaka*, 'the young of any animal' (103): final *s* becomes Visarga by 63. *Káka-mukhád*, 'from the beak (or mouth) of a crow,' genitively dependent member formed by the crude noun *káka*, 'a crow;' the last, by the abl. case of *mukha*, 'mouth,' noun of the first class, neut. (104); *t* being changed to *d* by 45. *Bhrashṭo*, 'fallen,' nom. case, sing. masc. of the past pass. part. of the root *bhraṃś* (544. *a*): *as* changed to *o* by 64. *Drishṭaḥ*, 'seen,' nom. case, sing. masc. of the past pass. part. of the root *dṛiś*: final *s* becomes Visarga by 63. *a*.

Third sentence.—*Tata*, 'then,' adv. (719): *as* changed to *o* by 64. *Dayá-yuktena*, 'touched with compassion,' instrumentally dependent compound (740); the first member formed by the crude noun *dayá*, 'compassion;' the last, by the instr. case of *yukta*, 'endowed with,' past pass. part. of the root *yuj* (670). *Tena*, see second sentence. *Muniná*, 'by the sage,' instr. case m. (110). *Nívára-kaṇaiḥ*, 'with grains of wild rice,' genitively dependent compound (743); the first member formed by the crude noun *nívára*, 'wild rice;' the second, by the instr. plur. of *kaṇa*: final *s* becomes Visarga by 63. *Saṃvardhitaḥ*, 'reared,' nom. case, sing. of the past pass. part. of causal of *vṛidh* with *sam* (549): final *s* becomes Visarga by 63. *a*.

Fourth sentence.—*Tad-anantaram*, 'soon after this,' compound adverb; the first member formed with the pronoun *tat*, 'this,' at 220; the second, by the adverb *anantaram*, 'after,' at 731 and 917. *Múshikam*, acc. case m. (103). *Kháditum*, 'to eat,' infinitive mood of the root *khád* (458, 868). *Anudhávan*, 'pursuing after,' 'running after,' nom. case, sing. masc. of the pres. part. Par. of the root *dháv*, 'to run,' with the preposition *anu*, 'after' (514). *Viḍálo*, 'a cat,' noun of the first class, masc. (103), nom. case: *as* changed to *o* by 64. *Muniná*, see third sentence. *Drishṭaḥ*, see second sentence.

Fifth sentence.—*Tam*, acc. case, masc. of the pronoun *tat* at 220, used as a definite article, see 795. *Múshikam*, see fourth sentence. *Bhítam*, 'terrified,' acc. sing. masc. of the past pass. part. of the root *bhí* (532). *Álokya*, 'perceiving,' indeclinable part. of the root *lok*, with the prep. *á* (559). *Tapaḥ-prabhávát*, 'through the efficacy of his devotion' (814), genitively dependent compound (743); the first member formed by the crude noun *tapas*, 'devotion,' *s* being changed to Visarga by 63; the second, by the abl. case of *prabháva*, noun of the first class, masc. (103). *Tena*, see second sentence. *Muniná*, see third sentence. *Múshiko*, nom. case: *as* changed to *o* by 64. *Balishṭho*, 'very strong,' nom. case, masc. of the superlative form of the adj. *balin*, 'strong' (see 193): *as* changed to *o* by 64.

Viḍālaḥ, see fourth sentence: final *s* becomes Visarga by 63. *Kṛitaḥ*, 'changed,' 'made,' nom. case, sing. of the past pass. part. of the root *kṛi* at 682: final *s* becomes Visarga by 63. *e*.

Sixth sentence.—*Sa*, nom. case of the pronoun *tat* at 220, used as a definite article (795): final *s* dropped by 67. *Viḍālaḥ*, see fourth sentence. *Kukkurād*, 'the dog' (103), abl. case after a verb of 'fearing' (855): *t* changed to *d* by 45. *Bibheti*, 'fears,' 3d sing. pres. tense of the root *bhī*, 3d c. (666). *Tataḥ*, 'upon that,' adv. (719): *as* changed to *aḥ* by 63. *Kukkuraḥ*, 'the dog,' nom. case (103): final *s* becomes Visarga by 63. *Kṛitaḥ*, see fifth sentence. *Kukkurasya*, 'of the dog,' gen. case (103). *Vyāghrān*, 'for the tiger' (103), abl. case after a noun of 'fear' (814. *e*): *t* changed to *n* by 47. *Mahad*, 'great' (142), nom. case, sing. neut.: *t* changed to *d* by 45. *Bhayam*, 'fear' (104), nom. case. *Tad-anantaram*, see fourth sentence. *Vyāghraḥ*, nom. case: final *s* becomes Visarga by 63. *Kṛitaḥ*, see fifth sentence.

Seventh sentence.—*Atha*, 'now,' inceptive particle (727. *c*). *Vyāghram*, acc. case. *Api*, 'even,' adv. *Mūshika-nirviśesham*, 'as not differing at all from the mouse,' relative form of dependent compound (762): the first member formed by the crude noun *mūshika*; the second, by the acc. case of the substantive *viśesha*, 'difference,' with *nir* prefixed: or it may be here taken adverbially, see 776. *Paśyati*, 3d sing. pres. tense of the root *dṛiś*, 1st c. (604). *Muniḥ*, see first sentence.

Eighth sentence.—*Ataḥ*, 'then,' adv. (719). *Sarve*, 'all,' pronominal adj., nom. case, plur. masc. (237). *Tatra-sthāḥ*, 'residing in the neighbourhood,' compound resembling a locatively dependent; the first member being formed by the adverb *tatra* (720), 'there,' or 'in that place;' the second, by the nom. plur. masc. of the participial noun of agency of the root *sthā*, 'to remain' (587): final *s* dropped by 66. *a*. *Janāḥ*, 'persons,' noun of the first class, masc. gend. (103), nom. case, plur.: final *s* remains by 62. *Tam*, acc. case of the pronoun *tat* (220), used as a definite article (795). *Vyāghram*, 'tiger,' noun of the first class, masc. gend. (103), acc. case. *Dṛishṭvā*, 'having seen,' indeclinable past participle of the root *dṛiś* (556). *Vadanti*, 'they say,' 3d plur. pres. of the root *vad*, 1st c. (599).

Ninth sentence.—*Anena*, 'by this,' instr. case of the pronoun *idam* at 224. *Muninā*, see third sentence. *Mūshiko*, nom. case: *as* changed to *o* by 64. *a*. *Ayam*, 'this,' nom case, see 224: the initial *a* cut off by 64. *a*. *Vyāghratām*, 'the condition of a tiger,' fem. abstract noun of the first class (105), acc. case, formed from the substantive *vyāghra*, 'a tiger,' by the affix *tā* (80. XXIII). *Nītaḥ*, 'brought,' nom. case, sing. masc. of the past pass. part. of the root *nī* at 532.

Tenth sentence.—*Etat*, 'this,' acc. case, neut. of *etat* at 223: *t* changed to *c* by 49. *Ćrutvā*, 'overhearing,' indeclinable participle of the root *śru* (676 and 556): see 49. *Vyāghraḥ*, nom. case: final *s* becomes Visarga by 63. *Sa-vyatha*, 'uneasy,' relative form of indeclinable compound, formed by prefixing *saha* to the fem. substantive *vyathā* (769): *as* changed to *a* by 64. *a*. *Acintayat*, 'reflected,' 3d sing. impf. of *cint*, 10th c. (641): the initial *a* cut off by 64. *a*.

Eleventh sentence.—*Yāvad*, 'as long as,' adv. (713): *t* changed to *d* by 45.

Anena, see ninth sentence. *Jívitavyam*, 'to be lived,' nom. case, neut. of the fut. pass. part. of the root *jív* (569, 905. *a*, 907). *Távat*, 'so long,' adv. correlative to *yávat* (713. *a*). *Idam*, 'this,' nom. case, neut. of the demonstrative pronoun at 224. *Mama*, 'of me,' gen. case of the pronoun *aham*, 'I,' at 218. *Swarúpákhyánam*, 'story of my original condition,' genitively dependent compound (743); the first member formed by the crude noun *swarúpa*, 'natural form' (see 232); the second, by the nom. case of *ákhyána*, noun of the first class, neuter (104): *n* retained by 60. *Akírti-karam*, 'disgraceful,' accusatively dependent compound (739); the first member formed by the crude noun *akírti*, 'disgrace;' the second, by the nom. case, neut. of the participial noun of agency *kara*, 'causing,' from *kri*, 'to do' (580). *Na*, 'not,' adv. (717. *a*). *Paláyishyate*, 'will die away,' 3d sing. 2d fut. Átm. of the compound verb *paláy*, formed by combining the root *i* with the prep. *pará* (783).

Twelfth sentence.—*Iti*, 'thus,' adv. (717. *e*: see also 928). *Samálokya*, 'reflecting,' indeclinable part. of the compound verb *sam-á-lok* (559), formed by combining the root *lok* with the prepositions *sam* and *á* (784). *Munim*, acc. case. *Hantum*, 'to kill,' infinitive mood of the root *han* (458, 868, and 654). *Samudyatah*, 'prepared,' nom. case, sing. masc. of the past pass. part. of the compound verb *sam-ud-yam*, formed by combining the root *yam* with the prepositions *sam* and *ud* (545).

Thirteenth sentence.—*Munih*, nom. case: final *s* remains by 62. *Tasya*, 'of him,' gen. case of the pronoun *tat* (220). *Ćikírshitam*, 'intention,' acc. case, neut. of the past pass. part. of the desiderative base of the root *kri*, 'to do' (550 and 502), used as a substantive (896. *b*). *Jñátwá*, 'discovering,' indeclinable part. of the root *jñá* (556 and 688). *Punar*, 'again,' adv. (717. *a*): *r* remains by 71. *c*. *Múshiko*, nom. case: *as* changed to *o* by 64. *Bhava*, 'become,' 2d sing. impv. of the root *bhú* (585). *Ity* answers to inverted commas, see 927. *a*: the final *i* changed to *y* by 34. *Uktwá*, 'saying,' indeclinable part. of the root *vac* (556 and 650). *Múshika*, nom. case: final *s* dropped by 66. *Eva*, 'indeed,' adv. (717).

SENTENCES AND FABLE TO BE TRANSLATED AND PARSED.

933. Note—The numbers over the words in the following sentences and fable refer to the rules of the foregoing grammar.

स आगच्छतु । तौ आगच्छतां । आवाम् आगच्छाव । ते उपविशन्तु । तौ शृणुतां । ते शृण्वन्तु । अहं तिष्ठानि । युवां तिष्ठतं । वयम् उत्तिष्ठाम । स करोतु । त्वं कुरु । वयं करवामहै । स चिन्तयतु । त्वम् अवधेहि । ते ददतु । यूयं दत्त । भवान् एतु । कुत्र भवान् वसति । यूयं कुत्र वसथ । भवान् शेतां । ते शेरतां । नरः स्वपितु । ते सर्वे सुषुपुः ।

नरो गृहं याति । युष्माभिः किञ्चिद् भोक्तव्यं । वयं शास्त्रम् अध्ययामहे । अस्माभिः शास्त्राण्य् अध्येतव्यानि । त्वम् अन्नं भुङ्क्ष्व । मयान्नं भुज्यतां । त्वया दुग्धं पीयतां । यूयं जलं पिबत । यद् अहं जानामि तद् युष्मान् अध्यापयिष्यामि । मा दिवा स्वाप्सीः । नदीं मा गाः । मा शब्दाद् बिभीत । मा मां निरपराधं बधान ॥

रात्रिशेषे विद्यार्थी शयनाद् उत्तिष्ठेत् ॥

मातापित्रोस् तुष्ट्या सर्वस्य तपसः फलं प्राप्यते ॥

ईरिणे बीजम् उप्त्वा कर्षकः फलं न प्राप्नोति ॥

रात्रिर् भूतानां स्वप्नार्थं भवति दिनं च कर्मानुष्ठानार्थं ॥

बहिःशौचं मृद्वारिभ्याम् अन्तःशौचं रागद्वेषादित्यागेन क्रियते ॥

न जातु कामः कामानाम् उपभोगेन शाम्यति ॥

व्यसनस्य च मृत्योश्च व्यसनं कष्टम् उच्यते ॥

आमृत्योः श्रीसिद्ध्यर्थम् उद्यमं कुर्यात् ॥

अद्भिर् गात्राणि शुध्यन्ति मनस् तु निषिद्धचिन्तादिना दूषितं सत्याभिधानेन ॥

934. ॥ कथा ॥ FABLE.

कस्मिंश्चिद् अधिष्ठाने चत्वारो ब्राह्मणपुत्राः परं मैत्रीभावम् उपागता निवसन्ति स्म । तेषां त्रयः सर्वशास्त्रपारगाः परं बुद्धिरहिताः । एकस् तु शास्त्रपराङ्मुखः केवलं बुद्धिमान् । अथ कदाचित् तैर् मिलित्वा मन्त्रितं । को गुणो विद्याया यदि देशान्तरं गत्वा भूपतीन् परितोष्यार्थोपार्जना न क्रियते । तत् सर्वेषां सर्वे देशान्तरं गच्छाम

इति । तथानुष्ठिते किञ्चिन् मार्गं गत्वा तेषां ज्येष्ठतरः प्राह । अहो अस्माकम् एकश् चतुर्थो मूढः केवलं बुद्धिमान् । न च विद्यां विना राज्ञां प्रतिग्रहः केवलबुद्ध्या लभ्यते । तद् अस्मै स्वोपार्जनाविभागं न दास्यामः । तद् एष निवृत्य स्वगृहं गच्छतु । अथ द्वितीयेनाभिहितं । अहो सुबुद्धे विद्याहीनस् त्वं । तद् गच्छ गृहं । ततस् तृतीयेनाभिहितं । अहो न युज्यते कर्तुम् एवं । यतो वयं बाल्यात् प्रभृत्येकत्र क्रीडिताः । तद् आगच्छतु । महानुभावो ऽस्मदुपार्जितस्य वित्तस्य संविभागी भवतु । तथानुष्ठिते तैर् मार्गम् अतिक्रामद्भिर् अटव्यां मृतसिंहास्थीनि दृष्टानि । ततश्चैकेनाभिहितं । अहो पूर्वाधीतविद्यायाः प्रत्ययः क्रियते । किञ्चिद् एतन् मृतसत्त्वं तिष्ठति । तत् सदभ्यस्तविद्याप्रभावेण प्रत्युज्जीवयामः । ततश्चैकेनाभिहितं । अहम् अस्थिसञ्चयं कर्तुं जानामि । द्वितीयेनाभिहितं । चर्ममांसरुधिरं प्रयच्छामि । तृतीयेनाभिहितं । अहं सञ्जीवनं करोमि । तत एकेनास्थिसञ्चयः कृतः । द्वितीयेन चर्ममांसरुधिरैः संयोजितः । तृतीयो यावज्जीवितव्यं योजयितुं लग्नः । तावत् स बुद्धिमता निषिद्ध उक्तश्च । एष सिंहः । यद्येनं सञ्जीवं करिष्यसि तत् सर्वान् अप्यस्मान् व्यापादयिष्यतीति । ततस् तेनाभिहितं । धिग् मूर्ख नाहं विद्यां विफलतां नेष्यामि । ततश्च तेनाभिहितं । तर्हि क्षणं प्रतीक्षस्व यावद् अहम् एनं समीपतरुम् आरोहामि । तथानुष्ठिते यावत् सञ्जीवः कृतस् तावत् त्रयोऽपि ते तेनोत्थाय व्यापादिताः । स च बुद्धिमान सिंहे स्थानान्तरे गते वृक्षाद् अवतीर्य गृहं गतः ॥

SCHEME OF THE MORE COMMON SANSKRIT METRES.

1st class of Metres, consisting of two lines, determined by the number of SYLLABLES *in the half-line* (*Vṛitta*).

Note—It may be useful to prefix to the following schemes of metres a list of technical prosodial terms: पाद = the fourth part of a verse; मात्रा = an instant or short syllable; गण = four instants; यति = a pause; गुरु or ग = a long syllable (–); लघु or ल = a short syllable (⏑); गग = a spondee (– –); लल = a pyrrhic (⏑ ⏑); गल = a trochee (– ⏑); लग = an iambus (⏑ –); म = a molossus (– – –); भ = a dactyl (– ⏑ ⏑); न = a tribrach (⏑ ⏑ ⏑); य = a bacchic (⏑ – –); र = a cretic (– ⏑ –); स = an anapæst (⏑ ⏑ –); त = an antibacchic (– – ⏑); ज = an amphibrach (⏑ – ⏑).

Śloka or *Anushṭubh* (8 syllables to the half-line or Páda).

935. THE commonest of all the infinite variety of Sanskrit metres is the Śloka or Anushṭubh. This is the metre which chiefly prevails in the great epic poems.

It consists of four half-lines of 8 syllables or two lines of 16 syllables each, but the rules which regulate one line apply equally to the other; so that it is only necessary to give the scheme of one line, as follows:—

1	2	3	4	5	6	7	8	‖	9	10	11	12	13	14	15	16
·	·	·	·	⏑	⏒	⏒	·	‖	·	·	·	·	⏑	–	⏑	·

Note—The mark · denotes either long or short.

The 1st, 2d, 3d, 4th, 9th, 10th, 11th, and 12th syllables may be either long or short. The 8th, as ending the half-line, and the 16th, as ending the line, are also common. Since the line is considered as divided into two parts at the 8th syllable, it is an almost universal rule that this syllable must end a word, *whether simple or compound**.

The 5th syllable ought always to be short. The 6th may be either long or short; but if long, then the 7th ought to be long also; and if short, then the 7th ought to be short also. But occasional variations from these last rules occur.

The last 4 syllables form two iambics; the 13th being always short, the 14th always long, and the 15th always short.

Every Śloka, or couplet of two lines, ought to form a complete sentence in itself, and contain both subject and predicate. Not unfrequently, however, in the Rámáyaṇa and Mahá-bhárata, three lines are united to form a triplet.

936. In the remaining metres determined by the number of *syllables* in the half-line, each half-line is exactly alike (*sama*); so that

* There are, however, *rare* examples of compound words running through a whole line.

it is only necessary to give the scheme of one half-line, or quarter of the verse (Páda).

Note, that in printed books each quarter of the verse, if it consist of more than 8 syllables, is often made to occupy a line.

937. *Trishṭubh* (11 syllables to the half-line).

Of this there are 22 varieties. The commonest are—

	1	2	3	4	5	6	7	8	9	10	11	
938. *Indra-vajrá*,	—	—	◡	—	—	◡	◡	—	◡	—	.	‖
939. *Upendra-vajrá*,	◡	—	◡	—	—	◡	◡	—	◡	—	.	‖

There is generally a cæsura at the 5th syllable.

Note—The above 2 varieties are sometimes mixed in the same stanza; in which case the metre is called *Upajáti* or *Ákhyánakí*.

	1	2	3	4	5	6	7	8	9	10	11	
940. *Rathoddhatá*,	—	◡	—	◡	◡	◡	—	◡	—	◡	—	‖

941. *Jagatí* (12 syllables to the half-line).

Of this there are 30 varieties. The commonest are—

	1	2	3	4	5	6	7	8	9	10	11	12	
942. *Vanśa-sthavila*,	◡	—	◡	—	—	◡	◡	—	◡	—	◡	⏓*	‖
943. *Druta-vilambita*,	◡	◡	◡	—	◡	◡	—	◡	◡	—	◡	⏓	‖

944. *Atijagatí* (13 syllables to the half-line).

Of this there are 16 varieties. The commonest are—

	1	2	3	4	5	6	7	8	9	10	11	12	13	
945. *Mañju-bháshiṇí*,	◡	◡	—	◡	—	◡	◡	◡	—	◡	—	◡	⏓	‖
946. *Praharshiṇí*,	—	—	—	◡	◡	◡	◡	—	◡	—	◡	—	⏓	‖
947. *Rućirá* or *Prabhávatí*,	◡	—	◡	—	◡	◡	◡	◡	—	◡	—	◡	⏓	‖

948. *Śakvarí* or *Śakkarí* or *Śarkarí* (14 syllables to the half-line).

Of this there are 20 varieties. The commonest is—

	1	2	3	4	5	6	7	8	9	10	11	12	13	14	
949. *Vasanta-tilaká*,	—	—	◡	—	◡	◡	◡	—	◡	◡	—	◡	—	⏓	‖

950. *Atiśakvarí* or *Atiśakkarí* or *Atiśarkarí* (15 syllables to the half-line).

Of this there are 18 varieties. The commonest is—

	1	2	3	4	5	6	7	8		9	10	11	12	13	14	15	
951. *Máliní* or *Mániní*,	◡	◡	◡	◡	◡	◡	—	—	‖	—	◡	—	—	◡	—	⏓	‖

There is a cæsura at the 8th syllable.

* The mark ⏓ is meant to show that the last syllable is long at the end of the half-line, but long or short at the end of the line.

952. *Ashṭi* (16 syllables to the half-line).

Of this there are 12 varieties; none of which are common.

953. *Atyashṭi* (17 syllables to the half-line).

Of this there are 17 varieties. The commonest are—

	1	2	3	4	5	6	‖	7	8	9	10	11	12	13	14	15	16	17
954. *S'ikhariṇí*,	⏑	–	–	–	–	–	‖	⏑	⏑	⏑	⏑	⏑	–	–	⏑	⏑	⏑	⏓

Cæsura at the 6th syllable.

	1	2	3	4	‖	5	6	7	8	9	10	‖	11	12	13	14	15	16	17
955. *Mandákrántá*,	–	–	–	–	‖	⏑	⏑	⏑	⏑	⏑	–	‖	–	⏑	–	–	⏑	–	⏓

Cæsura at the 4th and 10th syllables.

	1	2	3	4	5	6	‖	7	8	9	10	‖	11	12	13	14	15	16	17
956. *Hariṇí*,	⏑	⏑	⏑	⏑	⏑	–	‖	–	–	–	–	‖	⏑	–	⏑	⏑	–	⏑	⏓

Cæsura at the 6th and 10th syllables.

957. *Dhṛiti* (18 syllables to the half-line).

Of this there are 17 varieties; one of which is found in the Raghu-vaṃśa—

	1	2	3	4	5	6	7	8	9	10	11	12	13	14	15	16	17	18
958. *Mahá-máliká*,	⏑	⏑	⏑	⏑	⏑	⏑	–	⏑	–	–	⏑	–	–	⏑	–	–	⏑	⏓

959. *Atidhṛiti* (19 syllables to the half-line).

Of this there are 13 varieties. The commonest is—

	1	2	3	4	5	6	7	8	9	10	11	12	‖	13	14	15	16	17	18	19
960. *S'árdúla-vikríḍita*,	–	–	–	⏑	⏑	–	⏑	–	⏑	⏑	⏑	–	‖	–	–	⏑	–	–	⏑	⏓

Cæsura at the 12th syllable.

961. *Kṛiti* (20 syllables to the half-line).

Of these there are 4 varieties; none of which are common.

962. *Prakṛiti* (21 syllables to the half-line).

	1	2	3	4	5	6	7	‖	8	9	10	11	12	13	14	‖	15	16	17	18	19	20	21
963. *Sragdhará*,	–	–	–	–	⏑	–	–	‖	⏑	⏑	⏑	⏑	⏑	⏑	–	‖	–	⏑	–	–	⏑	–	⏓

Cæsura at the 7th and 14th syllables.

964. Of the remaining metres determined by the number of syllables in the half-line, *Akṛiti* has 22 syllables, and includes 3 varieties; *Vikṛiti* 23 syllables, 6 varieties; *Saṅkṛiti* 24 syllables, 5 varieties; *Atikṛiti* 25 syllables, 2 varieties; *Utkṛiti* 26 syllables, 3 varieties; and *Daṇḍaka* is the name given to all metres which exceed *Utkṛiti* in the number of syllables.

965. There are two metres, however, peculiar to the Vedas, called *Gáyatrí* and *Ushṇih*. The first of these has only 6 syllables to the quarter-verse, and includes 11 varieties; the second has 7 syllables to the half-line, and includes 8 varieties.

a. Observe, that when the half-line is so short, the whole verse is sometimes written in one line.

b. Observe also, that great license is allowed in Vaidik metres: thus in the

966. *Gáyatrí*,

which may be regarded as consisting of a triplet of 3 divisions of 8 syllables each, or of 6 feet of 4 syllables each, generally printed in one line, the quantity of each syllable is very irregular. The following verse exhibits the most usual quantities:

1		2		3	
a	b	a	b	a	b
· · · ·	⏑ – ⏑ · ‖	· · · ·	⏑ – ⏑ · ‖	· · · ·	⏑ – ⏑ · ‖

but even in the *b* verse of each division the quantity may vary.

2d class of Metres, consisting of two lines, determined by the number of SYLLABLES* *in the* WHOLE LINE *(each whole line being alike, ardha-sama).*

967. This class contains 7 genera, but no varieties under each genus. Of these the commonest are—

968. *Vaitálíya* (21 syllables to the *whole* line).

1	2	3	4	5	6	7	8	9	10	11	12	13	14	15	16	17	18	19	20	21
⏑	⏑	–	⏑	⏑	–	⏑	–	⏑	– |	⏑	⏑	–	–	⏑	⏑	–	⏑	–	⏑	· |

There is a cæsura at the 10th syllable.

969. *Aupacchandasika* (23 syllables to the *whole* line).

The scheme of this metre is the same as the last, with a long syllable added after the 10th and last syllable in the line; the cæsura being at the 11th syllable.

970. *Pushpitágrá* (25 syllables to the *whole* line).

1	2	3	4	5	6	7	8	9	10	11	12	13	14	15	16	17	18	19	20	21	22	23	24	25
⏑	⏑	⏑	⏑	⏑	⏑	–	⏑	–	⏑	–	– |	⏑	⏑	⏑	⏑	–	⏑	⏑	–	⏑	–	⏑	–	· |

There is a cæsura at the 12th syllable.

3d class of Metres, consisting of two lines, determined by the number of FEET *in the whole verse (each foot containing generally four instants or mátrás).*

This class of metres is called *Játi*.

971. *Note*—Each foot is supposed to consist of four instants, and a short syllable is equivalent to one instant, a long syllable to two. Hence only such feet can be

* This class of metres is said to be regulated by the number of feet or instants in the line, in the same way as the 3d class. But as each line is generally distributed into fixed long or short syllables, and no option is allowed for each foot between a spondee, anapæst, dactyl, proceleusmaticus, and amphibrach, it will obviate confusion to regard this class as determined by syllables, like the 1st.

used as are equivalent to four instants; and of this kind are the dactyl (– ∪ ∪), the spondee (– –), the anapæst (∪ ∪ –), the amphibrach (∪ – ∪), and the proceleusmaticus (∪ ∪ ∪ ∪); any one of which may be employed.

Of this class of metres the commonest is the

972. *Áryá* or *Gáthá*.

Each line consists of seven and a half feet; and each foot contains four instants, excepting the 6th of the second line, which contains only one, and is therefore a single short syllable. Hence there are 30 instants in the first line, and 27 in the second. The half-foot at the end of each line is generally, but not always, a long syllable; the 6th foot of the first line must be either an amphibrach or proceleusmaticus; and the 1st, 3d, 5th, and 7th feet must not be amphibrachs. The cæsura commonly takes place at the end of the 3d foot in each line, and the measure is then sometimes called *Pathyá*. The following are a few examples:

1	2	3	4	5	6	7	
– –	∪ – ∪	∪ ∪ –	– ∪ ∪	– ∪ ∪	∪ – ∪	– –	–
∪ ∪ –	∪ – ∪	∪ ∪ –	– –	∪ ∪ –	∪	– –	∪
– –	∪ ∪ –	– –	– –	– ∪ ∪	∪ – ∪	– ∪ ∪	–
∪ ∪ –	– ∪ ∪	∪ ∪ –	∪ – ∪	– –	∪	– ∪ ∪	–
∪ ∪ –	– ∪ ∪	– –	∪ ∪ –	– ∪ ∪	∪ – ∪	– –	∪
∪ ∪ –	∪ ∪ ∪ ∪	– ∪ ∪	– –	∪ ∪ –	∪	– –	–
– ∪ ∪	∪ – ∪	∪ ∪ –	– ∪ ∪	– ∪ ∪	∪ – ∪	– –	–
– –	∪ – ∪	– –	∪ ∪ ∪ ∪	∪ ∪ –	∪	– –	–
– ∪ ∪	– –	– ∪ ∪	– –	– –	∪ ∪ ∪ ∪	∪ ∪ –	–
∪ ∪ ∪ ∪	∪ ∪ ∪ ∪	– –	– –	∪ ∪ –	∪	– –	∪

973. The *Udgíti* metre only differs from the *Áryá* in inverting the lines, and placing the short line, with 27 instants, first in order.

974. There are three other varieties:—In the *Upagíti*, both lines consist of 27 instants; in the *Gíti*, both consist of 30 instants; and in the *Áryágíti*, of 32.

INDEX I.

OBSERVE—The numbers refer to the number of the rule.

INDEX II.

OBSERVE—The numbers refer to the number of the rule.

LIST OF COMPOUND CONSONANTS.

CONJUNCTIONS OF TWO CONSONANTS.

क्क *kka*, क्ख *kkha*, क्ण *kṇa*, क्त *kta*, क्थ *ktha*, क्न *kna*, क्म *kma*, क्य *kya*, क्र or क्र *kra*, क्ल *kla*, क्व *kva*, क्ष *ksha*. ख्य *khya*, ख्व *khva*. ग्घ *ggha*, ग्ध *gdha*, ग्न *gna*, ग्भ *gbha*, ग्म *gma*, ग्य *gya*, ग्र *gra*, ग्ल *gla*, ग्व *gva*. घ्न *ghna*, घ्य *ghya*, घ्र *ghra*, घ्व *ghva*. ङ्क *ṅka*, ङ्ख *ṅkha*, ङ्ग *ṅga*, ङ्घ *ṅgha*, ङ्भ *ṅbha*, ङ्म *ṅma*.

च्च *ćća*, च्छ *ććha*, च्ञ *ćña*, च्म *ćma*, च्य *ćya*. छ्य *ćhya*, छ्र *ćhra*. ज्ज *jja*, ज्झ *jjha*, ज्ञ *jña*, ज्म *jma*, ज्य *jya*, ज्र *jra*, ज्व *jva*. ञ्च *ñća*, ञ्छ *ñćha*, ञ्ज *ñja*.

ट्ट *ṭṭa*, ट्ठ *ṭṭha*. ठ्य *ṭhya*. ड्ग *ḍga*, ड्ड *ḍḍa*, ड्ण *ḍṇa*, ड्ढ *ḍḍha*, ड्भ *ḍbha*, ड्य *ḍya*, ड्र *ḍra*. ढ्य *ḍhya*, ढ्र *ḍhra*. ण्ट *ṇṭa*, ण्ठ *ṇṭha*, ण्ड *ṇḍa*, ण्ढ *ṇḍha*, ण्ण *ṇṇa*, ण्म *ṇma*, ण्य *ṇya*, ण्व *ṇva*.

त्क *tka*, त्त *tta*, त्थ *ttha*, त्न *tna*, त्म *tma*, त्य *tya*, त्र *tra*, त्व *tva*, त्स *tsa*. थ्न *thna*, थ्य *thya*, थ्व *thva*. द्ग *dga*, द्घ *dgha*, द्द *dda*, द्ध *ddha*, द्न *dna*, द्ब *dba*, द्भ *dbha*, द्म *dma*, द्य *dya*, द्र *dra*, द्व *dva*. ध्न *dhna*, ध्म *dhma*, ध्य *dhya*, ध्र *dhra*, ध्व *dhva*. न्त *nta*, न्थ *ntha*, न्द *nda*, न्ध *ndha*, न्न *nna*, न्म *nma*, न्य *nya*, न्र *nra*, न्व *nva*, न्स *nsa*.

प्त *pta*, प्थ *ptha*, प्न *pna*, प्प *ppa*, प्फ *ppha*, प्म *pma*, प्य *pya*, प्र *pra*, प्ल *pla*, प्व *pva*, प्स *psa*. ब्ज *bja*, ब्द *bda*, ब्ध *bdha*, ब्ब *bba*, ब्भ *bbha*, ब्य *bya*, ब्र *bra*. भ्य *bhya*, भ्र *bhra*, भ्व *bhva*. म्ण *mṇa*, म्न *mna*, म्प *mpa*, म्फ *mpha*, म्ब *mba*, म्भ *mbha*, म्म *mma*, म्य *mya*, म्र *mra*, म्ल *mla*.

य्य *yya*, य्र *yra*, य्व *yva*.

र्क *rka*, र्ख *rkha*, र्ग *rga*, र्घ *rgha*, र्च *rća*, र्छ *rćha*, र्ज *rja*, र्ण *rṇa*, र्त *rta*, र्थ *rtha*, र्द *rda*, र्ध *rdha*, र्प *rpa*, र्ब *rba*, र्भ *rbha*, र्म *rma*, र्य *rya*, र्व *rva*, र्श *rśa*, र्ष *rsha*. र्ह *rha*.

ल्क *lka*, ल्ग *lga*, ल्ड *lḍa*, ल्प *lpa*, ल्ब *lba*, ल्भ *lbha*, ल्म *lma*, ल्य *lya*, ल्ल *lla*, ल्व *lva*, ल्श *lśa*, ल्ह *lha*.

व्न *vna*, व्य *vya*, व्र *vra*, व्ल *vla*, व्व *vva*.

श्च *śća*, श्न *śna*, श्य *śya*, श्र *śra*, श्ल *śla*, श्व *śva*. ष्क *shka*, ष्ट *shṭa*, ष्ठ *shṭha*, ष्ण *shṇa*, ष्प *shpa*, ष्म *shma*, ष्य *shya*, ष्व *shva*. स्क *ska*, स्ख *skha*, स्त *sta*, स्थ *stha*, स्न *sna*, स्प *spa*, स्फ *spha*, स्म *sma*, स्य *sya*, स्र *sra*, स्व *sva*, स्स *ssa*. ह्ण *hṇa*, ह्न *hna*, ह्म *hma*, ह्य *hya*, ह्र *hra*, ह्ल *hla*, ह्व *hva*.

CONJUNCTIONS OF THREE CONSONANTS.

क्क्ण or क्क्ण *kkṇa**, क्ष्ण *kshṇa*, क्थ्न *kthna*†, क्ष्म *kshma*, क्क्य *kkya*, क्ख्य *kkhya*, क्त्य *ktya*, क्थ्य *kthya*, क्ष्य *kshya*, क्त्र *ktra*, क्त्व *ktva*, क्ष्व *kshva*. ग्घ्य *gghya*, ग्ध्य *gdhya*, ग्न्य *gnya*, ग्भ्य *gbhya*, ग्र्य *grya*, ग्ध्व *gdhva*. ङ्क्त *ṅ-kta*, ङ्क्य *ṅ-kya*, ङ्ख्य *ṅ-khya*, ङ्ग्य *ṅ-gya*, ङ्घ्य *ṅ-ghya*, ङ्क्ष *ṅ-ksha*.

च्च्य *ććya*, च्छ्य *ććhya*, च्छ्र *ććhra*, च्छ्व *ććhva*. ज्ज्ञ *jjña*, ज्ज्व *jjva*. ञ्च्य *ñćya*, ञ्छ्य *ñćhya*, ञ्च्व *ñćva*, ञ्ज्व *ñjva*.

ट्ट्य *ṭṭya*. ड्ड्य *ḍḍya*, ड्भ्य *ḍbhya*. ण्ट्य *ṇṭya*, ण्ठ्य *ṇṭhya*, ण्ड्य *ṇḍya*, ण्ड्र *ṇḍra*.

त्क्र *tkra*, त्न्य *tnya*, त्प्र *tpra*, त्त्म *tma*, त्त्य *ttya*, त्थ्य *tthya*, त्म्य *tmya*, त्र्य *trya*, त्स्य *tsya*, त्त्र *ttra*, त्त्व *ttva*, त्र्व *trva*, त्स्व *tsva*. द्द्य *ddya*, द्ध्य *ddhya*, द्भ्य *dbhya*, द्र्य *drya*, द्व्य *dvya*. ध्व्य *dhvya*‡, ध्न्व *dhnva*. न्द्ध *nddha*, न्त्म *ntma*, न्द्म *ndma*, न्ध्म *ndhma*, न्त्य *ntya*, न्थ्य *nthya*, न्द्य *ndya*, न्न्य *nnya*, न्त्र *ntra*, न्द्र *ndra*, न्ध्र *ndhra*, न्त्व *ntva*, न्द्व *ndva*, न्ध्व *ndhva*, न्न्व *nnva*, न्त्स *ntsa*.

प्त्न *ptna*, प्त्य *ptya*, प्स्य *psya*, प्त्र *ptra*, प्ण्व *pṇva*, प्त्व *ptva*, प्ल्व *plva*, प्स्व *psva*§. ब्ज्य *bjya*, ब्ध्य *bdhya*, ब्भ्य *bbhya*, ब्भ्र *bbhra*,

---

* As in [illegible] from [illegible].

† [illegible] from [illegible] at 182.

‡ [illegible] from [illegible] at 187.

§ [illegible] from [illegible].

ब्ध्व *bdhva.* भ्र्य *bhrya.* म्प्य *mpya,* म्ब्य *mbya,* म्ब्ल *mbla,* म्भ्य *mbhya,* म्प्र *mpra,* म्भ्र *mbhra.*

र्क्ष *rksha,* र्ष्ट *rshṭa,* र्ण्ण *rṇṇa,* र्त्त *rtta,* र्द्ध *rddha,* र्ग्य *rgya,* र्घ्य *rghya,* र्च्य *rćya,* र्ण्य *rṇya,* र्त्य *rtya,* र्प्य *rpya,* र्ब्ब *rbba,* र्य्य *ryya,* र्ष्ण *rshṇa,* र्ह्म *rhma.*

ल्क्य *lkya,* ल्ग्य *lgya,* ल्प्त *lpta,* ल्प्य *lpya.*

श्च्य *śćya,* श्र्य *śrya.* ष्ट्य *shṭya,* ष्ण्य *shṇya,* ष्ट्र *shṭra,* ष्ट्व *shṭva.* स्त्य *stya,* स्त्र *stra,* स्त्व *stva,* स्थ्न *sthna,* स्थ्य *sthya,* स्न्व *snva,* स्म्य *smya,* स्र्य *srya,* स्र्व *srva.* ह्न्य *hnya,* ह्म्य *hmya,* ह्र्य *hrya.*

CONJUNCTIONS OF FOUR CONSONANTS.

क्त्र्य *ktrya,* क्ष्म्य *kshmya.* ङ्क्ष्ण *ṅ-kshṇa,* ङ्क्ष्म *ṅ-kshma**, ङ्क्त्य *ṅ-ktya,* ङ्क्ष्य *ṅ-kshya,* ङ्क्त्र *ṅ-ktra,* ङ्क्ष्व *ṅ-kshva.* ण्ड्र्य *ṇḍrya.* त्त्र्य *ttrya,* त्स्न्य *tsnya,* त्स्म्य *tsmya.* द्ध्र्य *ddhrya.* न्त्र्य *ntrya,* न्त्स्य *ntsya,* न्त्स्व *ntsva,* न्ध्र्य *ndhrya.* प्त्र्य *ptrya.* र्क्ष्य *rkshya,* र्त्त्य *rttya,* र्त्र्य *rtrya,* र्त्स्य *rtsya,* र्द्ध्र *rddhra.* ल्प्त्य *lptya,* ल्प्स्म *lpsma,* ल्प्स्य *lpsya.* ष्ट्र्य *shṭrya.*

CONJUNCTIONS OF FIVE CONSONANTS.

ङ्क्ष्ण्व *ṅ-kshṇva* †, ङ्क्त्र्य *ṅ-ktrya* ‡. र्ङ्क्ष्म *rṅ-kshma* §, र्ङ्क्ष्व *rṅ-kshva* §, र्त्स्न्य *rtsnya* ‖, र्द्ध्र्य *rddhrya.*

---

* चाकङ्क्ष्मि intens. of काङ्क्ष्. † दङ्क्ष्ण्वोः from दङ्क्ष्णु.

‡ सङ्क्त्र्योः from सङ्क्त्री. § As in अताङ्क्ष्म, अताङ्क्ष्व, from root तृंह्.

‖ As in कार्त्स्न्यं.

NOTES AND CORRECTIONS.

Page 28, rule 38. *b*. This rule would be more clearly expressed by omitting 'and आ *ā*;' thus, "Particles, when simple vowels, and *o*, as the final of an interjection, remain unchanged." But *ā* is, of course, included under particles consisting of a single vowel. Not, however, when it is used adverbially in the sense 'slightly,' as in *ā* + *ushṇa* = *oshṇa*, 'slightly warm.'

P. 32, r. 41. *b*. With reference to पितापितृभ्याम्, see p. 98 note.

P. 45, r. 70. With reference to this rule, compare r. 175. *d*. Add also, an exception to 70. *b*. in the root *sīv* preceded by *prati* (प्रतिसीव्यति). Compare also r. 500. *f*, which does not apply if a prep. is prefixed; thus अभिसिषेविषति is correct from root *siv* with *abhi*.

P. 47, 2d col. of the table, for 17. *e*. read 71. *e*.

P. 110, r. 208, l. 2, for '*sarva* and the pronominals' read '*śiva*;' l. 4, for '*śiva* (103)' read '*sarva*'

P. 120, r. 239, l. 2, read 'follow *śiva* and optionally *sarva* in certain cases, &c.'

P. 120, r. 240, l. 2, after पञ्चतय 'fivefold' add 'and all in *taya*'

P. 120, r. 240, l. 2, read 'follow *śiva* at 103; but may make their nom. voc. plur. masc. in *e*'

P. 138, l. 6, for 249 read 247.

P. 149, r. 304. *a*, compare r. 62. *b*.

P. 163, l. 17, for 397, 398, read 392.

P. 165, l. 5, for चौ *au* read चो *o*

P. 168, r. 381, compare r. 48. *e*.

P. 169, l. 12, for 371 read 367. *b*.

P. 174, r. 393, compare note to 627.

www.ingramcontent.com/pod-product-compliance
Lightning Source LLC
Chambersburg PA
CBHW022010110726
47901CB00006B/1462
* 9 7 8 3 7 4 1 1 7 8 7 6 4 *